THE
PROSECUTOR

ONE MAN'S BATTLE TO BRING NAZIS TO JUSTICE

JACK FAIRWEATHER

WH
ALLEN

WH Allen

UK | USA | Canada | Ireland | Australia
India | New Zealand | South Africa

WH Allen is part of the Penguin Random House group of companies
whose addresses can be found at global.penguinrandomhouse.com

Penguin Random House UK
One Embassy Gardens, 8 Viaduct Gardens, London SW11 7BW

penguin.co.uk
global.penguinrandomhouse.com

First published by WH Allen in 2025

1

Printed and bound in Great Britain by Clays Ltd, Elcograf S.p.A.

The authorised representative in the EEA is Penguin Random House Ireland,
Morrison Chambers, 32 Nassau Street, Dublin D02 YH68

A CIP catalogue record for this book is available from the British Library

Hardback ISBN 9780753558102
Trade Paperback ISBN 9780753558119

Penguin Random House is committed to a sustainable future
for our business, our readers and our planet. This book is made
from Forest Stewardship Council® certified paper.

THE PROSECUTOR

ALSO BY JACK FAIRWEATHER

The Volunteer

The Good War

A War of Choice

For Big Jack and Betty, and for Hedi

The pang, the curse, with which they died,
Had never passed away:
I could not draw my eyes from theirs,
Nor turn them up to pray.

—*The Rime of the Ancient Mariner,*
  Samuel Taylor Coleridge[1]

Contents

Part I

Part II

Part III

Part IV

Introduction

I MAGINE A HISTORY of the twentieth century in which the Holocaust is only a footnote to the Second World War. Where the encyclopedia entry for Auschwitz describes the flourishing chemical industry in the nearby town but omits the gas chambers. Where school textbooks describe Hitler as "gifted in a variety of ways" and limit the discussion of the mass murder he orchestrated to just forty-seven words, concluding that "no more than a hundred people knew about it." This isn't an abstract thought experiment. This was West Germany in the years following Hitler's defeat, when the Holocaust was all but forgotten and the Allies sanctioned the return of millions of former Nazis to forge a new country to serve as a bulwark against Communism. It was time, in the words of West German chancellor Konrad Adenauer in 1949, to "let bygones be bygones."[1]

This book is the story of Fritz Bauer, the remarkable Jewish prosecutor who with a small band of activists, lawyers, and survivors resolved that Germany and the world should not forget. This is also the story of Bauer's battle against the West German state that sought to stop him, as represented by its head of intelligence, Reinhard Gehlen, and the chancellor's right-hand man, Hans Globke, who both had their own reasons for covering up the past. Above all, this is the story of how the German people were made to face their complicity in the industrialized mass murder of Europe's Jews, and how the Holocaust came to define our collective sense of humanity.

Note on Text

THIS IS A WORK OF NONFICTION.

In reconstructing Fritz Bauer's life, I was privileged to interview many who knew him and to be granted access to unpublished family papers and correspondence. These sources, along with the thousands of pages of interviews, speeches, and journalistic and legal writings Bauer left behind, are the the basis for my descriptions of his thinking and many of his experiences. Scenes that it's clear Bauer would have observed have been re-created from testimonies, memoirs, and newspapers. I additionally drew from more than five thousand sources taken from forty-nine archives in Austria, the Czech Republic, Denmark, Germany, Great Britain, Israel, Italy, Poland, Russia, Sweden, and the United States.

Sources appear in the endnotes in the order in which they appear in each paragraph. I have not provided sources for information that is widely available. Archival sources are cited in full in the endnotes; books, articles, and other secondary sources appear in full in the bibliography, along with URLs for online sources. Quotations have been edited for spelling and punctuation but otherwise remain unchanged. I avoid acronyms unless they are commonplace, such as the SS for Schutzstaffel. I also use SS as an umbrella term encompassing the Sicherheitsdienst. West Germany and the Federal Republic are used interchangeably. For place names, I have retained national usage except where there are common anglicized versions. I use the name Oświęcim for the town and Auschwitz for the camp but refer to other Nazi death camps in Poland by their common Polish names. I have also used national letters in most circumstances, an exception being the German Eszett, which I've replaced with "ss."

All translations were carried out by my brilliant researche rs, Ingrid Pufahl, Harriet Phillips, Anna Schattschneider, Florine Miez, Sine Maria Vinther, Morten Baarvig Thomsen, Christian Kjellsson, Jonathan Cahana-Blum, and Katarzyna Chiżyńska, unless otherwise noted.

Prologue

Occupied Germany

Summer 1948

F RITZ BAUER GLANCED around the crowded carriage as the train reached the German border with Denmark near Flensburg. The painful dissonance of returning home as a German and a Jew—as though it were still possible to be both—pressed in on him as he showed his documents to a British guard. He was forty-five, a small man in a neatly tailored suit, his face prematurely lined and careworn. He had once been the youngest district judge in Germany, recognized as a rising voice in defense of the Weimar Republic, which claimed one of the most liberal constitutions in Europe. The Nazis had destroyed that vision when they seized control and enlisted the country in the industrialized mass murder of his people. Of the roughly half a million Jews who had lived in Germany in 1933, a third had been murdered and most of the remainder had fled. Bauer understood why many, including his surviving family, chose not to return to rebuild their shattered lives. Indeed, the World Jewish Congress had declared a few weeks earlier in June 1948 that it was "the determination of the Jewish people never again to settle on the bloodstained soil of Germany."[1]

Looking at his fellow passengers, Bauer wondered who among them had joined the cheering crowds that greeted Hitler's motorcade. Who had killed, or watched others kill? For Bauer, these were pressing questions not simply because of the danger he faced returning to a country where many might still wish him harm.[2]

They were questions he had to ask because he sought justice.

The anger that compelled him onto that train came from the knowledge that the Germans, the Allies—the world—seemed to think that
justice had already been served. The Allies had made it clear at the International Military Tribunal in Nuremberg in 1945 that they considered the crimes of the Nazis to have been carried out by Hitler and his
inner circle. Twenty-two Nazi leaders were convicted the next year and
several thousand more senior officials in subsequent trials and military
tribunals. It was the case that the Allies had attempted a broader scrutiny of German society through special denazification panels intended
to bar incriminated individuals from employment. But the effort had
largely petered out by 1948, as attention shifted to the Cold War.[3]

Bauer was staggered by the number of perpetrators who walked
free. Among them were Adolf Eichmann, the man who had transported Europe's Jews to the death camps; Josef Mengele, the SS doctor
who had performed selections for the gas chambers on the ramp in
Auschwitz; and Hans Globke, the bureaucrat who had helped create
the legal framework for what was to become known as the Holocaust.
But it wasn't simply the architects and implementers of the genocide
who remained at large. Hitler had enlisted the German people in a
national effort to persecute, plunder, and finally kill the entirety of Europe's Jews. Eight and a half million Germans had joined the Nazi
Party. More than 250,000 had served in the SS, which had operated the
death camps of Auschwitz, Majdanek, Treblinka, Bełżec, Chełmno,
and Sobibór and staffed special murder squads known as Einsatzgruppen. Tens of thousands of soldiers had committed atrocities on the
front lines. Countless civil servants had participated in the vast bureaucratic machinery of industrialized murder. And yet most of these
people had simply slipped back into German society and resumed
their lives as if nothing had happened.[4]

Bauer hoped to prosecute at least some of these men. He was returning to Germany for an interview to become attorney general in
the city of Braunschweig. But even if he got the job, he faced a struggle. Braunschweig was a provincial backwater, and he'd only have a
small team of prosecutors. He was painfully aware, too, that the courts

were stacked with Nazi-era judges who had enforced Hitler's racial laws, and that former SS men ran the police. In his optimistic moments, Bauer imagined provoking a wave of prosecutions that might ultimately bring thousands to justice. But even then, he knew that millions more who had aided and abetted Nazism would go free. His idea—incomplete and seemingly impossible—was to use the justice system to force a national reckoning. If he could compel his countrymen's attention through enough prosecutions, he might succeed in forcing them to confront their own complicity in the Nazis' crimes. Only then could Nazism be expunged from German culture, and his family and other survivors might begin to believe the horror would not be repeated.[5]

His train came to a halt in Flensburg. The city had escaped the worst of the bombing but not the postwar upheavals. The station was packed with passengers hauling bags or sitting on piles of luggage, wives in patched dresses searching for news of husbands missing since the war, runaway children, ticket touts, and the destitute begging. The humid air smelled of unwashed bodies and cigarette smoke. Half the country was still displaced, with tens of thousands of refugees from Soviet-occupied territory streaming to the West each month. Trains were overflowing with those desperate for passage, who clambered through carriage windows—even three years after the war, many still had no glass—or onto the roofs for more space.[6]

Bauer had no doubt seen images of Germany's ruined cityscapes on newsreels, but he was shaken as they passed the still-charred remains of the Altona-Nord and St. Georg neighborhoods outside Hamburg. Gray puddles had formed in the craters between rain-slicked piles of rubble, overgrown in places by grass and weeds, and piles of meticulously cleaned and salvaged bricks. He would need to find allies in this wasteland—not only like-minded judges, prosecutors, and politicians, but also ordinary Germans who hadn't succumbed to Nazism or abandoned their hope in the progressive promise of the Weimar years.[7]

His thoughts inevitably took him back to the country he had left more than a decade ago. He had believed in 1933 that he could rally the workers to resist Hitler in the name of a freer and more just Germany. He had nurtured this faith in his countrymen during his exile by banishing the memories of what they had done to him. But as the train carried him steadily back toward the scene of so much suffering, he knew that he, like his fellow Germans, needed to confront the past.[8]

Part I

1

Home

Ludwigsburg

February 1933

FRITZ BAUER KNEW the Nazis were watching them from the
moment he and his fellow marchers unfurled their flags and
stamped through the cold, shuttered streets of Ludwigsburg on Sunday, February 26, 1933. A week before, the new chancellor, Adolf Hitler, had called an election to gain a majority for the Nazi Party in the
German parliament, the Reichstag. Bauer and his small band of sixty
aging World War I veterans and factory workers had taken to the
streets to rally support for the country's democratic order they had
sworn to protect as members of the Reichsbanner militia. Bauer did
not know if Hitler would follow through on his threats to overturn the
constitution to rid the country of Jews and socialists. But he didn't
doubt that if Hitler won, then the Nazis would pursue their enemies
and that he, as a Jewish judge and outspoken critic, was surely one of
them.[1]

The twenty-nine-year-old had already come to their attention after
being appointed chairman of the Reichsbanner in the state of Württemberg and taking to the smoky auditoriums, men's clubs, and beer
halls of Stuttgart to rally against Hitler. "Bauer," observed one Nazi informant, "[has] with genuine Jewish impudence agitated against the
National Socialist movement at every opportunity. His weapons . . . :
hatred, lies, and slander."[2]

Bauer was certainly an impressive speaker. Away from a stage, he
could be shy and diffident, a slim delicate man in a suit that seemed too

Fritz Bauer, c. 1920s
Courtesy of Marit Tiefenthal

big for him, his head invariably stuck in a book as he walked down the
street dodging lampposts. Indeed, when Bauer had first offered to
campaign for the Social Democrats, the main progressive party of the
Weimar Republic, the local leader, Kurt Schumacher, noted Bauer's law
doctorate, soft jawline, and propensity to quote Goethe and declared:
"Workers don't like intellectuals." But Bauer had persisted, and Schumacher, impressed by his quiet charisma and evident sensitivity to the
plight of others, agreed to let him speak at a few rallies. He was surprised by the result: Placed before a crowd, Bauer grew fierce and im-
passioned; his transformation onstage was so surprising, recalled one
contemporary, that his words felt like a jolt of electricity.[3]

Bauer sensed his men's unease as he led them past the prim, swastika-
lined shop windows in Ludwigsburg. Nazis were likely already watching them, noting who was there and mobilizing the local Brownshirts,
Hitler's paramilitary, to confront them. Bauer roused his men as best
he could at rallies in the working-class districts of Pflugfelden, Eg-
losheim, Hoheneck, and finally Ossweil, where they chanted "Hail
Freedom" and their breath rose in a cloud in the chill evening air. Defending the Weimar Republic, Bauer believed, was worth the risk. The
republic's constitution, established in the aftermath of World War I,
had granted universal suffrage and rights to freedom of expression and
assembly. Workers had gained protection for the eight-hour day and

better access to healthcare, while the country's gay rights movement was openly calling for the decriminalization of homosexuality.[4]

Yet the republic's darker side was never far from Bauer's mind. As a Jewish student in Munich in the early 1920s, he'd been barred from joining most fraternities. He'd watched his right-wing classmates flock to Hitler's beer hall speeches and then spill out onto the streets looking for socialists and Jews to beat up. These experiences had pushed Bauer to find his political voice, first by rallying students on campus to embrace a "tolerant way of life" and then by joining the Social Democratic Party as his legal career began in Stuttgart and support for the Nazi party surged following the Great Depression of 1929.[5]

Night fell and the marchers made their way back through Nazi territory toward Ludwigsburg train station. Bauer registered the police as they passed the market square. Then he heard an angry cry and suddenly a red-faced, slick-haired gang of Brownshirts was upon them. Bauer was caught in a flailing press of bodies as the Nazis beat the Reichsbanner down the hill to the station, where the police finally blew their whistles to intervene.[6]

The next morning, a Monday, back in Stuttgart, Bauer shaved, brushed his hair, and got ready for court. He was lucky that he bore no marks from the confrontation, but that seemed a minor concern as he considered what would happen if the Nazis won the election. Was he prepared to keep fighting or even go to jail for his beliefs? His thoughts turned uncomfortably to the reasons why the Nazis would come for him. Political activism wasn't a crime, at least not yet. His love life was a different matter. He didn't think they knew he was gay—a secret he had shared with only a few friends—although he couldn't be sure; the police regularly surveilled popular hookup spots in parks and public urinals.[7]

Bauer also worried about his parents, with whom he still lived in a generous apartment on Wiederholdstrasse. He'd tried to shield them from the Nazi vitriol he'd already attracted, both for their own sake and because his father, Ludwig, did not appreciate his son's socialist convictions. Ludwig was a short man with a thrusting jaw, clipped

Bauer with a friend, c. 1920s
Courtesy of Marit Tiefenthal

mustache, and beady eyes who at age forty-five had volunteered for the front lines of the Great War. He was proud of the way Jews like himself had fought for Germany and made sure to pass on his faith in the fatherland and belief in duty and obedience to Bauer and his younger sister, Margot. As a child, Bauer had sat in dread at the dining room table, awaiting a thrashing for some transgression—a hand moving too soon or a word spoken out of turn. Ludwig, now sixty-three, disliked Hitler's crude talk about the Volk and racial purity, and was offended by the Nazis' refusal to acknowledge the sacrifices of Jewish soldiers. But he was skeptical of democracy—at least the Weimar kind—which he felt was an imposition of the Allies following the country's defeat, and thoroughly un-German. Like many Jews, he was confident that the Nazis' antisemitic fervor would pass, and broadly agreed with Hitler's promise to end political factionalism and restore the glory of the Reich.[8]

Ludwig's values reflected the politics of an earlier generation that had come of age following German unification in 1871. Chancellor Otto von Bismarck had imposed an authoritarian style of government on an otherwise fractious array of German states and princely holdings and promoted the German language and culture as a unifying force. Jews were granted full legal equality, and families like the Bauers took advantage of rapid industrialization and the emergence of a mass soci-

Ludwig Bauer, c. 1920s   *Ella Bauer, c. 1920s*
Courtesy of Marit Tiefenthal   Courtesy of Marit Tiefenthal

ety to grow their businesses. For Ludwig, Hitler represented the return
of order.[9]

Bauer was close to his mother, Ella, eleven years Ludwig's junior, a
quietly determined woman who comforted young Fritz after her husband's rages. Ella came from a family of rabbis in Tübingen, and while
she had allowed Ludwig's secular views to prevail, her spiritualism
filled the household. The family were members of the local synagogue
and observed Passover and other high holidays; Bauer spoke regularly
at a liberal Jewish organization and was treasurer of its youth group.
Bauer felt that Ella trusted his judgment, and he shared with her most
things, even his homosexuality.[10]

He often found Ella in the kitchen in the mornings with coffee ready,
which he took with a cigarette by way of breakfast. Then he was off to
work down the hill, past the family's textile business on Seestrasse, and
across Kriegsbergstrasse, the city's main thoroughfare, to the Schloss-
garten, an elegant park lined with poplars and plane trees. Stuttgart
was the largest city in southwest Germany, provincial compared to
Berlin, but no less transformed by the forces of modernity. The city
had erected its first skyscraper, the sixteen-story Tagblatt Tower, with a
high-speed elevator and viewing gallery where visitors could admire
the panorama: the half-timbered buildings of the old town, the grand
city hall, the gleaming glass edifice of the Jewish-owned Schocken

Bauer and university friends, 1920s
Courtesy of Marit Tiefenthal

department store, and the low hills on all sides, topped with vineyards and forests where Bauer liked to hike. Those who could afford distractions filled the cafés and restaurants under the linden trees or "briskly jazzed" at the Regina and Residenz Cafés.[11]

Most of Bauer's colleagues in the staid sandstone courthouse on Archivstrasse were older than him and deeply conservative. Several of his superiors supported Nazism and as Hitler rose to prominence, they had sought to push Bauer out. Two years earlier, someone had leaked a story to the *NS-Kurier,* the local Nazi newspaper, that Bauer had passed on court details to a left-wing journalist. This in itself was not illegal, but the *NS-Kurier* had seized on the case as an example of perfidious Jewish infiltration of the judiciary. Bauer sued for libel and won, but he was still demoted to the civil courts and limited to handling minor offenses. He could have joined a lucrative private practice, but he felt that even in a lesser role inside the court he still had more value to the Left as a source of intelligence and counsel to activists targeted by the police.[12]

On this Monday, with the fate of the Republic in the balance, such incremental resistance seemed futile. Bauer hurried from the courthouse after work to join Schumacher at their usual spot in the crowded lobby of Hotel Zeppelin by the train station. Bauer looked to the thirty-seven-year-old Schumacher for political guidance and moral clarity. Like many Social Democrats in Stuttgart, Bauer was rather daunted by the Reichstag representative who had lost an arm in the war.[13]

Kurt Schumacher, 1936
AdsD/FES, 6/FOTA008945

Schumacher "had a face like a shrivelled apple, lips as thin as if they had been cut into his face with a razor blade, and ice-cold green eyes," noted one of Bauer's political friends, Fred Uhlman. "You could feel his willpower and his unconditional belief in the absolute rightness of his cause. . . . I was afraid of him."[14]

Schumacher had been among the most outspoken critics of the country's rightward shift since the Nazis had become Germany's largest party in 1932. For the first time in German history, he told the Reichstag, the Nazis had "managed to fully mobilize human stupidity." But his words were no counter to Hitler's evident appeal to the country. People across the political spectrum seemed to read into Hitler their own aspirations. Industrialists thought that behind his performative fury was someone who would protect their money. Socialist revolutionaries saw a firebrand prepared to confront the aristocracy. There was even the Association of German National Jews, which supported Hitler because they shared some of his animus toward Jewish immigrants from Eastern Europe. Schumacher had reluctantly come to see that Hitler's rise to power was inevitable, but he hoped that because the Nazis lacked an outright majority their radicalism would be contained by more mainstream governing partners. He supported the decision of the Center Party of conservatives to form a coalition with the Nazis, which gave Hitler the chancellorship in January 1933. "We'll box Hitler in," Center Party leader Franz von Papen had promised. "In two months, we'll have pushed Hitler so far into a corner that he'll squeal." Hitler immediately called an election for March 5 in a clear sign he meant to dispense with any constraints from his governing partners. And to Schumacher's alarm, the Reich president Paul von Hindenburg and his fellow conservatives went along with Hitler's desire to upend the democratic order.[15]

As Schumacher and Bauer met that evening of February 27, 1933, the news broke that someone had set fire to the Reichstag. Hitler, arriving at the flaming wreckage at 10:00 P.M., immediately blamed the Communists. There would be "no mercy now," he declared. "Anyone who stands in our way will be cut down." Dozens of leading Communist politicians were arrested in the early hours of the morning. The next day, Hindenburg granted Hitler emergency powers to suspend habeas corpus, freedom of the press, the right to public assembly, and the right to free association. The measures were meant to target the Communist Party, but it soon became clear that the Nazis would use these new powers to prevent a free and fair election. In Stuttgart, the police descended on left-wing rallies and seized socialist publications. Four Social Democrats burst into the recording studio of the city's radio station to declare, "Down with Hitler! Long live freedom—vote for the SPD [Social Democrats]!" and were promptly arrested.[16]

Schumacher was not to be intimidated. So long as there was an election, there was a chance. He held a rally on Saturday, March 4, the eve of the vote. Fourteen thousand supporters crowded in front of the city hall beneath a poster of Karl Marx and joined in an old revolutionary song: "Black is the powder, red is the blood, golden flickers the flame."[17]

That night, leading activists, some armed, gathered at the law offices of Bauer's friend Uhlman near the courthouse. Bauer, in a wild mood, thought he should summon two thousand Reichsbanner men to take to the streets. Others suggested calling a strike or seizing the train station and bringing southern Germany's railway to a halt. Schumacher, however, feared that any mass action would lead to clashes and perhaps even spark a civil war if socialists in other parts of the country did the same. He advised them to vote the next morning and trust that democracy would prevail.[18]

Results were announced on Monday, March 6. The Nazi Party won 43.9 percent of the vote, forty-two seats short of a majority. But Hitler still claimed he had a mandate to suspend the constitution entirely and henceforth rule by decree. The impending dictatorship scarcely seemed to register in the mainstream press, where editors chose to be cautiously optimistic. "Calm Election Process," reported the *Badische Presse*. It was now time, ran its editorial, for the new government to bring the people together with "impartiality and justice." The Nazi press, by contrast, was euphoric. "The chains have fallen, the people are free," triumphed the *NS-Kurier*. Bauer was devastated; the democracy had all but collapsed.[19]

The Nazis moved to consolidate power and eliminate freedoms faster than Bauer had feared possible. Brownshirts took control of the city's main radio station, the Süddeutsche Rundfunk AG, within hours of the election results being announced. They ordered the station's employees to assemble in the courtyard of the building. One of the technicians, a short, heavyset man dressed in a balaclava and black leather trench coat, with a revolver, and a pair of binoculars around his neck, appeared at a balcony overlooking the courtyard and delivered a blazing speech about the dawn of a new era. Staff were ordered to greet one another with "Heil Hitler" and encouraged to apply for party membership.[20]

The next day, the Nazis installed a special state commissioner in Stuttgart, as they did in other regions, with the powers to bypass the municipal council. The new governor ordered the occupation of the police barracks and the seizure of weapons. Heavily armed Brownshirts were soon standing guard outside most government buildings, and a swastika flag hung from the city hall. By the end of the week, the Nazis had closed the city's cabaret and the Schauspielhaus, where an operetta staged by a Jewish director had attracted their ire. Brownshirts also picketed the city's three largest department stores, all owned by Jewish families, handing out flyers that read "Germans! Buy only in German shops."[21]

Bauer was terrified by his countrymen's apparent acquiescence. He continued to work in the courthouse but stayed at different friends'

SWEDEN

Baltic Sea

LATVIA

Riga

LITHUANIA

Neman

Kovno

Königsberg

EAST
PRUSSIA

Stettin

DANZIG

Narew

Vistula

Bug

Oder

Warta

Warsaw

Łódź

Lublin

POLAND

Breslau

Kraków

Prague

Oświęcim

CZECHOSLOVAKIA

Carpathians

Danube

Vienna

Bratislava

AUSTRIA

HUNGARY

Budapest

*Central
Europe, 1933*
John Gilkes

houses most nights for his parents' safety. It seemed only a matter of time before he would be arrested. On Friday, March 10, two hundred Communists were rounded up in Stuttgart and placed in "protective custody," a Nazi euphemism for detainment without trial. Hundreds more were arrested over the following week, including the first Social Democrats. Stuttgart's prisons couldn't process the influx of so many prisoners, and rumors circulated that the Nazis were preparing a concentration camp outside the city. Bauer had heard of such camps: The British had used them during the Boer War, rounding up whole villages to stop them from supporting rebels, and the Soviets had built camps following the 1917 revolution in order to isolate political opponents. But he'd never imagined they would be used by Germany to imprison its own people.[22]

Some activists fled to Switzerland and Czechoslovakia, but Schumacher made it clear that he intended to stay and urged Bauer and his comrades to do the same. They had a duty to resist.[23]

．　．　．

Bauer was in his office on March 23, a cloudy Thursday, when he heard a knock at the door. Several officers from Württemberg's political police department entered, confirmed his identity, and declared him under arrest. His fellow judges watched silently as he was led down the corridor and out of the building to a waiting police van for the short drive to the prison on Büchsenstrasse, where he was crammed into a cell with ten inmates. Bauer had hardly settled when Dietrich von Jagow, the newly appointed Nazi police chief who had led the Brownshirts in Württemberg, opened the door. "We don't just arrest small people," he gloated. "We've also got district court judge Bauer with us."[24]

Bauer understood that his arrest was part of a national campaign to crush the opposition and recognized others in his cell as left-wing activists and trade unionists. Indeed, that evening Hitler fulfilled his promise to suspend the constitution by forcing a so-called Enabling Act through the Reichstag that effectively granted him unlimited power.

Nothing now held the Nazis back. Social Democratic members of the parliament who bravely voted against the measure were led away into waiting police vans. Tens of thousands of political opponents were seized over the following weeks and held in makeshift camps converted from restaurants, pubs, hotels, castles, and sports grounds, where violence and abuse were widespread.[25]

A few days after Bauer's arrest, the guards loaded him and his cellmates onto a truck. They headed south on a road Bauer knew well—it passed Tübingen, where he had once played as a child amid the rolls of fabric in his grandfather's textile shop. Then they began to climb steadily into the Swabian hills and finally arrived at a newly instituted concentration camp on the glittering icebound Heuberg plateau.[26]

The trucks pulled up to a row of a dozen three-story white buildings set sideways to the street and separated into pairs by rolls of barbed wire strung out on wooden posts. The buildings had served as a children's recreation home, and some of the property, separated by a fence, was still in use; children could be seen playing nearby. A crowd of Brownshirts waited for the prisoners, several of whom knew of Bauer from street brawls with the Reichsbanner.[27]

Bauer was led to the commandant's office, where he was stripped of his valuables and registered as a category III prisoner: an "irreconcilable" enemy of the regime. Max Kaufmann, the commandant, explained matter-of-factly that Bauer was unlikely ever to be released. The guards separated Bauer and the other category III prisoners and led them to block 19a, one of a pair of buildings for the irreconcilables set back from the street with a small courtyard between them that was enclosed by a fence. The first two floors of the building contained the prisoners' rooms with thirty to forty men in each. The guards had a room to themselves next to the entrance.[28]

At some point that evening or the next, Bauer heard footsteps on the stairs. Guards burst in and dragged him upstairs to the building's narrow attic, where he saw several other prisoners huddling on the floor. Wilfred Acker, a Communist, was the first to be savagely beaten by the guards. Bauer's turn soon came. The only time he'd been assaulted like

Heuberg concentration camp, 1933
Creative Commons

this had been in the schoolyard as a six-year-old when he'd made the mistake of answering a question a fellow student had gotten wrong. As his classmates had punched and kicked him, they'd shouted, "You and your family killed Jesus."[29]

Bauer awoke the next morning to another beating, and then another. He tried to keep track of time by the light from a small window. But when one of his cellmates was caught peering through to the courtyard, the head guard threatened to shoot them all and the window was painted over, leaving them in virtual darkness.[30]

After what Bauer guessed was several more days, he was released to join the other prisoners. Category I and II prisoners from the other blocks spent their days laboring around the camp, but Bauer and the other "irreconcilables" kept to their rooms—work could not redeem them, according to the commandant. Mealtimes were the only highlight, usually little more than a broth of cabbage and noodles with a lump of hard black sausage or cheese. On occasion they received soup with swastika-shaped pasta pieces, to "renew us . . . from the inside out," noted one prisoner.[31]

Then, in early April, Bauer was summoned to the commandant's office. He didn't know whether to steel himself for more abuse or if some sort of ruling had been made in his case. Commandant Kaufmann was at his desk. A man in a suit, who introduced himself as Edmund Taylor, the Paris correspondent for the *Chicago Tribune,* sat before him. The

Reich's new propaganda minister, Joseph Goebbels, eager to ensure that Nazi rule was accepted across Europe and the United States, had invited journalists like Taylor to visit the new concentration camps on the assumption that some aspects of prisoner life—the roll calls and regular meals—would appear normal.[32]

"Do you know why you're here?" Taylor asked.[33]

Bauer looked at him warily, suddenly conscious of his own appearance: thin, dirty, dressed in the same clothes he'd worn on the day of his arrest. He knew he shouldn't say too much.

"Yes. I am a socialist and vice president of the Reichsbanner organization in Stuttgart."[34]

"How are you treated?"[35]

"Humanely, and in a manner corresponding to the situation," Bauer answered carefully. "Nothing more could be done for the prisoners under the present conditions."[36]

"What's the worst feature of prison life for you?" Taylor asked.[37]

Bauer said he missed his family and the monotony of prison was maddening.[38]

"But the worst," he said, "is the feeling that my life has crumbled to pieces under me. I feel mentally crushed. I am beaten by my environment."[39]

Taylor later described the camp in his story as "halfway between a health resort and Devil's Island." Bauer, he noted, looked like a "furtive-eyed piece of human wreckage . . . [who] wore the stamp of prison as if he had been serving for years."[40]

. . .

Bauer tried to keep track of events outside the camp through the steady stream of new arrivals. Thus he learned that one of the Führer's first measures was to ban Jews from the civil service and the judiciary, effectively ending Bauer's hope of ever going back to work. The Social Democratic Party was outlawed in June. There was no word of any resistance and the surest sign of the Nazis' growing sense of impunity was their ever harsher treatment of prisoners. A new commandant named Karl Buck, a committed Nazi with a toothbrush mustache and a peg leg, introduced a special ritual for new prisoners: The entire garrison assembled to form two rows between which the prisoners were forced to pass while the guards pushed, kicked, and spat on them. On the block, guards began lashing out at the smallest provocation and brutal little games developed: They chased prisoners on the way to the latrines or lined them up beside the block facing the building to have their faces smacked against the wall.[41]

One morning in late July, Bauer noticed the guards cutting swatches of stinging nettles beside the fence. He learned what they were for later that day when a truck pulled up with a batch of new prisoners. Kurt Schumacher got out and staggered down the line of guards as they whipped him with the nettles until he reached a waiting Commandant Buck.[42]

"Why are you here, Schumacher?" Buck asked.[43]

"Because I belong to the defeated party," Schumacher replied.[44]

He was then pushed and harried toward Bauer's block.[45]

"Why don't you hang yourself? You'll never get out of here!" a camp guard yelled at him.[46]

"No, you'll have to take responsibility for that yourself," said Schumacher, catching the eyes of his fellow prisoners.[47]

Bauer snatched a hurried reunion later. "I'll be here until Nazism is gone," Schumacher told him, "and Nazism won't be gone until war breaks out, which it inevitably will. I reckon it will take ten, eleven years; that's how long I'll be here." Bauer, who had been three months in the camp and just turned thirty, despaired at the prospect.[48]

The guards took a special pleasure in harassing Schumacher that sweltering summer and Bauer was also singled out for humiliating tasks like cleaning out the latrine. So far, he'd been targeted for his politics, but he noticed that guards had started to single out prisoners for their Jewishness. In September, a forty-five-year-old Jewish man named Simon Leibowitsch, who worked for the national railway, arrived in Heuberg and was beaten so badly that he had to be carried to his room in Bauer's block. When the guards ordered the prisoners to fetch firewood that afternoon, Leibowitsch, still incapacitated, stayed in bed. Buck was summoned and ordered Leibowitsch brought to the water trough outside for a "washing." Two guards proceeded to scrub Leibowitsch down with a rough brush while kicking him and repeatedly holding his head underwater. His shuddering screams between dunkings rang out over the square.[49]

"Don't act like that, you filthy Jewish pig!" yelled one guard.[50]

"Jews have to be scrubbed so they don't stink anymore," cried the other.[51]

Leibowitsch, insensible, was finally released. But the next morning, the guards set on him again, dragging him down the stairs of the block so his head hit one step at a time. By the time they reached the bottom, Leibowitsch was dead.[52]

.   .   .

A few weeks later, as the autumn of 1933 began, Bauer and some other "irreconcilables" were transferred to a former garrison prison sixty miles away in the city of Ulm. He was given his own cell with a bed, a relief after the overcrowding of Heuberg. The prison jailer, Gotthilf Knäuer, a long-serving police officer and not a Nazi, called the prisoners "gentlemen," gave Bauer a job in his office processing censored letters, and prevented nighttime harassment of the inmates by taking home the only key to their cells. The reason for Bauer's move to Ulm soon became clear. While working in Knäuer's office, Bauer learned that he and the other irreconcilables were to be released if they agreed to pledge loyalty to the regime.[53]

The news caused a sensation among the selected prisoners, many of whom had come to believe the commandant's promise that they would be imprisoned for life. Bauer knew Schumacher wouldn't condone renouncing their party or beliefs. But then again, he wasn't a Jew. Bauer agreed to sign, as did many of the others. In advance of his release, the Nazis issued a press statement on October 22, 1933. Bauer was reported to be "joyful" at the opportunity for reconciliation with the Nazi regime and to now "stand unreservedly on the side of the Fatherland in the German struggle for honor and peace."[54]

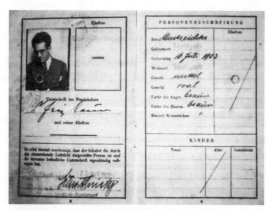

Bauer's passport, 1932
Courtesy of Marit Tiefenthal

The truth was that Bauer was shattered by his six months in the camp—just as the Nazis had intended. He still had the presence of mind to locate his prisoner file in the office, remove his passport, and slip it into an envelope addressed to his parents. But he looked a broken figure as he emerged from the prison gates on November 27 in his ragged suit, head freshly shaved in a final degrading act by the authorities to whom he would have to report regularly. His sister, Margot, and her husband, Walter, brought him home in their car.[55]

Bauer didn't want to talk about the camp with his family, so they discussed the worsening situation instead. The Nazis had promulgated a disorientating array of anti-Jewish measures during his incarceration: The number of Jewish students at German schools and universities had been restricted; Jewish doctors were barred from practice and Jewish civilian workers fired from the army. In Stuttgart, the local Nazis had escalated their boycott of Jewish businesses into a citywide campaign that included painting the word *Jude* in red on shop windows. Dozens of Jewish families had already fled the city for life outside Germany. Indeed, Walter, a twenty-seven-year-old textile merchant and keen amateur photographer, was making plans to relocate to Copenhagen with Margot and their two young sons. Margot, usually high-spirited, seemed overwhelmed at the thought of breaking up the family. But Ludwig had no intention of leaving. He still believed Hitler when he said that Jewish veterans would not face persecution. Besides, his business was booming; Hitler's drive to rearm the country meant Stuttgart's factories had full order-books.[56]

The conversation turned to what Bauer would do for work now that he could no longer practice law. Bauer realized he had little choice but to agree to his father's invitation to join him in the warehouse. He began filing paperwork and keeping accounts a few days later. Otherwise he was a virtual recluse, overwhelmed with guilt for his act of submission and almost paralyzed by fear of others. On his way to visit relatives, Bauer somehow slipped and fell, breaking a couple of ribs, which he put down to his enfeebled condition. "Released prisoners know," Bauer would later write, "that punishment does not end at the prison or even the penitentiary gate." He thought about leaving Germany, but he also couldn't imagine a life in exile.[57]

Adding to his alienation, the city's inhabitants seemed to carry on as if nothing had changed. As Christmas approached, the market square filled with stalls selling hutzelbrot and springerle cookies embossed with designs, string sausages, and peanuts. Girls from the newly renamed Adolf Hitler School sang carols. Bauer played a little with his sister's children when they came over, performing an ironic show in which Ludwig the policeman arrested Bauer the criminal. "Very impressive was his face behind bars," observed Margot.[58]

As the winter of 1933 deepened, Bauer forced himself to reach out to a few friends. One, Werner Fleischhauer, had joined the Nazi Party, having decided that liberalism was dead and the future lay with the Volk. An old intimate, Helmut Mielke, offered encouragement and possibly a more tender connection, but the thought of pursuing sexual encounters was far from Bauer's mind. The Nazis had made it clear that gay men—like Jews, Roma, Sinti, and "asocial" types that included the homeless, sex workers, and pacifists—were to be especially targeted. In May, Brownshirts and far-right students in Berlin had attacked the Institute for Sexual Science set up by the gay rights pioneer Magnus Hirschfeld, burning its books and arresting staff. More reprisals were feared.[59]

Bauer felt sufficiently recovered as the weather warmed in 1934 to meet some youth activists from the now-outlawed Social Democratic Party. They went hiking outside the city and spoke of their

Bauer, c. 1934
Courtesy of Marit Tiefenthal

disappointment with the older generation, whom they blamed for not doing more to stop Hitler's rise to power. One young man, Hans Gasparitsch, said he had arranged for leaflets denouncing Hitler to be stashed in school toilets.[60]

"Do you see the goal toward which Hitler is marching?" he wrote in one. "German youth, do you want war and Germany's destruction?"[61]

Bauer thought they were taking dangerous risks. The country had increasingly come to resemble a police state. Heinrich Himmler, the head of Hitler's personal protection squad, known as the Schutzstaffel or SS, had taken over the old political police of the Weimar Republic and was in the process of rebranding it the Geheime Staatspolizei—secret police—or Gestapo for short. Under his direction, the force had rapidly built up a network of informants. Every block and apartment building now had its spies. The summer months passed in a state of anxiety for Bauer. While the Nazis released many of those they had detained the year before, the Gestapo had begun a new wave of more targeted arrests. Several of the youth activists were detained during Christmas, ending even this limited underground work.[62]

That spring of 1935, Bauer's thoughts turned to joining the thousands of Jews fleeing the country. Margot and Walter had managed to secure residency permits in Denmark and invited him to join them. Bauer still couldn't fully imagine leaving Germany—even this Germany—for good. Instead, he booked an exploratory trip to Copenhagen, arriving in the Danish capital by train on the evening of June 1. Outside the main station, the northern sun was only just dipping, but the colorful lights of Tivoli, Copenhagen's amusement park, were already lit. He felt a weight lift as he walked along Vesterbrogade to Rådhuspladsen, where the red bricks of the town hall glowed in the soft amber light, the neon advertising boards flicked on, and crowds of workers, shopgirls, and town officials queued for trams beside vendors selling sausages, cigarettes, and bunches of flowers. The first strains of jazz came from the bars and restaurants on Strøget. Copenhagen was a city of "some sad rectangular lakes with artificial bird islands, banal ugly bridges and screaming seagulls," observed the left-wing writer Mogens Klitgaard, although he did concede it had a quiet and easy charm.[63]

Walter and Margot Tiefenthal, c. 1930
Courtesy of Marit Tiefenthal

Indeed, the Copenhagen Bauer discovered was buzzing with the arrival of hundreds of German political refugees. Under the terms of their asylum, they were forbidden from speaking out publicly against the Nazi regime, but German activists prepared reports on conditions in Germany for dissemination in Britain and America without getting into trouble. Walter Hammer, a left-wing publisher, handed anti-Nazi flyers to surprised German tourists outside Tivoli. Bauer valued the general spirit of tolerance he found in Denmark toward Germans, even Jewish ones. He took a liking to one of the bars, Café Mokka, near

Rådhuspladsen, that was popular with emigrés and played jazz until the early hours. Denmark seemed to Bauer everything that Nazi Germany was not: It had a Social Democratic government and minority rights, and sex between men over the age of eighteen was legal.[64]

He returned to Germany at the end of June 1935, hoping to convince his parents to move with him to Copenhagen. But Ludwig was determined to remain, even after Hitler announced at a party rally in Nuremberg in September that Jews were to be stripped of their citizenship, their right to vote, and most of their basic legal protections. A further decree outlawed sexual relations and marriage between Jews and people "of German or related blood." Up until that point, anti-Jewish legislation had been piecemeal. But the Nuremberg Race Laws, as they became known, represented the Nazis' first systematic attempt to isolate Jews from the rest of German society.[65]

Hitler's decrees also overrode his earlier promise to protect Jewish veterans. And yet Ludwig still refused to leave, holding on to the increasingly flimsy excuse that he had his business to run. Bauer had made his mind up to go, but he hesitated at the thought of leaving without his parents. Then, in January 1936, he was picked up again by the police for a day of questioning about a soldier he'd met at the train station. The Gestapo suspected him of resistance work, which was lucky, because the real reason for the rendezvous was possibly sexual. Himmler had passed legislation that branded gay men "a danger to the national health" and made any suspicious contact between men punishable by five years' hard labor. A further decree proposed forced sterilization and castration.[66]

Upon his release, Bauer hastily arranged his application for asylum in Denmark. He returned to a frigid Copenhagen on March 15, 1936, with several hundred reichsmarks from his father and plans to write for social democratic and Jewish newspapers. He found a comfortable ground-floor apartment in Amager, a short walk from his sister's place and the beach. His political asylum application was sponsored by a left-wing organization, the Matteotti Committee, on condition he refrain from provocative statements.[67]

But now that he was free, a reckless mood had seized him. He wrote a scathing opinion piece on how the German national character had led to Nazism, but no papers would run it. Undeterred, he started work on a political satire of Germany provisionally titled "Dirt Shines When the Sun Shines."[68]

One evening in April, Bauer finished up his drink at Café Mokka and walked the short distance down Strøget to Rådhuspladsen. It was cold and wet and the neon advertising billboards cast a sheen over the stones. Bauer felt a nervous thrill at the shape of the young man approaching him. He had a sly smile and big brown eyes that seemed to both mock Bauer and ask for his sympathy. His price was four kroner, around twenty dollars today.[69]

Bauer sought out the young man again a few nights later. He was hungry, so Bauer bought him something to eat and this time they talked. His name was Gordon Torp. He'd grown up poor, one of six, and been a sailor for a while, but now he was trying to make a living as a craftsman. Torp had been in prison for a few months for theft and prostitution. He wasn't just interested in money, he suggested to Bauer, a little coyly perhaps.[70]

They met again on April 16. This time Bauer brought Torp back to his apartment. He knew he would be opening himself to blackmail—but he longed to lie with Torp in his own bed.[71]

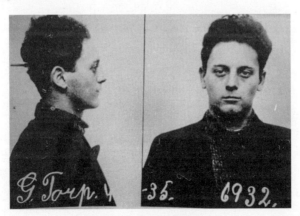

Gordon Torp, 1945
Poul Christensen / Danish National Archive

The yellow trams to Højdevej in Amager left Rådhuspladsen every fifteen minutes. It was then a short walk back to his apartment. Bauer led the way along the garden path to his door.[72]

He beckoned Torp inside. No one would be awake in the upstairs apartment. In the sudden stillness of the building, he could hear Torp breathing, as well as his own shallow breaths. Bauer brought Torp to his bedroom and began to undress, the younger man watching but not touching. Bauer turned off the light and in the darkness reached for Torp.[73]

2

Flight

B AUER TRIED TO settle into life in Denmark that summer of 1936 but was often frustrated. As a political refugee, he was unable to work officially and could earn only a pittance writing for newspapers and selling lace for his brother-in-law's company. Despite his best efforts to learn the language and seek out friends among Danish Social Democrats, he was often made to feel unwelcome. Neighbors and local shopkeepers threw him suspicious glances on the street and the police hassled him constantly. Indeed, the day after bringing Gordon Torp home, he had been summoned to police headquarters for questioning. A police inspector, it emerged, had been watching him and Torp from the bushes of his garden. Bauer at first tried to claim that Torp was teaching him Danish but then openly admitted to being gay and having given Torp food and money. He knew they couldn't arrest him for sleeping with a man, but that didn't stop the police from hauling him in again after he moved in with another lover. This time his brother-in-law, Walter, was also summoned. A usually affable man, Walter stammered out that Bauer was a bookworm and a scholar of an impractical nature who wasn't "interested in women and not at all in men."[1]

Bauer tried to ignore the harassment as best he could, but he felt a deeper unease over the following months. Danish life was too insular and self-contented. The Danes "eat their Smørrebrød, drink their few bottles of beer with schnapps, skip no opportunity for coffee and cake in the afternoon and evening and at night [ask], 'are we really doing so well?'" he observed. Meanwhile, thousands languished in German concentration camps and Hitler was openly preparing for war.[2]

Part of Bauer's anger came from the powerlessness he felt at being unable to help his parents as Nazi terror increased. A Reich ministry official named Hans Globke had written a commentary for the Nuremberg Race Laws in November 1936 to guide the courts and the police as to who should be classed as a Jew. A raft of new measures to isolate, exploit, and persecute Jews had swiftly followed over the next year. Bauer's parents were restricted to shopping in Jewish stores and barred from public parks and most clubs and societies. Under one Interior Ministry law written by Globke, Ludwig and Ella had to add *Israel* and *Sara* to their names to ensure they could not pass as "Aryan." Then in October 1938, Ludwig's textile business was "Aryanized"—that is, sold to ethnic Germans for next to nothing.[3]

Bauer was struck particularly hard by the news that the family had been forced to sell his grandfather's textile shop in Tübingen. Bauer fondly remembered his grandfather, a rabbi with a bushy mustache and kindly manner who used to read him the Torah. The apartment had seemed "bathed in a mysterious dusky light." He loved to nestle into the floral brocade of his grandparents' sagging sofa and gaze at portraits of past generations. He remembered one book in particular, *The Flowers of Jerusalem,* which contained pressed blossoms from the Holy Land: olive, orange, and violets from Nazareth and Tiberias. Now this world was gone.[4]

Bauer feared it might be too late for his parents to escape to Denmark. Countries across Europe were closing their borders to Jews as thousands continued to flee each month. In July 1938, the League of Nations had hosted a summit in Évian, France, to discuss the plight of tens of thousands of refugees, mostly Jews, fleeing the Third Reich. Little was achieved. Sweden and Switzerland announced they would no longer accept being Jewish as a valid claim for asylum and agreed to a proposal from the Nazi Interior Ministry that German Jews were to have a red *J* stamped in their passports. The Danish government imposed its own restrictions, requiring Jews to show proof of their intention to return to Germany. Bauer hoped to make a case to the Danish authorities that his parents were being persecuted because of him and therefore should be considered political asylees. He had himself been stripped of his German citizenship that summer. He wasn't sure how he felt about being stateless. If he wasn't a German, then what was he? A Jew? He'd always resisted defining himself according to his Jewishness, but perhaps that had been naïve.[5]

Then disaster struck. On November 7, 1938, Herschel Grynszpan, a seventeen-year-old Polish-German Jew, shot a German embassy official in Paris, who died two days later. The Nazis used the killing as a pretext for a mass pogrom that started on the evening of November 9. In Stuttgart, the city's fire chief broke into the main synagogue on Hospitalstrasse, doused the interior with benzine, and set the building ablaze. Crowds watched as gangs of Brownshirts in civilian clothes looted Jewish businesses on Königstrasse. The violence escalated over the next few days. Eight hundred Jewish men were dragged from their homes in the city, including Bauer's uncles Arthur and Leopold Hirsch, for deportation to concentration camps. Bauer's fourteen-year-old nephew, Erich, was attacked by a gang of Nazis in the Jewish orphanage where he lived while his mother worked. He managed to escape and ran ten miles through the driving rain to the Bauers' apartment in Stuttgart.[6]

At least ninety-one Jews were killed and thirty thousand interned in the camps during the pogrom. Bauer wasn't able to reach his parents, but he didn't wait, and pushed for a meeting with the Danish justice minister, Karl Kristian Steincke, to arrange their visas. Steincke, a fellow Social Democrat, agreed to see him, only to issue a flat refusal. How could he make an exception for Bauer's family, Steincke wanted to know, without opening the country to the whole of German Jewry?[7]

Then give my parents permission to go to Greenland, Bauer snapped. Denmark's frozen territory might be inhospitable, but if his parents went there, at least "I would know that [they] are alive!"[8]

Steincke, perhaps startled by Bauer's outrage, relented and agreed to authorize visas. Bauer knew that the politician might very well have saved Ludwig and Ella's lives—still, the arbitrariness of the decision left him shaken.[9]

Walter telegrammed Ludwig and Ella the news, but by then the German government had imposed fresh restrictions. Fleeing Jews now had to surrender their savings, which for Ludwig included the proceeds from the sale of his company and the liquidation of the family's securities. There were additional Reich flight taxes, an emigration tax, and an inspection of valuables by the City Pawn Office.[10]

Bauer waited for their paperwork to be approved and watched with growing unease as Hitler began to subjugate the continent. The Führer had annexed Austria and German-speaking parts of Czechoslovakia in 1938. He seized what remained of Czech territory in March 1939. Then, on September 1, he attacked Poland in the name of greater Lebensraum or "living space" for the German people. Britain and France declared war three days later, marking the start of World War II.[11]

As German forces smashed through Polish defenses, Hitler moved quickly to impose a brutal new racial hierarchy. Einsatzgruppen death squads followed regular German soldiers into the country to eliminate the educated classes. Fifty thousand Polish nationals were murdered within the first four months of the occupation. Ethnic Germans and settlers from the Third Reich were granted special privileges as the so-called master race. They seized the best homes, looted artwork from museums, and claimed exclusive access to parks, theaters, and cinemas. Ethnic Poles—the weaker Slavic race—were to serve as slave labor. Jews, considered a parasitic subspecies, were to be contained in newly constructed ghettos.[12]

Bauer could only glean a few of these details in the Danish press. But it was clear the outbreak of war had led to a new and more radical phase of the Nazi campaign against Jews. In Stuttgart, Ludwig and Ella received orders to evacuate their home in order to be rehoused in special apartment buildings, or "Judenhäuser." Ella hastily sold the family china and cutlery, silver serving plates, bowls, her wristwatch, even her diamond wedding ring, saving only a photograph album, an inlaid box, and clothes as Ludwig desperately paid the ever increasing flight taxes. They finally secured second-class tickets for the train journey to Copenhagen on December 31, 1939, with three months of living expenses to their name. They were some of the last Jews allowed to leave.[13]

Bauer traveled to the border crossing at Padborg on New Year's Day 1940 to meet them. He stood in the brutal cold—minus fifteen degrees Fahrenheit—as their train pulled in, still unsure if they had been allowed to board. He finally saw his father struggling through the crowd, head bowed and limping, startlingly unsure of himself. His mother had put on weight and looked unwell. Bauer shared a look with her as he helped them onto the next train. Ludwig had been wrong about many things, but now wasn't the time to discuss their differences.[14]

. . .

Over the next few weeks, they settled into family life. Ludwig and Ella moved into the Tiefenthals' apartment building in Maltagade. On Walter's insistence they celebrated a belated Christmas in order to "fit in." He had raised a goose in a neighboring yard for the occasion. Opa, as Ludwig was affectionately known to his two grandsons, was grumpier than ever; Ella worried about the children. Bauer moved into an apartment nearby and began work on a book about the Danish economy. It was a dry topic, but the Jewish newspaper he'd mainly been writing for in Berlin had closed and the alternative was working as a full-time lace salesman for Walter. At least they were safe.[15]

Then, on the morning of April 9, 1940, Bauer was awoken by a deep and steady rumble overhead that set the glassware clinking. He hastened onto the street with his neighbors to discover a vast phalanx of airplanes passing low in the direction of the airport. The swastikas on their tail fins were clearly visible. "Are the bombers coming now?" cried one woman as pale green flyers fluttered from the sky calling for calm in misspelled Danish. Nobody seemed sure whether to run or go

Bauer's parents after their escape, c. 1940
Courtesy of Marit Tiefenthal

about their day. But by the start of the morning commute, it was evident that Germany had invaded Denmark and seized Copenhagen with little resistance from the Danish authorities. A German troop transport docked at the harbor as if it were a regular tourist boat. By midmorning, the Danish king announced the country's formal capitulation over the radio: "May God have mercy on you all."[16]

Bauer learned from a friend a few hours later that the Gestapo had raided the offices of the Danish Labor movement that morning looking for lists of German exiles in the country. He hurriedly packed his apartment, knowing they might come for him at any moment. There seemed little chance of escaping to Sweden or even getting out of Copenhagen with the Germans in control of the port and train stations. He simply needed to hide.[17]

It was growing dark by the time he made it onto the eerily deserted streets. The Germans had driven around the city with a loudspeaker announcing a 7:00 P.M. curfew. The streetlights were out, a sign that Copenhagen was now a target of Allied bombing. He decided to try Paul Wagner, an activist he had met at a workshop for Social Democratic youth. Bauer liked the tall, angular, and slyly humorous twenty-two-year-old; they had bonded over their shared idealism, Bauer enjoying the role of the older man, showing off his learning. Bauer wasn't certain Wagner would risk hiding him, but he needn't have worried. Wagner greeted him warmly, quickly grasped the situation, and said Bauer could stay in the living room of his one-bedroom apartment. There was a little patio hidden from view by raspberry bushes at the back where they smoked and listened out for trouble.[18]

Paul Wagner, c. 1940
Courtesy of Helle Wagner

Copenhagen was quiet in the days after the invasion. Unlike in Poland, Hitler allowed the Danish authorities to stay in place, as he considered Danes to be of good Nordic blood and capable of following orders. The Danish government encouraged citizens to resume their lives and avoided persecuting domestic dissidents and the country's seven-thousand-strong Jewish community. The SS, however, wanted German political refugees known to be troublemakers arrested for deportation. A Danish officer and a German soldier soon came knocking on Walter and Margot's apartment door asking for Bauer. Their six-year-old son, Peter, blurted out in Danish, "I know where Uncle Fritz is!" But the men either didn't hear or chose to ignore it.[19]

Bauer kept off the streets as much as possible, other than a brief visit back to his apartment to pick up the manuscript of his finance book. He lived in constant fear of arrest. But the risk of fleeing seemed greater that spring. Walter Hammer, the German anti-Nazi pamphleteer who'd become a friend of Bauer's, was caught boarding a yacht for Sweden; he slashed his wrists in prison but upon recovery was deported to Germany. Even if Bauer could get out of Denmark, it wasn't clear if anywhere in Europe was safe as Hitler moved rapidly to bring the continent under his control. German forces seized the Netherlands and Belgium in May 1940, and then broke through French lines the following month on their way to capturing Paris and routing the British at Dunkirk.[20]

Finally, Bauer could no longer stand the tension in Copenhagen. On September 11, he made a dash for Korsør, where the ferries left for the neighboring island of Fyn. The Danish police caught him almost immediately and brought him to Vestre Prison in Copenhagen. It was now only a matter of time before he was handed over to the Germans. At midnight, a guard opened the door of his narrow stone cell and offered him some food.[21]

"Do you want something to read?" the man asked, seemingly as an afterthought. Bauer said no. But the guard closed the cell door and stepped toward him. Bauer tensed for a blow, only for the man to tenderly embrace him.[22]

"I will think of you," said the man, and then, just as inexplicably, left.[23]

On September 19, a Thursday, Bauer was transferred to a temporary internment camp outside the village of Horserød. He was registered and led to one of the two crowded, single-story wooden barracks, which smelled of mildew and sweat. The camp commandant, a Dane called Alfred Klaudius Bentzen—"a small arrogant psychopath, who acted like Mussolini in front of the inmates," noted one prisoner— informed them that inmates were expected to cook, clean, and work on the barracks while they awaited their fate. Bauer's only encouragement was that so long as he remained in Danish hands, his brother-in-law, Walter, might be able to secure his release.[24]

The following morning, Bauer wrote to Walter to alert him of his arrest and arrange a prison visit. Walter arrived with Bauer's sister, Margot, for a supervised meeting a few days later. He agreed to contact various Danish Social Democrat politicians on Bauer's behalf. Bauer asked the same of Paul Wagner when he visited the following week. Ludwig came, too, hobbling into the room alongside Margot, which

Bauer's mugshot, 1940
Danish National Archive

touched Bauer. Several weeks passed with no word. Bauer distracted himself with wood carving.[25]

Then one day, without warning, Bauer was released. His economist neighbor, Henry Grünbaum, had persuaded the president of Denmark's National Bank that Bauer was an important thinker on the financial system who must be spared. The German authorities were prepared to make some concessions to the Danish government to maintain good relations. Bauer was free to return to his apartment to complete his book provided he reported weekly to the Danish police. It was a lucky escape. A week later, forty-nine of his fellow prisoners, mostly minor dissidents, were deported to Germany and almost certain death.[26]

. . .

Bauer tried to return to his earlier life, moving back in with Wagner, editing his book, and meeting his parents most days for lunch or a walk in the park. Sometimes he picked up his nephews from the nearby Montessori school for ice cream. The quirk in Hitler's racial policy that had left Danes in charge meant that Jews in Denmark continued to avoid restrictions. But outside the country the Nazis' persecution of Jews reached a new, terrifying level. On June 22, 1941, Germany attacked the Soviet Union to destroy what Hitler called the "Jewish

Wooden dinosaur carved by Bauer in Horserød, gifted to Paul Wagner
Courtesy of Helle Wagner

powerholders of the Bolshevik Center in Moscow." Bauer was soon
reading fragmentary accounts of shootings in the uncensored Swedish
press that circulated in Denmark, but nothing seemed certain.[27]

Bauer and his nephews, Rolf and Peter Tiefenthal, c. 1930s
Courtesy of Marit Tiefenthal

*   *   *

What Bauer could not know was that these killings marked the Nazis'
first steps toward the Holocaust. Einsatzgruppen murder squads had
followed German troops into Russia with orders to kill Soviet political commissars and "Jewish partisans." The SS units took this as an

opportunity—rapidly endorsed by the Nazi leadership—to round up Jewish men, women, and children and execute them en masse. Seven hundred thousand Jews were murdered mostly by machine gun in the first six months of the German invasion, pushing the SS to consider more efficient methods of killing. Under a program to euthanize mentally ill and disabled Germans, the Nazis had already pioneered the use of carbon monoxide to kill. Special gassing trucks that pumped their exhaust into sealed cargo bays were deployed to occupied parts of the Soviet Union in November and Chełmno in Poland the following month. In Auschwitz, Commandant Rudolf Höss had begun to experiment with the use of pesticide to kill sick prisoners and Soviet POWs, while in Lublin, the SS police chief had suggested building a dedicated gas chamber to kill Jews from local ghettos.[28]

By the winter of 1941, no single order had been given for the systematic murder of Europe's Jews, but many of the elements for industrialized killing were already in place. Adolf Eichmann, the head of the SS's special Jewish "evacuation" department, was the desk officer who brought the killing strands together. He had risen to prominence in Nazi circles for managing the mass emigration of Jews in annexed Austria and Czech territory. That winter, he was tasked with deporting German Jews to the ghettos of occupied Poland and the Soviet Union, among whom were Bauer's aunt Paula and nephew Erich. The ghettos were soon overflowing. To solve the problem, Eichmann paid a hurried visit to Chełmno to see a gassing truck in operation, then to Auschwitz, where he and Höss discussed potential sites for a killing facility, and to Lublin, where work had already begun on a gas chamber. Finally, he traveled to Minsk to observe a mass shooting in which women clutching their babies were gunned down in front of him.[29]

Eichmann and his superiors quickly grasped that these ad hoc methods of mass murder could become the basis for a program of extermination for the entirety of Europe's eleven million Jews. On January 20, 1942, Eichmann and a dozen other high-ranking Nazi officials met around a long oak table in a villa in the Berlin suburb of Wannsee to coordinate the initiative under the name of the "Final Solution to the Jewish Question." All levels of the German state would

Adolf Eichmann, 1942
Creative Commons

now be involved. Reinhard Heydrich, the head of the Reich Security Main Office, and SS officials from each of the occupied territories were present. So, too, were representatives from the ministries of foreign affairs, justice, and the interior, the latter to advise on who counted as a Jew. Others not present but who were to be enlisted included the Reich railway officials who'd arrange the transports, the manufacturers needed to build ovens for the crematoria and produce Zyklon B, the pesticide used for the gas chambers of Auschwitz, and the staff of the death camps, who'd operate facilities. Eichmann's office was to play a special role in coordinating the operation, an elevation in power he and Heydrich toasted with cognac in the villa's paneled fireroom afterward.[30]

Eichmann returned to Auschwitz in the spring of 1942 to observe the arrival of the first transports. Fit and healthy Jews were selected to be worked to death; the rest were gassed immediately. The SS escorted them to a converted farmhouse, the interior of which had been disguised to look like a shower room, and ordered them to strip. Those who guessed what was to come and made a fuss were hastily singled out and shot around the back of the building. The rest were locked inside and the Zyklon B administered. Eichmann was "completely obsessed" with killing Jews, noted Höss. The Auschwitz commandant was no less fanatical. On one occasion, he observed two children playing in the changing room and let their games continue. But when the time

*Richard Baer, Josef Mengele, and Rudolf Höss in
Auschwitz, 1944*
USHMM / Creative Commons

came, he ordered his men to scoop them up and throw them inside. Their mother, sobbing, followed.[31]

. . .

When Bauer learned of British foreign secretary Anthony Eden's statement in December 1942 that the Germans were carrying out a "bestial policy of cold-blooded extermination" against the Jewish people, he struggled to grasp the enormity of the horror. But as news reached him that Jews were being deported from Norway, France, and the Netherlands to be "resettled in the East," it was clear his family was in increasing danger, especially as relations between the Danish government and the German occupation authorities broke down. The catastrophic defeat of German forces in Stalingrad in February 1943 and the possibility that Germany might lose the war emboldened the Danish resistance movement into a campaign of strikes, sabotage, and targeted killings. The Danish government refused to intervene and finally withdrew its cooperation with Germany in August. Hitler responded by imposing a state of martial law, disarming and in some cases arresting Danish forces. Bauer, as a ward of the Danes, now had no protection at all. In desperation, he accepted a marriage proposal from Anna Maria Petersen, the headmistress of the Montessori school his nephews attended, to help secure him Danish citizenship. The marriage did little to ease his nerves.[32]

Then, on September 29, 1943, Rosh Hashanah, the city's acting chief rabbi, Marcus Melchior, interrupted his evening service to warn his congregation that he had learned of German plans to detain every Jew in the country. The Gestapo had raided the offices of Denmark's main Jewish organization, Mosaisk Troessamfund, and seized lists of the names and addresses of many of the country's seven thousand Jews. The rabbi urged everyone to share the news and to hide or flee the country at once.[33]

Bauer, who heard the warning that evening, knew he only had hours to save his family. He hastily gathered his clothes, writings, and a few books, and once again turned to his friend Paul Wagner. They needed to escape Denmark, but the only country that they could conceivably reach was Sweden—neutral but unwelcoming to refugees, especially Jewish ones. Simply getting there would involve a clandestine crossing of the Øresund strait, which separated the two countries. Wagner promised to help if he could, but Bauer would need to hide his family in the meantime.[34]

Bauer hurried to collect his mother from the hospital in which she was recovering from surgery for breast cancer, still unclear what to do. On the recommendation of Ella's doctor, Bauer arranged to check himself, his parents, Walter, Margot and their two boys, Rolf and Peter, into a sanatorium in Skodsborg, where they waited, ill at ease among its wealthy patrons, for news from Wagner.[35]

The roundup of Jews began on the evening of October 1. German police and soldiers spanned the country, going house to house, but the rabbi's warning had worked. Only 202 people were captured. The rest had gone into hiding in the spare rooms, attics, basements, broom cupboards, and summer cottages of their Danish friends. Scores of fishing boats had already started secretly ferrying families to Sweden across the Øresund.[36]

Wagner got in touch a few days later to say he had arranged a safe house for Bauer with the family of a mutual friend, Jørgen Jørgensen, in the northern Danish port town of Rørvig. It was farther away from

Sweden than other ports and would require an eight-hour crossing to reach the nearest Swedish harbor. No other Jewish families had taken the route. Finding a fisherman might be difficult.[37]

Jørgensen accompanied them on a tense train ride from Copenhagen to the station closest to Rørvig and then on to his family's home on Fjordvænget. His mother, Ingeborg, a stout fifty-four-year-old widow and mother of five, insisted that they hide in a broom cupboard under the stairs during the day.[38]

Ingeborg Jørgensen, c. 1940
Courtesy of the Jørgensen family

It took a week for Jørgensen to find a fisherman, Tage Møller. He wanted two thousand kroner for the crossing, about ten thousand dollars today. It was almost everything Bauer's family had left.[39]

On the cold, clear evening of October 9, they set off with Ingeborg to the meeting spot, several miles outside the town on a secluded beach. Rørvig was on the narrow mouth of a large, shallow fjord, tucked behind a peninsula of low dunes and scrub pine forest along the coast where they hoped to meet the fisherman. They walked in single file along a sandy track past the darkened windows of wooden summer cottages and villas on the outskirts of the town. One of the houses held the local German commander and his men. Ludwig was the slowest, leaning heavily on his cane. No one spoke, not even the boys.[40]

They encountered a German sentry as soon as they entered the woods. He passed them without a word. Bauer glanced back over his

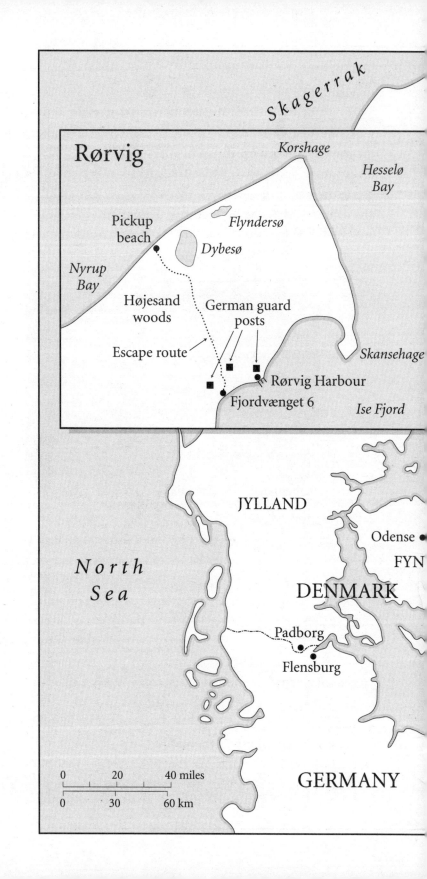

● Göteborg

SWEDEN

Kattegat

Mölle
●

Rørvig Horserød ●   ● Helsingborg

Skodsborg ●

Copenhagen ●

SJÆLLAND

● Korsør

● Malmö

Øresund

*Baltic
Sea*

Denmark, 1943
John Gilkes

*Pickup beach,
Rørvig*

shoulder. The soldier paused and turned. With a surge of panic, Bauer hurried his family on. When he looked again, the soldier had gone.[41]

The dense pine trees soon gave way to stunted oaks and rowan shrubs. The path rose to meet a low dune, and then suddenly they saw the waves rushing over the white sand. A full moon glinted off the dark water beyond.[42]

They soon heard the hum of Møller's two-stroke Hundested engine and then saw the boat's black outline gliding toward them. The fisherman pulled up just short of the shore. Bauer waded toward the boat as Møller leaped into the icy water to help them aboard. Ludwig had to be lifted over the side of the boat, and he cursed loudly when one of the boys sat on his hat.[43]

They had hardly left the coast when they heard the throb of a larger vessel and then saw the dark shape of a German destroyer gliding over the water. Møller urged them into the hull with the wet fishing nets and steered straight for the Germans to allay suspicion. Bauer heard him shouting and the German crew responding. And then they moved on.[44]

3

Mission

I T WAS STILL DARK when they pulled into the harbor of Mölle, Sweden, on October 10, 1943. A few lights shone in the town that rose above them on the hillside. The stone pier was empty, as was the small customs house—a wooden shed beside the quay. They felt dull with exhaustion. The two boys slept on the ground beside the hut. Bauer watched the sky turn gray and the first seagulls alight on the quay.[1]

A police officer in a tight-fitting uniform and cap, clipboard in hand, approached the family at 8:00 A.M. sharp and asked if they were Jewish. The coast had been inundated with thousands of Jews over the past week, he explained. The Swedish government, in a reversal of its earlier position, had agreed to grant asylum and was even paying for their accommodation while their cases were processed. He took down the family's details and directed them up the hill to the Grand Hotel Mölle, where a few hours later Bauer finally collapsed into bed.[2]

Bauer occupied himself over the following weeks with the practicalities of settling in Sweden. He soon found a Swedish family in Gothenburg who were willing to vouch for their presence in the country and helped them rent a summer home for Ludwig, Ella, Walter, Margot, and the children. Bauer decided not to join them; he needed work, and as his mind turned back to politics, he knew that he wanted to be near the Swedish capital, where leading members of Europe's intelligentsia

Bauer's Swedish identity card, 1943
Courtesy of
Marit Tiefenthal

and figures in the Jewish Diaspora were gathering in anticipation of Germany's defeat to discuss the country's future. Since Stalingrad, the Red Army had rapidly pushed back German forces. Through Bauer's contacts in the Social Democratic Party, he found a professor to sponsor research on a Swedish edition of his finance book, a university position that included travel papers and salary enough to pay for a room at the Hotel Astoria in central Stockholm.[3]

Bauer arrived in the Swedish capital on November 25, 1943. He made his way to the Astoria through the rain, possibly catching sight of the redbrick city hall on the other side of the gray Riddarfjärden. Sweden had eased its neutrality and strict monitoring of dissent. The press openly discussed Hitler's downfall, and rumors of secret peace negotiations taking place in Stockholm were widespread.[4]

Bauer spent his first days connecting with the German exile community, which, to his frustration, was riven by political infighting. The only thing Social Democrats and Communists could agree upon was the inevitability of German defeat and Allied occupation, but what sort of country should emerge was the subject of fierce ideological debate. The Allies themselves were equally divided. U.S. secretary of war Henry Stimson favored restoring the German economy to aid in European reconstruction. Treasury Secretary Henry Morgenthau—the only Jew in Roosevelt's cabinet—wanted Germany reduced to agrarian subsistence to ensure it could never wage war again. The Soviet Union, meanwhile, had designs on large swaths of German land as a form of reparation. It wasn't clear what role, if any, émigrés would be asked to play in administering the country, but the various factions in Stockholm each acted as if only they could be trusted as the true representatives of the anti-Hitler resistance.[5]

Bauer was careful to avoid taking sides. He recognized that underlying the debates was the question of justice. How should the country's Nazi regime be punished for laying waste to a continent, and to what extent should Germans be held collectively responsible? The Americans were considering an international tribunal for Nazi war criminals, but the British, citing the failed attempt at prosecuting Germans after 1918, wondered how the piecemeal and oftentimes untested international law could be used. They were in favor of court-martialing Nazi leaders. Stalin, meanwhile, wanted wider and immediate retaliation, possibly to avoid a court drawing attention to his alliance with Hitler at the start of the war. At the Allied conference of December 1943 in Tehran, the Soviet leader proposed that the entire German General Staff of fifty thousand officers should simply be shot.[6]

Bauer believed that all Germans needed to accept some responsibility for not having done more to stop Hitler—even principled opponents like himself. But this view was condemned by many Social Democrats as denigrating their own sacrifices and inviting Allied retribution. Even those like the thirty-year-old socialist Willy Brandt, who agreed with Bauer's view of collective guilt, worried about the rise in anti-German sentiment among the Allies as ever more Nazi atrocities were revealed. Indeed, Brandt feared the mounting horror would lead to a more punitive vision of justice, which would, in turn, drive German resentment and make his countrymen less responsive to democratic ideas. He thought it necessary, therefore, to remind the Allies that a progressive foundation had been laid during the Weimar years that could be built upon.[7]

Bauer, however, questioned whether the Weimar experiment, which had not been strong enough to resist the Nazis, should be used as a model for a new state. He had come to think that Hitler's rise to power reflected a deeper flaw in German culture. How else to explain why millions had endorsed Nazism and tens of thousands participated in the killings? Indeed, he'd started to ask himself whether the writers and thinkers who'd inspired him as a young man might have unwittingly masked darker forces and served, as the writer Thomas Mann suspected, as a "shield and spearhead of the absolutely monstrous." Could anyone read German Enlightenment thinker Immanuel Kant again without considering the ways in which the Nazis had co-opted his ideas about duty and moral order to idolize Hitler?[8]

Bauer wasn't sure what form a national reckoning should take or how to go about provoking one. He agreed to join the Free German Cultural Association that Brandt was setting up to promote a progressive agenda, although he often appeared frustrated by the vague and self-serving terms of the debate in Stockholm. "I don't want to waste my time on your idealistic rubbish," he told one discussion group.[9]

Bauer preferred to lose himself in preparing the Swedish edition of his finance book while enjoying his newfound freedom. In December, he moved into a generous apartment on Storgatan, a street that also happened to be a vibrant cruising area for gay men, rent boys, and soldiers looking to supplement their salaries. "I have not yet visited them," he wrote to Paul Wagner, "since I cannot afford this pleasure"— perhaps alluding to the danger faced if he was caught. Sweden was in the process of liberalizing its anti-gay laws, but sex work remained a crime.[10]

Bauer was thinking of writing another book about planned economies when he attended the opening event of Brandt's Free German Cultural Association on January 28, 1944. A large crowd had assembled inside a hall on Kungsgatan, specially rented for the occasion that was to feature a performance of a scene from *William Tell* and Beethoven's *Pathétique Sonata*.[11]

Max Hodann, one of the organizers, opened proceedings. He was a physician and sex educator who had worked as a counselor at Magnus Hirschfeld's Institute for Sexual Science in Berlin. The Nazis had labeled Hodann "the sex Jew of the Weimar Republic." His work in exile had continued to focus on advocating for sexual reform in a future Germany. But on this evening, he dispensed with whatever remarks he

Max Hodann, 1928
Magnus-Hirschfeld-
Gesellschaft

might have prepared on the matter. He had just met with Adolf Folkmann, a Polish Jew who had escaped from the final liquidation of the
Lwów Ghetto in August 1943, reaching Stockholm a few months later.
Folkmann had related to Hodann the harrowing story of the ghetto's
liquidation in the Bełżec death camp. Some of Folkmann's details were
wrong—he himself had never been to Bełżec, only hearing accounts
secondhand from the few who had escaped. But the fractured scenes
Folkmann described—one transport of Jews following another, dark
halls packed with naked people, and the crematoria chimneys belching
smoke—conveyed the horror and urgency. While the rest of the world
was planning for life after the war, the Nazis' industrial killing machine
was operating at full capacity.[12]

A wild-eyed Hodann informed the room that "what has occurred in
recent years and is continuing to happen day after day in the name of
Germany is worse and much bigger than the most profoundly criminal imagination could think up." Millions had died at the Nazis' hands
and Jews were "being killed by mass executions. . . . They are being
gassed."[13]

"These are the facts," Hodann declared. "Mere protest" was no longer enough.[14]

Bauer listened in stunned silence. He had heard stray details of the
killings before, and if he stood back and took in the whole of his experience, the genocidal intentions were all there. But those pieces, large

and small, at turns vague and terrifyingly real, had never cohered for him into the picture he saw in this moment.[15]

The rest of Hodann's speech didn't seem to register with Bauer. His mind raced with self-recrimination. What had he done, except save his own life and the lives of his closest family? Then anger took hold. The rain had turned to snow by the time he set off for home. The flurries obscured the shop fronts, and a glowing nimbus of flakes surrounded the lampposts. Hodann was right. Protests were not enough; they had never been enough.[16]

Bauer's thoughts turned to the law. It hadn't been able to prevent the Nazis' crimes, but perhaps it could be used to ensure the horror was never repeated. He saw in that moment the fundamental flaw in the Allies' plans to administer justice. Unless the Germans were empowered to address the Nazis' crimes and see the roots of Nazism in themselves, there was a danger that the evil would return. And that, he swore, must never happen.[17]

Bauer began setting his thoughts down over the following days, writing on an Underwood typewriter that cost him two weeks' wages, and was soon so engrossed in his work that the embers from his pipe were burning holes in his jacket. His book—he knew instinctively it would be one—opened with a stark imagining of what Germany might look like after the war: a country in denial with war criminals hidden by their communities and survivors unwilling or too scared to appear in court. "Perhaps the Nazi terror has not been completely broken," he imagined. "Perhaps there are still fears of assassination and reprisals."[18]

He then plunged into the legal theory of how war crimes had been punished from the battles of antiquity to the downfall of Napoléon Bonaparte. A consensus against wars of aggression had clearly developed in international law, he observed. The Hague Conventions of 1899 and 1907 offered protections for civilians and POWs from abuse and murder; the Kellogg-Briand Pact of 1928 outlawed wars of aggression. No single law, however, addressed the industrialized mass murder of a people, and Bauer was open to the idea of expanding international law to address the unprecedented nature of the Nazis' crimes. Indeed, concepts like "genocide" and "crimes against humanity" would be coined only that year by the Jewish lawyers Raphaël Lemkin and Hersch Lauterpacht, respectively.[19]

But Bauer felt that in the first instance, existing laws needed to be enforced. This was particularly true for Germany, which had signed most international treaties while maintaining its illiberal and authoritarian legal tradition which held that the country had the sovereign right to do as it pleased. What the German judiciary—the German people—needed was a "lesson in international law and basic human rights," he believed. Only then would the courts be able to "open the eyes of the German people to what has happened."[20]

As Bauer wrote that June, the Allies announced plans for a tribunal of forty-one major war criminals, mostly members of Hitler's inner circle. Extending the list further, they explained, would make it "practically impossible to distinguish between general political responsibility and responsibility of professionals who are merely carrying out regime orders." No German was to serve as a judge or prosecutor.[21]

Bauer was dismayed by the news but kept writing throughout the summer of 1944 as the continuing retreat of German forces across Europe revealed ever greater crimes. The Red Army liberated the Nazi camp of Majdanek outside Lublin in eastern Poland on July 23, 1944. The SS had fled without destroying its gas chambers or the warehouses containing the clothes, belongings, and suitcases of murdered Jews. Vast burial pits around the camp were revealed to contain the bodies of sixty thousand Jewish victims. A deeply affected Bauer concluded his manuscript with the words "No crime committed during wartime should be more serious than this mass extermination, as it is evidence of the most cynical contempt for human life."[22]

Bauer's book, *War Criminals on Trial,* was published on November 15, 1944. At a book launch hosted by the Free German Cultural Association, he declared to a gathering of eighty-five people that new battle lines were being drawn. On the one side were those who wanted to narrow the scope of justice and uphold German legal tradition. On the other were those who believed that the German legal code had been so thoroughly corrupted by the Nazis that it should be entirely replaced with "revolutionary law." He knew which side he stood on. Only the elimination of Nazism in the legal system could allow "peace and human dignity" to prevail, he declared, to a round of applause.[23]

Bauer, after so many years on the run, had rediscovered his political voice. That December, he and Willy Brandt helped establish a newspaper, the *Sozialistische Tribüne,* to give émigrés like themselves a platform as the war entered its final months. The Allies were yet to announce any occupation plans, but Bauer was starting to imagine a role for himself in the new Germany, joking with a colleague at one point that he hoped his lost party membership card would "not interfere with my future plans in Germany, should there be any question of the distribution of ministerial posts!!"[24]

That he would go home Bauer never seemed to doubt, although some did ask him how he, a Jew, could consider returning. His parents were settled in Sweden and had no intention of leaving. Their family home and factory in Stuttgart had been destroyed by Allied bombing, and the Nazis had killed Ella's sister and nephew and Ludwig's brother. The thought of being in Germany made Bauer "shudder," but he also couldn't imagine continuing a life in exile.[25]

In January 1945, Soviet forces entered German territory and reached the Oder, about forty miles east of Berlin. By March, the Red Army had surrounded the German capital and the Allies had crossed the Rhine in the West. Then, on April 30, with Soviet soldiers less than five hundred meters from the Führerbunker below the chancellery building, Hitler bade his staff farewell and retreated to his private quarters with his wife, Eva Braun. He and Braun each took a cyanide capsule that contained the same killing compound used in the gas chambers. Just to make sure, Hitler took out his Walther PPK 7.65mm pistol and shot himself in the head as he bit down on the pill. Germany's surrender was finally announced on May 7 shortly after 2:00 P.M.[26]

Bauer joined the vast crowd on Kungsgatan, the air filled with confetti cast by well-wishers from the windows above. "Kungsgatan is ankle-deep in paper, and everyone seems to have gone crazy," the novelist Astrid Lindgren noted in her diary. But Bauer felt his sense of joy tempered by a renewed pang of guilt over how little he had done to oppose the Nazis, as well as a new anxiety. What would happen when he returned home to confront the people who had attempted the industrialized murder of Europe's Jews?[27]

4

Survivors

A S THE THIRD REICH collapsed in a final paroxysm of violence in the spring of 1945, Nazis at all levels of the regime sought to cover up their crimes and escape retribution. SS squads had already dismantled the death camps of Bełżec, Treblinka, and Sobibór and exhumed and burned hundreds of thousands of bodies from mass graves over the preceding two years. In January 1945, they blew up the gas chambers of Auschwitz and shot the Jewish prisoners who had operated them. As the Red Army closed in on Berlin, Nazi Party members torched files and destroyed their identification cards. Some senior figures like SS deportation specialist Adolf Eichmann, Auschwitz commandant Rudolf Höss, and the race law expert Hans Globke fled to the countryside. Others slipped through Allied lines, bound for Italy, Spain, the Middle East, and South America. Thousands killed themselves out of fear of punishment or because they felt unable to live in a world without Hitler. At a final concert by the Berlin Philharmonic on April 12, 1945, members of the Hitler Youth handed out capsules of cyanide to the Nazi elite as they headed to the exit. On May 1, the day after Hitler's suicide, propaganda chief Joseph Goebbels administered cyanide to each of his six children in the Führerbunker, then ordered an SS man to shoot him and his wife. Himmler was caught by the British in northern Germany after his last followers had deserted him. During his medical examination, he too bit down on a cyanide capsule.[1]

Reinhard Gehlen, Hitler's former head of military intelligence for

Reinhard Gehlen,
c. 1940s
Courtesy of Dorothee
Gehlen-Koss

the eastern front, however, had a different plan. When word reached him of the Third Reich's surrender on May 8, 1945, he was camped with a few of his men in a small pine glade where the sun had melted the snow on the Maroldschneid in the Bavarian Alps. The war was over. But the forty-three-year-old Gehlen understood enough about Stalin's intentions to realize that the struggle for Germany was just beginning. The Soviets, who had lost 27 million lives to the war, would attempt to seize control of the country. And Gehlen knew that as one of the key planners of the eastern offensive, if he fell into their hands, he would be interrogated, likely tortured, and almost certainly executed.[2]

He had fled to the Alps knowing that his best chance of survival was to surrender to the Americans and make himself useful. Yet he tarried on the ridge for several days, reading a book on art history, sketching a little, living off canned food as the spring sun played across the valley. He thought of his family, who he'd last seen in Silesia in January 1945. He'd sent an officer to rescue them from the advancing Red Army in April but had heard nothing since. His mind drifted back to when he'd first met his wife, Herta, at a country ball in 1929 and his rise through the military had begun. He was a slender man with pale blue eyes and delicate skin who could be awkward and diffident with those he did not trust. But Herta von Seydlitz-Kurbach found him to be warm, effusive, and quite dashing beneath the chandelier in his parade dress and gold tassels, shoes polished to a dark luster. The match caused a stir within her family. The Gehlens were of decent enough stock from Breslau, where his father, a military man, ran a publishing company. The von Seydlitzes, by contrast, were Silesian nobility. Nonetheless, they were married in 1931. Gehlen's promotion to the General Staff, the military elite, followed.[3]

Gehlen never joined the Nazi Party. Like many officers, he disliked the crude racism. But after what he saw as the national humiliation of the Weimar years, Gehlen had embraced Hitler's promise to restore German prestige through strength of arms. Some of his colleagues saw soldiering as a spiritual calling—what the militarist writer Ernst Jünger called "the yearning for great experience." But Gehlen viewed war as a means to an end, which was how he could support Hitler's drive to subjugate the continent without feeling himself to be motivated by ideology or racial hatred. During the German invasion of Poland in 1939, he served as the staff officer for an artillery unit sent in to secure the rear. He saw the bombed-out towns and the corpses of civilians strewn in the fields and knew that massacres were being carried out. SS units nearby were rounding up hundreds of Poles for summary execution. Soldiers from his own unit burst into a house in Poddębice and shot the family cowering inside, including a ten-year-old girl. But he considered bloodshed to be the unavoidable cost of war.[4]

Gehlen first learned about the genocidal nature of Hitler's plans for the Soviet Union in March 1941 while working as a planner for the chief of the German Army High Command, General Franz Halder. Hitler summoned Halder to the chancellery on March 17 to lay out his vision for a "war of extermination." This was not the Final Solution—that would come later—but another murderous scheme to starve to death as many as thirty million Slavs to clear Soviet lands for German settlement. Part of this plan involved the stripping of provisions from captured territories to feed the military. Gehlen was to organize logistics, making sure that units received the supplies they needed.[5]

Six months into the invasion, Gehlen had a chance to see for himself the impacts of the starvation policy when he visited the front lines with Halder. The campaign was not going well. After advancing rapidly, the

Planning Operation Barbarossa
B 206 Bild-GN13-16-37, Bundesarchiv

Germans had stalled outside Moscow. The scale of the killing was staggering. Halder had issued an order at Hitler's behest to summarily execute anyone suspected of being a Soviet commissar, while SS units were rounding up and shooting entire villages of Jews. At the same time, tens of thousands of Soviet POWs were being starved to death in camps. Gehlen and Halder visited one such camp in Molodechno where the prisoners were on rations of one hundred grams of bread a day. Gehlen saw a vast crowd of sticklike men with grossly distended bellies and sunken eyes standing beside piles of corpses. "Picture of human misery," Halder noted in his diary. By the following year, more than three million Soviet POWs would be dead.[6]

The mass murder made no sense to Gehlen from a military perspective, but he still believed in the war itself. In 1942, Halder promoted Gehlen to the role of intelligence chief for the eastern front. Gehlen won Hitler's approval to raise a Russian force of committed anti-Communists, along with a network of spies composed of Soviet POWs and nationalist groups, like the Iron Guard in Romania, which had already carried out pogroms at the behest of the SS. Instead of reducing the killing, the information Gehlen supplied to the SS on the location of Soviet-backed partisans only contributed to a frenzy of bloodletting as whole villages were wiped out. By the end of the war, Gehlen had become profoundly disillusioned with Hitler, who dismissed his reports of massive buildups of Soviet forces and called him "crazy General

Gehlen," a "storyteller," and a "fool." Gehlen was removed from his post in April 1945. But by then, he had already begun making preparations to pitch his services to the Americans as an intelligence expert with extensive knowledge of the Red Army.[7]

. . .

Gehlen rose early on the morning of May 21, 1945, as the clouds rolled in. He shaved and dressed in his gray-green Wehrmacht uniform from which he'd carefully removed the red arabesque along the collar and the gold and silver epaulets that marked him out as a general. He had no idea whether his plan would work. Even if he succeeded in persuading the Americans that he wasn't a war criminal, the Soviet Union would almost certainly seek his extradition. Gehlen could only hope that their alliance would not last and that at some point Washington would realize that Stalin meant to claim the whole continent for himself. Then Gehlen would be an asset that the Americans would want to protect.[8]

The Maroldschneid

After breaking camp, Gehlen and his men set off down the northern face of the Maroldschneid, around the edge of the broken face of the Rotwand, and then toward the lake, Spitzingsee, where the fields lower down were spotted with purple and white crocuses and patches of forget-me-nots. They stopped every so often to scan the terrain with binoculars. It was imperative that they avoid patrols—the Soviets controlled the Austrian border nearby, and there was no telling whom they might run into before they reached an American officer capable of grasping the proposal. At one point, they spotted a French detachment of infantry near a small settlement on the Lower Schönfeld Alp. Gehlen thought they could slip past, but one of the French soldiers suddenly opened a window of a farmhouse they were passing and spotted them. "Bonjour, monsieur!" Gehlen called out and kept walking. The man returned the greeting, apparently satisfied.[9]

They reached the village of Fischhausen at nightfall, where one of his men had family. They were given supper and learned that the Americans had taken over the largest building in town as their headquarters. It was Pentecost the following day, so they stayed over the weekend to eat pancakes with the family. Gehlen thought again of his wife and children.[10]

Gehlen family, c. 1940s
Courtesy of Dorothee Gehlen-Koss

Then on Monday morning, he turned himself in and met his first American officer. Gehlen introduced himself as a major general of the German army headquarters, in charge of intelligence gathering in the East. But as the young American lieutenant spoke no German and Gehlen's English was limited, he said no more. The Americans separated him from his men and transferred him to Wörgl, an hour's drive into Austrian territory, where he was screened by an American officer who did speak German. Gehlen revealed he had information to share

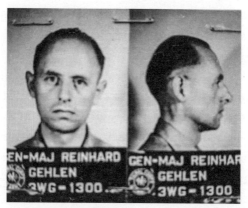

Gehlen as a prisoner of war, c. 1945–1946
NARA / Creative Commons

of the highest importance to the Allies. But the officer waved the story away as if he'd heard it before and checked Gehlen's name against the Allied registry of more than sixty thousand war criminals. Gehlen wasn't listed, a sign that the Soviets weren't looking for him yet, which meant he had a little more time to make his case.[11]

He languished in a hotel on the outskirts of Salzburg for several days. "We forgot all about you!" exclaimed the officer who finally brought him to the U.S. Seventh Army's main interrogation center in the Bärenkeller suburb of Augsburg, back in Germany. Gehlen guessed the camp of two dozen cordoned-off houses contained roughly a hundred POWs, mostly officers, which he took as a sign that his value would be recognized. He was assigned a bare mattress in one of the rooms with several other men. They were expected to keep to their quarters but could talk across stairwells or the exercise yard. Mostly they argued and complained about conditions in the camp—"One doesn't treat a captive general like this!" fumed one panzer commander, Georg-Hans Reinhardt—and argued over who was to blame for the war. Few spoke openly about the mass killings of Jews in which many had played a role in ordering victims ferried to murder sites. They didn't want to implicate themselves and were already on guard from Allied attempts to expose Germans to Nazi crimes: A magazine about atrocities titled *Guilt* was being distributed around POW camps, while in nearby Dachau, U.S. troops had made Germans in the surrounding area bury the camp's victims, many of whom had died from sickness and disease after liberation.[12]

Gehlen was summoned for questioning in early June by another young American officer, who identified himself as Lieutenant Drake. His German was excellent, which raised Gehlen's suspicions; it was known in the camp that the Americans had a cadre of German Jewish interpreters looking for war criminals to add to their list. Still, Gehlen felt he had no choice but to reveal his role as Hitler's intelligence chief in the East. Drake wrote everything down, his expression inscrutable.[13]

A few days later, Gehlen was woken roughly.[14]

"Get packed, get packed!" a guard shouted.[15]

He was shoved into the rear of a truck with several prisoners. Had he miscalculated? Was he being turned over to the Soviets after all? He was relieved when they turned west. The roads were clogged with refugees, demobilized soldiers, and former forced laborers, everyone ragged, dirty, hungry. That summer, seventy-five million people— more than half the country—were uprooted from their homes. A further ten million foreigners lived in displaced persons camps.[16]

Gehlen's convoy skirted the ruins of Stuttgart and then Frankfurt, where they passed over one of the few bridges still standing across the Main, giving him a view of the city's rubble-strewn interior with only the blackened spire of the cathedral breaking the skyline.

Frankfurt, 1945
World War II Images collection,
San Diego Air & Space Museum / Creative Commons

Almost a third of homes across Germany had been destroyed. The *Nürnberger Nachrichten* speculated that if the country's 500 million cubic meters of rubble were piled onto Nuremberg's Nazi Party parade ground, it would make a snowcapped peak two and a half miles high.[17]

They finally reached their destination, Wiesbaden, by nightfall. The truck pulled up to a drab prison building on Albrechtstrasse and Gehlen was hauled out. He discovered the reason for his rough handling upon registration: Lieutenant Drake had put him down as a Gestapo general. He felt the guards eyeing him up and feared he might be in for a beating. They were taking him to a cell when Gehlen was hailed in the corridor by his former superior, General Franz Halder. The two men shared a surprised embrace as Halder, sporting a fresh buzz cut and pince-nez spectacles, explained that he was now working for the American military to write a history of the war from the German perspective as part of a lessons-learned exercise.[18]

Halder had been lucky. As Hitler's chief planner for the invasion of the Soviet Union, he had been party to some of the war's worst atrocities. But the failure of the campaign had led to a falling-out with Hitler, who had removed Halder from his post and imprisoned him in a concentration camp. Upon his liberation by the Americans, Halder was able to claim that he had opposed the Führer. The American request to write a campaign history was another stroke of fortune. He planned to use the task to exonerate the German military and hide his own crimes by blaming the atrocities on Hitler and the SS.[19]

As it happened, Halder was visiting the prison to look for former officers who might help and was therefore delighted to find Gehlen. Halder assured the Americans that Gehlen was not a Gestapo general but a talented officer with vital insight into the Russian campaign. Gehlen was swiftly transferred to a nearby villa on Bodenstedtstrasse, where Halder had assembled a small staff of officers to sift through captured German documents. The villa, which had once belonged to the Vatican's representative in Germany, contained a grand dining room and terrace that opened onto a decorative garden. Gehlen shared his second-floor bedroom with several generals and was told he was welcome to roam the house and grounds, although he had to steer clear of a shed in the bushes, where the Americans had locked up Ernst Kaltenbrunner, former head of Himmler's feared Reich Main Security Office—a reminder to Gehlen of the stakes involved if he didn't make himself indispensable to the Americans.[20]

The following afternoon, Gehlen was napping in his bedroom when he was awoken by an American officer. Gehlen roused himself, in his britches, embarrassed. The man told him to take his time. Gehlen dressed and made his way downstairs to the terrace, where the American introduced himself in fluent German as Captain John Boker, a thirty-two-year-old Yale-educated intelligence officer from New York. He was tall and assured, and Gehlen suspected he probably had some German blood.[21]

Indeed, Boker was more than a little German. His father was from Duisburg in the Ruhr valley, which had given Boker a different perspective to his colleagues as they interrogated German POWs. The stories told by East Prussian officers of how wives and children had been raped, homes plundered, and families driven from land now claimed by Moscow disturbed him. But when Boker tried to raise concerns about Stalin's brutal, expansionist ambitions, his superiors weren't interested. The U.S. military was in the midst of a massive drawdown of its forces in Europe, and its leadership was determined to see Stalin as an ally. To change minds, Boker knew he would need evidence of the Soviet threat, which was why he'd sought out Gehlen after he learned that the intelligence chief was in U.S. custody.[22]

Gehlen, realizing that he'd at last found an American capable of grasping his proposition, revealed that his office's entire collection of intelligence files—everything the Americans would need to understand the threat posed by the Red Army, from descriptions of units to profiles of individual commanders and analysis of military-industrial capacity—were hidden in the Alps. If Boker reconnected Gehlen with his men, together they could help the Americans exploit the files.[23]

Boker understood both the value and the risks of taking Gehlen up on his offer. Gehlen was asking him to endorse one of Hitler's own to his superiors for a collaboration that would provoke Soviet wrath if

John Boker, c. 1950s
Harmers International,
New York

they ever learned about it. Boker made discreet inquiries over the next few days. The Soviets, he learned, had begun to hunt for Gehlen. He consulted with his commander, Colonel William R. Philp, who agreed the offer sounded interesting. However, Philp thought it best not to bother Washington until they had retrieved Gehlen's Soviet files.[24]

As a first step, Boker arranged for Gehlen's name to be removed from the list of internees in U.S. custody in order to hide him from the Soviets. Then he tracked down Gehlen's deputy, Gerhard Wessel, his chief recruiter, Hermann Baun, and six intelligence officers in other camps and brought them to the villa. In return, Gehlen revealed the location of his files. Boker recovered five stores of material hidden in the Alps and learned that the British had found three others. So he forged a requisition order, showing up at the warehouse where they were stored and collecting them in a four-ton truck.[25]

In mid-July, Gehlen gave his first presentation on Soviet military tactics to Philp over drinks at the villa. The meeting was an informal affair, but Gehlen knew that Philp's buy-in was necessary for his case to be pushed higher up the chain of command. Philp, wineglass in hand, proved considerably less demanding than Hitler and instructed Gehlen to continue with his work.[26]

As a reward, Boker helped Gehlen and his men contact their families. Gehlen's wife, Herta, and his four children were found, unharmed, in a Bavarian manor. Their flight from the Red Army had taken them through Dresden, which they left only days before the British and Americans dropped 3,900 tons of explosives and incendiaries on the city, igniting a firestorm that killed more than twenty thousand Germans. Boker helped Gehlen pass on a message to his family as well as care packages of goods from the American military store, which was well stocked with canned macaroni and packets of Lucky Strikes for bartering.[27]

Over the following month, Gehlen's team settled into a rhythm at the villa, writing reports for Boker during the day to the sound of rubble being cleared from the streets outside by work squads of former SS men and in the evenings sitting outside on the veranda to talk more informally. Boker, who liked a drink, opened up about his stamp collecting and interest in astrology. Gehlen, a teetotaler, remained on guard and preferred to parse the latest news. The Allies had announced plans following the Potsdam Conference of July 1945 to divide Germany into four zones of occupation, with the Soviets taking the eastern part of the country, the Americans the south, the British the north, and the French the west. Stalin had, at the same time, formally annexed the northern part of East Prussia and given forty thousand square miles of German territory to Poland. All Germans in these territories—some twelve million in total—had been ordered from their homes. Gehlen's hometown, Breslau, was now the Polish city of Wrocław.[28]

Gehlen shared his views with Boker that Stalin would only see the borders between the occupation zones as provisional. He suspected that the Soviets had already begun to infiltrate agents into local German government and the offices of newly established newspapers and radio stations in Allied zones. Such "cultural bolshevism," he believed, was intended to weaken Allied efforts to rebuild the country and pave the way for Soviet control. But he had a solution, which he'd been holding back, unsure of how Boker would respond. To combat Soviet machinations, Gehlen wanted the Americans to let him rebuild his network of intelligence officers, SS men, and Nazi collaborators.[29]

Boker, however, was unfazed. He agreed that the United States needed a more robust spy operation in Europe. The American drawdown meant that it would lose most of its military intelligence officers while the Office of Strategic Services, which had overseen a network of

Central
Europe, 1945
John Gilkes

agents, was due to be disbanded. Boker thought that Gehlen's men might be useful, vital even, if the Soviets were intent on penetrating Western Europe. But there was no question that the Pentagon must now be informed.[30]

Nervous weeks followed for Gehlen as Boker waited to hear back from Washington. Gehlen wasn't sure precisely what Boker had shared with his superiors, and he feared his wartime record was coming under scrutiny at the worst possible moment as news reached the villa in August that the Allies were establishing an international military tribunal for Nazi war criminals in Nuremberg that would indict not only the Nazi leaders but also the organizations that had supported them. The SS, the Brownshirts, and—to Gehlen's dismay—the General Staff, to which he belonged, were to be indicted as criminal entities, previous membership in which would become a crime. Several senior officers in the villa, including Halder, were placed back under arrest and taken to Nuremberg.[31]

Finally Boker informed Gehlen in mid-August that he and six of his intelligence evaluators had been summoned to the Fort Hunt interrogation center outside Washington, DC, for further assessment. Boker was frustrated. He had hoped to start rebuilding Gehlen's network at once, but Gehlen was sanguine. Given the news about Nuremberg, he was relieved to be getting out of Germany.[32]

. . .

It was overcast on August 21, 1945, as Gehlen and six staff members, accompanied by Boker, made their way to the military airport outside Frankfurt. They had agreed that Gehlen's deputy and his chief recruiter would stay behind to reactivate the intelligence network, should permission be given. Gehlen hated flying, which added to his agitation as the DC-3 plane lifted off and he saw the ruins of Frankfurt, bleached white over the summer. They touched down briefly in the Azores and then in Newfoundland. Gehlen tried to sleep while the others talked in hushed voices. For most it was their first journey to America, the country that had decisively turned the war against them.[33]

The following day was clear and sunny as they crossed into American airspace. The pilot dropped low over Maine to waggle the wings for the benefit of his girlfriend. Boker pointed out the Manhattan skyline as they passed New York. They finally descended over the Potomac, past the Capitol and Washington Monument, lit up against the darkening sky, and landed with a jolt at National Airport in Washington. After a medical inspection in a terminal building, they were led to a Black Maria van and ordered into its stifling, windowless hold. Boker promised he'd see them again soon. Half an hour later, the van pulled up outside a cell block behind a barbed-wire-topped fence, where Gehlen and his men were locked up in cells on the second floor.[34]

It was several days before Boker reappeared with a slightly built officer with thinning red hair and an intense blue-eyed stare whom he introduced as Eric Waldman, a thirty-one-year-old lieutenant from the War Department. Boker explained that Waldman would now be taking over Gehlen's case and left the two men to talk alone. Waldman spoke German with an Austrian accent. When Gehlen asked, Waldman said only that he was from Vienna originally and added that he had lost his parents in the war. Waldman was in fact Jewish, although he rarely mentioned it. He had fled Austria in 1938 and become a naturalized American citizen five years later, too late to save his parents. His father was murdered by the Gestapo in 1939 and his mother deported to the Łódź Ghetto and then Chełmno extermination camp, where she was later killed. Gehlen assured Waldman he was no Nazi, and warily fielded questions about his wartime record. He gave nothing away, and he was relieved when the discussion turned to the safer subject of his files.[35]

Waldman returned to the prison on Sunday, September 2, to announce the start of work. He was initially only interested in updating a handbook on the Red Army and creating an index for the documents that had accompanied Gehlen to the United States. But after several weeks of filing reports, Waldman started bringing Gehlen U.S. military intelligence on Soviet troop dispositions for his analysis. Gehlen took it as a sign that he was gaining Waldman's trust, which appeared to be confirmed in October, when he and his men were moved from their

Eric Waldman, 1946
N46/2, BND-Archiv

cells to chalets in a forested area of the same compound, where they
were free to walk to a military supply store to buy cigarettes and drink
in a club usually reserved for American officers.[36]

Gehlen decided to broach again the idea of his intelligence network.
Waldman said he was interested and allowed Gehlen to establish contact with his subordinates in Germany. But before they could discuss
his return, trust between the two men was damaged by Gehlen's discovery of a series of listening devices artfully hidden in his chalet.
Gehlen confronted Waldman and threatened to withdraw his cooperation. Waldman seemed genuinely taken aback and promised to bring
the matter up with his superiors. Gehlen was unconvinced. One of his
men was certain that Waldman—"the Viennese Sow Jew," he called
him—intended to set them up for prosecution. His comments were
caught by the listening devices.[37]

Tensions between Gehlen and Waldman ran still higher as the
Nuremberg trial convened in November, with the head of the military's high command and its operations chief in the dock. The prosecution's first witness, a former senior intelligence officer named Erwin
von Lahousen, testified about the German army's orders to kill Soviet
commissars and to assist the SS in the mass murder of Jews. At some
point, Waldman asked Gehlen directly if his proposed spy network
contained men who had taken part. There would be a political storm
if the American public, gripped by the revelations of Nuremberg,

learned that the U.S. military was bankrolling a bunch of Nazi killers. Waldman also drew a personal line at working with incriminated
SS men.[38]

Gehlen assured him that his organization was clean, and Waldman seemed prepared to offer him the benefit of the doubt, given
the growing concerns in Washington about the Soviet threat. Stalin's
brutal subjugation of central and eastern Europe was gathering pace,
and Moscow was actively thwarting attempts at joint administration of
Germany. Indeed, the country increasingly seemed divided into two
armed camps: a million Red Army soldiers on one side against 200,000
Americans with a nuclear arsenal on the other. It was, wrote George
Orwell, "a peace that is no peace"—a "cold war."[39]

As a gesture of goodwill, Waldman gave Gehlen a radio to play at
full volume to hide his conversations with his men and took them
Christmas shopping. It was a bitterly cold winter back in Germany and
Gehlen wanted to send his family thermal underwear, but all he could
find was lingerie. Waldman also made a point of inviting Gehlen home
to his modest rowhouse in northwest Washington, ostensibly for a
Christmas dinner. Waldman had recently divorced his first wife, an
Austrian Jew, for an American, Jo Ann, who served Gehlen southern
fried chicken. It was an odd moment at the table: the German officer
and the Jewish survivor, both eager to move on from the war, albeit for
very different reasons. They shared little of their wartime experiences,
but the relaxed setting further eased tensions.[40]

Waldman informed Gehlen over their next few meetings that there
was no chance of his returning to Germany while the public remained
outraged over Nuremberg. The U.S. military was, however, ready to
approve Gehlen's network. As 1946 began, Gehlen was in regular contact with his subordinates in Germany. His head of recruitment had
already reached out to several former colleagues and was ready to
begin hiring. Gehlen had particular views on who to enlist. Contrary
to what he told Waldman, he wasn't concerned about former SS men
with dark pasts so long as they were convinced "down to the last corner
of their soul" about the evil of Communism. For the first time he also
set down in writing the new organization's mission to "eliminate all

personalities who pose a danger for the future." He was particularly alarmed by reports about the growth of "antifascist" groups in Germany made up of members of the anti-Hitler resistance and camp survivors, which he suspected were being directed from Moscow to ruin Germany's reputation and prevent an alliance forming with the West. He considered the Nuremberg trial to be little more than propaganda driven by Soviet animus. The sooner he got back the better.[41]

That March, in 1946, Winston Churchill gave a speech in Fulton, Missouri, where he spoke grimly about the "Iron Curtain" descending across Europe. He condemned Moscow's imposition of totalitarian governments across Central and Eastern Europe, along with the expulsion of millions of Germans from their ancestral lands. "This is certainly not the liberated Europe we fought to build up," he declared. "Nor is it one which contains the essentials of permanent peace." The U.S. military was actively planning for a Soviet invasion of Western Europe. Many feared that war was inevitable.[42]

Gehlen kept pressing his case until finally, in June 1946, he received permission to return home. On June 30, he and his men boarded a troop transport bound for the French port of Le Havre. Waldman was concerned that the French might arrest Gehlen upon arrival for his wartime role, so he arranged for the entourage to travel disguised as German scientists. Waldman, who had gone ahead of the party, was also waiting for them at the dock on July 9 in case of any difficulties. Upon their arrival. Waldman whisked them away in three cars to Orly airport outside Paris, and from there, they flew to Frankfurt. The next day, they drove an hour north to Oberursel, a small town in the Taunus hills where the Americans had established an intelligence facility named Camp King. Gehlen was finally reunited with his family after Waldman personally fetched them from the Bavarian Alps. It had been over a year and a half since he'd last seen them. Felix-Christoph and Katharina were now teenagers with whom he shook hands while his two little daughters, Dorothee and Marie-Therese, hugged him around his knees.[43]

Then on Monday, July 15, 1946, Gehlen held his first meeting of a dozen staff in the cramped living room of the half-timbered house assigned to him and his family. The men comprised the core of his old military headquarters. His recruiter, Baun, had carefully stationed his recent SS hires in an old carpet factory in Karlsruhe. Gehlen set out his vision for the network as a security apparatus dedicated to battling Communism. They were working for the Americans, but he saw them as fighting for a greater Germany. He didn't need to warn them of the danger posed by the massing forces of leftists and Communists. He simply said they should consider themselves back on the front lines.[44]

5

Nuremberg

As Bauer formulated his ideas for a reckoning over the summer of 1945, the Allies revealed their vision for justice with plans for a military tribunal in Nuremberg. Twenty-four Nazi leaders, including Hitler's deputy Hermann Göring, military commanders, senior SS officers, youth and labor leaders, and members of the conservative elite who had facilitated the Nazi rise to power were to be tried for waging a war of aggression and committing war crimes. Robert Jackson, the U.S. Supreme Court justice who would lead the prosecution, had pushed the tribunal to adopt radical new laws such as Crimes against Humanity to address Nazi atrocities. The mass murder of Europe's Jews—the term "Holocaust" was not yet current—fell under this law but was not to be a focus of the trial. For Jackson, the tribunal's principal aim was to establish a global rules-based order to deter future warmongers.[1]

For Bauer, the tribunal represented the affirmation and expansion of the kind of international law he had proposed in his book. But he also saw a potential flaw in the symbolism of charging only a handful of Nazis for a crime that had required the acquiescence of a nation. What's more, he worried that Allied provisions to pursue future prosecutions were not as robust as they appeared. Jackson had insisted on indicting the Gestapo, the SS, the Brownshirts, and the General Staff as criminal organizations. If the tribunal was successful, former members of these groups would then become liable to prosecution. This was closer to Bauer's broader vision of justice, but it was unclear how—or if—such a ruling would be put into practice.[2]

The Americans and British had established denazification panels that theoretically had sweeping powers to bar Germans from work and refer them for prosecution depending on where they fit on a scale of complicity. Category I (war criminals) and II (activists, militarists, profiteers) could expect immediate arrest. Category III (minor incrimination), IV (fellow traveler), and V (uncompromised) would be allowed to return to their old lives. The trouble was that the panels relied on Germans to self-report Nazi affiliations, allowing the guilty to reassimilate with ease.[3]

The Allies' efforts to rebuild a German justice system capable of handling the sheer volume of prosecutions that Bauer wanted seemed willfully negligent. The country's judiciary had been destroyed—literally, in the case of its bombed-out courthouses, but also morally as an institution. Under Hitler, German judges had enforced the systematic persecution of political opponents, Jews, Roma, Sinti, disabled people, and gay men and issued more than eighty thousand death sentences through a parallel system of special courts across Germany and the occupied territories. Bauer assumed that such judges would be under arrest or barred from having anything to do with the law again. He was disturbed therefore by a British ruling that in the name of expediency, up to half the judges employed in their zone could be former Nazi Party members provided they had been "denazified." Even more galling for Bauer was the antisemitism that stymied his own efforts to find a job. When he had approached the U.S. legation in Stockholm that May, they informed him that "it would be inopportune for Jews to undertake work that is in any way public." Bauer had then gone to Copenhagen in June to try his luck. This time his job application was rejected without explanation and even his request to travel to Germany to look for work was turned down. Seemingly out of options, he took a stopgap position on Denmark's Price Control Council and tried to settle.[4]

Copenhagen was eerily intact beyond the bombed ruin of the Gestapo's old headquarters, and he found his parents' apartment exactly as they had left it the night they fled. But the mood was tense. Danish resistance fighters with blue-white-and-red-striped armbands patrolled the streets, looking for collaborators. Some had already been summarily shot. Nearly a quarter of a million refugees and ex-soldiers who had escaped the advancing Red Army languished in requisitioned schools, sports halls, and German transport ships in Copenhagen's harbor. Movement for Germans was restricted, and they received little medical attention. By July, more than four thousand had perished. "They have suffered what they themselves have caused," said one Danish woman, whose son had been tortured by the Gestapo.[5]

Bauer's frustration at being sidelined peaked as the Nuremberg trial approached that autumn of 1945. He had started a side job editing a newspaper for refugees, and decided to visit the main German refugee camp in Copenhagen to hear what they thought of the Nazis' crimes. The camp housed more than seventeen thousand people, mostly women, children, and the infirm, in a fenced enclosure of rudimentary wooden barracks that contained little more than peat stoves and bunks. The majority of the refugees had fled from East Prussia, where Soviet abuse of civilians had been brutal. Most still wore the patched-up clothes they had escaped in. To Bauer, they looked like typical Prussian peasants, who had been among Hitler's most avid supporters. No one he spoke to claimed to be a Nazi, but they didn't condemn Nazism either. "We had it . . . good under Hitler," said one. "The anti-Nazis are to blame for the death of our sons," claimed another. Many still seemed to believe they belonged to a German master race. As the trial began on November 20, 1945, Bauer wondered how the Allies hoped to convince these people of their own complicity.[6]

He read coverage of the tribunal in the grand tearoom of the Hotel D'Angleterre with growing trepidation. The trial was one of the first to be filmed, which meant Bauer could also observe the crowded interior of the Nuremberg courtroom and the raised dais for the Allied judges opposite the wooden pen holding the defendants: the once-portly Hermann Göring in his pale gray Luftwaffe uniform, stripped of all decorations, now strikingly gaunt from a prison diet and sharp-eyed after being weaned off his addiction to painkillers; the Wehrmacht generals Wilhelm Keitel and Alfred Jodl in their army dress, stiff martinets; the Interior Minister Wilhelm Frick, fidgeting in a new suit provided by the authorities. Hitler's former deputy, Rudolf Hess, grinned mania-

Defendants' dock, Nuremberg trial, c. 1945–1946
NARA / Creative Commons

cally at the press box. Many court observers were baffled that these frail-looking men had at one time held Europe under their sway.[7]

The fifty-three-year-old Jackson, a commanding presence with a fine baritone voice, dominated the first day with his reading of the sixty-five-page indictment, which introduced Raphaël Lemkin's term *genocide* to a global audience, as well as a staggering array of Nazi crimes from the murder of POWs and the annihilation of whole towns to mass shooting and gassing of people in concentration camps. Jews were mentioned as one of several groups that had faced persecution. The integrity of the global order rested on these proceedings, stated Jackson. The wrongs of which the court would hear were "so calculated, so malignant and so devastating that civilization cannot tolerate their being ignored, because it cannot survive their being repeated." Yet Jackson also argued that the German people were not responsible for the Nazis' crimes. They, too, had suffered under Hitler. He urged them to become partners in restoring the country's ruined reputation and establishing a moral and legal code that could unite the world against future wars. With these brief words, Jackson had realized Bauer's worse fear: the unearned exoneration of the German people.[8]

Other problems with Jackson's approach soon became apparent. He had pushed to include on the indictment criminal conspiracy to wage war, but the concept drawn from American law to prosecute gangsters hardly seemed to apply to the workings of a nation-state. At the same time, Jackson appeared overwhelmed by the sheer volume of evidence his prosecutorial team had assembled. Despite the Nazi regime's final orders to destroy incriminating paperwork, some officials had ignored the directive, and material had been uncovered in the most unlikely of places: at private addresses across the Alps, in old castles, and at the bottom of salt mines. All told, Nuremberg's document room contained 110,000 captured documents, 19 miles of film, and 25,000 photographs. But Jackson and his team had no historical framework to guide them, and even with a team of 365 civilian lawyers, clerical staff, and translators, they failed to process all the material. Jackson's glaring lack of knowledge of how the Nazi regime had functioned was soon apparent. Göring, who approached the trial with the belief that he would "defend the honor of the Third Reich" by denying everything, delighted in baiting Jackson as his prosecutors misinterpreted documents and stumbled over archaic German script. The evidence produced was still devastating—an hour-long film of the liberation of Bergen-Belsen and Dachau showed an endless stream of corpses that stunned the room and wiped Göring's self-satisfied grin off his face.[9]

Nuremberg document room, c. 1945–1946
Harry S. Truman Library & Museum / Creative Commons

Bauer wasn't worried that Jackson might fail to secure convictions against the defendants. His concern was that the tribunal wasn't persuading even open-minded Germans that further trials were needed in the country's domestic courts. There was a growing conviction among Germans that the tribunal was victors' justice. One poll of 150 Germans in December 1945 suggested that while most were happy to see senior Nazis prosecuted, a third didn't trust the evidence and half simply weren't interested. The trial might as well have been "taking place on the moon," observed a German member of the defense; it felt so removed from most people's struggles to find food and shelter amid the rubble. Hundreds were dying each week from sickness and malnutrition, and 1.5 million soldiers were still interned or missing.[10]

Bauer was alarmed by the apparent readiness of his countrymen to dismiss the trial. The sooner Germans stopped seeing the Allies as the enemy and understood the need to "clean out the pigsty" the better, he observed. "It would be terrible if the German people were so selfish that they thought only of themselves, if they forgot what immense suffering and misery the Nazis brought upon hundreds of millions of innocent people, if they did not understand what these millions feel and think beyond Germany's borders."[11]

. . .

Bauer took a break from the trial that December to visit his terminally ill father in Gothenburg for his seventy-fifth birthday. Bauer's nephews put on a little play that made fun of Ludwig's once-fearsome temper. Ella good-humoredly admonished Bauer for not being in Nuremberg to observe the trial. Two weeks later, after Bauer had returned to Copenhagen, Ella wrote that Ludwig had passed away. Bauer did not attend the funeral, probably because of the difficulty of getting travel papers. He had never fully reconciled with his father. Ludwig's last letter to Bauer was a simple offer to send him tobacco.[12]

Bauer continued to follow the trial closely as the new year began, and Soviet prosecutors presented evidence of Nazi war crimes on the eastern front. But any hope Bauer had that the tribunal would foreground the mass murder of the Jews was dashed. The Soviet prosecutors seemed more interested in scoring political points. They framed the German violence in the East as being perpetrated against the Soviet people in a transparent effort to justify their seizure of most of Central and Eastern Europe. Still, fragmentary insights into the genocide emerged. Otto Ohlendorf, an Einsatzgruppen officer awaiting trial, spoke to his role in killing ninety thousand Jews in occupied areas of the Soviet Union. An SS "deportation specialist," Dieter Wisliceny, also facing charges, described his orders to carry out the "biological annihilation of the Jewish people" and how his superior, Adolf Eichmann, had declared he'd "leap laughing into the grave" at the thought of the six million Jews they'd killed. But the systemic nature of the murder program was rarely addressed.[13]

The problem continued when French prosecutors presented the Nazi crimes committed on the western front and proved equally focused on their own agenda, which highlighted German crimes against the French resistance. French survivor Marie Claude Vaillant-Couturier described the arrival of Jewish families to Auschwitz and their selection for the gas chambers. But prosecutors chose not to examine the camp's role at the center of the Final Solution.[14]

Then in March 1946, Rudolf Höss, the former commandant of Auschwitz, was captured on a farm outside Flensburg. Höss's wife had given him away when British soldiers threatened to hand her eldest son over to the Soviets. The British roughed Höss up, but once brought for interrogation, he was perfectly willing to speak about his crimes.[15]

Rudolf Höss after capture, 1946
Courtesy of Cross family

Höss took the stand on April 15, 1946, in a dark suit and coolly confirmed his statement to the British that he had overseen the murder of more than 2.5 million people—he wasn't sure of the exact number. He then detailed how men, women, and children were tricked into undressing and entering the sealed chambers, thinking they were to have a shower, only for the pesticide Zyklon B to be administered instead. The prosecution then read out sections from a sworn affidavit Höss had provided. The method of killing was remarkably efficient, he confirmed. Zyklon B took the form of blue pellets infused with hydrogen cyanide, which reacted with warm air to form a poisonous gas. Five to seven kilograms of Zyklon B was enough to kill 1,500 people, stated Höss, and sometimes as many as 2,000 people could be squeezed into the larger gas chambers.[16]

The New York Times described the scene as the "crushing climax to the case." In Britain, *The Times* said of Höss's affidavit: "Its dreadful implications must surpass any document ever penned." At lunch in the prisoners' canteen, Hans Frank, the former governor-general of occupied Poland, told one of the U.S.-appointed psychologists who was monitoring the defendants that "to hear a man say out of his own mouth that he exterminated two and a half million people in cold blood . . . is something that people will talk about for a thousand years." The next day, Frank became the first defendant to confess to his own role in the killings. The others continued to maintain their innocence but seemed deflated and depressed, especially Göring, who had for long periods tried to rally his fellow defendants but now appeared to have given up. "They are like burnt-out embers," observed *The New York Times* correspondent, "so empty when power is squeezed out of them that it is incredible that they lit a fire that scorched the world."[17]

For Bauer, Höss's and Frank's testimony had finally spoken to the evil at the heart of the Nazi enterprise. Overall, he was impressed by how the tribunal had established a "moral record" of the Nazis' crimes. He saw in the mass of evidence, including 16,793 pages of court transcripts, the material that he and other German prosecutors might need to pursue further cases in domestic courts. But he also recognized that the tribunal had singularly failed to persuade the German people that a deeper reckoning was necessary. Indeed, many seemed to think the trial meant the past had been dealt with and took umbrage at any suggestion otherwise. When the pastor Martin Niemöller told a church gathering of young people in Erlangen in 1946 that the only way to a new life for Germans was to confess their guilt to victims, he was met with loud boos. The philosopher Karl Jaspers, who argued against collective guilt, still received a barrage of abuse for suggesting that Germans needed to address their individual responsibility. It wasn't guilt that Germans needed to feel, observed an exasperated fellow philosopher, but shame.[18]

● ● ●

The Nuremberg verdict, issued on October 1, 1946, saw twelve of the defendants sentenced to death and all but three of the others given long prison sentences. Göring committed suicide with a hidden cyanide capsule the day before he was due to be executed. The rest were hanged in the prison gymnasium in the early hours of October 15. They were led one at a time to the gallows, where a small group of journalists recorded their final moments as they climbed the scaffolding and shouted out short statements. Some insisted they were innocent; others that they had only ever done their duty. Their bodies were later reported to have been cremated in the ovens of Dachau, their ashes joining those of the camp's 39,000 victims. President Harry S. Truman declared that the proceedings had blazed "a new trail in international justice" that would long be remembered. *The New York Times* heralded a trial that had presented "stern and exact justice, not vengeance"; *The Times* of London declared that it was surely "the most momentous legal judgment in history."[19]

Further trials were planned in Nuremberg under Allied direction, targeting major offenders within government ministries, the military, the medical profession, and among industrialists. The occupation authorities were also increasingly turning to the newly reconstituted German courts to pursue cases against lesser offenders. This was precisely the shift Bauer was advocating, and on the surface there seemed to be some appetite for trials. Indeed, the following year, 1947, saw nine hundred prosecutions. But Bauer was unimpressed by their limited scope, as they mainly focused on local acts of violence associated with Hitler's rise to power and the regime's brutal final months. The Allies were partly to blame for the courts' restraint, as they had reserved the right to prosecute those accused of crimes beyond Germany's borders, given Cold War sensitivities. Many of the crimes relating to Nazi atrocities in Eastern Europe consequently fell outside the purview of the German judiciary.[20]

Even where the courts were authorized to pursue perpetrators, judges sought to limit charges or issue the lightest of sentences. German judges in the British zone were permitted to use the novel laws of Nuremberg to try state-sponsored mass murder as a crime against humanity. Most judges, however, insisted on sticking to the traditional German penal code that only allowed defendants to be tried for individual cases of murder to avoid the appearance of retroactive justice. Further complicating the matter, the German code included a Nazi-era provision that required proof of base, cruel, or sadistic motives in murder cases to provide cover for those who killed in the name of the state. The courts were allowing hundreds of perpetrators to walk free simply by claiming they had only been following orders.[21]

For Bauer, it was clear such leniency stemmed from the Allies' original decision to bring back Nazi-era judges at the expense of committed resisters like himself. Given the Allies' apparent lack of concern and German readiness to move on—one bishop suggested the church just forgive everyone—the prospect of delivering meaningful justice for the Nazis' victims seemed vanishingly distant.[22]

Bauer, whose job search continued to go nowhere, wrote in desperation to his old mentor Kurt Schumacher in May 1947. Schumacher had miraculously survived twelve years of Nazi incarceration—just as he had said he would—to emerge as leader of the Social Democratic Party, which he had started to rebuild from his new headquarters in Hannover. Given his moral standing, Schumacher was widely tipped to be the chancellor of a future Germany. The letter exchange between the two men didn't result in an immediate job offer but did at least

Drawing of Bauer, 1947
Courtesy of Marit
Tiefenthal

reconnect Bauer with party circles. Then, in the spring of 1948, he applied for the position of attorney general in the small city of Braunschweig, where the first local elections since 1933 had installed a Social
Democratic council. The attorney general's office oversaw seventeen
prosecutors and the entire gamut of cases brought before the city's
courts. The office also had the power to direct its own investigations
and initiate trials. An interview and visa were arranged for July in Hannover.[23]

But even as Bauer packed his bag that summer of 1948, he had to
wonder if his plans had any real purpose, given the looming threat of
war. Stalin had sent troops to blockade Allied-controlled areas of West
Berlin in June. His aim was to force the Allies to withdraw and cede
him their enclave behind the Iron Curtain. The Allies decided instead
to stage a massive airlift of 480 planes, bringing 2,500 tons of supplies
daily to the capital. It wasn't clear how long Berliners could hold on
or if the Americans and British would have to send in troops. At the
very least, a division of Germany seemed increasingly likely as Stalin
made moves to turn his zone into a single state by forcing through
the merger of the local branches of the Social Democratic Party with
their Communist rivals. Bauer would need to visit Schumacher to get
his read on Germany's future, if it even had one.[24]

6

Enemy Territory

THUS, BAUER FOUND HIMSELF on a train back to Germany toward the end of July 1948, observing the scenes of devastation rolling by and, just as keenly, his fellow passengers. He thought he detected a hostility toward him, though he wasn't sure if it was because people suspected him of being an exile or of being a Jew. "The émigrés reminded people of things they wanted to repress," he later observed. "People were afraid of questions that might be asked of them."[1]

He was doubting the wisdom of returning as he took a car for the last leg of his journey from Hamburg to Hannover. Lost in thought as night fell, he spotted a young hitchhiker beside the highway and on a whim asked the driver to stop. His new companion talked only of himself, but Bauer was happy to avoid politics and simply enjoyed hearing a young person share his hopes for the future. They pulled into Hannover ahead of the 11:30 P.M. curfew imposed by the British, and Bauer set off to find accommodation. Most of the city's big hotels had been destroyed, as well as much of the old town. The train station had an air-raid shelter where for ten pfennigs, a bench seat could be rented for the night. The Luisenhof hotel, a short walk away, offered slightly more comfortable bunk beds, which were probably more to Bauer's liking. People scurried among the piles of rubble or lingered on street corners, too hot and restless to sleep.[2]

Bauer found the fifty-two-year-old Schumacher propped up in bed in his home, which doubled as the party headquarters. He was startlingly frail. Doctors had been forced to amputate his left leg just above

Kurt Schumacher,
c. late 1940s
U.S. Army / Creative
Commons

the knee because of arterial disease, and he lived on a diet of milk and biscuits due to crippling stomach ulcers. His staff, tapping away on old typewriters in an adjoining room, didn't appear much fitter—the average weight of a German man in his twenties was just fifty-two kilograms in 1948. Yet Bauer found himself once again moved by Schumacher's energetic vision for Germany. His mentor accepted that the country would be partitioned but believed that the western zones could be rebuilt as a progressive socialist republic. The launch of a new currency and massive American aid program under the Marshall Plan promised a reconstruction boom. Businesses were reopening and shops restocking their shelves with goods.[3]

What's more, Schumacher saw signs of democratic renewal. The Allies had embarked on a large-scale program for reeducation through cultural exchanges and town hall–style meetings where Germans were encouraged to express their opinions and share responsibility for community decisions. This did not always come easily. Mayors and teachers still liked to hold forth while others approached the debating like a "wrestling match." But it clearly made an impression on the young. Schools were required to teach citizenship, and many encouraged their pupils to form their own councils. One such council in Lower Saxony suggested changing the popular motto from "Talking is silver, silence is golden" to "Talking is silver, debating is golden." The press, too, was flourishing, with more than forty newspapers and radio stations licensed in the U.S. zone of occupation, allowing for cautious debate about the past. Jewish Auschwitz survivor Fritz Benscher produced radio programs about the liberation of the camps for Radio Munich while startling neighbors with repeated cries of "Führer," the name he had given to his dog. The popular author Ernst Wiechert, who had published one of the first camp memoirs about his imprisonment in Buchenwald, shocked lecture audiences by proclaiming that camp survivors were the only true heroes of the war.[4]

But Schumacher was also worried about the forces set against his progressive vision. Attempts at denazification had all but ended after the occupation authorities had handed over the running of the assessment panels to German officials. The certificates of exoneration had earned the moniker *Persilschein* after the washing detergent that had the power to remove all stains. Indeed, Germans increasingly saw themselves as victims of the war. Former soldiers returning from POW camps, or families who'd been driven from their homes that now lay in Poland and Czechoslovakia, talked bitterly about their losses. The "unspeakable guilt" of the Germans was "evaporating," observed Jewish sociologist Theodor Adorno upon his return to Germany that year. Meanwhile, those who spoke out about the past were sidelined or vilified. The attacks against the philosopher Karl Jaspers, both in the press and through his letterbox, had become so vicious that he and his Jewish wife, having endured all twelve years of the Nazi regime in Germany, were emigrating to Switzerland.[5]

Schumacher was particularly concerned about the resurgence of the Right. The newly formed Christian Democratic Union Party, whose predecessor had been disbanded for helping Hitler to power, quickly won support among conservatives and religious groups. Several far-right political parties had also sprung up and were polling well as former Nazis continued to return to their prewar jobs in government and across civil society. Even Schumacher's own British-appointed security detail contained former SS men. Bauer, Schumacher advised, needed to be careful.[6]

Bauer said goodbye to Schumacher, unsure what, if anything, to reveal about his prosecutorial vision in the job interview. As it turned out, he was never given the opportunity. The two officials he met with informed him that the post of attorney general had been temporarily filled. They wanted Bauer to take a more junior role as a court director, where he would be one of fourteen judges presiding over cases without any power to investigate. They were quick to promise that he would remain the principal candidate for the attorney general position once it reopened. Bauer suspected that the officials wanted to keep him "more controllable," he wrote to Schumacher, while they worked out if he could be trusted.[7]

Bauer was still ready to accept the position. Despite the setback, and the undeniable hardship of life in Germany, he was surprised to feel happy to be home. He might rationalize his return according to his mission. But it was the small things that gave him a sense of belonging, like the restaurant he tracked down that served his favorite Swabian dish—spätzle—egg noodles tossed in butter. He stole the menu as a keepsake before his return to Copenhagen.[8]

Two months followed without progress, and Bauer began to suspect that his Jewishness and left-wing background had once again thwarted him. On a follow-up visit in November, the justice minister for Lower Saxony informed him that the administration harbored "professional and personal reservations" against him. Bauer could hardly have been surprised. The minister was himself a wanted war criminal accused of abuse and murder in Poland. Finally Bauer's application was approved that winter and a date set for him to take up his new position in April 1949.[9]

He packed up quickly and bade farewell to his Danish friend Paul Wagner. He had hoped to resume their friendship after the war, but the younger man, a newlywed, had drifted away. Bauer, who had been reading *Sexual Behavior in the Human Male* by the American sexologist Alfred Kinsey, which included the controversial findings that as many as one in ten Americans were gay, and a third of all men had had same-sex experiences, wrote Wagner a short note. "I've just finished Kensey's [*sic*] report . . . and learned that for 75.4389 percent of Americans, marriage means nothing epochal in their lives," he wrote somewhat bitterly. "This likely also goes for you."[10]

Bauer arrived in Braunschweig in April 1949. The high-ceilinged room he'd rented on Adolfstrasse was to his liking. He was lucky to have found it; 90 percent of the town center had been destroyed by bombing. Almost half the city was still living in former army barracks, bunkers, school buildings, and prefabricated huts, with scores of refugees arriving daily from the Soviet-controlled zone a few miles to the east. In the filthy conditions of the displaced persons camps, where Germans were obliged to live alongside Poles, Jews, and the French, anger regularly flared.[11]

On April 12, Bauer set off across the fields of rubble for his first day in the office. Only a quarter of the debris had been cleared, but he could see the outlines of the once-prosperous trading center in the few half-timbered buildings tottering over the medieval streets. The city had succumbed early to Nazism, voting the party into government in 1930. Indeed, Braunschweig had featured in Nazi lore as the place that had offered the Austrian Hitler a local government job so that he could qualify for German citizenship. Upon his rise to power, the Brownshirts had hunted down left-wing activists and journalists with such ferocity that Himmler had admonished the local leadership for its excessive brutality. At least twenty-six people had died in the violence. A handful of the city's high-level Nazis had been prosecuted after the war, notably Dietrich Klagges, Braunschweig's former Nazi premier, on charges of murder, abuse, extortion, and the deportation of the city's Jews. But of the 985 postwar investigations of Nazis in Braunschweig, only 83 had reached court by 1949, and most received light sentences. Indeed, when twenty-nine former Brownshirts and SS men were charged with assaulting political opponents and Jews in 1947, twenty thousand residents took to the streets to demand their release.[12]

Bauer entered the imposing courthouse on Münzstrasse and donned his black robe for the first time since 1933. A glimpse in the mirror showed his receding hairline and sagging jowls of the years lost to exile and war. He was forty-five years old, and there was a coarseness to his features he hadn't seen before and a hardness around the eyes. The district court president led him through his oath to use his "powers for the

Braunschweig ruins, c. late 1940s
Courtesy of Eckhard Schimpf

good of the German people." He was then shown to his office and introduced to his colleagues. Down the hallway was Walter Ahrens, who had
ordered beheadings of French laborers for minor offenses. Wilhelm
Hirte, the city's former chief public prosecutor, who worked in the
building opposite, had approved of the killing of fifteen thousand mentally ill patients as part of a Nazi euthanasia program. Over at police
headquarters, the superintendent was a former SS-Hauptsturmführer
in Kraków who had deported Poles to Auschwitz.[13]

Bauer recognized some of the names or quickly found out who they
were. They shook his hand and smiled, but the look in their eyes said it
all. They knew who he was, and he knew what they'd done. The hardest
part of his homecoming, Bauer was starting to appreciate, wasn't being
surrounded by such men and the feeling that every time he left his office he was stepping into enemy territory; it was knowing that he must
seek the good graces of former Nazis if he was to gain promotion.[14]

The first serious case he adjudicated must have felt like a test of his
politics. It concerned the appeal of the sole surviving partner of a
Jewish-owned linen firm called A. J. Rothschild and Sons, who was
seeking to overturn a verdict from 1938 for trying to take money out of
the country during the mass "Aryanization" of Jewish businesses. The
company's four directors had been arrested, and two subsequently perished in the camps.[15]

Compensation for Jewish companies like Rothschild and Sons was left to a patchwork of Allied- and German-run local administrations and so-called Wiedergutmachung—"making good again"—committees. The results had so far been desultory. The Nazis had requisitioned around 12 billion reichsmarks—$48.75 billion today—from Germany's half a million Jews, three-quarters of the community's wealth. An occupation law gave regional authorities power to confiscate property and impose special levies on Nazi families to compensate victims. However, by June 1948 only 104 million reichsmarks had been collected, and most of the money had gone to supporting the 700,000 Jewish survivors and war refugees from around Europe housed in displaced persons camps as they waited to emigrate to Israel or the United States. Many Jewish families were also cautious about seeking compensation and stirring German resentment. The sole surviving partner of Rothschild and Sons, Josef Schoenbeck, simply wanted himself and his dead partners exonerated of any wrongdoing. Such cases were rare, given the small number of Jewish survivors in Germany, few of whom were prepared to take to the courts.[16]

Bauer no doubt had his own family's experience in mind as he plunged into the casework that July. He'd missed the hush of the legal chamber, the stacks of files on his desk, the smell of old paper and musty filing cabinets. One of his first discoveries was that his colleague Wilhelm Hirte, the euthanasia jurist, had in fact led the 1938 prosecution of Schoenbeck and his business partners. Bauer guessed Hirte would be watching him closely, but he wasn't going to bend on the law. A month later he issued his ruling: a scathing critique of the earlier judgment and a call for the case to be reopened and Schoenbeck to be exonerated. To Bauer's surprise and disappointment, no one—not even Hirte—seemed to pay much attention. His position was too junior and he was isolated. If his purpose was to bring the nature of the Nazi state to light, then he would need allies and a case to capture attention.[17]

Leaving work one day, Bauer noticed two young journalists from the *Braunschweiger Zeitung* outside the courthouse. They looked as if they wanted to speak but were hanging back. "What can I do for you?" he asked.[18]

Bauer, c. 1950
Courtesy of Till
Ausmeier

The shorter of the two, Heinz Meyer-Velde, twenty-three, with bright red cheeks and thick glasses, got up the courage to ask Bauer for an interview.[19]

"There's no more time today: We still have consultation," said Bauer matter-of-factly. "But tomorrow we can meet at 5:00 P.M. in the café next door."[20]

The next afternoon, Bauer peppered the young men with questions over coffee: How long had they been living in Braunschweig? When had they found work? And, more importantly, what were young people talking about nowadays?[21]

Meyer-Velde was able to confirm what Bauer had already sensed was a new cultural permissiveness that had arisen since the collapse of Nazism. Women ran many households now—their husbands, if they returned at all, were often shells of men who struggled to reassert their authority. Some women explicitly blamed them for losing the war— indeed for being the cause of war—and they wanted greater agency in the bedroom and beyond. Women's magazines appealing to the zesty spirit of the age proliferated, while mail-order companies distributed birth control and sex advice pamphlets that talked about female pleasure.[22]

At the same time, the conservative backlash against increased freedoms for women, and the broader liberalization of the culture was considerable. The Volkswartbund, a Roman Catholic organization that had flourished under Hitler, railed against men's loss of status and feared that young people were being corrupted by dangerous outside influences like jazz music and erotic literature; five hundred tons of smutty magazines had reached Bavaria over the Alps that summer, according to one report. To counter the danger, police departments in Lower Saxony and other states reestablished vice squads—last deployed by Himmler—to monitor newsstands and bookshops. Gay men, who had enjoyed greater freedom in the immediate aftermath of the war, were also targeted. One of the few Nazi-era edicts that the Allies had left in place was a clause targeting gay men for any form of questionable contact. More than three thousand were arrested in 1948. One, Karl Gorath, was sentenced to five years by the same judge who had condemned him to the camps before the war. "Ah, you again!" the judge had exclaimed upon seeing him.[23]

Bauer must have been reminded of Weimar and the feeling of a society at war with itself. He wanted to speak out, but he knew that as a judge he must avoid politics. Instead, he limited himself to writing an article on prison reform and meeting several more times with Meyer-Velde for coffee and a pastry. He felt profoundly alone. When he took the long way home from the courthouse to Adolfstrasse, he passed the park near the city theater, which had reopened with a production of the Nazi favorite *Carmina Burana*. His eye was inevitably drawn to the men gathered under the trees. But it would have been foolhardy for him to linger and risk the job he'd waited so long to regain.[24]

Bauer looked to the national stage for a decisive political shift. On May 12, the Soviets lifted their blockade of Berlin. A few weeks later, the Allies announced elections across their zones of occupation to create a West German state to be known as the Federal Republic of Germany. The Allies would remain in charge of national security and foreign policy while the West German government managed domestic matters. Bauer was initially optimistic. Schumacher was the early favorite to become chancellor, and a German-led commission had produced a new constitution that enshrined a range of human rights into law. But as the election campaign progressed that summer, it became clear that Schumacher's socialist vision was failing to connect with voters. By contrast, the conservative seventy-three-year-old Konrad Adenauer, a Catholic former mayor of Cologne and opponent of Hitler, was surging in the polls with a promise to restore order. On August 14, 1949, Adenauer's center-right Christian Democratic Party narrowly won the election with the support of the country's eight million former Nazi Party members. Bauer feared what type of order the new chancellor would impose at their behest.[25]

Part II

7

Restoration

H ANS GLOBKE, a skilled bureaucrat of the Third Reich, was
tempted when Konrad Adenauer asked him to run his administration in September 1949. He did not know the new chancellor,
but he appreciated the older man's staunch conservatism, Rhineland
background, Catholic faith, and sympathy for those of good character and Christian values who had fallen in line with Nazism. As Adenauer's chief of staff, Globke would be uniquely placed to shape the
country, in charge of determining the chancellor's legislative agenda,
staffing ministries, and rebuilding the country's institutions as it
emerged from totalitarianism. Globke was flattered but keenly aware
of the danger he faced in accepting the offer after narrowly escaping
prosecution as a war criminal.[1]

Hans Globke, 1940
bpk Bildagentur /
Deutsches
Historisches Museum /
Liselotte Orgel-Köhne
(Purper) /
Art Resource, NY

Few in government had known how to put Hitler's racial ideology into practice when, in 1935, the Führer had announced his intention at Nuremberg to exclude Jews from the life of the nation. Half a million Jews needed to be identified and stripped of their rights and citizenship as a result of the so-called Nuremberg Race Laws, which defined a Jew as a person with three or more Jewish grandparents. First-degree "Mischlinge," or "half-breeds"—those with two Jewish grandparents—were also to be treated as full Jews if they still practiced Judaism or were married to a Jew. Globke, a senior civil servant in the Reich Interior Ministry, saw that it would be technically difficult to enforce these laws. So he and a colleague drafted a commentary to provide a legal rationale and guidelines for policymakers and the courts, which earned praise in Nazi circles for its "scientific" thinking on the danger of "alien blood" and "racial defilement." Globke's advice was soon in high demand as the Reich expanded. He introduced additional measures to mark Jews out: They were forced to adopt the middle names *Israel* and *Sara* if their own didn't sound Jewish enough and to have their passports stamped with a red *J*. Reich interior minister Wilhelm Frick recommended Globke's promotion in 1938 for his "outstanding" work on the race laws as well as his "loyalty and constant readiness for duty."[2]

When the war began, the Nazi leadership was keen to export its model for persecution to the puppet regimes of occupied Europe. So Globke and Frick traveled to Bratislava, Slovakia, in September 1941. Globke usually wore a suit and tie at the ministry, but Frick had introduced a uniform for official visits that included a peaked black cap emblazoned with the eagle and swastika and a double-breasted black jacket with another swastika on the sleeve. The dozen-strong German delegation paraded through the town center, pausing in front of the waiting cameras to receive a bouquet of flowers from two girls belonging to the Slovak branch of a Nazi youth organization.[3]

Then they got down to business. The Slovaks were offering to send Jews to Germany for forced labor on the understanding that they

Globke in Slovakia, 1941
B 183-78475-0001, Bundesarchiv

would never return. The Germans were ready to oblige. Globke was able to provide expert advice on how to strip Slovak Jews of their rights. Four days later, the Slovak newspapers announced the government's intention to eliminate Jews from the economic life of the country. By the following spring, most were in ghettos, and SS deportation specialist Adolf Eichmann arranged for a first batch of twenty thousand Jews to be deported to Auschwitz.[4]

Globke was not directly involved in the conception of the Final Solution, although his co-commentator played a leading role in discussions at the Wannsee Conference in 1942 over whether to deport or sterilize first-degree "Mischlinge." Globke focused instead on adjudicating on the cases of Jews married to ethnic Germans, who had thus far received a measure of protection. Following Stalingrad, however, Goebbels wanted them gone. He gave a speech in the Berlin Sportpalast on February 18, 1943, in which he called for their "complete and radical extermi—" before catching himself and saying "elimination." Nine thousand were subsequently rounded up. Globke fielded desperate pleas from the wives of Jewish men. He instructed one woman to divorce her husband. When she declined, he refused her appeal to save the man. Another woman sat in Globke's office begging him to prevent the deportation of her half-Jewish son. Globke asked her if she had divorced her husband yet, and when she, too, said no, he scoffed, "Then you're still stuck with the Jew!" and did not prevent the boy's arrest.[5]

Globke and Frick were both arrested after the war. Frick was charged with crimes against humanity, in part for his role in implementing the Nuremberg Race Laws. But Globke was lucky. His application to the Nazi Party had been turned down due to his previous allegiance to the conservative Center Party. He used the rejection to cast himself as a mere functionary and shrewdly claimed that his legal guidebook had helped to protect people with a quarter or less Jewish blood. "I do not think that Globke's record is black enough to prevent his being employed in an advisory capacity, under supervision," observed Brigadier C.E.D. Bridge during Globke's denazification proceedings in 1945. Globke then cooperated with prosecutors to incriminate Frick, who was subsequently hanged at Nuremberg.[6]

In 1946, the British appointed Globke chief treasurer of his native Aachen, a city near the border with Belgium and the Netherlands. He lived in a generous apartment with his wife and three school-age children, seemingly just another bureaucrat with graying hair, stooped shoulders, and time on his hands to indulge in his passion for stamp collecting, Agatha Christie novels, and Armenian history. But he understood that his comfortable life was contingent on remaining outside the public eye and keeping his past hidden.[7]

Globke was open with Adenauer about his past as he explained that he would be a political liability at the center of the administration. But Adenauer read Globke's record differently. He wanted Globke precisely because his status as a senior figure of the Third Reich, combined with his knowledge of the inner workings of government, uniquely qualified him to help weave the nation back together. Adenauer did not condone Nazism. He supported punishing the "truly guilty" and privately recognized that the German people had been complicit in the "great cruelties" carried out in concentration camps, and by the SS and the army in Poland and the Soviet Union. Adenauer had himself suffered under the Nazis. He'd been dismissed as mayor of Cologne, arrested twice by the Gestapo, and constantly harassed. His wife had

Globke, 1951
B 145 Bild-
F000024-0042,
Bundesarchiv

attempted suicide with painkillers while in prison and died in 1948
from lingering complications. Yet Adenauer was prepared to follow the
edict of his church and forgive, which also made good political sense.
It was time, he believed, to end the division of Germans into the "objectionable" and the "unobjectionable" and enlist the millions who had
diligently served the Third Reich in rebuilding the country. The scale
of the task remained daunting: Rubble still choked city centers, food
was rationed, and millions were entering their fifth year living in shel-
ters and displaced persons camps. The entire machinery of government needed to be rebuilt. And in Globke, Adenauer believed he had
found a man of rare organizational talents with a strong desire to move
the country on from the past.[8]

In September 1949, Globke moved to the provisional West German
capital of Bonn, where he took an office next to the chancellor's, first in
a temporary hotel and then in the Palais Schaumburg, a villa on the
banks of the Rhine. Adenauer, a fierce, austere man with few interests
outside politics beyond the beds of roses he cultivated at home, soon
invested complete trust in Globke as a guide and intellectual partner.
The two men took walks together on a prescribed route around the
chancellery grounds most afternoons at 3:30 P.M. Adenauer, stiff and
tall, was instantly recognizable by his favorite homburg hat and wiz-
ened features, with Globke usually a half step behind, his gold-rimmed

Konrad Adenauer, 1952
Katherine Young /
Creative Commons

spectacles catching the light whenever he leaned forward to listen or share his views.[9]

Adenauer laid out his Nazi reintegration policy on September 20, 1949, in his first address to the Bundestag in the former gymnasium of a local teaching academy.[10]

"In the belief that many have subjectively atoned for a guilt that was not heavy," he told the packed session, "[the Federal Republic government] is determined, where it appears acceptable to do so, to put the past behind us." It was time to "let bygones be bygones" he declared, to shouts of "Bravo."[11]

A motion calling for an immediate end to denazification was overwhelmingly agreed to in the Bundestag. Globke then moved swiftly to usher through a general amnesty for offenses committed during the war and in the immediate postwar period. There was some debate as to where to draw the line of forgiveness, but the final bill stated that anyone with a sentence of a year or less—some 792,176 people—would be pardoned. This figure included 30,000 war criminals who had already benefited from light sentences.[12]

The amnesty bill passed in December 1949 with a large majority that included support from the Social Democrats. Globke pressed ahead with plans to reverse denazification entirely by offering to reinstate the 265,000 former members of Hitler's regime who had lost their jobs and pension rights and who referred to themselves as Entnazifizierungsgeschädigten, or "those damaged by denazification." Further proposals included a quota for the compulsory employment of former Nazis in each ministry. Globke was also keen to recognize other types of victims and offer them compensation: disabled veterans, war widows, expellees, those who had lost their homes to bombing, and returning POWs, who were paid for time served irrespective of any crimes they might have committed. Given the numbers involved—potentially 80 percent of the country—a special tax would be needed.[13]

By contrast, the compensation Globke was prepared to offer Nazi victims was limited. Only German Jews and those who could prove they had been politically persecuted—some 300,000 people, all told—would be eligible. There would be no recognition for forced laborers, gay men and lesbians, Sinti and Roma, those forcibly sterilized, or any of the millions of victims, Jewish or otherwise, outside Germany who had not formerly been citizens. Adenauer argued in the Bundestag that considering the shattered German economy, Wiedergutmachung—"making good again"—could not extend to everyone. But he hoped that the government's overall assumption of responsibility for the war would be recognized in itself as an important act of public accountability. Guilt had been removed from the conscience of individuals and reduced to a bureaucratic process.[14]

Criticism of the policies was pointed. Schumacher accused Adenauer of failing to issue a clear condemnation of the Third Reich. The Social Democrat Adolf Arndt attacked Globke's position as proof that "National Socialism had its central seat in the Federal Chancellery itself." The press picked up on this idea, calling Globke variously a "quietly treading sphinx," the "gray eminence," and the "spider in Bonn's web." But Adenauer stood firmly behind Globke—"You don't throw away dirty water until you have clean water"—and the attacks died down except from a few survivor groups that the chancellor was happy to ignore.[15]

Crucially, the Allies made no official comment. Indeed, from Washington's perspective, Adenauer had masterfully contained the anger of former Nazis and army veterans while doing just enough to recognize the rights of victims. By 1949, the Truman administration had come to see West Germany as the vanguard of its rapidly escalating confrontation with Moscow. The Soviet Union had successfully tested an atomic bomb the year before, canceling out the United States' nuclear advantage against the numerically superior Red Army. The Soviets had also announced the creation of their own proxy state in East Germany and were moving to rapidly build up German military police units to supplement their own forces along the border with the Federal Republic. The imbalance in troop numbers and the increasing cost of defending Europe had even led Washington to support the idea of rebuilding the West German military.[16]

This was precisely the policy Adenauer wanted to pursue on principle—West Germany would only be sovereign when it had its own army—and out of necessity to ward off a Soviet attack. Adenauer made rearmament his priority as 1950 began. He understood that it was a sensitive topic with some of the Allies; the French were adamant that it was still too soon to be handing weapons to the Germans. Rearmament was also deeply unpopular in the Federal Republic; polls suggested two-thirds were opposed in a nation tired of war. "We would rather have healthy people in healthy houses be bolshevized than cripples in holes in the ground," declared the Social Democrat politician Carlo Schmid.[17]

Adenauer didn't feel the country could wait for a shift in public opinion, so he asked Globke to quietly cast around for former military figures to begin planning rearmament. There was no shortage of generals looking for work, eager to restore, as they saw it, the lost honor of the Wehrmacht. The German General Staff as an organization had been found not guilty of war crimes at Nuremberg, but the final judgment had called them a "disgrace to the honorable profession of arms" and dozens of senior officers had been convicted of war crimes in subsequent tribunals. The obvious person for Globke to turn to was Reinhard Gehlen, whose U.S.-backed spy network preserved an entire branch of the Wehrmacht. The Americans insisted that all contact with Gehlen go through them, but Globke got in touch anyway and learned that Gehlen's relationship with his U.S. overseers was under strain and he was eager to start working for the West German government. Globke saw the potential of Gehlen's group to serve as a ready-made security solution for the fledgling republic.[18]

. . .

Reinhard Gehlen was indeed disgruntled. The newly formed CIA had taken over his organization in 1949 and set him up in a dedicated facility in Pullach outside Munich as his network expanded to more than four thousand agents across the Federal Republic and Soviet-occupied Eastern Europe. The Americans were principally concerned with Moscow's broader military ambitions and had tasked Gehlen with monitoring Soviet troop movements in the Eastern Bloc. Gehlen's priority, however, was the domestic threat. He remained obsessed with the idea that Moscow was constructing a red underground of West German socialists, writers, journalists, and left-wing activists to weaken national resolve and create discord with the Allies by exposing West Germany's links to the Nazi past.[19]

Gehlen found some sympathy for his idea among the Americans, who were themselves gripped with paranoia after the discovery of real-life Soviet spies like the German physicist Klaus Fuchs, who had been caught stealing American nuclear secrets. The CIA had sanctioned Gehlen's spying on thousands of West Germans, including agents in most government ministries, and surveillance of opposition politicians. They even agreed to raid the home of Buchenwald survivor Eugen Kogon, who had written an influential history of the concentration camp system and spoken out against rearmament.[20]

But James Critchfield, the CIA officer overseeing the operation in Pullach, was concerned about the growing number of former Nazis in Gehlen's employ. The thirty-three-year-old midwesterner didn't oppose the use of ex-Nazis per se, but he feared Gehlen was being unscrupulous in his recruitment practices. When Critchfield asked Gehlen to supply him with a detailed list of his agents, Gehlen refused. So,

Critchfield set up a secret camera in Pullach to monitor the German's office and soon discovered that his counterintelligence operation was almost entirely staffed with ex-Gestapo and SS men. They included Emil Augsburg, a former member of an Einsatzgruppe that had killed hundreds of Poles and Jews in Poland and the Soviet Union, and Rudolf Oebsger-Röder, the head of an Einsatzkommando that had murdered thousands more.[21]

Critchfield summoned Gehlen to a series of showdown talks. But Gehlen brazenly denied that he employed any former SS men, exposing the fundamental weakness of Critchfield's position: If he fired Gehlen, he'd face awkward questions from his superiors and possible public scrutiny. Critchfield complained bitterly to Washington that Gehlen was "difficult," "suspicious," and wouldn't take orders. He backed down nonetheless. Privately he wondered how Gehlen failed to see the danger he was creating for himself by hiring people who might be exploited and compromised by the Soviet Union if their identities became known. Critchfield didn't know if it was arrogance on Gehlen's part or a deeper moral blindness that meant he neither saw his complicity in Hitler's war nor recognized the guilt in others.[22]

From Globke's perspective, Gehlen was a man who understood the dangers posed by the past and was dedicated to fighting Germany's enemies. There was no sign the Americans would allow Adenauer to assume control of Gehlen's organization while the Allies discussed West Germany's overall security arrangements. But Globke was confident that some sort of arrangement could be reached. Meanwhile, in early 1950, the Allies announced a plan to create a German-run domestic intelligence service—the Bundesamt für Verfassungsschutz, or Federal Agency for the Protection of the Constitution—to monitor internal threats. Gehlen was the obvious candidate for the role. But when Adenauer put his name forward, he and Globke were surprised to find the Allies united in opposition. The Americans did not want to give up a useful asset, while the British were alarmed by the idea of Gehlen combining his current network of agents across Europe with a domestic operation, which would have borne an un-

James Critchfield,
1951
N46/2, BND-Archiv

comfortable resemblance to Himmler's all-powerful Reich Security
Main Office. The position went instead to London's pick: Otto John, a
former senior lawyer for Lufthansa who had been part of the anti-
Nazi resistance that attempted to assassinate Hitler in 1944 and had
subsequently assisted the British prosecution of Nazi war criminals.
Adenauer took an immediate dislike to John and remained determined to make use of Gehlen.[23]

On June 21, 1950, Globke paid Gehlen a visit in Pullach. The enclosed compound had originally been built as a settlement for the Nazi
Party elite, with several single and semidetached houses for staff families, as well as an amply stocked canteen, a hair salon, an outdoor
swimming pool, a clubhouse with a bar and dance room, and, in the
complex's old air-raid shelter, a bust of Hitler, left there by the Americans as a curiosity.[24]

The two men met in Gehlen's offices in the former villa of Martin
Bormann, the Nazi Party chancellery head. The villa had been dubbed
the "White House" because the CIA was also stationed there. Globke
seemed to loom over an agitated-looking Gehlen as they entered an
oak-paneled room with a grand piano in the corner. As one CIA observer later noted, "Gehlen's behavior toward Globke was like that of a
small schoolboy in the presence of a powerful master."[25]

Globke asked to see the centerpiece of Gehlen's intelligence operation: a vast card index system of more than sixty thousand names,

Gehlen's headquarters, Pullach
Olaf Kosinsky / Creative Commons

arranged alphabetically, that allowed Gehlen to keep tabs on people on both sides of the Iron Curtain. Globke could see that Gehlen maintained files not just on Communists and Social Democrats but also on prominent former Nazis, along with their wartime records, aliases, and current roles in government.[26]

Globke asked Gehlen if he had a file on him. He did. Globke's role in shaping the Nuremberg Race Laws was public knowledge, but he had managed to keep quiet his involvement in the murder of the Slovakian Jews, as well as how his office had fielded pleas from Germans to spare their Jewish spouses or "half-breed" children from deportation. Globke did not take offense that Gehlen had been digging around in his past. He knew as well as Gehlen that power lay in knowing others' secrets. Indeed, he saw the potential for Gehlen's organization to serve Adenauer politically by gathering material on his opponents.[27]

Globke moved on to his news: The West German government had agreed to take on some of the costs of Gehlen's organization from the Americans. But in return Globke expected regular reports from Gehlen on matters of concern to the chancellery. And one other thing—Globke would be taking his own dossier home with him.[28]

. . .

Gehlen, 1949
N46/2, BND-Archiv

That summer of 1950, the Cold War rapidly escalated with the outbreak of fighting in Korea. Communist forces in the North, aided and
abetted by Stalin, almost succeeded in seizing the entire peninsula
from the U.S.-backed regime in the South. The Truman administration
feared the attack was a prelude to a Soviet invasion of Europe. Adenauer pushed again for rearmament and this time, with Washington's
support, secured French agreement to begin work on a treaty to rearm
West Germany.[29]

Adenauer was encouraged but knew that the German public still
needed to be won over. In particular, he needed the support of the former soldiers and officers he was counting on to staff the new army.
Thus far, veteran groups had been almost unanimous in declaring that
they would not support rebuilding the military while so many of their
comrades were serving long sentences for war crimes. A flashpoint was
Landsberg Prison near Munich, where the Americans held hundreds
of military officers. A veterans' campaign to free the soldiers, who were
portrayed as "political prisoners" unjustly punished for their service to
the fatherland, had united conservatives and nationalists. Adenauer
made the pragmatic decision to back the drive, and the U.S. High
Commissioner John J. McCloy reluctantly agreed to a review in December 1950 that resulted in 102 prisoners being pardoned and the
sentences of 158 others being reduced.[30]

Adenauer's support for the campaign won him public acclaim and the backing of many former soldiers for rearmament. Landsberg had, however, also given fringe voices from the Far Right a boost. Otto Ernst Remer of the Socialist Reich Party, a former general revered in Nazi circles for his role in thwarting the plot to blow up Hitler in 1944, seized the moment to push Nazi ideas back into the mainstream. Tall and gaunt—"cadaverous," *The Washington Post* called him—Remer was a compelling speaker, who mannered his style on Hitler, right down to the one-armed salute. He was careful to avoid open antisemitism. A nationalist member of the Bundestag had been ejected from his party for asserting that "it is possible to have differing opinions about the question of whether gassing the Jews was the means of choice. Maybe other ways could have been found to get rid of them." Instead Remer spoke to packed halls of ex-soldiers and former Nazi Party members in not-so-subtle code that he shared the same "blood group" as the Nazis. Uniformed guards flanked the podium as Remer came loping into the room, usually to the sound of Hitler's favorite marching tune, the *Baden-weiler*.[31]

The Socialist Reich Party gained more than 350,000 votes in Lower Saxony in the local elections of 1951; or, as the *Frankfurter Allgemeine Zeitung* put it, every tenth representative in the state parliament belonged to a party that was an avowed successor to National Socialism. Adenauer didn't consider Remer to be a direct threat; his party was too fringe. The problem was that Washington thought otherwise. An undersecretary at the U.S. State Department was investigating whether Remer was planning a coup, and U.S. High Commissioner McCloy had warned Adenauer that the United States was prepared to intervene militarily if necessary.[32]

The last thing Adenauer wanted was to jeopardize West Germany's path to full statehood. Clearly he needed to put Remer back in his box. The West German state had no legal means for banning political parties until the creation of a constitutional court, which wasn't scheduled to happen until the following year. And Adenauer didn't trust the domes-

Otto Ernst Remer,
1949
DER SPIEGEL

tic spy chief Otto John to handle the matter. So he was pleased when his justice minister, Robert Lehr, came up with an elegant solution to discredit Remer. During an election rally in Braunschweig in May 1951, Remer had called those involved in the attempt to assassinate Hitler traitors. Lehr himself had been part of the resistance circle involved in the plot and suggested to Adenauer that he now sue Remer for slander. Adenauer knew they would need to proceed cautiously; many Germans, especially in military circles, still saw the assassination

Robert Lehr, 1950
B 145 Bild-P004377,
Bundesarchiv /
Creative Commons

plot as a betrayal that had undermined the German war effort. Few wanted to admit that fighting for Hitler had been wrong. Lehr thought the public needed a stern lesson in civic duty. He assured Adenauer that the new attorney general in Braunschweig was just the man to deliver it.[33]

8

Resistance

B AUER WAS PROMOTED to attorney general of Braunschweig in August of 1950 and immediately stated his intention to pursue Nazis. "The people's impartial sense of justice demands punishment and I, for my part, fully endorse it," he told an audience of senior judges and lawmakers at his inauguration. The former Nazis in the room might shift in their seats, but Bauer knew they were well protected under Adenauer, whose rapid reintegration of former Third Reich officials and drive for rearmament had emboldened the right flank of his coalition. Bauer could already feel the effects in Braunschweig, where support for the ex-Nazi general Otto Ernst Remer was surging among the army veterans and refugees crowding the camps on the city's edge. Braunschweig, he wrote to a friend, had become a "hotbed" of fascism.[1]

Bauer began his tenure with a flurry of investigations into Braunschweig's former Nazis. Mostly he reopened cases against defendants who'd been treated leniently by the courts or who'd had their proceedings dropped following public outcry. He ran into immediate resistance. When he indicted the city's deputy Gestapo chief in autumn 1950, the court dismissed the case on the grounds that the man's campaign of murder and abuse was in fact legal under the Nazis, so he had simply been doing his duty. The few cases Bauer did bring to court provoked a furious backlash. His office was inundated with complaints, and his friend Meyer-Velde reported back to him mutterings in town that the Nazis should have gassed him, too. Worse still, his work felt insignificant compared to the national debates shaping future prosecutions of war criminals. The Bundestag was discussing a measure to prevent German courts from implementing Allied laws such as crimes against humanity; no one was paying attention to the prosecution of a few Nazis in the provinces.[2]

It was all the more frustrating, therefore, to see the ease with which the former Nazi general Remer had turned his local election campaign into a national spectacle. His speeches attracted ever bigger crowds in Lower Saxony ahead of the state elections of May 1951. Bauer's neighbors—housewives, teachers, shopkeepers, and off-duty policemen—flocked to hear Remer speak. Three days before the polls, Remer addressed a raucous evening rally in Braunschweig's shooting club. Eight hundred people had crammed into the hall, while guards in red armbands, black trousers, and leather boots held back another four hundred outside.[3]

To cheers from the crowd, Remer declared that those who had tried to kill Hitler in 1944 had betrayed their country: "The time will come," he stated, "when people will shamefully conceal the fact that they were part of the 20 July 1944 [plot to assassinate Hitler]. You can bet your life that the traitors will one day have to answer to a German court."[4]

The Socialist Reich Party's modest return in the state elections in Lower Saxony was much less than some had feared, but alarming nonetheless. Bauer was therefore pleased when Interior Minister Robert Lehr's criminal complaint against Remer for slander landed on his desk that June 1951. The crime was minor; a conviction might even burnish Remer's credentials with the Far Right. But as the charge took shape in Bauer's mind, he saw a means to turn the case into an indictment of the Third Reich as a whole. The plotters couldn't be considered traitors because the Nazi regime itself had been illegal, starting from the moment that Hitler suspended the constitution in 1933. If Bauer could establish that idea in court, he might be able to undermine the defense of Nazi perpetrators that they had only been following state orders.[5]

Equally important, the trial was sure to command public attention, given Remer's profile and the sensational nature of the the plot itself.

Some of the most prominent families in the country had been involved in the attempt to kill Hitler. At the center of the plot was Count Claus Schenk von Stauffenberg, a member of the General Staff who in 1944 concluded that the war was lost and the bloodshed must be stopped. He was ready to sue for peace with the Allies and had secretly established contact with them.[6]

The circle of plotters he assembled proved so small that he was required to plant the timed bomb in Hitler's Wolf's Lair headquarters in East Prussia himself, before rushing back to Berlin to rally his fellow officers to arrest the Nazi leadership. The plan almost immediately came undone when Hitler's morning briefing was unexpectedly brought forward. Stauffenberg, who had lost an eye, his right hand, and two fingers on his left fighting in North Africa, managed to arm only one of his two bombs, which he concealed in his briefcase. He entered the briefing hut to find Hitler already at the conference table, surrounded by senior officers. Space was made for Stauffenberg near Hitler. He slid his briefcase under the table.[7]

Claus von Stauffenberg,
c. 1940s
Creative Commons

Stauffenberg made an excuse to leave, waited in a neighboring building for the bomb to detonate, and then fled to Berlin. But as he began issuing orders to arrest the Nazi leadership, news emerged over the radio that Hitler had survived. That was when Remer, instructed by the plotters to arrest Joseph Goebbels, was persuaded by the propaganda chief to detain Stauffenberg instead. The count was shot that evening. Over the following days, a special "People's Court" sentenced 4,980 people to death and dispatched hundreds more to concentration camps.[8]

By a quirk of fate, Bauer had known Stauffenberg personally—they had gone to the same school in Stuttgart and even taken part in a production of Schiller's *William Tell*. Bauer understood that Stauffenberg, like so many of his social class and profession, had once supported the Nazi regime. Stauffenberg's decision to turn against Hitler had not been in reaction to atrocities on the eastern front but because Germany was losing the war; his principal concern was to prevent the "destruction of the material and blood-based substance" of the nation. By coming to Stauffenberg's defense, Bauer knew he was in danger of validating a mindset that had aided Hitler's rise to power. But he also saw that Stauffenberg's journey to resistance offered a story of redemption for his fellow countrymen—if they were prepared to listen to a Jewish socialist.[9]

Bauer began his Remer investigation that autumn by contacting the few members of Stauffenberg's inner circle who had survived, either by going into hiding or thanks to blind luck. Fabian von Schlabrendorff had been in a courthouse waiting to receive a death sentence when an Allied bomb fell on the building, killing the judge and disrupting proceedings until the end of the war. Schlabrendorff, like many of those connected to the plot, had been subjected to public criticism in the years since for betraying the country. Bauer was heartened when Schlabrendorff and several of the plotters' families agreed to testify to the patriotism and moral vision of the plotters, which he planned to supplement by calling several leading theological and ethical scholars to speak to the Christian duty to resist in the face of evil.[10]

As Bauer built his case, he anticipated that Remer's defense would sidestep the issue of whether it was morally right to kill Hitler by arguing that the plotters' contact with the Allies was their real treason. From there the defense could draw parallels with left-wing members of the anti-Hitler resistance who had sided with Moscow—a move that would almost certainly play to current fears of Soviet infiltration.

Bauer planned to counter this argument by calling Otto John—the new domestic spy chief who had served as the plotters' liaison to the British—to make the point that all resistance to a despotic and criminal regime was legitimate.[11]

. . .

With the Remer case poised to capture national attention that autumn of 1951, Bauer began to think more broadly about how to oppose the conservative order taking shape under Adenauer. Bauer was naturally on guard against the return of fascism as Hans Globke moved to reintegrate Nazis across government. But this wasn't his principal fear. Adenauer, it seemed to Bauer, wanted to unify the country by enforcing strict social conformity. Nowhere was this more evident than in the prosecution of men under the anti-gay laws contained within Article 175 of the German penal code. As attorney general, Bauer was in the invidious position of overseeing its application. Yet he thought he saw an opening that October to overturn the statute with the inauguration of the Federal Republic's version of the U.S. Supreme Court. Bauer believed the law violated Article 2 of the new constitution, which guaranteed the "right to free development of [one's] personality." A sympathetic judge might be persuaded to appeal a case to the court.[12]

Bauer was encouraged in his thinking by a shift in German attitudes toward homosexuality. The previous year, police had detained a seventeen-year-old rent boy named Otto Blankenstein in Frankfurt and coerced him into becoming an informant. Officers then drove Blankenstein around the city to point out his customers. More than two hundred people were investigated as a result, and fifty were arrested and interrogated. One man leaped to his death from the Goethe Tower after receiving a court summons; another poisoned himself in a cinema; a dental technician and his friend gassed themselves. The proceedings were overseen by a judge named Kurt Ronimi, who, as public prosecutor under the Nazis, had zealously gone after gay men and who had continued his crusade as a judge postwar. He had created a special court to try Article 175 cases that reminded many of Nazi-era justice and prompted backlash in the press. The *Frankfurter Rundschau* questioned the role of Article 175 and opened its letter pages for debate, where at least some respondents called for tolerance and expressed revulsion at Ronimi's crusade. *Der Spiegel* pointed out the absurdity of attempting to prosecute the one million homosexuals it calculated lived in West Germany. Growing public disquiet led to the dissolution of the special court and Ronimi's own transfer to another district.[13]

Otto Blankenstein,
1950
Creative Commons

Liberal Frankfurt was one thing, but Bauer knew he would need to build a compelling argument to win over a judge in the provinces. He began that September by informing his seventeen prosecutors that he wanted all Article 175 cases brought to his attention. In particular, he wanted to find a recent prosecution of a gay man using the Nazi-era clauses, which he thought the constitutional court would be more likely to repeal. Next he connected with some of the leading gay-rights campaigners who had resurfaced postwar. The movement remained fractured and mostly concerned itself with helping gay men facing prosecution. Bauer met several like-minded lawyers at a conference in Stuttgart to discuss legal strategy and also reached out to the thirty-year-old doctor Hans Giese, who had founded the Institute for Sexual Research in his parents' Frankfurt apartment, for the latest scientific articles proving that homosexuality was not a mental or moral sickness.[14]

By October, Bauer had half a dozen cases on his desk of recently prosecuted gay men in Braunschweig's parks, cafés, train station, and private residences. It was impossible not to read his own experiences into some of them, a stark reminder of the danger he faced if he ever gave in to longing. Bauer chose two cases: The first concerned a merchant accused of playing with the genitals of an eighteen-year-old and asking for anal sex. The second involved another trader caught engaging in mutual masturbation with a rent boy. There was nothing unique about either prosecution; indeed, in many ways they were typical, which may have been why he chose them.[15]

On October 22, Bauer filed motions to appeal the convictions on the grounds they were unconstitutional. Two weeks later, he received a report from the judge overseeing the first case, a former Nazi, who failed to see how Article 175 impinged upon human dignity as in fact it was homosexuality that was "unnatural and abnormal." Furthermore, he ruled, the clauses added to the law during the Third Reich could no longer be considered Nazi because German society itself was no longer Nazi. A similar verdict was delivered by the judge in the second case, who claimed that none of Bauer's arguments could detract from the fundamental indecency of gay sex. Bauer was disturbed—if not surprised—by the vehemence of their response. It was the illiberal mindset he needed to attack if Article 175 was ever to be repealed—and that began with Remer.[16]

. . .

Public interest in the Remer case steadily built in anticipation of the March start date. Bauer held a press conference in January 1952 to explain his argument that Germans had had a duty to resist the Nazi state. The journalists, however, seemed mainly interested in whether the plotters were "oath breakers." This was a particularly contentious question for military officers, who maintained that the pledge of loyalty Hitler had demanded from soldiers exonerated them from any wrongdoing.

Bauer retorted that as the oath to Hitler had been immoral in the first place, it hardly mattered. His office was inundated with letters. "It is really the worst thing here that the memory of the fallen is being questioned," one woman whose son had died on the eastern front wrote to him. A member of parliament went further: "Your conception of the sanctity of the oath must be very bad, Mr. Prosecutor, if you have a whole battery of theologians to prove that a person can break an oath on his own without becoming a criminal. Your blunt thinking and your Jew-loyal views cannot come to any other conclusion."[17]

February passed in a rush of preparations as Bauer wrote and rewrote his arguments, corresponded with witnesses like Otto John, and lobbied the press. He had recently moved to a new flat on Jasperallee, which bore testament to the intensity of his work: not a scrap of food in the house, overflowing ashtrays, and books and papers scattered everywhere—Meyer-Velde remembered seeing an antique copy of Schopenhauer with its pages ripped out because Bauer had wanted to use some quote from it and didn't want the bother of carrying a book around.[18]

The trial began on Friday, March 7, 1952. Interest had grown so intense that the court had issued tickets and a queue snaked around the block. The Socialist Reich Party had turned out in force: twenty-five of its members occupied the front row of the visitors' gallery. They glowered at Bauer as he took his seat in the packed courthouse. The room suddenly hushed as Remer, looking haggard in his dark brown suit and red tie, made his way to the dock, photographers at his heels. He draped himself over the small chair in the defendant's box beside his two lawyers and stared theatrically at the crowd. Next came the chief judge, Joachim Heppe, in his black robes and tricolor hat, a small man with glassy blue eyes and near-translucent skin. He was a Nazi-era judge, had served in Stalingrad as an officer, and had only been released from Soviet captivity a year earlier.[19]

The German legal system was inquisitorial rather than adversarial. Unlike the Anglo-Saxon model with defense and prosecution arguing opposing sides, German trials were led by judges, who questioned wit-

Remer in the dock, 1952
picture alliance / dpa | dpa

nesses to establish the facts of the case for the jury. Bauer and the defense lawyers could intervene during testimony to seek clarification but would only present their arguments in closing statements. This limited role wouldn't stop either side from trying to steer proceedings through pointed comments and objections.[20]

Judge Heppe began the trial by directing the defendant to answer the charge of slander. Remer unfolded himself slowly and, tucking his left hand into his suit jacket, declared that he stood by his statements and would say the same again. Bauer then called his first witness, a fifty-year-old editor for the German Press Agency who'd reported on Remer's speech in May. Remer smiled sardonically, leaning forward to whisper comments to his defense counsel. The court grew restless as more eyewitnesses spoke. Bauer intervened at one point with an ironic aside that Remer had, by all accounts, acted "more or less laudably." Remer's lawyers leaped on the comment, obliging Judge Heppe to request that both sides refrain from further derogatory remarks. It was a small moment, but the journalists picked up on Bauer's "hot devotion to the cause"—this was also a battle between the Nazi general and the Jewish prosecutor.[21]

Then Otto John took the stand. The dapper forty-two-year-old measured his words carefully. Every day that the war continued, he explained, brought more death and destruction. Indeed—although John

Otto John, c. 1950s
picture-alliance / dpa | Peter Wichman

didn't say it—the last ten months of the war had led to the slaughter of 2.5 million German soldiers, half the total war dead. To end the war meant removing Hitler, stated John. It had only been prudent, therefore, to gauge the Allies' reaction. The defense tried to attack John's motives in their cross-examination but in the end appeared to concede the point that at least some members of the resistance might have been acting for the greater good of Germany in trying to kill Hitler—a major victory for Bauer.[22]

Next up were two theologians from the University of Göttingen, who jointly argued for the moral right of Christians to resist in the Protestant tradition, citing Martin Luther and the Gospel. A professor at the Philosophical-Theological University of Freising argued that an oath of allegiance to a leader who had become a tyrant was no longer valid because Christians were morally bound to defend the greater good. Bauer appreciated this public rebuke, especially given the churches' earlier endorsement of Nazism. More important, it provoked Remer's lawyers into arguing for the Third Reich's legitimacy, which was precisely the battle Bauer wanted to fight.[23]

The testimony on the second day of the trial turned to Stauffenberg's motivation. His colleague Fabian von Schlabrendorff gave a passionate defense of their mission. Several family members spoke powerfully to the plotters' patriotism and sacrifice. A retired general and chairman of

Bauer at the Remer trial, 1952
bpk Bildagentur / Deutsches Historisches Museum /
(Gerhard Gronefield) / ArtResource, NY

a veterans' association said that he didn't think Remer's sentiments were shared by other soldiers and wished that he would stop politicizing the war.[24]

The defense called their witnesses as the second day of the trial drew to a close. They wanted the convicted war criminal General Erich von Manstein, a popular figure among veterans, to take the stand, along with one of the Nazi judges who had sentenced the plotters to death. But Bauer objected to the obvious attempt to politicize the trial and Heppe said that he didn't see their relevance. In the end, Remer's lawyers managed to call only two witnesses of the May 1951 speech, to make the point that Remer had been speaking in response to a question from the audience, and that his words had been taken out of context. It was a risible defense and they knew it.[25]

Bauer delivered his closing statement the next day to a hushed courtroom. He began by presenting the court with a simple question: Did the plotters of July 20 act as traitors? For Bauer, the answer was clear. "I don't think there is anyone in this room," he said, "who would have the courage to say that one of the resistance fighters did not act with the holy intention of serving his German fatherland."[26]

The Third Reich had been a criminal and unjust state, he explained. In a country that was killing tens of thousands of people each day,

Bauer, c. 1952
Otto Hoppe, Courtesy
of Eckhard Schimpf

resistance was a duty, whether that meant rising up against Hitler or providing "emergency aid to the threatened Jews or the threatened intelligentsia abroad." Bauer went on to quote thirteenth-century German law under the Holy Roman Empire, the Icelandic Edda, and even Hitler's own words in *Mein Kampf* on the right to rebel.[27]

The courage of the men who tried to overthrow the Nazi state should be an inspiration now for the new Germany, he declared: "What the resistance fighters achieved was the greatest national act with which we Germans could confront the Allies at the end of the war."[28]

Finally, Bauer concluded with a quotation from the Rütli scene from *William Tell* that he and Stauffenberg had once taken part in—words which now echoed around the courtroom: "There's a limit to the despot's power!"[29]

Bauer, flushed and exhilarated, took his seat. It was the defense that noticed he had forgotten to present the actual criminal complaint. Rather wryly, he got back up to state the charges.[30]

The defense presented their basic argument next: The soldier's oath could not be broken, no matter how criminal the orders; therefore the plotters' actions were treasonous. Remer, who had remained silent throughout the proceedings, jumped to his feet to reiterate that he would not retract a word of his statement.[31]

It was now Judge Heppe's turn to speak. Bauer's words had moved him, he said, even plunged him into a crisis of conscience. As a prisoner of the Soviet Union after Stalingrad, he had seen some of his fellow officers join the Soviet-backed anti-Hitler force. He had considered them traitors, but Bauer had forced him to reexamine how he thought about resistance.[32]

"We, your colleagues, know that you have a warm heart for the law, for the fighters for justice and truth," Bauer responded. "I beg you, do not let that warm heart . . . grow cold through your terrible memory of the Siberian expanses."[33]

As the court broke up, the families of the resisters in the audience approached Bauer to shake his hand. Over the next few days, Bauer's office was flooded with letters. "Your words have renewed my confidence that a democracy can develop in Germany after all, and that the law is still there," wrote one respondent. The press was equally laudatory, with the *Neue Zeitung* declaring that Bauer's plea was historically significant because it had "clearly proven in legal terms that Hitler's state was not a state under the rule of law, but a state of injustice."[34]

Heppe delivered his verdict on March 15: Remer was guilty; he would serve three months in prison and pay for the trial costs. More important, he ruled that Nazi Germany could no longer be considered a just state. It was, said Heppe, a "bitter and difficult" finding for any who had served under the Nazis. He stopped short of affirming that all acts of resistance to the Nazi regime were legitimate. But the legal implications were potentially profound: Nazi perpetrators might struggle to claim they had only been following orders when the orders themselves had been criminal. Other courts were under no obligation to accept Heppe's ruling, but a precedent had been set, and Bauer had proof that his ideas might take hold.[35]

Bauer continued to receive dozens of letters that spring, around half of which were supportive. One in particular caught his eye. It was from the father of a dead soldier, who wrote that he could never accept that his son had acted immorally by fighting for Germany. Bauer wrote back by quoting from the letter of a young farmer to his parents begging for their forgiveness after he'd been sentenced to death for refusing to join

Bauer in Sweden with Ella, c. 1950s
Courtesy of Marit Tiefenthal

the SS. "Many parents will lose their children. Many SS men die as well," he wrote. "[But] if I fell in the war with a guilty conscience, that would be sad for you too."[36]

Bauer had no solace to offer. The past offered none.

That summer of 1952, Bauer took some time off to visit his terminally ill mother, Ella, in Sweden. She was proud of his success and encouraged him to use his newfound prominence to land a bigger role. He returned to Braunschweig to begin his job search only to learn in August that Kurt Schumacher had died of a heart attack. The two men had drifted apart as Schumacher had increasingly tried to appeal to nationalist sentiments. He had backed the release of war criminals in Landsberg, a stance Bauer could not support. But as hundreds of thousands thronged the Autobahn to observe the hearse on its way to Hannover, strewing the road with flowers, Bauer felt like he'd lost his last connection to his youthful idealism.[37]

He was also practical: Schumacher's death meant he needed to find a new patron to further his career. So he began reaching out to old friends and emerging left-wing politicians. He knew he couldn't be alone in his desire to hold former Nazis to account, but who would back him?[38]

9

Front Line

THE OUTCOME OF the Remer trial in March 1952 was precisely what Adenauer needed to assure the Allies that the country had rejected Nazism and could be trusted to rearm. The actions of an "incorrigible" few posed no threat to West Germany's democratic order, he told Western leaders. The Socialist Reich Party was banned a few months later. Adenauer offered further proof that the Federal Republic was taking responsibility for its Nazi past by agreeing to pay $14.5 billion—$170 billion today—in reparations to Israel and the Conference on Jewish Material Claims Against Germany. He hoped the money would help ease "the way to the spiritual settlement of infinite suffering." The agreement was met with protests in Israel, where the idea of accepting what might be construed as blood money was repulsive for many. Nationalists in the Federal Republic also reacted angrily, denouncing the deal as a form of appeasement. But with Globke's help, Adenauer pushed the reparations bill through the Bundestag in March 1953 and earned—as he knew he would—praise from the international community.[1]

The story Adenauer told his own country was, however, quite different. Germans were also victims of Nazism, he asserted at rallies for federal elections in 1953. The fate of more than 1.5 million soldiers missing in the Soviet Union featured prominently in his campaign as a symbol of the nation's suffering. Adenauer announced an annual day of remembrance for the men and had their stories incorporated into the school curriculum. Public radio broadcast music was chosen by the

relative of a POW every Sunday, and an association for returnees organized more than ten thousand demonstrations that year calling for the
prisoners' release.[2]

Some on the left criticized Adenauer for neglecting to commemo-
rate the victims of Nazi persecution and obscuring the soldiers' role in
mass murder. He responded by suppressing voices of dissent. Globke
pushed through legislation in July 1953 which, under the guise of protecting young people from obscene or subversive literature, effectively
curtailed freedom of speech. Novels that mentioned the mass murder
of Jews were censored along with gay magazines and sex education
manuals. The author of *All Quiet on the Western Front,* Erich Maria
Remarque, whose sister had been beheaded by the Nazis for opposing
the war, saw his latest novel excised of passages referring to German
soldiers as murderers. Several states led drives to bury offending books
in so-called Schmökergräber, or "pulp-fiction graves."[3]

In the background, Globke used Gehlen and his U.S.-backed organization to slander critics in the press as Soviet spies or else paint them
as their unwitting stooges. Gehlen's surveillance of opposition parties
also served a political purpose. By bugging politicians' phone lines, he
was able to collect "bedroom secrets and the like" to feed to the press.
Adenauer boasted to a party executive that he had gained access to his
opponents' inner workings "by all kinds of crooked means." The Social
Democrat Adolf Arndt—himself under surveillance—referred to Adenauer's subordinates as the "federal security main office," a reference
to Himmler's feared intelligence apparatus.[4]

Adenauer won a resounding victory in the federal elections of
September 1953. But while he had secured his power at home, he felt
the country was dangerously exposed. Stalin's death in March had
done little to ease tensions between the Soviet Union and the United
States, as both sides continued to expand their nuclear arsenals. Adenauer was particularly concerned that Moscow was using its East German proxies to destabilize his government and undermine Allied
support for rearmament. The propaganda flowing from East Germany's state-controlled media to the West was often crude: Adenauer was

presented as a henchman of imperialist America who sought the resurrection of the Third Reich. But some of their attacks claiming that the chancellor wanted a new war resonated in West Germany. Adenauer's push for rearmament still faced considerable domestic opposition. Two million had taken to the streets to protest his plans. In Munich, demonstrators carried a black cross topped with a helmet and a placard that read "U.S. Adenauer."[5]

Instead of addressing the protestors' concerns, Adenauer blamed the dissent on East German propaganda and tasked Gehlen with countering its impact. Gehlen was well aware of the danger. His organization was already a target of the East German secret police, known as the Staatssicherheitsdienst, or Stasi, which had begun searching for compromising material on the Nazi pasts of West German officials. Gehlen suspected it had been responsible for blowing his cover in 1952 when the journalist Sefton Delmer published a piece in *The Daily Express* titled "Hitler General Now Spying for Dollars." Delmer accused Gehlen of meddling in politics and using "all sorts of former Nazis" to become "an immense underground power."[6]

"Watch out for a name that promises bad things," Delmer wrote. "It stands for what, in my opinion, is the most dangerous political explosive in Western Europe today. This name is Gehlen."[7]

Gehlen was able to dismiss the allegations as propaganda and created a public relations department to rebut stories. But the Stasi danger extended beyond spreading negative press coverage. It was uniquely poised to infiltrate and expose his organization because its operatives came from the same backgrounds as his own men, in many cases shared Nazi pasts, and knew exactly what blandishments to offer over drinks in smoky West Berlin clubs—money, women, boys—or what threats to use if Gehlen's men refused to cooperate, from detaining family members living in East Germany to exposing extramarital flings or particularly dark Nazi pasts. Even Gehlen had to be careful, as he was having an affair with one of his employees.[8]

Rumors of a mole in Gehlen's headquarters began to circulate in early 1953. A staff member accused one of his counterintelligence operatives, Heinz Felfe, of being a Communist spy. Gehlen thought it was just spiteful gossip. Felfe, a balding, gregarious thirty-five-year-old whose face regularly broke out in hives, had worked for the Gestapo in Dresden and, Gehlen was sure, would never side with the Soviet Union. But the Stasi were clearly getting closer. On one occasion, Gehlen was shot at in the woods as his driver stopped to change the number plates. On another they were chased by two cars.[9]

Heinz Felfe, 1954
5157_Teil2, BND-Archiv

Then, in the autumn of 1953, one of his key operatives in Berlin, Hans Joachim Geyer, went missing. Had he been kidnapped, killed, or, worse, defected? The answer came a few days later when Geyer reappeared under the glare of flashbulbs at an East German press conference: He was a Soviet double agent. Geyer, a former Nazi Party member and crime novelist who wrote under the pen name Henry Troll, told reporters that as the deputy head of Gehlen's branch in Berlin, he'd photographed hundreds of files, including agent lists, courier routes, and the locations of radio transmitters. Several such devices were on display at the back of the room.[10]

Over the next few months, some of Gehlen's most important operations—such as an underground telegraph line he'd built with the Americans that ran between East and West Berlin—were uncovered by the Stasi and publicly revealed in show trials of some of his captured men. At his office Christmas party in 1953, Gehlen appeared visibly shaken as he took the floor with his reputation in tatters. He wasn't sure who to trust. He bugged his own office to listen in on his colleagues, and even checked the fittings of Globke's Bonn townhouse for devices.[11]

His attention soon turned to the obvious enemy within: the domestic spy chief Otto John. An informant in the Social Democratic Party headquarters revealed that John was passing on details of Gehlen's intelligence operation to the opposition. Gehlen concluded that John was also supplying material to the East Germans and sympathetic Western journalists. These suspicions were at least partly true—John, a committed democrat, had started gathering material on former Nazis in government. With Globke's approval, Gehlen set about engineering John's dismissal by planting stories in the press about his financial dealings, flamboyant lifestyle, and possible homosexuality. A German parliamentary inquiry soon accused John of seeking too much publicity and not putting his office first. His superior noted he was romantic and weak-willed. "For some time, we have had misgivings because John drinks," wrote the British high commissioner Sir F. Hoyer Millar; "despite warnings, he maintains some contacts which are dubious for a man of his position. He is also prone to indiscretions and talks too much whether he is drunk or sober."[12]

Under pressure, John cracked. On July 20, 1954, he attended a commemoration in Berlin for those who had been executed following the failed plot to assassinate Hitler ten years earlier. Later that evening, he sneaked out of his hotel and took a car with a doctor friend known for his Communist sympathies to dinner at a villa in the Eastern Sector, where a senior KGB official was waiting for him. As the wine flowed, John aired his frustrations at the rise of old Nazis in the West and asked the KGB for documents that would prove the war crimes of people like Hans Globke.[13]

What happened next is unclear. According to John's later accounts, he was drugged, detained by the Stasi, and coerced into switching sides. Other accounts suggest that a drunken, fired-up John willingly betrayed his country. Either way, he was next heard from in an East German radio broadcast on July 23, declaring that he was joining the

Gehlen, 1954
DER SPIEGEL 39/1954

Communist cause. At a press conference in East Berlin on August 11, he told a roomful of three hundred journalists he would be able to work more effectively for the German nation in the East, as the political elite in Bonn was riddled with former National Socialists. Now he would have the freedom to expose their influence, he declared.[14]

Unforeseen by John, his defection directly strengthened Gehlen's hand. After all, his organization might be getting the worst of the spy war with the Stasi, but at least Gehlen's loyalty could be counted on. "Once a traitor, always a traitor," Gehlen commented sardonically, in reference to John's earlier role in resisting Hitler.[15]

Gehlen seized the moment to reestablish his reputation by inviting a reporter from *Der Spiegel* magazine to profile him in September 1954. He opened the interview by dismissing the notion that he had staffed his organization with former SS men and spoke proudly of his war record. He was careful to present himself as a middle-class family man. The Gehlens had moved to a summer house overlooking Lake Starnberg in 1951. Gehlen's wife, Herta, had hired help, and his security man, who lived with them, doubled as the gardener. His seventeen-year-old son liked riding motorbikes and wanted to become an engineer. On the weekends, the family attended church and Gehlen swam in the lake.[16]

Gehlen alluded to some of the Soviet danger lurking behind this portrait of quiet prosperity, revealing that he carried a six-shot pistol as

Gehlen family, c. 1950s
Courtesy of Dorothee Gehlen-Koss

he traveled to and from his office at high speed in his Mercedes. He wanted to illustrate the risks but at the same time reassure the German public that he and his organization had the situation under control and that, as their future spy chief, they could rely on him.[17]

That autumn of 1954, Globke passed on the news that Gehlen had long been waiting for. After months of deliberation, the Allies had agreed to grant the Federal Republic full independence the following year. West Germany would be admitted into NATO and allowed to build a new army, and Gehlen's organization would become the Federal Republic's official intelligence service, to be known as the Bundesnachrichtendienst, or BND. It had taken almost a decade, but Gehlen's transition from wanted war criminal to linchpin of West Germany's security was almost complete.[18]

The Stasi let him know what they thought of the new arrangement that December. Gehlen received a warning from his office that the East Germans had moved a special task force into the area to seize him. He hurried home and had his driver set himself up in the kitchen with a machine gun. The family spent an anxious night waiting. Nothing happened. Had the threat been real, or were they just playing games with him? He wondered where their next attack would fall.[19]

10

Breakthrough

BAUER FINALLY GAINED his promotion in April of 1956 when Georg August Zinn, the reformist premier of Hesse, the largest state in West Germany, appointed him attorney general. The job represented a vast expansion of Bauer's powers and profile. He would manage almost two hundred prosecutors from Frankfurt, the country's financial capital and the center of an economic boom fueled by reconstruction. The city resembled a building site when Bauer arrived. Workers had torn up medieval streets to make way for highways and gleaming office blocks, while new stores on the Zeil offered the excitement of self-service aisles and escalators. Bauer approved of the modernist style even if, as he noted to a friend, the sewers remained the same. He knew that far from a fresh beginning, the city's veneer of wealth had simply covered over the past—quite literally in the case of the petrol station on Börnestrasse, which was built over the site of a synagogue that had been burned down by Nazi mobs in 1938.[1]

Bauer was not alone in feeling troubled by the city's unacknowledged crimes. Zinn, a one-time Reichsbanner member imprisoned by the Nazis, backed the pursuit of perpetrators as part of an overhaul of the state government and promised him political cover. Bauer also found allies in the philosophers Max Horkheimer and Theodor Adorno, who had reopened their Institute for Social Research in Frankfurt in 1950 to explore German views on the legacy of Nazism. Adorno had designed a questionnaire, featured in his book *The Authoritarian Personality*, that he claimed could reveal an individual's

Theodor Adorno, 1964
Ilse Meyer Gehrken, TWAA Fo 018, Akademie der Künste, Berlin

predisposition toward fascism. This so-called F-Scale attracted controversy from right-wing commentators—why was there no Communist
scale, they wanted to know—as did the institute's research in 1955 into
German guilt, which found that a decade after the war, most Germans
continued to avoid or reject any suggestion of complicity. "Why should
Germans be forced into collective self-accusation for years on end?"
exclaimed the prominent Hamburg sociologist Peter Hofstätter.
Adorno shot back that Hofstätter's comments made it clear: In the
house of the hangman "you should not speak of the rope."[2]

Bauer rented a two-bedroom flat in a new apartment building overlooking a park and botanical gardens of steamy, palm-filled glass-
houses in the formerly Jewish Westend district, where Horkheimer
and Adorno also lived. The city had once been home to thirty thousand Jews. Barely a hundred remained upon liberation, and the Westend's fire-ravaged synagogue was the only one still standing. Adorno,
acerbic and portly, hosted weekly gatherings at which he liked to serve
his favorite Rheingau wines, play his own anarchic compositions on
the piano, and discuss the latest trends. The ideas flew back and forth
"like ping pong balls," recalled one guest.[3]

Young people were a pressing topic after a series of riots that summer by teddy boys with quiffs—or, as the German press called them,
Halbstarke, or "half-strong." In Frankfurt, they gathered in the evenings along the stretch of the Main River known as "Nice" for its

waterfront and pontoon promenade, or outside the jazz clubs that had sprung up to cater to U.S. forces headquartered in the city. Conservative commentators blamed the influence of American culture and films like *Rebel Without a Cause* for the twin epidemics of "growing sexualization in our cultural life" and rowdiness among the young. Frankfurt was deemed worryingly Americanized, earning the nickname "Mainhattan." More than two thousand young people were arrested across the country that summer as the police threatened to show them the "meaning of discipline." Liberals were equally concerned about the new generation's values. The broadcaster Norddeutscher Rundfunk had played one of Hitler's speeches to a group of young people to gauge their reaction. They found Hitler turgid and boring—"Were our parents fools?" they asked—but no one commented on the speech's incitement to murder Jews. Did this disturbing absence of conscience reveal Adenauer's success in burying the genocide?[4]

Bauer shared the liberals' concerns but thought the younger generation should be treated with compassion. In Braunschweig, he had made a point of visiting young offenders in prison and learned that many had lost fathers in the war and turned to crime as children to provide for their families. Yet under Adenauer, these so-called delinquents were punished with the same severity and callousness that Bauer had seen applied to minors during the Weimar years. Was it any wonder that such young people were alienated from society and inured to the crimes of the state?[5]

Their plight reaffirmed Bauer's belief that the courts had a special role to play in building a more tolerant society. But his first priority was to use the law to address the Nazi past. Bauer certainly had more power to go after perpetrators in his new position. The question was whether the courts were prepared to cooperate. The signs were not good: Bauer was outnumbered by former Nazi officials and sympathizers in the criminal justice system while indictments against Nazi perpetrators nationally had fallen from 3,975 in 1949 to just 27 in 1955. Prosecutors sat on cases for years, local police tipped off suspects ahead of planned arrests, and witnesses and documentary evidence of wartime crimes

Bauer, c. 1950s
Courtesy of Marit
Tiefenthal

were hard to find as the West German authorities had imposed an embargo on contact with Eastern Bloc countries, where many of the worst
atrocities had taken place. Even motivated officials struggled to bring
cases to court. When prosecutors in Frankfurt tried to press charges in
the summer of 1956 against the city's former police chief, Adolf-Heinz
Beckerle, who had overseen the Nazis' brutal rise to power and, as an
envoy to Sofia, Bulgaria, the deportation of twenty thousand Jews to
Auschwitz, they were informed by police investigators that "in most
respects [Beckerle] had acted correctly."[6]

Bauer understood that the failure of the German justice system reflected a deeper urge to move on from the past that extended beyond
Germany. Intellectuals and journalists in Britain and America were focused on the Cold War; Jewish thinkers on the creation of Israel; and
survivors everywhere on rebuilding their lives. A handful of academics
were attempting to establish the historical record. Bauer had read *The
Final Solution* by Gerald Reitlinger, a British Jew and art historian, and
was likely familiar with *Harvest of Hate* by Léon Poliakov, chief archivist
at the Contemporary Jewish Documentation Center in Paris. Ota Kraus
and Erich Kulka, two Czech Jews who survived Auschwitz, had written
a documentary history of the camp titled *The Death Factory*. But the
wider public wasn't listening. "Nowadays it is bad taste to speak of the
concentration camps," noted Auschwitz survivor Primo Levi in 1955.[7]

What Bauer needed was a case that would capture German—and global—attention by putting the system of genocide as a whole on trial.

. . .

Bauer made his presence felt in the office that summer of 1956 as he began his search. He peppered colleagues with questions and ideas in a "breath-taking" manner and quickly identified the younger members of staff whom he could trust because they didn't have Nazi pasts to hide. They were summoned to Bauer's office up a flight of green marble steps to the second floor of the grand justice building, where two secretaries with hair stacked in beehives guarded the door. Inside, Bauer was to be found chain-smoking, ready to give them the once-over, a small man, noted a contemporary, with a mighty head, a rumbling voice, and an alarmingly provocative manner.[8]

Bauer's first thought was to review every charge against Nazis filed with his office since 1933 that his predecessors had either failed to pursue or abandoned. Most cases consisted of Nazi crimes against Germans committed during their rise to power or at the end of the war, when harsh punishments were meted out for desertion. Bauer was examining the former police chief Beckerle's case—he needed to start somewhere—when the Hesse Justice Ministry informed him in October 1956 that it was assigning thirteen Nazi war criminal cases to his office. The men were all from Austria and had initially fallen under Viennese jurisdiction. The newly independent Austrian state was, however, eager to shed its connections to Nazism and was therefore passing on as many prosecutions as it could to Germany. As Bauer scanned the list, he spotted a familiar name: Adolf Eichmann.[9]

Eichmann had first risen to international prominence at Nuremberg as the man who claimed he would "leap laughing" to his grave at the thought of the six million Jews he'd helped to kill. The historian Léon Poliakov had since documented Eichmann's role in organizing the deportation of Jews from across Europe to the death camps of Nazi-occupied Poland, including the dispatch of more than 400,000 Hungarian Jews to Auschwitz in the summer of 1944, the Nazis' single largest act of mass murder. Here, at last, was a war criminal whose prosecution might reawaken Germans to the scope of the genocide and give lie to the belief that guilt was limited to Hitler and his inner circle.[10]

Bauer moved quickly that November to issue a warrant for Eichmann's arrest on suspicion of murder in an "insidious, cruel manner and for base motives in a large number of cases which cannot be precisely determined." Actually finding and arresting Eichmann was another matter. The Austrian file on him was thin. The Viennese police had made little effort to track him down beyond collecting several news clippings attesting to sightings, which at least suggested he was alive. Some were outlandish or impossible to verify—like the claim he was a guest of the grand mufti in Cairo or roaming the Alps searching for hidden Nazi gold. The only real lead in the case had come from the self-styled Nazi hunter Simon Wiesenthal, who was obsessed with finding Eichmann. Wiesenthal, a survivor originally from Buchach in what had been part of the Austro-Hungarian empire, had settled in Linz, Austria, after the war and built up his own bureau to investigate Nazis in the region. In 1952, he had hired a private investigator to stake out Eichmann's family home in the Altaussee region of Austria. He discovered that Eichmann's wife, Vera, had disappeared with her three children to Argentina. Wiesenthal believed Eichmann was there, too. Argentina's authoritarian leader, Juan Perón, had welcomed twelve thousand fleeing Nazis after the war, and the country had remained a haven for Nazism even after Perón's fall in 1955.[11]

It wasn't much, but Bauer had little else to go on. He placed a request with the German federal criminal police to add Eichmann's name to the Interpol search list, although he doubted the case would go far. Indeed, it was possible Eichmann was being protected by former colleagues in the Adenauer administration. In all events, the case would require extreme sensitivity, so he assigned it to Arnold Buchthal, one of the few older prosecutors he could trust. Buchthal was a Jewish former district magistrate who had been forced from office in

Dortmund and then into exile. As a translator at Nuremberg, Buchthal had helped the court understand what the Nazis had meant by terms like "Untermensch"—"subhuman"—and later prosecuted Nazi bureaucrats at a follow-up trial. The balding, earnest, fifty-six-year-old Buchthal immediately grasped the delicacy of the assignment. He agreed to lock away the Eichmann casework in a safe each night and to only communicate developments to Bauer when they were sure they weren't being overheard.[12]

Arnold Buchthal,
c. 1930s
Courtesy of Dame
Stephanie Shirley

Buchthal's first move was to scrap the Viennese file and visit the Nuremberg State Archives to examine trial records. They provided him with several key testimonies given by Eichmann's associates.[13]

Buchthal assumed that most of his staff were either dead or in hiding. He was surprised, therefore, to discover through a routine police search that Eichmann's former deputy, Hermann Krumey, was living under his own name and ran a drugstore and a tent-rental and sack-sewing business in the town of Korbach, two hours outside Frankfurt. Krumey had even received 24,000 deutschmarks in government grants to set up his business and was the local representative of the Federation of Expellees, an organization that represented the interests of Germans displaced during the war. Buchthal passed on the discovery to Bauer. They both agreed that Krumey was not just a potential witness against Eichmann but a major war criminal in his own right who could presumably be brought to justice much sooner than his former superior.[14]

With Krumey in his sights, Buchthal began searching for witnesses. He knew he would need dozens to build up the picture of an operation that deported hundreds of thousands from Hungary to Auschwitz. A key figure was Joel Brand, a textile merchant and leading Zionist who had helped Jews flee to Budapest up until the Nazi occupation of Hungary in March 1944. Buchthal learned of Brand's story through the publication in December 1956 of his biography, in which Brand described his disturbing first encounters with Eichmann. On April 25, 1944, Brand had been summoned to meet the SS officer in Budapest's Hotel Majestic, perched on a hill overlooking the city. Eichmann had recently issued orders for the country's Jews to be put into ghettos in advance of their "resettlement" to the East.[15]

"I expect you know who I am," he declared, hands on hips. "I was in charge of the 'actions' in Germany, Poland, and Czechoslovakia. Now it is Hungary's turn."[16]

Brand did not understand precisely what that meant, but he knew enough to be alarmed.[17]

Eichmann had an offer to make. "I am prepared to sell you one million Jews," he announced "Money for blood, blood for money."[18]

When Brand protested that he didn't have that kind of money, Eichmann suggested he make the payment in kind and then turned threatening. "Today I am able to sit at a table with you and discuss business," he said. "Tomorrow, maybe, I shall have to talk in a different tone."[19]

Eichmann informed Brand at their next meeting that he wanted ten thousand trucks for use on the eastern front, eight hundred tons of tea, eight hundred tons of coffee, two million bars of soap, two hundred tons of cocoa, and a million dollars. Brand had no idea how to acquire these items, but Eichmann nonetheless dispatched him to Turkey to try and arrange their purchase. Brand's meeting with the Jewish Agency in Istanbul was unsuccessful; he was subsequently detained by the

Joel Brand, 1961
National Photo
Collection of Israel /
Creative Commons

British as a possible spy. In the end, Brand's colleague in Budapest, Rezső Kasztner, negotiated the safe passage of a single train carrying 1,684 Jews, including 273 children, which left Budapest in exchange for a thousand dollars per person. Brand's eighty-year-old mother was meant to be on board, but at the last minute Krumey had her hauled off under orders from Eichmann. She died in Bergen-Belsen shortly after liberation. In total Eichmann transported 438,000 Hungarian Jews to Auschwitz, the majority of whom were gassed upon arrival.[20]

Buchthal invited Brand to testify in Frankfurt in March 1957. He was a small, animated man with wispy, thinning hair that seemed to float around his head, naturally jovial but clearly haunted by guilt. He had moved to Israel after the war, where he had hoped to find understanding for his collaboration, only to face a barrage of criticism from fellow survivors. Brand spoke frankly about his dealings with Eichmann, but Buchthal, eager to make an arrest, focused on Krumey and his role in organizing deportations to Auschwitz. Brand recalled him to be a venal, brutal man, well aware that he was sending thousands to their deaths, but ultimately more interested in extorting money from Jewish leaders. He liked to disguise his demands for payments and gifts, telling them: "Well, I'm helping you too, so you can do something for me!"[21]

Buchthal felt that Brand's testimony against Krumey was compelling enough to arrest the former SS man. He didn't trust the local po-

Hermann Krumey, 1960
Hessisches Hauptstaatsarchiv, 461, 32744/3

lice in Korbach to carry out the task, so, shortly after 9:00 A.M. on
Monday, April 1, 1957, Buchthal accompanied officers to the small
pharmacy on Bahnhofstrasse to find fifty-one-year-old Krumey at
work in a neatly pressed jacket and tie. He had lined, pinched features
and seemed unsurprised to see the police—at least he made no attempt
to flee. Buchthal handed him a copy of his arrest warrant and then
brought him to the waiting car for the drive back to Frankfurt's Hammelsgasse Prison, a grim brick building from the days of the Kaiser,
which echoed with the din of prison life.[22]

Buchthal took advantage of the moment to begin interrogating
Krumey at once. The former Nazi denied everything: He claimed not
to have known what the Final Solution meant upon his arrival in
Hungary in March 1944 and that he'd been unaware, until Jewish
leaders themselves told him, that the transports he was arranging
were bound for Auschwitz. He expressed his sadness at the news that
Kasztner, the rescue train organizer, had recently been shot dead outside his home in Tel Aviv following a high-profile court case over his
collaboration. But the next day, Krumey struggled to answer Brand's
accusations that he had extorted money from Jews and admitted that
he and an accomplice received three million Hungarian pengő in a
suitcase.[23]

Buchthal felt that he had what he needed to press charges against
Krumey for aiding and abetting the murder of over 400,000 Hungarian

Jews. But nothing Krumey had said advanced the Eichmann investigation. Bauer and Buchthal reluctantly agreed it was time to publicly announce their search in the hope of generating a tip on Eichmann. It was a risky move: Nazi networks in the Federal Republic might try to thwart the investigation or alert the former SS man. But they needed a lead.

At a packed press conference on April 3, 1957, Buchthal announced Krumey's arrest. Then he revealed that his main target was Adolf Eichmann, who was believed to be alive and well and living in South America.[24]

In the weeks that followed, Bauer considered the implications of pursuing Eichmann. What if his investigation triggered a backlash? Adorno and Horkheimer's research had shown that knowledge of Nazi crimes tended to provoke instinctive defensiveness in the average German. Even more troubling were findings suggesting that exposing the mass murder of Jews might in fact provoke a resurgence of antisemitism. "We have nothing against the Jews" was a common refrain, "so long as they don't take actions that conflict with the national interest." As it was, synagogues and Jewish cemeteries were routinely defaced and daubed with swastikas. Indeed, Horkheimer was so worried about Nazism remanifesting that he regularly sent a young lawyer to meet Bauer for information on members of the city's administration. Horkheimer feared he was under surveillance by Gehlen's men in the

*Bauer smoking,
c. 1950s*
Courtesy of Marit
Tiefenthal

BND—he was—and theorized that the only reason Bauer remained safe was because he had files on the crimes of officials. "Let us think of those who will have to die under a future Gestapo," Horkheimer warned colleagues at the opening of a new office for his institute.[25]

Bauer, for his part, made a point of showing that he wasn't afraid, sitting up late into the night at the elegant, gilded Café Kranzler on the Hauptwache square with a glass of wine, a cigar, and a stack of newspapers. Yet he knew that prosecuting the likes of Eichmann and Krumey would place him under intense scrutiny, for his Jewishness, his socialism, and—if it was ever revealed—his homosexuality. A further effort by reformers to overturn Article 175 had led to a disastrous ruling by the federal court in 1957 that "same-sex activity clearly violates the moral law," effectively ending attempts at judicial reform. So he was careful to reserve any liaisons for his trips back to Denmark.[26]

As he contemplated the risks he faced, Bauer attended a conference of more than forty Auschwitz survivors in late spring 1957. The camp was an obvious component of the Eichmann investigation, yet the site where over one million Jews had perished hardly appeared in public discourse. *Night and Fog,* a 1956 French documentary about the Nazi concentration camp system, had featured Auschwitz and been shown—despite a West German government effort to restrict distribution—to schools and youth groups, leading to a stirring of interest. But it was still the case that Germans who looked up Auschwitz in the *Brockhaus*

Encyclopedia found details concerning the camp's industrial capacity but nothing on genocide.[27]

The organizer of the Auschwitz conference, Hermann Langbein, had made it his mission to raise awareness about the camp. A wiry, bald Austrian and longtime Communist with nicotine-yellowed teeth and an old corduroy suit, Langbein clearly made an impression on Bauer. He had fought in the Spanish Civil War and spent four years in the Nazi camps, first in Dachau then Auschwitz, where he had been forced to work as the chief doctor's secretary. Langbein had risked his life to document the Nazis' crimes for the camp resistance and since the war had worked tirelessly to help survivors seek compensation through his organization, the International Auschwitz Committee, which was partly funded by the Polish government. He had scant regard for petty rules and niceties; such things hadn't mattered over "there"—in the camps, that is—and he wasn't going to live by them now. He refused to use crosswalks, going around them instead, and had once brought a woman to tears after she had asked about the fate of a prisoner—only for Langbein to baldly state he'd seen him hanged on the roll call square. "Well, who broke this news gently to me?" he stated.[28]

Langbein considered it an outrage that Auschwitz was not better known. The Nazis' genocidal project could not be understood, he believed, without an understanding of the camp's role as a site of experimentation for mass murder. The camp had initially been established in a former artillery barracks outside the small Polish city of Oświęcim in 1940 to crush resistance in occupied Poland. The conditions were so harsh that its rudimentary hospital was quickly overwhelmed, leading to the SS euthanizing sick and dying prisoners, first with lethal injections and then with the pesticide Zyklon B in the camp's first gassing experiments. Following the Wannsee Conference in January 1942 to organize the Final Solution, the SS converted two farmhouses near Auschwitz into gas chambers as part of a new camp to be known as Birkenau. Jews deemed capable of labor would be admitted to the camp to be worked to death. The rest would be murdered upon arrival.

Hermann Langbein, c. 1960s
Günther Schindler

Four more gas chambers with attached crematoria were built the following year to increase the camp's killing capacity to over five thousand people per day.[29]

Langbein had convened the conference in Frankfurt in part to draw
attention to the upcoming trial of Auschwitz doctor Carl Clauberg,
who had conducted gruesome sterilization experiments on Jewish
men and women in the camp. Langbein had enlisted the help of the
Frankfurt lawyer and Dachau survivor Henry Ormond, who'd made
his name suing the chemical conglomerate IG Farben for its use of inmate slave labor, to gather evidence for the case. Ormond, also at the
conference, had just come back from a fact-finding mission to Auschwitz and shared some of his disquieting experiences with attendees.
The camp had been turned into a museum in which the main exhibition contained little reference to Jewish suffering, and the rise of Nazism was blamed on American capitalism.[30]

Bauer had never been among such a large group of survivors or
heard so many speak about their experiences. It was their voices, he
realized, that were almost entirely absent from the public debate. They
needed to be heard. The group attended a ceremony with Frankfurt's
chief rabbi to receive an urn of ashes from Auschwitz at the Jewish
cemetery on Eckenheimer Landstrasse. They then watched a stage
adaptation of Anne Frank's diary in the Frankfurt municipal theater.

Henry Ormond, c. 1960s
Günther Schindler

Bauer was familiar with the diary and no doubt noted that the play had been stripped of all reference to deportations and gas chambers. It ended with Anne's saccharine remark that "in spite of everything, I still believe that people are really good at heart." Bauer could appreciate the call to a common humanity. But for him it would remain a dangerous platitude until Germans understood where they had sent Anne Frank.[31]

11

Rebels

G EHLEN KNEW PRECISELY where Adolf Eichmann was hiding in Buenos Aires and the pseudonym he was living under, but he had no particular interest in bringing him to justice. As far as Gehlen was concerned, Eichmann was just one of dozens of German war criminals that the BND tracked in South America, mostly to make use of their business and political connections. Eichmann appeared to be leading a quiet life in Argentina, working as a line manager at a Mercedes Benz factory and spending his evenings with Willem Sassen, a Dutch former SS propagandist and lead writer for *Der Weg*, a far-right newspaper that claimed that the mass murder of the Jews was a hoax to extort money from Germans. Sassen had enlisted Eichmann's help in 1957 for a revisionist history project to prove that there had been no systematic program to kill Jews. He and Eichmann had recorded dozens of hours of interviews over drinks in the living room of his villa, often in front of a small audience of former Nazis, while his two daughters played in the adjoining room. Unfortunately for Sassen, Eichmann had no intention of downplaying the Final Solution. The deportation of more than 400,000 Hungarian Jews to their deaths in Auschwitz was, he believed, "an achievement that has not been matched before or since."[1]

Gehlen, who had a number of informants among Sassen's associates, could only conclude that the project was destined for failure. But Bauer's investigation into Eichmann did give Gehlen pause for thought. In March 1958, he sent an agent to consult with the CIA.

The Americans shared Gehlen's view that the former Nazis of Buenos Aires posed no real threat. Neither did they deem it necessary to alert Bauer to Eichmann's hiding place. Indeed, they agreed with Gehlen that the Nazi past was chiefly a concern because of Moscow's growing efforts to weaponize it to destabilize West Germany. The Stasi had set up a special research department in 1956 to scour Eastern Bloc archives for evidence of West German officials' wartime crimes. It had initially targeted hundreds of Nazi-era judges still in office who had enforced racial laws and handed down summary death sentences for minor offenses. One East German press conference followed another as Communist officials released the names of incriminated jurists—more than four hundred by 1958—and published booklets containing page after page of genuine wartime execution orders. The Federal Republic could not be trusted, East German officials stated, because the judiciary tasked with rooting out Nazis was itself stacked with them.[2]

The campaign had made headlines in West Germany and provoked a debate in the British parliament, emboldening the Stasi. Globke was an obvious target. Stasi operatives were reported to be gathering a vast tranche of evidence against the man they labeled the "Jew murderer"; plans were announced in the state-run media for a special court to try him. Newspapers ran stories speculating on what crimes might come to light. Adenauer was once again forced to defend Globke on national radio. "The carelessness with which people's good names are currently being treated," he stated, "is likely to endanger the democratic life of our country, which has risen from the ruins." Privately he, too, feared that his right-hand man might be forced from office. "I don't know of anyone who could replace Globke," he confided to friends.[3]

Gehlen worked to keep the Stasi campaign out of the newspapers through his special public relations department. At the same time, he used his network to get advance warning of Stasi attacks. Spycraft at that stage of the Cold War remained rudimentary: phone taps and the secret copying of documents using miniature Minox cameras.

Messages were sent on plastic reels from Ultravox Dictaphones and material exchanged via dead-letter boxes. Gehlen had a fondness for innovative techniques to bring information across the Iron Curtain. Lists of Stasi targets and evidence of Nazi crimes might be smuggled in specially designed dry compartments in cans of sausages. Japanese silk was used for writing down longer messages and folded away into a matchbox. His men even trained a swan on Glienicker Lake in Potsdam to carry material in small plastic bags under its wings from the East German side to the West.[4]

Gehlen was reasonably confident he could shield Globke, but each successive Stasi allegation risked sparking debate in West Germany about Adenauer's reintegration of millions of Nazis into society. For more than a decade, Adenauer had relied on Germans' collective desire to avoid talking about the past. But by the mid-1950s, the subject of the Final Solution was resurfacing in ways that Gehlen couldn't anticipate or control. Anne Frank's diary became a national bestseller upon its release as a paperback in 1955. Historians like Léon Poliakov had opened up the study of the Final Solution by publishing commentaries on Nazi documents. And a new generation of pioneering journalists was exposing the role institutions like the German Foreign Office played in the killing.[5]

Then, in June 1958, public attention was seized by the trial in the southern German city of Ulm of Einsatzgruppen commander Bernhard Fischer-Schweder for the murder of 5,502 Lithuanian Jews. Fischer-Schweder's crimes had first attracted the interest of prosecutors in 1955 after the former SS man had filed a complaint over his dismissal from a refugee agency for his Nazi record. The investigation, like so many others, had stalled as local police tipped off the man's accomplices and the Cold War embargo on contact with Eastern Bloc countries prevented access to key witnesses and records. But Erich Nellmann, the attorney general for the state of Baden-Württemberg, persisted and eventually gathered enough evidence to bring Fischer-Schweder and nine members of his killing squad to trial. The press was filled with accounts of the tearful confession on the stand of Wilhelm

Gerke, one of the squad's members. Gerke, not on trial himself, described rounding up Jews in the small town of Gargždai, forcing them to dig their own graves, and then lining each prisoner up for Fischer-Schweder to shoot in the head. Gerke collapsed after speaking. Upon coming around, he was immediately arrested.[6]

Commentators expressed outrage that Fischer-Schweder and his colleagues hadn't been brought to justice sooner. "Trial of Horror," declared one West German newspaper. "After the Shots in the Neck They Drank Schnapps," ran another. "A Hard Day for the Gestapo," went a third.[7]

The trial precipitated precisely the sort of national push for reform that Gehlen feared would empower the government's internal enemies. That October, justice ministers in left-leaning states pressured Adenauer into agreeing to the creation of the Central Office of the State Justice Administrations for the Investigation of National Socialist Crimes, tasked with examining atrocities committed outside Germany that had thus far evaded scrutiny. The new office represented a direct threat to Gehlen. He employed more than two dozen Einsatzgruppen members and hundreds of former SS officers, any of whom might be investigated. The prospect of one BND employee after another being dragged through the courts worried Adenauer enough that he told lawmakers in a closed-door meeting that he had "strong reservations" about Gehlen's continued employment of former SS men.[8]

Gehlen, however, insisted to Adenauer that SS expertise on the Soviet Union was indispensable for containing East Germany's propaganda offensive. A case in point was Heinz Felfe, the star counterintelligence operative and former Gestapo officer from Dresden. Felfe had cultivated an agent inside East Germany's largest publishing house, which was responsible for producing the Stasi brochures that named West German officials with Nazi pasts. Gehlen was able to anticipate and therefore mitigate some of the damage. His reliance on Felfe raised some concerns among his staff, and rumors of perfidy continued to swirl around the ex-Gestapo man, who had moved into a three-bedroom apartment in Munich and bought land in the Alps that demonstrably exceeded a civil service paycheck. But Gehlen trusted in the anti-Communist fervor of all the former SS men on his staff. And besides, Adenauer was demanding the sort of information that only Felfe could provide.[9]

What Gehlen could not anticipate was how the Stasi campaign and breakthrough prosecutions like the one in Ulm were shaping the politics of the younger generation. The conservative press was already worried about the disaffected youth. His eldest daughter had for a time also worn jeans and danced to Elvis Presley, before settling down to marry one of his men, a former officer twenty years her senior. But Gehlen's concerns deepened in 1959 as he read reports about young people who had been radicalized by Stasi propaganda.[10]

Two stood out. The first was a twenty-eight-year-old philology student at the Free University in West Berlin named Reinhard Strecker. His mother was from a Jewish family and had narrowly escaped deportation; as a teenager, Strecker had spent the last year of the war in a concentration camp. He belonged to a socialist student group whose members believed that the Federal Republic was engaged in a conspiracy to cover up Nazi crimes. But unlike his peers, Strecker appeared determined to do something about it. He initially approached the Federal Ministry of Justice to review its files on Stasi-incriminated jurists. When the ministry refused, he contacted the East German government and received an invitation in January 1959 to visit the East Berlin offices of the "Committee for German Unity," from where the Stasi was coordinating its campaign. West Germans were still permitted to travel freely to the East, and the Communist authorities readily provided Strecker copies of three thousand files on West German judges.[11]

The fact that Strecker had become—to Gehlen's mind—an unwitting dupe of the Stasi was bad enough. But then word reached him that summer of 1959 that Strecker and his fellow students were planning an exhibition about Nazi judges based on the Stasi documents, which was due to open in the town hall of the southern German city

Reinhard Strecker, 1959
Courtesy of Heidi
Strecker

of Karlsruhe on November 27, 1959, a short distance from the Federal
Constitutional Courthouse. A local magistrate—probably at Gehlen's
request—bypassed free-speech protections to order the exhibition
closed the day after its opening. Strecker, undaunted, moved it to a
nearby pub, the Krokodil, where he gave a speech to journalists. "The
whole [Nazi] epoch lives on," he said, and it was the duty of every citizen to be "responsible for the maintenance and expansion of the rule of
law." He announced plans to tour the exhibition around West Germany.[12]

Gehlen could explain Strecker as an outlier: He was half-Jewish, and
Gehlen's agents described him as "very self-absorbed, politically im-
mature and obviously strongly impressed and influenced by the 'docu-
mentaries' of Eastern propaganda." But the second man Gehlen was
tracking was more disturbing because of his impeccable pedigree.
Thomas Harlan was a twenty-eight-year-old playwright whose father,
Veit, had been a leading film director in the Third Reich. The Nazi propaganda chief Goebbels had praised Veit Harlan's movie *Jud Süss* as "an
antisemitic film as we could only wish for"; it was made obligatory
watching for all SS men and played at their barracks in Auschwitz.
Thomas Harlan, however, seemed determined to rebel against his father's legacy. He and an actor friend, Klaus Kinski, had sailed to Israel
in 1953 on forged Turkish passports to make a documentary provisionally titled *I Want to Go to the Jews*. There they met survivors of the

1943 Warsaw Ghetto uprising in which a small group of Jewish underground members had held off a German force of two thousand SS men, tanks, and artillery for almost a month. Harlan had been inspired by the meetings to write a play, partly in Yiddish, about the events titled *Myself and No Angel*, which opened in West Berlin in September 1958.[13]

Thomas Harlan and Klaus Kinski, 1955
INTERFOTO / Alamy Stock Photo

The production came to Gehlen's attention when, at its fiftieth performance, Harlan took to the stage to announce that he was launching a petition against the rehabilitation of Nazi war criminals in West Germany. He had learned from a journalist friend about two mass murderers pursuing successful postwar careers. The first, Heinz Jost, the former head of an Einsatzgruppe responsible for murdering 100,000 Jews, had been released after serving only a few years of a life sentence and was working as a real estate agent in Düsseldorf. The second, Franz Six, a former department head in the Reich Main Security Office, another pardoned lifer, had become the director of a publishing firm. Harlan demanded that both men "be brought before a proper German court immediately to correct the impression for the German and foreign public that murder is a career in Germany."[14]

Harlan's stunt posed a material threat to Gehlen. Six was a sometime adviser to the BND and personally knew most of the Einsatzgruppen men whom Gehlen employed. It would be disastrous if he appeared in court and exposed the BND's Nazi links to public scrutiny. The next day, Harlan was summoned to the Culture Ministry in West Berlin, where officials told him that his petition and its unfounded accusations against Jost and Six were "unlawful, if not immoral" and ordered him to desist. Harlan refused. The next night, a group of right-wing students armed with stink bombs stormed the stage and shouted antisemitic slurs at the audience in the first of a series of attacks against the production.[15]

Six's attorney next threatened Harlan and the theater with a lawsuit. Harlan, realizing he might need to back up his claims in court, contacted the Polish Jewish writer Krystyna Żywulska for access to the archives in Warsaw. Żywulska had attended a performance of his play and been impressed by its depiction of Jewish suffering. She was herself an Auschwitz survivor, as was her husband, a senior figure in the Communist regime's state security service, who arranged for Harlan to visit the Polish capital and provided an assistant to help him sift through captured SS records. Harlan started compiling lists and came up with a plan, backed by the Communist authorities, to write a book called The Fourth Reich that would "prove that the National Socialists [now] exercised even greater power than they had in Hitler's time."[16]

Gehlen had reached the conclusion, by the time Harlan returned to the Federal Republic in early 1960, that the young playwright was unhinged. The student activist Strecker might genuinely be motivated by an "urge for absolute truth." Harlan, by contrast, appeared to be a volatile mix of motivations. "Egotistical psychopath with criminal tendencies . . . a lot of charm . . . [and a] father complex," according to one source. It wasn't clear what his research in Poland had uncovered— Gehlen recruited a journalist from Harlan's circle to monitor him closely and learned with growing alarm that Harlan had reached out to Strecker to suggest they collaborate. Furthermore, Harlan had written to attorneys general across the Federal Republic with offers to share his findings. Gehlen could expect most to dismiss Harlan as an attention seeker or propagandist. But a few left-leaning prosecutors might take him seriously: Erich Nellmann, who had overseen the Ulm prosecution, was one. Fritz Bauer in Frankfurt was another. So far, Bauer's efforts to gather evidence for his investigations had been limited by the Cold War embargo. But Bauer—a "leftwing idealist" according to his BND file—might enlist Harlan and Strecker to bypass official channels and conduct covert investigations behind the Iron Curtain. What's more, he had the power to turn their findings into damaging trials.[17]

Gehlen ordered Bauer placed under surveillance. The Frankfurt prosecutor, he soon learned, had established contact with Israel for undisclosed reasons and was harboring dangerous anti-German sentiments.[18]

Part III

12

Sylvia

B AUER HEARD BACK from the federal criminal police about
Eichmann in July of 1957, months after he requested their assistance in his investigation. It was impossible, they said, to initiate a
search because Eichmann's crimes were of a "political and racial character." Bauer knew the police had no right to determine which murders
were appropriate to investigate; he also knew the force was full of former SS men. He let the matter go but was still left with the challenge of
investigating further. Eichmann could be hiding anywhere.[1]

Then that autumn a letter landed on Bauer's desk, postmarked from
Coronel Suárez, Argentina. The writer introduced himself as Lothar
Hermann, a "half-Jew by birth from Germany." Hermann had read
about Krumey's arrest in a local newspaper and understood that prosecutors in Frankfurt were looking for Adolf Eichmann. "By chance,
reliable information reached me about the hiding place of the former
SS officer," he wrote. "Eichmann lives under an alias, together with his
wife, Vera Liebl Eichmann, his son Dieter and a younger son, about
five years old, at Calle Chacabuco 4261, Olivos, Buenos Aires."[2]

Wild rumors of the whereabouts and dealings of ex-Nazi leaders
routinely reached Bauer's office. The idea that a source hailing from a
small town in the Argentine Pampas—according to the map, Coronel
Suárez was a ten-hour train journey from Buenos Aires—had simply
handed him Adolf Eichmann's home address seemed fantastical. But
Bauer noted Hermann's Jewishness, his factual tone, and the lack of
conditions, and wrote back for more details. Some weeks later, he

received a reply. Hermann had traveled to Buenos Aires and visited Eichmann's alleged house. He said that a middle-aged gentleman who spoke German and resembled Eichmann lived there; he also confirmed the birthday of one of Eichmann's sons.[3]

Bauer knew he couldn't trust the federal criminal police, but he still needed someone to pursue the lead on the ground in Argentina. The only people he could think to turn to were the Israelis. It was a risk: He had no contacts inside the country and he couldn't count on finding interest. The Final Solution didn't feature prominently in Israeli public debate as the new state focused on its survival and forging a story of heroic self-determination. The risks for Bauer were also grave—should news get out that he had tried to enlist the help of a foreign government to find Eichmann, he would probably lose his job and the power to pursue any other war criminals. Still, he didn't see another option.[4]

Bauer reached out first to Frankfurt's chief rabbi, who put him in touch with Felix Shinnar, Israel's trade envoy and effective ambassador in the absence of an official mission. They met on September 19, 1957, at the Metropol Hotel in Frankfurt, a grand old building near the train station. Bauer took in the crowd and lights in the lobby and suggested that they go back to their cars. They reconvened an hour later at a roadside inn off the highway to Cologne.[5]

"Eichmann has been traced," Bauer stated at once.[6]

Shinnar, a round-faced, balding lawyer originally from Stuttgart, took a moment to process.[7]

"He's in Argentina," continued Bauer, and explained that the German authorities could not be trusted to arrange his extradition. "I see no other [option] but to turn to you." Bauer said he was ready to share what information he had on the condition Shinnar help arrange for Eichmann's capture by the Israelis.[8]

Shinnar was noncommittal, other than promising to keep their exchange secret. Bauer supplied Eichmann's address and alias but declined to share Hermann's name, in part to protect his source but also to avoid revealing how little he knew about him.[9]

Some weeks later, in early November, Shinnar met Bauer at his

apartment to update him on progress. He had been to Israel and spoken personally to the head of Mossad, Isser Harel. The Israeli intelligence chief had at first refused to expend resources chasing down leads
for Eichmann when Israel faced tangible threats from Arab neighbors.
Israel's ten-year anniversary was approaching in 1958, and he expected
attacks. But Shinnar had finally persuaded Harel to open an investigation, arguing that Bauer was "known to be a man of balanced judgment."[10]

· Bauer saw Shinnar again on November 7, this time accompanied by
a lanky Mossad agent with striking green eyes named Shlomo Cohen-
Abarbanel, a watercolorist by training who still used painting as a
cover for his spy work in Paris. He was one of the few Mossad agents
committed to hunting Nazis, and he pushed Bauer on his source. He
wanted to know the person's motivations for coming forward.[11]

"I know nothing beyond what he himself has offered," said Bauer.
"He may be afraid of reprisals, so perhaps he feels he is taking less of a
risk by passing on only part of the information."[12]

Cohen-Abarbanel asked what Bauer wanted to happen next. Bauer
thought that was obvious. Mossad needed to send an agent to Argentina to stake out the address.[13]

"If we manage to prove that the man really is Eichmann," Cohen-
Abarbanel mused, "we may run into insurmountable difficulties in trying to get him extradited."[14]

"I'm worried about that too," Bauer replied, "and I don't oppose the
idea of your getting him to Israel in your own way."[15]

Bauer met Cohen-Abarbanel again on January 21, 1958. He was
prepared to hear that Hermann was simply mistaken. Instead, he was
shocked by Mossad's lackluster investigation. A local agent had visited
the address on Calle Chacabuco. It was a modest home in a poor section of the neighborhood. The agent had seen a stout, unkempt, vaguely
European-looking woman in the yard and dismissed the possibility
that an SS officer of Eichmann's standing could live there. Bauer was
incredulous. Hermann might be wrong about the man's identity, but
the investigation had proven nothing either way. It was poor police
work.[16]

Cohen-Abarbanel admitted he was struggling to engage his colleagues' interest. The key to unlocking the case, he thought, was to find out what else Bauer's source knew. If they could prove he was legitimate, then Cohen-Abarbanel felt his bosses would commit more effort. A police colleague of his, Efraim Hofstetter, who ran the criminal investigation unit in Tel Aviv, would be in the Argentine capital next month to attend an Interpol conference. Cohen-Abarbanel thought he could be persuaded to meet with Hermann.[17]

Bauer handed over Hermann's name, but to avoid any awkwardness, he suggested that Hofstetter pretend to be working for him. He dashed off a letter for him to carry and sent a duplicate to Hermann.[18]

. . .

Efraim Hofstetter had his doubts about the mission as he and a colleague boarded a train packed with farmers and prospectors in Buenos Aires bound for Coronel Suárez in March 1958. Hermann had refused to travel to meet him and Bauer's information on the man was practically nonexistent. For all he knew, Hermann was a hoaxer or, worse, a Nazi looking to lure a Jew into the wilderness. The forty-seven-year-old had lost his family in Poland to the Final Solution and usually avoided dwelling on the past. But the thought that Eichmann's crimes had gone unpunished nagged at him, even if he did wonder what a long, hot train journey through the Argentine night, throbbing with the sound of cicadas, might possibly achieve.[19]

Coronel Suárez felt deserted when they pulled into its dilapidated station the next morning. A single unpaved road lined with shacks led into the distance. The few locals they approached eyed their suits suspiciously, and it took some time to find a taxi to drive them down the dirt road to a modest house on Avenida Libertador San Martín. Hofstetter knocked on the door while his colleague waited nearby in case of trouble. The blinds of the house were already drawn against the heat. After a pause, a middle-aged man opened the door. He was short and balding, in sunglasses despite the home's darkened interior. Hofstetter introduced himself as Bauer's representative and Hermann ushered

Efraim Hofstetter, c. 1950s
ISA

him into a sparsely furnished room with a couple of chairs and a table, where they took their seats.[20]

"I have brought a copy of Dr. Bauer's last letter," said Hofstetter. "He thought it might be useful to establish who I was."[21]

But, to Hofstetter's consternation, Hermann ignored the proffered document. Instead, he summoned his wife and asked her to read it. In a flash, Hofstetter realized that the man who was meant to have seen Eichmann was blind. The entire mission had surely been a waste of time.[22]

He tried to conceal his disappointment as Hermann began speaking.

"Don't think that I started this Eichmann business through any desire to serve Germany," Hermann said. "My only purpose is to even the score with the Nazi criminals who caused me and my family so much agony and suffering." Hermann had survived three months in Dachau and had also lost relatives to the Final Solution.[23]

"I don't even want any reward or any other sort of compensation for my efforts," he insisted and then launched into his story.[24]

The family had moved to Coronel Suárez only eighteen months ago, he explained. Before that, he, his wife, and their sixteen-year-old daughter, Sylvia—"You'll meet her, she'll be home soon"—had lived in Buenos Aires in the same neighborhood as the house on Calle Chacabuco.[25]

Lothar Hermann, 1958
Yad Vashem

One day, Sylvia had brought home a young man named Nick Eichmann, whom she'd met on a Saturday-afternoon outing to Cine York, the neighborhood cinema. Hermann's wife, Martha, wondered at the young Eichmann's accent, which had no regional inflection. Nick explained that his father had been a high-ranking military officer and that the family had followed him around Europe. His father had "done his duty for his fatherland," he declared. On a further visit, the young Eichmann casually mentioned that it was a shame that the Nazis hadn't wiped out all of the Jews.[26]

Hermann wasn't particularly alarmed—Sylvia had clearly not mentioned that her father was Jewish, and antisemitism was common enough in Buenos Aires, especially among Germans. So he thought nothing more of it until a few months later, when Sylvia read him an article in the local German-language newspaper about the arrest of Hermann Krumey and the ongoing investigation into Adolf Eichmann. He'd written to the Frankfurt prosecutor's office at once and been encouraged by Bauer's response to believe the Eichmann he had met might indeed be the son of the war criminal. By then, the Hermann family had moved to Coronel Suárez. Bauer's requests for more information had obliged Hermann to travel back to Buenos Aires twice with Sylvia.[27]

Just then Sylvia walked in. She had dark, wavy hair and was confident, playful, and obviously devoted to her father.[28]

Sylvia Hermann, 1953
Yad Vashem

"In two months, she's going to study at a university in America," said Hermann proudly.[29]

"Father must have told you," Sylvia began, "that Nick never let me know his address. When we went to Buenos Aires, I asked a friend to help me find his house. I knocked at the door and it was opened by a woman. I asked her in German if this was the house of the Eichmann family."[30]

Sylvia recounted how the woman had paused, but then a middle-aged man in glasses with a long, thin nose had appeared. She'd held her nerve.[31]

"I asked him if Nick was at home. He said no, Nick was working over-time," said Sylvia. "I asked if he was Mr. Eichmann. No reply. So I asked if he was Nick's father. He said he was, but only after a long hesitation."[32]

Hermann said that he wasn't asking for any money except to cover the expense of his and Sylvia's travel.[33]

Hofstetter assured Hermann that he would reimburse any costs. Hermann wanted to return to Buenos Aires straightaway to establish Eichmann's identity further and perhaps secure a photograph of him. Hofstetter asked him to hold off. The story sounded credible, but he would need to consult his superiors. He gave a New York address for one A. S. Richter for future correspondence—in reality a Mossad dead-letter box—and promised to be in touch.[34]

. . .

Bauer, c. 1958
Courtesy of Marit
Tiefenthal

Bauer flew to Israel on March 17, 1958, shortly after learning about Hofstetter's breakthrough. His official purpose was to participate in a government junket for German officials to learn more about the country. But Shinnar had arranged meetings for him, and it's likely one was to be with Mossad director Isser Harel to discuss how to bring Eichmann to justice.[35]

Bauer arrived on a blustery, warm spring morning. He was intrigued to see Israel for himself. Bauer had been skeptical of Zionism in his Weimar days; he'd never wanted to be defined by his Jewishness. But it was impossible not to consider how many lives might have been saved had a Jewish homeland existed sooner. The Final Solution cast its shadow over the new state. The population had tripled since 1945 as refugees and survivors of ghettos and concentration camps flooded in from Europe and the Soviet Union. Nonetheless, the mass murder of Europe's Jews was rarely openly addressed. Indeed, the memorial and museum Yad Vashem was deliberately placed outside Jerusalem so that when it opened in 1953, people wouldn't be confronted with a constant reminder of a trauma that so many had experienced firsthand.[36]

What struck Bauer was how modern the country felt, particularly Tel Aviv with its gleaming tower blocks and breezy openness. He stayed at the Dan, a luxury hotel on the coast with a heated pool and manicured beach that had just hosted a fashion show featuring models in the latest shift dresses from America. It was nothing like the fusty, exotic world of his grandfather's books. Bauer was taken to a new town with Bauhaus-style social housing in the Negev desert. The country had embarked on a massive housing and infrastructure campaign following its war of independence, in which around 12,000 Palestinians had been killed and more than 700,000 displaced. Thirty new towns and more than four hundred kibbutzim and moshavim communities had been built, in many instances, where Palestinians' homes had once stood, although that was almost certainly not alluded to in the town Bauer visited. Instead, they offered to make him the town's mayor if he moved there—most likely, he noted wryly, because his unruly hair, which had recently turned white, made him look like Israeli prime minister David Ben-Gurion.[37]

Bauer met with Israeli officials, hoping to be briefed on a plan to seize Eichmann. He knew the risks would be considerable—he took it for granted that they would need to bypass the Argentinian authorities to avoid the risk that Eichmann would be tipped off. Mossad would then have to stage a kidnap operation in a city filled with one-time Nazis and their sympathizers, and even if they succeeded in capturing him, Eichmann would still need to be spirited across the Atlantic. But Bauer soon realized that the Israelis did not share his sense of urgency. Mossad director Isser Harel had ruled that even though Hermann seemed legitimate, it was too early for Mossad to intervene. Instead, he proposed to let the Hermann father-daughter team continue their investigations that spring. The idea of leaving the discovery to a blind concentration camp survivor and his teenage daughter made it clear that Harel wasn't taking the case seriously. Bauer had no choice but to return to Frankfurt and hope Hermann succeeded.[38]

13

Witnesses

ISRAEL'S RELUCTANCE TO pursue Eichmann that summer of 1958 was particularly frustrating to Bauer, as his own prosecution of Hermann Krumey had stalled. A judge had ruled that Krumey couldn't have known that sending Jews to Auschwitz meant death, and he'd been released pending fresh charges. Soon afterward, Bauer was forced to remove Buchthal from the investigation after the latter caused controversy by trying to indict the right-wing press for slandering opposition politicians. Bauer was exasperated not least because he sensed a change in West Germany in the wake of the ground-breaking Ulm trial of Einsatzgruppen killers that year. West Germans had started to speak about the mass murder of Jews without reflexively mentioning their own suffering. Church groups called for reconciliation with Jews through an annual "week of brotherliness" and arranged for survivors to visit classrooms to share their experiences. To mark the twentieth anniversary of the 1938 pogrom, 2,500 young people joined survivors that November in marching to Dachau.[1]

In search of allies and a new case that could have national impact, Bauer met Erwin Schüle, the director of the new Central Office for the Investigation of National Socialist Crimes. Bauer had been skeptical of the agency's limited remit to investigate rather than prosecute. Schüle was himself a compromised figure: a Nazi lawyer and officer, he'd been sentenced to death by a Soviet court for allegedly shooting three people in custody outside Leningrad and had only been released in 1950. But the fussy, sometimes querulous forty-five-year-old, with pale blue eyes and bushy eyebrows had surprised his colleagues by taking up the prosecution of the Ulm defendants with a passion that seemed like fury at times—he claimed to have felt personally betrayed by their crimes.[2]

Whatever Schüle's motives, Bauer was impressed by his evident sense of urgency in pursuing other Einsatzgruppen units as a twenty-year statute of limitations for manslaughter loomed that would prevent charges being brought against thousands of perpetrators. Bauer offered his unreserved support and sent one of his best men to Ludwigsburg to help gather evidence and identify potential targets for prosecution in Frankfurt. Bauer's eye was drawn to one of Schüle's cases in particular: Stuttgart police had arrested Wilhelm Boger, deputy head of the Gestapo in Auschwitz, the previous October. With the help of Austrian activist Hermann Langbein, prosecutors had tracked down several witnesses to Boger's crimes. Schüle's office had taken over the case in early 1959 as new suspects came to light and the evidence grew. Schüle had compiled a list of ninety more camp perpetrators that included brutal guards, camp orderlies involved in euthanizing sick prisoners, and SS doctors who'd selected Jews for the gas chambers.[3]

As Bauer learned more about the case, a bold idea began to take shape in his mind. The problem with applying German law to the crimes of the Final Solution was that the German criminal code did not recognize state-sponsored mass murder. Perpetrators could be convicted only for individual murders, and even then their intent to kill had to be established. But what if, instead of trying camp personnel separately, an array of functionaries were brought together under a single indictment that had the potential to reveal the role of each individual in the killing apparatus? Bauer would still have to marshal evidence against the individual defendants. Yet such a trial had the potential to implicate thousands in the running of the camp and expand the legal definition of murder to include anyone who had knowingly participated in the machinery of genocide.[4]

Schüle agreed to hand over the investigation to Bauer in April 1959. There were grumblings in Bauer's office about taking on such a large case. Bauer, never popular with older staff, had provoked outright hostility for backing investigations against dozens of Hessian jurists following

the East German propaganda campaign. So he made a point of selecting two young lawyers for the Auschwitz investigation who'd served as
teenage conscripts in the war. Georg Friedrich Vogel was a sometimes-
morose, portly thirty-five-year-old, awkward around people but with
a flair for organization. He was not a man to skewer a suspect in the
interrogation room, but he did know how to doggedly build a case. He
was complemented by the fiery and quick-witted Joachim Kügler, who
was the same age but looked a decade younger with his ruddy cheeks,
cropped ginger-blond hair, and sly schoolboy grin. Kügler could argue
for hours for the pleasure of it, obstreperous and perhaps a little con-
ceited, but also capable of charming a courtroom. His colleagues suspected he was gay, but he, like Bauer, was careful to keep his private life
to himself. Neither Kügler nor Vogel knew much about the Final Solution, and they appeared unfazed when Bauer summoned them to his
office that June and told them: "Now you're doing Auschwitz."[5]

Kügler and Vogel made it their first task that July to visit Schüle at
his headquarters in an Italianate villa in Ludwigsburg, where they
learned that in addition to Boger, four other former SS men had already been detained. Furthermore, two notorious guards and the camp
pharmacist who'd supplied Zyklon B to the gas chambers had been located. Schüle was keen to underscore the challenges they faced: The
crime scene itself was out of bounds in Soviet-controlled Poland, along
with most of the camp's records. Schüle had some books about Ausch-

Joachim Kügler, 1964   *Georg Friedrich Vogel, 1964*
Günther Schindler   Günther Schindler

witz; he recommended that they read a short history of the camp written by the Polish judge who had investigated commandant Rudolf Höss in 1947. The bulk of the investigation would, however, rely on them finding witnesses prepared to speak about their experiences.[6]

To aid their search, Schüle encouraged Kügler and Vogel to meet the Austrian Communist Hermann Langbein with the caveat that the press might accuse them of peddling Soviet propaganda. Langbein had already helped investigators contact dozens of witnesses. Many proved reluctant to engage with the German authorities or felt overwhelmed with survivor's guilt. Post-traumatic stress disorder was hardly recognized beyond a small circle of medical practitioners, who called the condition "KZ-Syndrome," after the German word for concentration camp, *Konzentrationslager*. But Langbein had succeeded in persuading forty survivors to testify, including a woman so traumatized from working as Boger's secretary that she had a gallbladder attack after being interviewed by the Berlin police. It was later revealed that Boger had coerced her into having sex with him in return for preferential treatment, which, it went without saying, meant sparing her from the gas chambers.[7]

Upon their return to Frankfurt, Bauer's young prosecutors set about arresting the two guards accused of murdering prisoners. On July 21, Vogel and two armed officers picked up the first, Oswald Kaduk, from a hospital in Berlin where he worked as a nurse and was fondly known as "Papa Kaduk." The same day, Kügler arrested the second, Heinrich Bischoff, a sickly fifty-five-year-old former miner, in his rundown cottage outside Essen. Both men denied the charge of murder. Kügler had arranged for a survivor, Fritz Hirsch, to pick Bischoff out of a lineup a few days later. Afterward, Hirsch testified to how he'd been supervising a work detail in the camp when he heard a shot ring out. A moment later, he saw a Jewish prisoner stagger in his direction and then collapse on the floor. He rushed over to help the man, when Bischoff appeared, ordered him aside, and shot the stricken man in the neck. "The blood gushed a meter high," recalled Hirsch.[8]

Kügler steeled himself to delve deeper into the camp's horrors as three Polish survivors traveled to Frankfurt in semi-secret on tourist

visas that autumn to give evidence against the pharmacist Viktor Capesius. They had worked in the camp pharmacy and regularly observed
Capesius arranging for canisters of Zyklon B to be loaded into an am-
bulance that he personally delivered to the gas chambers of Birkenau.
He would return a few hours later with suitcases stuffed with money
and valuables and, on one occasion, a box of teeth containing gold fillings removed from the mouths of the dead. The Polish testimony was
enough to order Capesius's arrest on suspicion of murder that December in Göppingen, where he'd gone back into business as a pharmacist
after the war. But Kügler knew that to substantiate the charges, he
needed to find witnesses who could speak to the murderous operation
of the gas chambers.[9]

14

Capture

As the Auschwitz investigation expanded that winter of 1959, Bauer's attention turned to Eichmann. The cases were closely connected in his mind: Eichmann's prosecution would reveal how the Nazi bureaucracy had delivered victims to the slaughter; the Auschwitz trial demonstrated the scale of German complicity in running an industrial killing machine. But as far as he could tell, the Israelis had dropped the Eichmann investigation. Nazi hunters like Tuviah Friedman had begun to question publicly why more wasn't being done to look for Eichmann in Argentina. The longer the delay, the greater the chance that Eichmann would go to ground. Josef Mengele, an SS doctor who'd carried out hundreds of gruesome experiments in Auschwitz and was under investigation in Freiburg, had disappeared without a trace in Buenos Aires in October 1958 after a tip-off. Around that time, a former SS man in the police informed Bauer that Eichmann was definitely not in Argentina and that he should look elsewhere. Did that mean they already knew where he was? Bauer, in desperation, asked Schüle to feed Friedman a line that Eichmann was suspected to be in Kuwait, knowing that the Nazi hunter would inevitably inform the press—which he duly did—and give the impression the prosecution was on the wrong track.[1]

Then, that November, Bauer received a call from a military bishop, who informed him that one of his pastors, a chaplain named Giselher Pohl, might know something of Eichmann's whereabouts. So, on a gray

Giselher and Rosemarie Pohl, c. 1950s
Courtesy of Sigrid Wobst

day with a light mist hanging over the hills, Bauer made the two-and-a-half-hour drive on the Autobahn to Unna, a small town near Dortmund, where Pohl lived in a modest semidetached with his wife and two children. Pohl, a kindly looking thirty-three-year-old who'd served as a teenage recruit with an antiaircraft flak unit, ushered Bauer into his living room. His wife, Rosemarie, served coffee in a white porcelain pot.[2]

Bauer was naturally suspicious. Even if Pohl did have crucial information, he warned that "you, as a clergyman, will not receive any reward money."[3]

"I don't even think of it being about money," Pohl responded curtly. "I see it as my duty."[4]

Pohl explained that a month earlier he'd met up with an old university friend, Gerhard Klammer, who had worked as a geologist studying locations for a hydroelectric plant in the remote province of Tucumán in Argentina. One of the surveyors on the project was a thin, ironic man with a bitter streak who went by the name of Ricardo Klement. But everyone on the team knew his real name: Adolf Eichmann.[5]

Klammer had tried to alert the authorities, but no one had been interested. In the end, he left Tucumán, and the company went bust with the fall of Perón. It was just by chance, on a recent trip to Buenos Aires,

Adolf Eichmann and Gerhard Klammer in Tucumán, c. 1950s
ISA

that Klammer had spotted Eichmann again, getting off a bus. On a whim, Klammer followed him to his modest house on Calle Chacabuco.[6]

Bauer listened, thinking the story was almost too good to be true. Then Pohl handed him a photograph taken in Tucumán of his friend Klammer standing next to a man Bauer recognized at once. It was Eichmann.[7]

Bauer was welcome to take the photograph, said Pohl. His friend Klammer asked only that every effort be made to protect his identity, as he still worked in South America.[8]

Bauer shot back to Frankfurt, elated by the discovery and angry again at Harel's failures. He reached out to Cohen-Abarbanel to demand a meeting with Harel and booked a ticket to Israel, arriving in the early hours of December 3, 1959. After a brief rest, he took a car from his hotel to the Ministry of Justice to meet Harel and State Attorney Haim Cohen, who would be in charge of overseeing any trial against Eichmann in Israel. Harel was late, so Bauer discussed legal matters with Cohen while they waited. Bauer explained he wouldn't seek Eichmann's extradition to the Federal Republic, despite the outstanding arrest warrant. He knew that Eichmann would likely only get a few years, given the leniency of West German courts toward former Nazis. Cohen, however, was concerned a Mossad kidnap operation would breach international law and call into question the legitimacy of any subsequent trial in Israel. It would be easier, Cohen conceded, to simply kill the former SS man. Bauer told him they needed to focus on finding Eichmann first.[9]

The brash, balding Harel finally appeared with several staff members in tow. Bauer tried to strike a collaborative tone but couldn't hide his frustration with the Mossad director as he presented the latest evidence from Pohl, which, he pointed out, only confirmed what Hermann had been telling them for two years.[10]

Harel responded defensively by asking Bauer whether he had considered the possibility that Klammer and Hermann might be working together.[11]

Isser Harel, c. 1950s
National Library of
Israel / Creative
Commons

"This is simply unbelievable!" Bauer exploded. Any "second-class policeman" should be able to follow the leads he had provided, he declared. "Just go and ask the nearest butcher or greengrocer and you will learn all there is to know."[12]

If Harel didn't take action this time, Bauer threatened, he would file an extradition request with the Argentinian authorities. They both knew this would lead to Eichmann's escape. Harel responded by introducing Zvi Aharoni, a thin, reserved member of his staff, as Mossad's chief interrogator. Aharoni would now lead a "comprehensive investigation," first visiting Bauer in Frankfurt to gather the latest intelligence, then flying on to Buenos Aires. Bauer left the meeting without retracting his extradition threat, and Harel felt obliged to inform the Israeli prime minister, David Ben-Gurion.[13]

"Prevent Bauer from taking this step," Ben-Gurion said. "If Eichmann is there, we will capture him in order to bring him here."[14]

• • •

Bauer returned to Frankfurt as Christmas approached, and West Germany saw the worst outbreak of antisemitism since the war. On December 24, 1959, two young men painted huge swastikas and "JUDEN RAUS" ("JEWS OUT") across the walls of a new synagogue and on a memorial to those who had resisted Hitler in Cologne. Over the following days, hundreds of synagogues and Jewish cemeteries were daubed with swastikas and Nazi slogans. These were not isolated incidents. Similar attacks had taken place two years previously in a dozen towns. In a 1956 poll, a quarter of respondents said Germany would be better off without Jews; half the country was undecided on the matter. Nonetheless, the sheer scale of the attacks in 1959 alarmed Jewish leaders in the Federal Republic for whom the vandalism evoked memories of the pogrom of November 1938.[15]

At the same time, the far-right German Reich Party, a successor to Remer's Socialist Reich Party, had made gains in state elections, and nationalist organizations were proliferating. Their members shared a hatred of the "Bonn democracy" and a desire to "correct the accepted facts" about Hitler and German war guilt. One right-wing activist wrote a pamphlet that gained national attention in which he claimed that the Final Solution had been carried out by the Jews themselves in collusion with the Nazis.[16]

On December 31, Adenauer delivered an emergency radio address that the antisemitic attacks were not to be tolerated and that Nazi ideas had "no roots in the German people." But it was plain that much more was needed to address the rise of what the press now called "neo-Nazism." Bauer attended a commemoration with Adenauer and a small group of survivors and officials at the Bergen-Belsen concentration camp in January 1960. He stood on the frigid square that had once been stacked with corpses as the chancellor spoke of the Jewish dead. "Things are going haywire at my place," Bauer confided to his old friend Meyer-Velde. "I'm hardly ever here, but constantly on the road; the work is getting out of control and the resistance is very great."[17]

Bauer disagreed fundamentally with Adenauer's interpretation of the attacks. He had believed since his exile days that Nazism was deeply embedded in the German psyche. The idea was controversial, he knew, and ran counter to the emerging consensus among historians who had begun to explain Hitler's rise to power as a result of Germany's defeat in World War I and the unrest of the Weimar years. From Bauer's perspective, these historians were willfully ignoring the centuries of German thought that had steadily eroded an ethic of personal responsibility. He found it telling that when American and French writers were espousing revolutionary democratic ideas, Immanuel Kant, Germany's leading philosopher of the Enlightenment, was arguing that peace was the citizen's highest duty. The result was a state that appeared to guarantee order with its "forest of laws, commandments and prohibitions," reflected Bauer, but was in fact readily exploited once the Nazis took power because people had been taught to idolize order over their convictions. Some form of moral reconstruction was needed to achieve a cultural reckoning. But Bauer feared the courage to look inward was lacking. "We have not even examined the concentration camp murderers, the little Eichmanns, for their mental state or tested them," he observed. "Although a policy of prevention is not possible without knowledge of the source of the illness, the fear and timidity of 'know thyself' has been prevalent in Germany."[18]

The ultimate rebuke to Nazism, Bauer felt, would come when society approached criminals with understanding and compassion. If the courts could help offenders recognize the fear, unhappiness, and loneliness that drove them to commit crimes, then some form of redemption was possible. He wanted to believe this was true of Nazis, too. Yet what if he were wrong? At one point, he summoned from prison Werner Heyde, a euthanasia doctor arrested for his role in orchestrating the gassing of tens of thousands under the so-called T4 program. It was highly unusual for an attorney general to meet a defendant, let alone in his own office. Heyde was a sallow-faced man with pursed lips and a closely cropped mustache, who eyed Bauer suspiciously. Bauer asked him directly: Why had he—educated and worldly—allowed himself to become a killing tool of the Nazis? Did he not feel a sense of remorse? But Heyde hardly seemed to comprehend the question and took umbrage at being singled out.[19]

*   *   *

Bauer finally heard from Zvi Aharoni at the end of January 1960. He wanted to see Bauer's Eichmann file, including his SS service photograph, for identification. It was too risky for Bauer to meet Aharoni in person, so they planned for Bauer to supply an office key and leave the files on his desk. On the agreed evening, a Mossad agent sneaked into the building carrying a camera and a lamp. As the agent began work in Bauer's office, he heard a shuffling sound in the marble-floored corridor. He scrambled under the desk. It was the cleaning lady dragging her mop bucket. She paused outside Bauer's office and then moved on.[20]

Bauer heard little for weeks, beyond a few more questions about his second source. He feared Mossad was letting Eichmann slip away. In March, he contacted the U.S. consulate in Frankfurt to ask if they could assist in extraditing war criminals. No response. In the first week of

Zvi Aharoni, c. 1950s
Courtesy of Avner
Avraham

May, he wrote to Cohen-Abarbanel, his original Mossad contact, demanding news, but again, there was no response.[21]

What Bauer didn't know was that Cohen-Abarbanel was in Buenos Aires with Aharoni preparing to seize Eichmann. Indeed, Aharoni had already staked out the house at Calle Chacabuco, only to discover that the Eichmann family had moved several weeks before. Undeterred, he sent a young agent to the garage where Eichmann's son, Nick, worked, with a story that he had a gift for him. One of the mechanics directed him to a house on the outskirts of town. It was a desolate area, with few neighboring houses and little traffic. Aharoni drove over and immediately spotted a middle-aged man in the yard bringing in the laundry. He returned with a pickup truck and lay in the back under a tarpaulin with a hole cut in it to observe more closely. The next time the man appeared in the yard, Aharoni sent an agent to approach him with the ruse that he was looking for land to buy. They chatted casually as the Mossad man snapped pictures with a camera concealed in his briefcase. When compared against Eichmann's SS file headshot, the photographs removed any lingering doubt. They had found their man.[22]

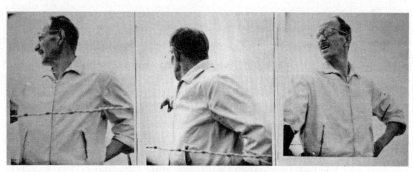

Mossad's secret photographs of Eichmann, 1960
Courtesy of Avner Avraham

Over the next few weeks, Aharoni observed the house and Eichmann's comings and goings from the Mercedes-Benz factory where he worked in San Fernando. He was a man of routine, taking the same bus each morning and returning each evening at 7:40 P.M., the obvious time to seize him as he walked the few hundred yards from the bus stop to his home. Aharoni wanted two cars for the operation: one to transport Eichmann to a safe house, the other as backup in case of trouble. By then, Harel had conceived an audacious plan to bring Eichmann to Israel via El Al airlines, which launched its first direct flight to Buenos Aires on May 11, 1960. The return journey would be reserved for Eichmann.[23]

That same day, shortly after sunset, Aharoni and the other Mossad agents pulled up in sight of the bus stop near Eichmann's home, in which a single light shone. The two agents traveling with Aharoni in the first car got out and raised its hood, leaned over the engine, and pretended to fix it. The backup car stopped thirty meters away. Aharoni craned around in the driver's seat with a pair of binoculars to scan the bus stop. The air was hot and humid with an approaching storm. The first two buses from San Fernando drove past without stopping. No sign of Eichmann. The minutes ticked by. The longer they waited, the more suspicious they seemed and the greater the likelihood they would be discovered. Aharoni watched, tense, as the next bus lumbered into view shortly after 8:00 P.M. This time two figures got out. The first, stout and short and obviously a woman, turned off the street almost at once. The second passenger, a man, silhouetted against the light, walked toward them.[24]

"Someone's coming," whispered Aharoni in the waiting car, "but I can't see who it is." On cue, the headlights of the second car, facing the street, flicked on.[25]

They recognized Eichmann at once, the collar of his coat upturned against the wind, which had picked up, and his right hand in his pocket.[26]

One of the agents at the front of the car, Peter Malkin, stepped into view and started toward Eichmann. As he passed the driver's seat, Aharoni hissed that Eichmann might have a gun.[27]

Malkin kept walking along the dusty side of the road. The sky overhead suddenly streaked with lightning. At the last moment, he stepped directly into Eichmann's path.

"Un momentito, señor," he said.[28]

Then his and Eichmann's eyes locked. Eichmann stepped back as

Malkin grabbed his right arm. The two men stumbled into the shallow, muddy ditch beside the road. Malkin reached for Eichmann's mouth but couldn't stop him from shouting out. Aharoni revved the engine to drown out the noise. Another agent ran over to help. In the struggle, Eichmann rolled on top of Malkin and tried to regain his footing, now screaming at the top of his lungs. The second agent grabbed Eichmann by his legs as Malkin freed himself and pinioned the former SS man. Almost at once his body went slack and he fell silent, surrendering to the inevitable.[29]

They bundled him into the back seat of the car. Malkin had his gloved hand over Eichmann's mouth while the other man closed the car's hood, clambered in on the other side of the former SS man, and covered his eyes with a pair of motorcycle goggles with blacked-out lenses.[30]

"Sit still and nothing will happen to you," shouted Aharoni in German as they sped into the night. "If you resist, we will shoot. Do you understand?"[31]

Malkin eased his hand off Eichmann's mouth. They drove in silence until finally Eichmann said, "I am already resigned to my fate."[32]

For the next ten days, Mossad agents questioned Eichmann in a safe house as they made preparations to drug and bundle him onto a flight to Israel disguised as an El Al air steward. Bauer was the only West German official whom Israel briefed upon Eichmann's safe arrival. On May 22, a Mossad agent called Bauer with instructions to meet at a restaurant in Cologne the following day at 1:00 P.M. The man arrived late, his hands black with rubber from a blown tire. Eichmann had been caught, he blurted out. Bauer leapt to his feet to embrace the stranger, tears in his eyes.[33]

15

Fallout

M ONDAY, MAY 23, 1960, started like any other day for Reinhard Gehlen. His desk was stacked with reports concerning the
resignation of one of Adenauer's cabinet ministers, a former Nazi,
whom the East Germans had tried in absentia for his role in instigating
pogroms in Ukraine. Other matters were more humdrum. The West
German navy was carrying out radio surveillance in the Baltic on behalf of the BND but apparently didn't have enough boats. Gehlen wrote
a memo, finished a light lunch, and was preparing for a customary nap
when he heard a commotion next door.[1]

Israeli prime minister Ben-Gurion had just informed the Knesset
that "a short time ago one of the most notorious Nazi war criminals,
Adolf Eichmann . . . was discovered by the Israeli Security Services.
Adolf Eichmann is already under arrest . . . and will shortly be placed
on trial in Israel under the terms of law for the trial of Nazis and their
helpers." No further details were given. The first news reports speculated that Eichmann had been apprehended in an Arab country: Egypt
or Syria, or possibly Kuwait. Gehlen, of course, knew exactly where
Eichmann had been seized. But the kidnapping had caught him un-
awares. Eichmann, whom he had dismissed as just another Nazi fugi-
tive eighteen months earlier, was suddenly front-page news around the
world as the press offered sensational accounts of his capture and
raised awkward questions over why the West Germans had not brought
him to justice themselves.[2]

The kidnapping was an immediate political embarrassment to

Adenauer. But Gehlen saw a greater crisis looming if Eichmann was brought before a court and allowed to speak in public: The former SS man might then reveal his links to Globke. Gehlen had done his research into the chancellor's chief adviser and didn't think he was hiding any great crimes beyond those already on record. But the danger was that in the volatile atmosphere, public opinion might suddenly shift and Globke's crimes would catch attention and make his position in government untenable. And if Globke was forced out, would any former Nazi in Adenauer's administration be safe?[3]

Globke called Gehlen on Wednesday, May 25, clearly shaken. The East Germans were already accusing the Adenauer administration of having known Eichmann's whereabouts all along and of working to prevent a trial and scrutiny of his connections to Globke. "Globke is Bonn's Eichmann," declared one East German radio station. Gehlen was confident they could rebuff such headlines as propaganda and limit their impact in West Germany. Still, his agents were already reporting rumors from Israel that Eichmann possessed documents detailing his connections to current German officials. Anything coming from Eichmann was sure to make headlines, and there was no telling what he would say to save himself. Globke and Gehlen agreed they needed to keep their distance from Eichmann publicly to avoid the press drawing any more connections, while gaining a handle on what he might reveal.[4]

Gehlen put one of his best men on the case. Kurt Weiss was a forty-four-year-old former journalist whom Gehlen had hired in 1952 to run his public relations department. Weiss had quickly demonstrated his value by creating a network of reporters and editors with whom he exchanged information in return for favorable coverage. He was a jovial workaholic who spent his spare time composing humorous rhyming couplets about his colleagues that he read out at office Christmas parties. His political advice, which Gehlen had come to rely on, was usually delivered in "print-ready German" with a theatrical flourish.[5]

Weiss's first step was to contact the Eichmann family in Buenos

Kurt Weiss, c. 1950s
N13/7, BND-Archiv

Aires to find out what had actually happened. By then, the press had homed in on the city as the site of the kidnapping, and a diplomatic war of words had broken out between Argentina and Israel, during which the latter admitted that a group of "Jewish volunteers, including several Israelis" was behind the capture. Argentina had referred the matter to the United Nations as a breach of international law, and anti-Jewish riots had broken out across the country.[6]

Eichmann's wife, Vera, told Weiss what little she knew about the kidnapping. Her sons had found Eichmann's broken glasses in the ditch, so they suspected he'd been taken with a struggle. They'd then rallied every far-right activist they could find to scour the city on motorbikes. Guns tucked into their belts, they'd broken into a Jewish synagogue to search the basement, but they hadn't found anything. Vera was looking for a lawyer to establish contact with her husband. She promised to stay in touch.[7]

Weiss focused next on what information the Israelis might extract from Eichmann about current West German government officials or uncover during their investigation. He assembled a small team of six researchers to explore every facet of Eichmann's career in the archives. They also coordinated with the Foreign Ministry, which held notes from dozens of wartime meetings between Eichmann's office and almost every branch of the German government. Weiss surmised that

Globke had sat in hundreds of meetings that discussed the Final Solution—routine bureaucratic meetings, any one of which might, in the current situation, be blown out of all proportion. The Foreign Ministry agreed to close public access to its archives and carry out a cull of incriminating documents.[8]

Weiss was still coming to grips with the material when a new threat appeared. The BND had kept Fritz Bauer under watch for several months and already noted that he appeared to have been "informed in advance of [Eichmann's] arrest." Then, in June 1960, Weiss received intelligence that Max Merten, a former military administrator in Greece and a convicted war criminal, had visited Bauer with a story that implicated Globke in Eichmann's deportation of Greek Jews to Auschwitz. Merten claimed that the International Committee of the Red Cross had approached him in 1943 with a proposal to rescue twenty thousand Greek Jews by sending them to British-controlled Palestine. Merten had taken the proposal to Eichmann in Berlin, who had liked the idea of causing trouble for the British. "All these Jewish women should get themselves impregnated by some men before their departure," Eichmann had declared. "[Then] the English would have quite a large increase in Jews."[9]

Eichmann, Merten alleged, had then called Globke. After a brief conversation, Eichmann passed on Globke's advice: The Führer's orders were clear. No Jews were to be saved.[10]

Max Merten, 1959
INTERFOTO /
Alamy Stock Photo

Weiss didn't know how seriously to take Merten's story or, more important, whether he had given Bauer substantiating evidence. Merten had reasons to lie: He might be after money or protection from further prosecution. But if Merten could prove his story, then Globke might find himself in a Frankfurt court.

Weiss sent agents to rifle through Bauer's office papers. They found a letter from Merten explaining that he had no evidence to back his claims, but that he would look for supporting documents. Weiss could only assume that Bauer would try to get Eichmann to implicate Globke directly, either by coordinating with the Israelis or by collaborating with the former SS man's defense team.[11]

By July, Weiss had the name of Eichmann's counsel: Robert Servatius, a thick-necked bruiser from Cologne with a nervous disposition who had served as a defense attorney at Nuremberg for Fritz Sauckel, Hitler's head of slave labor. Servatius had not been a Nazi Party member—which would have barred him from work in Israel—but Mossad still considered him to have "militaristic and right-wing inclinations." Weiss knew to keep his distance from Servatius to avoid any suggestion of government involvement in Eichmann's defense. So he ordered his agents to break into Servatius's office to examine his correspondence. There was nothing from Eichmann yet, but they found letters from Bauer, Merten, and an alarming list of Nazi war criminals offering their services in Eichmann's defense. They included

Robert Servatius, 1961
National Photo
Collection of Israel /
Creative Commons

Eichmann's deportation expert in Greece, Alois Brunner, another man who could presumably implicate Globke. Brunner had gone into hiding in Syria but, to Weiss's alarm, had resurfaced that summer in Cairo with a plan to break Eichmann out of jail or kidnap the president of the World Jewish Congress for a prisoner exchange.[12]

As if the situation wasn't combustible enough, the Dutch former SS propagandist Willem Sassen showed up in Hamburg that summer, looking to sell more than eight hundred pages of transcript from his conversations with Eichmann in Buenos Aires. Weiss could only assume that Eichmann had named collaborators in the interviews. He hurriedly cut a deal to pay Sassen 60,000 deutschmarks—around $150,000 today—for the material, only to then learn that the Dutchman had already sold a selection to *Life* magazine for the same amount. Weiss examined his copy of the transcript and asked the CIA that September to stop *Life* from publishing the interviews. The agency informed him that the U.S. government had no power to censor the magazine but agreed to have a quiet word with its publisher, Henry Luce. Three days later, the Americans gave the all-clear. The material contained only a single obscure Globke reference, which *Life* agreed to omit. Weiss was relieved to report that of the four hundred names mentioned in his own copy, none were of serving government officials.[13]

Weiss finally gained some control over the situation that autumn of 1960 when his agents recruited Servatius's new assistant, Dieter Wechtenbruch, an earnest, baby-faced twenty-nine-year-old law graduate from Munich, who was tasked with keeping close tabs on what Eichmann said. One of his first assignments for Servatius that September was to meet Bauer, ostensibly for advice on archival sources. Wechtenbruch's mission for the BND was to uncover Bauer's thinking about Globke.[14]

Wechtenbruch reported back to his BND handler that Bauer was "very reserved" when they met, eyeing him suspiciously from behind his desk through a haze of cigarette smoke. Bauer advised the young lawyer to read up on the Final Solution and gave him some archival pointers. He had no plans to try to bring Eichmann to West Germany.[15]

Then, unbidden, Bauer turned to the subject of Globke. A number of people were very interested in the outcome of Eichmann's trial for personal reasons, Bauer observed. Indeed, he explained, Max Merten had told him "the most fantastic things" in connection with the chancellor's right-hand man. But Bauer revealed nothing more about his intentions.[16]

16

Pathétique

Bauer's phone in his apartment echoed and clicked throughout the summer of 1960. He knew that Gehlen was listening in and probably had been since the start of his Globke investigation. He suspected he had a BND mole in his office. In May, he had opened cases against ninety-nine Nazi-era judges and prosecutors in the Hessian judiciary, any one of whom might be a paid informer looking to share details of his investigation. Bauer had the backing of the Social Democratic administration in Hesse, so he didn't fear losing his job. But he understood that the BND was stacked with former SS men who might have few qualms about using violence to stop him. That March, Bauer had ordered the arrest of Richard Schweizer, a BND agent who had belonged to a unit that had killed 137,346 Jews in Lithuania. Bauer bought a 6.35mm-caliber pistol.[1]

Yet a familiar mood of recklessness had seized him ever since Max Merten walked through his office door. Merten's story linking Globke and Eichmann together in the mass murder of Greece's Jews was unsubstantiated and might be entirely fabricated for all he knew. Still, the charges were new and justice demanded he try to prosecute Globke.[2]

The obvious place to start was Eichmann. Bauer put in a formal request to the Israeli Justice Ministry that June to question him and then met Felix Shinnar in Cologne to make his case. Shinnar had just come from seeing Eichmann for himself. The SS man was being held in an old British fort in the hills outside Haifa, where three guards kept watch at all times: one inside Eichmann's cell to prevent suicide attempts, another outside to ensure the first guard didn't try to kill the prisoner, and a third to watch the second guard. Eichmann had been cooperative at first, informing the chief interrogator, Avner Less, that he was "prepared, unreservedly, to say everything I know." He recounted the shootings and gassings he had witnessed, which Israeli police investigators, cross-referencing against the archival evidence they were gathering, confirmed to be accurate. Less, whose father had died in Auschwitz—a fact he did not reveal—even received a confession of sorts from Eichmann that summer. "I do not ask for mercy because I am not entitled to it," the former SS man declared. "I would even be prepared to hang myself in public as a deterrent example for antisemites of all the countries on earth." On one occasion, Less had escorted him to see the judge for a court arraignment, only for an agitated Eichmann, who was apparently convinced that he was about to be shot, to declare in transit, "But Captain, I haven't told you everything yet!" Yet when pressed to describe his own role in the killings or to name collaborators, Eichmann was evasive.[3]

Deposition of Eichmann, 1960 (Avner Less to his right)
ISA

Shinnar told Bauer that he thought the Justice Ministry might grant him access to Eichmann once Abraham Selinger, the head of Bureau 06, the police unit building the case against Eichmann, completed his investigation. Bauer immediately followed up with Selinger, who agreed to a secret meeting in Paris on September 3, 1960. Bauer was visibly agitated as they searched for a café in Montmartre. Selinger wanted Bauer's advice on accessing additional Nazi records from archives across Europe to aid their fact-checking. The Eastern Bloc countries had refused to provide material unless Israel publicly foreswore capitalism, and the Israelis were reluctant to collaborate with the Germans. Bauer warned Selinger that on no account should he contact the West German police.[4]

Bauer turned the conversation to Merten's accusations and asked when he could get access to Eichmann. Selinger said it was out of the question. What he didn't say was that Ben-Gurion had issued orders not to investigate any living Nazis associated with Eichmann and that any incriminating material that Selinger uncovered was to be put in a separate folder for the eyes of his superiors only.[5]

But Bauer suspected the truth: The Israelis wanted to protect their relationship with Adenauer, even if it meant shielding Globke. His misgivings were further confirmed on September 10 when he met the Israeli justice minister, Meir Rosenne, in Zurich. Rosenne informed Bauer that the Knesset had decided to delay his access to Eichmann until after the trial, when the political stakes—the very stakes Bauer hoped to make use of—would be reduced. Bauer suggested that one of his experienced prosecutors could join the Israeli investigation and act as a liaison, but Rosenne rejected this idea as well. At most he could send a trial observer. Bauer felt personally affronted. He could make sense of Adenauer's desire to protect his chief of staff, but he still couldn't grasp why the Israelis would allow one of the key administrators of the Nuremberg Race Laws to remain in power unchallenged.[6]

The answer to which Rosenne was certainly privy lay in a secret $500 million West German aid package that Adenauer had negotiated with Ben-Gurion a few months earlier to fund Israel's nuclear program over the next decade. "You cannot undo what Hitler did," Ben-Gurion was reported to have told the chancellor. "But you can help us achieve the means to rebuild Israel."[7]

•   •   •

Bauer needed fresh leads. The Stasi were scouring the Polish archives for material on Globke, but Bauer had no way of accessing the files for himself. He was intrigued, therefore, to receive an offer of assistance from the Nazi film director's son, Thomas Harlan, who had spent six months in the Warsaw archives gathering evidence of Nazi crimes. Bauer was familiar with his father, Veit. He had urged the Hamburg prosecutors' office in 1949 to press charges against the director for crimes against humanity, only to see him acquitted twice, a frustration Bauer undoubtedly shared when he and Harlan met for dinner in Frankfurt on September 15, 1960. Harlan was accompanied by the elegant Polish Jewish writer and Auschwitz survivor Krystyna Żywulska, Harlan's chief supporter in Poland and more recently his lover despite being fifteen years Harlan's senior. Bauer wasn't entirely surprised. Harlan was handsome, with sandy hair, pale blue eyes, and a coy smile and seemed to know it. They discussed Harlan's research and his plans to write a book that would expose the Nazi underpinnings of the Federal Republic. He had already compiled the names and current occupations of hundreds of former Einsatzgruppen members and death camp operators. Indeed, Harlan was on his way back to Warsaw from a visit to the archives in Paris, where he had found "over three thousand documents . . . [and] quite incredible Eichmann material." He was eager to search the Polish archives on Bauer's behalf.[8]

Bauer was charmed by Harlan's enthusiasm and evident need for approval. He also appreciated the groundbreaking nature of Harlan's research—few from the West had explored the Polish archives before. Most of Harlan's findings were beyond the scope of his own work. On the spur of the moment, Bauer suggested Harlan accompany him the next day to Ludwigsburg to meet Dietrich Zeug, a prosecutor he had seconded to the Central Office for the Investigation of National Socialist Crimes in order to pursue the Einsatzgruppen. It was a two-hour drive, but Bauer wanted Harlan to connect with Zeug, compare notes, and learn about the risks he was taking.[9]

They found the thirty-year-old Zeug at his desk, typically stressed and tetchy. The office didn't have enough prosecutors to process the vast amounts of evidence they were uncovering, and the material itself

Harlan, c. 1950s
IPN

had led to some staff feeling so distressed they had quit. Zeug was also under pressure from the BND to drop investigations after he'd discovered at least nine members of the killing squads were on its payroll. In one case, the BND had gone so far as to secure a list of witnesses to dissuade them from testifying. Bauer seemed to want Harlan to understand the scale of state interference he was likely to face. He and Zeug had a measure of protection from Gehlen's operatives on account of their official roles. Harlan, however, would be dangerously exposed.[10]

On the way back to Frankfurt, Bauer appeared to relax. He tended not to invite people to his apartment; neighbors might gossip, and he couldn't afford rumors about his personal life reaching the office. Nonetheless, he brought Harlan back to his place and they sat in the living room smoking. Bauer usually had an open bottle of wine in the kitchen but no food. Harlan noted that he had a record player in the corner with a stack of discs—Tchaikovsky's overwrought *Pathétique* was usually on top—and papers and books strewn everywhere.[11]

It was the first of several meetings that deepened their personal and political connection. Harlan shared some of his experience growing up in the Berlin of the Nazi elite. Goebbels had been a regular houseguest, and as a child Harlan would climb into bed with him in the mornings. "I loved him," Harlan was known to confess, because—unlike his father—Goebbels treated him like a son. For one of Harlan's birthdays, the propaganda chief had shown up at their villa late in the evening

Dietrich Zeug, c. 1960
Courtesy of Andreas Zeug

and whisked Harlan away to an "Aryanized" department store to select a model railway.[12]

Bauer was interested in what had triggered Harlan's moral awakening. Harlan explained that he had begun to reject his Nazi upbringing after he and his siblings were sent to a country estate in Pomerania in 1943 to escape the Allied bombardment. The manor belonged to a German aristocrat who subtly let his opposition to Hitler's regime be known to Harlan, until one morning his wife took Harlan aside and revealed to him that she was Jewish and might need his help. Harlan knew about the persecution of Jews at that point. It wasn't until after the war, when Veit stood trial in Hamburg in 1949, that he learned just how complicit his father had been in the genocide; his film *Jud Süss* had used Jewish extras drawn from ghettos who were sent to their deaths after filming. Overcome with a violent sense of self-loathing— but for Hitler's defeat, he would have been "one of them"—Harlan confronted his father. Veit denied any wrongdoing and simply repeated his trial defense, that he had been coerced into making antisemitic films. Veit was acquitted, but not in Harlan's eyes. The two men had shared a fraught relationship since, with Harlan making use of his father's connections to stage his play about the Warsaw Ghetto uprising while castigating him for his failure to confess.[13]

Bauer had his own thoughts on the role of abusive fathers and authoritarian homes in Hitler's rise to power. German children were so browbeaten into accepting their fathers' authority that once they reached adulthood, they were too scared to take a stand or trust their own judgment. Hitler had played upon these insecurities by telling the German people they needed a firm hand. Bauer feared the same pattern was repeating itself in the Federal Republic. He'd recently lent a book about the liberation of the Bergen-Belsen concentration camp to a high school student. The boy had returned it the next day after his father had shouted at him, "Such books should be . . . banned today because they only pollute the air!" Bauer wasn't sure which depressed him more, the angry father in denial about the "poisonous clouds of the gas chambers" or the son who so meekly handed the book back. This was why Harlan's awakening was so meaningful; it suggested that at least some of his generation was prepared to confront the crimes of their parents.[14]

17

Bauer's Boys

BAUER TOOK A short break to Palermo, Sicily, in early October 1960, where the hordes of tourists at the beach oppressed him no less than the lawyers did in Frankfurt's courthouse. His spirits fell further upon his return when he learned from the Israelis about the disappointing outcome of Robert Servatius's first meeting with Eichmann. After being mobbed by reporters at the airport, Servatius had been whisked away by the police to his hotel and then to Eichmann's secret hilltop location. He'd been searched and brought into a large room divided by a glass wall with a telephone fixed to each side. Eichmann stood opposite him in light-colored trousers and a white shirt. Servatius held up a note, warning his client to be careful in what he said as the room was probably bugged. He needn't have worried. The defense Eichmann offered was the same used by almost every Nazi since Nuremberg: While he personally regretted the killings, he felt duty-bound to carry out his "harsh orders" because they had been mandated for "political reasons" by the Nazi leadership. At their second meeting, Servatius probed deeper: Who, he asked, had given Eichmann his orders? The former SS man refused to say. Servatius asked about Merten's allegation against Globke. Eichmann shrugged: The name Globke meant nothing to him, at least in connection with the "mission of the Final Solution."[1]

Bauer wasn't surprised. Eichmann might be telling the truth. Just as likely, he was keeping quiet from a sense of loyalty, thinking that the

West German government would come to his assistance. The trouble was that Bauer had no way of determining what Eichmann knew, while the Israelis were keeping him at arm's length.[2]

The impasse highlighted the growing importance of the Auschwitz trial, which, by focusing on the crimes of lower-ranking Nazis, had so far avoided state interference. The scope of the investigation had rapidly expanded over the past year. His boys, as Bauer sometimes referred to Kügler and Vogel, had assembled a list of 599 suspects based on their interviews with dozens of witnesses and the hundreds of questionnaires they had sent to those unable or unwilling to travel to Frankfurt. Indeed, one of Bauer's primary considerations was how to whittle down the number of potential defendants to a more manageable twenty to thirty people. Some were obvious inclusions, like Richard Baer, the last commandant of Auschwitz; the camp adjutants Robert Mulka and Karl Höcker, who had overseen the daily operation of the camp; and the SS doctor Josef Mengele, if he could be found. So, too, those already in custody, such as SS guards Bischoff and Kaduk and the camp pharmacist Viktor Capesius.[3]

Bauer wanted the remaining names on the list to reflect different aspects of how Auschwitz had functioned. No job in the camp should be considered too lowly, he told Kügler, because every SS man had contributed to the systematic killing. Indeed, to consider any activity in Auschwitz as discrete from the collective endeavor was absurd. A truck driver in Birkenau wasn't simply driving a truck if he was transporting Jews to the gas chamber.[4]

"Everyone who worked within this killing machine, regardless of what they did, was guilty of complicity in murder," Bauer believed.[5]

Landing this argument, however, would be a challenge, since German law did not recognize state-sponsored mass killing as a crime. To bring murder charges against defendants who didn't have actual blood on their hands, his prosecutors needed to build up a complex picture of how the camp's genocidal system operated, thereby proving each defendant's role in the killing. Kügler and Vogel had already set about gathering the documentary evidence and found a clever work-around to the fact that most surviving camp records were stored behind the Iron Curtain in Auschwitz's archives. They enlisted Jan Sehn, the Polish judge who'd investigated Rudolf Höss in 1947, to travel to Frankfurt in March 1960 on a tourist visa with documents hidden in his luggage. Sehn, a dapper man with an ironic sense of humor, showed up wearing an Eden hat and chamois gloves, carrying the files.[6]

"What took you so long?" he said to Bauer when the two men sat down to dinner. Bauer took the point good-humoredly. He knew that Sehn had been investigating Nazi crimes in Auschwitz since 1945. Indeed, Sehn had arrived in the camp within weeks of its liberation to find Soviet troops drunkenly dancing atop the flat roof of the crematorium beside the main gate, looters ransacking buildings and digging holes around the ruined gas chambers looking for Jewish gold, and crucial SS documents floating in cesspits where they'd been hurriedly dumped. Sehn had saved what he could and pushed the Soviet authorities to protect the site.[7]

Jan Sehn, 1952
IPN

Sehn was ready to provide anything Bauer might need from the tens of thousands of documents kept in the museum's archives; despite the Communist regime's insistence on an ideological reading of the camp, he and the former prisoners who ran the museum had considerable freedom to gather and share material. At Sehn's insistence, Kügler and Vogel repeated the tourist visa trick and visited Auschwitz that summer of 1960 to assess the files. Kügler found copious evidence of how the camp was run but little to directly implicate the defendants, beyond several signed orders from Mulka for extra shipments of Zyklon B gas and for trucks to transport infirm Jews from the trains to the gas chambers. The SS had been careful to disguise their crimes in official paperwork. Gassings were described as "special treatment" and individual murders as "shot while escaping" or "heart failure."[8]

The trip made it clear to Kügler that the bulk of the evidence would need to come from survivors who could attest to the actions of specific SS men. But the interviews Kügler and Vogel conducted were exhausting for all involved. The questions they put to witnesses—Which SS men stood on the ramp? How many prisoners did the guard shoot?— seemed, to many of them, beside the point compared to what they had lived through. Langbein was usually on hand to comfort them afterward. But even Langbein could be shaken by the work. In June 1960, Kügler arrested Josef Klehr, an SS orderly who was notorious for selecting prisoners for lethal injection and had personally administered hundreds if not thousands of shots straight into the hearts of his victims. Langbein offered to pick him out of the police lineup himself. He hadn't witnessed Klehr killing in person, but he knew of the SS man's sadism from his work as a hospital clerk. In one notorious incident, Klehr's prisoner assistant had burst into tears after dragging out a corpse from the operating room. When Klehr asked why he was crying, the man explained that Klehr had just killed his father. Langbein had himself come close to death at Klehr's hand upon falling sick with typhus in 1943, but Klehr had inexplicably spared him. Langbein recognized Klehr immediately as he lumbered into the interrogation room, coughing and sniffling from some illness. That night, Langbein dreamed he was back in the block again.[9]

Kügler was increasingly disturbed by the work. He found himself glaring at older passengers on the tram ride back to his one-bedroom apartment. Surely they had known about the killing—how could they

Josef Klehr, 1960
HHStAW, 544, 1414

simply go about their lives now as if nothing had happened? But he reserved his special fury for the former SS men he hunted. Klehr had been relatively easy to trace to Braunschweig, where a neighbor whose brother had been denounced by Klehr and arrested by the Gestapo reported that he was working as a chassis builder. Other discoveries were accidental. In September of 1960, he stumbled across a newspaper article in *Die Welt*. The Olympics were under way in Rome, and the paper had a short article on a bronze medal–winning sailor named Rolf Mulka, whose father, Robert, it turned out, was the missing adjutant of Auschwitz. That November, Kügler arrested Mulka senior in his office in Hamburg, where he ran a lucrative glass shipping business. The sixty-eight-year-old peered disdainfully down his nose at Kügler before being led away.[10]

But most targets required extensive legwork that increased the chances that they might get tipped off. To dodge the suspected moles in the office, Kügler sent telexes from a greengrocer around the corner. He avoided the police altogether, preferring to investigate clues in person, and when their presence was unavoidable for an arrest, he often traveled at his own expense to accompany officers, sleeping in the stations' mess rooms, and on one occasion on a park bench, to save money.[11]

Commandant Baer proved among the most challenging of the Auschwitz men to track down. Kügler first retrieved his photograph from the Berlin Document Center and published it in the mass-market newspaper *Bild* that December with a request for tips and the offer of a

Kügler, c. 1950s
Nachlass Joachim Kügler, FBInst

reward. He received hundreds of replies, mostly from cranks and jokers. "There's smoke coming from our neighbor's chimney, they've got a fireplace," read one. "I think you should come and check it out." But a letter from a forester outside the small town of Dassendorf, near Hamburg, sounded more authentic. The writer thought the picture looked like a man he worked with who went by the name Karl Neumann. On December 13, Kügler took the train to Hamburg, where he met two officers, who drove him to Dassendorf. By the time they reached the local police station, it was after 9:00 P.M. and snowing hard, but Kügler insisted on tracking down the forester, who lived in a neighboring town. They roused him from bed to confirm that the man in the SS photo resembled Neumann.[12]

The next morning, Kügler visited the town's registration office to examine Neumann's paperwork. Kügler recognized Baer's handwriting from his SS personnel file and set off with the police to search for him in a dense pine forest. The fog had yet to clear as they trekked through the snow. They heard men working, then saw two lumberjacks in a clearing and the outline of a heavyset man in overalls a little farther on. The police rushed forward with their pistols drawn, but the man offered no resistance. He identified himself as Karl Neumann. Kügler corrected him, "Your name is Baer and you were the last commandant of Auschwitz." It was only after they cuffed him and brought him back to the car that Kügler noticed that the forty-nine-year-old had soiled

Richard Baer, 1960
HHStAW

himself. They stopped at his cottage so he could clean himself up. All the while, he continued to insist his name was Neumann. Kügler finally snapped that he had more than enough evidence to prove his identity. "Fine, I am Richard Baer," he conceded, and then, seeming to take note of the fresh-faced prosecutor, added, "Please, treat me accordingly." Kügler planned to.[13]

18

Bikini Decree

B AUER'S OFFICE ANNOUNCED the arrest of Richard Baer at
a press conference on December 21, 1960. Bauer was impressed
by his young prosecutor's dedication—Kügler seemed particularly
driven. But Bauer couldn't join in the jubilant mood when so many of
his other cases were threatened. New regulations protecting judges had
forced him to concede defeat in his investigation into the Hessian judiciary. Hermann Krumey's lawyers kept stalling. As for Globke, Bauer
hadn't heard from Harlan since his return to Poland earlier in the year,
and he was getting anxious both for Harlan's safety and about the fad-
ing prospect of implicating the chancellor's right-hand man. The only
remaining option was to turn to the East Germans. Following Eichmann's capture, the Stasi had published a pamphlet based on their research in Eastern Bloc archives titled "Globke and the Extermination
of the Jews," which was light on detail but promised more revelations.
A documentary film containing newsreel footage of Globke in Slovakia
was also in the works. In desperation, Bauer reached out to the Stasi
through a trusted journalist and was informed that the Communist
authorities would share their findings—provided he agreed to a formal
meeting with two of their prosecutors, which they would no doubt use
for political gain. It was a steep price to pay; Bauer risked being labeled
a Communist stooge, and the Stasi might feed him little more than
propaganda. But if he wanted to bring Globke to justice, he needed to
pursue every lead.[1]

He received a large packet of Stasi documents on January 5, 1961.

They looked genuine enough—and incriminating. Globke's trip to Slo-vakia in 1941 to advise its puppet administration on how to impose the race laws was documented in full, including letters from Globke to a Slovak official in which he fondly recalled his "beautiful days in Slova-kia" and hoped "that the trip will also show practical results." The of-ficial wrote back that he had already sent one of the richest Jews in Slovakia to a concentration camp. The most damning piece of evidence was the 1938 letter from Nazi interior minister Wilhelm Frick com-mending Globke's work persecuting Jews "to an outstanding degree."[2]

Taken together, there wasn't enough evidence to press charges, but Bauer decided to go ahead anyway and launch a full-scale investigation into Globke. It would be a high-stakes bluff. Bauer hoped that by call-ing out Globke, he might generate fresh evidence or even enough pub-lic pressure to force the chancellor's confidant from office before the state could mobilize against him.[3]

Bauer announced his investigation the next day to the press. Globke was forced into an immediate denial of any wrongdoing as the chancel-lery sent its allies to attack Bauer. The chairman of the Christian Dem-ocratic Union Party in Hesse accused Bauer of collaborating with Communists and demanded his dismissal. Then the two East German prosecutors showed up in Bauer's office for their publicity stunt and held a press conference in the Frankfurter Hof hotel that ended in a shouting match between them and the West German reporters. Bauer was rapidly becoming "the most controversial political person in [the state]," noted the U.S. envoy in Frankfurt.[4]

Bauer weathered the attacks with the help of the Hessian state pre-mier, Georg August Zinn, who invited Bauer to join him at a press conference at his official residence in Wiesbaden. Zinn insisted Bauer had acted correctly and backed his investigation. Indeed, Bauer almost seemed to be enjoying himself as he announced plans to question Alois Brunner, Eichmann's deportation specialist in Greece, to prove Globke's hand in the mass murder of Greek Jews. "If something were to happen to me, it would make big waves abroad," he told one reporter, "and the Nazis know that too."[5]

The pushback came soon thereafter. Adenauer sent Zinn a thinly veiled threat that he would publicly denounce him and seek Bauer's dismissal if the Globke investigation was not handed over to Bonn prosecutors—in other words, shelved. Zinn faced a "political conflict which will only be of use to the Communist opposition," warned Adenauer. As for Bauer, he risked being "dragged into the shadows."[6]

Nonetheless, the pressure was starting to tell on Globke. He complained to colleagues of stomach pains he'd last experienced during the war as more revelations emerged. A small news outlet in Saarland discovered an order from Globke in 1944 that prospective Czech brides from the Protectorate of Bohemia and Moravia seeking to marry German citizens send his department photographs of themselves in swimsuits so that their "Aryan" characteristics could be examined. "If a swimsuit is not available in individual cases," Globke decreed, "please ensure that the photographs showing the applicant in her unclothed state are attached to the file in a sealed envelope so that they are accessible only to the officials directly involved." An earlier decree calling for exclusively naked photographs had been in effect since 1941. The national press seized on the "bikini decree," which appeared to cause Globke more damage than any revelation of his role in mass murder to date. Conservative politicians began to discuss in private whether it might not be in the chancellor's interest, after all, to jettison his confidant with elections approaching in the autumn. There was no telling what might emerge from a prospective trial, or what might be released by the Communists.[7]

On February 17, Globke was forced into a further statement to the press in which he explained that his bikini decree was in fact meant to stop the photographs from being circulated and "misused" by colleagues. He denied entirely Max Merten's accusations that he'd sent twenty thousand Greek Jews to their deaths. He had only ever seen Eichmann once in passing, he claimed, and they had certainly never discussed deporting Jews.[8]

Bauer could have left the investigation open for a few more weeks in the hope of further damaging Globke, but he recognized the pressure Zinn was under. Adenauer could not order Zinn to remove Bauer, but

Hamburger Echo

„Ik weiß jar nich, wat die von Ihnen wolln, lieber Jlobke, schließlich haben Se doch nur dafür jesorcht, dat bei den Nazis de Moral nich jänzlich unterjejangen is ..."

Cartoon from Hamburger Echo, *1961:*
"I honestly don't know why they're after you, my dear Globke—after all,
you only saw to it that Nazi morale didn't take a complete nosedive."
Creative Commons

it was not clear what would happen if the chancellor publicly called for Bauer's sacking. In mid-February, Bauer informed Zinn that he would hand the Globke case over to Bonn, effectively ending the investigation. He had spoken out against Globke and the chancellor's man had been humiliated in public. He also informed Wayland B. Waters, the U.S. consul general in Frankfurt, that he wasn't ruling out filing fresh charges against Globke. After all, the trial against Eichmann was due to begin, and no one knew what he would say on the stand.[9]

19

Jerusalem

REINHARD GEHLEN DID his best to neutralize Fritz Bauer as 1961 began. In January, he arranged for the Stasi documents in the attorney general's office to be secretly copied and brought back to BND headquarters in Pullach for assessment. Then he isolated Bauer from his sources. Gehlen had his press man, Kurt Weiss, reach out to Globke's accuser, Max Merten, to find out how much it would cost to buy his silence. The amount—around 25,000 deutschmarks or $60,000 today—was less than expected. Gehlen also approached Eichmann's associate Alois Brunner in Syria, who might be tempted to cooperate with Bauer in exchange for immunity from prosecution if he returned to West Germany. Gehlen sent him funds "through other channels" and brought one of Brunner's contacts onto the BND payroll.[1]

Gehlen, c. 1961
Courtesy of Dorothee Gehlen-Koss

But Gehlen understood that gaining control over Bauer's investigation did nothing to lessen the danger posed by Eichmann. The trial in Jerusalem was starting to look like it would be a global phenomenon. Hundreds of foreign journalists had requested credentials, including representatives of every major West German newspaper in what was shaping up to be the greatest Nazi war crimes trial since Nuremberg, and the first to focus exclusively on the mass murder of the Jews. There was no way to ensure that Eichmann would stick to his claims of ignorance regarding Globke. The former SS man was already showing worrying signs that he might crack under pressure. If "everything is blamed on me," he declared to Servatius at one point, "I will come clean." Gehlen also didn't know what evidence the Israelis had dug up. One thousand five hundred documents would be submitted in court, any one of which might incriminate Globke.[2]

Adenauer decided to take matters into his own hands and send Ben-Gurion a not-so-subtle message. The prime minister had expected to receive the first tranche of the $500 million West German grant for Israel's secret nuclear program in early 1961. No money was sent. And if that wasn't clear enough, Adenauer sent a personal envoy, a thirty-nine-year-old journalist named Rolf Vogel, to meet Ben-Gurion in March. The Israeli prime minister, who was on holiday, met Vogel at the Sharon Hotel in Herzliya in his dressing gown, as his wife served tea and biscuits. Vogel, himself half-Jewish, blustery and self-assured in an ill-fitting suit, turned straight to the topic of Globke.[3]

Ben-Gurion offered assurance if not exactly an endorsement of the chancellor's right-hand man: "Whomsoever Konrad Adenauer has with him, he has examined more than we ever could." He undertook to keep Globke's name out of the trial.[4]

Adenauer professed himself to be satisfied but decided to hold back the money until after the verdict. There were other ways the trial might prove damaging: If the proceedings sensitized the West German public to the genocide, it might shatter the postwar consensus to bury the past. Exposing the horror was precisely what Gideon Hausner, Israel's chief prosecutor, appeared intent on doing. He had been influenced by

David Ben-Gurion and
Rolf Vogel, 1961
ISA

Gideon Hausner, 1961
mauritius images / TopFoto

Rachel Auerbach, a Warsaw Ghetto survivor and the director of testimony collection at Yad Vashem, who wanted the voices of survivors, so
long neglected, to be at the heart of the trial. Hausner planned to summon 110 witnesses to tell their stories and provide catharsis for themselves and the nation.[5]

There was little Adenauer could do to alter the facts. Instead he
asked Vogel to return to Israel at the head of a dozen-strong delegation
that would try and spin proceedings in West Germany's favor. A secret
"Eichmann Working Group" would prepare talking points that were to
downplay and even deny German responsibility for the mass murder
of the Jews. The group commissioned a report from the Institute for
Contemporary History in Munich to show that the Final Solution was
"a) . . . carried out by a small circle of people and b) . . . surrounded by
such secrecy that people who were not directly involved could not have
any knowledge of events." Furthermore, the guards of concentration
camps were to be presented as coming predominantly from Ukraine
and the Baltic republics.[6]

As the April 11 trial date approached, Vogel and his team arrived
in Jerusalem and ensconced themselves at the grand old King David
Hotel with most of the press corps. Each morning, Vogel pored over
newspaper copy and flagged awkward comments in telegrams back

to Bonn. In the afternoons and evenings, he manned the bar or held forth on the veranda with its sweeping view of the limestone walls of the Old City and the graveyards of Mount Zion. He made a point of singling out Israeli journalists for "tough discussions that cannot be conducted with excuses." The other West German delegates sometimes allowed the free-flowing alcohol to get the better of them— one member had to be carried out by the head waiter—which, together with their crude spinning of the mass murder of the Jews, generally made a "devastating impression," according to one reporter.[7]

Fortunately for Vogel, the press's only real interest was Eichmann. In March, the Israeli authorities had given journalists access to his cell. The former SS man was not present, so they breathlessly reported on the slippers neatly placed beneath the single bunk, the table stacked with books about the Final Solution, and the notes that Eichmann was apparently making for his defense. Page after page of newsprint considered the nature of the man who had sent millions to their deaths. The West German press seemed unsure what to make of him. Was he a monster driven to kill by his hatred of Jews? If this was true, speculated one reporter, it might be enough to lock him up, along with the other Nazi ideologues. But if he had only been following orders as an obedient civil servant, perhaps a wider reckoning was needed. The idea that Eichmann might just be an "average guy"—an everyman—was a disturbing thought for another journalist, who noted that "people with 'typewriter souls,' in contrast to absolute evil, are not merely isolated abnormalities; they existed—and exist in quantities." Everything hinged on what Eichmann had to say.[8]

· · ·

The trial opened on the bright, cool morning of April 11, 1961. Eichmann had been moved from his hilltop prison to a secure room on an upper floor of the fenced-off courthouse. Dozens of armed police in

Eichmann trial, 1961
National Library of Israel / Creative Commons

green caps patrolled the nearby rooftops. A few boys in yarmulkes played tag on the cobbled streets outside the courthouse while a house-wife peeked out the window at the line of visitors stretching around the block, waiting to be frisked. The judges had agreed that the proceedings should be filmed, although most Israelis didn't own televisions. They crowded around radio sets to listen as the country ground to a halt.[9]

By 9:00 A.M., the courtroom was packed with hundreds of journalists and several dozen survivors. Adenauer's emissary, Vogel, found his seat near the front as the room fell silent and a visibly nervous Eichmann entered through a side door dressed in a blue suit and cross-striped tie. He made his way to a bulletproof booth flanked by two guards. Vogel thought he looked haggard under the neon lighting of the windowless hall, like a "harmless civil servant who is on trial because some mistakes have accumulated in his books of figures, or who is to be questioned here as to why the building permits are taking so long." He wasn't alone in this assessment. Elie Wiesel, writing for *The Jewish Daily Forward,* observed that Eichmann looked "no different to other humans."[10]

The three judges entered next and took their seats on a raised dais. The presiding judge, Moshe Landau, originally from Germany and somber in his black robes, brought the room to order with a slap of

his gavel. He then began to read out the indictment in Hebrew. Eichmann was asked to rise and answer the charges. He gave the same
reply to each count that Göring had used at Nuremberg: "In the sense
of the indictment, no." He stood to attention at first but slowly
slumped, biting his lower lip as the names of various death camps
were read out.[11]

Servatius immediately challenged the jurisdiction of the court on
the basis that the crimes had been committed prior to Israel's creation,
against people who had no connection to the country. He also challenged the trial's legitimacy, given Eichmann's kidnapping and the par-
tiality of the Jewish judges.[12]

Chief Prosecutor Hausner, a short, delicate man with a receding
hairline and thick glasses, responded at length. Reporters grew restless
and retreated to the snack bar to follow the breaking news that the
Soviets had just launched the cosmonaut Yuri Gagarin into orbit. Spectators dozed and even the judges grew impatient.[13]

It wasn't until the fourth day that Hausner made his opening address and laid out the moral vision behind the trial.[14]

"As I stand here before you, . . . Judges of Israel, to lead the prosecution of Adolf Eichmann, I do not stand alone," declared Hausner, a
Polish-born Jew who had lost most of his family to the Nazis.[15]

"With me in this place and at this hour, stand six million accusers.
But they cannot rise to their feet and point an accusing finger toward
the man who sits in the glass dock and cry: *J'accuse.*' For their ashes
were piled up in the hills of Auschwitz and in the fields of Treblinka, or
washed away by the rivers of Poland; their graves are scattered over the
length and breadth of Europe. Their blood cries out, but their voices
are not heard. Therefore, it falls to me to be their spokesman." Vogel
was impressed. "There is hardly anyone in the courtroom—apart from
the defendant himself—who is not stirred by what Hausner is saying
here," he reported back to Adenauer.[16]

Vogel noted that Hausner made sweeping claims against the Germans, namely that "antisemitism was not an invention of the Nazis"
and that Hitler had only "exposed the hatred of Jews that was hidden in

the soul of wide circles of the German people." Furthermore, Hausner argued that Eichmann's accomplices were not "gangsters and figures of the underworld"; rather, they were Germany's leaders, its intellectuals, its doctors and lawyers—an entire society had conspired to commit the greatest of horrors. These were damaging assertions, but at least he did not mention Globke.[17]

Hausner proceeded to call his witnesses. First on the stand was Eichmann's chief interrogator, Police Inspector Avner Less. The gallery listened in rapt silence as Hausner played extracts from Less's interrogations from a tape recorder on his desk and Eichmann's thin, reedy voice filled the room. Eichmann flatly described a killing he had observed outside the village of Chełmno in Nazi-occupied Poland. A crowd of Jews was forced into the sealed hold of a truck into which the exhaust pipe had been fitted. The driver's cabin contained a peephole. Eichmann watched as the driver revved his engine and the gas enveloped those inside. They kicked and screamed for a time, beating on the doors to get out.[18]

Eichmann then accompanied the truck into a forest to a specially prepared pit. The doors were opened and the disfigured bodies, covered in blood and excrement, tumbled out of the back. "The most horrible thing that I had ever seen in my life," admitted Eichmann. He continued watching as a civilian crew opened the mouth of each corpse and used pliers to rip out gold fillings. The courtroom was silent except for the occasional sob. Eichmann sat fidgeting throughout, coughing into his handkerchief and jotting down notes. He looked even more tired than he had at the start of the trial, thought Vogel.[19]

At the end of the first week, the court adjourned early for Israel's Independence Day, which was observed with vast crowds on the streets and a military parade. The trial resumed with witness testimony on April 21. The first to speak were those who had known Eichmann in Vienna as the preening, power-hungry head of the Central Agency for Jewish Emigration. Others described life in the ghettos into which they'd been driven by Eichmann's men once the war began. Then witnesses began to describe the killings. A forty-six-year-old Ukrainian-born Jew

Rivka Yoselevska, 1961
Creative Commons

named Rivka Yoselevska, the sole survivor of a massacre outside Pinsk, Belarus, in 1941, took to the stand on May 8. She had been due to appear the previous week but had suffered a heart attack. Against her doctor's orders, Yoselevska had insisted on testifying. In Russian-accented Yiddish, she described how she and her family had been brought from a ghetto with several hundred other Jews to a low rise in a forest clearing, ordered into rows, and told to strip. At the base of the hill Yoselevska glimpsed a pit that already contained a dozen bodies.[20]

"What are we waiting for? Come, let's escape," whispered her six-year-old daughter, Merke. Even as she spoke, the shooting began, one row at a time, the whole column shuffling forward, getting ever shorter. Merke began to shake with fear. Yoselevska's family reached the brow. Her father refused to fully undress. The guards beat him and then dispatched him, still in his underwear. They shot Yoselevska's mother, her grandmother, her nieces, and her sister. One of the guards turned to Rivka as Merke clung to her side. "Who shall I shoot first?" he asked. When she didn't answer, he seized Merke and fired at point blank range. Then he grabbed Yoselevska by the hair and pulled the trigger. She felt herself topple forward.[21]

"I thought that I was dead, but that I could feel something even though I was dead. I couldn't believe that I was alive," she told the court.[22]

By the time she recovered her senses, other bodies had landed atop her. Some were still alive but in their death throes. She fought her way up through the twitching pile. "People were dragging me down, biting and scratching and pulling, while I made my way up," she said. By the time she surfaced, the Germans had gone. A few children, bloodied and injured, ran around the edge of the pit. Yoselevska tried to care for them with another woman who emerged from the pile. Then the Germans came back and shot them but unaccountably left Yoselevska, clawing at the earth beside the grave, begging to join the dead. "I called out to my parents, 'Why have I been left alive? What did I do to deserve this? What should I do now? I have no one.'" She was eventually rescued by a Polish peasant and, after the war, had rebuilt her life in Israel, where she had two children.[23]

The audience filed out of the courtroom in stunned silence. "Hausner's going to turn us all to stone," observed a young lawyer once they got outside.[24]

Servatius declined to cross-examine Yoselevska or any of the other witnesses, pointing out that in many cases his client had not been involved.[25]

Vogel, like almost everyone in attendance, was moved by the power of survivor testimony, but he didn't deem it concerning from a West German perspective. He shared his growing confidence with Bonn that they had successfully navigated the trial's opening. The court adjourned for a week in June to allow Servatius time to finish submitting affidavits from defense witnesses. Servatius's assistant and BND informant, Dieter Wechtenbruch, had interrogated Krumey and Baer in their cells in Frankfurt, which meant their statements could be carefully vetted at BND headquarters before being passed along to Servatius. The witnesses seemed mostly interested in self-exoneration; crucially, there was no mention of Globke.[26]

Then on the morning of June 20, Eichmann finally took the stand. It was the moment Vogel had long feared. But Eichmann's long, rambling answers, filled with non sequiturs and irrelevant details, gave him hope that the former SS man was focused on presenting himself as a mere

functionary and not about to expose his co-conspirators. Eichmann repeatedly claimed to have had no ability to direct events and denied
playing a leading role at the Wannsee Conference in 1942. He recalled
sharing a glass of cognac with his superior Reinhard Heydrich afterward, but any happiness he felt at the time, Eichmann explained, came
from relief in the knowledge that he was in no way responsible for the
awful "solution." When there were written orders for killings that bore
his signature, he said there must have been a mistake in the memo because the matter lay "far beyond my area of competence." At one stage,
to derisive laughter from the audience, he insisted that he was no anti-
semite and had in fact "worked with Jews" to extricate them from the
problems they faced.[27]

The New York Times reported that Eichmann did not appear "sullen
or defiant," just "dull," a man who "reveled in bureaucratic phrases" and
was not even "worth hating." Hannah Arendt, covering the trial for *The
New Yorker,* later coined the phrase "the banality of evil" to describe
how a man who appeared "neither perverted nor sadistic" but "terrifyingly normal" could take part in mass murder. Only occasionally did
the mask slip, when Servatius mixed up a document and Eichmann
corrected him sharply. "The cold snarl, the bark that many of the witnesses remembered was there, one tone beneath what we heard," noted
the *Atlantic* correspondent Martha Gellhorn.[28]

Servatius did ask Eichmann one question about Globke, concerning
a meeting they had both attended in 1941 to discuss the application of
the Nuremberg Race Laws: Had Globke, the ranking official, invited
Eichmann to attend? This was the moment for Eichmann to reveal all.
Instead, he said he couldn't remember the details. Hausner avoided the
subject altogether in his cross-examination. The moment made headlines in the West German press, but only a few commentators called for
Globke to step down.[29]

From Vogel's perspective the testimony was a major victory. The
only other danger was the antics outside the courtroom of the East
German prosecutor Friedrich Karl Kaul, who had been sent to politicize the trial. At a press conference, the grandiloquent, double-chinned

Kaul accused West Germany of conspiring to cover up Globke's role in the mass murder of Jews and claimed to have a dossier of incriminating material for the prosecution, a few pages of which he handed out to those present. Vogel took advantage of the situation to quietly break into Kaul's room at the King David Hotel with a journalist from the *Bild* newspaper. The two men quickly rifled through Kaul's things and found the dossier. The documents concerned the role of the German navy in deporting Norwegian Jews to Auschwitz and weren't particularly damning. Kaul had been bluffing.[30]

Friedrich Karl Kaul,
c. 1960s
Deutsche Fotothek /
Christian Borchert

With only the closing statements to come, Vogel flew back to Germany to meet Adenauer. Bonn was in turmoil over Moscow's decision to erect a wall around West Berlin to stem the flow of easterners to the West. The chancellor was, however, in a surprisingly reflective mood. He explained that some of the witness testimony had affected him deeply. He'd read about one survivor's account of the deportation of four thousand children from an internment camp near Drancy, France, to Auschwitz. It was in the early days of the Final Solution, when working-age Jews were initially deported without their families, which had led to a surfeit of children without parents—a procedural blunder the SS soon fixed by sending entire families to Auschwitz. In the meantime, the children in Drancy were dragged onto the trains, some too young to say their names, others crying out for their parents, all destined to be gassed in a few days' time. Adenauer said he couldn't imagine sitting through such testimony.[31]

"How do you actually stand it?" he asked Vogel.[32]

Part IV

20

Indictment

BAUER FINALLY RECEIVED Israeli permission for his trial observer Dietrich Zeug to interrogate Eichmann in August 1961 as the former SS man awaited sentencing. Bauer wasn't sure what to expect with Eichmann's fate all but decided. His best hope was that the prospect of execution would push the former SS man to name his superiors and prove he was the minor bureaucrat he claimed to be. Zeug found Eichmann responsive and clearly relieved the trial was over. When it came to Globke, however, he stuck to his line that he could not remember any details of their interactions and certainly nothing about a request to rescue Greek Jews.[1]

The verdict was announced in December of 1961 to a packed courtroom in Jerusalem. Judge Landau emphasized Eichmann's personal responsibility for the Final Solution: "Even if we had found that the Accused acted out of blind obedience, as he argued, we would have said that a man who took part in crimes of such magnitude as these over years must pay the maximum penalty known to the law. . . . But we have found the Accused acted out of an inner identification with the orders that he was given and out of a fierce will to achieve the final objective. . . . This Court sentences Adolf Eichmann to death."[2]

It was a poignant moment for Bauer. Adenauer—with Ben-Gurion's help—had managed to prevent the trial from damaging the West German government. Nonetheless, Bauer saw that the proceedings had lodged the Holocaust—the term had started to be used by survivors and historians—in the global conscience. What's more, there were signs of a dawning awareness of Nazi crimes in West Germany. "We cannot free ourselves from what happened by suppressing it or remaining silent about it," observed the center-right *Die Welt*. "Only in the effort to become clear about the monstrous, to want to understand it, can history be 'worked through' at all." The younger generation wanted to "know the sober facts and make sense of them," argued the liberal *Süddeutsche Zeitung*. "They insist on their right to an unencumbered new beginning, on their unbreakable chance, admittedly also their duty: to do better." The *Frankfurter Rundschau* hoped that the shock of the trial would purge West Germany of "anti-democratic and anti-humanist ideas." These sentiments were beginning to surface in opinion polls. Ninety percent of Germans reported that they had heard about the trial and 50 percent viewed it as justified. The latter figure represented an important change since Nuremberg. Even so, for most Germans the mass murder of Jews remained the crime of a few, committed far away during a war of national survival. The question weighing on Bauer as he turned his attention to the Auschwitz proceedings was how to apply the lessons of the Eichmann trial to close this gap between recognition and responsibility.[3]

Hausner, in Bauer's view, had succeeded in connecting his audience emotionally to the story of the Holocaust by giving witnesses a platform to share their experiences. It was their raw emotion that cut through public indifference and compelled attention. One survivor, Yehiel Dinur—better known by his pen name, KZ-nik, for the abbreviation of *Konzentrationslager*—declared that he served as a bridge to the dead, who continued to exist in another dimension he called "Planet Auschwitz." The efforts of the presiding judge and prosecutors to bring him back on track ended with KZ-nik falling unconscious in the witness box to gasps from the audience and sensationalist press coverage the next day.[4]

Another survivor, Joseph Buzminsky, recounted how he'd seen a boy being whipped in the Przemyśl Ghetto. "Usually, fifty lashes were enough to kill a young man," Buzminsky recalled. "But he was able to hold on, and after eighty lashes they told him to run. . . . That saved his life."[5]

"Do you recognize that boy in this courtroom?" Judge Hausner asked.[6]

"Yes, he is the police officer sitting next to you!"[7]

Hannah Arendt, covering the trial for *The New Yorker*, regarded such theatrics as a distraction from the legal case. She shared her thoughts with Bauer during a visit to his office. But Bauer couldn't have disagreed more. From his perspective, the spectacle was the point. Trials needed to immerse people in the experience of the crime in order to generate an emotional response that resonated beyond the courtroom.[8]

Where Hausner had gone wrong, Bauer believed, was in mischaracterizing Eichmann as the mastermind of the Final Solution. The former SS man was in many ways the venal bureaucrat he made himself out to be. He might be a true believer and an important facilitator of the Holocaust—but equally, he was one component of a national enterprise that had involved all levels of the state.[9]

Bauer intended to take a different approach. Auschwitz itself was the crime he planned to prosecute; the defendants were simply the willing hands needed to run the death factory. They were ordinary Germans, and therein lay the trial's power to implicate German society as a whole. It was true that the defendants had committed monstrous acts individually—Klehr the lethal injector, Kaduk the rapist and murderer, Capesius the supplier of gas. Bauer wanted to evoke their deeds in excruciating detail through witness testimony. But he also wanted his countrymen—the world—to see how their crimes fitted together to make industrial murder possible. No defendant had acted alone. They needed the camp, a community, an entire culture, to support them. That was why it wouldn't just be a selection of defendants in the dock, but the whole nation.[10]

.   .   .

Eichmann's trial provided one final moment of drama in March 1962 after he'd appealed his death sentence. His lawyer, Servatius, handed him a book by the student activist Reinhard Strecker detailing Globke's work on behalf of the Nazi state. Eichmann wrote a flurry of notes confirming that Globke had served as a key legal adviser on matters of Jewish citizenship during the Holocaust, along with the plaintive observation "here, secretary of state . . . ; there, sentenced to death."[11]

Servatius filed a final petition to summon Globke to give evidence. The Israeli government had no wish to see that happen, and the judges rejected both the petition and Eichmann's appeal.[12]

Just before midnight on June 1, 1962, guards escorted Eichmann to a specially constructed gallows in one of the cells of his prison. He ascended the wooden platform, where a rope hung from an iron frame. A curtain in one corner hid the release mechanism for the trapdoor. Eichmann spotted an Israeli police inspector who had interrogated him among the officials and journalists in attendance. "I hope, very much, that it will be your turn soon after mine," he told the man as his legs were bound and the rope placed around his neck. "Long live Germany. Long live Argentina. Long live Austria," he declared. "I had to obey the laws of war and my flag. I am ready."[13]

The trapdoor dropped and the rope snapped taut. His body was then placed on a stretcher under a gray wool blanket and carried to a nearby orange grove, where a guard who had once worked at a concentration camp crematorium had stoked a fire in a waiting furnace. It was still dark when the ashes were retrieved, placed in a nickel canister, and brought to the port of Haifa to be taken out to sea.[14]

Two weeks later, Dieter Wechtenbruch, the defense lawyer turned BND spy, appeared at Bauer's office. The young man was visibly shaken. He had suffered a breakdown during the trial, he said. One of Hausner's assistants had found him sobbing in a bathroom. Fellow guests at his hotel had overheard him saying, "I can no longer believe anything Germans of that generation say. I now know the truth."[15]

Wechtenbruch had returned to legal practice in Munich but found he couldn't concentrate. He was thinking of moving to Israel. Bauer was pleased by Wechtenbruch's moral awakening, which seemed to confirm his theory that confronting his countrymen with the Holocaust could spark a new sensitivity.[16]

.   .   .

By the summer of 1962, Bauer's prosecutors had narrowed down the number of possible defendants for the Auschwitz trial to twenty-four. They represented a cross-section of West German society, as Bauer had intended. Many came from solidly middle- or lower-class backgrounds and claimed that they served in Auschwitz out of a sense of patriotism or as a professional requirement. Almost all had returned to the jobs they had done prior to joining the SS or had found respectable employment elsewhere: Camp adjutant Robert Mulka had his lucrative glass business; SS doctor Franz Lucas ran the obstetrics and gynecology department of a hospital; gas chamber operative Hans Stark was a lecturer at the Cologne Chamber of Agriculture. Bauer had developed his own classification for Nazis—the believers, the obedient, and the beneficiaries—and placed most of the defendants in the last category: men who might never have killed but for the rise of Nazism. Bauer hoped the proceedings would confront his fellow Germans with a disturbing question: How were they any different from these men?[17]

But Bauer's lofty ambitions for the trial almost immediately ran up against the more straightforward concerns of Hermann Langbein, who felt the list of defendants was neither long nor comprehensive enough. What's more, Langbein considered the court's decision to release five of the perpetrators from custody during the pretrial investigation a gross miscarriage of justice that boded ill for the trial itself. He knew the ruling was out of Bauer's hands but thought the attorney general could do more to intervene. "Someone who murdered Auschwitz prisoners," Langbein complained bitterly to Bauer's office, "is not treated according to the same standards as someone who murders other people."[18]

Langbein went public with his criticism of the prosecution. Bauer tried to mollify him, knowing Langbein's help persuading witnesses to come forward was vital to the investigation. Bauer understood the sacrifices he was making. The Polish government had forced him out of his job as general secretary of the International Auschwitz Committee in 1960, in part for his refusal to follow the regime's agenda to politicize the camp and minimize Jewish suffering. As a result, he could only afford to heat a single room in the small house in Vienna that he shared with his wife, who served as his unpaid amanuensis, and their two small children. He still spent whatever money he could scrape together from writing about Auschwitz on traveling to Frankfurt to chaperone witnesses. But from Bauer's perspective, Langbein's public outbursts were undermining the prosecution. Indeed, Vogel and Kügler were so furious that they had stopped sharing information with him.[19]

Bauer could see that his young prosecutors were also nearing a breaking point. He assigned junior prosecutor Gerhard Wiese to assist his team as they sifted through thousands of pages of documents and witness transcripts to prepare the indictment. But that could not alleviate the underlying stress they all faced from daily exposure to the material. "You'd better do something else," Kügler thought to himself as he drank alone in the pub below his apartment. His pay was so low that he had to borrow money from friends at the end of each month and he suspected his chances of promotion were slim, given how unpopular his work was in the judiciary. Vogel, for his part, was so disturbed by accounts of the murders of children in Auschwitz that he struggled to keep his composure in the presence of his own daughter.[20]

Bauer wasn't doing much better and found himself exploding in fits of rage at colleagues. He had aged visibly and complained of chronic pains. When asked by a reporter how many cigarettes he got through per day, he told the man to divide his eighteen-hour workday by the number of minutes it took him to smoke a cigarette. The result was a hacking cough and regular bouts of bronchitis. He rarely talked to friends or family about his own past and found himself avoiding the survivors who visited his office for reasons he couldn't explain. To escape his general sense of oppression, he'd started traveling to more exotic locations: Athens, Istanbul, Tangier, where William S. Burroughs had written *Naked Lunch* about his sexual adventures with young Moroccan men.[21]

Perhaps the only people he felt at ease with during this period were the young inmates he visited in prison. He had set up an organization

called "Free Time" to offer education and vocational training to offenders. On several occasions he secured their early release. Bauer
found work for one ex-offender as Max Horkheimer's chauffeur. Other
times Bauer simply sat with the prisoners and asked them about their
lives. One thief, Peter Kuper, thought Bauer was some kind of pastor.
But at other times it seemed like Bauer was seeking their forgiveness
for the system that had let them down and the deeper feeling of guilt
that he could not shake.[22]

Meanwhile, the Auschwitz perpetrators struck Bauer as remarkably
unencumbered by their crimes. Those who remained in custody met
regularly in the prison exercise yard to renew their bonds and shape
their stories. Auschwitz pharmacist Viktor Capesius had gone so far as
to enlist an associate to travel the country and bribe former SS men to
testify in his favor. Their indifference stood in contrast to the shame
felt by so many survivors that Bauer understood so well. Every survivor had suffered alone in the camp, while the SS had acted together in
their crimes. It was this collective identity that seemed to prevent any
form of individual conscience from emerging.[23]

The defendants' failure to recognize their crimes made Bauer fear
he had underestimated how deeply the country continued to affirm
the Nazi mindset. He had seen fleeting signs of change, but intolerance, reinforced by Adenauer's conservative policies, endured. This
was particularly evident in the ongoing persecution of gay men. Police harassment was on the rise, and groups of "concerned" citizens
were monitoring bars for suspicious behavior such as men dancing together. The Adenauer administration proposed new measures in 1962
that would, under the guise of partially decriminalizing homosexuality, introduce a raft of more repressive laws that penalized gay men
for any perceived affront to public morality. Bauer responded with his
first public call for the full repeal of Article 175 in a collection of essays
he edited, which included contributions from other prominent writers
and activists. But he remained pessimistic. The freedoms enshrined in
the constitution didn't exist in any meaningful way, he told a Danish
reporter. Schools were "the most authoritarian institutions in Germany

today," while Jews were subjected to constant abuse. They were no longer called "pigs"; instead they were told, "We forgot to gas you."[24]

"A new Hitler would have an easy job today," ran the headline. "Attorney General Dr. Fritz Bauer, the German leading the hunt for Nazi
leaders, says a new Hitler wouldn't be stopped."[25]

His comments were picked up by the German press, triggering a furious backlash. Perhaps the most insulting was the *Rheinischer Merkur*'s
false pity. One needed to "make allowances for the fact that he was persecuted on racial grounds, that he endured the concentration camp."[26]

Bauer felt under constant attack. His phone rang at regular intervals
through the evening. "My Nazis still haven't grasped that I'm not in
bed before midnight!" he joked to a friend. But the harassment was
exhausting and he was finding it difficult to distinguish real danger
from paranoia. One evening in December 1962, as his driver Heinz
ferried him to a talk in Loccum, a village near Hannover, the car, a
black Opel Kapitän, careened off the road, overturned, and hit a tree.
Bauer emerged with only minor abrasions, but Heinz was gravely injured. Bauer went ahead and gave his talk—he didn't know what else to
do—and was devastated to learn a few days later that Heinz had died.
Had it been sabotage, as he intimated in a tribute to Heinz that he published in the *Frankfurter Neue Presse*?[27]

Bauer still longed for a human connection and thought often of
Harlan, who had last visited Frankfurt in May 1961. The young activist
had then gone silent for nearly a year, only to confess in a letter that he
was struggling with his book project. He had tried to pull together ten
thousand discrete biographies of perpetrators and their current jobs in
West Germany. But his two-thousand-page manuscript was almost
unreadable. To make matters worse, the Poles had started to suspect
that the money he had persuaded them to invest in his research might
not deliver. He was "lost in the documentation," noted his Polish secretary, who also worked for the Communist secret police. The authorities
briefly detained Harlan and then ordered him to leave the country—
without his manuscript.[28]

Bauer's heart went out to the young man. "I don't only want to hear

Bauer, 1963
AdSD/FES, 6/
FOTA025083

from you because it is 'proper for a man to write,' " he wrote to Harlan,
but because "I am also concerned when one wonders for almost a year
how you are doing."[29]

· · ·

Some of Bauer's unease over the defendants' lack of repentance
stemmed from the legal dilemma the prosecution faced in proving
their intent to kill. Only three of the twenty-four accused had admitted
to murder: Heinrich Bischoff confessed to shooting one prisoner, Hans
Stark to killing "five to six" more, and Franz Johann Hofmann to pushing people into the gas chambers. They, along with the rest of the group,
had rallied around the pharmacist Capesius to claim that they had only
been following orders. To some extent their defense contributed to
Bauer's goal to present them as ordinary Germans who had enacted
Hitler's genocidal policies. But to secure convictions, German law required him to prove motivation and show that each man had willingly
played their part in operating the killing machine. The surest way to
establish the defendants' agency was to have other SS men speak to
their moral choices in the camp. Kügler and Vogel had interviewed
over two hundred during the investigation. Most of the steady stream
of former camp guards and officials that came to Bauer's offices had

been cagey about incriminating themselves or others. But he thought that one man in particular, a former SS doctor named Hans Münch, might be persuaded to state in court that SS men in the camp could refuse to take part in the killing without facing sanction.[30]

Münch had stood trial in Kraków in 1947 and been acquitted in part because he protected those who worked for him in the camp's so-called Hygiene Institute, where he researched cures for infectious diseases by conducting medical experiments on prisoners. Yet what set Münch apart, from Bauer's perspective, was that he refused to join medical staff in so-called "ramp duty" in which they were expected to select Jews from newly arrived transports for the gas chamber. The first time Münch visited the ramp as a bystander he'd vomited. "That will pass," a doctor colleague had tried to reassure him. "It happens to everyone. . . . Don't make such a fuss about it."[31]

But Münch was determined to avoid selections and boarded a night train to Berlin to make his case directly to the head of his institute, who intervened on his behalf. Calling Münch to the stand was risky. He had told Vogel during questioning that Viktor Capesius had approached him to speak in his defense. What's more, Münch appeared to still identify closely with the SS. He maintained that Josef Mengele was "the most decent colleague," which suggested that his objection to the killing had more to do with his personal distaste for witnessing it than with the policy of genocide. Indeed, he made no effort to help the young doctor, Hans Delmotte, who took his place on the ramp and was similarly disturbed by the killing. Delmotte ended up succumbing to his colleagues' blandishments and later shot himself.[32]

Bauer understood the moral hazard of recruiting former Nazis as witnesses and shared Langbein's conviction that every SS man who had worked in the camp should be charged with murder. But he felt that SS witnesses were essential, both for proving intent and for revealing the role of each defendant in the system of killing.

Kügler and Vogel had already pieced together a devastating picture of the camp's operation from their interviews with former SS men. The process began from the moment the commandant's office received a coded message from Berlin announcing the arrival of a transport for

Hans Münch, 1945
Creative Commons

"special treatment." The camp adjutant immediately began preparing the reception party. First he rang the barracks for guards to provide a cordon around the ramp and a detachment to clear the trains; then he contacted the camp Gestapo for an officer to receive transport lists and the hospital for a doctor to perform selections and oversee the gassing operation. Lastly he instructed the motor pool to provide trucks to transport the Jews who were too sick to walk to the crematoria. By the time the transport came to a shuddering halt at the ramp, around seventy SS men and prisoner functionaries were typically gathered beside the railway tracks, which from May 1944 ran directly into the camp in Birkenau.[33]

Emptying the train was usually a noisy, chaotic affair: Some people collapsed once they got out; others didn't want to leave their luggage by the sidings as instructed and were beaten; screaming, hungry children ran around. As the doctors performed their selections, separated families called to one another or snatched hurried embraces. Eventually two columns were formed of five people abreast: workers to the left; women, children, and the elderly to the right. The second group was then loaded onto waiting trucks or led on foot to the crematoria a short distance away, hidden behind fences and a screen of trees. This was the most sensitive moment of the operation, as flames from the incineration pits were often visible and the unmistakable smell of burning flesh permeated the air. Jewish prisoners forced to work in the gas chambers—the squad was known as the Sonderkommando—guided people into the changing rooms, persuaded them to undress, and then ushered them into a long, dimly lit room with showerheads in the ceiling. Once everyone was inside, the doors were screwed shut, the lights turned off, and the signal given to the SS disinfectors to empty their cans of Zyklon B pellets through chutes into the chamber, to the sound of thuds and screams.[34]

A doctor was meant to stay until the end of the process—around fifteen minutes—to confirm that everyone was dead. But they usually left early to avoid the scene that was revealed when the doors were opened and the fans switched on: a press of bodies around the door and in the corners as people had climbed over one another to try to get away from where the pellets had landed. One Sonderkommando unit hastily cleared out the bodies and washed blood and excrement from the floors; another checked the mouth of each corpse for gold fillings and shaved off women's hair for use as cheap insulation elsewhere in the Reich. Then the bodies were either dragged to the oven room or incineration pits for burning. The whole killing process, from the moment the coded message arrived to the dumping of the ashes in the nearby river, might take only a few hours. During the mass murder of Hungarian Jews in the summer of 1944, up to ten trains had arrived around the clock and queues formed from the ramp to the gas chamber.[35]

No single witness could speak to the entire operation, but one SS man came close. Konrad Morgen was a Frankfurt lawyer and former SS judge who had been sent to Auschwitz in 1943 to investigate corruption in the camp. The influx of transports had created a vast black market in Jewish goods; Himmler was concerned that not enough plunder was reaching the Reich coffers and that the moral probity of the SS men—as he saw it—was being undermined. A short, bald man with a nervous, florid disposition, Morgen explained that the starting point for his investigation had been the discovery of three large lumps of dental gold in a package that one of the SS men in the camp had addressed to his wife. On a private tour of the gassing facilities, Morgen realized where the gold had come from, and that the real

Konrad Morgen, c. 1940s
Nachlass Konrad Morgen,
FBInst

crime he should be investigating was the mass murder of the Jews, which was of course out of the question. From the prosecution's perspective, Morgen's position as a dispassionate, if morally dubious, onlooker and his yearlong investigation of the camp made him an ideal witness.[36]

Morgen's testimony complemented other pieces of SS evidence Kügler and Vogel had already gathered, including a seventy-page account that the defendant Pery Broad had given the British in 1946. Broad, a multilingual, jazz-loving Gestapo officer, had been careful not to implicate himself, but he had described gassing operations in vivid detail and the sadistic pleasure, megalomania, and greed that drove his colleagues to kill. A further source was the diary of the SS doctor Johann Paul Kremer, written after performing shifts on the ramp or supervising gassings. Kremer, a lecturer at the University of Münster who'd volunteered for the SS after being overlooked for a promotion to a professorship, had welcomed the opportunity to perform experiments on "fresh human material" in the camp. In one entry from September 5, 1942, Kremer described how, "most horrible of all horrors," a group of emaciated female prisoners had begged for their lives at the gas chamber doors but were driven in anyway. "[My colleague] was right when he said we are located here at the anus mundi [anus of the world]," he noted. The next day, Kremer recorded himself sitting down to an excellent Sunday lunch: "Tomato soup, one half chicken with potatoes and red cabbage (20 grams of fat), dessert and magnificent vanilla ice-cream."[37]

Another extraordinary piece of SS evidence was a set of photographs showing the arrival of several Hungarian transports in late May 1944. They had apparently been taken by an SS photographer to record the process for Berlin, but unaccountably, an album containing the pictures had been left behind in a nightstand in an SS barracks of another concentration camp during the German retreat in 1945. There it was discovered by a newly liberated Auschwitz survivor named Lili Jacob, herself from Hungary. Leafing through the pages, she was horrified to discover some of the photographs were of her own transport arriving in the camp and included pictures of herself and her family, who were gassed a short time later. Jacob later shared the album with a Czech archive, where it was uncovered by an amateur historian, Erich Kulka, who realized at once the photos' value not only as visual evidence of the Nazis' genocidal machine but also as a possible means for identifying SS men. Kulka sent copies to Vogel and to dozens of survivors to try and identify perpetrators.[38]

.   .   .

Bauer was pleased with how the case was taking shape. Langbein, however, remained unimpressed by the prosecution's increasing reliance on SS testimony and continued to push for more survivors to be heard. The prosecutors, in his view, had not done enough to capture voices from outside Germany. He was particularly concerned they had failed to gather testimony from members of the Jewish Sonderkommando, who had operated the gas chambers. They alone could speak to the horror at the heart of Auschwitz; they alone had come closest to the experience of what Primo Levi called being true witnesses to the camp, those who had touched bottom, the "drowned" who by definition could not speak. Less than 100 of the 873 Sonderkommando members working Auschwitz's gas chambers in 1944 had survived the war: Two thirds had died during an attempted uprising in one of the crematoria in October 1944, and the SS had killed the rest soon after

Auschwitz album, 1944: "Women upon arrival"
Yad Vashem / Creative Commons

Auschwitz album, 1944: "Sorting"
Yad Vashem / Creative Commons

as "bearers of secrets." The writings of some of the unit's leaders, buried in jars beside the crematorium before the uprising and retrieved after the war, attested to the unspeakability of what they had endured.[39]

One water-damaged page, almost decipherable, read:

[ ] may all the heaven be ink [ ]
[
[
[
[ ] were [ ]
[
[
[
[ ] written with blood in the world [ ]
[
[

[ ] terrible [ ]
[
[
[ ] in order to find out [ ]
[
[
[
[⁴⁰

Other evidence included four photographs of a gassing taken by a
Sonderkommando member on a stolen camera. The images had been
smuggled out of the camp to the Polish resistance. One blurred shot
showed naked Jewish women from a Hungarian transport running
toward the gas chambers. Another was taken afterward from inside a
gas chamber, showing a heap of bodies and smoke rising from an incineration pit.[41]

Sonderkommando photos, 1944
Creative Commons

Langbein was adamant that at least one Sonderkommando member
testify to make it clear that the gassing process, far from being a bureaucratic operation, was a form of murder every bit as ghastly as those
carried out by Boger and Kaduk. The Austrian was scarcely on speaking terms with the prosecution at this point, but he had connected with
Heinz Düx, the examining magistrate whose job it was to assess the

charges on behalf of the court, and found him receptive to his ideas. Langbein then reached out to Filip Müller, a Slovak Jew who had been forced to work for more than two and a half years in the gas chambers. Müller had testified in the Kraków Auschwitz trial in 1947 but had otherwise been silent, tired of the public incredulity his story provoked and the outright hostility from those who saw him as a Jew who had killed other Jews in order to survive. He had spent much of the past ten years in a sanatorium because of poor health, the vision of the piled corpses and flickering flames never far from his mind. He was reluctant to testify again, he informed Langbein through a friend, sure he would once again be "badly written off for surviving this commando."[42]

Filip Müller, 1964
Günther Schindler

But Langbein persisted and finally Müller agreed to share his story with Düx. He described seeing the piles of corpses on his first day in the gas chambers in 1942—he'd realized at once that to survive he would have to follow orders without hesitation. He carried out his terrible tasks for over two years until one day in 1944, unable to bear it any longer, he had slipped into the gas chamber with a throng of naked people. He knew that when the Zyklon B pellets dropped into the room and the choking, searing pain began, everyone would rush to the door in a frenzy to escape. So he had drifted to the back of the dank, two-hundred-foot-long room and waited for the door to be sealed in the hope that he could die in peace.[43]

Just then a group of young women had recognized Müller in his prison uniform as a camp functionary and urged him to save himself. "Return to the camp and tell everyone about our last hours," they had insisted. Even then he hadn't wanted to go, but they had dragged him to the entrance, where an SS guard had spotted him and punched him to the ground.[44]

"You bloody shit, get it into your stupid head: *We* decide how long you stay alive and when you die, and not you. Now piss off!"[45]

Düx was so disturbed by Müller's story that his daughter found him weeping over his files one evening. Langbein thought the testimony would "hit like a bomb" in court.[46]

. . .

Kügler and Vogel worked over the Easter weekend to finish the indictment. The final version was 763 pages long. Seventy copies needed to be prepared for submission to the court, the defense lawyers, and the defendants. The young prosecutors dictated each page to the office secretaries, who typed it onto wax paper before hand-cranking it through a mimeograph press. Vogel had the stacks of pages laid out on a long table. The wax master paper kept deteriorating, and so it had to be dictated again, but steadily the piles on the office table grew, as did the men's sense that they were on the cusp of confronting the country with the Nazis' greatest crimes. Afterward, they shared a glass of cheap champagne.[47]

Bauer would not be leading the prosecution; it would have been unusual for him to do so as attorney general, and he was concerned about drawing attention to his background as a survivor, which might call into question the trial's impartiality. Kügler and Vogel would be his representatives in court while he focused on explaining the trial's meaning to the public. He liked the symbolism of his young prosecutors taking on the aging Nazis and their lawyers, and Kügler, for one, appreciated Bauer's trust. He fully subscribed to Bauer's idea that the trial was a tool with which to educate the German public about the Nazis' crimes. But as he and Vogel prepared to submit the indictment in April 1963, he was keenly aware of the difficulties they faced in se-curing convictions. The basic structure of the trial as laid out in the indictment was straightforward enough. First came the charges against the defendants, then a description of the camp's history and its place in the Nazis' genocidal project. Bauer had commissioned several histori-ans to serve as expert witnesses. The rest of the indictment detailed the evidence to be used against each defendant, primarily made up of statements from survivors.[48]

But here was the problem: Laid out in the indictment, the testimony appeared well-argued and cogent. In the courtroom, however, the wit-nesses would be under pressure to share their most harrowing experi-ences, face down their abusers, and fend off questions from defense lawyers trying to undermine their credibility. Bauer welcomed the "primordial ground of feeling" the survivors' voices would stir up. Küg-ler, though, worried that the strain might lead to emotional outbursts, which the defense would surely exploit. As a prosecutor, Kügler's role was limited to questioning witnesses and objecting to leading ques-tions by the defense. He could only hope that the judges and jury would be as moved as he had been by the survivors' courage and determina-tion to speak the truth.[49]

21

Reckoning

GEHLEN KNEW HE was in serious trouble well before the end of the Eichmann trial in August 1961. The Americans had informed him earlier in the year that they strongly suspected he had a Soviet mole in his headquarters. Gehlen's first thought had been his counterintelligence operative, Heinz Felfe. The former Gestapo man had long attracted suspicion in the organization, both for his ability to cultivate rare sources within the East German leadership and for his extravagant lifestyle. Unsure of whom to trust, Gehlen turned to his adviser Annelore Krüger to set up a secret unit to tail Felfe and tap his phone lines over the spring. The truth soon became clear: Felfe had been spying for the Soviets for over a decade and, together with two other BND double agents, had stolen thousands of documents and compromised countless operations, dozens of which involved the Americans.[1]

Gehlen knew that he couldn't cover up a security breach on this scale. Felfe and his accomplices would have to be arrested as spies, which meant the story would inevitably reach the press and expose the BND's Nazi links at the very moment the public had been newly sensitized to the past through the Eichmann trial. What's more, Gehlen was no longer sure he could count on Adenauer's backing. The eighty-five-year-old chancellor had lost his outright majority in federal elections that September and was under pressure to retire.

At Gehlen's request, Felfe was summoned to Pullach on the morning of November 11, ostensibly to discuss an East Berlin operation.

Felfe arrived, briefly disappeared to get a pastry, and then Wolfgang Langkau, Gehlen's deputy, called him into his office. As they took their seats, Langkau explained that he had good news: Felfe was to receive the St. George medal for ten years of loyal service. Moments later, the compound's head of security burst into the room with three plain-clothes officers, seized a startled Felfe, and quickly patted him down. Felfe made no effort to resist, but once in the car outside, he ripped out his wallet, took out a small capsule, and tried to swallow it. One of the policemen intervened just in time. The capsule turned out to be a roll of Minox film containing his latest stolen files.[2]

Gehlen gave Globke a report of Felfe's confession on November 9, along with those of his two accomplices, who had been arrested the same day. Felfe freely admitted to spying for Moscow since 1951. He was from Dresden, he explained, the city that had been devastated by Anglo-American incendiary bombs at the end of the war. He disliked the Allies, and the Soviets had offered him an opportunity to get back at them. Felfe revealed little about the information he had stolen, other than to insist he had not harmed anyone.[3]

With Felfe behind bars, Gehlen traveled to Bonn a week later to explain himself to a furious Adenauer. The chancellor sat glowering behind his vast dark oak desk as Gehlen tried to assure him that he had the situation under control. Every intelligence organization had double agents, he explained. Catching Felfe should be seen as the successful neutralization of a known threat. Adenauer didn't look convinced. So far, Gehlen had managed to keep news of the arrest out of the press, but that would be impossible once Felfe's trial began. He understood that he had until then to regain control.[4]

Gehlen's first thought was not to start ridding the organization of former SS men but to monitor his headquarters for internal dissent and potential leaks. It wasn't edifying. Felfe's arrest was an open secret. Staff gossiped about how much longer Gehlen would last. Several younger officers complained that he was surrounded by former SS men who might also be compromised. At the same time, those with Nazi pasts feared that Gehlen was too weak to protect them from prosecutors like Fritz Bauer. Everyone seemed to think the organization was in decline.[5]

Increasingly withdrawn and distrustful, Gehlen was unsure of how to address the growing unrest. He hoped to repair his relationship with Adenauer, believing that the chancellor's unequivocal backing would restore his authority. But Adenauer was dealing with his own problems in a fractious coalition, as well as growing street protests against his rule. In June 1962, riots broke out in the bohemian Schwabing district of Munich after the police moved along several buskers and tried to break up a knot of a hundred or so onlookers. For several nights in a row the protestors blocked off streets, threw beer bottles, and shouted "Gestapo" and "Nazi police." The police responded by charging them with batons and dragged dozens into prison trucks. Unrest quickly spread to college campuses, where students staged protests against police brutality and the stationing of American nuclear weapons in West Germany.[6]

Schwabing riots, 1962
Rudi Dix, FS-NL-RD-2076B02, Stadtarchiv München

The riots were an embarrassment to a chancellor who had built his reputation on law and order. Adenauer's downfall, however, stemmed from the very authoritarian instincts that had defined his rule. In October 1962, *Der Spiegel* ran a story criticizing the combat readiness of the new German military, the Bundeswehr, as the Cuban missile crisis brought the world to the brink of war again. Recruitment for the Bundeswehr had barely reached a quarter of the 500,000-strong force originally intended, and morale among the men was low, reported *Der*

Spiegel. West German defense minister Franz Josef Strauss, furious that
the *Spiegel* article appeared to contain information from sources inside
his own ministry, pushed the police to search *Der Spiegel*'s newsrooms
and arrest its publisher, its editor-in-chief, and the story's reporter on
charges of treason. But, far from silencing the affair, the arrests provoked an unprecedented pushback in the media as well as nationwide
protests against what many saw as a Nazi-style assault on the freedom of
the press. Adenauer came under heavy criticism for his political judgment, which some attributed to his age, and for his rigid style of governing, which many felt was outdated. His coalition partners demanded his
resignation, and he reluctantly agreed to step down the following year.[7]

Adenauer was furious at the change in his fortunes, but instead of
turning on Strauss, he accused Gehlen of orchestrating *Der Spiegel*'s
story, after it emerged that one of his men had provided a background
briefing for the piece. Gehlen was summoned to the chancellor's office,
where he found Adenauer flanked by the federal minister of justice and
a senior prosecutor. Adenauer told Gehlen that he intended to have
him arrested for treason and demanded that he confess to conspiring
to take down Strauss. Gehlen denied knowledge of the leak, which was
true. Adenauer didn't believe him and ordered Gehlen to remain in
Bonn for questioning. He was released two days later when it became
clear that they had nothing to hold him on. It was obvious Gehlen's
relationship with Adenauer was damaged beyond repair. Gehlen had
no intention of quitting, but to survive he would need to navigate the
Felfe trial, which was due to begin in July 1963.[8]

Gehlen took a few days off with his family as he awaited the trials. His youngest daughter, Dorothee, was studying psychology in
Bonn and was back home for the summer. Gehlen was upstairs when a
neighbor called to inform him that a young man was walking through
the local town of Berg asking where Dorothee lived. Gehlen thought
little of it—Dorothee was nineteen now and had her friends. Then
he heard a stranger's voice in the kitchen. He knew his live-in guard
and gardener was on hand to deal with intruders and hurried downstairs to find a neatly dressed young man with a mustache standing by
the kitchen stove with his wife, Herta, and Dorothee. He introduced

Gehlen, 1962
Quick

himself as Jobst Koss. Dorothee's flushed expression made it clear that he was her boyfriend. It was unconventional but there was nothing for it: Koss would have to stay for dinner.[9]

Koss revealed a little more about himself as they ate: He, too, was studying psychology; his family were former Prussian landowners who'd fled the Soviet occupation. He asked Gehlen what he had done during the war. Gehlen explained that he had been an officer, but something in Koss's tone made Gehlen realize that he wasn't interested in his career. He wanted to know whether Gehlen had been involved in atrocities. Gehlen denied any involvement, sensing the troubling gap between them. This new generation asked questions when none had been necessary before. Gehlen had his people check out Koss, probing his background and politics for Communist links. But they found nothing suspicious, and when Dorothee asked if she and Koss could stay together that summer in the little cottage the family rented across the road, he agreed.[10]

The Felfe trial began on July 8, 1963, in Karlsruhe. The East Germans, sensing an opportunity to cause maximum political embarrassment, had announced that they would hold a show trial of Globke at the same time in East Berlin. Globke was due to leave office with Adenauer, so this was their last chance to embarrass him, but they had no fresh revelations, and the press largely ignored the proceedings. Instead, dozens of reporters, including the international press corps, at-

Jobst Koss, c. 1970s
Courtesy of Dorothee
Gehlen-Koss

tended the opening of the Felfe trial. Details of the scale of the breach
had started to emerge. Felfe and two other BND associates—both former SS men—had stolen more than fifteen thousand documents during a decade-long spying career, one of the greatest espionage
operations of the Cold War. Gehlen, who'd spent those years cultivat-
ing the image of a mysterious, all-knowing spymaster, was exposed as
the incompetent head of an organization riddled with disgruntled former Nazis, any one of whom could be a potential blackmail target of
the Soviets. "During these days a Karlsruhe courtroom has witnessed
the destruction of a legend and a good name which has been carefully
preserved for the last fifteen years," wrote *The New York Times*. "The
legend of the superior capabilities of the [BND] and the reputation of
General Gehlen." The attacks against Gehlen grew so personal that
Globke stepped in to give an interview on July 14, assuring the public
that the mistakes of the past would not be repeated.[11]

Felfe was sentenced to fourteen years in prison on July 23, 1963.
Gehlen tried to counter some of the bad press in a friendly interview
with the deputy editor of *Die Zeit,* East Prussian countess Marion Grä-
fin Dönhoff. People heard about spy services only when things went
wrong, he complained, but never about their successes. He dismissed
the idea that the BND was full of former SS officers and claimed that
the few who had been employed were thoroughly vetted to ensure
that none had blood on their hands. Still, Gehlen knew he was barely

Globke, 1963
Renate Patzek, B 145
Bild-F015051-0001,
Bundesarchiv

hanging on. Following the trial, Adenauer wanted him to submit a full report on the Felfe affair and demanded that all BND employees be checked for connections to the SS. Gehlen insisted that a review was not necessary, as he had already identified the fifty-odd members of his staff with SS pasts. They had "for the most part engaged in defensive tasks" and followed the law at all times.[12]

Adenauer was incredulous and sounded out the U.S. ambassador, George McGhee, about firing Gehlen. McGhee said that Gehlen clearly lacked judgment in his employment practices. However, the CIA was worried that any move to get rid of Gehlen would expose Washington to charges of sponsoring and protecting Nazis. It would be an "intelligence disaster," confessed the ambassador, far worse than Felfe's double-crossing.[13]

Adenauer, set to resign in October, was nonetheless determined that Gehlen would not outlast him in office and instructed senior civil servant Günter Bachmann to visit Pullach and assess the BND's employment records. Gehlen hurriedly ordered his staff to doctor files and ensure that those presented to Bachmann appeared less incriminating. Emil Augsburg, the former Einsatzgruppen member and formulator of genocidal policies at the Wannsee Institute, had his role in the killing squad removed and his work at the institute labeled "scientific." Others, like the former police chief in the Alpine region who had ordered the shooting of hundreds of Italians, were described as "purely professional leader[s]." Bachmann spent two days in Pullach and submitted a final report in September that failed to provide Adenauer with sufficient evidence to oust Gehlen.[14]

Adenauer dined with Globke on October 12, 1963, the eve of his resignation. He then headed to a reception where three thousand guests had been invited to celebrate his fourteen years in power. His accomplishments were undeniable. He had overseen West Germany's economic recovery and its integration into the Western alliance under the constant threat of a Soviet attack. More remarkably, he and Globke had brought millions of Germans who had subscribed to Nazism and genocide back to constitutional democracy.[15]

"We Germans may carry our heads upright again," Adenauer announced at his last session of the Bundestag on October 15, in a statement that captured his vision of a Germany that had found redemption without acknowledging its greatest crime. Three days later, he and Globke said goodbye to their staff in the Palais Schaumburg.[16]

Gehlen was hardly sorry to see Adenauer go; in his final days in office he had insisted on a further investigation of the BND that the new chancellor, Ludwig Erhard, had endorsed. Gehlen had no choice but to carry out a purge. He brought together a small group of junior staff members too young to have Nazi pasts to draw up a list of incriminated colleagues and collect evidence against them from the Berlin Document Center and the Central Office in Ludwigsburg. Gehlen guessed he would have to retire hundreds of agents; in 1955, around one in ten of his employees had played an active role in Nazi atrocities. He just hoped to do so without attracting any attention.[17]

For many on the team, it was their first time engaging with Nazi crimes, and they were deeply affected by their work. Thirty-year-old Hans-Henning Crome, the group's leader, examined records of a dozen employees who had belonged to the Einsatzgruppen responsible for mass murder in Lithuania and Ukraine. Some had already been prosecuted or left the service; others still worked in Pullach. Crome found it difficult to sleep at night after reading survivor testimony. Once he had compiled enough evidence, Crome summoned each man to his office for interrogation. One of those he questioned turned pale and

Hans-Henning Crome,
c. 1960s
Jan Roeder

started shaking as he confessed to his role in the killing. Most, however, denied the charges against them and confessed only when confronted with hard evidence.[18]

As he dug deeper, Crome also uncovered evidence of attempts by Gehlen's headquarters to interfere with judicial investigations, including those of Fritz Bauer's office in Frankfurt. The file for Richard Schweizer, the former SS man who'd played a key role in the mass murder of Lithuania's Jews, clearly showed how Crome's colleagues had tampered with witnesses and leaned on prosecutors to drop the case. Schweizer had even tried to bribe a survivor into giving false testimony. It was illegal activity and explosive, should details ever come to light. Crome wasn't sure how much truth Gehlen wanted to hear.[19]

22

Trial

BAUER ROSE EARLY for the opening of the Auschwitz trial on Friday, December 20, 1963. It was still dark as he dressed and hurried through the cold to his waiting car. He had imagined a moment like this since the evening nearly twenty years earlier when Max Hodann took the stage in Stockholm and announced that Germany was carrying out the mass murder of Europe's Jews. Mere protest, Hodann had said, wasn't enough. The Auschwitz trial was Bauer's response: a stage to display the worst crimes of the Nazi regime. Five years in the making, it would be the largest trial in West German history. More than three hundred witnesses from a dozen countries would take the stand to evoke the camp's horrors and force the country to consider how such evil had come to be. More than a hundred journalists from every major newspaper and radio station in the Federal Republic and the foreign press corps would record the survivors' words and share them with the world. Yet, as Bauer was driven down Frankfurt's snowy streets to the courtroom in the old city hall, he remained filled with doubts as to whether the trial would provoke his fellow Germans into recognizing their complicity in the genocide.[1]

He had reason to worry. The prosecution had suffered several setbacks in the months leading up to the trial. Richard Baer, the last commandant of Auschwitz, had died of a heart attack in June at the age of fifty-one, and three other defendants had been removed from the indictment at the last moment because Kügler and Vogel felt the evidence against them wasn't compelling enough. Far more damaging, however, had been the convening court's decision to downgrade the charges from murder to accessory to murder for half the remaining defendants, including the camp's senior leadership—the adjutants Robert Mulka and Karl Höcker. Only those who had killed with their own hands could be considered murderers, ruled the court, in a direct rebuke to Bauer's argument that every SS man in Auschwitz was guilty of genocide, regardless of his role.[2]

Bauer had hoped the decision could be reversed following the appointment of Hans Forester as presiding judge that autumn. Forester was part Jewish and his brother had been killed in Majdanek. At the very least he would bring sensitivity and perspective to the task. Yet Forester had recused himself almost at once after the defense raised doubts about his impartiality, and the press and some Jewish advocates agreed that his presence on the bench would undermine the trial's legitimacy. The court had replaced him with Hans Hofmeyer, a Nazi-era military judge whom Bauer had tried to have fired for his wartime role ordering summary executions. Now the fate of a trial designed to expand the definition of the Nazis' guilt rested in the hands of a man who had willingly served their cause.[3]

Hans Hofmeyer, c. 1960s
Günther Schindler

Bauer fretted over how his young prosecutors would handle the hardened older judge and the defense lawyers, many of whom had spent their careers helping Nazis avoid conviction. He would advise Kügler and Vogel from the sidelines, and they would also be backed in the courtroom by senior prosecutor Hanns Grossman and the Frankfurt lawyer Henry Ormond, who had been admitted to proceedings as a civil counsel on behalf of fourteen survivors. Bauer knew, however, that the ultimate success of the trial would depend on the public's response, and that his chief task was to explain the proceedings' deeper meaning to the press.[4]

In the cold, gray light of that December morning, he wondered how he'd manage. The past few months had exhausted him. He had two other major trials scheduled to begin around the same time: the long-delayed prosecution of Eichmann's deputy, Hermann Krumey, and a trial of euthanasia doctors for which he'd personally written the 833-page indictment. Bauer had hoped to make use of this convergence of trials to show the entirety of the Nazi project, but the other proceedings were proving a source of stress and distraction. Bauer veered from manic energy to inertia. "You brought so much dynamism that we were both wide awake for hours after you left," wrote Gisela, the wife of his friend Meyer-Velde, in October. "You come—and it is as if a grandiose firework went off, one of the kind that remains vivid for a long time. You leave—and what remains is this tremendous enthusiasm." At other times Bauer felt "dead tired" and under constant attack. His apartment building had been defaced with swastika posters that summer, and his phone rang through the night with threatening calls. Sometimes he wished he could just disappear.[5]

It was a short drive to the red sandstone city hall, which was flanked by the covered stalls of the Christmas market and a makeshift car park on an old bomb site. Bauer walked past the queue of survivors and members of the public and headed up the steps to the foyer that led to the council chamber where the trial was to take place. A crowd of journalists had gathered, chatting and smoking "as if at a book fair." The smell of coffee and cervelat sausages wafted in from the small cafeteria. A sign handwritten in red pencil beside the entrance to the chamber announced, "Proceedings against Mulka and Others." Red begonias for the magistrate's office Christmas party overhung the doorway. Few in the crowd noticed they were mingling with the defendants out on bail: Mulka in a tailored black lounge suit, chauffeured from his room at the grand Frankfurter Hof hotel; Schatz, the camp dentist, freshly pomaded, sharing a cigarette with his attorney. "They look like everyone else of course," noted one reporter, "well-fed, well-dressed gentlemen advanced in years: academics, doctors, businessmen, craftsmen, caretakers, citizens of our affluent new German society."[6]

A gong sounded and Bauer joined the press of people entering the lofty, wood-paneled chamber with inlaid floors and green drapes. Floodlights lit the raised stage where the judges would sit, facing four rows of wooden school desks bearing numbers for each defendant. A nine-by-sixteen-foot map of Birkenau and a smaller one of Auschwitz stood on easels at the far end of the room. Bauer took a seat in the front row opposite his prosecutors as film crews and photographers bustled around. Hofmeyer had ruled that no cameras would be allowed after the initial swearing-in, as he considered them to be beneath the dignity of the court. The entrance of East German lawyer Friedrich Karl Kaul— who was seeking to join the trial as a civil counsel on behalf of nine East German plaintiffs—created a stir as he paused theatrically in the doorway for the cameras. Everyone knew his presence meant Cold War drama. Then excited whispers began to filter around the room that the prison vans carrying the nine incarcerated defendants had arrived at the rear of the building. Flanked by police officers, Boger, Kaduk, and the others entered to the pop of flashbulbs, hiding their faces and scowling as they took their seats.[7]

Finally, Hofmeyer, a stout, bald man with coarse features and sharp, intelligent eyes, appeared with his two assistant judges, each resplendent in a black gown and cap with a gold stripe. The jury followed— three housewives, a warehouse worker, a technical employee, and a laborer—along with five substitute jurors. They were quickly sworn in and the defendants' names then read out; some responded with a loud "Here"; others just raised their hands. The photographers retreated, the spotlights were turned off, and Hofmeyer declared over a tinny loudspeaker that the trial was now open.[8]

Bauer at the Auschwitz trial, Dec. 20, 1963
picture alliance / ASSOCIATED PRESS

He began by addressing Kaul's presence. The East German argued he had every right to serve as civil counsel to survivors from East Germany, given that his counterpart Ormond had already been admitted. Hans Laternser, a lawyer for the defense who had argued the case for the Wehrmacht High Command at Nuremberg, immediately objected. The back-and-forth between them took up most of the day's proceedings, which ended with Kaul being ejected from the court until he could produce documents proving that his clients were indeed related to camp victims.[9]

Bauer didn't mind the drama. Kaul's antics were sure to make headlines and preserve the public's attention through the first procedural days of the trial, which would be limited to Hofmeyer's basic questions about the defendants' résumés. Indeed, Bauer was pleased with the initial coverage. No one doubted the need for the trial. Most correspondents seemed shocked that these ordinary-looking Germans could have been involved in such crimes. "Could [the killers] have functioned," wondered one letter writer to the *Frankfurter Rundschau*, "without the hundreds of thousands, the millions who 'knew something' or 'guessed' but couldn't summon the courage to ask: What is happening to our neighbors? Only if we dare to answer these questions openly and honestly, and understand the consequences, can we determine whether we have really overcome this terrible past." Another letter writer questioned how any earthly court could deal with "the mountain of guilt" the trial was sure to uncover.[10]

Formal charges were finally read out on January 6, 1964. The list, a shocking chronicle of everyday violence in the camp, took more than an hour to get through. The defendants then took the stand to answer the charges and present their side of the story. On January 9, Mulka was the first to testify and face Hofmeyer's questions about his role in running the camp's day-to-day operations on behalf of Commandant Höss. Key to the charge against Mulka and other members of the SS headquarters was establishing their knowledge of the gassing operation as well as their role in staffing the ramp in Birkenau, where the trains had arrived, and supplying transport to bring the old and infirm to the gas chambers. Mulka, hard of hearing and craning forward, irritably dismissed the charges, claiming he had never set foot in the main camp, let alone Birkenau, had seen nothing of the killings, and had only heard rumors that Jews were being gassed.[11]

"Didn't you know that there were gas chambers there?" asked Hofmeyer.[12]

Mulka paused. "Yes, but I had no reason to ask about that. I would say that there was no one whom one could have asked."[13]

"The commandant?" suggested Hofmeyer, with a flash of annoyance.[14]

"He was an opaque man. I refrained from asking him things."[15]

Mulka said he had heard—but only through rumor—of "three or four" transports of Jews arriving in the camp for special treatment. But the matter did not concern him, and besides, he went on, the Third Reich had ordered the removal of Jews.[16]

The second accused adjutant, Karl Höcker, followed Mulka on the stand and explained that Jews were sent to the camp for public safety.[17]

"Could you possibly believe that innocent children were murdered in order to protect the public against acts of violence?" asked Hofmeyer.[18]

"Well, there [sic] were the Jews," came the response.[19]

One denial followed another as each defendant took the stand. Pery Broad, the Gestapo officer who had spoken in detail about gas-

Robert Mulka, 1962
Fotosammlung Auschwitz-Prozess, FBInst

sing operations to the British in 1945, insisted he hadn't been personally involved. Wilhelm Boger, the camp's chief torturer, refused to answer any questions, as did the brutal block leader Oswald Kaduk, accused of strangling and murdering prisoners. When Kaduk's turn to speak came, he strolled up to the front, "a ghost of a smile lurking in the corner of his pinched mouth," according to the journalist Bernd Naumann, clicked his heels before the judges, and bowed slightly, mockingly.[20]

Some defendants made a point of ignoring the questions of Henry Ormond, possibly because they knew he was Jewish. On one occasion, a snickering Höcker made Kügler leap to his feet in frustration. "Your Honor, I request that you point out to the defendant Höcker that he may possibly find out here that he has nothing to laugh about," said Kügler.[21]

Others sought to elicit the court's sympathy by presenting themselves as conscientious and law-abiding citizens who had only ever done what was asked of them. The former SS man Hofmann broke into tears over the injustice of the charges against him. Another, Willy Frank, an "old fighter" who had taken part in the Beer Hall Putsch in Munich, claimed that before the war Jews had frequently been guests at his family home and that he had always spoken up for everyone in the camp.[22]

"Yes, yes, I have yet to meet anyone who did anything in Auschwitz,"

Oswald Kaduk, 1964
IMAGO / United Archives

observed Hofmeyer facetiously. "The commandant was not there, the officer in charge only happened to be present, the representative of the Political Department only carried lists, and still another one only came with the keys."[23]

Nonetheless, the sum effect of these obfuscations was to earn sympathy in the press. One commentator wondered whether the defendants could even be called perpetrators and suggested they were at worst accomplices. "If everything [Mulka] said was true," mused one Hamburg reporter, "then the Frankfurt court will not be able to do much." A law professor named Paul Bockelmann wrote that as far as he could see, the defendants had been perfectly "socially adapted people, good family men, good husbands, who had rebuilt their professional lives without murdering and maltreating." He failed to see the point of the trial.[24]

Bauer did not return to the courtroom after the opening day as he focused on engaging the public in the proceedings. The defendants' apparent normalcy was precisely what should alarm people, he told students at Frankfurt University on February 5, 1964. Don't be deceived by their appearance of civility, he warned the audience. He repeated the message onstage at another event with Hermann Langbein and a Jewish camp survivor on February 18.[25]

Bauer also tried to generate press interest in the testimony of four historians who took the stand next. Their job was to lay out the camp's history and genocidal function, but the journalists seemed uninterested in their analysis. Bauer felt himself straining to get his message across and inadvertently thrust himself into the limelight through a stray remark to *Der Spiegel* that when he drove past the camp where he had been imprisoned, "I stop, get out of the car and refresh my memories." The comments were seized upon in the press as evidence that Bauer was harboring a deep-seated malice. He wrote a weary letter to the editor explaining that he had been misquoted. But the incident clearly exhausted an already overwrought Bauer. He appeared "nervous, cigarette-smoking, jumping up from his chair every now and then," observed a reporter at one press conference. The British journalist Sybille Bedford thought him "kindly, brilliant, excitable, shining with a sort of nonconformist goodness" but clearly "wearing himself out over the case."[26]

Bauer at a press conference, 1964
picture alliance / Roland Witschel | Roland Witschel

Meanwhile, the trials against Krumey and the euthanasia doctors were facing further difficulties as they headed to court that spring. The Krumey trial was also going to be overseen by a Nazi-era judge, while the proceedings against the doctors were close to collapse after one of the defendants, on remand, fell to his death from the eighth floor of a high-rise building in Cologne. The next day, another euthanasia defendant, Werner Heyde, whom Bauer had once summoned to his office to interrogate, hanged himself with his belt from the radiator in his cell in

Hammelsgasse Prison. On the table was a suicide note addressed to his attorneys that singled out Bauer for using the trial to seek attention and carry out his "malign desires for revenge."[27]

Heyde's suicide led to a hurried meeting between Bauer's prosecutors and the prison director to discuss what measures could be taken to prevent any of the Auschwitz defendants from following suit. The prisoners, however, appeared to be drawing strength from one another in their collective defiance. More than half remained at liberty and often strolled to the court together, chatting and smoking, and terrified any witnesses they ran into. Even those in prison seemed to make a point of demonstrating that they were enjoying themselves. Pharmacist Viktor Capesius ordered lavish lunches from the Frankfurter Hof hotel that he ate in the cafeteria between sessions with evident pleasure. He liked to complain that he was being treated worse than an Auschwitz inmate in prison.[28]

Wilhelm Boger and Viktor Capesius, 1963
INTERFOTO / Alamy Stock Photo

Bauer shared his disquiet with a young writer friend one evening over coffee. "I have often asked myself and am asking myself more and more often," he reflected, "Why did I ever come back to Germany?"[29]

His spirits improved at the end of February 1964, when Otto Wolken, the first survivor witness, took the stand. He was a sixty-year-old Austrian Jew from Vienna, a slender, unobtrusive man, who'd survived almost four years in the camp working as an orderly in Birkenau's

Otto Wolken, 1964
Günther Schindler

hospital block, caring for the sick and staying on after the camp's liberation to assist Soviet forces. The prosecutors had chosen Wolken to testify first not only because he had witnessed some of the worst horrors of the camp but also because he had powerful supporting evidence for his memories through a secret record he had kept.[30]

The packed room fell silent as Wolken took the stand. He spoke softly and with restraint. For the first time, the life of prisoners in the camp came into focus: the squalor of the barracks in which hundreds were packed on filthy pallets; the fleas and rats that gnawed at the corpses left on the floor and those too sick to fend them off. The hunger was so terrible, said Wolken, that at mealtimes when bowls of slop were dispensed, the prisoners would fight each other to lick the spills off the filthy floor. The SS guards beat and tormented them. One of the defendants, Stefan Baretzki, even staged "rabbit hunts" in which he'd force the prisoners to run on all fours while he shot at them.[31]

They were the fortunate ones, Wolken told the room, who had been selected to work in the camp and thus had a chance at life. The rest—the elderly, women with young children—went straight to the gas chambers.[32]

Wolken held the court in thrall for two hours with little interruption from Hofmeyer or even the defense.[33]

Horst Krüger, a young journalist whom Bauer had urged to attend the trial, was deeply moved as Wolken described in his second day of

Stefan Baretzki, 1960
HHStAW

testimony a conversation he'd had with a small boy who'd caught scarlet fever and was due to be gassed the next day. The child was weak and tired.[34]

"Aren't you afraid?" Wolken had asked.[35]

"No, I'm not afraid. It's all so terrible here, it can only be better up there," the boy had replied. One of the female jurors burst into tears at that.[36]

The longer Wolken spoke, the more slowly his words emerged. "Pauses of memory for the speaker, pauses of embarrassment for the listeners," noted Krüger. "Everywhere there are embarrassed faces, downcast silence, German shock—at last." A window at the back of the hall had been opened—it was an unseasonably warm day—and Krüger heard a tram rattle by.[37]

The session adjourned for ten minutes, and Krüger staggered into the foyer with the others, disoriented and disgusted. He noticed two older lawyers in black silk robes leave the bathroom, one stopping to adjust his tie, another getting a Coca-Cola from the cafeteria, then re-uniting to laugh at some joke. "The broad, stolid faces of the Frankfurt bourgeoisie, the hearty laughter that you hear in Sachsenhausen, tipsy and pleasure-loving," Krüger observed with disdain.[38]

The lead defense lawyer, Hans Laternser, saw the damage being done by Wolken and complained at one point that he appeared to be reading from a prepared statement, which was, in reality, Wolken's notes written in Birkenau. Hofmeyer ruled this was perfectly in order. Another defense lawyer asked if he could identify the SS man he had described hunting inmates like rabbits. Wolken said he could and proceeded to walk along the row of defendants, looking at each in turn and then stopping at Baretzki's desk at the back. For Krüger, the disturbing proximity of perpetrators to victims suddenly felt like a revelation. Baretzki shifted uncomfortably in his seat as Wolken stood over him.[39]

"Aren't you confusing me with block leader Meier?" Baretzki asked. "Take a good look at me, take a good look."[40]

"As you see, I recognized you. I am sorry," Wolken replied.[41]

One of the defense lawyers expressed doubt, but Wolken cut him off: "He wasn't the innocent lamb he makes himself out to have been. I can still see him, riding through the camp on his bicycle, and how the prisoners left and right scattered out of fear as he approached."[42]

.   .   .

Bauer felt the trial was going according to plan as Wolken finished speaking on February 27. Defense lawyers like Laternser had mostly kept quiet, and Hofmeyer's input had been scrupulously correct. But Bauer's sense of progress started to change when the first SS witnesses took the stand. The SS doctor Hans Münch, who Bauer hoped would prove that SS men could refuse to kill without censure, was the first to testify, on March 2. Yet Münch was reluctant to tell his story when facing his former colleagues in court. He knew several of the defendants well. None had performed their duties with great enthusiasm, he stated. Instead he recalled that they'd tried to rationalize the killing and had agreed that of the various means of death that Jews faced in the camp, "it is without doubt more humane, if one sends those not capable of work, even if they are children, to the gas chambers." Münch tried to downplay his decision not to take part in selections. The "normal ability to react in Auschwitz was extinguished very, very soon," he explained. And he spoke with professional pride of his "scientific work" on inmates, some of whom had been selected by Josef Mengele. He had even devised a formula to predict how long prisoners would live given the limited amount of food they received. Münch's testimony, far from damning the defendants for their actions, seemed to explain them away as unavoidable.[43]

Then Konrad Morgen, the SS judge who had been sent to Auschwitz in 1943 to investigate camp corruption, took the stand on March 9. Morgen opened his testimony about the camp with a description of the ramp and gas chamber. He knew the killing of Jews was a crime, he admitted, his voice breaking. But he had no authority to intervene when the order to kill came from the Führer. All that he could do, he said, was identify instances when SS men had strayed from the camp rules.[44]

Hofmeyer followed up in a collegial tone with a seemingly innocuous question. Was Morgen aware that under the German military penal code it was illegal to carry out an order which constituted a criminal offense?[45]

Morgen agreed but said it wasn't for individual SS men to refuse an order based on their moral standpoint. "If an order comes from the corresponding superior authority . . . then he has to carry it out without objection." But what if they had been instructed to throw babies onto a fire, as some said had happened in Auschwitz? Hofmeyer persisted.[46]

The SS never promoted or required sadistic cruelties, "despite everything that is said about them," replied Morgen. Of course, there were a few bad apples in Auschwitz who took advantage of their positions, but otherwise the SS had been very orderly and correct.[47]

Morgen was one of four former SS men who spoke that March, and they all subtly reinforced his point that Auschwitz had been run according to the rules, which, however objectionable, still had to be followed.[48]

Kügler didn't seem to see the danger. He thought Hofmeyer's line of questioning had simply drawn out the logic of the German legal code that only those with base or sadistic motives could be considered murderers. But for Bauer, Hofmeyer had intentionally led the jury to the conclusion that regular camp functionaries could not be held responsible for the killing. Bauer was distressed that the trial might end up, in effect, legitimizing mass murder. The idea seemed to trigger a deeper reaction in him. Suddenly, the months—years—of fighting against the system, the office sniping, the threatening calls each night, the constant living with the horror of the Nazis' crimes and the injustice of a society bent on forgetting them, proved too much for him. He was convulsed with cramps and felt on the verge of a collapse. By March 13, he was unable to get out of bed and had broken down completely. He lay listlessly in his apartment, knowing he was needed but unable to find any motivation.[49]

"I can't get anything done anymore," he confessed to Thomas Harlan. "That is not bad in itself. But I have doubts about the sense of it, and the great resistance that is constantly growing clearly confirms this. Sometimes I feel like throwing in the towel, but the only thing that speaks against it is the joy of others at such a step."[50]

Whatever his physical ailment was, it had turned into a feeling of depression that he couldn't seem to shake.[51]

By the time Bauer, still recovering, returned his attention to the trial in April 1964, the defense had grown emboldened. The courtroom had changed location on April 3 to the Haus Gallus community center, a larger space that could accommodate more spectators, including groups of schoolchildren. Witnesses now sat exposed in the middle of the room with the defendants to one side, a mass of black shadows against the light from the windows. Laternser, imposing and self-assured, seemed to relish attacking survivors, questioning what they had seen, their ability to remember at such a remove, even their motives in testifying. He wanted to keep details of how the camp functioned as vague as possible, so that he could claim the defendants had only "heard" about the gas chambers and couldn't therefore be said to have knowingly taken part in mass murder. Whenever he succeeded in bullying a survivor into an outburst of exasperation or frustration, he claimed their judgment was clouded or that they were motivated by revenge.[52]

Women were made to feel especially uneasy. Dounia Wasserstrom, one of the Gestapo officer Boger's former secretaries, described the

Courtroom sketch, 1964
Erich Dittmann, Courtesy of Werner Dittmann

Press and public outside Haus Gallus, c. 1964–1965
Günther Schindler

arrival of a truck carrying Jewish families to the gas chamber, visible from her office window. She watched Boger meet them and approach a little boy in the group with an apple in his hand. Suddenly he grabbed the boy's ankles, flipped him up, and swung him around so his head smashed open against the wall. Then he picked up the apple, which he later ate in the office.[53]

Laternser immediately saw the power of the story, which threatened to lodge with the jury in a way that descriptions of large groups being

Hans Laternser, c. 1964–1965
Günther Schindler

killed did not. He leaped on the fact that Wasserstrom had not mentioned this incident in her pretrial testimony.[54]

Wasserstrom explained that she had kept silent because the scene had left her so traumatized that she could no longer look at children without crying. She'd even aborted her only pregnancy after the war because she feared being reminded of the incident.[55]

Kügler and the other prosecutors objected when they could to Laternser's questions, but they had no power to stop them. Hofmeyer could have intervened to protect the witnesses. Instead he seemed to encourage Laternser's attacks through his own rough interrogations and evident lack of sympathy for the strain survivors were under. After her raw testimony, Wasserstrom was called back again by Hofmeyer because he doubted the story of Boger's smashing a child's head against the wall.[56]

"Is what you have told us the absolute truth?" he asked.[57]

She was obliged to repeat that it was.[58]

The defendants themselves were also growing increasingly rowdy. Many showed an evident delight at being recognized in court by the witnesses. They nodded and smiled at them, sometimes bowing as if meeting an old acquaintance. Other times they reacted with theatrical anger. German witness Ludwig Wörl, a stocky fifty-eight-year-old greengrocer from Munich who hadn't been to the doctor in years for fear of being lethally injected, testified that he had seen Oswald Kaduk drive twelve children into the gas chambers at gunpoint. Kaduk leaped

Dounia Wasserstrom and Hermann Langbein, 1964
Günther Schindler

to his feet to scream out his denial and lunged toward Wörl. Several police officers grabbed hold of Kaduk.[59]

Wörl, however, was not to be cowed.

"Kaduk, you are no longer facing me with a pistol in your hand," he yelled, and also had to be restrained.[60]

Someone in the audience shouted at Kaduk: "Why don't you beat him to death?"[61]

The treatment of witnesses outside the courtroom was almost as bad. Bauer had assigned Gerhard Wiese from his team to see to their welfare, but neither he nor anyone else seemed to have given the task much thought. Those arriving from abroad frequently had to make their own way from the airport or train station. The Rex Hotel, where Wiese had arranged for many of the survivors to stay, was also used to host those defendants still at liberty, their families, and former SS men serving as witnesses, leading to distressing scenes as survivors and abusers bumped into each other at the breakfast buffet or in the lobby.[62]

The Austrian activist Hermann Langbein had testified in March and was thereafter present at every court session to take notes for a book he planned to write. He also offered moral support to survivors and advised them on how best to answer the court's questions. "They had to pour their hearts out to someone," he explained. He was hauled before the court for his troubles to answer defense charges that he was witness tampering.[63]

Bauer was increasingly alarmed by the trial's drift. Hofmeyer's focus on crimes that could be shown to have "exceeded orders" had brought out the sheer gruesomeness of the camp and made it appear less a microcosm of German society under Nazi rule and more like a bizarre and terrifying aberration that few if any German citizens would have sanctioned, much less participated in. Press headlines proclaimed: "Women Thrown Alive into the Fire," "Soup and Mud Stuffed into Their Mouths," "Deathly Ill Gnawed on by Rats," "Chicken and Vanilla Ice Cream for the Executioners," "The Devil Sits on the Defendants' Bench," "Just Like Beasts of Prey." In this sensationalist telling, Auschwitz became a dark pit of horror that defied comprehension. The writer Martin Walser feared the portrayal was once again allowing the German public to blame Nazi crimes on a few sadistic murderers. "I do not feel my part in Auschwitz, that is quite certain," he confessed. "There is an upper limit to human comprehension," admitted the *Neue Zürcher Zeitung,* "beyond which compassion quickly turns into dullness and resignation."[64]

With Bauer apparently incapacitated, Langbein was determined to gain control of the trial's public message. Auschwitz wasn't hell, he told a room of students in April, but a real place that had been built by a German government. Likewise, the majority of the defendants were not sadists or inherently criminal but "ordinary men" who had sunk to appalling depths after being corrupted by the Nazi system.[65]

The civil counsel Henry Ormond also stepped in with the bold suggestion to bring the court to Auschwitz for an official site inspection. The visit would corroborate witness statements and establish the reality of the camp for the court and wider public. Ormond had been in touch with the Polish former judge Jan Sehn, who'd promised the support of Poland's Communist government.[66]

Hofmeyer dismissed the idea. German courts rarely decamped themselves to other countries, and certainly not to one that had been brutally occupied by Germany in recent memory. Given the extreme Cold War tensions and the embargo on East-West judicial contact, there seemed little chance of success.[67]

Bauer despaired. He had hoped that the proceedings might trigger cultural and political change. But as the weeks passed, all he appeared to have done was retraumatize survivors, while the institutions he wanted to expose to the horror—the courts, the government, the German press—had closed ranks. He didn't know how to bridge the gap between what he needed the trial to signify and the grinding reality of the court. His mind turned to Harlan and the thought of escape. In April, Bauer persuaded the younger man to join him on a vacation to the coastal town of Djerba, Tunisia.[68]

"It's quiet there, so you can do enough work. . . . I won't disturb you," he wrote. "I am already satisfied if I can and may drink Turkish coffee or Tunisian tea with you in the afternoon. . . . And if I get on your nerves (see above over coffee or tea), then chase me into the water."[69]

Bauer left for Tunisia at the end of April. The hotel he had reserved sat on a desolate strip of sand surrounded by a few date palms. Harlan sent word he was delayed by the death of his father, Veit.[70]

"All of us have a relationship with our fathers that is not without tension," Bauer wrote back, "and you in particular have loved and suffered through it."[71]

When they finally united, Bauer met Harlan on the beach with a bouquet of the bright yellow sand clover that grew along the shore. He insisted they swim and plunged into the water as Harlan stripped off to join him.[72]

Djerba, 1964
Creative Commons

Bauer swam hard without stopping, straight out to sea, and when he finally turned to head back, he discovered that he could barely make out the people on the shore. He tried to strike out toward the beach but couldn't make headway against the current. Harlan caught up and swam over, only for Bauer, in a panic, to grab him, forcing them both under. It was just by chance that they had stopped over a sandbank. Harlan gained a footing and helped Bauer to the surface. They huddled for the next three hours in the chest-deep water as the Tunisian sun beat down relentlessly, until they were finally spotted by a fishing boat. Bauer was horribly burned, in great pain, and feverish. When they finally got back to the hotel, he retreated to his room, surfacing only briefly the next day for breakfast without saying a word and then retiring again.[73]

A short time later, Harlan was at his door. In his hand he had a bunch of tomatoes. He knew an old Bedouin cure for sunburn, he explained. As Bauer lay on his front, his raw and blistered back exposed, Harlan crushed one of the tomatoes in his hands, letting the juice run through his fingers, and the smell of the ripe fruit filled the room. Gently he pressed the broken flesh into Bauer's back, which made him wince at first, until he relaxed under Harlan's firm touch. Harlan massaged one shoulder and then the other, slowly and tenderly.[74]

Bauer stirred after a few hours. It was afternoon now, and the blinding sunlight had softened. He came to sit down next to Harlan on a covered veranda.[75]

"Thomas," he said, "I have been touched [like that] by a human being only three times in my life. The first time by my nanny, I was five years old, she always hugged me so much that she almost broke my bones; she loved me so much!" The next time had been in his prison cell in Denmark, when the guard had wrapped him in his arms. And now this.[76]

Harlan was shocked. Bauer seemed "fatally lonely, without love always full of love . . . and here now, with his pain, his eyes suddenly start to give away something of it," he wrote to his lover, Krystyna Żywulska.[77]

Bauer and Harlan talked about art and poetry and the younger man's writing over the next few days. "The conversations go from

Mondrian to Aristotle; caste theory of sociology, Roman history, biology and genetic code," Harlan related to Żywulska. "If I didn't have [my] poems, which he seems to love as much as me, I'd be standing there like a real idiot."[78]

They also discussed personal matters, although even now Harlan felt Bauer's "almost agonizing reticence" in talking about their feelings for each other. Harlan was direct: They could get a house together on Capri, a retreat for writing and thinking and being together. But Bauer wasn't ready to say what he wanted. It seemed enough for him just to bask in the company of someone who understood and loved him.[79]

23

Fugue

B AUER RETURNED TO Frankfurt in May 1964, still feeling unstable, but with a better understanding of where the trial had gone wrong. The court, he felt, had a clear sense of Auschwitz's genocidal purpose, but press accounts of gruesome murders had created a disconnect that was preventing the public from engaging. Somehow he needed to ground the trial in the reality of the camp. Bauer and Ormond agreed they should push Hofmeyer to bring the court to Auschwitz by filing a formal motion. Bauer's only other idea—to stage an exhibition of camp photographs and artifacts—didn't seem capable of bridging the gap.[1]

In the meantime, the court appeared bound by Hofmeyer's view that only those who had killed with their own hands could be considered murderers, which was most jarringly reflected in his decision to allow half a dozen defendants to remain at liberty. The case of Hans Stark was particularly galling: He was accused of operating the main camp's gas chamber and shooting prisoners in the penal company. Hofmeyer, however, had accepted Stark's youth as a mitigating factor—he had left school aged sixteen to join the SS under pressure from his father. The fact that he had a reputation for singling out Jewish women before gassings to shoot them in the genitals was disturbingly discounted.[2]

Bauer was surprised therefore to learn that during his absence, Stark had been rearrested on the basis of a single devastating testimony. On May 15, Józef Kral, a former camp functionary from Poland, described

Hans Stark, 1959
HHStAW

Józef Kral, 1964
Günther Schindler

in halting words how Stark had beaten his friend to death with a shovel. Kral was trembling so badly at one point that he asked the court for an adjournment so that he could take valerian drops to ease his nerves. But his testimony left the room in no doubt that Stark was a murderer, and Hofmeyer duly ordered the former SS man detained at the end of the session.[3]

Stark's arrest was proof for Bauer that witness testimony had the power to change the court's perception of defendants. But it didn't indicate a fundamental shift in Hofmeyer's approach: Stark was in custody because he had wantonly murdered, not for his role in following genocidal orders. Neither had the treatment of witnesses in the stand improved. Laternser had been allowed to savage Kral at his next court appearance. The defense lawyer accused him of being a murderer and summoned two Ukrainian witnesses to back his claim. For several hours they offered a rambling and contradictory account of Kral's maltreatment of prisoners without actually accusing him of killing anyone.[4]

Worse was to come. During an intermission, two men approached Kral and threatened to beat him up. Kral, at this point too scared to alert the court, asked a fellow Polish witness, Józef Seweryn, for help. Seweryn had himself received death threats after the press published the address of the house where he was staying in Frankfurt. "Bolshevik scum be careful what you say," read one. "True German justice will sooner or later mete out the punishment you have avoided." The text was accompanied by a hand-drawn gallows. Seweryn led Kral to the train station to escape to Poland, never to return.[5]

Bauer recognized he had been naïve to think that witnesses would be treated with sensitivity for their suffering, but he remained at a loss for how to respond. He worried that if he appeared to take their side too strongly, the press would seize upon his background as a Jew and a former convict and accuse him of seeking vengeance. No doubt the lingering effects of his depression and his reluctance to talk about his own experience stopped him from reaching out to survivors.[6]

While Bauer remained silent, the treatment of witnesses had at least started to gain public attention. The center-right *Die Welt* ran a piece castigating the prosecution for failing to support its witnesses. A group of Red Cross volunteers that included Emmi Bonhoeffer, the wife and sister-in-law of executed resistance fighters, took it upon themselves to help. They brought survivors from the airport or train station to their hotels, chaperoned them to the trial, and sat through their testimony. Afterward, they offered walks in the park or, in the case of twenty-seven-year-old sociology student Peter Kalb, fried chicken and beer at a local fast-food chain.[7]

Red Cross volunteers and witnesses, 1964: witness Stanisław Kamiński, volunteers Emmi Bonhoeffer and Barbara Minssen, interpreter Wera Kapkajew, witness Paul Pajor Günther Schindler

At the same time, Kügler increasingly gave voice to his frustration at the defendants' denials and the overall conduct of the trial. On one occasion he kept interrupting a defense lawyer as the latter sought to undermine a witness's credibility, and Hofmeyer was obliged to ask them both to express themselves in a more "gentlemanly fashion." Kügler shot back that he would object whenever he needed to. Then, during the cross-examination of an Israeli witness, he ended up in a shouting match with defense lawyers of such vitriol that Hofmeyer threatened to clear the courtroom. Kügler also snapped over Mulka's repeated references to himself as a soldier, declaring in July that the camp adjutant was in fact a "member of a uniformed murder squad." Mulka promptly refused to answer any further questions from him. "You are a mendacious coward," Kügler retorted. When Hofmeyer asked him to apologize, he refused. Bauer called Kügler into his office the following day for a quiet word after receiving a formal complaint from the court about his behavior. "One should not say something like that," Bauer admonished him, though he undoubtedly shared his young prosecutor's sentiments.[8]

Yet even as the prosecution's anxiety grew, the accumulation of witness testimony was starting to have an effect. On August 17, 1964, Mauritius Berner, a physician and Hungarian Jewish survivor, arrived from Israel to testify against the pharmacist Viktor Capesius, who claimed he had never been involved in selections on the ramp and that he had been mistaken for another SS man. Capesius appeared so confident he would be exonerated that he had taken to openly mocking witnesses. That was, until the mild-mannered Berner took the stand. He explained in gravelly, lilting tones that he had known Capesius in Romania before the war, when the pharmacist had worked as a sales representative for IG Farben. Berner went on to describe arriving in Birkenau in May 1944 with his wife; twelve-year-old daughter, Suzi; and nine-year-old twins, Helga and Nora, after spending four days packed into a filthy cattle transport with little food or water. Berner, disoriented and blinded by the sunlight as he stepped out of the train, was almost immediately ordered into a different column from his family. Just then he spotted Capesius in an SS uniform by the ramp and

Mauritius Berner,
1964
Günther Schindler

called out to him. Berner explained that he wanted to stay together
with his girls, particularly the twins, and pointed them out. Capesius
appeared to understand and took Helga and Nora over to an SS doctor,
who shooed the girls away; Capesius returned them to their original
column.[9]

Berner testified that he began to sob as his wife and children disappeared back into the throng.[10]

"Don't cry," Capesius had said in Hungarian. "They're just having a
bath. You'll see each other again in an hour."[11]

Berner later learned that the SS doctor was in fact Josef Mengele,
who selected twins from transports for gruesome medical experiments. Perhaps, he told himself, they'd been fortunate to escape that
fate. Nonetheless, he was tormented by the thought that he'd abandoned his wife and children. All he had left were a few photographs
he'd retrieved from his luggage at the last minute, which he offered to
share with the court.[12]

Berner had clearly, irrefutably identified Capesius as working on
the ramp, another moment, along with Kral's testimony, when the
emotional impact of a survivor account aligned with the dictates of
German law in revealing defendants' complicity at the scene of their
crimes.

Then came the testimony of the Sonderkommando survivor Filip
Müller on October 5, 1964: a crucial test of how the court would treat

the subject of genocide. The heart of the killing operation—the gas chambers themselves—had yet to feature prominently in proceedings. No one could speak more intimately about how families like the Berners had been ushered to their deaths than Müller, given his two and a half years working in the crematoria. The forty-two-year-old with thick black hair and a gentle charisma was clearly nervous as he took the stand. Hofmeyer interrupted him repeatedly, growing exasperated by Müller's decision to speak in German, which he struggled with under pressure.[13]

When Kügler directed Müller to describe the gas chambers, Hofmeyer stepped in to say he didn't see the point.[14]

"But Mr. Prosecutor, we have already heard all that," he said.[15]

"We have not yet heard it from a witness who saw it himself," Kügler insisted. "I think it is not unimportant to establish what it was actually like."[16]

Hofmeyer allowed Müller to complete his account of the gas chambers. The effect was so powerful that even the Nazi-era judge seemed moved at times into a strange synchronicity with the witness. Müller, when asked by the defense why bodies in the morgue were covered in blood, replied that the gassing took time.[17]

> Müller: "It lasted seven, eight, ten, even more minutes, and the people . . ."
> Hofmeyer: "Had a death struggle . . ."
> Müller: "From them all the blood goes . . ."
> Hofmeyer: "From their noses and ears . . ."
> Müller: "And that was terrible, how the people suffered."[18]

At which point Stark's lawyer tried to get them both back on track by asking Müller if he had any specific allegations he wanted to make. Müller didn't appear to register the lawyer's dismissive tone. He replied simply that he did. After all, he had witnessed, he guessed, half a million people being gassed during his two and a half years in the Sonderkommando. Müller's account would not have been believable had it been given at the beginning of the trial, observed one reporter afterward. But now Bauer felt a shift in the court's attitude as Hofmeyer ordered first one of the at-large defendants to prison and then another, culminating with the detention of Mulka himself that autumn.[19]

Then on October 27, Hofmeyer made the unexpected announcement that the court would be visiting Auschwitz. Ormond had skillfully played the German Foreign Ministry against the judge by informing ministry officials that the Polish government had provisionally backed the visit. The ministry, fearing the Poles would weaponize the court's refusal for propaganda, had pushed Hofmeyer to agree to the visit, provided several conditions were met. The first was that the visit would only verify witness statements; new evidence that couldn't be vouchsafed in court would not be accepted. Second, the visit should be strictly limited to trial participants—there would be no place for Bauer there. Crucially, the Polish authorities needed to guarantee delegates' safe passage. Hofmeyer was concerned that the defendants—and possibly he himself—might be arrested. In any event, he made it clear that attendance would be voluntary and that he would not be going. His deputy, Walter Hotz, a man without a Nazi past, would take his place instead. This was the opportunity Bauer had been waiting for to confront Germans—and the world—with the reality of Auschwitz, in the hope they would not be able to look away.[20]

24

Auschwitz

THE TWENTY-THREE MEMBERS of the delegation met for the court visit to Auschwitz at Frankfurt Airport on the afternoon of December 12, 1964. They chatted amiably while waiting for the heavy fog to clear. A single defendant, SS doctor Franz Lucas, had agreed to attend. He had been the only one to acknowledge some feeling of guilt although he denied taking part in selections, despite several witnesses claiming to have seen him on the ramp in Birkenau. The rest of the party included Hofmeyer's deputy Hotz, the jury and prosecutors, a police officer, the court interpreter Wera Kapkajew, and half a dozen defense lawyers. Seventeen journalists accompanied them. The mood was strangely festive, noted the reporter Inge Deutschkron.[1]

"An innocent observer could have thought yesterday that at the Frankfurt Airport, a national football team had gathered to reap victories in foreign countries," she wrote in her dispatch for the Israeli newspaper *Maariv*. All the cameras were trained on the defendant Lucas, the "star player," she noted. Deutschkron and Ormond—the two Jews—kept apart.[2]

The flight was finally canceled at 4:00 P.M. The party boarded a bus to try to catch a flight from Stuttgart, where the holiday spirit continued at the bar. "The fronts that had been hard against each other in the courtroom for 121 days are dissolving," observed *Der Spiegel* reporter Gerhard Mauz. "[We] can finally talk to each other." They joked awkwardly about Auschwitz: "Let's get ready for the selection" and "Are you ready for an injection from Klehr?"[3]

They flew to Vienna, where they overnighted, and then took a chartered flight to Warsaw the next day, where the lawyer Jan Sehn met the group as the Polish government's representative. The mood grew somber as they traveled through Warsaw. The picturesque old town, leveled by the Germans after the Polish uprising of 1944, had largely been rebuilt, but the city center remained a building site of drab modernist structures dominated by Stalin's forty-two-story Palace of Culture and Science, built over part of the ruined ghetto. Poland's Communist leadership had eased some of its Stalinist dogma in the years since the dictator's death, but an all-powerful state security apparatus continued to police dissent. The regime pushed a crude form of nationalism in which Poles were seen as the prime victims of German aggression, and there was still little or no reference made to the fate of the country's Jewish population. Anxiety ran high that Germans would one day seek to reclaim their lost territories.[4]

The party stopped briefly to freshen up and collect more journalists before continuing on two buses for the 180-mile drive to Hotel Francuski in Kraków, where they would be staying. A special center had been set up in the hotel for the press corps, which had grown to over a hundred reporters.[5]

Jan Sehn (standing) and Walter Hotz (seated to the right), 1964
Georg Bürger, FAP/BUR 000002, FBInst

"Dance music, beer, vodka, excitement about rooms in which most of them later find themselves in twos and threes," wrote Mauz. "The night is long for most of them." Lucas was, awkwardly, put in a room next to Ormond's, but there was no chance of changing quarters, as they had been carefully bugged by the Polish secret police, with dedicated snoopers for each room.[6]

The next morning, they were up at 6:00 A.M. to get ready. It was gray and bitterly cold, with snow forecast later in the day. Someone had daubed "German pig" on the hood of one of the reporters' cars. Sehn, genial and immaculately dressed, ushered the court members, Lucas, and the reporters onto a bus for the two-hour drive to the camp. A freezing rain was falling as they drove past the soot-blackened factories with barbed-wire-topped walls on the outskirts of the town of Oświęcim, which neighbored the camp. They pulled up at the museum's administrative offices housed in the old SS headquarters. The crematorium where Stark had worked stood opposite, covered in frozen sod, its single chimney silhouetted against the sky. The wooden hatches in its roof, through which SS men had dropped the gas pellets, were still visible. Beside the crematorium, on the remains of the interrogation barracks, stood the gallows upon which Commandant Höss had been hanged in 1947.[7]

The museum director, Kazimierz Smoleń, a forty-four-year-old former prisoner with a determined air, ushered them to an office on the ground floor, which had been set up like a courtroom with a table for the judges and benches for the jurors, defense, and prosecution. Sehn gave a short speech. There had been rumblings among the lawyers that he was a Communist agent. Sehn said simply that he saw the chance to forge an understanding between the two countries by acknowledging the crimes of Auschwitz. The plan for the visit was to inspect the main camp and then Birkenau. Hotz had produced a list of thirty-two questions for the court to consider, mostly concerning the sight lines of witnesses. Given the snowy forecast, Sehn suggested they confine themselves to a brief walk around the main camp and then inspect the more exposed site of Birkenau.[8]

They set off for the entrance with its trellis and iron lettering: *ARBEIT MACHT FREI*. Beyond were twenty-eight brick barracks laid out in three rows, surrounded by a barbed-wire fence. This was the

*Auschwitz main camp
crematorium, 1964*
22 442/36 DZ. III/3,
Auschwitz-Birkenau
Museum

Auschwitz main gate, 1964
Georg Bürger, FAP/BUR 000008, FBInst

oldest section of the Auschwitz complex that had held more than fifteen thousand political prisoners, mostly Poles. Prisoners weren't expected to last more than three months through a combination of
starvation rations and brutal labor. The crematorium, able to incinerate 340 bodies a day, attested to the murderous regime. As the camp
had expanded with the building of Birkenau and more than forty sub-
camps, the SS had conscripted political prisoners into the camp's administration as clerks, cleaners, and sick-bay orderlies, improving their
survival chances. But death was still a constant presence, whether in
the form of epidemics that ravaged the camp, leading to large-scale
euthanizing of the sick, or executions carried out by the camp Gestapo.

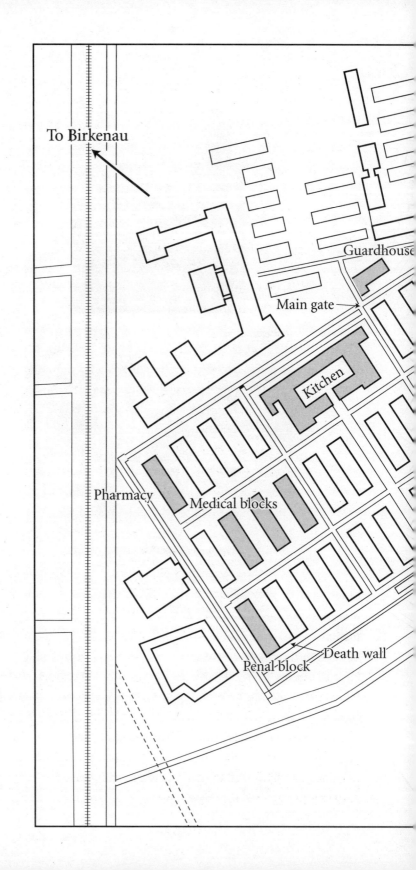

To Birkenau

Guardhouse

Main gate

Kitchen

Pharmacy

Medical blocks

Penal block

Death wall

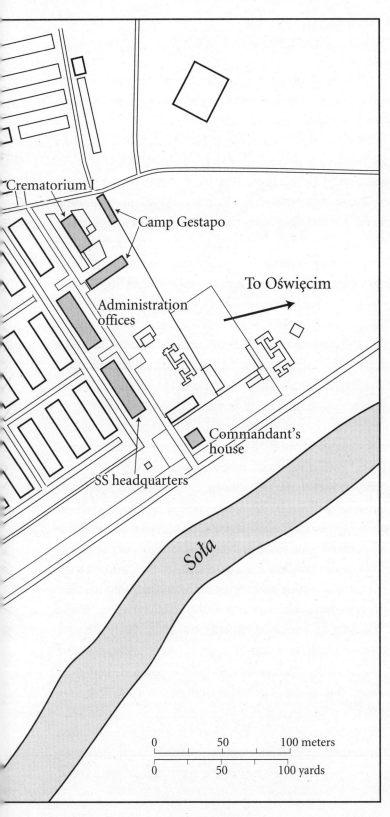

Crematorium I

Camp Gestapo

To Oświęcim

Administration offices

Commandant's house

SS headquarters

Soła

| 0 | 50 | 100 meters |

| 0 | 50 | 100 yards |

Auschwitz main camp, c. 1944
John Gilkes

Around eighty thousand political prisoners quartered in the main camp had died, a thought that lingered with the visitors as they walked the streets of what felt like a small abandoned town.[9]

Smoleń led them first to the kitchen where Kaduk had drowned some of his victims in a water trough and then to the sick bay where Klehr had administered his injections. The journalist Deutschkron was struck by the dimensions of the original camp—barely three hundred by three hundred meters. Everything felt so close and cramped. She could hear the sound of trains clanking and shunting through the nearby town of Oświęcim. "It must have been quite easy to follow what was happening, wherever it was happening," she reflected.[10]

The group stopped again in the penal block courtyard to observe a minute of silence in front of the "death wall" of cinder blocks against which SS men like Boger and Broad had executed thousands of prisoners. Press photographers climbed onto the sealed windowsills for a better shot; one dragged a metal trash can over and clambered up. Lucas was a special object of interest as he bowed his head, soft felt hat in hand. "Lucas from the front. Lucas in profile, Lucas against the background of floral wreaths at the Black Wall," observed the Israeli journalist Amos Elon. "Perfect for mass circulation magazines."[11]

Then they headed back to the bus to begin their inspection of Birkenau before the snow arrived. It was a two-mile drive. No one spoke much. They pulled up at a parking lot some distance from the entrance and then followed on foot the single railway track, overgrown with yellowed grass in places, under the arched gatehouse to the camp, its windows just then catching a stray shaft of sunlight, to the ramp beyond. Birkenau, built on malarial swampland near the Polish village of Brzezinka in 1941, was originally intended to hold 100,000 Soviet POWs for the construction of a vast agricultural and industrial enterprise that included a synthetic rubber factory for the chemical giant IG Farben in nearby Monowice. But as the war had turned in the East, Jews had been sent instead.[12]

As the visitors entered the camp, they saw to their right the wooden horse barracks for those selected to work stretching into the distance across the half-frozen plain. Survival in the crowded, unheated, and

Death wall, 1964
Georg Bürger, FAP/BUR 000012, FBInst

disease-infested blocks was usually measured in weeks. All that remained of many were the chimney columns, the wood having been salvaged by locals. Fences divided the barracks into enclosures for Roma prisoners and a short-lived family camp. To the left were dozens of brick buildings that had constituted a camp for women. The visitors' gaze was, however, inevitably drawn along the line of the track to the half-mile-long ramp where the selections had taken place.[13]

Judge Hotz summoned Lucas to confirm it still looked the same. Lucas, who up until that point had appeared relaxed, chatting to officials and journalists as if he were conducting a tour, turned stiff.[14]

"I don't remember—it was so long ago."[15]

Where on the ramp were the selections made, Kügler asked more pointedly, and where had Lucas stood? Lucas repeated that he couldn't remember. His defense lawyer objected, and Hotz waved the question away.[16]

The group then worked through Hotz's questions. A twenty-five-year-old German police sergeant took out a tape measure to record distances. Hotz asked one of the Polish sentries if they could take pictures of him from one of the nearby barracks to ascertain whether or not it was possible to recognize a face from that distance, but he refused to imitate an SS man. Finally, prosecutor Gerhard Wiese and one of the defense attorneys agreed to do it. "Herr Hollen, please record,"

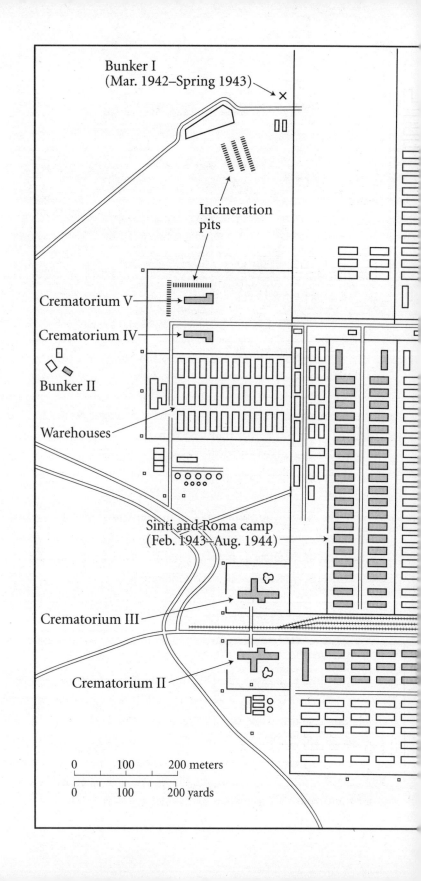

Bunker I
(Mar. 1942–Spring 1943)

×

Incineration
pits

Crematorium V

Crematorium IV

Bunker II

Warehouses

Sinti and Roma camp
(Feb. 1943–Aug. 1944)

Crematorium III

Crematorium II

0   100   200 meters

0   100   200 yards

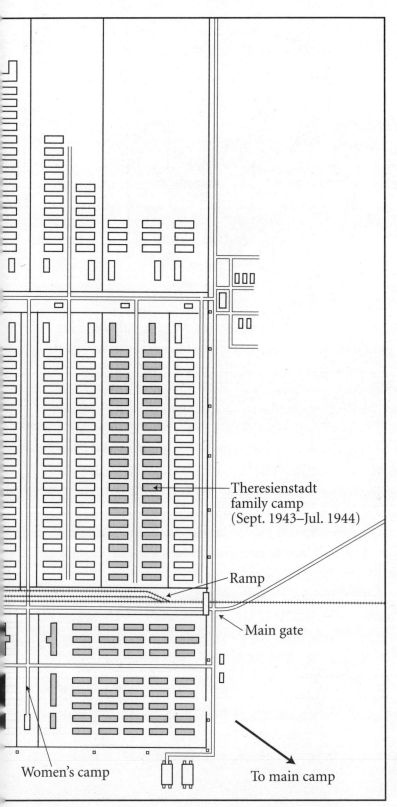

Theresienstadt
family camp
(Sept. 1943–Jul. 1944)

Ramp

Main gate

Women's camp

To main camp

Birkenau, c. 1944
John Gilkes

Franz Lucas at Birkenau ramp, 1964
Georg Bürger, FAP/BUR 000042, FBInst

Hotz dictated to the court stenographer, "the sky is slightly overcast. The view is good. The two men can easily be recognized."[17]

Next they walked along the side of the ramp for half a mile to the remains of Birkenau's crematoria and gas chambers. As the camp's genocidal function had grown, the SS had decommissioned its earlier gas chambers in former farmhouses and constructed four custom facilities, each with the capacity to kill 2,000 people, as well as ovens that could incinerate 184 bodies an hour. A small memorial had been built at the end of the railway line, in front of the ruins of Crematoria II and III. They walked over to the latter, where the steps leading down to the changing rooms were still clearly visible. Some of the jurors climbed onto its collapsed roof or gingerly tried the steps. The museum director Smoleń then led them to a large ditch beside the building, where bodies had been burned when the ovens couldn't process them quickly enough. "Thereupon the Court went to the trenches in which corpses were burned," Hotz dictated to the stenographer.[18]

"Shouldn't it say '. . . in which corpses were allegedly burned'?" one of the defense lawyers objected. Hotz hastily corrected the record.[19]

Smoleń pulled back a layer of sod beside the ditch to reveal the ash below, mixed with bone fragments and the rotting pages of a prayer book.[20]

He led them along the camp's perimeter to a second pit beside Crematorium IV, this one filled with brackish water. He bent down and scooped up a handful of whitish-gray matter. "That is the ash of the dead," he said.[21]

"Well that might be true," defense lawyer Fritz Steinacker interjected, chewing on some gum. "But it really should be examined by a chemist."[22]

None of the others followed his lead. Hotz whispered quietly to Jan Sehn: "I would have revealed my reactions much more, had the defendant not been with us."[23]

The journalists themselves seemed equally affected. One Swedish reporter found a five-pfennig coin from 1940, another a ball of human hair. Gerhard Strecker of the *Neue Ruhr Zeitung* noted it would take "two thousand years for humanity to forget these crimes." A Belgian reporter seemed at a loss for how to capture what he was looking at. "You need to see it," he said. "Only then you can imagine the magnitude of the crime."[24]

They returned to the main camp for a short break and then began to inspect one of the blocks nearby. But darkness was already falling, making it impossible to check the sight lines. So after a late buffet lunch in a small cafeteria in one of the blocks, the group drove back to Kraków. The journalists hurried to file their pieces, everyone claiming that the UPI reporter was deliberately hogging the telex printer. A group of Polish survivors held a press conference at a nearby dining club to attest to Lucas's role on the ramp and decried his haughty attitude and refusal to confess.[25]

Meanwhile, the defense lawyers gathered in their hotel rooms, where their reflections were caught on tape by the Polish secret police. Most were in a state of shock. One suggested that the Poles might have altered the camp to make it look worse than it was. Kaduk's lawyer, Anton Reiners, said he felt ashamed. In the trial they had been talking only about individual crimes, noted another; now they could see the murderous whole.[26]

The inspection resumed the next morning a little after 9:00 A.M. Fresh snow covered the mound of the crematorium and capped the roofs of the unheated blocks. The delegation checked the sight lines from various barracks to verify witnesses' claims they had seen Klehr injecting victims in the hospital block or Boger shooting prisoners at the death wall. Ormond and one of the defense lawyers volunteered to stand against the wall while others climbed up to the attic window of an opposing block. The window itself had been deliberately boarded up by the SS, but on closer inspection the delegation noticed that prisoners had created a peephole by removing the mortar around one of the bricks.[27]

Hotz wanted to test witness Georg Severa's claim that one of the defendants, Bruno Schlage, had ordered that a prisoner be starved to death in the so-called standing cells of the camp's penal block. There were three of these narrow, sealed flutes, in which prisoners were forced to stand for days and sometimes weeks in darkness, according to their punishment. Severa testified that he had learned of Schlage's order from the condemned man while he was being held in an adjoining cell. For several days, Severa heard him singing to keep his spirits up, his voice getting weaker and weaker until finally, with a whimper, he'd died. At Hotz's insistence, the delegates crowded into Severa's cell to test whether it was possible to hear someone speaking next door. There was an uncomfortable silence as a police officer crawled through the opening to one of the standing cells. Then they heard his voice, muffled but clear. He was singing a Goethe poem turned into a popular song by Schubert: "Once a boy saw a little rose standing / Little rose on the heathland."[28]

That afternoon, Kügler held a press conference at the camp where he fielded some awkward questions, mostly from Polish reporters, as to why it had taken the Federal Republic so long to hold Auschwitz perpetrators to account. His answer—that they hadn't had enough evidence—felt hopelessly inadequate.[29]

The delegation returned to the camp for a third day of inspections. A thick fog hung over the buildings. Several witnesses had accused the defendant Hans Stark of drowning prisoners in ditches during the construction of the foundations of one of the blocks. Stark denied the allegations, claiming the buildings had no foundations. To prove the survivors' point, Polish workmen had dug down a couple of meters at the base of the wall of block 15 to reveal the stonework. Dirty water had pooled at the bottom. Finally, the group visited Mulka's office, where his desk had overlooked a prisoner block less than twelve meters away on the other side of the barbed-wire fences. The idea that Mulka had been unaware of what was happening in the camp now seemed preposterous.[30]

Once the inspection was complete, Smoleń led the group to the auditorium of the camp museum, where they watched a short documentary featuring scenes shot by liberating Soviet forces of piled corpses and emaciated prisoners. They then visited the camp's exhibition to see sacks of human hair and piles of dentures, bags, suitcases, and children's shoes. A tag on one of the bags read: "Clara Sara Nadelmann. Berlin. W. 15. Xantenerstrasse 2." Judge Hotz left the viewing room with his hat in his hands, muttering, "It's horrible, horrible." Kaduk's lawyer Reiners burst into tears and wept throughout the drive back to the hotel.[31]

"Some of the defense attorneys continued to stubbornly fight for their clients during the examinations," noted Deutschkron. "But at the sight of the hair of the camp victims and the children's shoes . . . their last resistance, which they created for themselves in an effort not to believe in the crimes of the mass murderers, was broken." Reiners later confided to Deutschkron that he would like to return with his fourteen-year-old daughter so she could "learn in time what Nazism 'espoused.'" Mulka's lawyer apologized to a Polish witness who had traveled with the party as a journalist for asking him such "insolent questions" during the hearings.[32]

"It is now clear," wrote Deutschkron, "these attorneys would have refused to defend the mass murderers if they understood the true meaning of the Auschwitz trial as they now perceive it." Gerhard Mauz, *Der Spiegel*'s reporter, thought the court's visit was a form of confession to "the dead and the survivors" on behalf of the German people. The group left Kraków for Warsaw the next morning and spent an afternoon sightseeing in the capital, where they were shown the remains of the ghetto and a film about the city's destruction at the hands of the Germans. They overnighted at the Hotel Europejski, where the reception desk fielded calls all night threatening to kill Lucas. The party was back in Frankfurt by the following afternoon.[33]

· · ·

For Bauer, the trip to Auschwitz confirmed his view that redemption could begin only with facing the reality of the crime. He had thought that the survivors' testimony would be enough—that anyone who listened to Kral, Berner, or Müller would be confronted with the horror of the Nazis' crimes. Unfortunately, Adorno had been right: Human beings instinctively sought to deny uncomfortable truths. The defense lawyers had used that impulse to their advantage in the courtroom to discredit survivors. But no one who joined the delegation could dispute the sheer physicality of the camp. The change in thinking was reflected in the West German press and echoed in the shaken sentiments of the defense lawyers. It also proved to be a turning point for Lucas, who upon returning to the stand in the new year finally admitted that he had taken part in selections, explaining that his fear of imprisonment had led him to mislead the court.[34]

"There's nothing left of the man who was hiding his knowledge about Auschwitz for so long, pretending to be calm and cool," noted the Polish reporter Mieczysław Kieta. "Now his face is gray as dust." Lucas was subsequently detained.[35]

Bauer wrote a note of appreciation to Jan Sehn, reflecting on the trip's success. But as the trial wound down, Bauer knew that its outcome still lay with Hofmeyer. The former Nazi judge would guide the jury to its verdict and his judgment would shape the trial's legal impact. If he ruled that all who served in the camp had taken part in a single genocidal enterprise, he would set a powerful precedent for other courts to follow. Bauer knew that those who had visited Auschwitz had seen how murder had dominated every aspect of the camp. Hofmeyer, however, had pointedly refused to go.[36]

25

Verdict

J OACHIM KÜGLER ROSE from the prosecutors' bench on
May 13, 1965, to deliver his closing argument to a packed courtroom. Over the course of six years of immersion in Auschwitz, he had
come to know every facet of the camp and the murderous routines of
each defendant. More so than the other prosecutors, the press had
come to see him as Bauer's surrogate and an embodiment of a new
generation taking on the crimes of their past. His colleagues had already put forward the prosecution's basic premise and taken turns presenting arguments against individual defendants. Kügler, however,
wanted to take a step back from the simple parameters of the law to
confront the court with the question of German complicity. What had
struck him while listening to the 360 witnesses who had testified over
sixteen months was how the vast killing operation had involved all levels of German society.[1]

"The taking of evidence," Kügler began, "has shown with crystal-clear
harshness that we are dealing with Auschwitz, a murder center of un-
imaginable horror, and that its functioning depended on the conscious
and deliberate collaboration of the accused and thousands of others."[2]

Kügler understood that it was the scale of the complicity that had
compelled the West German government to try to dismiss the Nazis'
crimes as the conspiracy of a few and an aberration of history. But he was
asking the court and the country not to turn away from the horror.[3]

"[The Nazis'] atrocities were of such unbridled and at the same time
factually and bureaucratically organized unkindness, malice, and

murderousness that no one can reflect on them without deep shame that human beings are capable of such things. Auschwitz was a hollow space of complete cultural deprivation."[4]

He reminded the court of their visit to the camp, where they had seen for themselves the barrack blocks, the injection rooms, the gate adorned with the lettering *ARBEIT MACHT FREI*, the ramp, the gas chambers. The horror remained tangible. "You can still grasp it with your hands today," he said, "and if you bend down over the incineration pits or at that sinkhole between the crematoria . . . in Birkenau, then slide your hands through the water, you will grasp nothing but human ash, white human ash, and in between here and there a bleached bone. Homo sapiens."[5]

The defense lawyers began their closing arguments on May 31 by claiming that their clients had been unfairly singled out. They had not conceived of Auschwitz or been responsible for its overall operation. It would be absurd to blame ordinary Germans for state policy. "One cannot simply label and condemn as a murderer, everyone who was in some way incorporated into this machinery of mass extermination," argued Mulka's lawyer, Hermann Stolting II, himself a former Nazi. He then questioned whether the trial could be considered fair, given the intense press coverage that had at times presented the defendants' denials "in a satirical light." Finally, Stolting attacked Bauer for his "inappropriate" interventions outside the courtroom to influence public thinking. Laternser asked whether the witnesses could be relied upon, given what he called their overemotionality. Many, it seemed to him, were motivated by feelings of revenge. Survivors from Poland might even have had their testimony scripted by the Communist government. He asked the jury to discount the prejudice shown against his clients and recognize that the men who selected Jews on the ramp for labor had actually saved lives.[6]

The defendants followed with short statements. Mulka bemoaned the "unfortunate situation" that had landed him in Auschwitz in the first place. Lucas explained that he was indeed "haunted by the memory" of his time on the ramp, but having now confessed to his involvement and having sworn that he had tried to keep as many Jews alive as possible, he hoped that the verdict would allow him to "re-open a way to life." Only Stark offered something nearing a confession.[7]

"I participated in the killing of many people," he admitted. "After the war I often asked myself whether I had thereby become a criminal. I have not found an answer that is satisfactory for me. I believed in the Führer, I wanted to serve my people. At that time, I was convinced that what I was doing was right. Today I know that the ideas I believed in are wrong. I very much regret the error of my ways at that time, but I cannot undo them."[8]

Bauer was unimpressed. None of the defendants had recognized the suffering they had caused or offered anything like an apology.[9]

Hofmeyer and his deputies swept into the Haus Gallus courtroom on the humid, overcast morning of August 19, 1965, to deliver their decision. The defendants rose and bowed their heads, except for Kaduk, who stood tall, chin thrust forward. Hofmeyer read out the verdicts and sentences: Boger, Kaduk, Klehr, Hofmann, and Baretzki were among those found guilty of murder and received life sentences. Stark was also convicted of murder but got only ten years. Ten defendants were convicted as accessories: Mulka received fourteen years; Lucas, three and a quarter. Five were acquitted or released for time served. The defendants showed no emotion as they were sentenced. Kügler, however, was hit with a fresh wave of anger that Mulka—whom he considered one of the main facilitators of the mass murder in the camp—had only ever been charged as an accessory to murder.[10]

Hofmeyer acknowledged that many people wished for a "comprehensive presentation of the events of that time." However, he cautioned, "the court was not called in order to confront the past" or to pass judgment on Nazism. To do so, he suggested, would be to transform the proceedings into a show trial. Then he set out to dismantle Bauer's argument that Auschwitz represented a collective act of mass murder. The Final Solution, he said, had fallen outside the law, which was why the German judiciary had not prosecuted it at the time and could not

Bauer, 1965
Stefan Moses,
Münchner
Stadtmuseum

do so here. Only near the end of his remarks did Hofmeyer acknowledge the mass murder of Jews was a crime.[11]

The trial had been emotionally hard on jurors, the defense, the civil counsels, and the police, he observed, but he made no reference to the witnesses. "There will probably be many among us who for a long time will no longer be able to look into the joyful and trusting eyes of a child," Hofmeyer said, as his voice broke, "without seeing the hollow, questioning and uncomprehending, fear-filled eyes of the children who met their end in Auschwitz."[12]

Bauer met the verdict with anger. Hofmeyer had pointedly rejected his argument that all who served in the camp were guilty of murder. Instead, the judge had encouraged the court to see Auschwitz as a series of discrete crimes that obscured the camp's genocidal function and fed the "wishful thinking" that only the Nazi leadership was guilty. The short sentences made a "mockery of the victims," Bauer felt. He suspected the real reason why the courts had consistently failed to recognize the Holocaust was because jurists like Hofmeyer didn't want to confront their roles in the system of killing. The lion, he observed in an article that autumn, needed to look in the mirror.[13]

But Hofmeyer's limited verdict had not denied Bauer his victory. For the better part of two years, the trial had captured the West German public's attention and forced it to contend with the killing. The press alone had published more than nine hundred stories about the proceedings. Some of the commentary was critical. The writer Martin Walser recognized that he was supposed to see himself "entangled in the Great German crime." But he was repelled by the media's focus on gratuitous violence and felt the prosecution should have done more to implicate Germans in the day-to-day mechanisms of the camp. "Auschwitz wasn't hell," he reflected. "It was a German concentration camp." The Jewish writer Ralph Giordano worried that the trial would allow Germans to claim they had "dealt" with the past, in contrast to the experience of survivors who could never escape the burden. "We, the surviving victims," could never "see blood, feel pain or catch sight of a tattoo ... without thinking of Auschwitz." But it was clear to Bauer that the trial had lodged the camp in the public consciousness. According to one poll, 83 percent of West Germans were aware of or had followed the trial. "Auschwitz is no longer 'far away, somewhere in Poland,'" noted the journalist Bernd Naumann, who had reported daily for the *Frankfurter Allgemeine Zeitung*. "It has come close to us."[14]

The trial had also gained global recognition. *The New York Times* declared it to be an "edifice of total truth." Germans might have dismissed the Nazis' crimes chronicled in Nuremberg as the "exaggerations of vengeful victors applying ex post facto laws," wrote American prosecutor Benjamin Ferencz. But the Auschwitz trial meant that "even the German criminal law has now confirmed" international standards of law and morality. Sybille Bedford, writing in *The Observer*, noted the presence of so many young people in the visitors' gallery, looking no different from teenagers in Manchester or Chicago and yet ready to confront the crimes of their parents' generation. It moved Bedford to reflect on how the trial, in giving survivors a platform to speak, had reminded the world of its duty to listen. "We, too, should hear and not forget," she wrote.[15]

And it was the witnesses themselves who seemed to value the trial most profoundly. Some remained angry at their treatment in the courtroom. Yet for Stanisław Kamiński, the act of confronting his abusers was transformative. "For the first time in my life I felt very good," he told volunteer chaperone Peter Kalb, with whom he became lifelong friends. Hans Frankenthal noticed the difference upon returning to his hometown after testifying. Neighbors started coming up to him to ask if he wanted to talk. "About what?" he asked. "So that tomorrow you'll tell me again that you don't believe me? There is plenty of literature about it, go read it." But their interest meant something to him: The silence had been broken. The profoundest change for witnesses sometimes came within their own families. Seventeen-year-old Cilly Kugelmann learned that her two older siblings and her grandparents had been gassed in Auschwitz only after reading about her father's trial testimony in the newspaper. For the Kugelmanns, reckoning with the past meant helping each other share some of the pain.[16]

And for the Austrian activist Hermann Langbein, the trial's conclusion marked the start of a renewed mission to explain the camp to West Germans. He embarked on a lecture circuit, funded by the Hessian Department of Education, to speak in schools and at town hall–style events across the state. Older attendees continued to deny any complicity. "Why did the Jews allow themselves to be deported without a fight?" asked an elderly attendee in one small town. We should probably have taken to the square to protest, admitted another. "So why didn't you?" a student challenged them. The young, noted Langbein, didn't offer excuses. Instead they asked: "What can be done? How can we stop this from ever happening again?"[17]

Bauer recognized that the trial had filled the gap in public knowledge about the mass murder of Jews. West Germans had begun to acknowledge their own complicity in the killing. But the reckoning Bauer was looking for involved more than a public recognition of wrongdoing; true atonement meant people seeing their relationship to the world differently. And that change still seemed far away.[18]

26

Protest

THE AUSCHWITZ TRIAL had earned Bauer national fame, and in the months that followed the verdict in August 1965, he experimented with new ways to engage the country in the legacy of the camp. He had considered commissioning a film about the trial and was delighted when the German Jewish writer Peter Weiss reached out to say he was working on a play. Like Bauer, Weiss had escaped Nazi persecution by fleeing to Sweden, and he was haunted by the thought that he was meant to have died in the camp. Weiss had spent months following the proceedings, but it was only when he'd joined the court visit to Auschwitz that the idea for a play had taken shape. He imagined it as a dramatic poem of eleven cantos in which survivors laid out their accusations against the defendants for each of the camp's murderous functions. Weiss had used the witnesses' words wherever possible, but as there was no court transcript, he had leaned on the extensive shorthand notes of the reporter Bernd Naumann to produce what he called a "concentrate."[1]

The Investigation opened in fourteen cities across West and East Germany on October 19, 1965, to a blaze of publicity. Bauer attended the Stuttgart performance on October 24 at the Württemberg State Theater. He was struck by the discordant tone of the production, which was performed in the Brechtian style, without props or staging. Weiss had eschewed characterization, and actors switched between playing defendants and witnesses. The latter had numbers instead of names

Peter Weiss, c. 1965
imageBROKER.com
GmbH & Co. KG /
Alamy Stock Photo

and stood in a group like a Greek chorus, speaking without emotion as one defendant after another appeared before the chorus to justify or deny his actions. Weiss wanted their disembodied affect to reflect the impossibility of ever approaching the horror of the camp. The whole production was set to a grueling score by the Italian composer Luigi Nono featuring choirs of women and children, electronic music, and the sound of detonations and screams.[2]

Afterward, Bauer joined Weiss and the writer Erich Kuby onstage to discuss the ethics of portraying Auschwitz in art. Kuby doubted that the play had succeeded in helping the audience engage with the reality of the camp. Bauer agreed, but he put it differently: Weiss's decision to stick closely to the legal proceedings invited the audience to judge the crime and, for this reason, the play suffered from the same limitations as the trial itself. "The judge in our criminal law looks backwards and he really only sees deeds," Bauer noted. "Unfortunately, he does not see the sources, the causes of the deeds." Bauer wanted a play that would plunge its audience into the evil of the camp itself, so "we are all filled and shaken, and Auschwitz is now a living experience."[3]

Bauer was buoyed in his thinking about cultural change that autumn through his conversations with Thomas Harlan, who had all manner of ideas for plays and films. Bauer's love for the younger man had burgeoned that summer. After years of moving cautiously in his personal life to protect his work, Bauer felt a new sense of freedom. Bauer had visited Harlan in June, before the verdict, at his home in Ascona, where they sat in the sun beside Lake Maggiore and talked about Harlan's latest project—a script about an ostracized Jew in post-war Germany—while Bauer showered him with fatherly praise. Their relationship was intimate without perhaps becoming physical.[4]

"You are an ocean of feelings and of thought," Bauer wrote after the visit. "One must feel lucky to know you and to be able to like you." He was thinking of Harlan in his bed, "the pages [inscribed] with the blood-red pen" piling up beside Harlan as he wrote. "Now I know where you are and what you are doing. That is good. Everything is in front of me, and believe me, my warmest wishes and my heartfelt greetings are in your room."[5]

They met again in Zurich, after which Harlan wrote suggestively: "You will say that I am bombarding you with letters. In reality I am showering you with something else."[6]

As his feelings for Harlan deepened, Bauer found himself drawn to West Germany's nascent gay rights movement. He was encouraged that earlier attempts to impose more restrictions on homosexuality in the name of public morality had stalled and gay life increasingly featured in radio and television. *Quick,* one of West Germany's largest magazines, asked him to participate in a story for an issue dedicated to homosexuality in the Federal Republic. He agreed, aware that his presence would likely be construed as an acknowledgment of his sexuality. The issue was published under the provocative headline "Article 175 in Germany: How They Live, What They Fear, How They Camouflage Themselves." Still, the stories featured some of the first nuanced and unbiased reporting on West German gay life. One article described the Schnurrbart-Diele—the Mustache Hall—in West Berlin, a bar for younger trendsetters in Frankfurt, and an exclusive salon curated by a wealthy middle-aged man in Hamburg. Another featured profiles of gay men across Germany, with only passing references made to "abnormal dispositions." Bauer stopped short of declaring his sexuality in the magazine but shared his thoughts on why gay sex was misunderstood.[7]

Quick: "To what do you attribute the average citizen's general
aversion to homosexuals?"

Bauer: "Partly to ignorance of the nature of homosexual
intercourse. In the vast majority of cases, this takes place in a
completely different way than is generally assumed—less
repulsive. In addition, there is a considerable amount of
hypocrisy and prejudice."[8]

Bauer saw this new sexual openness as connected to the student
protests against the Vietnam War and police brutality, movements that
were made possible, he believed, by the postwar generation's vehement
rejection of fascism. The crimes of the Nazis featured at their rallies but
usually as a point of comparison to current injustices. Student activists
likened Vietnam to Auschwitz. Bauer probably shared some of the
Jewish writer Ernst Fraenkel's reservations about drawing such moral
equivalences. "I think Berlin students would do well to avoid the impression that they are equating L.B. Johnson's America with Adolf Hitler's Germany," Fraenkel observed.[9]

Nonetheless, Bauer felt moved to contribute his own radical argument for overturning antigay legislation. As long as Article 175 was on
the statute books, Germany could not be said to have overcome its
authoritarian past, he wrote in an essay for *Die Zeit.* "The pluralism of
our society," he declared, requires the protection of "the opinions of
our minorities."[10]

Bauer also took to the road to give a series of student talks advocating for a reduction in the age of consent for gay sex, removal of fines for
adultery, and access to contraception. "It is part of the intimate sphere
of the human being," he concluded, "to decide whether he wishes to
have children and what meaning he wants to attach to his eros and
sexus."[11]

Bauer's outspoken views led to a growing celebrity among young
intellectuals. He featured in a novel about the trial by the writer Robert
Neumann, and the director Alexander Kluge approached him to appear in a cameo role as himself in an avant-garde film about a young
Jewish woman caught in the Federal Republic's judicial system. The

Bauer, 1967
picture alliance / AP

film, *Yesterday Girl,* went on to win the Silver Lion at the Venice Film Festival. As Bauer pointed out to Kluge, the last German film to do so had been Veit Harlan's *Jud Süss.*[12]

. . .

Bauer ran into Hofmeyer at a closed meeting of jurists in Königstein in April 1966. Bauer was in a pugnacious mood, telling the jurists they could make his life easier by simply instituting a mandatory three-year minimum sentence for all the SS men who'd served in concentration camps. Hofmeyer accused Bauer of advocating summary justice and, predictably, argued that no change in the law was necessary. "Mammoth trials" such as Auschwitz were a bad idea, claimed Hofmeyer, both for their length and for their reliance on witnesses, whom he deemed "the weakest form of evidence." He could point to other proceedings staged by Bauer that had not gone well, including the Krumey trial, which had ended with Krumey being convicted in 1965 to just five years in prison for the mass murder of Hungarian Jews. He was immediately released for time served.[13]

The bad-tempered meeting ended without resolution. In a letter to Harlan, Bauer described the strain of working with people "who think I'm a bastard" and having to listen to their objectionable opinions. He wished he could simply dismiss the views of people like Hofmeyer, but he knew they still held the upper hand in West Germany. That December of 1966, Kurt Georg Kiesinger, a former Nazi who had worked on antisemitic propaganda at the foreign ministry, became chancellor. The BND was still run by Reinhard Gehlen. His investigation into the organization's Nazi past had led to fifty-five former SS men of the hundreds he employed being fired, enough to assure the chancellery that the past had been dealt with. Gehlen was thinking of retiring and writing his memoirs. Hans Globke continued to advise the government behind the scenes and appeared to be enjoying himself as a star defense witness for war criminals. The only inconvenience he faced was being forced to sell his retirement home on Lake Geneva after the local parliament declared him persona non grata and stripped him of his residency permit.[14]

Bauer recognized the Auschwitz trial had at best stirred the German conscience. Further prosecutions of Nazis were needed. In October 1967, he launched a trial against eleven members of an Einsatzgruppe involved in the single greatest atrocity on the eastern front: the mass murder of thirty-three thousand Jews in Babi Yar, Ukraine. The case was controversial because of the rarely scrutinized role of the German military in facilitating the killing across Eastern Europe. The small courtroom in Darmstadt was uncomfortably packed as chilling details of the massacre emerged from the defendants: the Jews who had sung as they were led to be machine-gunned into ravines; the children made to lie with their parents to be shot in the back of the head; the "mountain" of belongings left behind. One of the defendants, Viktor Trill, broke down on the stand as he described entering the ravine to search among the corpses—"the flabby stuff"—for any survivors in order to dispatch them. The SS had attempted to set fire to some of the bodies and the air was filled with smoke and the reek of burnt flesh. A few were still alive, moaning in pain. "I saw someone lying there and shouting, 'Finish me off!'" Trill recalled.[15]

Then the defendant Adolf Janssen shocked the courtroom by testifying that senior army officers in Kyiv had initiated some of the killings, citing the rationale that as Jews were dying anyway in the ghettos, they should be "brought to an expedient end." Another defendant described the Wehrmacht's subsequent role in transporting Jews to the ravines, standing guard over the slaughter, and shooting anyone who tried to escape.[16]

Bauer, following the proceedings closely through the press, noted the initial impact of Janssen's testimony. "Joint responsibility of the Wehrmacht?" asked the *Darmstädter Echo.* The Wehrmacht leadership certainly approved of the killing, explained *Der Spiegel,* which pointed out that Janssen had also worked for a time in Gehlen's intelligence headquarters during the war. Some officers "made no secret of their distaste," noted the newspaper. "Rarely, however, did aversion turn into resistance."[17]

But to Bauer's disappointment, the trial hardly seemed to register with the public at large. *The New York Times* visited the trial in February 1968 and commented on the general indifference, noting that only four seats in the gallery for the public and members of the press were taken. Babi Yar might be a symbol of Nazi atrocities, noted its correspondent, but in "West Germany now, the Babi Yar proceedings are just another trial."[18]

Bauer was feeling increasingly exhausted from his eighteen-hour days on a diet of instant coffee and cigarettes. Kügler had decided to leave the office to take up work as a defense lawyer after becoming disillusioned over his poor pay and lack of promotion. In truth, Kügler was burned out, as they all were. Still, Bauer was shocked to discover that his star prosecutor had joined the firm of Auschwitz defense lawyer Hans Laternser and was now working for the very war criminals Bauer was seeking to convict. Bauer struggled to sleep, his phone ringing most nights with death threats. He learned of at least one plot by three delusional neo-Nazis to plant a bomb under his car or kidnap him on his way to work and shoot him in a forest. He thought about stepping down with his sixty-fifth birthday approaching, the legal age of retirement in Germany, but chose to extend for a further three years "if things go well." If they don't, he reflected, "I could be ill or dead."[19]

He looked for comfort from Harlan and nurtured the idea of the two

of them running off to the mountains. But Harlan was distracted. He'd
moved in with another man in Switzerland, a relationship that didn't
seem to bother Bauer, who appeared more troubled by the discovery
that Harlan had simultaneously had a fling with a woman who was
now pregnant. "Thomas, write to me. Two lines are enough. I can't
tousle your mop of hair," he wrote, and then a little later, "You promised to write me a doctor's letter on how I should treat myself more
tenderly. Unfortunately it did not come. So I have not yet been able to
learn 'tenderness' toward people, including myself." When Harlan did
resurface, it was to bombard him with requests for money to buy a
house—not just for himself and Bauer but also for Harlan's male lover.
Bauer was offered a room of his own. He finally broke off contact with
Harlan.[20]

Bauer felt the loss keenly just as he needed Harlan's help to understand the emerging counterculture of the late 1960s. Bauer liked the
rebelliousness and instinctive antiauthoritarianism of many young
people. They talked about conscience not as an innate and private quality framed through religion but as a political force they were personally
responsible for upholding. "The highest authority is conscience, and
not a parliamentary majority," proclaimed Konrad Tempel, a Quaker
primary schoolteacher and antiwar campaigner who took part in
the increasingly large protests against nuclear armament. "Better active today than radioactive tomorrow!" was a popular slogan. Bauer
was no doubt touched to learn that church chaplains had started to
organize youth groups, known as the Aktion Sühnezeichen—"Action
Atonement"—to visit Auschwitz and help the museum with site maintenance. One group had pulled up weeds from the train tracks leading to Birkenau; another uncovered the foundations of the ruined gas
chambers. Yet Bauer was also troubled by the students' individualism—
which struck him at times as a form of egotism and intolerance for differing views—and the calls by some on the radical fringes to overthrow
the government.[21]

Bauer's mood grew darker as violence flared in the spring of 1968.
In response to the shooting of student leader Rudi Dutschke in Ber-

lin on April 11, protests broke out in cities across the country. The government's intention to amend the constitution to allow rule by decree in the event of an emergency—a provision found in the constitutions of most Western democracies—was another flashpoint because of its association with the Nazis' rise to power. Students staged sit-ins and stopped traffic. One group blockaded the printing operations of the newspaper publisher Springer, blamed for abetting the right-wing establishment. Another group set fire to a department store in Frankfurt. Arson attacks were common—"A new demonstration method" intended to introduce "American napalm" to a European audience, according to one radical flyer. The police responded with tear gas and truncheons, arresting more than five thousand in just a few weeks.[22]

Meanwhile, the Far Right had coalesced around a new leader, Adolf von Thadden, an urbane former artillery officer who refused to accept German war guilt and skirted around Holocaust denial. Thadden's National Democratic Party had done well in state election polls and was expected to gain seats in the Bundestag. Bauer was appalled by Thadden—he called him "Adolf II"—and the growing polarization of German society. Democracy still felt fragile to him. Young people needed to engage with institutions and change them from the inside, he argued in a lecture on resistance at Munich University that summer. What he feared most was that the government would use the unrest as an excuse to clamp down on debate. "Look at today's politics and the emergency laws that have been introduced. Line up a ruler. What direction is it pointing? Toward the right!" he told a friend. "Where's it all going to lead in the long term? To a dystopia at best! Thankfully we're old. We won't live to see it." Helga Einsele, a prison director close to Bauer, thought he had grown more cynical and disillusioned. "He no longer believes in anyone or anything," she noted in her diary, "[but] can't give up waiting and wanting."[23]

Bauer's old friend Heinz Meyer-Velde , whom Bauer had persuaded to pursue a career in the prison service, also noticed a change when the attorney general visited him at the correctional facility he ran. Bauer

Bauer, 1967
Courtesy of Marit
Tiefenthal

insisted on meeting inmates and sat listening patiently to the concerns of a convicted murderer, looking drained. A new bill under discussion in the Bundestag threatened to make most Nazi-era crimes subject to the statute of limitations, which amounted to a virtual amnesty. Bauer was determined to fight the measure.[24]

"Why are you doing this to yourself?" Meyer-Velde asked him afterward. "It's all too much, isn't it?"[25]

"Nobody else is doing it," Bauer replied.[26]

.   .   .

Bauer took a much-needed break to Naples in June, determined to unwind and consider an entirely different type of project. He had long been interested in the story of Oscar Wilde's sensational trial and imprisonment in 1895 on charges of gross indecency for his liaisons with young men. Wilde, under cross-examination, had given an unapologetic defense of his desire when asked to explain what his young lover Alfred Douglas had meant when describing their relationship in a poem as "the love that dare not speak its name."[27]

Wilde said that Douglas was writing about the "great affection of an elder for a younger man as there was between David and Jonathan, such as Plato made the very basis of his philosophy. . . . It is in this century misunderstood, so much misunderstood that it may be described as the 'Love that dare not speak its name' and on account of it I am placed where I am now. It is beautiful, it is fine, it is the noblest form of affection. There is nothing unnatural about it."[28]

Bauer began to conceive of a play about the trial and Wilde's imprisonment in Reading Gaol. On his return to Frankfurt, Bauer enlisted playwright and gay rights activist Rolf Italiaander to help him develop the story and approached the Hebbel Theater in Berlin about staging the play as soon as September 1968, in time for a groundbreaking debate in the Bundestag to reform and potentially repeal Article 175. Bauer missed Harlan at moments like this, but he held back from contacting him. He was used to being alone.[29]

The journalist Horst Krüger visited Bauer in June and found him restless and discontented. However, when Ole Grünbaum, the son of the man who had rescued Bauer from the Horserød concentration camp in Denmark, met him a few weeks later, Bauer was in excellent spirits. The twenty-three-year-old wild-haired revolutionary had written a bestselling book extolling the virtues of pot smoking and free love that featured drawings of large multicolored penises. They talked about the old days when Ole had known Bauer as "Uncle Fritz" and used to run over to his apartment for sweets. He rather nervously asked Bauer what he thought of his book.[30]

Ole Grünbaum,
c. 1960s
Courtesy of Ole
Grünbaum

"I like your style," Bauer replied warmly.[31]

On June 28, 1968, a Friday, Bauer gave a lecture to students at the University of Karlsruhe on his ongoing work tracking down war criminals and stayed chatting with participants until well past midnight. Afterward, he had a drink with the magazine editor Christof Müller-Wirth at the bar of his hotel. He returned home the following day and spent the long, warm evening on his balcony with his neighbor, Lucie Schöpf. They spoke about his family and the ongoing student protests. He asked her to bake him a new batch of biscuits, as he'd run out. Bauer went inside when a friend called around 11:00 P.M. He then heated up a pair of sausages for himself and Schöpf, and served them with mustard on the balcony.[32]

They said good night and he went to run himself a bath. He took five Veronal sleeping pills, a strong dose, but he was used to them. He let the warm water envelop him. Then he closed his eyes and slipped away.[33]

Epilogue

B AUER'S BODY WAS discovered in his bath on Monday, July 1, 1968, after he failed to show up for work and his office ordered a search of his apartment. His deputy Ulrich Krüger realized questions were inevitable and requested a forensic autopsy. Indeed, Thomas Harlan feared that Bauer had taken his own life in despair over the failure of the courts to deliver justice, or worse, that he'd been murdered. But there was no evidence to suggest that Bauer had died of anything other than a heart attack. "Everyone who knew him could see there was a fire burning inside him," the *Frankfurter Allgemeine Zeitung* wrote on July 2, "a fire that ultimately consumed him."[1]

On Wednesday morning, thirty of Bauer's friends and family made their way through a summer downpour to a small chapel in Frankfurt's main cemetery, where his body lay in a coffin decorated with palm leaves. Theodor Adorno swayed gently to the strains of Beethoven's string quartet No. 13 in B-flat major, a piece he had chosen for the ceremony. Bauer had requested no speeches in his will, but Ilse Staff, a jurist and friend, was moved to speak to the sense of difference Bauer had felt during his childhood and the isolation of his later years. He had looked for human connection, in law and in life, she said. "What did we do? In many important and not-so-important ways, we allowed him to die infinitely alone, infinitely depressed, infinitely sad." An official memorial service followed the next day, attended by government ministers and a motley crew of old Reichsbannermen, Swedish Social Democrats, off-duty police officers, and even, Harlan noted, a few rent boys. State Justice Minister Johannes Strelitz stood before them and pledged to serve Bauer's mission to uphold human dignity.[2]

It was a hollow promise. Three months after Bauer's death, the legislation time-barring the prosecution of Nazi crimes came into force, limiting the courts to trying cases only where murderous intent could be proven. Prosecutors quickly grasped that the new law prevented them from pursuing the vast majority of Germans who had participated in the Final Solution. Two hundred and eighty-two former Nazis saw their cases dropped that year. Horst Gauf, Frankfurt's new attorney general, who lauded Bauer as a "great role model, a titan a hundred years ahead of his time," shelved Bauer's attempt to prosecute those involved in the Nazi euthanasia program and waved through early releases of camp adjutant Robert Mulka and pharmacist Viktor Capesius. By the time SS doctor Franz Lucas was acquitted on appeal in 1970, Bauer's radical vision of mass complicity appeared all but lost.[3]

And yet to measure Bauer's success by the number of convictions he helped secure would be to miss his larger significance. At the time of his death, Bauer's vision of a collective reckoning had helped to inspire a new generation of jurists, activists, journalists, writers, and educators. Their efforts were perhaps felt most profoundly in German schools. From the forty-seven words devoted to the Final Solution in the textbooks of 1956, the subject steadily expanded throughout the 1970s to dominate the teaching of modern German history. The growth in knowledge led to a quiet moral awakening that was bolstered by increasing depictions of Nazi atrocities in books and film. In 1979, twenty million West Germans—half the adult population—watched the American miniseries *Holocaust* about a fictional Jewish family in Berlin starring Meryl Streep. Thousands called in to an accompanying hotline staffed by historians to express outrage at their own country.[4]

The shift in German attitudes was most evident in the public acknowledgment of survivors. They found themselves increasingly invited to schools, interviewed at commemoration events, filmed and recorded for oral history databases and local history projects. Filip Müller, the Slovak Sonderkommando survivor who'd broken years of self-imposed silence at the Auschwitz trial, published a memoir and featured prominently in Claude Lanzmann's 1985 film *Shoah*, a ground-breaking documentary that brought home Jewish trauma to West Germans. The emergence of second-generation survivor organizations in the 1980s and 1990s encouraged more families to share their experiences. Other groups who had been persecuted by the Nazis, including Roma and Sinti, forced laborers, "asocials," and finally gay men, began to be recognized. A profusion of Holocaust commemoration sites followed, from Berlin's grand "Memorial to the Murdered Jews of Europe" to hundreds of brass plaques embedded in sidewalks around Germany, known as Stolpersteine, or stumbling stones, to remind passersby of the names of former residents who were Nazi victims. Bauer's work came full circle in 2011, when his long-sought ambition to have state-sponsored mass murder recognized was achieved with the conviction of the Ukrainian-born death camp guard John Demjanjuk as an accomplice to murder for having served in Sobibór.[5]

There is little doubt that Germany's reckoning with Nazism has exceeded some of Bauer's expectations. But he would also have been troubled by the pockets of silence and shame that persist within many German households that have connections to Nazism. When I interviewed Hans Globke's son Werner and daughter Marianne in 2021, they insisted that he had tried to help Jews through his commentary on the Nuremberg Race Laws. Reinhard Gehlen's daughter Dorothee told me that he had no choice but to follow orders to help plan and implement Hitler's genocidal Soviet campaign. She didn't believe her father had known about the Nazi pasts of those he hired. I share these anecdotes not to argue that these men indoctrinated their children. They are well-versed in their fathers' war records and would be the first to say that they abhor Nazism. Rather it is to observe that the ripple effects of Adenauer, Globke, and Gehlen's project to exonerate the millions who enacted Nazism in the name of national unity continue to be felt within many German households. A 2014 study found that only 1 percent of Germans polled believed their own families had been active supporters of Nazism. Two contradictory narratives seem to exist for these children and grandchildren of the war generation. They recognize the Holocaust as a national crime. But they cannot reconcile its horrors with the picture they hold of their family members—or of themselves.[6]

Bauer would not have been surprised by the partial nature of Germany's reckoning. History is never settled, he believed, and each generation must struggle with the meaning of the Holocaust. For Bauer, that meant engaging in a sustained examination of the cultural roots of Nazism. But it was essential to him that this exercise be grounded in the question the Holocaust asks each of us to consider: How could ordinary people come to be enlisted in perpetrating such a crime? He knew that to begin answering that question required a willingness to understand the killers themselves.[7]

On December 8, 1964, shortly before the court visit to Auschwitz, Bauer appeared in a live debate for Hessian television in which he tried to explain his thinking to a group of young people. The idea that even Nazi killers required some form of empathy proved too radical for many in the audience, and they pressed him to draw a distinction between those who had murdered with their own hands and those who had not. Bauer became exasperated. He acknowledged that the Auschwitz defendants had shown no remorse, but this, he felt, could be explained by the court's failure to explore their mindset.[8]

Bauer himself was never able to satisfactorily answer the question as to why so many of his countrymen had killed, perhaps because to empathize with Nazis felt dangerously close to forgiving them. But he wasn't seeking their redemption. Instead, he wanted his trial to push us to examine ourselves, in the belief that the strength of democracy and the guarantee that Nazism will never return lies not in the lines society draws, which can be breached, nor in institutions, which can be corrupted. Rather it lies in our commitment to seek connection with those we struggle to understand.

Acknowledgments

THIS BOOK WOULD not have been possible without my brilliant editor at Crown, Kevin Doughten, who has shared my passion for Fritz Bauer's story over the past five years and helped me bring him to life. I'm grateful to my publisher, Gillian Blake, and the Penguin Random House team for pulling the book together: Amy Li and Jess Scott, the assistant editors; Dustin Amick and Jessica Heim, the production managers; Aubrey Khan, the text designer; and Patricia Shaw and Craig Adams, the production editors. Patricia and Craig's incorporation of edits for the galleys was exceptional. I feel fortunate to have worked with Jamie Joseph at Ebury for the U.K. edition. He is one of the best publishers in the business. The book was first conceived of with the help of my wonderful agents, Larry Weismann and Sascha Alper. I am indebted to Clare Alexander, my U.K. agent, for her advice and backing over the past fifteen years. I've worked with Jacob Levenson on my last three books and he helped craft every page. He is, as Bauer would say, a true comrade.

Ingrid Pufahl, Katarzyna Chiżyńska, and Sine Maria Vinther led my research team. Ingrid is one of the finest researchers I've worked with, and the book is filled with the details she so painstakingly tracked down and the insights she shared over the course of countless conversations. Katarzyna performed the remarkable feat of pulling together the source material for the endnotes and bibliography. She has been my longtime guide and companion throughout my research into Auschwitz. Sine is a remarkable organizer and networker who uncovered Bauer's hidden life in Denmark and attempted to cross the Øresund with me. I'm especially grateful to Harriet Phillips, who worked on every stage of the book's production, from archival research in six languages to shaping the narrative threads, especially the Auschwitz investigation, and critiquing endless drafts. Many thanks to the rest of my amazing team: Florine Miez, Anna Schattschneider, Jan Tattenberg, Anne Uhl, Morten Baarvig Thomsen, Christian Kjellson, Jonathan Cahana-Blum, Catherine Mullier, Francesca Teal, Isabel Blankfield, and Ester González Martín. The following interns also made important contributions: Jonathan Fridman, Matthaios Amanatiadis, Maria Klein, Marína Kováčová, Chantelle Leiderman, Helena Brann, Charlotte Boreham, and Malene Sølvdahl Clemmensen. Wojciech Kozłowksi and Hanna Radziejowska of the Pilecki Institute provided support for the research from its inception. It was hearing Hanna speak glowingly about Fritz Bauer while preparing our Witold Pilecki exhibition in Berlin that first drew my attention to his story. Almut Schoenfeld, Klára Švecová, Jennifer Lauxmann, Luiza Walczuk, Agnieszka Mazurczyk, Iris Yael Blum Cahana, and Hanna Renke provided invaluable research assistance. Ingrid's mother, Hedi Rosskamp, performed the almost impossible task of deciphering handwritten Sütterlin. Special thanks to Emma Widdis and Stanley Bill at Cambridge University and Nicholas Stargardt at Oxford University for their help finding talented researchers.

No book about Fritz Bauer can be written without reference to the work of his outstanding German biographers, Irmtrud Wojak and Ronen Steinke, along with the brilliant scholarship of Werner Renz. I am grateful for their encouragement and Renz's guidance on the manuscript. I would also like to thank the following archivists on behalf of the team: Christian Carlsen at Stasi-Unterlagen Archiv, Tarek Strauch at Deutsche Kinemathek, Volger Kucher at VVN-Archiv Stuttgart, and Johannes Beermann-Schön at the Fritz Bauer Institute. I feel privileged to have had a superb set of manuscript reviewers: Robert Jan van Pelt, Klaus Dietmar Henke, Mary Fulbrook, Therkel Stræde, Clayton Whisnant, Sieglinde Geisel, Wolfgang Hörner, Devin Pendas, Gerhard Sälter, Filip Gańczak, Bettina Stangneth, Daniel Cowling, Jochen Böhler, Suzannah Lipscomb, Frank McDonough, Mark Klamberg, Peter Edelberg, Helen Torr, Aviva Davidson, Jen Banbury, Jesse Wegmann, Kyra Wegmann, Rachael Cerrotti, Anthony Lipmann, and Dave Booker. I also appreciated the insights and support of: Piotr Setkiewicz, Magdalena Gawin, Maria Bormuth, Kevin Ruffner, Annette Hess, Annette Weinke, Jean-Pierre Stephan, Avner Avraham, Philipp Kratz, Jan Pietrzak, Gerd Biegel, Heinrich Gerdes, Julia Noah Munier, Ralf Bogen, Raimund Wolfert, Elke Banabak, Helmut Kramer, Uwe Meier, Minna Steffen Pedersen, Vojtěch Kyncl, Ilona Ziok, John v. Jensen, Halfdan Höner, Sigrid Corry, Matt Walker, Frank Bøgh, Paul Hartis, Kirsten Larvick, and Alvydas Nikzentaitis. I appreciated those who shared material during lockdown: in particular Matias Ristic, Helmut Müssener, Peter Kessler, and Clara Glynn. Thank you to François Jeandet and Adrianna Wojcik Muffat Jeandet for their hospitality.

I am immensely grateful to Bauer's extended family for their support, insights, and trust. Marit Tiefenthal opened up her family archive to Harriet and me, fielded my questions, and read an early draft of the manuscript. On a particularly memorable day, Marit joined Sine, Therkel Stræde, and Jack Kliger of the Museum of Jewish Heritage on a trip to Rørvig, from where both Marit's and Jack's families escaped. Special thanks to Mi and Pernilla Tiefenthal, Eric Hirsch, and Karyn Hirsch. My team and I were also fortunate to interview those who worked closely with Bauer—prosecutors Gerhard Wiese and Johannes Warlo—and many who shared insights into his life and mission. They include: Reinhard Strecker, Alexander Kluge, Thomas Ormond, Sylvia Düx-Heiseler, Chester Harlan, Bastian Gnielka, Sigrid Wobst, Monica von Rosen, Irmgard Lauer-Seidelmann, Liliana Hermann, Jerzy Łabędź, Jacek Andrzejewski, Tadeusz Andrzejewski, Philip Zinn, Peter Kalb, Arthur Sehn, Finn Rowold, Nils Nygaard, Leif Møller, Carina Birgersson, Caroline Compton, Måns Lönnroth, Inger Grünbaum, Ole Grünbaum, Ralph Dobrawa, Eckhard Schimpf, Till Ausmeier, and Esther Velde-Posters. Helle Wagner entrusted Sine and me with Bauer's letters and the dinosaur he carved in Horserød. Helle and her sister Lis also shared the painful story of their father, whose role in saving Bauer's life I have tried to honor.

It was a privilege to interview survivors Bent Melchior and Daniel

Passent, along with the families of witnesses who testified at the Frankfurt Auschwitz trial. They included Maria Pankowska, Barbara Paczuła, Tadeusz Hołuj, Kazimierz Kłodziński, Jan Fejkiel, Danuta Mikusz-Oslislo, Jan Mikusz, Tadeusz Mikusz, Evelyn Dürmayer, Klaus Dirschoweit, Daniel Bergmann, Zenon Kowal, Sheldon Piekny, Ze'ev Raz, Hella Matalon, Tomasz Kulka, Michael Kraus, Eilat Negev, and the extended family of Mauritius Berner. Harriet and I were welcomed into the home of Ilona Porębska, the daughter of Henryk Porębski, one of the most extraordinary figures of the resistance in Auschwitz, who also featured in my last book, and about whom, I hope, more will be written. Kurt and Daniel Langbein brought home the personal cost of Hermann Langbein's commitment to chronicling and educating the public about Auschwitz. Cilly Kugelmann and Micha Brumlik shared their experiences of interviewing Bauer and growing up as the children of survivors in Frankfurt.

I have been touched by the openness and kindness of Reinhard Gehlen's family, in particular Dorothee Koss-Gehlen, Jobst Koss, their daughter Wega, and Christina Gehlen. A simple question to Chris Waldmann—was your dad Jewish?—sparked a wonderful voyage of discovery that united two sides of Eric Waldman's family. I felt honored to share insights with Chris, Jane Storace, and Greta Mari Storace. I would also like to thank Werner and Marianne Globke for their reflections; Dörthe Dylewski, the daughter of Klaus Dylewski; Ursula Boger, the granddaughter of Wilhelm Boger; and Axel Eisser, the grandson of Victor Capesius. Lois Critchfield, Joan Shisler, and Barbara Wüster also shared memories and reflections.

One of the joys of research was following in Bauer's footsteps with the help of expert guides and local historians. In Stuttgart I'd like to thank Roland Maier and Sigrid Brüggemann for showing us Bauer's neighborhood, Fritz Endemann for discussing the courthouse, and Elfriede Krüger and Walter Mugler for taking me around the outskirts of Ludwigsburg. Peter Edelberg guided Sine and me through gay Copenhagen and provided insights into Bauer's experience with the Danish police. Helle Hvidtfeldt Jensen and her family kindly showed us around Ridder Stigsvej, Torben Gulnov the Horserød concentration camp, and Bruno Nielsen the sanatorium at Skodsborg. Bo Braestrup deserves an extra special mention for uncovering Bauer's escape route in Rørvig. Thanks also to Michael Kastrup, Ulla Jørgensen, Marianne Hansen, and her sisters Helle and Nina. Florine and I were shown around Braunschweig by the inimitable Udo Dittmann. Christian Setzepfandt brought us to Bauer's office in Frankfurt, the Römer, and a few back alleys. For revealing Reinhard Gehlen's journey from the mountains to American captivity, I relied upon Helmut Sankowski in Elendalm, Max Lohrmann in Augsburg, Manfred Kopp in Oberursel, and Rolf Faber in Wiesbaden.

Last, I'd like to thank my mum and dad for their support; my brother, Adam; and Chrissy and our girls, Amelie, Maz, and Tess, for whom this book is written.

Characters

Adenauer, Konrad (1876–1967)—Chancellor of West Germany (1949–1963).

Adorno, Theodor (1903–1969)—German Jewish sociologist and Bauer's neighbor in Frankfurt, whose research into German defensiveness toward Nazi crimes influenced Bauer's thinking.

Aharoni, Zvi (1921–2012)—Israeli Mossad agent who helped capture Adolf Eichmann.

Augsburg, Emil (1904–1981)—Einsatzkommando member who worked for Gehlen Organization and then BND. Dismissed in 1966 for his wartime role.

Baer, Richard [Karl Neumann] (1911–1963)—SS officer and last commandant of Auschwitz concentration camp. Postwar worked as forester. Arrested December 1960, died in custody.

Bauer, Ella [née Hirsch] (1881–1955)—Bauer's mother.

Bauer, Fritz (1903–1968)—German Jewish judge and prosecutor who orchestrated capture of Adolf Eichmann and instigated the Frankfurt Auschwitz trial.

Bauer, Ludwig (1870–1945)—Bauer's father.

Beckerle, Adolf Heinz (1902–1976)—Nazi diplomat and SS officer who supervised deportation of twenty thousand Bulgarian Jews to Auschwitz. Beckerle was Bauer's first target upon becoming attorney general in Frankfurt in 1956. Proceedings suspended June 1968.

Berner, Mauritius (1902–1976)—Hungarian Jewish physician and Holocaust survivor. Lost his wife and three daughters in Auschwitz, testified against defendant Viktor Capesius at the Auschwitz trial.

Boger, Wilhelm (1906–1977)—SS officer, deputy head of Gestapo in Auschwitz; infamous for his use of a torture device known as the Boger swing. Postwar worked as commercial clerk. Arrested October 1958, tried in the Auschwitz trial and sentenced to life plus five years in prison.

Boker, John (1913–2003)—CIA intelligence officer who became Gehlen's first supporter in the U.S. military, leading to the establishment of Gehlen's postwar spy network.

Brandt, Willy (1913–1992)—Socialist German émigré, friend of Bauer in Stockholm. Later first Social Democratic chancellor of West Germany (1969–1974).

Brunner, Alois [Georg Fischer] (1912–2001)—Austrian SS officer, Eichmann's deputy, oversaw deportation of over 100,000 Jews from Greece and other countries. Postwar fled to Egypt, then Syria.

Buchthal, Arnold (1900–1965)—German Jewish jurist and judge. Lead prosecutor in Hermann Krumey investigation.

Capesius, Viktor (1907–1985)—SS pharmacist in Auschwitz. Provided Zyklon B for gas chambers, participated in selections, and enriched himself from victims' belongings. Postwar opened a pharmacy in Göppingen. Arrested December 1959, tried in the Auschwitz trial, and sentenced to nine years in prison. Released in 1968.

Deutschkron, Inge (1922–2022)—Israeli journalist and Holocaust survivor. Reported on the Auschwitz trial and court visit to the camp for Israeli newspaper *Maariv*.

Eichmann, Adolf [Ricardo Klement] (1906–1962)—SS officer who oversaw mass deportation of Jews to death camps in Nazi-occupied Poland, including 438,000 Hungarian Jews to Auschwitz in summer 1944. Postwar fled to Argentina. Seized in Buenos Aires by Mossad in 1960 after a tip-off from Bauer. Tried in Jerusalem in 1961 and executed the following year.

Felfe, Heinz (1918–2008)—Gestapo agent; postwar BND counterintelligence operative and Soviet double agent. Arrested November 1961 for espionage, sentenced to fourteen years in prison. Released to Soviet Union in 1969 in prisoner exchange.

Gehlen, Herta [née von Seydlitz-Kurzbach] (1904–1993)—Gehlen's wife.

Gehlen, Reinhard (1902–1979)—Head of Foreign Armies East, responsible for gathering military intelligence on Soviet forces during WWII. Postwar head of Gehlen Organization (1946–1956) and BND (1956–1968).

Globke, Hans (1898–1973)—German lawyer and civil servant. Co-wrote commentary for Nuremberg Race Laws, which shaped implementation of Jewish persecution in Nazi Germany. Postwar served as secretary of state under Chancellor Konrad Adenauer (1953–1963).

Harel, Isser (1912–2003)—Head of Israeli intelligence service Mossad (1952–1963).

Harlan, Thomas (1929–2010)—German writer and filmmaker, son of Veit Harlan, and intimate friend of Fritz Bauer. Collaborated with Bauer to investigate former Nazis in the West German government.

Harlan, Veit (1899–1964)—German film director, collaborated with Nazis to produce the antisemitic propaganda film *Jud Süss*. Stood trial for war crimes in Hamburg in 1949 and 1951; acquitted both times.

Hausner, Gideon (1915–1990)—Israeli attorney general (1960–1963), lead prosecutor in Adolf Eichmann trial.

Hermann, Lothar (1901–1974)—German Jewish survivor of Dachau who emigrated to Argentina and helped to identify Adolf Eichmann.

Hermann, Sylvia (1942–)—Daughter of Lothar Hermann, also helped to identify Eichmann.

Heyde, Werner (1902–1964)—Psychiatrist, professor, and leading figure in the Nazi euthanasia program. Postwar lived under false identity and continued to practice medicine. Arrested 1959 and committed suicide in prison.

Hodann, Max (1894–1946)—German physician and sexologist whose Stockholm speech about the mass murder of the Jews was an impetus to Bauer's mission.

Hofmeyer, Hans (1904–1992)—SS military judge involved in summary executions; later presiding judge of the Auschwitz trial.

Hofstetter, Efraim (1911–1971)—Head of criminal investigation unit in Tel Aviv. Visited Lothar Hermann in Argentina in 1958 to gather information on the whereabouts of Adolf Eichmann.

Horkheimer, Max (1895–1973)—German Jewish sociologist and director of Institute for Social Research; explored the Nazi mindset with Theodor Adorno.

John, Otto (1909–1997)—German lawyer and member of German wartime resistance. Involved in July 20, 1944, attempt to assassinate Hitler and subsequently testified at the Remer trial. Head of West Germany's Office for the Protection of the Constitution (BfV) (1950–1954) until his defection to East Germany.

Kaduk, Oswald (1906–1997)—SS guard in Auschwitz notorious for his abuse and murder of prisoners. Postwar worked as hospital nurse. Arrested July 1959 and tried in the Auschwitz trial. Sentenced to life in prison, released in 1989.

Kaul, Friedrich Karl (1906–1981)—East German lawyer and judge who attended Eichmann trial and served as civil counsel in the Auschwitz trial.

Klehr, Josef (1904–1988)—SS orderly and head of the "disinfection squad" that operated the gas chambers in Birkenau. Postwar worked as chassis builder. Arrested September 1960 and tried in the Auschwitz trial. Sentenced to life plus fifteen years in prison and released in 1988.

Kral, Józef (1910—?)—Polish Auschwitz survivor. Following his testimony at the Auschwitz trial, defendant Hans Stark was arrested on suspicion of murder.

Krumey, Hermann (1905–1981)—SS officer responsible for orchestrating deportation of Hungarian Jews to Auschwitz, deputy to Adolf Eichmann. First arrested April 1957. Sentenced to five years in a penitentiary in 1965 and released for time served. Following an appeal by the prosecution, sentenced to life in prison in 1969; released in 1976.

Kügler, Joachim (1926–2012)—Prosecutor in Auschwitz trial who tracked down key defendants such as the last commandant of Auschwitz, Richard Baer.

Langbein, Hermann (1912–1995)—Austrian communist and Auschwitz survivor who played key role in raising awareness about the camp and organizing witnesses for the Auschwitz trial.

Laternser, Hans (1908–1969)—German lawyer, defended Nazi war criminals at the Nuremberg Military Tribunal and Frankfurt Auschwitz trial.

Lucas, Franz (1911–1994)—SS doctor in Auschwitz, participated in selections. Tried for aiding and abetting murder in the Auschwitz trial; only defendant to join the court visit to the camp in December 1964. Arrested March 1965, sentenced to three years and three months in prison and released in March 1968 upon appeal.

Mengele, Josef (1911–1979)—SS officer and doctor in Auschwitz, conducted lethal medical experiments on prisoners. Postwar fled to Argentina and then Paraguay.

Merten, Max (1911–1971)—Nazi military administrator in Greece, involved in the deportation of fifty thousand Greek Jews to Auschwitz. Sentenced to life in prison by a Greek court in 1959, extradited to West Germany the same year and released. Accused Hans Globke of playing a role in the Greece deportations.

Meyer-Velde, Heinz (1926–2016)—Journalist from Braunschweig and one of Bauer's closest friends; became director of several correctional facilities after Bauer persuaded him to join the prison service.

Morgen, Konrad (1909–1982)—German lawyer and SS judge who investigated corruption in Auschwitz. Key witness for the prosecution in the Auschwitz trial.

Mulka, Robert (1895–1969)—SS officer and adjutant to Rudolf Höss in Auschwitz. Postwar ran glass export business. Arrested November 1960 and tried in the Auschwitz trial. Sentenced to fourteen years in prison, released early in 1968.

Müller, Filip (1922–2013)—Slovak Jewish Auschwitz survivor, member of Sonderkommando, testified in the Auschwitz trial.

Münch, Hans (1911–2001)—SS doctor in Auschwitz, acquitted of war crimes during trial of Auschwitz perpetrators in Kraków in 1947. Testified at the Auschwitz trial, where he spoke of his refusal to take part in selections.

Ormond, Henry (1901–1973)—German Jewish lawyer, prosecuted Nazi war criminals. Civil counsel for survivors in the Auschwitz trial, instigated court visit to the camp in December 1964.

Pohl, Giselher (1926–1996)—German pastor who gave Bauer crucial information about Eichmann's whereabouts in Argentina.

Remer, Otto Ernst (1912–1997)—Wehrmacht officer, helped suppress July 20 plot against Hitler. Postwar became leading figure in the neo-Nazi Socialist Reich Party. Tried for slander by Bauer in 1952 and fled to Egypt.

Sassen, Willem (1918–2002)—Dutch SS propagandist, interviewed Adolf Eichmann in Argentina.

Schüle, Erwin (1913–1993)—West German lawyer and lead prosecutor in the Ulm Einsatzgruppen trial. Former Nazi accused of war crimes in the Soviet Union, first head of the Central Office for the Investigation of National Socialist Crimes.

Schumacher, Kurt (1895–1952)—Leader of Stuttgart branch of Social Democratic Party (1928–1933) and Bauer's political mentor with whom he spent time in the Heuberg concentration camp. Postwar leader of Social Democratic Party of Germany.

Sehn, Jan (1909–1965)—Polish lawyer and investigator of Nazi crimes. Investigated Auschwitz camp commandant Rudolf Höss and forty other members of the camp's leadership in Kraków in 1947. Supplied evidence to Frankfurt prosecutors for the Auschwitz trial, helped organize court visit to Auschwitz in 1964.

Servatius, Robert (1894–1983)—German jurist, Adolf Eichmann's defense lawyer during his trial in Israel.

Shinnar, Felix (1905–1985)—Head of Israeli Mission in West Germany. Bauer's first Israeli contact in his search for Adolf Eichmann.

Stark, Hans (1921–1991)—SS officer in Auschwitz, involved in gassing operations. Postwar worked as agriculture lecturer. Arrested in April 1959 and tried in the Auschwitz trial. Sentenced to ten years juvenile detention, released early in 1968.

Strecker, Reinhard (1930–)—German Jewish activist who organized an exhibition exposing Nazi-era judges still serving in the West German judiciary.

Tiefenthal, Margot [née Bauer] (1906–1992)—Bauer's sister.

Tiefenthal, Walter (1906–1976)—Bauer's brother-in-law.

Vogel, Georg Friedrich (1926–2007)—Prosecutor in the Auschwitz trial.

Vogel, Rolf (1921–1994)—German journalist and author; Konrad Adenauer's personal envoy to Israel during the Eichmann trial.

Wagner, Paul (1922–1958)—Danish Social Democrat and Bauer's close friend; helped Bauer and his family escape to Sweden in 1943.

Waldman, Eric (1914–2007)—Jewish U.S. military intelligence officer originally from Austria. Oversaw Gehlen's organization (1948–1949).

Wechtenbruch, Dieter (1932–)—German lawyer, Servatius's assistant during the Eichmann trial and BND agent.

Weiss, Kurt (1916–1994)—BND head of public relations.

Wessel, Gerhard (1913–2002)—Gehlen's deputy in Foreign Armies East during WWII. Played key role in establishing the BND. Gehlen's successor as head of BND (1968–1978).

Wolken, Otto (1903–1975)—Austrian Jewish physician and Auschwitz survivor, testified at the Nuremberg International Military Tribunal. First survivor witness to testify at the Auschwitz trial.

Yoselevska, Rivka (1915–?)—Ukrainian Jewish Holocaust survivor who testified at the Eichmann trial.

Zeug, Dietrich (1930–1997)—German prosecutor seconded by Bauer to Central Office for the Investigation of National Socialist Crimes. Questioned Eichmann on Bauer's behalf.

Zinn, Georg August (1901–1976)—German politician, minister-president of Hesse (1950–1969), who appointed Bauer attorney general in Frankfurt. Publicly supported Bauer in his pursuit of Globke for war crimes.

Żywulska, Krystyna (1918–1992)—Polish Jewish writer and Auschwitz survivor, supported Thomas Harlan's research into Nazi war criminals in postwar Poland.

Notes

EPIGRAPH

1. On several occasions Primo Levi compared himself to Coleridge's ancient mariner.

INTRODUCTION

1. "Town in Poland with 6700 inhabitants (1946) on the Upper Silesian Plateau; railway junction; zinc rolling mills and steam mills. Notorious Nazi concentration camp during World War II." (Brockhaus, *Der Neue*, p. 151). The favorable reference to Hitler was followed by a depiction of him as a madman who was solely responsible for the war (Sharples, *Postwar*, pp. 152–153). Borries, "The Third Reich," *Journal of Contemporary History*, 2003/38 (1), pp. 51–55; Frei, *Adenauer's*, p. 3.

PROLOGUE

1. For Bauer's visa requirements see: Note, Feb. 12, 1948. TNA, FO 1071/18, p. 331; Fritz Bauer, Letter to Kurt Schumacher, Sept. 14, 1948. AdsD, 2/KSAA000071, no pages. Ronen Steinke notes there is no evidence to support or deny the claim that Bauer was the youngest district judge in Germany (Steinke, *Fritz Bauer*, p. 54). Schwarz, *Juden*, p. 23; Anthony, *Ins Land*, p. 123. By 1955, there were just 15,000 Jews in Germany (Trentmann, *Out of,* p. 190).
2. Wojak, *Fritz Bauer*, pp. 10–11. Bauer's thoughts are based on his writings at the time and an interview he gave describing his return. For Bauer's sense of being surrounded by murderers see: Bauer, "Mörder," *Deutsche Nachrichten*, 1947/3, p. 2. On Bauer's hope for the future during his return journey in 1948 see: Bauer, "Heute," Dec. 8, 1964, in: Foljanty, Johst (eds.), *Fritz Bauer*, vol. 2, p. 1129
3. Bauer, "Der Nürnberger," Oct. 17, 1946, in: Foljanty, Johst (eds.), *Fritz Bauer*, vol. 1, pp. 223–240; Bauer, *Die Kriegsverbrecher*, pp. 82, 168, 210; Wachsmann, *KL*, pp. 607–613. The British-run Belsen trial was the first to pass judgment on camp perpetrators. Thirty were convicted, of whom eleven were sentenced to death on November 17, 1945, a few days before the International Military Tribunal at Nuremberg convened (Wachsmann, *KL*, p. 608).

4. Fritz Bauer, Letter to Kurt Schumacher, May 23, 1946. AdsD, 2/KSAA000064, no pages; Bauer, "Die Splitterrichter," Mar. 26, 1946, in: Foljanty, Johst (eds.), *Fritz Bauer,* vol. 1, pp. 190–191; Bauer, "Die Abrechnung," *Sozialistische Tribüne,* Feb. 2, 1945, pp. 11–13; Weinke, *Die Verfolgung,* pp. 32–39.

5. Wojak, *Fritz Bauer,* p. 224; Bower, *The Pledge,* pp. 156–157, 171–176; Bauer, *Die Kriegsverbrecher,* p. 211; Bauer, "Die Splitterrichter," Mar. 26, 1946, in: Foljanty, Johst (eds.), *Fritz Bauer,* vol. 1, pp. 190–192; Bauer, "Der Todestag," May 6, 1946, in: Foljanty, Johst (eds.) *Fritz Bauer,* pp. 192–194; Bauer, "Der Nürnberger," Oct. 17, 1946, in: Foljanty, Johst (eds.), *Fritz Bauer,* vol. 1, pp. 234–235; Bauer, "Mörder," *Deutsche Nachrichten,* 1947/3, p. 2. The position of attorney general is typically political in Anglo-American judiciaries. In the U.S. and U.K., the role of attorney general is usually a political appointment, whereas in the German system, the Generalstaatsanwalt holds a civil service position.

6. Bauer took one of three train routes from Copenhagen: the Nordexpress, the Skandinavien Express, or the Scandinavia-Switzerland Express. All routes went via Flensburg; the latter allowed for intra-Germany domestic travel between Flensburg and Hamburg-Altona. International express trains like Bauer's only allowed Germans on board the third-class compartment for some routes (Reichsbahndirektion München [ed.], Reichsbahn-Kursbuch, p. 68; Wilbrink, "Epoch III," 2005, dbtrains.com, online source). The Scandinavia-Switzerland Express also ran through Hannover, but Bauer indicates he stopped in Hamburg and traveled by car from there to Hannover (Bauer, "Heute," Dec. 8, 1964, in: Foljanty, Johst [eds.], *Fritz Bauer,* vol. 2, p. 1129). Jähner, *Aftermath,* pp. 84–87. For Bauer's understanding of the devastation before his return see: Bauer, "Freunde," June 3, 1946, in: Foljanty, Johst (eds.), *Fritz Bauer,* vol. 1, pp. 197–198.

7. Jähner, *Aftermath,* pp. 195–199; Hocke, "Streifzüge," in: Schoeller (ed.), *Diese merkwürdige,* pp. 305–310.

8. "Treugelöbnis," *Schwäbische Tagwacht,* June 28, 1932, cited in: Steinke, *Fritz Bauer,* p. 58; Steinke, *Fritz Bauer,* pp. 64–67; Bauer, "Mörder," *Deutsche Nachrichten,* 1947/3, p. 2.

1

HOME

1. "Ein Sonntag," *Ludwigsburger Kreiszeitung,* Feb. 27, 1933, no pages; Alfred Tischendorf, Letter to Fritz Bauer, Mar. 23, 1960. StAS, B 8600/172, no pages; "Treugelöbnis," *Schwäbische Tagwacht,* June 28, 1932, cited in: Steinke, *Fritz Bauer,* p. 58; "Wahlkundgebungen," *Ludwigsburger Kreiszeitung,* Feb. 27, 1933, no pages. For Nazi hit list of opponents from 1932 and growing Nazi aggression see: Mielke, "Die Zeit," in: Bregenzer, Pötzel, Ruggaber (eds.), *Unser Land,* pp. 61–62; Uhlman, *The Making,* pp. 151–152. For Hitler's intentions on coming to power see: McDonough, *The Weimar,* p. 403; Fritzsche, *Hitler's,* pp. 1–15, 161. Bauer's official title was Amtsrichter; his role was equivalent to that of a magistrate or district judge (Amtsgericht Stuttgart I. Übersicht über die Verteilung der Geschäfte der Abteilungen B und C im Jahr 1932, no date. StAL, F 304 Bü 4, no pages).

2. Fritz Bauer, *Als sie,* Interview by Renate Harpprecht, Westdeutscher Rundfunk, 1967; "Treugelöbnis," *Schwäbische Tagwacht,* June 28, 1932, no pages; Staatspolizeileitstelle Stuttgart, Aberkennung der deutschen Staatsangehörigkeit des

jüdischen Emigranten Dr. Fritz Max Bauer, July 12, 1938. Akten betreffend Ausbürgerungen A–L von 1937 bis 1939. PAAA, RZ214/099722, pp. 40–42.

3. M. R. Egeskov, Report, 1940. Fritz Bauer: udl. no. 53658, no date. RA Denmark,
1409: 53651–53681, no pages. For Bauer's personality see: Helmut Mielke, Interview by Irmtrud Wojak, June 2, 1997, in: Wojak, *Fritz Bauer,* p. 108; Jürgen Baumann, cited in: Horstmann, Litzinger (eds.), *An den Grenzen,* p. 136. The
question of Bauer's homosexuality has led to some debate among his previous
biographers (Renz, "Wider die Sittenwächter," in: Borowski et al. [eds.], *Jahrbuch,*
pp. 85–93). Bauer wrote extensively about gay rights but did not directly address
his own sexuality—understandable given Nazi-era anti-gay laws that endured in
the Federal Republic until 1968. Bauer, however, did state to the Danish police in
1936 that he was homosexual after being observed through his apartment window undressing with a male sex worker (H. Folmer Larsen, Report, Apr. 18,
1936. Fritz Bauer: udl. no. 53658, no date. RA Denmark, 1409: 53651–53681, no
pages). Bauer was under no obligation to volunteer this information. Homosexuality had been fully decriminalized in Denmark in 1930 with the legislation coming into force in 1933, but it was common for homosexual men to deny being gay
(Edelberg, *Storbyen,* p. 38). Fritz Bauer, *Als sie,* Interview by Renate Harpprecht,
Westdeutscher Rundfunk, 1967.

4. "Ergebnisse," *Ludwigsburger Kreiszeitung,* Mar. 5, 1933, no pages; "Treugelöbnis,"
Schwäbische Tagwacht, June 28, 1932, cited in: Steinke, *Fritz Bauer,* p. 59;
"Wahlkundgebungen," *Ludwigsburger Kreiszeitung,* Feb. 27, 1933, no pages; Hett,
The Death, p. 7.

5. Steinke, *Fritz Bauer,* pp. 33, 39–40; Wojak, *Fritz Bauer,* p. 44; McDonough, *The
Weimar,* p. 7.

6. "Wahlkundgebungen," *Ludwigsburger Kreiszeitung,* Feb. 27, 1933, no pages.
Tischendorf describes a rally on the Ludwigsburg market square but makes no
mention of a brawl; this is at odds with local press reports, which describe a confrontation with Brownshirts on the square (Alfred Tischendorf, Letter to Fritz
Bauer, Mar. 23, 1960. StAS, B 8600/172, no pages).

7. For Bauer's court schedule see: Amtsgericht Stuttgart I. Übersicht über die Verteilung der Geschäfte der Abteilungen B und C im Jahr 1932, no date. StAL, F 304
Bü 4, no pages; Fuchs, "Auseinandersetzungen," in: Fuchs (ed.), *Stuttgart . . . Die
Machtergreifung,* p. 262; Whisnant, *Queer,* pp. 117–118, 201. The Nazi Party itself
had an ambivalent attitude toward homosexuality; the leader of the Brownshirts
was himself rumored to be gay (Whisnant, *Queer,* p. 206).

8. Sellner, "In diesem Haus," *Stuttgarter Zeitung,* Aug. 25, 2023, p. 20; Marit Tiefenthal, Interview by Jack Fairweather, Mar. 30, 2022; Steinke, *Fritz Bauer,* pp. 20–
21. For Bauer's strict upbringing see: Bauer, "Heute," Dec. 8, 1964, in: Foljanty,
Johst (eds.), *Fritz Bauer,* vol. 2, pp. 1238–1239. Bauer, "Die 'ungesühnte,'" 1960, in:
Perels, Wojak (eds.), *Die Humanität,* p. 135; Trentmann, *Out of,* p. 45.

9. Baden and Württemberg granted Jews full equality before the law in 1861–1864,
legislation that was then adopted by the newly formed German empire in 1871.
Special thanks to Robert Jan van Pelt for his insights. Steinke, *Fritz Bauer,* p. 20.
Marit Tiefenthal, Interview by Jack Fairweather, Mar. 30, 2022.

10. Margot Tiefenthal, Walter Tiefenthal, Interview by Walter Fabian, July 18, 1973.
Deutsches Exilarchiv, EB 87/112, no pages; Steinke, *Fritz Bauer,* pp. 19–23; Ein-
stein, Bauer, Note on founding Jüdischer Jugendring in Stuttgart, *Gemeinde-
Zeitung für die israelitischen Gemeinden Württembergs,* Apr. 18, 1930, p. 26. Ella's

knowledge of Bauer's homosexuality is implied in a letter likely from his close friend Helmut Mielke, in which the letter writer describes his envy on learning from Ella that a young man has been visiting Bauer every night for a year (Author unknown [likely Helmut Mielke], Letter to Fritz Bauer, Oct. 31, 1937. Fritz Bauer: udl. no. 53658, no date. RA Denmark, 1409: 53651–53681, no pages). Special thanks to Ingrid Pufahl and Hedi Rosskamp for deciphering the Sütterlin. Johannes Warlo, Interview by Ronen Steinke, Oct. 9, 2012, cited in: Steinke, *Fritz Bauer*, p. 190; Benno Ostertag, Entschädigungsantrag Ella Bauer, Apr. 22, 1950. StAL, EL 350 I, BA 35321, p. 5; West, *So ist*, p. 28.

11. West, *So ist*, pp. 40–41, 58, 79, 82, 88–89; Ehrenburg, *Visum*, p. 106; Schweigard, *Stuttgart*, pp. 29, 35; Fuchs, "Arbeitslosigkeit," in: Fuchs (ed.), *Stuttgart . . . Die Machtergreifung*, p. 267; Stiefele, "Banditentum," in: Fuchs (ed.), *Stuttgart . . . Anpassung*, p. 539; Lilienthal, "Rassenhygiene," *Medizinhistorisches Journal*, 1979/1–2, p. 120. As Fuchs notes, Stuttgart's economy was more insulated from the impact of the depression (Fuchs, "Arbeitslosigkeit," in: Fuchs [ed.], *Stuttgart . . . Die Machtergreifung*, p. 267).

12. Bauer, "Scham," *Die Zeit*, Sept. 29, 1967, p. 3; Uhlman, *The Making*, pp. 151–154; Steinke, *Fritz Bauer*, p. 52. For Bauer's leniency in sentencing and membership in the Württemberg branch of the "red" Republican Association of judges see: Steinke, *Fritz Bauer*, pp. 52–53; Gerlach, "Ein jüdischer," *NS-Kurier*, June 5, 1931, p. 3; Urteil gegen Adolf Gerlach, Sept. 25, 1931. StAL, F 302 III Bü 51, p. 7; "Die Affäre," *NS-Kurier*, Sept. 26–27, 1931, p. 3; Akte des Amtsgericht Stuttgart I, Übersicht über die Verteilung der Geschäfte der Abteilung A für Zivilsachen im Jahr 1932. StAL, F 304 Bü 6, cited in: Steinke, *Fritz Bauer*, pp. 55–57. The only case of note for Bauer as a judge on the civil courts had been when his brother-in-law, Walter Tiefenthal, a rather staid businessman with whom he disagreed politically, had appeared before him to appeal a parking fine. Bauer had taken a dark pleasure in doubling the fine (Margot Tiefenthal, Walter Tiefenthal, Interview by Walter Fabian, July 18, 1973. Deutsches Exilarchiv, EB 87/112, no pages); Staatspolizeileitstelle Stuttgart, Aberkennung der deutschen Staatsangehörigkeit des jüdischen Emigranten Dr. Fritz Max Bauer, July 12, 1938. Akten betreffend Ausbürgerungen A–L von 1937 bis 1939. PAAA, RZ214/099722, pp. 40–42.

13. Helmut Mielke, Interview by Irmtrud Wojak, June 2, 1997, cited in: Wojak, *Fritz Bauer*, p. 109; West, *So ist*, p. 245; Uhlman, *The Making*, p. 156.

14. Uhlman, *The Making*, p. 157.

15. Fritzsche, *Hitler's*, p. 77; Merseburger, *Der schwierige*, pp. 61–62, 138–139. Schumacher, however, noted in November 1932: "One cannot ward off fascism if the people deprive us of the democratic basis for it" (Merseburger, *Der schwierige*, p. 140). Fritzsche, *Hitler's*, pp. 19–20. Hindenberg had, in fact, appointed Hitler chancellor on the understanding that if the Nazis won an outright majority at the upcoming election they would rewrite the constitution to create an authoritarian state (Fritzsche, *Hitler's*, pp. 6–8). Palmier, *Weimar*, p. 103; Wistrich, *Who's*, p. 177.

16. The democratic order had already been severely compromised between 1930 and 1932 when the chancellor of the time, Heinrich Brüning, began to govern by emergency measures. Wachsmann, *KL*, pp. 28–29; Hett, *The Death*, p. 6; Merseburger, *Der schwierige*, pp. 148–149; Fuchs, "Im Schweizer," in: Fuchs (ed.), *Stuttgart . . . Anpassung*, p. 410; Weinmann, "Das Oberlandesgericht," in: Stilz (ed.), *Das Oberlandesgericht*, p. 42.

17. Uhlman, *The Making*, p. 161; Merseburger, *Der schwierige*, pp. 148–149.

18. Uhlman, *The Making*, p. 163; Steinke, *Fritz Bauer*, p. 59; Abmayer, "Wir wollten," *Kontext: Wochenzeitung*, Mar. 1, 2023, online source; Merseburger, *Der schwierige*, p. 150; Ilona Ziok (dir.), *Fritz Bauer*, 2010.

19. Uhlman, *The Making*, p. 157; "Ruhiger," *Badische Presse*, Mar. 6, 1933, p. 4; Fuchs, "Zeugnisse," in: Fuchs (ed.), *Stuttgart . . . Die Machtergreifung*, p. 399. Two thousand Reichsbannermen did indeed gather in the forests outside Stuttgart on the evening of March 7, but the order for action was never given (Merseburger, *Der schwierige*, p. 150). Ilona Ziok (dir.), *Fritz Bauer*, 2010. Bauer, Letter to Margot Tiefenthal, no date. Material formerly in possession of Rolf Tiefenthal, cited in: Wojak, *Fritz Bauer*, p. 119.

20. Fuchs (ed.), "Am 6. März," in: Fuchs (ed.), *Stuttgart . . . Die Machtergreifung*, pp. 359, 364.

21. Fuchs, "Die neuen Herren," in: Fuchs (ed.), *Stuttgart . . . Die Machtergreifung*, p. 319; Müller, "Ein geräuschloser," in: Fuchs (ed.), *Stuttgart . . . Die Machtergreifung*, pp. 335, 331; Fuchs, "Die 'März-Ereignisse,'" in: Fuchs (ed.), *Stuttgart . . . Die Machtergreifung*, p. 355; Müller, "Ein geräuschloser," in: Fuchs (ed.), *Stuttgart . . . Die Machtergreifung*, p. 331; Fuchs, "Bühne," in: Fuchs (ed.), *Stuttgart . . . Die Machtergreifung*, p. 369; Müller, "Ein geräuschloser," in: Fuchs (ed.), *Stuttgart ... . Die Machtergreifung*, p. 338.

22. Fuchs, "Zeugnisse," in: Fuchs (ed.), *Stuttgart . . . Die Machtergreifung*, pp. 399–400, 402; Fritzsche, *Hitler's*, p. 118; Wachsmann, *KL*, p. 69; Teschke, *Hitler's*, p. 222. Concentration camps were also used by German authorities to suppress the indigenous population during the brutal colonial war in southwest Africa in 1904–1908 (Wachsmann, *KL*, pp. 7–8).

23. Mielke, "Die Zeit," in: Bregenzer, Pötzel, Ruggaber (eds.), *Unser Land*, p. 64; Röder, "Die politische," in: Krohn et al. (eds.), *Handbuch*, pp. 16–17, cited in: Wojak, *Fritz Bauer*, p. 121.

24. "Das Wetter," *Stuttgarter Neues Tagblatt*, Mar. 22, 1933, p. 3; "Das Wetter," *Stuttgarter Neues Tagblatt*, Mar. 23, 1933, p. 3; Weinmann, "Das Oberlandesgericht," in: Stilz (ed.), *Das Oberlandesgerichts*, p. 44; Foth, "Günther Wieland," in: Wieland, *Naziverbrechen*, p. 411; "Gefängnis," 2018. Hotel Silber, online source; Erwin Holzwarth, Testimony, Nov. 8, 1998. IWitness USC Shoah Foundation, online source; Fuchs, "Die neuen Herren," in: Fuchs (ed.), *Stuttgart . . . Die Machtergreifung*, p. 318; Erwin Holzwarth, Testimony, Nov. 8, 1998. IWitness USC Shoah Foundation, online source.

25. Kienle, *Das Konzentrationslager*, pp. 29, 32, cited in: Steinke, *Fritz Bauer*, p. 50; Wachsmann, *KL*, p. 69; Ewrin Holzwarth, Testimony, Nov. 8, 1998. IWitness USC Shoah Foundation, online source; Fuchs, "Die neuen Gesetze," in: Fuchs (ed.), *Stuttgart . . . Die Machtergreifung*, p. 320; Wachsmann, *KL*, p. 122; Fritzsche, *Hitler's*, pp. 156–157; Wachsmann, *KL*, p. 36.

26. Kienle, *Das Konzentrationslager*, p. 59; Fritz Bauer, Letter to Ella Bauer, summer 1938, cited in: Steinke, *Fritz Bauer*, p. 17; Heinz Meyer-Velde, Gisela Meyer-Velde, Interview by Ronen Steinke, Nov. 22, 2012, cited in: Steinke, *Fritz Bauer*, p. 18; Fuchs, "Zeugnisse," in: Fuchs (ed.), *Stuttgart . . . Die Machtergreifung*, p. 402; Kienle, *Das Konzentrationslager*, p. 62.

27. Taylor, "Eyewitness," *Chicago Tribune*, Apr. 7, 1933, p. 1; Steinthal, "Politiken's," *Politiken*, Apr. 23, 1933, p. 1; Marley, Roosevelt, World Committee for the Victims

of German Fascism, *The Brown Book*, p. 297; Kienle, *Das Konzentrationslager*, pp. 63–64, 62; Merseburger, *Der schwierige*, p. 169.

28. Kienle, *Das Konzentrationslager*, pp. 30, 64, 73, 81, 82; [Plank], Bericht des Genossen E. P., no date. A-DZOK, Rep. 2, 7, cited in: Steinke, *Fritz Bauer*, p. 65; Fuchs, "Zeugnisse," in: Fuchs (ed.), *Stuttgart... Die Machtergreifung*, p. 405; Merseburger, *Schumacher*, p. 170; Max Hartinger, Letter to Fritz Bauer, Apr. 20, 1965. VVN-BdA Baden-Württemberg Stuttgart, LKZ 12, no pages; Kienle, *Das Konzentrationslager*, pp. 63–64; Marley, Roosevelt, World Committee for the Victims of German Fascism, *The Brown Book*, p. 297.

29. Acker was not able to remember Bauer's name in his subsequent recollection of the interrogation, but he recalled that "a Social Democratic Jewish lawyer from Stuttgart" was among those selected for special treatment. Given that he and Bauer shared the same block, it seems likely the lawyer was Bauer (Wilfred Acker, *Kommandant*, Oct. 24, 1965. VVN-BdA, Baden-Württemberg Stuttgart, D 751, pp. 2–3). Fritz Bauer, *Als sie*, Interview by Renate Harpprecht, Westdeutscher Rundfunk, 1967; Bauer, "Im Kampf," Apr. 1955, in: Foljanty, Johst (eds.), *Fritz Bauer*, vol. 1, pp. 446–447.

30. Wilfred Acker, *Kommandant*, Oct. 24, 1965. VVN-BdA, Baden-Württemberg Stuttgart, D 751, p. 3.

31. Wilfred Acker, *Kommandant*, Oct. 24, 1965. VVN-BdA, Baden-Württemberg Stuttgart, D 751, p. 2; Kienle, *Das Konzentrationslager*, pp. 65–67, p. 74; Fuchs, "Tote," in: Fuchs (ed.), *Stuttgart... Die Machtergreifung*, p. 413; Wachsmann, *KL*, pp. 61–63; Kienle, *Das Konzentrationslager*, pp. 70–71.

32. Marley, Roosevelt, World Committee for the Victims of German Fascism, *The Brown Book*, p. 302; Garvey, *The Byline*, p. 46; Wachsmann, *KL*, pp. 71–72.

33. Taylor, "Eyewitness," *Chicago Tribune*, Apr. 7, 1933, p. 12.

34. Ibid. Elsewhere, Bauer claims he was president of the Stuttgart Reichsbanner (Fritz Bauer, *Als sie*, Interview by Renate Harpprecht, Westdeutscher Rundfunk, 1967).

35. Ibid.

36. Ibid.

37. Ibid.

38. Ibid.

39. Ibid.

40. Wachsmann, *KL*, p. 72; Taylor, "Eyewitness," *Chicago Tribune*, Apr. 7, 1933, pp. 1, 12.

41. For description of how news of the outside world reached the camp see: Erwin Holzwarth, Testimony, Nov. 8, 1998. IWitness USC Shoah Foundation, online source. Fuchs, *Zeugnisse*, in: Fuchs (ed.), *Stuttgart... Die Machtergreifung*, pp. 413, 405, 408; Steinke, *Fritz Bauer*, p. 65; Wojak, *Fritz Bauer*, p. 114; Fuchs (ed.), *Stuttgart... Die Machtergreifung*, p. 410; Hans Ruess, Heuberg und Kuhberg. Die Nazihöllen in Württemberg, no date. VVN-BdA Baden-Württemberg, D 21, p. 1; Kienle, *Das Konzentrationslager*, pp. 83–84, 80–81.

42. Bauer, "Im Kampf," Apr. 1955, in: Foljanty, Johst (eds.), *Fritz Bauer*, vol. 1, p. 448; Heinz Meyer-Velde, Gisela Meyer-Velde, Interview by Ronen Steinke, Nov. 22, 2012, cited in: Steinke, *Fritz Bauer*, p. 66.

43. Bauer, "Im Kampf," Apr. 1955, in: Foljanty, Johst (eds.), *Fritz Bauer*, vol. 1, p. 448.

44. Ibid.

45. Fritz Bauer, *Als sie*, Interview by Renate Harpprecht, Westdeutscher Rundfunk, 1967.

46. Steinke, *Fritz Bauer*, p. 64.

47. Ibid.

48. Fritz Bauer, *Als sie*, Interview by Renate Harpprecht, Westdeutscher Rundfunk, 1967.

49. Heinz Meyer-Velde, Gisela Meyer-Velde, Interview by Ronen Steinke, Nov. 22, 2012, cited in: Steinke, *Fritz Bauer*, p. 66. For description of how news of the outside world reached the camp see: Erwin Holzwarth, Testimony, Nov. 8, 1998. IWitness USC Shoah Foundation, online source. Fritz Bauer, Judiciary personnel file, no date. FBInst, Nachlass Fritz Bauer 08/03, p. 41, cited in: Steinke, *Fritz Bauer*, p. 68; Staatspolizeileitstelle Stuttgart, Aberkennung der deutschen Staatsangehörigkeit des jüdischen Emigranten Dr. Fritz Max Bauer, July 12, 1938. Akten betreffend Ausbürgerungen A–L von 1937 bis 1939. PAAA, RZ214/099722, p. 40; Kienle, *Das Konzentrationslager*, pp. 90–91.

50. Fuchs, "Tote," in: Fuchs (ed.), *Stuttgart . . . Die Machtergreifung*, p. 414.

51. Kienle, *Das Konzentrationslager*, p. 91.

52. Fuchs, "Tote," in: Fuchs (ed.), *Stuttgart . . . Die Machtergreifung*, p. 414; Kienle, *Das Konzentrationslager*, p. 91.

53. Kienle, *Das Konzentrationslager*, p. 38; Renz, "Geschichtsklitterung," 2015, FBInst, pp. 3–4; Karl Ruggaber, Fritz Hauer [*sic*], Erich Rossmann, Ernst Reichle, Johann Weisser, Eugen Wilme, Gustav Illguth, Heinrich Fackler, Letter to Reich Governor Wilhelm Murr, Oct. 22, 1933. AdsD, Emigration, SoPaDe, folder 114, no pages; Rossmann, *Ein Leben*, p. 85; Lechner, *Das KZ*, p. 49; Rossmann, *Ein Leben*, p. 86. Knauer has previously been identified in other accounts as Gnaier and Gneidig; neither name appears in the telephone book of the time (Lechner, *Das KZ Oberer Kuhberg*, p. 63; Rossmann, *Ein Leben*, p. 85). In Swabian dialect, /gn/ at the start of a word is pronounced /kn/, and /ei/ is pronounced /oi/, so Gneier becomes Knäuer. Gotthilf Knäuer is recorded in a 1949 address book, with the rank of Hauptwachtmeister, two levels above Oberwachtmeister, which was Knäuer's rank in 1933. (Gotthilf Knäuer, Personenakten, Polizeidirektion Ulm, LABW. HStAS, E 151/21 Bü 540, no pages). Many thanks to Ingrid Pufahl for the sleuthing. Although the Nazi leadership had an ulterior motive for transferring Bauer to Ulm, Knäuer appears to have been a genuinely kindly man who resisted the brutalization that many of his colleagues went through under Nazi rule. He "couldn't understand how a judge could be put in prison simply because of his affiliation with the Social Democrats and his leadership of the Reichsbanner Schwarz-Rot-Gold," according to Bauer (Fritz Bauer, Interview by Leni Yahil, Mar. 9, 1962. YVA, 0–27/13–5, p. 1). Knäuer was reprimanded in 1943 for treating prisoners too humanely (Redies, "Karl Ruggaber," Cannstatter Stolperstein-Initiative, 2021, online source).

54. Lechner, *Das KZ*, p. 44; Fritz Bauer, *Als sie*, Interview by Renate Harpprecht, Westdeutscher Rundfunk, 1967; Bauer, "Im Kampf," Apr. 1955, in: Foljanty, Johst (eds.), *Fritz Bauer*, vol. 2, p. 448; Redies, "Karl Ruggaber," Cannstatter Stolperstein-Initiative, online source; Rossmann, *Ein Leben*, p. 86; Steinke, *Fritz Bauer*, p. 67. A loyalty pledge titled "Treuebekenntnis einstiger Sozialdemokraten" was published on November 13, 1933 in the *Ulmer Tagblatt* (Kienle, *Das Konzentrationslager*, p. 115). The published declaration misspells Bauer's name as "Hauer." As Steinke points out, in old German typeface, "B" and "H" are often mixed up, and

in any case, there are no records of the existence of a prominent figure named Fritz Hauer. Bauer's release around the time of the publication of this "pledge" further indicates that his name was simply misprinted (Steinke, *Fritz Bauer*, p. 67 note 21). Karl Ruggaber, Fritz Hauer [*sic*], Erich Rossmann, Ernst Reichle, Johann Weisser, Eugen Wilme, Gustav Illguth, Heinrich Fackler, Letter to Reich Governor Wilhelm Murr, Oct. 22, 1933. AdsD, Emigration, SoPaDe, folder 114, no pages. Some Social Democratic Party members were critical of Bauer for his oath. "I am not self-righteous enough to throw stones at the comrades who made this declaration," wrote Erwin Schoettle, a party activist who had fled to Switzerland. "They will, even if they have received the reward for their loyalty, the freedom from the Third Reich, have to bear heavily enough on the contempt of our friends (Erwin Schoettle, Letter to Board of German Social Democratic Party in Prague, Nov. 17, 1933. AdsD, Emigration, SoPaDe, folder 114, p. 2). For further details on the debate surrounding Bauer's pledge see: Renz, "Geschichtsklitterung," 2015 FBInst, pp. 6–21.

55. Fritz Bauer, Interview by Leni Yahil, Mar. 9, 1962. YVA, 0–27/13–5, p. 1; Staatspolizeileitstelle Stuttgart. Aberkennung der deutschen Staatsangehörigkeit des jüdischen Emigranten Dr. Fritz Max Bauer, July 12, 1938. Akten betreffend Ausbürgerungen A–L von 1937 bis 1939. PAAA, RZ214/099722, p. 41. For head shaving on dismissal see: [Plank], Bericht des Genossen E. P., no date. A-DZOK, Rep. 2, 76, no pages. Kienle, *Das Konzentrationslager*, p. 115.

56. Mellenthin, "Chronologie," no date. Chronologie des Holocaust, online source; Kurz, "Mord," no date. Gegen das Vergessen: Stolpersteine für Stuttgart, online source. The Württemberg political police had, in fact, issued a statewide edict against boycotting Jewish businesses in September 1933, but local Nazi groups continued to take action throughout the year (Stiefele, "Banditentum," in: Fuchs (ed.), *Stuttgart . . . Anpassung*, pp. 538–540). Weinmann, "Das Oberlandesgericht," in: Stilz (ed.), *Das Oberlandesgerichts*, p. 43; Margot Tiefenthal, Walter Tiefenthal, Interview by Walter Fabian, July 18, 1973. Deutsches Exilarchiv, EB 87/112, no pages; Marit Tiefenthal, Interview by Jack Fairweather, June 16, 2022; Reichsgesetzblatt, part I, Reichsministerium des Innern, 1933, pp. 175, 188, cited in: Wojak, *Fritz Bauer*, pp. 117–118; Marit Tiefenthal, Interview by Jack Fairweather, Mar. 30, 2022.

57. Margot Tiefenthal, Walter Tiefenthal, Interview by Walter Fabian, July 18, 1973. Deutsches Exilarchiv, EB 87/112, no pages; Bauer, "Die Rückkehr," 1960, in: Foljanty, Johst (eds.), *Fritz Bauer*, vol. 1, p. 658; Margot Tiefenthal, Walter Tiefenthal, Interview by Walter Fabian, July 18, 1973. Deutsches Exilarchiv, EB 87/112, no pages.

58. "Der Goldene," *NS-Kurier*, Dec. 18, 1933, p. 8; Margot Tiefenthal, Walter Tiefenthal, Interview by Walter Fabian, July 18, 1973. Deutsches Exilarchiv, EB 87/112, no pages; Steinke, *Fritz Bauer*, p. 23; Margot Tiefenthal, Walter Tiefenthal, Interview by Walter Fabian, July 18, 1973. Deutsches Exilarchiv, EB 87/112, no pages. Rolf Tiefenthal was born on April 2, 1929; Peter Tiefenthal on August 26, 1933 (H. Wiene, Report, Sept. 25, 1936. Walter Tiefenthal: udl. no. 40604, no date. RA Denmark, 1153: 40552-40609, no pages).

59. Werner Fleischhauer, Spruchkammerakte, no date. HStAS, Nachlass Werner Fleischhauer (1903–1997), Q 2/21 BÜ 105, no pages. For gay cruising spots in early 1930s Stuttgart see: Munier, *Lebenswelten*, pp. 129–130. Whisnant, *Queer*, pp. 209, 210.

60. Longerich, *Himmler*, loc. 3171–3348; Burkhardt, "Hitler = Krieg," in: Fuchs (ed.), *Stuttgart . . . Anpassung*, p. 382. For a description by Bauer of his underground work see: Fritz Bauer (alias Frandsen), Letter to unknown recipient (likely Helmut Mielke), Nov. 11, 1936 Fritz Bauer: udl. no. 53638. RA Danmark, 1409: 53651–53681, no pages.

61. Burkhardt, "Hitler = Krieg," in: Fuchs (ed.), *Stuttgart . . . Anpassung*, p. 382.

62. Nachtmann, *Intensive*, in: Fuchs (ed.), *Stuttgart . . . Anpassung*, pp. 19–20; Hogenkamp, *Die Württembergische*, p. 357; Bauz, Brüggemann, Maier (eds.), *Die Geheime*, p. 172; Burkhardt, "Hitler = Krieg," in: Fuchs (ed.), *Stuttgart . . . Anpassung*, p. 383.

63. Benz, "Die jüdische," in: Krohn et al. (eds.), *Handbuch*, p. 5, cited in: Wojak, *Fritz Bauer*, p. 119; Barkai, *Jüdisches*, in: Meyer, Brenner (eds.), *Deutschjüdische*, vol. 4, p. 227, cited in: Wojak, *Fritz Bauer*, p. 119; Dähnhardt, Nielsen, "Einleitung," in: Dähnhardt, Nielsen (eds.), *Exil*, p. 30, cited in: Wojak, *Fritz Bauer*, p. 124; Lorenz, "Dänemark," in: Krohn et al. (eds.), *Handbuch*, p. 204, cited in: Wojak, *Fritz Bauer*, p. 124. Walter and Margot left Stuttgart in March 1934 (H. Wiene, Report, Sept. 24, 1936. Walter Tiefenthal: udl. no. 40604, no date, RA Denmark, 1153: 40552-40609, p. 3). Tiefenthal, *Doppelter*, in: Backhaus, Boll, Gross (eds.), *Fritz Bauer*, p. 75; H. Folmer Larsen, Report, Oct. 21, 1936. Fritz Bauer: Udl. no. 53658, no date. RA Denmark, 1409: 53651–53681, no pages. The likely route Bauer took from Stuttgart to Copenhagen went via Berlin and the ferry service at Warnemünde (Amtliches Kursbuch für das Reich. 15. Mai–5. Oktober 1935, no pages; Grieben Reiseführe, *Kopenhagen*, p. 12; Bruun-Petersen, Poulsen, *Internationale*, pp. 23, 25, 32; Danske Statsbaner. Danmarks Jernbaner: Køreplan. 15. Maj–30. September 1935, no pages). Special thanks to Halfdan Höner at the Danish Railway Museum in Odense. H. Folmer Larsen, Report, Apr. 18, 1936. Fritz Bauer: udl. no. 53658, no date, RA Denmark, 1409: 53651–53681; Kristensen, *Havoc*, pp. 44, 52, 80, 121, 313; "Gennem byen," *Aftenbladet (København)*, June 1, 1935, p. 2; "Pingvinerne," *Politiken*, June 2, 1935, p. 10; "Gøg," *Aftenbladet (København)*, June 1, 1935, p. 20; Klitgaard, *Der sidder*, pp. 17–18.

64. Wojak, *Fritz Bauer*, p. 124; Kolk, *Mit dem Symbol*, pp. 87–88; Buchwitz, *50 Jahre*, p. 157; Kjeldbæk, "Café," in: Lauridsen (ed.), *Over stregen*, p. 164; Bak et al., *Turen*, p. 31; H. Folmer Larsen, Report, July 5, 1936. Fritz Bauer: udl. no. 53658, no date. RA Denmark, 1409: 53651–53681, no pages; Wojak, *Fritz Bauer*, p. 124; Kolk, *Mit dem Symbol*, pp. 82–83; Hammer, *Musste*, p. 1; Bauer, "Rezept,"1968, in: Foljanty, Johst (eds.), *Fritz Bauer*, vol. 2, p. 1679; Kolk, *Mit dem Symbol*, pp. 90–91, 94; Pedersen, "Matteotti-Komiteen," *Årbog for arbejderbevægelsens historie*, 1990/20, pp. 305–319. In April 1937, the German immigrant community numbered 1,512 people, of whom 825 were identified as Jewish (Wojak, *Fritz Bauer*, p. 124). Buchwitz, *50 Jahre*, p. 155. For Danish liberalization of anti-gay laws see: Boll, "Als politischer," in: Backhaus, Boll, Gross (eds.), *Fritz Bauer*, pp. 58–59. Sex between men over eighteen years of age was legal. Only in cases of an authority relationship (e.g., teacher-student) did the age limit go up to twenty-one ("Forbrydelser mod Kønssædeligheden, §225," in: Krabbe, *Borgelig Straffelov af 15. April 1930*).

65. H. Folmer Larsen, Report, Apr. 18, 1936, Fritz Bauer: udl. no. 53658, no date. RA Denmark, 1409: 53651–53681, no pages; Wojak, *Fritz Bauer*, pp. 118–119; Stiefele, "Banditentum," in: Fuchs (ed.), *Stuttgart . . . Anpassung*, pp. 540–541. The

Nuremberg Race Laws of 1935 revoked the so-called *Frontkämpferprivileg*—frontline fighters' privilege—for state employees. Lommatzsch, *Hans Globke,* pp. 67–69.

66. Steinke, *Fritz Bauer,* p. 21; Wojak, *Fritz Bauer,* pp. 117–118. Bauer was also pulled in for questioning in December 1935 after a letter to a friend was intercepted by the police (H. Folmer Larsen, Report, Apr. 18, 1936. Fritz Bauer: udl. no. 53658, no date. RA Denmark, 1409: 53651–53681, no pages). Fritz Bauer, Letter to Max Horkheimer, Sept. 21, 1937. Universitätsbibliothek Frankfurt am Main, Nachlass Max Horkheimer, Na 1, 4—Korrespondenzen 1937–1939, p. 230; Fulbrook, *Reckonings,* pp. 30–31.

67. Bauer visited Margot and Walter Tiefenthal over Christmas 1935 (H. Folmer Larsen, Report, Apr. 18, 1936. Fritz Bauer: udl. no. 53658, no date. RA Denmark, 1409: 53651–53681, no pages). "Søndag," *Politiken,* Mar. 15, 1936, p. 1; Fritz Bauer, Interview by Leni Yahil, Mar. 9, 1962. YVA, 0–27/13–5, p. 1; H. Folmer Larsen, Report, Apr. 18, 1936. Fritz Bauer: udl. no. 53658, no date. RA Denmark, 1409: 53651–53681, no pages; Pedersen, "Matteotti-Komiteen," *Årbog for arbejderbevægelsens historie,* 1990/20, pp. 305–319; Wojak, *Fritz Bauer,* pp. 124–127.

68. H. Folmer Larsen, Report, Oct. 21, 1936. Fritz Bauer: udl. no. 53658, no date. RA Denmark, 1409: 53651–53681, no pages.

69. H. Folmer Larsen, Report, Apr. 18, 1936. Fritz Bauer: udl. no. 53658, no date. RA Denmark, 1409: 53651–53681, no pages; H. Folmer Larsen, Report, July 5, 1936. Fritz Bauer: udl. no. 53658, no date. RA Denmark, 1409: 53651–53681, no pages; "Lunefuld," *Aftenbladet (København),* Apr. 16, 1936, p. 2; Klitgaard, *Der sidder,* pp. 17–18; Peter Edelberg, Email to Jack Fairweather, Oct. 19 and 22, 2020. Special thanks to Peter Edelberg for helping reveal Bauer's gay experience in 1930s Copenhagen.

70. H. Folmer Larsen, Report, Apr. 18, 1936. Fritz Bauer: udl. no. 53658, no date. RA Denmark, 1409: 53651–53681, no pages; H. Folmer Larsen, Report, Apr. 18, 1936. Fritz Bauer: udl. no. 53651, no date. RA Denmark, 1409: 53651–53681, no pages; H. Folmer Larsen, Report, July 5, 1936. Fritz Bauer: udl. no. 53658, no date. RA Denmark, 1409: 53651 53681, no pages; Christensen, "Likvideringen," no date, Lokalhistorie fra Nordvestfyn, online source.

71. H. Folmer Larsen, Report, Apr. 18, 1936. Fritz Bauer: udl. no. 53651, no date. RA Denmark, 1409: 53651–53681, no pages; H. Folmer Larsen, Report, Apr. 18, 1936. Fritz Bauer: udl. no. 53658, no date. RA Denmark, 1409: 53651–53681, no pages; Peter Edelberg, Email to Jack Fairweather, Oct. 19, 2020.

72. H. Folmer Larsen, Report, Apr. 18, 1936. Fritz Bauer: udl. no. 53651, no date. RA Denmark, 1409: 53651–53681, no pages; H. Folmer Larsen, Report, Apr. 18, 1936. Fritz Bauer: udl. no. 53658, no date. RA Denmark, 1409: 53651–53681, no pages; Kristensen, *Havoc,* p. 133.

73. H. Folmer Larsen, Report, Apr. 18, 1936. Fritz Bauer: udl. no. 53651, no date. RA Denmark, 1409: 53651–53681, no pages; H. Folmer Larsen, Report, Apr. 18, 1936. Fritz Bauer: udl. no. 53658, no date. RA Denmark, 1409: 53651–53681, no pages.

2

FLIGHT

1. For a discussion of Denmark's illiberal tendencies in the 1930s see: Andersen, *Danmark,* pp. 165–203. Bauer's experience of being treated hostilely as an immi-

grant is captured in the Danish police reports. He was initially trailed after a tip-off from a shopkeeper (H. Folmer Larsen, Report, Apr. 18, 1936. Fritz Bauer: udl. no. 53658, no date. RA Denmark, 1409: 53651–53681, no pages). Bauer admitted "that he has had sexual relations—homosexuality—with a younger Danish person, whose address he does not know and whose name he does not remember at this moment" (H. Folmer Larsen, Report, Apr. 18, 1936. Fritz Bauer: udl. no. 53658, no date. RA Denmark, 1409: 53651–53681, no pages). For Walter Tiefenthal's visit to the police see: H. Folmer Larsen, Report, Oct. 21, 1936. Fritz Bauer: udl. no. 53658, no date. RA Denmark, 1409: 53651–53681, no pages. The Matteotti Committee was also informed of Bauer's homosexuality, leading to Bauer being denied entry to Sweden for work (Fritz Bauer, Visa application to Sweden, 1938. Material in possession of Helmut Müssener). One of the police officers involved in the surveillance of Bauer, Max Pelving, was exposed in 1939 to be a Gestapo agent who passed on details of German emigrants to the SS office in Flensburg. There is no evidence that Bauer's record was passed on by Pelving, who interrogated Bauer on various occasions (Vilhjáæmsson, *Medaljens*, pp. 286–288; Kirchhoff, Rünitz, *Udsendt*, pp. 59–60; Lund, "Transnational," *DBP Working Papers in Business and Politics*, 2016/91, pp. 1–24). Bauer met with Richard Schmid in Copenhagen in 1936 (Schmid, "Nachruf," *Kritische Justiz*, 1968/1, pp. 60–61; Sepp Laufer, Letter to Fritz Bauer [alias Erik Kaj Olsen], July 23, 1937. Fritz Bauer: udl. no. 53658, no date. RA Denmark, 1409: 53651–53681, no pages). Erik Kaj Olsen, Bauer's live-in partner, is described in the police report as "a pronounced heterosexual, weak-willed, and as a person who likes to spend his money on liquor" whom they suspect Bauer has slept with (H. Folmer Larsen, Report, Oct. 21, 1936. Fritz Bauer: udl. no. 53658, no date. RA Denmark, 1409: 53651–53681, no pages; M. R. Egeskov, Report, Feb. 14, 1938. Fritz Bauer: udl. no. 53658, no date. RA Denmark, 1409: 53651–53681, no pages; Author unknown, Letter to Fritz Bauer, Oct. 31, 1937. Fritz Bauer: udl. no. 53658, no date. RA Denmark, 1409: 53651–53681, no pages). As a sign of Bauer's closeness to Olsen, his friend Helmut Mielke began writing to Bauer, but using Olsen's name as a cover (see: Helmut Mielke, Letter to Fritz Bauer [alias Erik Kaj Olsen], July 23, 1937. Fritz Bauer: udl. no. 53658, no date. RA Denmark, 1409: 53651–53681, no pages).

2. Bauer, "Glückliche," Dec. 24, 1936, in: Backhaus, Boll, Gross (eds.), *Fritz Bauer*, p. 108.

3. Julius Bauer, Erhebungsbogen. Erhebungen über die jüdischen Einzelschicksale in alphabetischer Folge der Wohnorte: Stuttgart A–Bi. HStAS, EA 99/001 Bü 163, no pages; Wojak, *Fritz Bauer*, p. 135; Müller, "Der Branddirektor," in: Fuchs (ed.), *Stuttgart . . . Anpassung,* p. 490; Kurz, "Mord," no date. Gegen das Vergessen: Stolpersteine für Stuttgart, online source; Landesbezirksstelle für die Wiedergutmachung, Stuttgart, Note, Entschädigungssache Bauer, Ludwig, Apr. 2, 1952. StAL, EL 350 ES 5229, p. 46.

4. Fritz Bauer, Letter to Ella Bauer, no date. Material in possession of Marit Tiefenthal; Steinke, *Fritz Bauer,* p. 18; Fritz Bauer, Letter to Ella Bauer, summer 1938. Rolf Tiefenthal's personal archive, cited in: Steinke, *Fritz Bauer,* p. 15; Wojak, *Fritz Bauer,* p. 32.

5. For tightening Danish restrictions see: Lund, "Transnational," *DBP Working Papers in Business and Politics,* 2016/91, pp. 1–24; Wojak, *Fritz Bauer,* pp. 134–135; Fritz Bauer, Walter Tiefenthal, Letter to The Ministry of Justice, Jan. 11, 1939.

Ella and Ludwig Bauer: udl. no. 65430. RA Denmark, 1700: 65424–65442, no pages; Staatspolizeileitstelle Stuttgart. Aberkennung der deutschen Staatsange-hörigkeit des jüdischen Emigranten Dr. Fritz Max Bauer, led. Kaufmann, July 12, 1938. Akten betreffend Ausbürgerungen A–L von 1937 bis 1939. PAAA, RZ214/099722, p. 42. For Bauer considering assimilation issues see: Bauer, "Juden," Sept. 22, 1938, in: Foljanty, Johst (eds.), *Fritz Bauer*, vol. 1, pp. 86–89.

6. Samuel Honaker, Description of Anti-Semitic Persecution and Kristallnacht and Its Aftereffects in the Stuttgart Region, Nov. 12 and 15, 1938, in: Breitman (ed.), *German*, vol. 7, document 6, online source; Müller, "Der Branddirektor," in: Fuchs (ed.), *Stuttgart . . . Anpassung*, pp. 496–497; Nachtmann, "Wir haben," in: Fuchs (ed.), *Stuttgart . . . Anpassung*, p. 55; Walk et al. (eds.), *"Stuttgart." Encyclo-paedia*, vol. 2, online source; H. Wiene, Report, Nov. 23, 1938. Ella and Ludwig Bauer: udl. no. 65430, Nov. 23, 1938–Jan. 27, 1939. RA Denmark, 1700: 65424–65442, no pages; Fritz Bauer, Walter Tiefenthal, Letter to The Ministry of Justice, Jan. 11, 1939. Ella and Ludwig Bauer: udl. no. 65430. RA Denmark, 1700: 65424–65442, no pages; Wojak, *Fritz Bauer*, p. 135. Arthur died a few weeks later in Dachau (Klehr, "Arthur Hirsch," no date. Gegen das Vergessen: Stolpersteine für Stuttgart, online source; Zapf, *Die Tübinger*, pp. 200–201). Berta Beer, Report, in: Hahn, *Jüdisches*, p. 212; Heinz Alter, Report, in: Hahn, *Jüdisches*, p. 212.

7. Müller, "Der Branddirektor," in: Fuchs (ed.), *Stuttgart . . . Anpassung*, p. 503; Fritz Bauer, Interview by Lieselotte Maas, no date. Deutsches Exilarchiv 1933–1945, EB 2010/075, p. 11; Steincke, "Emigrantspørgsmålet," *Social-Demokraten*, Apr. 27, 1937, p. 11.

8. Bauer, No title, in: Sender Freies Berlin (ed.), *Um uns die*, pp. 31–32.

9. Ibid. A few days later, on November 18, Bauer learned from Ella how close the Nazis had come to seizing Ludwig. He responded by writing to the Justice Min-istry that his father had been targeted because of his past political work (Fritz Bauer, Letter to The Ministry of Justice, Nov. 18, 1938. Ella and Ludwig Bauer: udl. no. 65430, Nov. 23, 1938–Jan. 27, 1939. RA Denmark, 1700: 65424–65442, no pages).

10. Wojak, *Fritz Bauer*, p. 137; Benno Ostertag, Entschädigungssache Bauer, Ludwig, Apr. 22, 1950. StAL, EL 350 ES 5229, pp. 1–6; Bezirkstelle der Reichsvereinigung der Juden in Deutschland für Württemberg und Reg. Bezirk Sigmarigen, Entschädigungssache Bauer, Ludwig, Apr. 22, 1950. StAL, EL 350 ES 5229, pp. 28–29; Wojak, *Fritz Bauer*, pp. 138–139.

11. Chester Wilmot, Notes on interrogation of General Franz Halder, no date. LHCMA, LH 15/15/150/2. Liddell Hart Papers, cited in: Walker, *Poland*, p. 51 note 20; Kochanski, *The Eagle*, p. 90.

12. Fairweather, *The Volunteer*, pp. 19–20.

13. Walk et al. (eds.), *"Stuttgart." Encyclopaedia*, vol. 2, online source; Benno Oster-tag, Entschädigungssache Bauer, Ludwig, Apr. 22, 1950. StAL, EL 350 ES 5229, pp. 35–37; Benno Ostertag, Entschädigungssache Bauer, Ludwig, Oct. 15, 1954. StAL, EL 350 I BA 35321, no pages; Deutsches Kursbuch, Gesamtausgabe. 1. Dezember 1939–21. Januar 1940, no pages.

14. Marit Tiefenthal, Interview by Jack Fairweather, June 16, 2022; Benno Ostertag, Entschädigungssache Bauer, Ludwig, Oct. 15, 1954. StAL, EL 350 I BA 35321, no pages; Deutsches Kursbuch, Gesamtausgabe. 1. Dezember 1939–21. Januar 1940, no pages; Bernaerts, *War*, p. 37.

15. Marit Tiefenthal, Interview by Jack Fairweather, June 16, 2022; Author unknown,

Report, Aug. 19, 1939. Fritz Bauer: udl. no. 53658, no date. RA Denmark, 1409: 53651–53681, no pages; Wojak, *Fritz Bauer*, p. 139.

16. Marit Tiefenthal, Interview by Jack Fairweather, Mar. 20, 2022; Bergstrøm, *En Borger*, p. 116; Tiefenthal, *Doppelter*, in: Backhaus, Boll, Gross (eds.), *Fritz Bauer*, pp. 75–76; Raloff, *Ein bewegtes*, pp. 108–109; Buchwitz, *50 Jahre*, p. 167; Bergstrøm, *En Borger*, pp. 116, 119. Germany attacked Denmark with approximately forty thousand Wehrmacht soldiers, facing fewer than four thousand Danish soldiers, with the majority located in Jutland close to the border, where some Danish troops resisted until the surrender (Christensen et al, *Danmark*, pp. 93–112).

17. Kirchhoff, Rünitz, *Udsendt*, p. 109; Raloff, *Ein bewegtes*, p. 109; Aktenvermerk von der Gestapo Berlin Amt VI über die deutschen sozialdemokratischen Emigranten Dänemarks, no date. BA B, R 58/2258, Fonds Reichssicherheitshauptamt, Abt. IV: Geheime Staatspolizei, pp. 130–131; Pedersen, "Matteotti-Komiteen," *Årbog for arbejderbevægelsens historie*, 1990/20, pp. 305–319.

18. Bergstrøm, *En Borger*, p. 120; Helle Wagner, Interview by Jack Fairweather and Sine Maria Vinther, Oct. 10, 2021; Fritz Bauer, Letter to Paul Wagner, June 10, 1944. Material in possession of Helle Wagner; M. R. Egeskov, Report, Dec. 7, 1940. Fritz Bauer: udl. no. 53658, no date. RA Denmark, 1409: 53651–53681, no pages.

19. For Danish police handing over lists of foreigners on April 19 see: Stevnsborg, *Politiet*, pp. 283–285, and Lund, "Transnational," *DBP Working Papers in Business and Politics*, 2016/91, pp. 1–24. Pedersen, "Matteotti-Komiteen," *Årbog for arbejderbevægelsens historie*, 1990/20, pp. 305–319; Margot Tiefenthal, Walter Tiefenthal, Interview by Walter Fabian, July 18, 1973. Deutsches Exilarchiv, EB 87/112, no pages; Steinke, *Fritz Bauer*, p. 72.

20. Bauer, "Rezept," 1968, in: Foljanty, Johst (eds.), *Fritz Bauer*, vol. 2, pp. 1679–1680. Walter Hoesterey [Hammer]: udl. no. 47756, Nov. 23, 1938. RA Denmark, 1283: 47698–47756, pp. 1–14; Aktenvermerk von der Gestapo Berlin Amt VI über die deutschen sozialdemokratischen Emigranten Dänemarks, no date. BA B, R 58/2258, Fonds Reichssicherheitshauptamt, Abt. IV: Geheime Staatspolizei, p. 130; Kolk, *Mit dem Symbol*, pp. 93–94.

21. Christensen et al., *Danmark*, pp. 93–112; Margot Tiefenthal, Walter Tiefenthal, Interview by Walter Fabian, July 18, 1973. Deutsches Exilarchiv, EB 87/11, no pages; M. R. Egeskov, Report, Sept. 1940. Fritz Bauer: udl. no. 53658, no date. RA Denmark, 1409: 53651–53681, no pages; Bauer, "Lebendige," June 9, 1963, in: Foljanty, Johst (eds.), *Fritz Bauer*, vol. 2, p. 1071.

22. Bauer, "Lebendige," June 9, 1963, in: Foljanty, Johst (eds.), *Fritz Bauer*, vol. 2, p. 1071.

23. Ibid.

24. Clausen, Larsen, *De Forrådte*, pp. 111, 38; Max Schäfer, Testimony, Aug. 30, 1940, cited in: Clausen, Larsen, *De Forrådte*, pp. 150–152. For Horserød prisoner schedule see: Kirchhoff, Rünitz, *Udsendt*, p. 168. Margot Tiefenthal, Walter Tiefenthal, Interview by Walter Fabian, July 18, 1973. Deutsches Exilarchiv, EB 87/11, no pages; Kirchhoff, Rünitz, *Udsendt*, p. 166; Rasmus Bonde Larsen, Testimony, no date, cited in: Clausen, Larsen, *De Forrådte*, pp. 183–184.

25. Horserødlejren, no. 52: Fritz Bauer. Correspondence list, Sept. 9, 1940–Nov. 20, 1940. RA Denmark, 9: 1940–1941, no pages; Horserødlejren: Besøgsprotokol (1940–1941). RA Denmark, 9: 1940–1941, pp. 1–52; Margot Tiefenthal, Walter Tiefenthal, Interview by Walter Fabian, July 18, 1973. Deutsches Exilarchiv, EB 87/11, no pages; Wojak, *Fritz Bauer*, p. 142.

26. According to Bauer, he was released with the help of National Bank president Carl V. Bramsnæs and economist Professor Jørgen Petersen, who taught at Aarhus University. As neither features on his list of sent correspondence, it seems likely Grünbaum helped contact them. Grünbaum's daughter Inger claimed that he had been instrumental in rescuing Bauer (Fritz Bauer, Interview by Leni Yahil, Mar. 9, 1962. YVA, 0–27/13–5, p. 2; Ole Grünbaum, Interview by Jack Fairweather, Oct. 13, 2021). Wojak, *Fritz Bauer,* p. 142; M. R. Egeskov, Report, Dec. 7, 1940. Fritz Bauer: udl. no. 53658, no date. RA Denmark, 1409: 53651–53681, no pages. For number of prisoners deported see: Wojak, *Fritz Bauer,* pp. 141–143.

27. Bauer, *Penge,* pp. 6, 11–16, 42, 183, 251; H. P. Götrik, Letter to Andreas Boje, June 6, 1940. RA Denmark, Socialpolitisk Forening (1933–1955), no pages. Special thanks to Morten Baarvig Thomsen for a literary study of *Penge* and uncovering Bauer's correspondence with his publisher. Marit Tiefenthal, Interview by Jack Fairweather, Mar. 20, 2022; Stargardt, *The Germans,* pp. 158–159.

28. Dwork, van Pelt, *Auschwitz,* pp. 276–306; Zimmerman, *The Polish,* pp. 129–130, p. 134; Höss, *Commandant,* pp. 184–185.

29. Special thanks to Ingrid Pufahl for researching Paula and Erich's fate. Cesarani, *Becoming,* pp. 97–101; Zapf, *Die Tübinger,* pp. 53, 74, 89ff, 199ff.

30. Cesarani, *Becoming,* pp. 114–115, 112–113. Zyklon B was also used in Majdanek.

31. Höss, *Commandant,* pp. 148–154, 215. A second farmhouse was converted for use as a gas chamber in June 1942.

32. Danielsen, *Dansk,* p. 26; Gilbert, *Auschwitz,* p. 103. For Bauer knowledge of unfolding Holocaust see: Fritz Bauer, Interview by Leni Yahil, Mar. 9, 1962. YVA, 0–27/13–5, pp. 2–4. Bauer seems to have first encountered a limited presentation of the mass shootings of Jews on the eastern front via the so-called Molotov Note of January 6, 1942 (Bauer, *Die Kriegsverbrecher,* p. 11). The note downplayed the anti-Jewish nature of Nazi policy: It spoke of the mass murder of all "Ukrainians, Russians, and Jews who gave any sign of their loyalty to Soviet rule" ([Stepanenko] Степаненко, "Что происходит," *Правда,* Nov. 29, 1941, p. 3; [Molotov] Молотов, "Нота," *Известия,* Jan. 7, 1942, p. 2, cited in: Zeltser, "The Subject," Yad Vashem, online source). For the state of knowledge of the Holocaust in Denmark pre-October 1943 see: Danielsen, *Dansk,* pp. 24–36; Fritz Bauer, Interview by Leni Yahil, Mar. 9, 1962. YVA, 0–27/13–5, pp. 2–4. For Danish resistance see: Christensen et al., *Danmark,* pp. 496–508. Margot Tiefenthal, Walter Tiefenthal, Interview by Walter Fabian, July 18, 1973. Deutsches Exilarchiv, EB 87/112, no pages.

33. Herbert, *Best,* pp. 366–373; Marcus Melchior, Interview by Judith Goldstein, June 24, 1996. USHMM, 1996.A.0284, RG 50.030.0364, no pages; Wojak, *Fritz Bauer,* p. 149. Melchior was himself tipped off via a German official at the legation named Georg Duckwitz; Hedtoft, "Introduktion," in: Bertelsen, *Oktober,* pp. 7–9; Wojak, *Fritz Bauer,* p. 149.

34. Wojak, *Fritz Bauer,* p. 151.

35. Fritz Bauer, Interview by Lieselotte Maas, no date. Deutsches Exilarchiv 1933–1945, EB 2010/075, p. 4. Ella had surgery for breast cancer in August 1943 (Patientjournaler 2110. Sundby Hospital. Kirurgisk Afdelings Arkiv, 1943. KSA, 262271, no pages). Special thanks to Morten Baarvig Thomsen for tracking down Ella's hospital files. Ella's doctor may have been Hjalmar Trier (Rolf Tiefenthal

mentions a Dr. Trie), who regularly assisted the Danish underground and could have suggested the family stay at Skodsborg. Special thanks to Sine Maria Vinther for late-night inspiration regarding Trier's connection. Ulla Johansen, Interview by Sine Maria Vinther, Sept. 30, 2020; Tiefenthal, "Doppelter," in: Backhaus, Boll, Gross (eds.), *Fritz Bauer*, p. 78.

36. Bak, *Nothing*, pp. 17–18. In the days that followed, the number of Jews arrested rose to 481 (Wojak, *Fritz Bauer*, p. 149). Tiefenthal, *Doppelter*, in: Backhaus, Boll, Gross (eds.), *Fritz Bauer*, p. 79; Bak, *Nothing*, p. 38.

37. Ulla Johansen, Interview by Sine Maria Vinther, Sept. 30, 2020; Margot Tiefenthal, Walter Tiefenthal, Interview by Walter Fabian, July 18, 1973. Deutsches Exilarchiv, EB 87/112, no pages; Tiefenthal, "Doppelter," in: Backhaus, Boll, Gross (eds.), *Fritz Bauer*, pp. 75–81.

38. Tiefenthal, "Doppelter," in: Backhaus, Boll, Gross (eds.), *Fritz Bauer*, pp. 78–79; Ulla Johansen, Interview by Sine Maria Vinther, Sept. 30, 2020; Ulla Johansen, Interview by Bo Bræstrup, Nov. 2, 2020.

39. Fritz Bauer, Interview by Leni Yahil, Mar. 9, 1962. YVA, 0–27/13–5, p. 3; Ulla Johansen, Interview by Sine Maria Vinther, Sept. 30, 2020; Ulla Johansen, Interview by Bo Bræstrup, Nov. 2, 2020. The average cost of a crossing was one thousand kroner, but some fishermen charged up to fifty thousand (Bak, *Nothing*, p. 37).

40. Ulla Johansen, Interview by Sine Maria Vinther, Sept. 30, 2020; Tiefenthal, "Doppelter," in: Backhaus, Boll, Gross (eds.), *Fritz Bauer*, p. 79. Marit Tiefenthal, Interview by Jack Fairweather and Sine Maria Vinther, Oct. 11, 2020; Hansen family, Interview by Jack Fairweather and Sine Maria Vinther, Oct. 13, 2021; Ulla Johansen, Interview by Sine Maria Vinther, Nov. 6, 2020. Special thanks to Bo Bræstrup for uncovering Bauer's escape route and providing invaluable advice throughout the research. Thanks also to Michael Kaastrup for welcoming Sine and me to Fjorvænget 6.

41. Fritz Bauer, Interview by Lieselotte Maas, no date. Deutsches Exilarchiv 1933–1945, EB 2010/075, p. 4.

42. Observation from site visit to Rørvig, Oct. 13, 2021.

43. Leif Møller, Interview by Jack Fairweather and Sine Maria Vinther, Mar. 25, 2022; Tiefenthal, "Doppelter," in: Backhaus, Boll, Gross (eds.), *Fritz Bauer*, p. 79; Annie Danielsen, Email to Bo Bræstrup, Nov. 20, 2020; Leif Møller, Interview by Jack Fairweather and Sine Maria Vinther, Mar. 25, 2022.

44. Fritz Bauer, Interview by Lieselotte Maas, no date. German Exile Archive 1933–1945, EB 2010/075, pp. 4–5; Tiefenthal, "Doppelter," in: Backhaus, Boll, Gross (eds.), *Fritz Bauer*, p. 79; Annie Danielsen, Email to Sine Maria Vinther, Nov. 20, 2020; Leif Møller, Interview by Jack Fairweather and Sine Maria Vinther, Nov. 5, 2021.

3

MISSION

1. Tiefenthal, "Doppelter," in: Backhaus, Boll, Gross (eds.), *Fritz Bauer*, p. 81.

2. Bruno Johansson, Testimony, no date. Material in possession of Lennart Rasmusson. Many thanks to Lennart Rasmusson for sharing insights on Mölle and putting me in touch with Bruno Johansson's son. Fritz Bauer, Letter to Kurt Heinig, Oct. 12, 1943. ARAB, Heinigs församling, vol. 8, no pages.

3. Wojak, *Fritz Bauer,* p. 159; Fritz Bauer, Letter to Kurt Heinig, Oct. 12, 1943. ARAB, Heinigs församling, vol. 8, no pages; Bauer, "Natur, 15.10.1943," vol. E4: 208. Diverse äldre korrespondens 1943. Centrum för Näringslivshistoria, Natur och Kultur, pp. 1–5; Fritz Bauer, Letter to Kurt Heinig, Oct. 29, 1943. ARAB, Heinigs församling, vol. 8, no pages. It is not clear when Bauer's family moved to the Gothenburg area, but Gelbart suggests that he was still in Mølle with his family in December (Fritz Gelbart, Letter to Kurt Heinig, Dec. 10, 1943. ARAB, Heinigs församling, vol. 10, no pages). Fritz Max Bauer, 16.07.1903: statsl. tysk/m, Stuttgart, Jur.dr, Grosshandl, man. Kanslibyrån F1 AC-1932 Bauer, 1943–1954. RA Sweden, Utlänningskommissionen, no pages; Wojak, *Fritz Bauer,* pp. 159–164.
4. Fritz Max Bauer, 16.07.1903: statsl. tysk/m, Stuttgart, Jur.dr, Grosshandl, man. Kanslibyrån F1 AC-1932 Bauer, 1943–1954. RA Sweden, Utlänningskommissionen, no pages; Astoria hotel. Stockholm, Sweden [brochure]. "Astoria hotell— samling av trycksaker, 1933–1936." Royal Library, Stockholm; "Vädret," *Svenska Dagbladet,* Nov. 25, 1943, p. 10; "Vädret," *Svenska Dagbladet,* Nov. 26, 1943, p. 12; Agrell, *Stockholm,* p. 58.
5. Wojak, *Fritz Bauer,* pp. 164–168. In October 1943, the Allies had created a United Nations War Crimes Commission, which had begun to collect evidence of atrocities (Tusa, Tusa, *The Nuremberg,* pp. 63–68.)
6. Tusa, Tusa, *The Nuremberg,* p. 24.
7. Albert Friedmann, "Ärade," Oct. 26, 1970. ARAB, Helmut Müssener, Exilen samling, box 1122/2/6, folder Albert Friedmann, no pages; Fritz Bauer, Letter to Paul Wagner, Jan. 15, 1944. Material in possession of Helle Wagner. For an example of the rancorous debates between German exiles on the left see: Landesvertretung der Deutschen Gewerkschaften, Landesgruppe Schweden, Rundbrief nr. 2, Jahrg. 2, Feb. 1944. ARAB, box Walter Pöppel 1930–1988–479/1, Landesgruppe Deutscher Gewerkschaften, no pages; Brandt, *Links,* pp. 360–364; Merseburger, *Willy Brandt,* pp. 187–188; "Krigsförbrytare," *Dagens Nyheter,* Dec. 20, 1943, p. 11; Kochavi, *Prelude,* pp. 83–84, 69.
8. Mann, "Letter," *Prevent W.W.III Magazine,* Dec. 1945, p. 25.
9. "Det fria," *Aftonbladet,* June 4, 1944, p. 21; Landesvebtretung der Deutschen Gewerkschaften landesgruppe Schweden. Rundbrief nr. 2, Jahrg. 2, Feb. 1944. ARAB, Walter Pöppel 1930–1988–479/1—Landesguppes Deutscher Gewerkschaften Rundbrief, no pages; Albert Friedmann, "Ärade," Oct. 26, 1970. ARAB, Helmut Müssener, Exilen samling, box 1122/2/6, folder Albert Friedmann, no pages.
10. Wojak, *Fritz Bauer,* pp. 159–164; Carina Birgersson, Interview by Christian Kjellson, Aug. 20, 2021; Stamkort Nils Erik Eriksson, 19220706-0852, no date. Krigsarkivet, no pages; Mantalslängd Nils Erik Eriksson, O 40847, no date. Oscars församling, Stockholms Stadsarkiv, no pages; Parikas, "Identitet," in: Silverstolpe, Söderström (eds.), *Sympatiens,* pp. 541–543. Many thanks to Carina Birgersson for sharing Bauer's inscription to a book he gave to Eriksson. Parikas, "Identitet," in: Silverstolpe, Söderström (eds.), *Sympatiens,* pp. 522, 555; Rydström, *Sinners,* pp. 254–262; Fritz Bauer, Letter to Paul Wagner, Jan. 15, 1944. Material in possession of Helle Wagner; Fritz Bauer, Letter to Paul Wagner, Feb. 17, 1944. Material in possession of Helle Wagner.
11. Fritz Bauer, Letter to Andreas Boje, Jan. 28, 1944. RA Denmark, Socialpolitisk Forening (1933–1955), no pages; Landesvertretung der Deutschen Gewerk-

schaften, Landesgruppe Schweden, Rundbrief nr. 2, Jahrg. 2, Feb. 1944, p. 4. ARAB, box Walter Pöppel 1930–1988–479/1, Landesgruppe Deutscher Gewerkschaften, no pages.

12. Landesvertretung der Deutschen Gewerkschaften, Landesgruppe Schweden, Rundbrief nr. 2, Jahrg. 2, Feb. 1944, p. 4. ARAB, box Walter Pöppel 1930–1988–479/1, Landesgruppe Deutscher Gewerkschaften, no pages; "Det fria," *Aftonbladet,* June 4, 1944, p. 21; Wolff, *Max Hodann,* p. 61 and note 59; Szende, *Der letzte,* pp. 5–6, 282–285, 291–292. The Hungarian émigré Stefan Szende first met Folkmann in Stockholm in October 1943 and conducted an extensive interview with him, later published as a book in March 1944. Some details shared by Folkmann were secondhand and incorrect, such as the use of electrolysis to kill. Hodann met Folkmann in early 1944.

13. Max Hodann, Opening speech, Jan. 28, 1944. ARAB, box 1124, S—111 81, cited in: Wojak, *Fritz Bauer,* pp. 170–171;"Die Deutschen," *Politische Information,* Nov. 15, 1944, pp. 2–3.

14. Max Hodann, Opening speech, Jan. 28, 1944. ARAB, box 1124, S—111 81, cited in: Wojak, *Fritz Bauer,* p. 171.

15. Information about the Holocaust remained incomplete in Stockholm (Åmark, *Att bo,* p. 259; Svanberg, Tydén, *Sverige,* p. 242). See: [Stepanenko] Степаненко, "Что происходит," *Правда,* Nov. 29, 1941, p. 3; [Molotov] Молотов, "Нота," *Известия,* Jan. 7, 1942, p. 2, cited in: Zeltser, "The Subject," Yad Vashem, online source. By 1944, Bauer was also aware of the first Soviet war crimes trials of Nazi perpetrators in Kharkiv, Ukraine, in August 1943 (Bauer, *Die Kriegsverbrecher,* pp. 155–156). He cites Russian author Aleksey Tolstoy's statement at the trial in which he described the uncovering of mass graves of Jewish victims.

16. Vädret, *Svenska Dagbladet,* Jan. 28, 1944, p. 8; Vädret, *Svenska Dagbladet,* Jan. 29, 1944, p. 8. For an example of Bauer's response to emerging details of the Holocaust see: Bauer, *Die Kriegsverbrecher,* pp. 211–214.

17. Klamberg, "Raphaël Lemkin," *Genocide Studies and Prevention,* 2019/13 (1), pp. 65–82; Power, "A Problem," p. 42; Frieze (ed.), *Totally,* p. 5.

18. Fritz Bauer, Letter to Paul Wagner, June 10, 1944. Material in possession of Helle Wagner; Fritz Bauer, Letter to Dansk Forening for Social Oplysning, May 6, 1944. RA Denmark, Socialpolitisk Forening (1933–1955), no pages; Bauer, *Die Kriegsverbrecher,* p. 5.

19. Bauer, *Die Kriegsverbrecher,* pp. 28–40; Sands, *East,* pp. 107–115; Klamberg, "Raphaël Lemkin," *Genocide Studies and Prevention,* 2019/13 (1), pp. 65–82; Power, "A Problem," p. 42; Frieze (ed.), *Totally,* p. 5. In German Völkermord—the murder of a people—had been used prior to the Holocaust and was most commonly used to refer to the Armenian genocide.

20. Bauer, *Die Kriegsverbrecher,* p. 211.

21. Kochavi, *Prelude,* p. 78.

22. Bauer, *Die Kriegsverbrecher,* pp. 214, 212. Bauer read about the revelations the following month in an article by Alaric Jacob, a correspondent for the *Daily Express* in Moscow, who was one of a dozen reporters brought to Majdanek to attest to the Nazis' crimes (Bauer, *Die Kriegsverbrecher,* pp. 211–214).

23. "Die Deutschen," *Politische Information,* Nov. 15, 1944, pp. 2–3. The book was also well received by the Swedish press and a Swedish publisher wanted to bring out a German edition (G. -Dr, "Världshistorien," [Nov. 1944]. Centrum för Näringslivshistoria, Stockholm. Natur och Kultur, vol. Ö1b, Pressklipp 1920-20,

pp. 9–11). See also: "Buchbesprechung," *Politische Information*, Oct. 15, 1944, no pages.

24. Wojak, *Fritz Bauer*, p. 175; Bauer, Letter to Karl B. Frank. Mar. 2, 1945. IfZ, ED 213, 27, no pages; Bauer, Letter to Paul Wagner, May 12, 1945. Material in possession of Helle Wagner; Fritz Bauer, Letter to Kurt Heinig, Oct.–Nov. 1943. ARAB, Heinigs församling, vol. 8, no pages.

25. Bauer, Letter to Karl B. Frank. Mar. 2, 1945. IfZ, ED 213, 27, no pages; Bauer, Letter to Paul Wagner, May 12, 1945. Material in possession of Helle Wagner. Fritz Bauer, Letter to Kurt Heinig, Nov. 11, 1943. ARAB, Heinigs församling, vol. 8, no pages.

26. Bauer, "Zum 7.," May 1945, in: Foljanty, Johst (eds.), *Fritz Bauer*, vol. 1, pp. 159–160.

27. Ibid.; Lindgren, *War Diaries*, May 7, 1945, p. 130.

4

SURVIVORS

1. The exhuming of bodies began in 1942. The dismantling of the death camps outside Bełżec, Treblinka, and Sobibór took place in 1943. Auschwitz's gas chambers were blown up in January 1945 (Arad, " 'Operation Reinhard,' " *Yad Vashem Studies XVI*, 1984, online source; Wachsmann, *KL*, p. 315; Długoborski, Piper [eds.]. *Auschwitz*, vol. 5, pp. 33–34, vol. 3, pp. 144–145). Beevor, *The Fall*, pp. 108, 288–289; Labatut, *When We Cease*, pp. 4–6; Trentmann, *Out of*, p. 69; Lommatzsch, *Hans Globke*, p. 104.

2. Gehlen, *The Service*, pp. 113, 115; Müller, *Reinhard Gehlen*, pp. 406–407, 421–422; Höhne, Zolling, *The General*, p. 53.

3. Gehlen, *The Service*, pp. 113, 115; Dorothee Gehlen-Koss, Interview by Jack Fairweather, Sept. 18, 2021; Müller, *Reinhard Gehlen*, p. 406; Oskar Thielert, Interrogation, July 10, 1963. BA, MfS, HA IX/11, FV, Nr. 5/72, vol. 11, part 2, p. 369; Dorothee Gehlen-Koss, Interview by Jack Fairweather, Sept. 18, 2021; Meinl, Hechelhammer, *Geheimobjekt*, p. 149; Weapon registration form for Reinhard Gehlen, no date. NARA, RG 263, Reinhard Gehlen. NAID 139337808, vol. 1, p. 199; Müller, *Reinhard Gehlen*, pp. 29, 71–73, 857; Reese, *General*, p. 198; Critchfield, *Partners*, p. 83.

4. Dorothee Gehlen-Koss, Interview by Jack Fairweather, Sept. 18, 2021; Trentmann, *Out of*, pp. 7–9; Junger, *Storm*, p.1; Gehlen, *The Service*, p. 99; Müller, *Reinhard Gehlen*, pp. 117–119; Dorothee Gehlen-Koss, Interview by Jack Fairweather, Sept. 18, 2021; Böhler, *Auftakt*, p. 49. The 213th Infantry division, in which Gehlen served as a staff officer, killed nine civilians in the town of Poddębice. Among the dead were: Anna Adamowicz, thirty-six years old; Anna's son Mieczysław Adamowicz, sixteen years old; Anna's daughter Zdzisława Adamowicz, ten years old; Antoni Leśniak, forty-two years old, and his mother-in-law Cybulska (her first name is unknown). Anna's husband, Zygmunt Adamowicz, was wounded by four bullets, but survived by pretending to be dead (Pietrzak, "Mord," *Nad Wartą*, 2019/401, p. 14; Stanisława Kubiak, Interrogation, Aug. 16, 1968. IPN, Ld S 12/74, vol. II, p. 287; Bronisława Kubiak, Interrogation, Aug. 16, 1968. IPN, Ld S 12/74, vol. II, p. 288; Maria Błochowicz, Uzasadnienie, 1970. IPN, Ld S 12/74, vol. II, pp. 308–309). See also: Binder et al.,

"Ofiary," in: Binder et al. (eds.), *Świadkowie*, p. 153; Markowska et al., *Zbrodnie*, no pages. For Einsatzgruppen in the Łódź region see: Datner, *55 dni*, pp. 136–139.

5. For Gehlen's meeting with Quartermaster General Georg Thomas in January 1941 to suggest the deployment of SS and order police to rear areas see: Müller, *Reinhard Gehlen*, p. 198. Gehlen likely attended the March 1941 meeting with Hitler (Hürtler, *Hitler's*, pp. 1–13; Halder, *Kriegstagebuch II*, Mar. 30, 1941, p. 337, cited in: Stahel, *Operation*, p. 96). Thomas held a key meeting with senior Reich officials on May 2, 1941, at which Hitler's starvation policies for future occupied territories of the Soviet Union—developed by Herbert Backe of the Reich Ministry of Food—were outlined. The extent to which these plans were shared by Thomas with other senior officers is not clear. Following the invasion, the Army High Command issued orders for the mistreatment of Soviet Prisoners of War, as well as the so-called Commissar Order for the summary execution of Soviet political officers (Arnold, Lübbers, "The Meeting," *Journal of Contemporary History*, 2007/42 [4], pp. 613–626). For the Wehrmacht's subsequent complicity in genocide see: Stahel, *Operation*, p. 101. Despite the clear war crimes signaled by such policies, few officers like Gehlen complained. General von Haskell was rare in recording his personal objection that "[i]t makes one's hair stand on end to learn about and receive proof of orders signed by Halder and distributed to the troops as to measures to be taken in Russia, and about the systematic transformation of military law concerning the conquered population into uncontrolled despotism—indeed a caricature of all law" (Stahel, *Operation*, p. 101). Halder, *Kriegstagebuch III*, Nov. 10, 1941, p. 286, cited in: Müller, *Reinhard Gehlen*, p. 228.

6. Gehlen later claimed that Halder and other senior officers opposed the "Commissar Order" and that it was mostly not obeyed by the troops. There is no evidence to support this claim (Müller, *Reinhard Gehlen*, p. 209). According to Halder, German forces were "not obliged to supply Soviet prisoners-of-war with food corresponding in quantity or quality to the requirements of this regulation," because Moscow was not party to the Geneva Convention (Tusa, Tusa, *The Nuremberg*, p. 240). More than three million POWs died of starvation and sickness within six months of the invasion. See also: Förster, "Wehrmacht," in: Müller, Volkmann (eds.), *Die Wehrmacht*, pp. 958ff; Streit, "The German," in: Hirschfeld (ed.), *The Policies*, pp. 1–12; Stahel, *Operation*, p. 101; Halder, *Kriegstagebuch III*, Nov. 12, 1941, p. 286, cited in: Müller, *Reinhard Gehlen*, p. 228. Gehlen did not record the visit to Molodechno. He was not in a position to object to the prisoners' treatment, which clearly contravened basic laws of war, nor to take action to alleviate the suffering. Halder was, but did nothing. A week after the trip, Gehlen was put on administrative leave from his job. No reason was given, but it's possible his breakdown was the result of use of the amphetamine Pervitin, common among German officers and soldiers (Müller, *Reinhard Gehlen*, p. 99). Halder, *Kriegstagebuch III*, Nov. 10, 1941, p. 286, cited in: Müller, *Reinhard Gehlen*, p. 228. For Soviet testimony on Molodechno see: [Krasnopiorkin] Краснопёркин, "Молодечненский," Apr. 1, 1945. ГА РФ, фонд 7021, опись 89, дело 9, листы 96–105.

7. Müller, *Reinhard Gehlen*, pp. 235, 239. For Gehlen's use of SS for information-gathering and knowledge of massacres in connection with antipartisan warfare see: Pahl, *Fremde*, p. 107; Müller, *Reinhard Gehlen*, p. 297; Gehlen, *The Service*,

p. 99; Müller, *Reinhard Gehlen,* p. 258; Höhne, Zolling, *The General,* p. 45; Reese, *General,* p. 4; Müller, *Reinhard Gehlen,* pp. 355, 376.

8. Müller, *Reinhard Gehlen,* p. 424; Gehlen, *The Service,* pp. 115–116; Müller, *Reinhard Gehlen,* p. 423.

9. Gehlen, *The Service,* p. 115; Höhne, Zolling, *The General,* pp. 52–53; Gehlen, *The Service,* p. 116.

10. Gehlen, *The Service,* pp. 115–116. It is a German tradition to eat pancakes on Whitsun.

11. Gehlen, *The Service,* p. 3; Müller, *Reinhard Gehlen,* p. 424. For war crimes list see: Tusa, Tusa, *The Nuremberg,* p. 103; Stangneth, *Eichmann,* p. 67. Höhne and Zolling suggest the Wörgl meeting actually took place in Miesbach (Höhne, Zolling, *The General,* p. 54).

12. Gehlen, *The Service,* p. 4; Strik-Strikfeldt, *Gegen Stalin,* pp. 243–244; Reese, *General,* pp. 41–42. For camp description see: Brüggemann, *Männer,* pp. 36–37. Hermann Goering had stayed in Augsburg two weeks prior, bringing with him two suitcases full of paracodeine pills for his drug addiction (Manvell, *Goering,* pp. 471–474). Georg-Hans Reinhardt, Diary, June 14–17, 1945. BA-MA Freiburg im Breisgau, N 245/24, no pages; Trentmann, *Out of,* pp. 92, 95; Georg-Hans Reinhardt, Diary, June 7–9, 1945. BA-MA Freiburg im Breisgau, N 245/24, no pages; Adolf Heusinger, Gehlen's former superior on the general staff, was rare in addressing the Wehrmacht's "historical guilt" in allowing itself to be used by Hitler as well as the Führer's "mistakes" in trying to solve the Jewish question. "A thousand-year Reich cannot be created in six years" and "violence and injustice alone are a bad breeding ground," Heusinger wrote in a report for the U.S. military compiled during his time in Augsburg. The tenor of his report suggests only a partial reckoning (Meyer, *Adolf Heusinger,* p. 294). Gehlen submitted two reports to the U.S. military in Augsburg, neither of which addressed war crimes: "Russia's Military Policy Objectives in Europe," June 15, 1945, and "Notes on the Red Army—Leadership and Tactics," June 21, 1945, cited in: Müller, *Reinhard Gehlen,* p. 424; Silver, "Memories," *Studies in Intelligence,* 1994/37 (5), pp. 86–87; Wachsmann, *KL,* p. 598.

13. Müller, *Reinhard Gehlen,* pp. 423–424; Reese, *General,* p. 42; Gehlen, *The Service,* pp. 4–5.

14. Gehlen, *The Service,* p. 5.

15. Ibid.

16. Ibid.; Tusa, Tusa, *The Nuremberg,* p. 37; Kardorff von, *Berliner,* p. 351. Kardorff describes Halle, but this was a common scene across Germany at the time. Jähner, *Aftermath,* p. 39; Trentmann, *Out of,* p. 88.

17. Gehlen, *The Service,* p. 5; Drummer, Zwilling, "Die Befreiung," Jan. 1, 2012. *Institut für Stadtgeschichte,* online source; Jähner, *Aftermath,* pp. 13, 39.

18. Gehlen, *The Service,* p. 5.

19. Stahel, *Operation,* p. 101; Brüggemann, *Männer,* p. 317; Bor, *Gespräche,* pp. 230–231; Müller, *Reinhard Gehlen,* p. 428.

20. Boker, Report . . . May 1, 1952, in: Ruffner (ed.), *Forging,* vol. I, p. 23; Schröder, "Geschubse," *Wiesbadener Nachrichten,* Dec. 12, 2020, p. 18; Zaeske Architekten, "Neubau," no date. Zaeske, online source; Müller, *Reinhard Gehlen,* p. 428.

21. Reese, *General,* p. 45; Gehlen, *The Service,* p. 6.

22. Reese, *General,* pp. 43–44, 46; Gehlen, *The Service,* pp. 6–7; Boker, Report . . . May 1, 1952, in: Ruffner (ed.), *Forging,* vol. 1, pp. 19–23; Joan Shisler, Interview by Jack Fairweather, Aug. 24, 2020.

23. Gehlen, *The Service*, p. 7; Boker, Report . . . May 1, 1952, in: Ruffner (ed.), *Forging*, vol. 1, p. 23.

24. Reese, *General*, p. 47; Boker, Report . . . May 1, 1952, in: Ruffner (ed.), *Forging*, vol. 1, p. 25. After speaking with Boker, Gehlen sought out Admiral Karl Dönitz. Boker might not be seeking approval from his higher-ups, but Gehlen felt it necessary to get permission from the last Führer of the Third Reich, who duly gave his assent (Reese, *General*, p. 51). For Soviet interest in Gehlen see: Reese, *General*, pp. 40–41.

25. Boker, Report . . . May 1, 1952, in: Ruffner (ed.), *Forging*, vol. 1, pp. 25–26; Müller, *Reinhard Gehlen*, p. 430; Reese, *General*, pp. 47–48.

26. Reese, *General*, pp. 48–49; Boker, Report . . . 1 May 1952, in: Ruffner (ed.), *Forging*, vol. 1, pp. 27–28.

27. Dorothee Gehlen-Koss, Interview by Jack Fairweather, Sept. 18, 2021; Müller, *Reinhard Gehlen*, pp. 389–390.

28. Joan Shisler, Interview by Jack Fairweather, Aug. 24, 2020; Biographic Sketch on Reinhard Gehlen, no date. NARA, RG 263, Reinhard Gehlen, NAID 139337808, vol. 1, p. 3; USHMM, "Poland 1945," no date. USHMM, Holocaust Encyclopedia, online source; Statista Research Department, "Zahl der vertriebenen," Apr. 30, 2015. Statista, online source.

29. Sälter, *Phantome*, p. 60; Hermann Baun, Letter to Reinhard Gehlen, May 27, 1946. MGFA, box Gehlen, folder 69, cited in: Müller, *Reinhard Gehlen*, p. 465. For an extensive overview of Gehlen's perception of the Communist threat see: Gehlen, *The Service*, pp. 305–331; Sälter, *Phantome*, pp. 51–53, 99; Müller, *Reinhard Gehlen*, p. 452; Henke, *Geheime . . . Die politische Inlandsspionage der Organisation*, pp. 48–49.

30. Reese, *General*, pp. 46, 50–51. Boker describes a prearranged plan prior to Gehlen's trip to the United States to reactivate his network through Hermann Baun (Boker, Report . . . May 1, 1952, in: Ruffner [ed.], *Forging*, vol. 1, p. 33). Breitman (ed.), *U.S. Intelligence*, p. 382.

31. Reese, *General*, p. 48. For Nuremberg preparations see: Tusa, Tusa, *The Nuremberg*, pp. 61–62, 99–101. Halder avoided being charged as a war criminal, and served as a prosecution witness at Nuremberg (Brüggemann, *Männer*, p. 56). Gehlen learned only later that Halder's history project had done enough to ensure he appeared at the trial as a witness and not defendant.

32. Gehlen, *The Service*, p. 11; Boker, Report . . . May 1, 1952, in: Ruffner (ed.), *Forging*, vol. 1, pp. 28–30; Gehlen, *The Service*, p. 126.

33. Accompanying Gehlen were Konrad Stephanus, Horst Hiemenz, Hans Hinrichs, Karl Freiherr von Lütgendorf, Albert Schöller, and Herbert Fühner (Boker, Report . . . May 1, 1952, in: Ruffner [ed.], *Forging*, vol. 1, p. 30). Müller, *Reinhard Gehlen*, p. 430; Boker, Report . . . May 1, 1952, in: Ruffner (ed.), *Forging*, vol. 1, p. 30; Müller, *Reinhard Gehlen*, pp. 559, 881, 430; Gehlen, *The Service*, p. 1; Reese, *General*, pp. 52–53.

34. Reese, *General*, pp. 53–54; Müller, *Reinhard Gehlen*, p. 432; Reese, *General*, p. 55; Stern, Gajdosch, *U.S. Army*, p. 61.

35. Boker, Report . . . May 1, 1952, in: Ruffner (ed.), *Forging*, vol. 1, pp. 30–33; Müller, *Reinhard Gehlen*, pp. 433–434; Ruffner, Persons Mentioned: Waldman, Eric, in: Ruffner (ed.), *Forging*, vol. 1, pp. 40–41; Reese, *General*, pp. 56–57; Müller, *Reinhard Gehlen*, p. 432; Waldmann, Sofie. Last Letters from Łódź Ghetto, no date. USHMM, Holocaust Survivors and Victims Database; Chris Waldmann,

Interview by Jack Fairweather, Sept. 3, 2020, no pages. Special thanks to Eric Waldman's family for sharing their insights and discoveries into Eric's past.

36. Reese, *General*, p. 58; Müller, *Reinhard Gehlen*, pp. 433–436; Hechelhammer, Meinl, *Geheimobjekt*, p. 142; Reese, *General*, p. 58; Franz Gajdosch, Interview by Brandon Bies, May 6, 2010, and Oct. 25, 2010. Fort Hunt Oral History, P.O. Box 1142, National Park Service. By mid-November, Gehlen had produced 716 type-written pages and 68 maps and attachments, and dozens more reports on the Red Army's order of battle in Europe, as well as political and military intelligence (Müller, *Reinhard Gehlen*, pp. 434–435).

37. Boker says he facilitated contact between Gehlen and Baun to begin reestablishing his network that autumn. It's not clear when Hermann Baun began actively recruiting, but he had definitely begun by December 1945 (Boker, Report . . . May 1, 1952, in: Ruffner [ed.], *Forging*, vol. 1, p. 33; Müller, *Reinhard Gehlen*, p. 443). Eric Waldman, Interview, no date, cited in: Reese, *General*, p. 58; Müller, Gehlen, *The Service*, pp. 125–126; *Reinhard Gehlen*, p. 469; Reese, *General*, p. 58.

38. Müller, *Reinhard Gehlen*, p. 469; Tusa, Tusa, *The Nuremberg*, p. 115; Brüggemann, *Männer*, p. 85; Tusa, Tusa, *The Nuremberg*, pp. 177–178; Reinhard Gehlen, Letter to William E. Hall, Nov. 3, 1948. BND-Archiv, 1111, pp. 411–416, cited in: Müller, *Reinhard Gehlen*, p. 549. Gehlen suggests that prosecution witnesses were threatened to provide damning testimony and that the German Jewish prosecutor Robert Kempner was in the pay of the Soviets (Müller, *Reinhard Gehlen*, p. 550). Reese, *General*, p. 57.

39. Reese, *General*, p. 60; Müller, *Reinhard Gehlen*, p. 462; Reese, *General*, pp. 60–61; Müller, *Reinhard Gehlen*, pp. 467–468; Orwell, "You and the Atom," *Tribune*, Oct. 19, 1945. The Orwell Foundation, online source.

40. Reese, *General*, p. 95; Kevin Ruffner, Persons Mentioned: Waldman, Eric, in: Ruffner (ed.), *Forging*, vol. 1, pp. xl–xli; Reese, *General*, p. 58; Chris Waldmann, Interview by Jack Fairweather, Sept. 3, 2020.

41. Müller, *Reinhard Gehlen*, pp. 446–450, 440–445, 448, 453; Sälter, *Phantome*, p. 51; *Reinhard Gehlen*, Letter to William E. Hall, Nov. 3, 1948. BND-Archiv, 1111, pp. 411–416, cited in: Müller, *Reinhard Gehlen*, p. 549; Gerhard Wessel, Letter to Reinhard Gehlen, Mar. 5 and 8, 1946. BND-Archiv, N 1/1, cited in: Müller, *Reinhard Gehlen*, p. 454; Hermann Baun, Letter to Reinhard Gehlen, May 27, 1946. MGFA, box Gehlen, folder 69, cited in: Müller, *Reinhard Gehlen*, p. 465; Höhne, Zolling, *The General*, p. 157; Müller, *Reinhard Gehlen*, p. 467. For Gehlen's rivalry with Hermann Baun see: Müller, *Reinhard Gehlen*, pp. 491–498.

42. Müller, *Reinhard Gehlen*, p. 462; Tusa, Tusa, *The Nuremberg*, p. 245; Menand, "George," *The New Yorker*, Nov. 6, 2011, no pages. The latter had already reached out to several old contacts in the network (Müller, *Reinhard Gehlen*, pp. 448–450). Judt, *Postwar*, p. 197. For Waldman's support of the use of former Nazis for combatting "cultural bolshevism" see: Henke, *Geheime . . . Die politische In-landsspionage der Organisation*, pp. 64–68. Waldman played a role in the release of former Nazi theater director Fritz Fischer from American custody in Flensburg to infiltrate the theater scene and target, among others, the well-known writer Eric Kästner. Waldman insisted that Fischer was not involved in "operations" and that to his knowledge Gehlen did not employ major war criminals (Eric Waldman, Debrief, Sept. 30, 1968, cited in: Ruffner [ed.], *Forging*, vol. 1, p. 50; Reese, *General*, pp. 94–95). For Waldman's role in forging identity papers for Gehlen's staff see: Reese, *General*, pp. 86, 92.

43. Danko Herre, Statement, Apr. 8, 1953, Doc. 4, in: Ruffner (ed.), *Forging*, pp. 13–14; Reese, *General*, pp. 74–76; Hechelhammer, Meinl, *Geheimobjekt*, pp. 143–144; Hans Hinrichs, Statement, no date, cited in: Ruffner (ed.), *Forging*, vol. 1, pp. 9–10; Kopp, "Im Labyrinth," *Sonderdruck aus dem Jahrbuch des Hochtaunuskreis*, 2010/18, pp. 234–235; Dorothee Gehlen-Koss, Interview by Jack Fairweather, Sept. 18, 2021.

44. Müller, *Reinhard Gehlen*, p. 471; Müller, *Reinhard Gehlen*, p. 452; Henke, *Geheime . . . Die politische Inlandsspionage der Organisation*, pp. 48–49.

5
NUREMBERG

1. Fritz Bauer, Letter to Kurt Schumacher, May 23, 1946. AdsD, 2/KSAA 000064, no pages; Bauer, *Die Kriegsverbrecher*, p. 211; Fulbrook, *Reckonings*, pp. 212–214, 221; Tusa, Tusa, *The Nuremberg*, p. 131.

2. Bauer, *Die Kriegsverbrecher*, p. 211; Fulbrook, *Reckonings*, pp. 212–214, 221; Tusa, Tusa, *The Nuremberg*, p. 131.

3. Bower, *The Pledge*, pp. 156–157, 171–176; Jähner, *Aftermath*, pp. 311–312, 386; Trentmann, *Out of*, p. 122; "Elimination of Nazis from Political Posts," 1944–1945. TNA, FO 937/16, no pages; Bower, *Pledge*, p. 154; Trentmann, *Out of*, pp. 124, 112. Of the 12 million questionnaires issued in the American zone, only 631,000 were completed (Bower, *Pledge*, p. 172).

4. Fritz Bauer, Letter to Kurt Schumacher, May 23, 1946. AdsD, 2/KSAA 000064, no pages; Fulbrook, *Reckonings*, p. 251; Bauer, *Die Kriegsverbrecher*, p. 211; Bauer, "Brief," Sept. 1945, in: Foljanty, Johst (eds.), *Fritz Bauer*, vol. 1, p. 173. Some of his old friends from Stuttgart secured posts, so he could only assume it was his Jewishness that was the problem. Being a Nazi, by contrast, seemed less of an issue (Fritz Bauer, Letter to Richard Schmid, Oct. 7, 1946. HStAS, Q1/40 Bü 31, no pages; Fritz Bauer, Letter to Richard Schmid, Nov. 17, 1946. HstAS, Q1/40 Bü 31, no pages).

5. Fritz Bauer, Letter to Kurt Schumacher, May 23, 1946. AdsD, 2/KSAA 000064, no pages; Bauer, "Brief," Sept. 1945, in: Foljanty, Johst (eds.), *Fritz Bauer*, vol. 1, p. 173; Franz, *Kløvermarken*, 1947–1949. Archive of Arne Gammelgaards, Tyske Flygtninge, online source; Mix, *Deutsche*, p. 42; Wojak, *Fritz Bauer*, pp. 191–193; Mix, *Deutsche*, pp. 14, 16, 34–36.

6. Bauer is not explicit about which camp he visited, but it is highly likely it was Kløvermarken (Bauer, "Brief," Sept. 1945, in: Foljanty, Johst [eds.], *Fritz Bauer*, vol. 1, p. 173). Franz, *Kløvermarken*, 1947–1949. Archive of Arne Gammelgaards, Tyske Flygtninge, online source; Bauer, "Brief," Sept. 1945, in: Foljanty, Johst (eds.), *Fritz Bauer*, vol. 1, p. 173.

7. The Hotel D'Angleterre was a favorite hangout of Bauer's, and one of the few places in Copenhagen to stock an array of international newspapers. Bauer stayed there for a time upon his return to Copenhagen (Fritz Bauer, Letter to Paul Wagner, summer 1945. Material in possession of Helle Wagner). Tusa, Tusa, *The Nuremberg*, pp. 158–160; Kästner, "Streiflichter," *Die Neue Zeitung*, Nov. 23, 1945, in: Radlmaier (ed.), "Der Nürnberger," p. 69; Tusa, Tusa, *The Nuremberg*, pp. 161–162, 104. The number of defendants at the time of the trial stood at 21. Robert Ley, the German Labor Front leader, had committed suicide in his cell in October 25, 1945. The industrialist Gustav Krupp von Bohlen und Halbach was

deemed unfit to stand trial, and charges against him were later dropped. Martin Bormann, the head of Nazi Party chancellery was tried in absentia (he was in fact dead).

8. Bauer, "Recht," June 24, 1946, in: Foljanty, Johst (eds.), *Fritz Bauer*, vol. 1, p. 200; Tusa, Tusa, *The Nuremberg*, pp. 72–74; Fulbrook, *Reckonings*, p. 214; Tusa, Tusa, *The Nuremberg*, pp. 120, 167–169.

9. Tusa, Tusa, *The Nuremberg*, pp. 58–61, 87–91, 110, 171, 181–182, 103–106, 559. The film featured only camps liberated by Western Allied forces, and therefore not Auschwitz or the German Nazi death camps in Poland (Tusa, Tusa, *The Nuremberg*, pp. 173–174). Tusa, Tusa, *The Nuremberg*, pp. 272–273; Bauer, "Der Nürnberger," Oct. 17, 1946, in: Foljanty, Johst (eds.), *Fritz Bauer*, vol. 1, pp. 226, 234.

10. Bauer, "Recht," June 24, 1946, in: Foljanty, Johst (eds.), *Fritz Bauer*, vol. 1, p. 200; Tusa, Tusa, *The Nuremberg*, p. 269; Fulbrook, *Reckonings*, pp. 216–218; Trentmann, *Out of*, p. 35.

11. Bauer, "Freund," Feb. 11, 1946, in: Foljanty, Johst (eds.), *Fritz Bauer*, vol. 1, p. 186.

12. Per Tiefenthal, Rolf Tiefenthal, *Festspiel zu Opas 75. Geburtstag*, Nov. 11, 1945. Material in possession of Marit Tiefenthal; Bauer Ludwig, Bauer Ella, Letter to Fritz Bauer, Nov. 26, 1945. Material in possession of Marit Tiefenthal. The letter informing Bauer of his father's death has not survived but can be inferred.

13. Tusa, Tusa, *The Nuremberg*, p. 269; Otto Ohlendorf, Testimony, Jan. 3, 1946. Yale Law School. The Avalon Project. Nuremberg Trial Proceedings, vol. 4, online source; Dieter Wisliceny, Testimony, Jan. 3, 1946. Yale Law School. The Avalon Project. Nuremberg Trial Proceedings, vol. 4, online source; Stangneth, *Eichmann*, p. 61; Stangneth, *Eichmann*, p. 67; Pelt van, *The Case*, p. 246.

14. Fulbrook, *Reckonings*, pp. 214–215.

15. Harding, *Hanns*, p. 250.

16. Rudolf Höss, Testimony, Apr. 15, 1946. Nuremberg Trial Proceedings. Yale Law School. The Avalon Project, vol. 11, online source; Długoborski, Piper (eds.), *Auschwitz*, vol. 3, p. 170, p. 141. For Bauer's particular interest in Höss's testimony see: Bauer, "Der Nürnberger," Oct. 17, 1946, in: Foljanty, Johst (eds.), *Fritz Bauer*, vol. 1, p. 230.

17. Harding, *Hanns*, pp. 258–260; Tusa, Tusa, *The Nuremberg*, p. 327; McCormick, "Nuremberg," *The New York Times*, Sept. 29, 1946, p. 21. No other defendants followed Frank's lead in the end. Only Albert Speer, Hitler's armaments minister, expressed something like an apology without mentioning guilt or naming any victims other than the German people.

18. Bauer, "Der Nürnberger," Oct. 14, 1946, in: Foljanty, Johst (eds.), *Fritz Bauer*, vol. 1, p. 204; McCormick, "Nuremberg," *The New York Times*, Sept. 29, 1946, p. 21; Bauer, "Der Nürnberger," Oct. 17, 1946, in: Foljanty, Johst (eds.), *Fritz Bauer*, vol. 1, pp. 234–235; Trentmann, *Out of*, pp. 110, 112–113.

19. Fulbrook, *Reckonings*, p. 215; Tusa, Tusa, *The Nuremberg*, pp. 550–560. As Tusa and Tusa note, there is no official record of what happened to the defendants' bodies; however, many believe that they were driven to Dachau to be cremated (Tusa, Tusa, *The Nuremberg*, p. 557). Wachsmann, *KL*, p. 628; "Nuremberg," *The New York Times*, Oct. 13, 1946, p. 36; "The Nuremberg," *The New York Times*, Oct. 2, 1946, p. 28; "Judgment," *The Times*, Sept. 30, 1946, p. 4.

20. Eichmüller, "Die Strafverfolgung," Vierteljahrshefte für Zeitgeschichte, 2008/56 (4), p. 262; Fulbrook, *Reckonings*, pp. 224, 231, 235. A flurry of pros-

ecutions saw 2,011 Nazis convicted in 1948, but the number of active investigations had started to taper off. The following year 1,474 convictions were secured, and convictions dropped rapidly thereafter. In total, 13,600 trials were held between 1945 and 1949 (Fulbrook, *Reckonings,* p. 235). For a comparable breakdown of the falling number of proceedings in Hesse see: Eichmüller, "Die juristische," *Einsicht 12: Bulletin des Fritz Bauer Institutes,* Herbst 2014, pp. 42–49.

21. Bower, *Pledge,* p. 172. For West German judges protecting themselves from prosecution see: Fulbrook, *Reckonings,* p. 251. Bauer, "Mörder," *Deutsche Nachrichten,* 1947/3, p. 2; Trentmann, *Out of,* p. 134; Fulbrook, *Reckonings,* pp. 245–246. Gustav Radbruch, the prominent German legal scholar, a Social Democrat, a former minister of justice in the Weimar Republic, and an important influence on Bauer, argued in favor of Germany adopting novel laws used at Nuremberg such as crimes against humanity by invoking a higher universal law. This contravened the positivist principle against retroactive punishment that underlined the German penal code (Trentmann, *Out of,* p. 119). In the British zone, the Control Council Law 10 had the potential to discount the superior orders defense, but German courts rarely applied it. The Supreme Special Court (Oberster Spruchgerichtshof) notably ruled in several cases that the creation of concentration camps was a crime against humanity and that conviction could not be secured without evidence of personal brutality toward inmates (Trentmann, *Out of,* p. 134). Sohn, *Im Spiegel,* p. 150. On the problems arising from Control Council Law 10 and its retroactive application see: Pöpken, *Vergangenheitspolitik,* pp. 163–167.

22. Fulbrook, *Reckonings,* p. 251; Bauer, "Mörder," *Deutsche Nachrichten,* 1947/3, p. 2; Trentmann, *Out of,* pp. 124, 112.

23. Wojak, *Fritz Bauer,* p. 224; Biegel, *75 Jahre,* p. 13; "Braunschweig," *Braunschweiger Presse,* Nov. 5, 1949, p. 3; Wojak, *Fritz Bauer,* pp. 227–228; Fritz Bauer, Letter to Erwin Schoettle, Oct. 12, 1948. AdsD, Nachlass Erwin Schoettle, 1/ESAC000015, no pages; Fritz Bauer, Letter to Kurt Schumacher, Aug. 8, 1948. AdsD, 2/KSAA 000071, no pages. For Bauer's thoughts on the role of public prosecutor see: Bauer, "Im Kampf," Apr. 1955 in: Foljanty, Johst (eds.), *Fritz Bauer,* vol. 1, p. 446.

24. Jähner, *Aftermath,* pp. 197–198; Milton, *Checkmate,* p. 269. When the Allies suggested introducing a new currency that June to tackle the black market—the reichsmark was effectively worthless—Stalin rejected the idea; when Washington pressed ahead anyway, he sent in troops to blockade Allied-controlled areas of West Berlin (Jähner, *Aftermath,* pp. 195–199).

6

ENEMY TERRITORY

1. Wojak, *Fritz Bauer,* p. 225; Fritz Bauer, Letter to Kurt Schumacher, Aug. 8, 1948. AdsD, 2/KSAA000071, no pages; Bauer, No title, in: Sender Freies Berlin (ed.), *Um uns,* p. 69, cited in: Steinke, *Fritz Bauer,* p. 90.

2. Bauer, "Heute," Dec. 8, 1964, in: Foljanty, Johst (eds.), *Fritz Bauer,* vol. 2, p. 1128; Fritz Bauer, Letter to Erwin Schoettle, Oct. 12, 1948. AdsD, Nachlass Erwin Schoettle, 1/ESAC000015, no pages; Raloff, *Ein bewegtes,* pp. 140–141.

3. Fritz Bauer, Letter to Kurt Schumacher, Aug. 8, 1948. AdsD, 2/KSAA 000071, no pages; Merseburger, *Willy Brandt,* p. 272; Merseburger, *Der schwierige,* pp. 200,

207; Trentmann, *Out of,* p. 88; Merseburger, *Der schwierige,* pp. 202–203, 206; Jähner, *Aftermath,* pp. 199–200.

4. Trentmann, *Out of,* pp. 222, 225; Wachsmann, *KL,* p. 12; Trentmann, *Out of,* pp. 191, 102–103, 110. The American Jewish sociologist David Boder interviewed more than one hundred Jewish survivors in displaced persons camps with a tape recorder—cutting-edge technology at the time—but neither he nor those he spoke to seemed sure of the timeline of events or of their significance, as the first histories were only just being written (Fulbrook, *Reckonings,* p. 191; Cesarani, Sundquist [eds.], *After the Holocaust,* pp. 9–10). The first published account about Auschwitz was likely *Jag sjöng mig genom helvetet* by Freddy Bauer, which appeared in Sweden in September 1945. "The world won't believe me but it still has to know everything," he observed (Kilian, *"Ein leiser," Mitteilungen der Lagergemeinschaft Auschwitz,* 2014/34, p. 28). Jähner, *Aftermath,* p. 246. Benscher had his program "War, Never Again" canceled by the Americans in 1948 and was subsequently forced off the air in 1950 (Trentmann, *Out of,* p. 191).

5. Bower, *Pledge,* p. 154. In Bavaria, only a fifth of the principal offenders (Hauptbelastete) had been examined by the summer of 1947 (Trentmann, *Out of,* p. 128). Jähner, *Aftermath,* pp. 296–297; Müller-Doohm, *Adorno,* p. 550; Trentmann, *Out of,* p. 116.

6. Jähner, *Aftermath,* p. 213; Bower, *The Pledge,* p. 168. The German Right Party had won 15,000 of 24,000 votes in the elections for the Lower Saxony town of Wolfsburg, near Braunschweig, where Bauer was heading. The British authorities annulled the result. But a successor party still won almost half the vote in a follow-up election (Jähner, *Aftermath,* p. 213).

7. The judges Bauer met—Bruno Heusinger, Braunschweig's court president, and his colleague Wilhelm Kiesselbach—had not been Nazi supporters. Kiesselbach had been dismissed from his post in 1933. Heusinger had stayed on and seemed reserved; he'd been reprimanded for not being zealous enough in the punishments he issued. Heusinger and Kiessellbach had both advocated for the reinstatement of Nazi-era judges (Wojak, *Fritz Bauer,* pp. 224, 227). Wojak, *Fritz Bauer,* p. 228; Fritz Bauer, Letter to Kurt Schumacher, Aug. 8, 1948. AdsD, 2/KSAA 000071, no pages; Fritz Bauer, Letter to Kurt Schumacher, Sept. 17, 1948. AdsD, 2/KSAA000071, no pages.

8. Fritz Bauer, Letter to Kurt Schumacher, Aug. 8, 1948. AdsD, 2/KSAA000071, no pages.

9. Fritz Bauer, Letter to Erwin Schoettle, Oct. 12, 1948. AdsD, 1/ESAC000015, no pages; Wojak, *Fritz Bauer,* p. 227; Fritz Bauer, Letter to Fritz Heine, Oct. 28, 1948. AdsD, 2/KSAA000071, no pages; Wojak, *Fritz Bauer,* p. 228; Janusz Gumkowski, Chief Commission for the Prosecution of German Crimes in Poland, Letter concerning extradition of Wilhelm Kopf, Feb. 24, 1948. IPN, Gk 173/85, p. 16. See the letters Bauer sent to Heusinger, president of the Higher Regional Court, on January 19, February 13, March 9, and March 27, 1949 (cited in: Wojak, *Fritz Bauer,* p. 228).

10. Fritz Bauer, Letter to Paul Wagner, July 8, 1948. Material in possession of Helle Wagner; Kinsey, *Sexual,* p. 650; Cervini, *The Deviant's,* p. 18; Fritz Bauer, Letter to Paul Wagner, July 8, 1948. Material in possession of Helle Wagner. Bauer offered to divorce his nominal wife, Anna Maria Petersen, but she seemed happy to keep the arrangement if it helped provide him with further cover, presumably for

his homosexuality (Anna Maria Petersen, Interview by Irmtrud Wojak, Feb. 28, 1997, cited in: Wojak, *Fritz Bauer*, p. 228).

11. Fritz Bauer, Letter to Kurt Schumacher, Apr. 24, 1949. AdsD, Nachlass Kurt Schumacher, 2/KSAA000071, cited in: Wojak, *Fritz Bauer*, pp. 228–229; Dittmann, "Der private," *Schriftenreihe des "Fritz Bauer Freundeskreises,"* 2013, p. 1; Ehrhardt (ed.), *Aufbauzeit*, pp. 9, 148; Sauer, "Situation," no date. *Leben in Braunschweig*, online source; Biegel, *75 Jahre*, part 4, p. 14.

12. Sohn, *Im Spiegel*, p. 54; Dittmann, "Der private," *Schriftenreihe des "Fritz Bauer Freundeskreises,"* 2013, p. 2; Ehrhardt (ed.), *Aufbauzeit*, p. 9; Heitefuss, *Braunschweig*, p. 119; Ausmeier, *Klagges*, pp. 9–10, 25; "Dr. Bauer," *Braunschweiger Presse*, Aug. 2, 1950, p. 7; "Amtseinführung," *Braunschweiger Zeitung*, Aug. 2, 1950, no pages.

13. "Schlicht," *Braunschweiger Presse*, Nov. 17, 1949, p. 6. As Helmut Kramer notes, judges' robes were in short supply. "You could only order them from a special company, from a lawyers' association. There you could specify your measurements according to the regulations. Judges had to have them with a kind of fur trim and lawyers had a different trim. Many judges were thrown out at that time and many robes just lay there and then you could take one" (Helmut Kramer, Interview by Jack Fairweather and Florine Miez, Oct. 4, 2020). Richard Graefe of Lüdenscheid was one of the few businesses to make such robes ("Robe worn by Fritz Bauer." Object 54. Shared History Project. *Jüdisches Leben in Deutschland*. Leo Baeck Institute, 2021, online source). Wojak, *Fritz Bauer*, pp. 229–230; Kramer, "Die NS-Justiz," in: Kramer (ed.), *Braunschweig*, pp. 29–30; Kramer, "'Gerichtstag,'" in: Loewy (ed.), *NS-"Euthanasie,"* pp. 100–101; Klee, *Was sie taten*, pp. 250–251; Franz Brunke, NLA HA, Nds. 100 Acc. 2000/098 Nr. 3, no pages; Nationalrat der Nationalen Front des Demokratischen Deutschland (ed.), *Braunbuch*, online source.

14. Bauer told his friend Helga Einsele that "when I leave my office I feel as if I am in enemy territory," presumably referring to his time in Frankfurt but broadly representative of his experience since returning to Germany (Einsele, "Worte," in: Oberstaatsanwaltschaft at Frankfurt am Main Oberlandesgericht [ed.], *Fritz Bauer*, p. 21, cited in: Steinke, *Fritz Bauer*, p. 179).

15. Wojak, *Fritz Bauer*, pp. 244–247; Trentmann, *Out of*, pp. 155–156.

16. Trentmann, *Out of*, pp. 156, 91, 187; Wojak, *Fritz Bauer*, p. 245.

17. Bauer quoted antisemitic statements from the original case to prove the court had been prejudiced against the defendants. He also argued that the court had been unnecessarily harsh on them (II. Strafkammer des Landgerichts Braunschweig, Beschluss in der Strafsache gegen Schönbeck, Matzdorf, Wolff, Künstler, May 2, 1949. NLA WO, 62 Nds, Fb. 2 Nr. 502, pp. 189–194; Wojak, *Fritz Bauer*, pp. 246–247). Bauer's family made their own compensation claims in Stuttgart around this time (Entschädigungssache Bauer, Ludwig, no date. StAL, EL 350 I, BA 35321, no pages; Entschädigungssache Bauer, Fritz, no date. StAL, EL 350 I, Bü 8657, no pages).

18. Meyer-Velde, "'Dann machen's,'" in: Backhaus, Boll, Gross (eds.), *Fritz Bauer*, p. 235.

19. Ibid.

20. Ibid.

21. Meyer-Velde, "'Dann machen's,'" in: Backhaus, Boll, Gross (eds.), *Fritz Bauer*, pp. 235–236.

22. Meyer-Velde, "'Dann machen's,'" in: Backhaus, Boll, Gross (eds.), *Fritz Bauer*, p. 236; Jähner, *Aftermath*, pp. 92–93, 127, 123–127; Steinbacher, *Wie der Sex*, pp. 242–243.

23. On origins of the Volkswartbund and its wartime role see: Steinbacher, *Wie der Sex*, pp. 31–42; for Volkswartbund postwar activities see: Steinbacher, *Wie der Sex*, pp. 42–49. Poiger, *Jazz*, p. 57; Steinbacher, *Wie der Sex*, pp. 63, 27; Blessing, "Kulturpolizei," *Frankfurter Rundschau*, Dec. 1, 1949, p. 2; Newsome, *Homosexuals*, pp. 73–74. For Bauer's thinking on the repeal of anti-gay laws as part of his larger cultural reform agenda see: Renz, "Wider die Sittenwächter," in: Borowski et al. (eds.), *Jahrbuch*, pp. 70–93. The postwar debate about gay life remained deeply regressive and focused on a distinction between those who were believed to be innately homosexual and those who acquired the so-called proclivity through seduction, typically of younger men, which fed into public concerns about the general sexual promiscuity and immorality of the new generation. Giese's own work was constrained by his efforts to enlist the support of former racial hygienists and Nazi medical professionals who could "prove" the scientific basis of sex research (Whisnant, *Male*, pp. 71–111).

24. Bauer, "Warum," June 1949, in: Foljanty, Johst (eds.), *Fritz Bauer*, vol. 1, pp. 286–290; Meyer-Velde, "'Dann machen's,'" in: Backhaus, Boll, Gross (eds.), *Fritz Bauer*, pp. 236–237; Staatstheaterprogramm, *Braunschweiger Zeitung*, May 7, 1949, p. 20; Bormuth, *"Ein Mann,"* p. 33.

25. Lommatzsch, *Hans Globke*, p. 122. See Adenauer's opening speech to Bundestag as an example of his limited idea of German culpability (Frei, *Adenauer's*, p. 3).

7

RESTORATION

1. Lommatzsch, *Hans Globke*, pp. 152, 156–157; Schwarz, *Konrad Adenauer*, pp. 466–467; Biermann, *Konrad Adenauer*, pp. 324–326.

2. Globke drafted the commentary with his superior Wilhelm Stuckart, who was a state secretary in the Reich Interior Ministry. Stuckart played a more prominent role than Globke in implementing the Nuremberg Race Laws, and attended the Wannsee Conference on behalf of the Interior Ministry. He received a light sentence after the war. Two other commentaries were written on the Nuremberg Race Laws in 1936. Strecker (ed.), *Dr. Hans Globke*, pp. 95–100; Lommatzsch, *Hans Globke*, pp. 67–68; 75–76; Bästlein, *Der Fall*, pp. 15–16, 139–140. For Globke's role in introducing the *J* stamp in Jewish passports, see his self-incrimination: "Globke, [Interview]," *Der Spiegel*, May 9, 1961, online source. Frick's recommendation came in April 1938, before several of the measures described had been implemented.

3. Globke traveled to Slovakia in September 1941 as an adviser to Stuckart. Globke himself admitted at Nuremberg to discussing "legislation" during the trip. For Globke's role in advising on matters of citizenship, see the dossier prepared by Václav Král, a history professor at Prague University and the chair of a Communist-backed antifascist organization (see: Union of Antifascist Warriors press release. Dr. Václav Král, Press conference regarding Globke, Prague, Dec. 8, 1960. Abs, NSR, Západní Berlín, k.c. 3, 1960–1964, pp. 1900649–1900670). For correspondence between Globke and Ludwig Eugen (later Dollmann), secretary to Slovakian Nazi leader Franz Karmasin, regarding the trip to Slovakia see:

BStU, MfS ASt I-7-63 GA, vol. 79, pp. 97–111; Strecker (ed.), *Dr. Hans Globke,* pp. 193–194, 218–219. For a full list of countries visited by Globke to assist in the implementation of the Nuremberg Race Laws see: Bästlein, *Der Fall,* p. 21.

4. Dwork, van Pelt, *Auschwitz,* pp. 299–300; Hans Globke, Letter to Ludwig Eugen-Dollmann, Sept. 22, 1941. BStU, MfS ASt I-7-63 GA, vol. 79, p. 102; Hans Globke, Letter to Ludwig Eugen-Dollmann, Nov. 7, 1941. BStU, MfS ASt I-7-63 GA, vol. 79, pp. 108–110; Union of Antifascist Warriors press release. Dr. Václav Král, Press conference regarding Globke, Prague, Dec. 8, 1960. Abs, NSR, Západní Berlín, k.c. 3, 1960–1964, pp. 1900649–1900670; Dwork, van Pelt, *Auschwitz,* pp. 299–300.

5. There were some exceptions permitted for first-degree "Mischlinge." For Globke's work on antisemitic legislation during the war see: Bästlein, *Der Fall,* pp. 17–21. "Who Is Dr. Globke?" *Frankfurter Rundschau,* Nov. 9, 1949, no pages. NARA, Hans Globke, 640446, box 42, folder 6, pp. 21–22; Trentmann, *Out of,* p. 22; Strecker (ed.), *Dr. Hans Globke,* pp. 247–249; Foth, "Die Nürnberger," *Bulletin für Faschismus- und Weltkriegsforschung,* 2006/27, pp. 63–64. Typically, children with one "Aryan" parent were not deported. However, a different policy existed in German-annexed and -occupied Poland and the Soviet-annexed Baltic countries, where such children were classified as Jewish and subject to deportation. Globke's papers include a letter from a German woman, Grete Heide, who thanked Globke for helping her rescue her half-Jewish son in 1940 (Grete Heide, Letter to Hans Globke, Feb. 27, 1961, cited in: Hehl, "Der Beamte," in: Gotto [ed.], *Der Staatssekretär,* p. 276). Globke's denazification file contained statements attesting to his role in rescuing some Jews, but it omitted testimony that revealed his sometimes callous disregard for others.

6. Lommatzsch, *Hans Globke,* p. 106. For Globke's defense that he was moderating or helping Jews through his commentary and subsequent anti-Jewish legislation see: Globke, "Aufzeichnung," 1956, cited in: Hehl, "Der Beamte," in: Gotto (ed.), *Der Staatssekretär,* pp. 250–254. Lommatzsch, *Hans Globke,* pp. 112–113; Bästlein, *Der Fall,* pp. 9–10, 24. For Globke's work on antisemitic legislation as a junior bureaucrat for the Prussian state government in the 1920s, see: Lommatzsch, *Hans Globke,* pp. 59–61. For Globke's account of his ties to resistance circles see: Globke, "Aufzeichnung," 1956, cited in: Hehl, "Der Beamte," in: Gotto (ed.), *Der Staatssekretär,* pp. 256–257. "I was aware that just as the co-edition of the commentary could be misinterpreted later, so could my remaining in office," Globke wrote in 1956. "However, I once believed that I should not give up the possibility of helping, but that, on the other hand, my anti-national socialist activity would later be a sufficient explanation for my behavior" (Globke, "Aufzeichnung," 1956, cited in: Hehl, "Der Beamte," in: Gotto [ed.], *Der Staatssekretär,* pp. 258–259). Schwarz, *Konrad Adenauer,* pp. 466–467. At various points after 1945, Globke collected affidavits from former friends and colleagues who spoke in his defense. Robert Kempner, the German Jewish prosecutor at Nuremberg, wrote of his experience working with Globke at the Prussian Ministry of the Interior (1929–1933), when he heard him speak in defense of democratic institutions, and of his role as a witness for the defense and prosecution at Nuremberg, in which, Kempner adjudged, he spoke with candor (Kempner, "Begegnungen," in: Gotto [ed.], *Der Staatssekretär,* pp. 213–229). Otto Lenz, a member of the Goerdeler resistance circle, arrested after the July 20, 1944, attempt to kill Hitler, claimed that his fellow resisters had asked Globke to stay in the Interior Ministry

(Lenz, "Eidesstattliche," Jan. 3, 1946, cited in: Hehl, "Der Beamte," in: Gotto [ed.], *Der Staatssekretär,* pp. 260–262). Church leaders like Cardinal Konrad von Preysing, the bishop of Berlin, also wrote that Globke had used his position to give the church advance warning of Interior Ministry decrees against Jews (Konrad von Preysing, Erklärung, Jan. 18, 1946, cited in: Hehl, "Der Beamte," in: Gotto [ed.], *Der Staatssekretär,* pp. 266–267). Lommatzsch, *Hans Globke,* p. 114. For a text of Globke's statement to Kempner see: Strecker, *Dr. Hans Globke,* p. 86.

7.   Lommatzsch, *Hans Globke,* p. 107; Jacques S. Arouet, Memorandum to Office of Intelligence Analysts, Apr. 7, 1950. NARA, RG 263, Hans Globke, 640446, box 42, folder 6, NAID: 139340943, p. 24; Globke family, Interview by Jack Fairweather, Anna Schattschneider, and Harriet Phillips, Sept. 20, 2021; Lommatzsch, *Hans Globke,* p. 152.

8.   Biermann, *Konrad Adenauer,* p. 325; Schwarz, *Konrad Adenauer,* pp. 465–466; Williams, *Adenauer,* pp. 283–285, 317–323; Frei, *Adenauer's,* p. 3. Adenauer neglected to mention any of the other countries occupied by Germany (Franz, *Prinzipien,* in: Creuzberger, Geppert [eds.], *Die Ämter,* online source). For Adenauer's experience under the Nazis, when he was forced from office as mayor of Cologne and twice arrested, see: Williams, *Adenauer,* pp. 229–275. Frei, *Adenauer's,* p. 3; Lommatzsch, *Hans Globke,* p. 122; Schwarz, *Konrad Adenauer,* p. 336; Schwarz, *Konrad Adenauer,* p. 465.

9.   Lommatzsch, *Hans Globke,* p. 158; Biermann, *Konrad Adenauer,* pp. 322–323; Williams, *Adenauer,* p. 381; Schwarz, *Konrad Adenauer,* p. 468; Biermann, *Konrad Adenauer,* p. 326; Bästlein, *Der Fall,* p. 31.

10.   Frei, *Adenauer's,* p. 3; Trentmann, *Out of,* p. 152.

11.   Wittmann, *Beyond,* p. 27; Frei, *Adenauer's,* p. 3; Trentmann, *Out of,* p. 152.

12.   Frei, *Adenauer's,* pp. 5–18; Trentmann, *Out of,* p. 126.

13.   Frei, *Adenauer's,* pp. 16–17, 20, 28–30; Schwarz, *Konrad Adenauer,* pp. 87; 42; Trentmann, *Out of,* pp. 167–171, Steinke, *Fritz Bauer,* p. 3; "Ist benachrichtigt," *Der Spiegel,* Apr. 14, 1968, online source. The legislation for rehabilitating former Nazis, which became known as Article 131, was first discussed in 1950, coming into effect in 1952. Already by the summer of 1950, one third of all government employees—nearly a million people—were former Nazi Party members (Frei, *Adenauer's,* p. 42; Fulbrook, *Reckonings,* p. 148).

14.   Trentmann, *Out of,* pp. 178–179, 180, 181–182; Fulbrook, *Reckonings,* pp. 6, 184, 340–342; Trentmann, *Out of,* pp. 184, 186.

15.   Frei, *Adenauer's,* p. 30; "Böse," *Der Spiegel,* Apr. 3, 1956, online source; Biermann, *Konrad Adenauer,* p. 325; Fulbrook, *Reckonings,* p. 249.

16.   Biermann, *Konrad Adenauer,* p. 337; Schwarz, *Konrad Adenauer,* p. 534.

17.   Frei, *Adenauer's,* p. 87.

18.   Frei, *Adenauer's,* p. 147; Tusa, Tusa, *The Nuremberg,* p. 537. For the various machinations of competing officers for Adenauer's attention and Gehlen's rivalry with Theodor von Schwerin and Friedrich Wilhelm Heinz see: Müller, *Reinhard Gehlen,* pp. 660–701.

19.   Müller, *Reinhard Gehlen,* p. 585; Reese, *General,* p. 96; Müller, *Reinhard Gehlen,* p. 721; Reese, *General,* p. 84; Henke, *Geheime . . . Die politische Inlandsspionage der Organisation,* pp. 48, 63, 720; Sälter, *Phantome,* pp. 98–99; Henke, *Geheime . . . Die politische Inlandsspionage der Organisation,* pp. 79–81. Gehlen suspected journalist Erich Kästner to be a Soviet agent and had a cultural subversion agent, the former theater director Fritz Fischer, investigate him closely (Henke,

Geheime . . . Die politische Inlandsspionage der Organisation, pp. 63–69). For an extensive overview of Gehlen's perception of the Communist threat see: Gehlen, *The Service,* pp. 305–331; Sälter, *Phantome,* pp. 51–53, 99; Müller, *Reinhard Gehlen,* p. 452.

20. Henke, *Geheime . . . Die politische Inlandsspionage der Organisation,* pp. 48, 63, 720; Sälter, *Phantome,* pp. 98–99; Henke, *Geheime . . . Die politische Inlandsspionage der Organisation,* pp. 79–81.

21. Henke, *Geheime . . . Die politische Inlandsspionage der Organisation,* pp. 48–49. A document from 1949 lists around twenty-six former Nazis among a hundred headquarter staff members. As Sälter points out, the figure is likely to be higher, as the headquarters had around 250 members (Sälter, *NS-Kontinuitäten,* p. 89). Critchfield, *Partners,* p. 82; Reese, *General,* p. 111; Breitman (ed.), *U.S. Intelligence,* p. 392; Sälter, *Phantome,* pp. 65, 106, 128; Critchfield, *Partners,* p. 82; Breitman (ed.), *U.S. Intelligence,* p. 383; Sälter, *NS-Kontinuitäten,* pp. 96–97. Rudolf Röder complained that his death squad, which operated in Poland in 1939, was not able to kill people quickly enough. He later ran a unit of Russian collaborators that had killed and looted behind enemy lines (Sälter, *NS-Kontinuitäten,* pp. 218–222).

22. Müller, *Reinhard Gehlen,* p. 937; Critchfield, *Partners,* pp. 166–167, 207.

23. Müller, *Reinhard Gehlen,* p. 658; Hett, Wala, *Otto John,* p. 91; Müller, *Reinhard Gehlen,* p. 678; Hett, Wala, *Otto John,* pp. 86, 125; Janssen, "Der Fall," *Die Zeit,* Sept. 6, 1985, online source. "From the standpoint of our control of future German intelligence," noted one CIA report, "Utility [Gehlen's codename] is too powerful in his own right to be allowed to accept the position" (Report, May 1950. NARA, RG 263, Reinhard Gehlen, 640446, box 38, folder 5, NAID: 139337808, pp. 135–139). Adenauer was likely aware that Gehlen had been organizing gatherings of senior ex-Wehrmacht officers to deliberate on the future leadership of a German military. Among those considered was Adolf Heusinger, a former senior strategist for the invasion of the Soviet Union, who was now working for Gehlen (Müller, *Reinhard Gehlen,* p. 658).

24. Critchfield, *Partners,* p. 129; Müller, *Reinhard Gehlen,* pp. 657, 661; Author unknown, Note, July 21, 1950. BND-Archiv, 4314, and Heinz Herre, Diary, July 21, 1950. College of William and Mary, Digital Archive, pp. 244–246, cited in: Müller, *Reinhard Gehlen,* p. 663; Hechelhammer, Meinl, *Geheimobjekt,* pp. 149, 156, 192–195; Dorothee Gehlen-Koss, Interview by Jack Fairweather, Aug. 29, 2022.

25. Reese, *General,* p. 46; Müller, *Reinhard Gehlen,* p. 937.

26. Sälter, *Phantome,* pp. 365, 372; Müller, *Reinhard Gehlen,* p. 656; Hechelhammer, "Die 'Dossiers,'" in: Dülffer et al. (eds.), *Die Geschichte,* pp. 83–92.

27. Müller, *Reinhard Gehlen,* p. 1272; Lommatzsch, *Hans Globke,* pp. 67–68, 75–76; Union of Antifascist Warriors press release. Dr. Václav Král, Press conference regarding Globke, Prague, Dec. 8, 1960. Abs, NSR, Západní Berlín, k.c. 3, 1960–1964, pp. 1900649–1900670; Correspondence between Hans Globke and Ludwig Dostal-Dollmann. BStU, MfS ASt I-7-63 GA, vol. 79, pp. 97–111; Strecker (ed.), *Dr. Hans Globke,* pp. 193–194, 218–219; Strecker (ed.), *Dr. Hans Globke,* pp. 247–249; Foth, "Die Nürnberger," *Bulletin für Faschismus- und Weltkriegsforschung,* 2006/27, pp. 63–64.

28. Reinhard Gehlen, Memo to Hans Globke, Feb. 8, 1951. BND-Archive, 1110, pp. 92–93, cited in: Müller, *Reinhard Gehlen,* p. 704; Müller, *Reinhard Gehlen,* p. 1270.

29. Müller, *Reinhard Gehlen*, p. 657; Schwarz, *Konrad Adenauer*, p. 516. The Americans had already been leading discussions on German rearmament, partly in response to increasing Cold War tensions.

30. Frei, *Adenauer's*, pp. 147–149; Karlsruhe Chief of Station, Memo to Chief of Foreign Division M, Sept. 1, 1951. MGLA-8039, in: Ruffner (ed.), *Forging*, vol. 2, pp. 409–410; Frei, *Adenauer's*, pp. 103, 163; "Meine," *Der Spiegel*, Jan. 30, 1951, online source; "Sie mögen," *Der Spiegel*, Feb. 27, 1951, online source; Frei, *Adenauer's*, pp. 143–144, 152, 157. Other flashpoints included the trials of Wehrmacht generals Albert Kesselring (1947) and Erich von Manstein (1949).

31. Trentmann, *Out of*, p. 221. The nationalist German Party (Deutsche Partei) and German Right Party (Deutsche Rechtspartei) had twenty-two seats between them. Franz Richter was in fact Fritz Rössler, a former Nazi who'd worked under Goebbels in the Propaganda Ministry. After the war he'd managed to have himself declared dead, remarry his "widow" and adopt his own four children (Maxwill, "Rechtsradikale," *Der Spiegel*, Mar. 2, 2012, online source). Anglo-Jewish Association, *Germany's*, p. 21; Frei, *Adenauer's*, pp. 237–238. Hedler was subsequently acquitted on all counts (Frei, *Adenauer's*, pp. 239–240). Frei, *Adenauer's*, p. 252; Paulus, "Remer," *Braunschweiger Zeitung*, Sept. 6, 1949, p. 8. FBInst, Nachlass Fritz Bauer 54; "Nichts," *Der Spiegel*, Dec. 1, 1949, online source; Paulus, "Remer," *Braunschweiger Zeitung*, Sept. 6, 1949, p. 8. FBInst, Nachlass Fritz Bauer 54; Grigg, "Fuehrer," *The Washington Post*, Mar. 31, 1952, p. 2; "Nichts," *Der Spiegel*, Dec. 1, 1949, online source; Frei, *Adenauer's*, p. 252; Paulus, "Remer," *Braunschweiger Zeitung*, Sept. 6, 1949, p. 8. FBInst, Nachlass Fritz Bauer 54; Frei, *Adenauer's*, p. 251; Wolf, "Der Remer-Prozess," *Forschungsjournal Soziale Bewegungen*, 2015/4 (28), p. 197.

32. Middleton, "Neo-Nazism," *The New York Times*, July 1, 1951, no pages; Sethe, No title, *Frankfurter Allgemeine Zeitung*, May 8, 1951, cited in: Wojak, *Fritz Bauer*, p. 262; Frei, *Adenauer's*, pp. 263, 260.

33. Frei, *Adenauer's*, pp. 261–266; Wolf, "Der Remer-Prozess," *Forschungsjournal Soziale Bewegungen*, 2015/4 (28), p. 197. For Lehr complaint see: Der Strafantrag von Dr. h. c. Robert Lehr, Bundesminister des Inneren, June 20, 1951. NLA WO, 62 Nds. Fb. 3, Zg 51/1985, Nr. 2/1, no pages. Trentmann, *Out of*, p. 166. For Adenauer's belated statement on October 2, 1951, about the significance of anti-Hitler resistance and the July 20 plot see: Fröhlich, *"Wider die Tabuisierung,"* pp. 73–75. Gehlen had also established contact with the Socialist Reich Party. His staff was using one of Remer's colleagues, a Nazi judge who had signed execution orders against some of the July 20 plotters, as a source for their Red Orchestra investigations. It was clear that some of Gehlen's men sympathized with Remer's views on the plotters being traitors. Globke felt obliged to have a quiet word with Gehlen to make sure he understood that Remer's views were problematic (Sälter, *Phantome*, pp. 173–175, 194–198). Trentmann, *Out of*, p. 70. A motion to ban the Socialist Reich Party was submitted to the Bundesverfassungsgericht in November 1951 (Frei, *Adenauer's*, pp. 261–266). The domestic spy service was investigating the Socialist Reich Party from summer 1951 onward and supplied reports to Lehr (Frei, *Adenauer's*, p. 256, 261–266).

8

RESISTANCE

1. "Dr. Bauer," *Braunschweiger Presse*, Aug. 2, 1950, p. 7; "Amtseinführung," *Braunschweiger Zeitung*, Aug. 2, 1950, no pages. Bauer's opening remarks allude to the ongoing debate among West German jurists over whether to keep Allied laws such as those relating to Crimes Against Humanity. Bauer argues that they should be retained (Bauer, "Der Kampf," Oct. 1950, in: Foljanty, Johst [eds.], *Fritz Bauer*, vol. 1, pp. 297–301). Frei, *Adenauer's*, p. 252; Fritz Bauer, Letter to Fritz Heine, May 15, 1950. AdsD, SPD-PV, Sekr. Heine, 2/PVV 8, no pages.

2. Bauer had opened or reopened 289 investigations by the end of 1952. Special thanks to Jonathan Friedman for compiling data on Braunschweig investigations (Eichmüller, "Die Verfolgung, von NS-Verbrechen durch deutsche Justizbehörden seit 1945." [Database at Institut für Zeitgeschichte München]). Wojak, *Fritz Bauer*, p. 237. As deputy head of Braunschweig's Gestapo, Otto Diederichs had not only given the orders but also created the legal framework that allowed for the deportation of political prisoners and Jews in Braunschweig to their deaths in concentration camps. Charges filed against him in 1947 had been dropped on the grounds that protective custody was legal under Nazi law and that he could not have known about conditions in the camp. He was soon remanded to custody again and ended up serving a little over a year in prison for membership in the SS before being released on bail. Bauer's 1950 indictment of Diederichs was rejected by a judge who had previously served on a Nazi military tribunal. Bauer appealed and secured a conviction, which was then overturned by the district court in February 1953. It's not clear if Bauer knew that Diederichs had served as head of the SS administration in Riga during the mass murder of Latvian and German Jews, including Bauer's aunt and nephew (Sohn, *Im Spiegel*, pp. 190–197; Sohn, *Im Spiegel*, p. 206, cited in: Wojak, *Fritz Bauer*, p. 258). For a description of an aggressive comment against Bauer see: Ilona Ziok (dir.), *Fritz Bauer*, 2010.

3. Steinke, *Fritz Bauer*, p. 86; "Remer," *Frankfurter Allgemeine Zeitung*, May 5, 1951, cited in: Fröhlich, "Der Braunschweiger," in: Diercks, KZ-Gedenkstätte Neuengamme (eds.), *Schuldig*, p. 17.

4. Bericht über die öffentliche Kundgebung der SRP in Braunschweig, May 4, 1951. NLA WO, 62 Nds Fb 3 Zg 51/1985 2-1b, pp. 5–6.

5. Frei, *Adenauer's*, pp. 257–259, 263, 266; Fröhlich, "Wider die Tabuisierung," p. 32. Bauer handed Lehr's case to his chief prosecutor, Erich Topf, a former Nazi whose record Bauer had already looked into. Topf initially dismissed the case, citing Remer's claim that he hadn't known Lehr had been in the resistance and therefore had not intended to insult him. Bauer subsequently arranged for Topf's transfer to another prosecutor's office and took over the Remer case himself (Fröhlich, "Der Braunschweiger," in: Diercks, KZ-Gedenkstätte Neuengamme [eds.], *Schuldig*, pp. 19–20; Fröhlich, "Wider die Tabuisierung," pp. 34, 37; Wojak, *Fritz Bauer*, pp. 263–264). For Bauer's trial strategy see: Fröhlich, "Wider die Tabuisierung," pp. 34, 37.

6. Trentmann, *Out of*, p. 69; Hoffmann, *Stauffenberg*, pp. 368–369.

7. Hoffmann, *Stauffenberg*, pp. 447, 451, 454–462, 313, 449–451.

8. Hoffmann, *Stauffenberg*, pp. 451, 457; Steinke, *Fritz Bauer*, p. 87; Hoffmann, *Stauffenberg*, p. 467; Trentmann, *Out of*, p. 69.

9. Gerlach, "Männer," in: Heer, Naumann (eds.), *Vernichtungskrieg*, pp. 427–446; Bauer, "Der Generalstaatsanwalt," July 20, 1952, in: Foljanty, Johst (eds.), *Fritz Bauer*, vol. 1, p. 336; Steinke, *Fritz Bauer*, p. 102; Fritz Bauer, Letter to Karl B. Frank, Mar. 2, 1945. IfZ, ED 213, 27, no pages; Trentmann, *Out of*, p. 70.

10. Fröhlich, "Der Braunschweiger," in: Diercks, KZ-Gedenkstätte Neuengamme (eds.), *Schuldig*, pp. 25–26; Wojak, *Fritz Bauer*, p. 269; Wolf, "Der Remer-Prozess," *Forschungsjournal Soziale Bewegungen*, 2015/4 (28), pp. 198–200; "Remer Prozess," Buxus Stiftung, Fritz Bauer Archiv, no date, online source; Wojak, *Fritz Bauer*, p. 267.

11. Janssen, "Der Fall," *Die Zeit*, Sept. 6, 1985, online source; Fröhlich, "*Wider die Tabuisierung*," pp. 61–62, 96. Bauer's first letter to John about the case is dated February 1952, but the wording suggests prior contact (Fritz Bauer, Letter to Otto John, Feb. 7, 1952. NLA WO, 61 Nds. Fb. 1, Nr. 24/2, no pages). Bauer had been contacted by the widow of a member of another resistance group, the so-called Red Orchestra, whose members had been wrongly accused of Soviet collusion by the Gestapo. The widow, Annette Harnack, wanted to join as a plaintiff. Bauer had felt obliged to reject her, as he wanted to stick to the subject of the July 20 resistors and "not deviate from this line . . . to the detriment of the criminal case" (Annette Harnack, Letter to Fritz Bauer, Dec. 6, 1951. NLA WO, 62 Nds Fb. 3 Nr. 2/1, p. 108; Fröhlich, "Der Braunschweiger," in: Diercks, KZ-Gedenkstätte Neuengamme [eds.], *Schuldig*, p. 25; Fröhlich, "*Wider die Tabuisierung*," pp. 64–65).

12. Bauer, "Ein neues," Oct. 23, 1954, in: Foljanty, Johst (eds.), *Fritz Bauer*, vol. 1, pp. 376–377; Renz, "Wider die Sittenwächter," in: Borowski et al. (eds.), *Jahrbuch*, pp. 77–80; "Staatsanwalt," *Allgemeine Gerichtszeitung*, 1952/15 (3), p. 5; Schiefelbein, "Wiederbeginn," *Zeitschrift für Sexualforschung*, 1992/5 (1), pp. 60–61; Bormuth, "*Ein Mann . . .*," pp. 14–15.

13. Schiefelbein, "Wiederbeginn," *Zeitschrift für Sexualforschung*, 1992/5 (1), pp. 59, 64–67; "Eine Million," *Der Spiegel*, Nov. 28, 1950, online source.

14. Fritz Bauer, Letter to Erster Staatsanwalt Schulz, Sept. 10, 1951. NLA WO, 61 Nds Fb 1 Nr. 204, p. 1. In September 1951, Bauer attended a biannual conference for legal professionals outside Stuttgart that debated strategies for overturning Article 175—itself a sign of progress. Heinrich Ackermann, a Hamburg lawyer, proposed to the conference that instead of attempting to eliminate the law, they should try to limit its reach to sex with minors. Bauer wanted a complete repeal but found himself agreeing with this incremental strategy, which had a greater chance of gaining support and easing the suffering of gay men sooner (Heinrich Ackermann, "Thesen," Sept. 13–15, 1951. NLA WO, 61 Nds Fb 1 Nr. 204, p. 12; "Der 39.," *Juristenzeitung*, Oct. 15, 1951, pp. 663–667). Bauer subsequently requested a copy of Ackermann's lecture (Fritz Bauer, Letter to Heinrich Ackermann, Oct. 5, 1951. NLA WO, 61 Nds Fb 1 Nr. 204, p. 30). The lawyer's conference tabled a vote 14:11 in favor of Ackermann's approach ("Der 39.," *Juristenzeitung*, Oct. 15, 1951, p. 666). Bauer also met with a gay law professor from Cologne, Richard Lange, who had been a Nazi Party member and commentator on the Nuremberg Race Laws (Pauly, " 'Kämpferische,' [Review]," no date. koeblergerhard.de, online source). Lange had also written an article analyzing the failure of a previous federal court appeal against Article 175. He pointed out that Article 2 of the Basic Law, the German constitution, enshrined the right to "free develop-

ment of one's personality," which, in his view, could be interpreted to include sexual orientation. Another potential argument was that Article 175 discriminated by targeting only men, thus violating the right to equality. Lange further argued that restricting a person's sexuality was a form of totalitarianism, precisely the kind of oppression the constitution was designed to prevent (Lange, "Strafrecht," *Juristenzeitung,* Sept. 5, 1951, pp. 561–566). Fritz Bauer, Letter to Schulz, Sept. 15, 1951. NLA WO, 61 Nds Fb 1 Nr. 204, no pages; Hans Giese, Letter to Fritz Bauer, Sept. 29, 1951. NLA WO, 61 Nds Fb 1 Nr. 204, p. 27. Giese had been an active member of the Nazi Party and admitted postwar to having fond memories of the Nazi takeover (Whisnant, *Male,* p. 73). On Giese's life and work see: Whisnant, *Male,* pp. 71–79.

15. Eckhard Schimpf, Interview by Harriet Phillips, May 14, 2024; Erich Topf, Letter to Fritz Bauer, Oct. 4, 1951. NLA WO, 61 Nds Fb 1 Nr. 204, p. 30; Fritz Bauer, Motion, Oct. 22, 1951. NLA WO, 61 Nds Fb 1 Nr. 204, pp. 74–87; Fritz Bauer, Motion, Oct 22, 1951. NLA WO, 61 Nds Fb 1 Nr. 204, pp. 88–101.

16. Fritz Bauer, Motion, Oct. 22, 1951. NLA WO, 61 Nds Fb 1 Nr. 204, pp. 74–87, 88–101; Heinemann, Ruling, Nov 10, 1951. NLA WO, 61 Nds Fb 1 Nr. 204, pp. 111–113; Goltz, Ruling, Nov. 10, 1951. NLA WO, 61 Nds Fb 1 Nr. 204, pp. 115–118.

17. Fröhlich, "Der Braunschweiger," in: Diercks, KZ-Gedenkstätte Neuengamme (eds.), *Schuldig,* pp. 20–21; Fröhlich, *"Wider die Tabuisierung,"* pp. 78–80; Author unknown, Letter to Fritz Bauer, Feb. 6, 1952. NLA WO, 62 Nds Fb 3 Zg 51-1985 2-7, p. 1.

18. Wojak, *Fritz Bauer,* p. 265; Fritz Bauer, Letter to Otto John, Feb. 7, 1952. NLA WO, 61 Nds. Fb. 1, Nr. 24/2, no pages; Fröhlich, *"Wider die Tabuisierung,"* pp. 78–80; Meyer-Velde, "'Dann machen's,'" in: Backhaus, Boll, Gross (eds.), *Fritz Bauer,* p. 242; Dittmann, "Der private," *Schriftenreihe des "Fritz Bauer Freundeskreises,"* 2013, p. 1.

19. Wolf, "Der Remer-Prozess," *Forschungsjournal Soziale Bewegungen,* 2015/4 (28), p. 200; Fröhlich, *"Wider die Tabuisierung,"* pp. 69, 104; Buck, "Der 20.," in: Graf, Fiedler, Hermann (eds.), *75 Jahre,* p. 1; Buschke, "Der Braunschweiger," in: Buschke (ed.), *Deutsche,* p. 190; Fröhlich, *"Wider die Tabuisierung,"* p. 104; "Scharfe," *Die Welt,* Mar. 8, 1952, p. 1; Staatsanwaltschaft Braunschweig. Strafsache gegen Remer. Öffentliche Sitzung der 3. Strafkammer des Landgerichts, Mar. 7, 1952. NLA WO, 62 Nds Fb. 3, nr. 2/2, Zg 51-1985, no pages; Fröhlich, *"Wider die Tabuisierung,"* p. 65; Wolf, "Der Remer-Prozess," *Forschungsjournal Soziale Bewegungen,* 2015/4 (28), p. 200.

20. Wittmann, *Beyond,* pp. 33–36.

21. Molitor, "Die Schatten," *Die Zeit,* Mar. 13, 1952 (11), pp. 2–2a; Staatsanwaltschaft Braunschweig. Strafsache gegen Remer. Öffentliche Sitzung der 3. Strafkammer des Landgerichts, Mar. 7, 1952. NLA WO, 62 Nds Fb. 3, nr. 2/2, Zg 51-1985, p. 5; Fröhlich, *"Wider die Tabuisierung,"* p. 105; Staatsanwaltschaft Braunschweig. Strafsache gegen Remer. Öffentliche Sitzung der 3. Strafkammer des Landgerichts, Mar. 7, 1952. NLA WO, 62 Nds Fb. 3, nr. 2/2, Zg 51-1985, p. 8; Fröhlich, *"Wider die Tabuisierung,"* p. 105.

22. Staatsanwaltschaft Braunschweig. Strafsache gegen Remer. Öffentliche Sitzung der 3. Strafkammer des Landgerichts, Mar. 7, 1952. NLA WO, 62 Nds Fb. 3, nr. 2/2, Zg 51-1985, p. 4; Otto John, Interview by Hans Speier, May 23, 1952. Speier

Papers B9F2, LOG-40. M. E. Grenander Department of Special Collections and Archives, University at Albany, State University of New York; "Beginn," *Hannoversche Allgemeine Zeitung*, Mar. 8, 1952, no pages; Fröhlich, *"Wider die Tabuisierung,"* p. 116; Buschke, "Der Braunschweiger," in: Buschke (ed.), *Deutsche*, p. 191. The distinction between treason (*Landesverrat*) and high treason (*Hochverrat*) was first drawn by Remer under questioning the previous summer (Varel, Strafsache gegen Otto-Ernst Remer, Aug. 28, 1951. NLA WO, 2 Nds Fb 3 Zg 51-1985 2-1b, pp. 9–10).

23. Staatsanwaltschaft Braunschweig. Strafsache gegen Remer. Öffentliche Sitzung der 3. Strafkammer des Landgerichts, Mar. 7, 1952. NLA WO, 62 Nds Fb. 3, nr. 2/2, Zg 51-1985, p. 5; Fröhlich, *"Wider die Tabuisierung,"* pp. 89–90; Staatsanwaltschaft Braunschweig. Strafsache gegen Remer. Öffentliche Sitzung der 3. Strafkammer des Landgerichts, Mar. 7, 1952. NLA WO, 62 Nds Fb. 3, nr. 2/2, Zg 51-1985, p. 6; Fröhlich, *"Wider die Tabuisierung,"* pp. 88–89; Wolf, "Der Remer-Prozess," *Forschungsjournal Soziale Bewegungen*, 2015/4 (28), pp. 200–201; Fröhlich, "Der Braunschweiger," in: Diercks, KZ-Gedenkstätte Neuengamme (eds.), *Schuldig*, pp. 22–23.

24. Staatsanwaltschaft Braunschweig. Strafsache gegen Remer. Öffentliche Sitzung der 3. Strafkammer des Landgerichts, Mar. 8, 1952. NLA WO, 62 Nds Fb. 3, nr. 2/2, Zg 51-1985, p. 6. Schlabrendorff also made a lengthy rant against left-wing activists who had sided with the Soviet Union, declaring them to be the real traitors. The defense seized on his comments to claim that these were, in fact, the traitors Remer had been referring to all along. The point fell flat, however, given the earlier witness statements to the contrary (Fröhlich, *"Wider die Tabuisierung,"* pp. 112–113). Fröhlich, *"Wider die Tabuisierung,"* pp. 111–112; Fröhlich, "Der Braunschweiger," in: Diercks, KZ-Gedenkstätte Neuengamme (eds.), *Schuldig*, p. 23; Fröhlich, *"Wider die Tabuisierung,"* p. 84.

25. Fröhlich, *"Wider die Tabuisierung,"* p. 81.

26. Bauer, "Der Generalstaatsanwalt," July 20, 1952, in: Foljanty, Johst (eds.), *Fritz Bauer*, vol. 1, pp. 323, 325. For analysis of Bauer's closing argument see: Fröhlich, *"Wider die Tabuisierung,"* pp. 66–67; Wolf, "Der Remer-Prozess," *Forschungsjournal Soziale Bewegungen*, 2015/4 (28), pp. 202–203.

27. Bauer, "Der Generalstaatsanwalt," July 20, 1952, in: Foljanty, Johst (eds.), *Fritz Bauer*, vol. 1, pp. 329–331, 333–335.

28. Bauer, "Der Generalstaatsanwalt," July 20, 1952, in: Foljanty, Johst (eds.), *Fritz Bauer*, vol. 1, p. 326.

29. Bauer, "Der Generalstaatsanwalt," July 20, 1952, in: Foljanty, Johst (eds.), *Fritz Bauer*, vol. 1, pp. 335–336.

30. "Das Dritte Reich," *Hannoversche Presse*, Mar. 11, 1952, p. 2.

31. Fröhlich, *"Wider die Tabuisierung,"* p. 96.

32. Fröhlich, *"Wider die Tabuisierung,"* p. 66.

33. Fröhlich, *"Wider die Tabuisierung,"* p. 67.

34. "Remer Prozess," Buxus Stiftung, Fritz Bauer Archiv, no date, online source; Werner Höhne, Response to Fritz Bauer's plea, Nov. 3, 1952, cited in: "Remer-Prozess," Buxus Stiftung, Fritz Bauer Archiv, no date, online source; No title, *Neue Zeitung*, Mar. 12, 1952, cited in: Fröhlich, *"Wider die Tabuisierung,"* p. 99; Werner Höhne, Response to Fritz Bauer's closing argument, Nov. 3, 1952, cited in: "Remer-Prozess," Buxus Stiftung, Fritz Bauer Archiv, no date, online source. Bauer made a point of handing to the press the negative and threatening com-

ments he received from the likes of "Gestapo IV, Berlin" ("Braunschweiger," *Hannoversche Presse,* Mar. 19, 1952, p. 1).

35. Buschke, "Der Braunschweiger," in: Buschke (ed.), *Deutsche,* p. 193; Burghardt, "Vor 60 Jahren," *Journal der Juristischen Zeitgeschichte,* 2012/6 (2), pp. 50–51; Buschke, "Der Braunschweiger," in: Buschke (ed.), *Deutsche,* p. 193; "Drei Monate," *Hannoversche Allgemeine Zeitung,* Mar. 17, 1952, p. 2. Remer's lawyers immediately announced their intention to appeal ("Drei Monate," *Hannoversche Allgemeine Zeitung,* Mar. 17, 1952, p. 2).

36. "Braunschweiger," *Hannoversche Presse,* Mar. 19, 1952, p. 1; Walter Velten, Response to Fritz Bauer's plea, Mar. 11, 1952, cited in: "Remer-Prozess," Buxus Stiftung, Fritz Bauer Archiv, no date, online source; Fritz Bauer, Response to letter from Walter Velten, Mar. 19, 1952, cited in: "Remer-Prozess," Buxus Stiftung, Fritz Bauer Archiv, no date, online source; "Remer hatte," *Hannoversche Presse,* Mar. 20, 1952, pp. 2, 2a.

37. Merseberger, *Schumacher,* pp. 498–500, 523–528.

38. Wojak, *Fritz Bauer,* p. 277.

9
FRONT LINE

1. Frei, *Adenauer's,* pp. 287, 274. Adenauer's cabinet originally passed a motion to ban the Socialist Reich Party in November 1951. The constitutional court ban came into effect October 23, 1952 (Frei, *Adenauer's,* pp. 260–261, 264–266, 269–270, 274). Moeller, *War,* pp. 27–28, 26; Bergmann, "Sind die Deutschen," in: Bergmann, Erb (eds.), *Antisemitismus,* p. 114; Moeller, *War,* p. 27. For Globke's support for reparations see: Kempner, "Begegnungen," in: Gotto (ed.), *Der Staatssekretär,* p. 227. The threat of the Far Right had not disappeared. Indeed, the British arrested one of Joseph Goebbels's deputies, Werner Naumann, for a plot to infiltrate Nazi supporters into a mainstream right-wing political party in January 1953 (Frei, *Adenauer's,* p. 277). According to a report by the American military administration in Germany (Office of Military Government for Germany, United States, or OMGUS), "demonstratively antisemitic" sentiment increased from 10 percent in 1949 to 34 percent in 1952, when 37 percent still thought Germany would be better off without Jews, and 44 percent were undecided (Bergmann, "Sind die Deutschen," in: Bergmann, Erb [eds.]), *Antisemitismus,* pp. 113–115). West Germany passed its indemnity law (Bundesentschädigungsgesetz) in 1956, applied retroactively to 1953, which offered additional compensation for victims of political, religious, and racial persecution, but was again limited to those who could prove they held German citizenship at the time (Trentmann, *Out of,* p. 180).

2. Frei, *Adenauer's,* pp. 73, 308–309; Trentmann, *Out of,* pp. 387–388. The number of likely survivors he had recently reduced to just 100,000 (Trentmann, *Out of,* pp. 387–388). At the same time, Adenauer passed several laws to protect German businesses from any private claims for compensation brought by camp survivors in the courts. A former Auschwitz prisoner, Norbert Wollheim, had been awarded damages in 1953 against a company, IG Farben, that had used slave labor from the camp to build a chemical plant in Buna-Monowitz. The Wollheim ruling was later annulled (Fulbrook, *Reckonings,* pp. 254–255).

3. Whisnant, *Male,* pp. 105–107; Trentmann, *Out of,* pp. 201–202; Poiger, *Jazz,* p. 47.

4. Wolf von Kahlden, Note, Aug. 8, 1952. BND-Archiv, 104054, pp. 169–172, cited in: Müller, *Reinhard Gehlen*, p. 783; Henke, *Geheime . . . Die politische Inlandsspionage des BND*, pp. 548–549; "Böse," *Der Spiegel*, Apr. 3, 1956, online source.

5. Trentmann, *Out of*, p. 377; Jarausch, *After*, p. 39. Adenauer had gained the Allies' provisional approval for a 120,000-strong West German army the previous year with the signing of a European defense agreement, but actual rearmament could not begin until full independence was granted, which might be years away. In the meantime, the defense pact, known as the Treaty Establishing the European Defense Community, was signed in May 1952, but it was ultimately abandoned after its rejection by the French parliament in 1954.

6. Delmer, "Hitler," *Daily Express*, Mar. 17, 1952, cited in: Kellerhof, von Kostka, *Capital*, pp. 143–144.

7. Müller, *Reinhard Gehlen*, p. 763; Delmer, "Hitler," *Daily Express*, Mar. 17, 1952, cited in: Kellerhof, von Kostka, *Capital*, pp. 143–144.

8. For Gehlen's assessment of the East German threat see: Müller, *Reinhard Gehlen*, pp. 760–763. Dorothee Gehlen-Koss. Interview by Jack Fairweather, Sept. 18, 2021.

9. Henke, *Geheime . . . Die politische Inlandsspionage des BND*, pp. 375–378; Hechelhammer, *Spion*, p. 124; Müller, *Reinhard Gehlen*, p. 845; Hechelhammer, *Spion*, pp. 119–121; Gehlen, *The Service*, p. 157; Dorothee Gehlen-Koss, Interview by Jack Fairweather, Sept. 18, 2021; Müller, *Reinhard Gehlen*, p. 886.

10. Höhne, Zolling, *The General*, p. 196; Heidenreich, Münkel, Stadelmann-Wenz, *Geheimdienstkrieg*, p. 284; Höhne, Zolling, *The General*, pp. 195–196; Heidenreich, Münkel, Stadelmann-Wenz, *Geheimdienstkrieg*, pp. 287–288.

11. Müller, *Reinhard Gehlen*, p. 841; Globke family, Interview by Jack Fairweather, Anna Schattschneider and Harriet Phillips, Sept. 20, 2021; Müller, *Reinhard Gehlen*, p. 864.

12. Otto John, Interview by Hans Speier, May 23, 1952. Speier Papers B9F2, LOG-40. M. E. Grenander Department of Special Collections and Archives, University at Albany, State University of New York; Gehlen, *The Service*, pp. 153–154; James Critchfield, Memorandum, Nov. 6, 1952. NARA, RG 319, Entry 134A, Reinhard Gehlen, vol. 1, 20F3, pp. 60–62, cited in: Müller, *Reinhard Gehlen*, p. 793; Hett, Wala, *Otto John*, p. 125; Reinhard Gehlen, Note, Nov. 7, 1952. BND-Archiv, 1110, p. 360, cited in: Müller, *Reinhard Gehlen*, p. 794; Hett, Wala, *Otto John*, pp. 124–125; Müller, *Reinhard Gehlen*, p. 742. John was married to a classically trained Jewish opera singer ten years his senior with whom he had no children and was reported to have consorted with a gay Soviet sympathizer during the war (Henke, *Geheime . . . Die politische Inlandsspionage des BND*, pp. 445–446; Hett, Wala, *Otto John*, pp. 70–71). Schwartz, *Homosexuelle*, pp. 251–252; Otto John, Interview by Hans Speier, May 23, 1952. Speier Papers B9F2, LOG-40. M. E. Grenander Department of Special Collections and Archives, University at Albany, State University of New York; Gehlen, *The Service*, pp. 154–155; Henke, *Geheime . . . Die politische Inlandsspionage des BND*, pp. 439–440; Janssen, "Der Fall," *Die Zeit*, Sept. 6, 1985, online source; Schwartz, *Homosexuelle*, p. 250; Janssen, "Der Fall," *Die Zeit*, Sept. 6, 1985, online source. For antagonism between Gehlen and John see: Hett, Wala, *Otto John*, pp. 127–128; Goschler, Wala, *"Keine neue,"* p. 135.

13. Janssen, "Der Fall," *Die Zeit*, Sept. 6, 1985, online source; Hett, Wala, *Otto John*, p. 107.

14. Hett, Wala, *Otto John*, pp. 108–109; Janssen, "Der Fall," *Die Zeit*, Sept. 6, 1985, online source; Hett, Wala, *Otto John*, p. 112.
15. Schwartz, *Homosexuelle*, p. 252; Gehlen, *The Service*, p. 154; Janssen, "Der Fall," *Die Zeit*, Sept. 6, 1985, online source.
16. [Becker], "Des Kanzlers," *Der Spiegel*, Sept. 21, 1954, online source; Dorothee Gehlen-Koss, Interview by Jack Fairweather, Sept. 18, 2021.
17. [Becker], "Des Kanzlers," *Der Spiegel*, Sept. 21, 1954, online source.
18. Müller, *Reinhard Gehlen*, pp. 856, 898.
19. Müller, *Reinhard Gehlen*, p. 886; Dorothee Gehlen-Koss, Interview by Jack Fairweather, Sept. 18, 2021.

1 0
BREAKTHROUGH

1. "Zum Generalstaatsanwalt," *Frankfurter Rundschau*, Mar. 24–25, 1956, p. 4; No title, *Frankfurter Rundschau*, Apr. 9, 1956, p. 4; Wojak, *Fritz Bauer*, p. 278; Falk, *Entnazifizierung*, pp. 245–254. Zinn likely knew of Bauer through Kurt Schumacher or Karl Geiler, Bauer's former dissertation supervisor, who became the first postwar prime minister of Hesse (Philip-André Zinn, Interview by Jack Fairweather, Feb. 16, 2021). No title, *Frankfurter Rundschau*, Mar. 2, 1956, p. 4; Albrecht-Heider, Ahäuser (eds.), *Frankfurter*, vol. 2, pp. 14–38, 73–74; Gerhard Wiese, Interview by Domagała-Pereira, Dec. 23, 2019, cited in: Domagała-Pereira, Dudek, "'Meine Lebensaufgabe,'" *Deutsche Welle*, Dec. 6, 2019, online source; Meyer-Velde, "'Dann machen's,'" in: Backhaus, Boll, Gross (eds.), *Fritz Bauer*, p. 241; Bauer, "Die Stärke," Feb. 1954, in: Foljanty, Johst (eds.), *Fritz Bauer*, vol. 1, pp. 368–372; Renz, "Wider die Sittenwächter," in: Borowski et al. (eds.), *Jahrbuch*, p. 74.
2. Wojak, *Fritz Bauer*, p. 278; Müller-Doohm, *Adorno*, pp. 541, 472–477; Jeffries, *Grand Hotel*, pp. 269–271.
3. Steinke, *Fritz Bauer*, p. 156; "Zeitliste," 2021. Stadt Frankfurt, online source; Steinke, *Fritz Bauer*, p. 156; Freimüller, *Frankfurt*, pp. 29–31, 33, 36. The Westend synagogue had survived because it served as a stage warehouse for the Frankfurt opera house under the Nazis. The interior was gutted by incendiary bombs in March 1944 (Freimüller, *Frankfurt*, p. 36). Müller-Doohm, *Adorno*, p. 510;
4. Poiger, *Jazz*, pp. 80–81; Albrecht-Heider, Ahäuser (eds.), *Frankfurter*, vol. 2, p. 41; Poiger, *Jazz*, pp. 81, 107, 46; "Adolf Hitler," *Frankfurter Rundschau*, Mar. 1, 1956, p. 3; Müller-Doohm, *Adorno*, p. 541.
5. Bauer, "Im Kampf," Apr. 1955, in: Foljanty, Johst (eds.), *Fritz Bauer*, vol. 1, p. 455; Bauer, "Die Strafe," Sept. 24, 1949, in: Foljanty, Johst (eds.), *Fritz Bauer*, vol. 1, p. 292; Bauer, "Die Kriminalität," May 1951, in: Foljanty, Johst (eds.), *Fritz Bauer*, vol. 1, pp. 304–307; Bauer, "Widerstand," July 1956, in: Foljanty, Johst (eds.), *Fritz Bauer*, vol. 1, p. 465.
6. Fulbrook, *Reckonings*, p. 233; Stengel, *Die Überlebenden*, pp. 79–81. The trial of Gerhard Peters, managing director of the Zyklon B producer Degesch, the German Society for Pest Control, concluded with his acquittal. Two other trials focused on prisoner functionaries and not the SS men who had commanded them (Stengel, *Die Überlebenden*, pp. 79–80). "Prosecutor," *The Washington Post*, Dec. 21, 1958, p. A4. In January 1950, 595 judges and 147 public prosecutors

worked at Hessian courts. Of these, 228 judges (38.32 percent) were classified as "not affected" by denazification, 60 (10.08 percent) as "exonerated," and 307 lawyers (51.6 percent) as "followers." Fifty public prosecutors (34.01 percent) were found to be "not affected," 16 (10.38 percent) were "exonerated," and 81 (55.1 percent) were deemed "hangers-on" (Meusch, *Von der Dikatur,* p. 229). Stengel, *Die Überlebenden,* p. 80; Eichmüller, "Die juristische," *Einsicht 12: Bulletin des Fritz Bauer Institutes,* Herbst 2014, p. 42; Joachim Kügler, Interview by Werner Renz, May 5, 1998. FBInst, part 1; Stengel, *Die Überlebenden,* pp. 66–67; Wojak, *Fritz Bauer,* pp. 403–407; No title, *Frankfurter Rundschau,* July 27, 1956, p. 4. Beckerle's case was dropped in April 1957, due to either the statute of limitations or insufficient evidence (Wojak, *Fritz Bauer,* p. 407).

7. Bauer, "Das politische," Aug. 20, 1963, in: Foljanty, Johst (eds.), *Fritz Bauer,* vol. 2, p. 1053; Reitlinger, *The Final Solution,* pp. xiii–iv. Bauer had read Poliakov by 1959 at the latest (Renz, "Der 1 . . . Zwei Vorgeschichten," *Zeitschrift für Geschichtswissenschaft,* 2002/50 [7], p. 19). Poliakov, *Harvest,* p. 282; Levi, *The Black Hole,* p. 28; Wachsmann, *KL,* p. 12. There had been a precipitous drop in the number of memoirs being published from 1950 (Stengel, *Hermann Langbein,* p. 289).

8. Einsele, "Worte," in: Oberstaatsanwaltschaft at Frankfurt am Main Oberlandesgericht (ed.), *Fritz Bauer,* p. 20; Bauer, "Unbewältigte," Mar. 25, 1961, in: Foljanty, Johst (eds.), *Fritz Bauer,* vol. 1, p. 703; Joachim Kügler, Interview by Werner Renz, May 5, 1998. FBInst, part 1; Gerhard Wiese, Interview by Jack Fairweather and Florine Miez, Oct. 2, 2020; Wassermann, "Fritz Bauer," in: Glotz, Langenbucher (eds.), *Vorbilder,* pp. 296–298.

9. For the Bundesgerichthof's decision to award the Eichmann file to Bauer's office see: Entscheidung BGH, Oct. 26, 1956 (2 Ars 74/56). HHStAW, 461, 33532, pp. 163–164. Wojak, *Fritz Bauer,* pp. 282–283.

10. Poliakov, Wulf, *Das Dritte Reich,* p. 221.

11. Arrest warrant for Adolf Eichmann, Nov. 24, 1956. BA K, B141 21887, p. 32. The newspaper cuttings were included in Eichmann's investigation file, which was sent to Bauer in 1956 (Wojak, *Fritz Bauer,* p. 284). Stangneth, *Eichmann,* pp. 98–99, 155, 158. The Viennese police's scant findings noted that Eichmann was accused of multiple murders in the concentration camps. Their assertion that he was the commandant of Auschwitz was flat-out wrong (Sachverhaltsdarstellung, May 11, 1955. HHStAW, 461, 33531, pp. 2–4). Fulbrook, *Reckonings,* p. 263.

12. Baumann, et al., *Schatten,* pp. 69–75; Schenk, *Auf dem rechten,* pp. 125–130. Eichmann's name appears to have been formally placed on West Germany's "wanted" list at the start of 1957, but no further action was taken (Stangneth, *Eichmann,* p. 189). Gerhard Wiese, Interview by Almut Schoenfeld, May 20, 2020; Bauer, "Unbewältigte," Mar. 25, 1961, in: Foljanty, Johst (eds.), *Fritz Bauer,* vol. 1, p. 703; Einsele, "Worte," in: Oberstaatsanwaltschaft at Frankfurt am Main Oberlandesgericht (ed.), *Fritz Bauer,* pp. 19–22; Falk, *Entnazifizierung,* p. 369.

13. Dieter Wisliceny, Testimony, Jan. 3, 1946. Yale Law School. The Avalon Project. Nuremberg Trial Proceedings, vol. 4, online source.

14. Korbach Police, Letter to Frankfurt Prosecutor's Office, Nov. 23, 1956. HHStAW, 461, 33532, p. 173, "Der organisierte," *Frankfurter Rundschau,* Apr. 4, 1957, p. 2; Conversation with W. Grothe, cited in: Lilienthal, "Hermann Krumey," no date. Gedenkportal Korbach, p. 27; No title, no date. StadtA KB, cited in: Li-

lienthal, "Hermann Krumey," no date. Gedenkportal Korbach, p. 27; Hermann Krumey, Interrogation, Apr. 1, 1957. HHStAW, 461, 33533, p. 365; No title, no date. BA Bayreuth, ZLA 1, 15306115, pp. 150, 151, 153, cited in: Lilienthal, "Hermann Krumey," no date. Gedenkportal Korbach, p. 27; Hermann Krumey, Interrogation, Apr. 1, 1957. HHStAW, 461, 33533, p. 366; Uslar von, "Der ehrenwerte," *Die Zeit,* June 24, 1966, cited in: Lilienthal, "Hermann Krumey," no date. Gedenkportal Korbach, p. 28. Special thanks to Harriet Phillips for researching Krumey material.

15. Brand led the Va'adat Ezrah Vehatzalah (Aid and Rescue Committee) together with diamond merchant and jeweler Samu Springmann and journalist Rezső Kasztner. Brand helped Jewish refugees escape from Ukraine, Poland, and Slovakia to Budapest, where he provided them with false documents (Weissberg, *Desperate,* pp. 16–19). Yablonka, *The State,* p. 117; Fritz Schnellbögl, Letter to Arnold Buchthal, Dec. 5, 1956. HHStAW, 461, 33532, pp. 201R–201V; Georg Friedrich Vogel, Vermerk, Dec. 15, 1956. HHStAW, 461, 33532, p. 201R; Weissberg, *Desperate,* pp. 1–2. The first Hungarian transport left on May 15, 1944, three weeks after Eichmann's meeting with Brand.

16. Weissberg, *Desperate,* p. 91.

17. Weissberg, *Desperate,* pp. 91–95; Hansi Brand, Testimony, May 29, 1961. The Trial of Adolf Eichmann: session 56, The Nizkor Project, online source.

18. Weissberg, *Desperate,* p. 91.

19. Weissberg, *Desperate,* pp. 92–93.

20. Weissberg, *Desperate,* p. 104; Yablonka, *The State,* p. 117; Hansi Brandt, Testimony, May 31, 1961. The Trial of Adolf Eichmann: session 59, cited in: Zweig, *The Gold Train,* pp. 223–232, in: Cesarani, *Becoming,* p. 179; Pasternak-Slater, "Kasztner's," *Areté,* 2004/15, p. 13; Długoborski, Piper (eds.), *Auschwitz,* vol. 3, pp. 31–32. Krumey personally oversaw the so-called Kasztner transport. Under Eichmann's orders, Joel Brand's family was specifically not to be included (Margit Fendrich, Interview by Anna Porter, in: Porter, *Kasztner's,* p. 26; Joel Brand, Deposition, Mar. 21, 1957. HHStAW, 461, 33533, pp. 334–337). Joel Brand, Deposition, Mar. 14, 1957. HHStAW, 461, 33532, p. 332.

21. Kasztner was gunned down near his home in Tel Aviv on March 15, 1957. "Joel Brand," *The New York Times,* July 15, 1964, no pages; Wilkinson, "Hansi Brand," *Los Angeles Times,* Apr. 19, 2000, no pages; Douglas, *Rivka Yoselewska,* in: Freeman, Lewis (eds.), *Law,* vol. 2, pp. 289–290; Brand was questioned by Vogel on March 12, 13, 14, and 21, 1957, and then again on April 15 and 17, 1957—the deposition on April 17 was about Hunsche. The March 12–14 depositions can be found in: HHStAW, 461, 33532; the March 21 interrogation in: HHStAW, 461, 33533. The April depositions can be found in: Hansi and Yoel Brand Collection, YVA, file 22. Joel Brand, Deposition, Mar. 12, 1957. HHStAW, 461, 33532, p. 316; Brand, Deposition, Mar. 14, 1957. HHStAW, 461, 33521, p. 328.

22. Arnold Buchthal, Note, Apr. 1, 1959. HHStAW, 461, 33533, p. 362; Joachim Kügler, Interview by Werner Renz, May 5, 1998. FBInst, part 1.

23. Hermann Krumey, Interrogation, Apr. 1, 1957. HHStAW, 461, 33533, p. 368.

24. For coverage of Krumey's arrest see: "SS-Obersturmbannführer," *Frankfurter Rundschau,* Apr. 2, 1957. HHStAW, 461, 33694. Krumey, Hermann u.a.: Handakten, vol. 1, p. 12; "Der organisierte," *Frankfurter Rundschau,* Apr. 4, 1957. HHStAW, 461, 33694. Krumey, Hermann u.a.: Handakten, vol. 1, p. 13; "Wegen der Tötung,"

Frankfurter Allgemeine Zeitung, Apr. 4, 1957. HHStAW, 461, 33694. Krumey, Hermann u.a.: Handakten, vol. 1, no pages; "Früherer," *Frankfurter Neue Presse,* Apr. 4, 1957. HHStAW, 461, 33694. Krumey, Hermann u.a.: Handakten, vol. 1, p. 16; "Lkw und Geld," *Abendpost,* Apr. 4, 1957. HHStAW, 461, 33694. Krumey, Hermann u.a.: Handakten, vol. 1, p. 17; Stangneth, *Eichmann,* p. 313.

25.   Jeffries, *Grand Hotel,* pp. 269–271; Müller-Doohm, *Adorno,* pp. 631–633; Trentmann, *Out of,* p. 193; Alexander Kluge, Interview by Jack Fairweather, Sept. 2, 2021; Freimüller, *Frankfurt,* p. 85; Sälter, *Phantome,* pp. 432–433; Kluge, "Wer ein Wort . . . ," p. 8.

26.   Alexander Kluge, Interview by Jack Fairweather, Sept. 2, 2021; Bundesverfassungsgericht, Urteil, May 10, 1957. 1 BvR 550/52, OpenJure, online source.

27.   Stengel, *Hermann Langbein,* pp. 215–216, 418; Trentmann, *Out of,* pp. 196–199; Brockhaus, *Der Neue,* p. 151.

28.   Langbein, *People,* p. 491; Pendas, *The Frankfurt,* p. 25; Ilona Porębska, Interview by Harriet Phillips, Sept. 17, 2021; Daniel Langbein, Kurt Langbein, Interview by Florine Miez, Dec. 8, 2021; Stengel, *Hermann Langbein,* pp. 143–210; Langbein, *People,* pp. 480–481.

29.   The lack of widespread knowledge about Auschwitz was partly due to the circumstances surrounding its liberation. By January 1945, dozens of camps had already been freed and widely publicized and interest in Nazi atrocities was on the wane. Levi, *The Drowned,* p. 75; Dwork, van Pelt, *Auschwitz,* pp. 276–349. Estimates for the number of the camp's victims varied. The Communist authorities said four million. Commandant Höss had admitted to more than two million ("Der Vergaser," *Der Spiegel,* Dec. 2, 1958, online source).

30.   Stengel, *Hermann Langbein,* pp. 164, 181–182; "Auschwitz-Komitee," *Frankfurter Rundschau,* June 1–2, 1957; "Auschwitz-Komitee," *Frankfurter Rundschau,* June 3, 1957; Stengel, *Hermann Langbein,* pp. 161–164, 178–179; Fulbrook, *Reckonings,* pp. 253–255; Stengel, *Die Überlebenden,* pp. 135–138; Henry Ormond, Letter to E. G. Löwenthal, July 9, 1957, cited in: Witte, *Alles,* unpublished typescript, FBInst, p. 305; Rauschenberger, "Recht," in: Rauschenberger (ed.), *Rückkehr,* pp. 41–44; Stangneth, *Eichmann,* p. 387; Witte, *Alles,* unpublished typescript, FBInst, pp. 308–310. Henry Ormond was originally named Heinz Neumeyer. Like Bauer, he was dismissed from his position as a junior judge in 1933 for being Jewish. He was arrested during the November Pogrom in 1938 and imprisoned in Dachau until mid-1939, when he managed to escape to England. Interned in 1940, he later joined the British army after his release. Special thanks to Thomas Ormond for sharing his father's calendar and insights. Gańczak, *Jan Sehn,* p. 189. Langbein first reports a meeting with Bauer in February 1959, but it is highly likely they met at the International Auschwitz Committee conference in May 1957. It appears Ormond first met Bauer in July 1956, per Ormond's diary entry on July 5, 1956 (Henry Ormond, Diary 1959–1961, no pages. Material in possession of Walter Witte).

31.   Stengel, *Hermann Langbein,* p. 179; Freimüller, *Frankfurt,* p. 256; Bauer, "Lebendige," June 9, 1963, in: Foljanty, Johst (eds.), *Fritz Bauer,* vol. 2, pp. 1069–1075; Trentmann, *Out of,* pp. 204–206; Heimsath, "Trotz allem," p. 178. A memorial plaque for Anne Frank was also unveiled on Ganghoferstrasse, Frankfurt, where she was born (No title, *Frankfurter Rundschau,* June 1–2, 1957, p. 5).

1 1

REBELS

1. Wojak, *Fritz Bauer,* p. 291; Stangneth, *Eichmann,* pp. 114, 143; Sälter, *NS-Kontinuitäten,* p. 458; Stangneth, *Eichmann,* pp. 238, 151, 333, 241–257, 267. French journalist Maurice Bardèche picked up on the obfuscation of the SS at the time of the killings and in 1948 argued that only lice were ever gassed in Auschwitz, that most deaths were caused by epidemics and the prisoners killing each other. Furthermore, witness testimony could not be relied upon, coming as it did from "the mouths of Jews and Communists" (Igounet, *Histoire,* no pages).

2. Stangneth, *Eichmann,* p. 325. The domestic spy agency was apparently also interested in Eichmann's whereabouts and put in a request with the German embassy in Buenos Aires for more information. The embassy wrote back two months later that their inquiries had yielded no results. Gehlen also saw no need to look further (154, Request for information on whereabouts of Adolf Eichmann, Sept. 1, 1959. BND-Archiv, 100470, p. 35; 409/Ia, Letter to 154 on whereabouts of Adolf Eichmann, Sept. 8, 1959. BND-Archiv, 100470, p. 36; Stangneth, *Eichmann,* p. 325). "Naziblutrichter," *Neues Deutschland,* Jan. 26, 1956, p. 2; Miquel von, *Ahnden,* p. 28.

3. "Böse," *Der Spiegel,* Apr. 3, 1956, online source.

4. Müller, *Reinhard Gehlen,* p. 757; Hechelhammer, *Spion,* pp. 116, 153; Gehlen, *The Service,* p. 158; Geyer, *Am Anfang,* p. 95; Felfe, *Im Dienst,* p. 299; Geyer, *Am Anfang,* p. 96; Reese, *General,* p. 87.

5. Henke, *Geheime . . . Die politische Inlandsspionage des BND,* pp. 420–424. Anne Frank's diary was first published in German in 1950, but it wasn't until its 1955 paperback release and a 1956 stage adaptation that it reached greater resonance with the German public. See: Freimüller, *Frankfurt,* p. 246; "Im Hinterhaus," *Der Spiegel,* Oct. 9, 1956, online source. For analysis of German reception of Anne Frank's diary see: Heimsath, "*Trotz allem,*" p. 178.

6. Tobin, *Crossroads,* pp. 236, 119–125; Tobin, "No Time," *Central European History,* 2011/44 (4), p. 701; Fulbrook, *Reckonings,* p. 281; Tobin, *Crossroads,* pp. 280–281. For a description of events in Gargždai see: Tobin, *Crossroads,* pp. 5–17. "Nazi Officer," *Jewish Telegraphic Agency,* July 14, 1958, online source.

7. Weinke, *Eine Gesellschaft,* p. 19; Fröhlich, "*Wider die Tabuisierung,*" p. 316; Osterloh, Vollnhals (eds.), *NS-Prozesse,* p. 240; Hofmann, "*Ein Versuch,*" p. 49 note 108.

8. Fulbrook, *Reckonings,* p. 247; Hofmann, "*Ein Versuch,*" pp. 78–81; Müller, *Reinhard Gehlen,* p. 950.

9. Hechelhammer, *Spion,* pp. 125–126, 165.

10. Poiger, *Jazz,* p. 81; Moses, *German,* p. 58; Jaide, *Das Verhältnis,* p. 73; Müller, *Reinhard Gehlen,* pp. 940, 1069.

11. Z. Barcikowski, Note concerning Reinhard Strecker, Aug. 19, 1965. IPN, Bu 1218/34495, p. 3; Madajczyk, "Kim był," *Rocznik Polsko-Niemiecki,* 2018/26, pp. 131–132; Z. Barcikowski, Note concerning Reinhard Strecker, Aug. 19, 1965. IPN, Bu 1218/34495, p. 1; Glienke, "Die Ausstellung," Aktives Museum, Berlin. *Mitglieder-Rundbrief 83,* Aug. 2020, p. 9; Glienke, *Die Ausstellung . . . Zur Geschichte,* pp. 67–70; Reinhard Strecker, Interview by Anna Schattschneider, July 10, 2020; Gieseke, *The History,* pp. 49, 38; Lepiarz, "Bezkarni," *Deutsche Welle,* Aug. 31, 2019, online source.

12. Henke, *Geheime . . . Die politische Inlandsspionage des BND,* pp. 1011–1012; Glienke, "Die Ausstellung," Aktives Museum, Berlin. *Mitglieder-Rundbrief 83,* Aug. 2020, pp. 10–11; Glienke, "Die Ausstellung," in: Weisbrod (ed.), *Demokratische,* pp. 31–34; Rigoll, *Staatsschutz,* pp. 145–146.

13. Henke, *Geheime . . . Die politische Inlandsspionage des BND,* p. 1014; Harlan, *Veit,* pp. 134, 41; "Harlan," *AJR Information,* June 1955, p. 3; Harlan, *Hitler,* pp. 232, 59–64; Harlan, *Veit,* pp. 51, 111.

14. Harlan, *Hitler,* pp. 79, 85–87; Woelk, "Authenticity," in: Helfer, Donahue (eds.), *Nexus 3: Essays,* pp. 171–186; Harlan, *Das Vierte,* 1962. Kinemathek, Nachlass Thomas Harlan, 201312 LzK 4/47 4.019, pp. 3, 2. What Harlan did not know was that Gehlen was connected to both Jost and Six. At the time of Harlan's performance, Gehlen was considering hiring Jost, although he didn't take the job in the end. Six was already working for Gehlen and knew most of the SS men on his staff (NARA, RG 263, Second Release of Name Files, file: Franz Six, NAID: identifier: 139397970). Sälter, *NS-Kontinuitäten,* p. 148; Hachmeister, *Der Gegnerforscher,* p. 305; "Merkt euch," *Der Spiegel,* Dec. 29, 1949, online source. Six's exact relationship to the BND is unclear. According to CIA files, he was an employee. Hachmeister, however, quotes the then BND president Konrad Porzner as saying "that Prof. Six was neither a full-time nor a part-time employee and also not a source of the Federal Intelligence Service or its predecessor organization" (Hachmeister, *Der Gegnerforscher,* p. 305).

15. Harlan, *Das Vierte,* 1962. Kinemathek, Nachlass Thomas Harlan, 201312 LzK 4/47 4.019, p. 3; Woelk, "Authenticity," in: Helfer, Donahue (eds.), *Nexus 3: Essays,* pp. 171–186; Harlan, *Hitler,* pp. 86–87.

16. Harlan, *Hitler,* pp. 90–91; Ryszard Kwiatkowski, Doniesienie, Feb. 19, 1962. IPN, Bu 003273/17, vol. II, pp. 121–123; Janina Trojanowska, Doniesienie, May 3, 1962. IPN, Bu 003273/17, vol. II, p. 155; Janina Trojanowska, Doniesienie, July 20, 1961. IPN, Bu 003273/17, vol. II, pp. 19–20; Harlan, *Hitler,* p. 119.

17. Henke, *Geheime . . . Die politische Inlandsspionage des BND,* pp. 1014, 1028; Hermann Langbein, Letter to Thomas Harlan, Oct. 24, 1960. ÖStA, Nachlass Hermann Langbein, E/1797: 30, no pages; Glienke, *Die Ausstellung,* pp. 159–160. For what are likely Gehlen's first reports on Bauer see: Author unknown, Report on Fritz Bauer, no date. KAS, Nachlass Hans Globke 01-070-103/2, no pages. Special thanks to Anne Uhl for finding.

18. Author unknown, Report on Fritz Bauer, no date. KAS, Nachlass Hans Globke 01-070-103/2, no pages.

12

SYLVIA

1. Steinke, *Fritz Bauer,* p. 3; Stangneth, *Eichmann,* pp. 189, 317; Baumann et al., *Schatten,* pp. 69–75.

2. Lothar Hermann, Letter to Fritz Bauer, Aug. 23, 1957, cited in: Saidon, *Letters,* pp. 28–29.

3. Ibid.; Lothar Hermann, Letter to Fritz Bauer, June 25, 1960. AdsD, Nachlass Fritz Bauer, 1/FBAB 000001, no pages; Harel, *The House,* p.18.

4. Aharoni, Dietl, *Operation,* p. 78.

5. Saidon, *Letters,* pp. 70–71; Harel, *The House,* p. 3.

6. Ibid.

7. Deutschkron, *Israel,* p. 57, cited in: Marwecki, *Germany,* p. 232; Harel, *The House,* p. 3.

8. Harel, *The House,* p. 3.

9. Harel, *The House,* pp. 1, 4; Bascomb, *Hunting,* p. 105.

10. Harel, *The House,* pp. 4–5.

11. Harel, *The House,* p. 5; Bergman, *Rise,* pp. 33–34; Cohen-Abravanel, *Art,* pp. 9–10.

12. Harel, *The House,* p. 6.

13. Harel, *The House,* p. 7.

14. Ibid.

15. Ibid.

16. Stangneth, *Eichmann,* p. 318; Bascomb, *Hunting,* pp. 106–107; Harel, *The House,* pp. 10–12.

17. Harel, *The House,* pp. 12–13; Hemi, Lahis (eds.), *Bureau 06,* 2020, p. 26.

18. Harel, *The House,* pp. 12–13; Bascomb, *Hunting,* p. 107; Lothar Hermann, Letter to Fritz Bauer, June 25, 1960. AdsD, Nachlass Fritz Bauer, 1/FBAB 000001, no pages.

19. Harel, *The House,* pp. 12–14; Aharoni, Dietl, *Operation,* pp. 80–81; Saidon, *Letters,* p. 75; Stangneth, *Eichmann,* p. 318; Efraim Hofstetter, Memoir, Jan. 1, 1962. ISA, no pages; Bascomb, *Hunting,* pp. 107–108.

20. Harel, *The House,* p. 14; Saidon, *Letters,* pp. 20–21; Jorge Dukuen, Email to Ester Gonzales Martin, Nov. 17, 2021; Saidon, *Letters,* p. 76; "No soy," *El Imparcial,* Mar. 24, 1961, p. 1.

21. Saidon, *Letters,* p. 77; Harel, *The House,* p. 15.

22. Harel, *The House,* p. 15.

23. Bascomb, *Hunting,* p. 108; Saidon, *Letters,* p. 135; Harel, *The House,* p. 16.

24. Harel, *The House,* p. 16.

25. Ibid.

26. Saidon, *Letters,* p. 27; Harel, *The House,* pp. 16–17; Aharoni, Dietl, *Operation,* p. 81.

27. Harel, *The House,* pp. 16–18; Saidon, *Letters,* p. 26.

28. Saidon, *Letters,* pp. 21–24; Harel, *The House,* p. 18.

29. Harel, *The House,* p. 18. This is likely a misquote, as Sylvia was due to complete her high school studies while living with her aunt in San Francisco (Saidon, *Letters,* p. 25).

30. Harel, *The House,* p. 18.

31. Ibid.

32. Ibid.

33. Harel, *The House,* p. 19.

34. Harel, *The House,* pp. 19–20; Aharoni, Dietl, *Operation,* p. 81. Richter means "judge" in German (Bascomb, *Hunting,* p. 109).

35. Fritz Bauer, Personnel file, no date. HHStAW, 505, 2000, p. 36; Fritz Bauer, Postcard to Anna Maria Petersen, Mar. 17, 1958. Material in possession of Irmtrud Wojak, cited in: Wojak, *Fritz Bauer,* p. 290; Fritz Bauer, Postcard to Anna Maria Petersen, Apr. 1, 1958. Material in possession of Irmtrud Wojak, cited in: Wojak, *Fritz Bauer,* p. 290; Fritz Bauer, Letter to Shlomo Cohen-Abarbanel, Mar. 3, 1958. Mossad Archive; Fritz Bauer, Letter to Heinz Meyer-Velde, Apr. 14, 1958. FBInst, Nachlass Meyer-Velde 10.

36. Steinke, *Fritz Bauer,* p. 40; Shavit, *My Promised,* p. 148.

37. Fritz Bauer, Letter to Heinz Meyer-Velde, Apr. 14, 1958. FBInst, Nachlass Heinz Meyer-Velde 10, no pages; Fritz Bauer, Postcard to Anna Maria Petersen, Mar. 17, 1958. Material in possession of Irmtrud Wojak, cited in: Wojak, *Fritz Bauer,* p. 290; Vered, "Displays," Mar. 5, 1958, *HaOlam HaZe,* pp. 10–11; Steinke, *Fritz Bauer,* p. 15; Fritz Bauer, Letter to Heinz Meyer-Velde, Apr. 14, 1958. FBInst, Nachlass Meyer-Velde 10; Shavit, *My Promised,* pp. 150–151; Margot Tiefenthal, Walter Tiefenthal, Interview by Walter Fabian, July 18, 1973. Deutsches Exilarchiv, EB 87/112, no pages.

38. Aharoni, Dietl, *Operation,* p. 83; Stangneth, *Eichmann,* p. 319; Saidon, *Letters,* pp. 30–33.

13
WITNESSES

1. Staff, Eck, Weil, Decision, June 18, 1957. HHStAW 461, 33534, pp. 664–668; Lilienthal, "Hermann Krumey," no date. Gedenkportal Korbach, p. 29; "Der Mann," *Der Spiegel,* Oct. 15, 1957, online source; Tobin, "No time," *Central European History,* 2011/44 (4), pp. 684–710; Fulbrook, *Reckonings,* p. 281; Trentmann, *Out of,* pp. 198, 196.

2. Riess, "Fritz Bauer," in: Rauschenberger (ed.), *Rückkehr,* p. 141; Weinke, *Eine Gesellschaft,* pp. 24–26; Bauer, "Mörder," *Deutsche Nachrichten,* 1947/3, p. 2; Fulbrook, *Reckonings,* pp. 146, 164; Stangneth, *Eichmann,* p. 340; Steinke, *Fritz Bauer,* p. 130; Weinke, *Eine Gesellschaft,* pp. 87–99; Weinke, *"Bleiben,"* in: Osterloh, Vollnhals (eds.), *NS-Prozesse,* p. 276; Hofmann, *"Ein Versuch . . . ,"* pp. 31–37.

3. Weinke, *Eine Gesellschaft,* p. 35; Pendas, *The Frankfurt,* pp. 25–33; Riess, "Fritz Bauer," in: Rauschenberger (ed.), *Rückkehr,* p. 141; Pendas, *The Frankfurt,* pp. 45, 47.

4. Bauer, "Mörder," *Deutsche Nachrichten,* 1947/3, p. 2; Bauer, "Unbewältigte" Mar. 25, 1961, in: Foljanty, Johst (eds.), *Fritz Bauer,* vol. 1, p. 701; Bauer, "In unserem," 1965, in: Foljanty, Johst (eds.), *Fritz Bauer,* vol. 2, p. 1423; Bauer, "Prozesse," Jan.–Feb. 1964, in: Foljanty, Johst (eds.), *Fritz Bauer,* vol. 2, p. 1401; Pendas, *The Frankfurt,* p. 47; Wittmann, *Beyond,* pp. 64–67.

5. Bauer had no jurisdiction over Boger's case, as he had been arrested in Stuttgart, Baden-Württemberg. But then in January 1959 Thomas Gnielka, a journalist from the *Frankfurter Rundschau,* sent Bauer a stack of half-burned files from Auschwitz that the man had spotted in the home of a survivor, Emil Wulkan, during an interview. The *Frankfurter Rundschau* had published several articles about a reparations office in Wiesbaden where the assessors had been heard singing antisemitic songs. The article had touched a nerve with Wulkan, who had been seeking compensation without success. He was interviewed by Gnielka, who spotted the files in his home. Wulkan explained that a friend had saved them from the burning wreckage of the SS police headquarters in Breslau. The files contained the names of camp guards who had shot prisoners "trying to escape." They appeared genuine. After establishing contact with Schüle, Bauer formally applied via the Federal Supreme Court for the case to be transferred to him (Wolf, "Auschwitz," *Frankfurter Rundschau,* Dec. 17, 1963, p. 3; Gnielka, "Die Henker," *Metall,* 1961/16, p. 6; Emil Wulkan, Deposition, Apr. 21, 1959. HHStAW, 461, 37638/2, vol. 1a, pp. 73–80; cited in: Renz, "Der 1. Frankfurter . . . Zwei Vorgeschichten," *Zeitschrift für Geschichtswissenschaft,* 2002/50

[7], pp. 15–16; Wittmann, *Beyond,* pp. 63–65; Pendas, *The Frankfurt,* pp. 46–47). The East Germans had, by mid-1959, published four brochures—so-called "Brown books"—containing eight hundred names of incriminated Nazi-era judges. Bauer indicated his support for prosecutions to Social Democrat Adolf Arndt on July 6, 1959. By the end of the year, sixty-five Hessian jurists had been investigated (Meusch, *Von der Diktatur,* pp. 249, 259, 261–267). Steinke, *Fritz Bauer,* p. 149; Hanns Grossmann, Interview by Werner Renz, July 29, 1998. FBInst; Joachim Kügler, Interview by Werner Renz, May 5, 1998. FBInst, part 2; Gerhard Wiese, Interview by Almut Schoenfeld, May 20, 2020; Joachim Kügler, Interview by Werner Renz, May 5, 1998. FBInst, part 1; Gerhard Wiese, Interview by Florine Miez and Jack Fairweather, Oct. 2, 2020; Joachim Kügler, Interview by Werner Renz, May 5, 1998. FBInst, part 1; Bauer, "Im Namen," 1965, in: Perels, Wojak (eds.), *Die Humanität,* pp. 77–90; Ilona Ziok (dir.), *Fritz Bauer,* 2010; Bauer, "Unbewältigte," Mar. 25, 1961, in: Foljanty, Johst (eds.), *Fritz Bauer,* vol. 1, p. 703. Special thanks to Harriet Phillips for researching pretrial material.

6.   Joachim Kügler, Note, June 25, 1959. HHStAW, 461, 37638/243, vol. 1, pp. 33–36; Joachim Kügler, Interview by Werner Renz, May 5, 1998. FBInst, part 1; Renz, "Der 1 . . . Zwei Vorgeschichten," *Zeitschrift für Geschichtswissenschaft,* 2002/50 (7), p. 18. Wilhelm Boger, Franz Hofmann, Hans Stark, Klaus Dylewski, and Pery Broad were arrested between October 1958 and April 1959; Dylewski was then released on bail in May 1959. Hofmann's arrest warrant was issued by Frankfurt in July 1959, but he had already been in pretrial detention since April 1959 for crimes committed in Dachau.

7.   Stengel, "Boten," *Damals,* 2020/07, pp. 24–27; Langbein, *People,* pp. 483–488; Levi, *The Drowned,* p. 68; Szymusik, "Progressive asthenia," *Medical Review—Auschwitz,* 2017, pp. 23–29. The Danish psychiatrist was Paul Thygesen (Withius, Mooji, *Negotiating,* p. 121). Evidence of Langbein sourcing witnesses before Frankfurt took over the case can be found in the following folders: HHStAW, 461, 37638/1, vol. 1; 37638/3, vol. 2; 37638/4 vol. 3; 37638/5, vol. 4; 37638/6, vol. 5; 37638/9, vol. 8; 37638/10, vol. 9. Maryla Rosenthal, Deposition, Feb. 21–22, 1959. HHStAW, 461, 37638/5, vol. 4, pp. 507–515; Siegfried Rosenthal, Letter to Erwin Schüle, Mar. 2, 1959. HHStAW, 461, 37638/5, vol. 4, p. 516; Stengel, *Die Überlebenden,* pp. 318–319, p. 11; Siegfried Rosenthal, Letter to Hermann Langbein, Dec. 27, 1958. ÖStA, Nachlass Hermann Langbein, E/1797: 92, no pages; Stengel, *Die Überlebenden,* pp. 309–320.

8.   Arrest warrant for Oswald Kaduk, July 13, 1959. HHStAW, 461, 37638/11, vol. 10, p. 1495; Arrest warrant for Heinrich Bischoff, July 13, 1959. HHStAW, 461, 37638/11, vol. 10, p. 1496; Joachim Kügler, Interview by Werner Renz, May 5, 1998. FBInst, part 1; Joachim Kügler, Note, July 23, 1959. HHStAW, 461, 37638/11, vol. 10, pp. 1579–1580; Georg Friedrich Vogel, Note, July 22, 1959. HHStAW, 461, 37638/11, vol. 10, p. 1552; Langbein, *People,* p. 513; Oswald Kaduk, Interrogation, HHStAW, 461, 37638/11, vol. 10, pp. 1545–1551; Heinrich Bischoff, Interrogation, July 21, 1959. HHStAW, 461, 37638/11, vol. 10, pp. 1558–1567; Heinrich Bischoff, Interrogation, July 27, 1959. HHStAW, 461, 37638/11, vol. 10, pp. 1616–1622.

9.   Ignacy Golik, Deposition, Oct. 14, 1959. HHStAW, 37638/16, vol. 15, p. 2388. Capesius's arrest warrant was ultimately based on the testimony of Polish witnesses Ignacy Golik and Edward Pyś, as well as the testimony of German witness

Ludwig Wörl. All three witnesses traveled to Frankfurt to testify in October 1959 (Heinz Wolf, Application for arrest warrant for Viktor Capesius, Nov. 30, 1959. HHStAW, 461, 37638/20, vol. 19, p. 2967; Frankfurter Amtsgericht, Arrest warrant for Viktor Capesius, Dec. 3, 1959. HHStAW, 461, 37638/20, vol. 19, p. 2970). Joachim Kügler, Letter to Göppingen Kriminalpolizei, July 27, 1959. HHStAW, 461, 37638/20, vol. 19, p. 3042; Göppingen Kriminalpolizei, Letter to Joachim Kügler, July 29, 1959. HHStAW, 461, 37638/20, vol. 19, p. 3045; Joachim Kügler, Letter to Göppingen Kriminalpolizei, dated Sept. 24, 1959, sent Oct. 1, 1959. HHStAW, 461, 37638/20, vol. 19, p. 3047; Göppingen Kriminalpolizei, Letter to Joachim Kügler, Oct. 7, 1959. HHStAW, 461, 37638/20, vol. 19, p. 3048; Schlesak, *Druggist*, pp. 102, 129; Neumann, "Mit der lustigen," *Frankfurter Allgemeine Zeitung*, Jan. 27, 1979, p. 51; Erwin Schüle, Letter to Bauer, Aug. 12, 1959. HHStAW, 461, 37638/243, vol. 1, pp. 70–71; Axel Eisser, Interview by Jack Fairweather and Florine Miez, Sept. 16, 2021; Joachim Kügler, Note, Dec. 4, 1959. HHStAW, 461, 37638/20, vol. 19, p. 3003; Viktor Capesius, Interrogation, Dec. 4, 1959. HHStAW, 461, 37638/20, vol. 19, pp. 2987–3002.

14
CAPTURE

1. Aharoni, Dietl, *Operation*, p. 83; Stangneth, *Eichmann*, p. 335; Wojak, *Fritz Bauer*, pp. 303–306, 293; Stangneth, *Eichmann*, pp. 341–342.
2. The bishop's name was Hermann Kunst (Stangneth, Winkler, "Der Mann," *Süddeutsche Zeitung*, Aug. 20, 2021, no pages). "Wie Pfarrer," *Westfälischer Anzeiger*, Sept. 9, 2021, no pages; Sigrid Wobst, Interview by Harriet Phillips, May 7, 2024.
3. Stangneth, Winkler, "Der Mann," *Süddeutsche Zeitung*, Aug. 20, 2021, no pages; "Wie Pfarrer," *Westfälischer Anzeiger*, Sept. 9, 2021, no pages.
4. Stangneth, Winkler, "Der Mann," *Süddeutsche Zeitung*, Aug. 20, 2021, no pages; "Wie Pfarrer," *Westfälischer Anzeiger*, Sept. 9, 2021, no pages.
5. Stangneth, Winkler, "Der Mann," *Süddeutsche Zeitung*, Aug. 20, 2021, no pages; "Wie Pfarrer," *Westfälischer Anzeiger*, Sept. 9, 2021, no pages. It appears that Eichmann was identified to Klammer by a member of the group, Herbert Kuhlmann, who had traveled with Eichmann to Argentina and helped him get a job with the Capri company. Kuhlmann, a former SS officer himself, had fallen out with Eichmann (Goñi, *The Real*, pp. 297–301).
6. Stangneth, Winkler, "Der Mann," *Süddeutsche Zeitung*, Aug. 20, 2021, no pages; "Wie Pfarrer," *Westfälischer Anzeiger*, Sept. 9, 2021, no pages.
7. Stangneth, Winkler, "Der Mann," *Süddeutsche Zeitung*, Aug. 20, 2021, no pages; "Wie Pfarrer," *Westfälischer Anzeiger*, Sept. 9, 2021, no pages.
8. Stangneth, Winkler, "Der Mann," *Süddeutsche Zeitung*, Aug. 20, 2021, no pages; "Wie Pfarrer," *Westfälischer Anzeiger*, Sept. 9, 2021, no pages.
9. Assuming Bauer arrived in Jerusalem on Thursday, December 3, 1959, and that he left on Wednesday, December 2, he would have had to fly to Rome on Lufthansa, and then take the connecting El Al flight to Tel Aviv. He would have arrived in Israel at 00:10 A.M. (Lufthansa Flugplan, May 24, 1959. Airline Timetable Images, no date, online source; El Al Time Table, Oct. 18, 1959–Feb. 27, 1960 [UK version]. Airline Timetable Images, no date, online source). Saidon, *Letters*, p. 271; Haim Cohen, Interview by Irmtrud Wojak, Jan. 7, 1997, cited in: Wojak,

Fritz Bauer, pp. 294–296. Following Eichmann's arrest, Bauer did publicly state his desire to extradite Eichmann, but this seems to have been a tactic to undermine the Adenauer government after it preemptively ruled out such a move ("Bonn," *Frankfurter Rundschau,* May 28–29, 1960, p. 2).

10. Aharoni, Dietl, *Operation,* pp. 84–85; Harel, *The House,* p. 32; Bascomb, *Hunting,* pp. 121–126; Haim Cohn, Interview by Irmtrud Wojak, Jan. 7, 1997, cited in: Wojak, *Fritz Bauer,* pp. 294–296.

11. Harel, *The House,* p. 32.

12. Bascomb, *Hunting,* p. 124.

13. Ibid.; Aharoni, Dietl, *Operation,* p. 85; Bascomb, *Hunting,* pp. 125–126; Saidon, *Letters,* p. 36.

14. Bascomb, *Hunting,* p. 125.

15. No title, *Frankfurter Rundschau,* Dec. 22, 1960, p. 4; Bascomb, *Hunting,* p. 127; Trentmann, *Out of,* p. 193; Lengowski, "Die antisemitische," Hamburg Geschichtsbuch, no date, online source; Bascomb, *Hunting,* p. 127; Trentmann, *Out of,* p. 193; Bergmann, "Sind die Deutschen," in: Bergmann, Erb (eds.), *Antisemitismus,* p. 116; Bascomb, *Hunting,* p. 127. Between January 1948 and March 1957, 176 Jewish cemeteries were desecrated (Freimüller, *Frankfurt,* p. 164). The KGB was behind some of the graffiti as part of its campaign to discredit and embarrass the Adenauer government (Trentmann, *Out of,* p. 193).

16. Bascomb, *Hunting,* p. 127; Conze, *Das Amt,* p. 615; Bergmann, "Antisemitism," *Key Documents of German-Jewish History,* Sept. 22, 2016, online source. The pamphlet had gained national attention after an attempt to prosecute timber merchant Friedrich Nieland for anticonstitutional writings and libel was turned down by a judge who, it transpired, had written in praise of the Nuremberg Race Laws in the 1930s.

17. Hubner-Funk, "Jugend," in: Bergmann, Erb (eds.), *Antisemitismus,* p. 232; Adenauer, "Ansprache," in: Bundesregierung (ed.), *Die antisemitischen,* pp. 66–67; Weber (ed.), *Kabinettssitzung,* online source. Afterward, Bauer jotted a short note to Langbein: "When I was in Bergen-Belsen today, I also remembered the victims in Auschwitz" (Fritz Bauer, Letter to Hermann Langbein, Feb. 9, 1960. ÖStA, Nachlass Hermann Langbein, E/1797: 96, no pages). Fritz Bauer, Letter to Heinz Meyer-Velde, Jan. 9, 1960. FBInst, Nachlass Heinz Meyer-Velde 12, no pages; Meyer-Velde, "'Dann machen's,'" in Backhaus, Boll, Gross (eds.), *Fritz Bauer,* p. 237.

18. Bauer, "Wurzeln," 1960, in: Foljanty, Johst (eds.), *Fritz Bauer,* vol. 1, pp. 664–682; Bauer, "Die Wurzeln," 1961, in: Foljanty, Johst (eds.), *Fritz Bauer,* vol. 1, pp. 770–796; Bauer, "Deutsche," 1961, in: Foljanty, Johst (eds.), *Fritz Bauer,* vol. 1, pp. 691–694; Bauer, "Antinazistische," Jan.–Feb. 1964, in: Foljanty, Johst (eds.), *Fritz Bauer,* vol. 2, pp. 1390–1405. Bauer also criticized Hegel. His and Kant's "formal ethics of duty and idealisation of state morality . . . led directly to Auschwitz, Treblinka and Majdanek" (Bauer, "Antinazistische," Jan.–Feb. 1964, in: Foljanty, Johst [eds.], *Fritz Bauer,* vol. 2, p. 1399).

19. Bauer, "Im Kampf," 1955, in: Foljanty, Johst (eds.), *Fritz Bauer,* vol. 1, pp. 446–456; Bauer, "Deutsche," 1961, in: Foljanty, Johst (eds.), *Fritz Bauer,* vol. 1, pp. 691–694; Godau-Schüttke, *Die Heyde-Sawade-Affäre,* pp. 235–236. Heyde had also supervised the compulsory sterilization of "asocial" prisoners in the prewar concentration camps (Wachsmann, *KL,* pp. 150, 247).

20. Aharoni, Dietl, *Operation,* p. 85; "Feindliches," *Der Spiegel,* July 30, 1995, online source; Aharoni, Dietl, *Operation,* p. 86. Harel gives a different account of the break-in, in which Bauer and his driver accompanied the photographer, Michael Moar, and a Mossad agent named Haim Yitzhaki to the office. Bauer then led them to his room, opened the safe, and waited for them to finish photographing the documents. Given the fact that Bauer wanted the documents copied clandestinely and without association to himself, it seems unlikely he would have been in attendance at the scene.

21. Fritz Bauer, Letter to Shlomo Cohen-Abarbanel, May 3, 1960. Mossad Archive, no pages. Special thanks to Gabriel Saidon. Bascomb, *Hunting,* p. 146.

22. Bascomb, *Hunting,* pp. 131–157.

23. Bascomb, *Hunting,* pp. 165–218.

24. Bascomb, *Hunting,* pp. 220–225.

25. Bascomb, *Hunting,* p. 225.

26. Ibid.

27. Bascomb, *Hunting,* pp. 225–226.

28. Bascomb, *Hunting,* p. 226.

29. Bascomb, *Hunting,* pp. 226–227.

30. Bascomb, *Hunting,* p. 227.

31. Ibid.

32. Bascomb, *Hunting,* p. 228.

33. Bascomb, *Hunting,* pp. 230–295; Harel, *The House,* p. 274.

15

FALLOUT

1. Theodor Oberländer was Federal Minister for Displaced Persons, Refugees, and War Victims. He resigned on May 4, 1960. Reinhard Gehlen, Memo to Inspector of the Navy, May 23, 1960. BND-Archiv, 4324, cited in: Müller, *Reinhard Gehlen,* p. 988; *Reinhard Gehlen,* p. 1302.

2. Yablonka, *The State,* pp. 30–32; Lipstadt, *The Eichmann,* p. 3; Author unknown, Reports about Eichmann whereabouts and arrest, May 31, 1960. BND-Archiv, 100470, pp. 42–45.

3. Müller, *Reinhard Gehlen,* pp. 1000–1001.

4. Author unknown, Memo concerning Gehlen-Globke meeting in Bundeskanzleramt, May 29, 1960. BND-Archiv, 01227, no pages; 363/VI, Note for BK and AA concerning East German "Freiheitssender" reports on BND attempts to prevent Eichmann trial, May 1960. BND-Archiv, 100470, p. 38; Henke, *Geheime . . . Die politische Inlandsspionage des BND,* p. 1072; Krause, *Der Eichmann-Prozess,* pp. 104–105; Stangneth, *Eichmann,* p. 380; 181 [Weiss], Letter to 363 [Gehlen], June 8, 1960. BND-Archiv, 43132, p. 1753; Author unknown, Note, (June 1960?). BND-Archiv, 43132, p. 1754. The Foreign Ministry agreed that no effort would be made to extradite Eichmann or pay his legal fees, as was customary for German nationals arrested overseas (Krause, *Der Eichmann-Prozess,* p. 108).

5. For Weiss's background see: Henke, *Geheime . . . Die politische Inlandsspionage des BND,* pp. 374–380.

6. Author unknown, Report on Adolf Eichmann, June 1960. BND-Archiv, 100470,

pp. 42–43, 45; Bascomb, *Hunting*, pp. 235–236, 243; Aharoni, Dietl, *Operation*, pp. 168–170.

7. Author unknown, Report on Adolf Eichmann, June 2, 1960. BND-Archiv, 100470, p. 45; Aharoni, Dietl, *Operation*, p. 156.

8. Henke, *Geheime . . . Die politische Inlandsspionage des BND*, p. 1055.

9. Wiegrefe, "Der Fluch," *Der Spiegel*, Apr. 11, 2011, online source; Harel, *The House*, p. 274; Author unknown, Report on Adolf Eichmann, June 1960. BND-Archiv, 100470, p. 43; "Ein unbedeutender," *Der Spiegel*, Feb. 15, 1961, no pages; Breyer, *Dr. Max Merten*, p. 131; Henke, *Geheime . . . Die politische Inlandsspionage des BND*, p. 1144. For details of Merten's accusations see: Franz Drugh, Letter to Tel Aviv Local Court, Jan. 7, 1961. BND-Archiv, 43132, p. 1948; Archer, *The Merten*, pp. 26, 75, 71, 74; Breyer, *Dr. Max Merten*, pp. 93–94; Franz Drügh, Letter to Tel Aviv Local Court, Jan. 7, 1961. BND-Archiv, 43132, pp. 1949, 1951.

10. Breyer, *Dr. Max Merten*, pp. 93–94; Wayland B. Waters, Memo to Department of State, Washington, Feb. 7, 1961. Hans Globke, 0178, p. 3. CIA Electronic Reading Room, online source. On the difficulty of establishing the truth behind Merten's claims see: Breyer, *Dr. Max Merten*, pp. 93–95.

11. Globke's estate in the Konrad-Adenauer-Stiftung contains a list of material addressed to Bauer, including a letter from Max Merten and documents from Thomas Gnielka's mission to East Berlin that suggest an extensive level of surveillance (KAS, Nachlass Hans Globke 01-070-092/1) The most likely source was an informant in Bauer's own office. It's not been possible to identify them.

12. Weinke, "Der Prozess," in: Groenewold, Ignor, Koch (eds.), *Lexikon*, online source; Author unknown, Report on Dr. Robert Servatius, July 20, 1960. BND-Archiv, 100470, p. 83; "Wer zahlt?" *Der Spiegel*, Oct. 18, 1960, no pages; Yablonka, *The State*, p. 125; Orbach, *Fugitives*, pp. 164–166.

13. Henke, *Geheime . . . Die politische Inlandsspionage des BND*, p. 1074; 181 [Weiss], Note to 363 [Gehlen] concerning alleged revelations by Eichmann, June 8, 1960. BND-Archiv, 121099, p. 1751, cited in: Henke, *Geheime . . . Die politische Inlandsspionage des BND*, p. 1055; Henke, *Geheime . . . Die politische Inlandsspionage des BND*, pp. 1057–1064; CIA Director, Note to CIA office in Munich, Sept. 17, 1960. NARA, RG 263, Second Release of Name Files, 640446, box 30, folder 3, Adolf Eichmann, vol. 2, p. 346, NAID: 139331937; Henke, *Geheime . . . Die politische Inlandsspionage des BND*, pp. 1063 note 311, 1062–1063.

14. It appears that the BND fixer Hans Rechenberg arranged for Wechtenbruch's salary and expenses to be paid. It's possible Servatius was also aware of this, as seems clear from his questions relating to Wechtenbruch's meeting with Bauer (Robert Servatius, Letter to Dieter Wechtenbruch, Sept. 15, 1960. Material in possession of Bettina Stangneth). For Rechenberg's role in funding Eichmann's defense see: Henke, *Geheime . . . Die politische Inlandsspionage des BND*, p. 1073. Wechtenbruch's role as a BND agent was disclosed to the author privately.

15. Dieter Wechtenbruch, Report to Robert Servatius, Sept. 12, 1960. Material in possession of Bettina Stangneth; Dieter Wechtenbruch, Interview by Hanna Yablonka, June 13, 1995. Material in possession of Hanna Yablonka.

16. Dieter Wechtenbruch, Report to Robert Servatius, Sept. 20, 1960. Material in possession of Bettina Stangneth; Private source, Email to Jack Fairweather, Jan. 10, 2022.

16
PATHÉTIQUE

1. Dittmann, "Der private," *Schriftenreihe des "Fritz Bauer Freundeskreises,"* 2013, p. 3; Sälter, *Phantome,* pp. 273–325; Sälter, *NS-Kontinuitäten,* pp. 95–155, 213–274; Arrest warrant for Richard Schweizer, Feb. 29, 1960. HHStAW, 461, 32438/278, pp. 5977R–5977V; Sälter, *NS-Kontinuitäten,* pp. 240–242, 629–632; Jehoschua Rosenfeld, Deposition, June 4, 1959. HHStAW, 461, 32438/276, pp. 1081R–1081V. Bauer had bought his gun at some point before the start of the Auschwitz trial (Steinke, *Fritz Bauer,* p. 156).

2. "Ein unbedeutender," *Der Spiegel,* Feb. 15, 1961, online source; Breyer, *Dr. Max Merten,* p. 131.

3. Jørgensen, "Ich hätte," 1965, in: Foljanty, Johst (eds.), *Fritz Bauer,* p. 1337; Felix Shinnar, Letter to Meir Rosen, June 23, 1960. ISA-mfa-ReparationsGermany-000rh94, pp. 195–197; No title, *Haboker,* June 10, 1960, p. 1; Lipstadt, *The Eichmann,* p. 42; Cesarani, *Becoming,* p. 240; Hemi, Lahis (eds.), *Bureau 06,* 2020, pp. 23–29; Yablonka, *The State,* pp. 64–75; Lipstadt, *The Eichmann,* pp. 43–45, 67–68.

4. Felix Shinnar, Letter to Meir Rosen, June 23, 1960. ISA-mfa-ReparationsGermany-000rh94, pp. 195–197; Felix Shinnar, Letter to Meir Rosen, July 10, 1960. ISA-PMO-StateDocumentsDep-0003ym4, p. 364; Abraham Selinger, Report of meeting with Fritz Bauer, Sept. 3–4, 1960. ISA-IsraelPolice-EichmannTrial-000r682, pp. 35–38; Abraham Selinger, Letter to Yosef Nahmias, Sept. 4, 1960. ISA-IsraelPolice-EichmannTrial-000r682, pp. 109–110; Fritz Bauer, Letter to Heinz Meyer-Velde, no date, c. summer 1960. FBInst, Nachlass Heinz Meyer-Velde 12, no pages; Hemi, Lahis. (eds.), *Bureau 06,* 2020, p. 96.

5. Abraham Selinger, Report of meeting with Fritz Bauer, Sept. 3–4, 1960. ISA-IsraelPolice-EichmannTrial-000r682, pp. 35–38; Yosef Nahmias, Letter to Abraham Selinger, May 25, 1960. ISA-PMO-StateDocumentsDep-0011upa, p. 49. Selinger objected to this directive and wrote back to Nahmias (as well as to Cohen-Abarbanel) on October 13 that he must interrogate Eichmann about his accomplices regardless of whether they were living or dead. Nahmias answered on November 19 that there was probably a misunderstanding; Selinger was free to question Eichmann about his accomplices' wartime activities but wasn't to ask about their postwar fates (Abraham Selinger, Letter to Yosef Nahmias and Shlomo Cohen-Abarbanel, Oct. 13, 1960. ISA-IsraelPolice-EichmannTrial-000qy5j, p. 513; Yosef Nahmias, Letter to Abraham Selinger, Nov. 19, 1960. ISA-IsraelPolice-EichmannTrial-000qy5j, p. 511).

6. Abraham Selinger, Report of meeting with Fritz Bauer, Sept. 3–4, 1960. ISA-IsraelPolice-EichmannTrial-000r682, pp. 35–38; Fritz Bauer, Letter to Heinz Meyer-Velde, no date, summer 1960. FBInst, Nachlass Heinz Meyer-Velde 12, no pages; Hofmann, *"Ein Versuch,"* pp. 162–164; Bauer, "Das Ende," Sept. 15, 1960, in: Foljanty, Johst (eds.), *Fritz Bauer,* vol. 1, pp. 650–654. That July, Peter Kubainsky, a Cairo-based journalist and intelligence peddler with Nazi connections, got in touch to say he was friendly with Alois Brunner, the deportation specialist whom Eichmann had assigned to Greece. Bauer thought there was a chance that Brunner might also be able to corroborate Merten's story, though he also recognized Brunner as a major figure in the Holocaust. He took down Brunner's address and passed it on to a Mossad contact (Orbach, *Fugitives,* p. 172; Chen, *Clouds,* pp. 116–117).

7. Herman, *Furnace,* pp. 82–83.

8. Thomas Harlan, Telegram to Fritz Bauer, July 21, 1960. HHStAW, 461, 37638/245, vol. 3, p. 457; Stengel, *Hermann Langbein,* p. 365; Jørgensen, "Ich hätte," 1965, in: Foljanty, Johst (eds.), *Fritz Bauer,* vol. 2, pp. 1337–1338; Harlan, *Veit,* pp. 20–21; Kuhlbrodt, *"Jud," Mitteilungen des Hamburgischen Richtervereins,* 1991, online source. There is no evidence in Veit Harlan's prosecution files to show the exact nature of Bauer's intervention (StAHH, 213, 11, 77294-72300). It's possible that he intervened after the Social Democrat leadership in Hamburg initially rejected the idea of prosecuting Veit Harlan (Tormin, *Die Geschichte,* pp. 193–194). Special thanks to Anne Uhl for Hamburg research and Ingrid Pufahl for deduction work. It's possible Harlan and Bauer met earlier in Munich (Thomas Harlan, Letter to Fritz Bauer, Aug. 1 1960. HHStAW, 461, 37638/245, vol. 3, pp. 467–468). Thomas Harlan, Letter to Georg Friedrich Vogel, Sept. 22, 1960. HHStAW, 461, 37638/245, vol. 3, p. 528; Domagała, "Prawdziwe," *Deutsche Welle,* Aug. 30, 2014, online source; Harlan, *Hitler,* pp. 79, 101–104; Steinke, *Fritz Bauer,* p. 159; Stengel, *Hermann Langbein,* pp. 365–366; Thomas Harlan, Letter to Fritz Bauer, Aug. 1 1960. HHStAW, 461, 37638/245, vol. 3, pp. 467–468; Thomas Harlan, Letter to Hermann Langbein, Oct. 15, 1960. ÖStA, Nachlass Hermann Langbein, E/1797: 30, no pages. Among the documents Harlan found in Poland was the testimony of an SS officer named Kurt Gerstein, who, along with his colleague Wilhelm Hermann Pfannenstiel, had supervised gassings in Bełżec. Gerstein had committed suicide in French internment after the war, while Pfannenstiel was now working for a German pharmaceutical company. Harlan launched a private action against him (Thomas Harlan, Letter to Hermann Langbein, Nov. 5, 1960. ÖStA, Nachlass Hermann Langbein, E/1797: 30, no pages). Harlan also gathered material on the SS men who accompanied transports from France to Auschwitz (Thomas Harlan, Letter to Georg Friedrich Vogel, Sept. 28, 1960. HHStAW, 461, 37638/245, vol. 3, p. 536). Harlan does not appear to have uncovered any material about Globke in the Polish archives, but at some point he did look into Globke's financial dealings, employing a private investigation firm he regularly used to track down former Nazis (Harlan, *Hitler,* p. 98). Fritz Bauer, Letter to Thomas Harlan, Nov, 1963 in: Renz (ed.), *"Von Gott,"* p. 53.

9. Thomas Harlan, Letter to Fritz Bauer, Aug. 1, 1960. HHStAW, 461, 37638/245, vol. 3, pp. 467–468; Krystyna Żywulska, Deposition, Sept. 15, 1960. HHStAW, 461, 37638/39, vol. 38, pp. 6527–6530; Harlan, "Fritz Bauer," *Forschungsjournal Soziale Bewegungen,* 2015/4 (28), p. 284; Dietrich Zeug, Note, Sept. 14, 1960. Kinemathek, Nachlass Thomas Harlan 201312 LzK 13.013, no pages. Harlan later claimed he visited Ludwigsburg with Bauer on the "first day we met" in Frankfurt; earlier correspondence also indicates a meeting in Munich around this time (Harlan, "Fritz Bauer," *Forschungsjournal Soziale Bewegungen,* 2015/28 [4], p. 284; Thomas Harlan, Letter to Georg Friedrich Vogel, Sept. 22, 1960. HHStAW, 461, 37638/245, vol. 3, p. 528). It seems logical that Bauer and Harlan traveled to Ludwigsburg the day after their evening meeting. Among the list of names Harlan had compiled were eight former SS men who were employed by the BND in 1960. They included the SS killer Rudolf Oebsger-Röder (Sälter, *NS-Kontinuitäten,* pp. 218–222). Special thanks to Anna Schattschneider for compiling Harlan's list and to Harriet Phillips for cross-comparing with known former Nazis in the BND. For the material Harlan shared with Zeug see: Kinemathek, Nachlass Thomas Harlan, 201312 LzK 13.013. Ludwigsburg 1960–1961–1963.

10. Dietrich Zeug, Note, Sept. 14, 1960. Kinemathek, Nachlass Thomas Harlan 201312 LzK 13.013, no pages; Hofmann, *"Ein Versuch,"* pp. 162–164; Sälter, *NS-Kontinuitäten,* pp. 629–632. For challenges facing the Central Office see Barbara Just-Dahlmann's speech discussed in: Weinke, *Eine Gesellschaft,* pp. 43–44. Just-Dahlmann, a prosecutor in Mannheim, had been seconded to the Central Office in May 1960 to help process material in Polish, a language she spoke fluently. On November 30, 1960, she gave a speech in Loccum, attended by Bauer, in which she laid out her concerns about the role of former Nazis in the justice system, citing three examples of Einsatzgruppen members with senior positions as police investigators. Although Just-Dahlmann didn't name officials, they were readily identifiable, such as the former RSHA department head, Friedrich Pradel, who had developed the use of mobile gassing vans, escaped trial, and risen to the position of head of the police department at the Hannover Regional Council. She further explained that the Central Office had been forced to set up special commissions to investigate offenders, as police offices were "full of people who should be arrested by the Central Office." She also expressed concerns about threats made against staff working in the office. The press attacked her for improper discussion of court documents. Bauer called up Just-Dahlmann in the midst of the controversy to express his support after her own boss, Erwin Schüle, refused to speak up for her (Weinke, *Eine Gesellschaft,* pp. 39–46, 52). For examples of former Einsatzgruppen members working for the BND see: Sälter, *Phantome,* pp. 273–325; Sälter, *NS-Kontinuitäten,* pp. 95–155, 213–274. Rudolf Oebsger-Röder had already been the subject of one investigation in Munich but had been transferred to one of Gehlen's field stations in Indonesia to avoid arrest (Sälter, *NS-Kontinuitäten,* pp. 218–222).
11. Harlan, *Hitler,* p. 106; Dittmann, "Der private," *Schriftenreihe des "Fritz Bauer Freundeskreises,"* 2013, p. 1; Steinke, *Fritz Bauer,* pp. 157–158; Ole Grünbaum, Interview by Jack Fairweather and Sine Maria Vinther, Mar. 24, 2022.
12. Harlan, *Hitler,* pp. 7–8, 219–220. The store in question was likely kept open on December 20, 1937, which is not Harlan's birthday. Other children also attended (Noack, *Veit Harlan,* p. 123).
13. Harlan, *Hitler,* pp. 30–34; Noack, *Veit Harlan,* p. 279; Niven, *Hitler,* p. 169; Liebert, "Vom Karrierestreben," in: Henne, Riedlinger (eds.), *Das Lüth-Urteil,* pp. 111–146; Harlan, *Hitler,* p. 101; Stanisław Skrzeszewski, Ferdynand Chaber, Stanisław Marczewski, Note, Nov. 1962. IPN Bu 1585/2945, p. 72; Author unknown, Noe, Sept. 1962. IPN, Bu 1585/2945, p. 71; Noack, *Veit Harlan,* pp. 273–284.
14. Bauer, "Die 'ungesühnte,'" May–June 1960, in: Perels, Wojak (eds.) *Die Humanität,* pp. 134–135, 140; Bauer, "Wurzeln," 1960, in: Foljanty, Johst (eds.), *Fritz Bauer,* vol. 1, pp. 676–677; Bauer, "Die Wurzeln," 1961, in: Foljanty, Johst (eds.), *Fritz Bauer,* vol. 1, pp. 770–796.

17

BAUER'S BOYS

1. Fritz Bauer, Letter to Heinz Meyer-Velde, no date, c. summer 1960. FBInst, Nachlass Heinz Meyer-Velde 12, no pages; Fritz Bauer, Letter to Heinz Meyer-Velde, Oct. 30, 1960. FBInst, Nachlass Heinz Meyer-Velde 12, no pages; Servatius, *Verteidiger,* pp. 14–15; Henke, *Geheime . . . Die politische Inlandsspionage des BND,* pp. 1111–1112; Author unknown, Lecture notes from 181 [Weiss] to

363 [Gehlen], Oct. 20 1960. BND-Archiv, 43132, p. 1816; Henke, *Geheime . . . Die politische Inlandsspionage des BND*, p. 1111. Eichmann's response concerning Globke to Servatius was known to Merten and Wiesenthal by December. It is highly likely Bauer also knew (Simon Wiesenthal, Letter to Ephraim Hofstädter, Israeli Police, Dec. 7, 1960. ISA, "Adolf Eichmann," cited in: Archer, *The Merten*, p. 72).

2. Bauer, "Unbewältigte," Mar. 25, 1961, in: Foljanty, Johst (eds.), *Fritz Bauer*, vol. 1, p. 701; Bauer, "Mörder," *Deutsche Nachrichten*, 1947/3, p. 2.

3. Bedford, "The Auschwitz," *The Observer*, Jan. 26, 1964, p. 12; Joachim Kügler, List of Auschwitz suspects, Jan. 18, 1960. IIIIStAW, 461, 37638/24, vol. 23, pp. 3741 3810; Pendas, *The Frankfurt*, p. 48.

4. Mauz, "Ein Gedränge," *Der Spiegel*, Feb. 24, 1969, cited in: Steinke, *Fritz Bauer*, p. 143.

5. Ibid.

6. Joachim Kügler, Interview by Werner Renz, May 5, 1998. FBInst, part 1; Pendas, *The Frankfurt*, p. 47; Wittmann, *Beyond*, pp. 64–67; Bauer, "In unserem," 1965, in: Foljanty, Johst (eds.), *Fritz Bauer*, vol. 2, pp. 1422–1424. The closest analogy Bauer could think of was a law that recognized how some crimes involved multiple offenses and gave prosecutors the scope to identify an overarching violation under which other violations fall. The law in question, Article 73, had been used only once, in 1951, to prosecute a single case against Josef Hirtreiter, an SS functionary in the Treblinka death camp. The West German federal constitutional court had upheld the judgment against him, arguing that since Treblinka's sole purpose was mass extermination, anyone who worked there, regardless of their specific duties, was effectively a participant in an "organised mass crime" and should therefore be considered guilty of murder (Hoffmann, *Die Verfolgung*, pp. 226–227). Georg Friedrich Vogel, Note, Mar. 8, 1960. HHStAW, 461, 37638/28, vol. 27, pp. 4510–4512; Jan Sehn, Report, Mar. 31, 1960. IPN, Gk 162/ II/1945, pp. 1–22; Maria Kozłowska, *Tak było . . .* [Memoir], 1999. IPN, Kr 120/33, p. 13.

7. Gańczak, *Jan Sehn*, pp. 9–19; Maria Kozłowska, *Tak było . . .* [Memoir], 1999. IPN, Kr 120/33, pp. 1–23; Joachim Kügler, Note, June 29, 1960. HHStAW, 461, 37638/245, vol. 3, pp. 424–425.

8. Wojak, *Fritz Bauer*, p. 319; Jan Sehn, Eugeniusz Szmulewski, Wizja lokalna w Oświęcimiu-Brzezince, Feb. 5, 1965. IPN, Bu 2586/404, p. 2; Renz, "Der 1 . . . Zwei Vorgeschichten," *Zeitschrift für Geschichtswissenschaft*, 2002/50 (7), pp. 22–23; Joachim Kügler, Interview by Werner Renz, May 5, 1998. FBInst, part 1.

9. Stengel, *Hermann Langbein*, pp. 420–430; Stengel, *Die Überlebenden*, pp. 144–153; Ignacy Golik, Interview by Dagi Knellessen, June 9, 2005, online source; Witness questionnaire, no date. HHStAW, 461, 37638/23, vol. 24, p. 3600; Ignacy Golik, Interview by Dagi Knellessen, June 9, 2005, online source; Stengel, *Hermann Langbein*, pp. 369, 406–407; Arrest warrant for Josef Klehr, Apr. 12, 1960. HHStAW, 461, 37638/29, vol. 28, p. 4723; Josef Klehr, Interrogation, Sept. 17, 1960. HHStAW, 461, 37638/39, vol. 38, pp. 6533–6540; Joachim Kügler, Plädoyer gegen Klehr, Scherpe und Hantl, May 20, 1965. FBInst, Tonbandmitschnitte des Auschwitz-Prozesses (1963–1965), online source; Hermann Langbein, Letter to Georg Friedrich Vogel and Joachim Kügler, Sept. 14, 1959. ÖStA, Nachlass Hermann Langbein, E/1797: 96, no pages; Langbein, *People*, pp. 501, 231; Stengel, *Die Überlebenden*, pp. 279–280; Stengel, *Hermann Langbein*, pp. 55, 81; Joachim

Kügler, Note, Sept. 20, 1960, and Sept. 22, 1960. HHStAW, 461, 37638/39, vol. 38, pp. 6577R-6577V; Georg Friedrich Vogel, Note, Nov. 2, 1960. HHStAW, 461, 37638/245, vol. 4, p. 570. For more on Klehr's murderous operation see: Bartosz Oziemkowski, Letter to International Auschwitz Committee, July 21, 1959. HHStAW, 461, 37638/13, vol. 12, pp. 1845–1847; Joachim Kügler, Plädoyer gegen Klehr, Scherpe und Hantl, May 20, 1965. FBInst, Tonbandmitschnitte des Auschwitz-Prozesses (1963–1965), online source; Application for arrest warrant for Josef Klehr, Mar. 18, 1960. HHStAW, 461, 37638/28, vol. 27, p. 4677; Tadeusz Paczuła, Deposition, Oct. 28, 1959. HHStAW, 461, 37638/17, vol. 16, pp. 2572–2573; Joachim Kügler, Note, Sept. 20, 1960 and Sept. 22, 1960. HHStAW, 461, 37638/39, vol. 38, pp. 6577–6577R; Georg Friedrich Vogel, Note, Nov. 2, 1960. HHStAW, 461, 37638/245, vol. 4, p. 570; Langbein, *People,* p. 501; Stengel, *Hermann Langbein,* p. 505.

10. Joachim Kügler, Interview by Werner Renz, May 5, 1998. FBInst, part 1; Bickel, Wagner (dirs.), *Deutsche,* 1993; Joachim Kügler, Interview by Werner Renz, May 5, 1998. FBInst, part 3; Robert Mulka, Interrogation, Nov. 8, 1960. HHStAW, 461, 37638/41, vol. 40, pp. 696–697; Robert Mulka, Interrogation, Sept. 11, 1961. HHStAW, 461, 37638/55, vol. 54, pp. 9934–9936.

11. Joachim Kügler, Interview by Werner Renz, May 5, 1998. FBInst, part 1.

12. Kügler was specifically tasked with tracking down suspects of unknown whereabouts in summer 1960 (Joachim Kügler, Note, June 28, 1960. HHStAW, 461, 37638/245, vol. 3, p. 422). Joachim Kügler, Interview by Werner Renz, May 5, 1998. FBInst, part 2; Kügler, "Es hat," in: Wojak, Meinl (eds.), *Im Labyrinth,* pp. 297–298; Pendas, *The Frankfurt,* p. 48; Joachim Kügler, Interview by Werner Renz, May 5, 1998. FBInst, part 2; Joachim Kügler, Note, Dec. 21, 1960. HHStAW, 461, 37638/246, vol. 4, pp. 659–663.

13. Joachim Kügler, Note, Dec. 21, 1960. HHStAW, 461, 37638/246, vol. 4, p. 662; Joachim Kügler, Interview by Werner Renz, May 5, 1998. FBInst, part 2.

18

BIKINI DECREE

1. "SS-Führer Baer," *Frankfurter Rundschau,* Dec. 22, 1960, p. 1; Bedford, "The Auschwitz," *The Observer,* Jan. 26, 1964, p. 12; Bauer, "Die 'ungesühnte,'" in: Perels, Wojak (eds.) *Die Humanität,* p. 140; Bauer, "NS-Verbrechen," 1964, in: Foljanty, Johst (eds.), *Fritz Bauer,* vol. 2, pp. 1185–1187; Steinke, "Fritz Bauer," *Kritische Justiz,* 2016/49 (1), p. 131; Meusch, *Von der Dikatur,* pp. 265–276; Archer, *The Merten,* pp. 41–43; Mielke, Letter to the Minister of the Interior of Bulgaria Georgi Tsankov, July 11, 1960. BA, MfS AP 6545-76, vol. 1, p. 101ff; Lemke, *Instrumentalisierter,* in: Danyel (ed.), *Die geteilte,* pp. 70–71; Reinhard Gehlen, Letter to Hans Globke, Jan. 19, 1961. KAS, Nachlass Hans Globke 01-070-103/2, uSECRET\u2028, no pages; Bastian Gnielka, Interview by Florine Miez, Nov. 26, 2021.

2. Reinhard Gehlen, Letter to Hans Globke, Jan. 19, 1961. KAS, Nachlass Hans Globke, 01-070-103/2, uSECRET\u2028, no pages; Hans Globke, Letter to Ludwig Eugen-Dollmann, Nov. 7, 1941. BStU, MfS ASt I-7-63 GA, pp. 108–110; Hans Globke, Letter to Ludwig Eugen-Dollmann, Sept. 22, 1941. BStU, MfS ASt I-7-63 GA, p. 102; Ludwig Eugen-Dollmann, Letter to Hans Globke, Oct. 31,

1941, BStU, MfS ASt I-7-63 GA, p. 105; Bästlein, *Der Fall*, p. 11; Strecker (ed.), *Dr. Hans Globke*, pp. 193–194, 218–219. For documents likely brought back by Gnielka see: KAS, Nachlass Hans Globke, 01-070-092/1, no pages; Carlos Foth, Gerhard Enders, Staatsanwälte, Jan. 19, 1961, online source. Some of the material given to Bauer, like the Frick letter, had appeared in the earlier East German publication *Globke und die Ausrottung der Juden* (Berlin: Ausschuss für deutsche Einheit, 1960).

3. "Ermittlungsverfahren," *Frankfurter Rundschau,* Jan. 6, 1961; Carlos Foth, Gerhard Enders, Note, no date. BA B, DP/3/2344, no pages.

4. "Ermittlungsverfahren," *Frankfurter Rundschau,* Jan. 6, 1961, no pages Franz Drügh, the public prosecutor in Bonn, wrote to the Israeli authorities on January 6, 1961, requesting that Eichmann testify in an earlier damages claim brought by Globke and Adenauer in October 1960. The timing does not appear to be a coincidence (Franz Drügh, Letter to Tel Aviv Local Court, Jan. 7, 1961. BND-Archiv, 43132, p. 1948). Archer, *The Merten,* p. 70; "Statement," *Frankfurter Rundschau,* Jan. 28–29, 1961, p. 2; "Zonen-Staatsanwälte," *Frankfurter Allgemeine Zeitung,* Jan. 18, 1961/15, p. 4; Archer, *The Merten,* p. 70; Wayland B. Waters, Memo to Department of State, Washington, Feb. 7, 1961. Hans Globke, 0178, p. 2. CIA Electronic Reading Room, online source; "Stellungnahme Zinns," *Frankfurter Rundschau,* Jan. 28–29, 1961, p. 2; Carlos Foth, Gerhard Enders, Note, no date. BA B, DP/3/2344, no pages; Foth, "Günther Wieland," in: Wieland, *Naziverbrechen,* p. 412; Wayland B. Waters, Memo to Department of State, Washington, Feb. 7, 1961. Globke, Hans, 0178, p. 2. CIA Electronic Reading Room, online source. In his meeting with the East German prosecutors, Bauer suggested the idea of a house on the border between East and West Germany that would contain all documents from the Nazi era and could be freely entered from both sides (Foth, "Mein Anteil," in: Die Linkspartei PDS [ed.], *Konferenz,* online source).

5. "Stellungnahme Zinns," *Frankfurter Rundschau,* Jan. 28–29, 1961, p. 2; "Fahndung," *Frankfurter Allgemeine Zeitung,* Jan. 28, 1961/24, p. 3; Bauer, "Deutsche," 1961, in: Foljanty, Johst (eds.), *Fritz Bauer,* vol. 1, p. 693. *Life* magazine's publication of Sassen's interviews with Eichmann had also alerted Bauer to the existence of a transcript of their conversations that might further implicate Globke. Hermann Langbein suspected a copy of the transcript was kept at the Eichmann family law firm in Linz, Austria, and, according to Thomas Harlan, staged a break-in with the help of two former Auschwitz prisoners, whom Harlan referred to as "the locksmiths." Two Czech Jews named Erich Kulka and Ota Kraus fit the bill: They had survived the camp by working as locksmiths. Both had taken an active interest in documenting the camp's horrors in the years since and had written one of the first histories of Auschwitz that was familiar to Bauer. Kulka also had a sister-in-law in Linz with whom he could stay. It is also possible that the transcript was acquired in much less dramatic fashion. Simon Wiesenthal had made contact with Robert Eichmann's secretary, who might have supplied him with the material. Langbein suggested that the copy of the transcript that reached both Bauer and Gideon Hausner, the chief prosecutor for the Eichmann trial, came via this route. This copy proved important in the trial, as it had pages with Eichmann's handwritten notes down the edges. As Eichmann refused to recognize the transcripts in court, only the notes could be submitted (Passent, "Zbrodniarz," *Polityka,* Mar. 10, 2007, online source; Feltrinelli, "Il racconto," *La*

Repubblica, Mar. 11, 2022, online source; Segev, *Simon Wiesenthal*, p. 149; Stangneth, *Eichmann*, p. 388; Stengel, *Hermann Langbein*, p. 481; Kraus, "Ota Kraus," in: Rauschenberger et al. [eds.], *Investigating*, pp. 171–192; Hájková, "Israeli," *Tablet Magazine*, Oct. 30, 2014, online source; Stangneth, *Eichmann*, pp. 390, 383, 388; Lipstadt, *The Eichmann*, p. 67).

6. Konrad Adenauer, Letter to Georg August Zinn, Jan. 1961. KAS, Nachlass Hans Globke 01-070-092/1, pp. 51–52. For a draft with handwritten changes see pp. 53–54. Special thanks to Matias Ristic for the letter. It's not clear when or if this letter was passed on to Zinn, but its contents were evidently conveyed. The expression "dragged into the shadows" is a direct translation and carries the meaning "appear suspect."

7. Bästlein, *Der Fall*, p. 46; Strecker (ed.), *Dr. Hans Globke*, pp. 271–275; Müller, *Reinhard Gehlen*, p. 1005; "Ein unbedeutender," *Der Spiegel*, Feb. 15, 1961, online source.

8. Strobel, "Globke," *Die Zeit*, Feb. 17, 1961, online source; Archer, *The Merten*, p. 70.

9. Bästlein, *Der Fall*, p. 74; Wayland B. Waters, Memo to Department of State, Washington, Feb. 7, 1961. Hans Globke, 0178, p. 2. CIA Electronic Reading Room, online source.

19

JERUSALEM

1. Orbach, *Fugitives*, pp. 160–173, 206–211; Sälter, *NS-Kontinuitäten*, pp. 732–733. As mentioned earlier, Globke's estate in the Konrad-Adenauer-Stiftung contains a list of material received by Bauer from Thomas Gnielka's mission to East Berlin, suggesting an informant in Bauer's office. (KAS, Nachlass Hans Globke 01-070-092/1). It is not possible to ascertain Brunner's exact relationship with the BND because his file was destroyed due to a "mistake" (Sälter, *NS-Kontinuitäten*, p. 733). Brunner's associate Karl-Heinz Spaeth, who had been added to the BND's payroll, appears to have offered the payment to Merten for a public avowal of Globke's innocence (Sälter, *NS-Kontinuitäten*, p. 733).

2. Yablonka, *The State*, p. 62; Herman, *The Furnace*, p. 71; Hausner, *Justice*, p. 439; Henke, *Geheime . . . Die politische Inlandsspionage des BND*, p. 1164; 521, Memo to 181 [Weiss] concerning Operation Gleisdreieck, Mar. 23, 1961. BND-Archiv, 43132, pp. 2010–2014; Müller, *Reinhard Gehlen*, p. 1149.

3. David Ben-Gurion, Diary, Dec. 5, 1960. BG Archive, cited in: Herman, *The Furnace*, pp. 83–84; Wiegrefe, "Der Fluch," *Der Spiegel*, Apr. 11, 2011, online source; Segev, *A State*, p. 645; Conze, *Das Amt*, p. 614. West Germany had agreed to loan Israel 2 billion deutschmarks over the course of a decade; the first installment was for 100 million deutschmarks (Hermann, *The Furnace*, p. 83). Yablonka, *The State*, p. 53; Hermann, *The Furnace*, p. 71; Vogel (ed.), *Der Deutsch-Israelische*, p. 181; Wiegrefe, "Der Fluch," *Der Spiegel*, Apr. 11, 2011, online source. Vogel reported directly to Adenauer and Globke but was also "a longstanding special connection" of the BND (Henke, *Geheime . . . Die politische Inlandsspionage des BND*, pp. 1172–1174).

4. Wiegrefe, "Der Fluch," *Der Spiegel*, Apr. 11, 2011, online source. Ben-Gurion summoned Hausner to his office to discuss the Globke issue in early April (Hermann, *The Furnace*, p. 71).

5. Cohen, "Rachel Auerbach," *Polin: Studies in Polish Jewry,* 2007/20, pp. 199–215; Yablonka, *The State,* pp. 88–89, 88 note 1.

6. Wiegrefe, "Der Fluch," *Der Spiegel,* Apr. 11, 2011, online source; Vogel (ed.), *Der Deutsch-Israelische,* pp. 184–186; Henke, *Geheime . . . Die politische Inlandsspionage des BND,* pp. 1139–1140; Hans Gawlik, Note for Christian Raab, Feb. 9, 1961. PAAA, B 83, vol. 55, cited in: Conze, *Das Amt,* p. 613. The committee's chairman, Hans Gawlik, was a former Nazi lawyer who had supervised the Foreign Office's program of legal assistance to German war criminals ("Ist benachrichtigt," *Der Spiegel,* Apr. 14, 1968, online source). Conze, *Das Amt,* p. 614. Rather embarrassingly, Gawlik discovered that one of the judges in the Eichmann trial was German-born and had made applications for reparations that had not yet been resolved. The Foreign Office found this situation "particularly unpleasant" and urged the Interior and Justice Ministries to take action (Wiegrefe, "Der Fluch," *Der Spiegel,* Apr. 10, 2011, online source).

7. Vogel (ed.), *Der Deutsch-Israelische,* pp. 185; Vogel, "Der Prozess," *Deutsche Zeitung,* Apr. 22–23, 1961, p. 3; Wiegrefe, "Der Fluch," *Der Spiegel,* Apr. 11, 2011, online source.

8. "Berichterstatter," *Frankfurter Rundschau,* Mar. 3, 1961, p. 16; Schwelien, "Der Amtsgehilfe," *Frankfurter Allgemeine Zeitung,* Apr. 21, 1961, cited in: Krause, *Der Eichmann-Prozess,* p. 171; Strobel, "Wieder," *Die Zeit,* June 30, 1961, online source.

9. Minerbi, *The Eichmann,* p. 3; Lipstadt, *The Eichmann,* p. 42; Yablonka, *The State,* p. 57; Minerbi, *The Eichmann,* p. 6.

10. Lipstadt, *The Eichmann,* p. 56; Yablonka, *The State,* pp. 62–63; Minerbi, *The Eichmann,* p. 6; Vogel, "Der Prozess," *Deutsche Zeitung,* Apr. 22–23, 1961, p. 3; Lipstadt, *The Eichmann,* p. 56.

11. Vogel, "Der Prozess," *Deutsche Zeitung,* Apr. 22–23, 1961, p. 3; Hausner, *Justice,* p. 323.

12. Lipstadt, *The Eichmann,* pp. 58–59.

13. Ibid.

14. Lipstadt, *The Eichmann,* p. 60.

15. Lipstadt, *The Eichmann,* p. 61.

16. Lipstadt, *The Eichmann,* pp. 61–62; Vogel, "Der Prozess," *Deutsche Zeitung,* Apr. 22–23, 1961, p. 3.

17. Krause, *Der Eichmann-Prozess,* p. 53.

18. Lipstadt, *The Eichmann,* pp. 67–68; Minerbi, *The Eichmann,* p. 29; Cesarani, *Becoming,* p. 106.

19. Adolf Eichmann, Testimony, Apr. 19, 1961. Trial of Adolf Eichmann: session 10, The Nizkor Project, online source; Lipstadt, *The Eichmann,* p. 67; Minerbi, *The Eichmann,* p. 29; Vogel, "Eichmann," *Deutsche Zeitung,* Apr. 13, 1961, p. 2.

20. Minerbi, *The Eichmann,* pp. 31, 32; Rivka Yoselevska, Testimony, May 8, 1961. Trial of Adolf Eichmann: session 30, The Nizkor Project, online source; Yablonka, *The State,* p. 109; Minerbi, *The Eichmann,* pp. 69–70; Lipstadt, *The Eichmann,* p. 77; Yablonka, *The State,* pp. 111–112.

21. Rivka Yoselevska, Testimony, May 8, 1961. Trial of Adolf Eichmann: session 30, The Nizkor Project, online source; Minerbi, *The Eichmann,* pp. 69–71; Lipstadt, *The Eichmann,* p. 77; Yablonka, *The State,* pp. 111–112.

22. Douglas, "Rivka Yoselewska," in: Freeman, Lewis (eds.), *Law,* vol. 2, p. 298.
23. Rivka Yoselevska, Testimony, May 8, 1961. Trial of Adolf Eichmann: session 30, The Nizkor Project, online source; Gouri, *Facing,* p. 51.
24. Gouri, *Facing,* pp. 51, 52.
25. Yoselevska, Testimony, May 8, 1961. Trial of Adolf Eichmann: Session 30, The Nizkor Project, online source.
26. Hausner, *Justice,* pp. 375–377. Franz Six and Hermann Krumey both submitted statements to the court, but neither mentioned Globke (Krause, *Der Eichmann-Prozess,* p. 63).
27. Lipstadt, *The Eichmann,* pp. 107–109.
28. No title, *The New York Times,* June 21, 1961, cited in: Lipstadt, *The Eichmann,* p. 116; No title, *The New York Times,* June 25, 1961, cited in: Lipstadt, *The Eichmann,* p. 116; No title, *The New York Times,* June 26, 1961, cited in: Lipstadt, *The Eichmann,* p. 116; No title, *The New York Times,* July 9, 1961, cited in: Lipstadt, *The Eichmann,* p. 116; Arendt, "Adolf Eichmann," *The New York Times,* Feb. 8, 1963, no pages; Lipstadt, *The Eichmann,* pp. 107–109, 108, 109; Gellhorn, "Eichmann," *The Atlantic Monthly,* Feb. 1962, online source.
29. Kaul also held a press conference upon arriving in Jerusalem in May (Rolf Vogel, Memo to Foreign Office and Oberregierungsrat Baden in Bundeskanzleramt, May 1, 1961. PAAA, B 130 5571A, no pages). Krause, *Der Eichmann-Prozess,* p. 225; Hausner, *Justice,* p. 466; Moshe Tavor, Letter to Felix Shinnar, May 10, 1960. ISA-mfa-ReparationsGermany-000rh96, pp. 270–271; Vogel (ed.), *Der deutsch-israelische,* p. 187, p. 192; Moshe Tavor, Letter to Felix Shinnar, May 10, 1960. ISA-mfa-ReparationsGermany-000rh96, pp. 270–271; Adolf Eichmann, Cross-examination by Gideon Hausner, July 10, 1961. The Trial of Adolf Eichmann: session 90, The Nizkor Project, online source; "Adolf Eichmann," *Frankfurter Rundschau,* June 22, 1961, p. 1; No title. *Frankfurter Rundschau,* June 23, 1961, p. 1; No title. *Frankfurter Rundschau,* June 24–26 1961, p. 2.
30. No title, *HaOlam HaZe,* July 5, 1961, pp. 7–8; Wiegrefe, "Aktenklau," *Der Spiegel,* Sept. 2, 2010, online source; Preuschen, Memo to Foreign Office, June 29, 1961. PAAA, B 130 5571A, no pages.
31. Vogel (ed.), *Der Deutsch-Israelische,* p. 195; Wiegrefe, "Who Ordered," *Der Spiegel,* May 30, 2009, online source; Lipstadt, *The Eichmann,* pp. 77–79.
32. Vogel (ed.), *Der Deutsch-Israelische,* p. 195.

20

INDICTMENT

1. Zeug does not include Globke in the list of people he informs Rosen he will be asking Eichmann about, likely due to political considerations (Dietrich Zeug, Letter to Shabtai Rosen, July 17, 1961. ISA-justice-StateAttorney-000r1xw, pp. 138–142). Dan, "Bonn," *Maariv,* Oct. 22, 1961, no pages; Birn, "Ein deutscher," in: Renz (ed.), *Interessen,* p. 97.
2. Judgment, The Trial of Adolf Eichmann, vol. 9, p. 2218, cited in: Bascomb, *Hunting,* p. 316.
3. Nellessen, "Vor dem Prozess," *Die Welt,* Feb. 7, 1961, cited in: Krause, *Der Eichmann-Prozess,* p. 256; Wucher, "Die Eigene," *Süddeutsche Zeitung,* July 24, 1961, cited in: Krause, *Der Eichmann-Prozess,* p. 270; Ahlers, "Vor der Abrech-

nung," *Frankfurter Rundschau,* Apr. 11, 1961, cited in: Krause, *Der Eichmann-Prozess,* p. 258.

4. Yablonka, *The State,* pp. 88, 109–111.
5. Minerbi, *The Eichmann,* p. 56.
6. Ibid.
7. Ibid.
8. Their frank exchange of views left Arendt ruffled. "[Bauer's] different, of course," she noted of their meeting, "but even so, not exceptionally intelligent and apart from that, he's Jewish" (Hannah Arendt, Letter to Leni Yahil, July 23, 1961. " 'Dear Hannah Arendt,' " Sept. 24, 2010, Eurozine, online source).
9. Lipstadt, *The Eichmann,* pp. 64, 117–124.
10. Bauer, "Mörder," *Deutsche Nachrichten,* 1947/3, p. 2; Bauer, "Unbewältigte," Mar. 25, 1961, in: Foljanty, Johst (eds.), *Fritz Bauer,* vol. 1, p. 701; Bauer, "In unserem," 1965, in: Foljanty, Johst (eds.), *Fritz Bauer,* vol. 2, p. 1423; Bauer, "Prozesse," Jan.–Feb. 1964, in: Foljanty, Johst (eds.), *Fritz Bauer,* vol. 2, p. 1401; Pendas, *The Frankfurt,* p. 47; Wittmann, *Beyond,* pp. 64–67; Fritz Bauer, Extracts from letters to Melitta Wiedemann, no date, *Gewerkschafliche Monatshefte,* 1968/19, pp. 490–492, cited in: Steinke, *Fritz Bauer,* p. 127.
11. Henke, *Geheime . . . Die politische Inlandsspionage des BND,* pp. 1169, 1990, 1201, 1193–1195. For the genesis of Strecker's book see: Söhner, Zombory, "Accusing," in: Bourhis Le, Tcherneva, Voisin (eds.), *Seeking,* pp. 362–373.
12. Henke, *Geheime . . . Die politische Inlandsspionage des BND,* pp. 1197–1201.
13. Bascomb, *Hunting,* pp. 318–319; Aharoni, Dietl, *Operation,* pp. 172–173.
14. Bascomb, *Hunting,* p. 319.
15. Bareli, "Letter to the reader," *HaOlam HaZe,* Aug. 15, 1962, p. 2.
16. Ibid.
17. Renz, "Auschwitz," 2013, FBInst, Tonbandmitschnitte des Auschwitz-Prozesses (1963–1965), online source; Henry Ormond, Closing argument, May 24, 1965. FBInst, Der Auschwitz-Prozess, DVD, pp. 33982-34102; Bauer, "Antinazistiche," Jan.–Feb. 1964, in: Foljanty, Johst (eds.), *Fritz Bauer,* vol. 2, pp. 1393–1401.
18. Stengel, *Hermann Langbein,* p. 429. Bischoff was released in November 1959 for health reasons, Uhlenbroock in November 1960 on bail, Broad in December 1960, and Mulka in March 1961 following a reappraisal of their guilt. Dylewski was released in March 1961 on bail and for health reasons. Mulka was rearrested in May 1961 and released again in December 1961 on bail following another reappraisal of his guilt (Joachim Kügler, Note, Nov. 27, 1959. HHStAW, 461, 37638/19, vol. 18, p. 2960; Opper, Decision, Nov. 29, 1960. HHStaW, 461, 37638/42, vol. 41, p. 7168; Opper, Decision, Dec. 23, 1960. HHStAW, 461, 37638/43, vol. 42, pp. 7417–7419; Opper, Decision, Mar. 22, 1961. HHStAW, 461, 37638/47, vol. 46, pp. 8189–8190; Joachim Kügler, Note, May 29, 1961. HHStAW, 461, 37638/51, vol. 50, p. 9010; Landgericht 3. Strafkammer, Decision, Dec. 13, 1961. HHStAW, 461, 37638/59, vol. 58, pp. 10872–10873). Hermann Langbein, Letter to Joachim Kügler and Georg Friedrich Vogel, Feb. 5, 1960. ÖStA, Nachlass Hermann Langbein, E/1797: 96, no pages.
19. Stengel, *Hermann Langbein,* pp. 436–437; Pendas, *The Frankfurt,* pp. 38–39; Stengel, *Hermann Langbein,* pp. 449–455, 487–488; Daniel Langbein, Kurt Langbein, Interview by Florine Miez, Dec. 8, 2021; Stengel, *Hermann Langbein,* pp. 462–468; Daniel Langbein, Kurt Langbein, Interview by Florine Miez, Dec. 8, 2021;

Joachim Kügler, Note, June 28, 1960. HHStAW, 461, 37638/244, vol. 2, pp. 422–423; Kügler, Interview by Werner Renz, May 5, 1998, part 1, FBInst.

20. Bauer, "Unbewältigte," Mar. 25, 1961, in: Foljanty, Johst (eds.), *Fritz Bauer*, vol. 1, p. 703. Kügler likely began writing the indictment in October 1962 (Henry Ormond, Letter to Hermann Langbein, Nov. 2, 1962. ÖStA, Nachlass Hermann Langbein, E/1797: 106, no pages). Steinke, *Fritz Bauer*, p. 178; Joachim Kügler, Interview by Werner Renz, May 5, 1998. FBInst, part 1; Gerhard Wiese, Interview by Jack Fairweather and Florine Miez, Oct. 2, 2020; Steinke, *Fritz Bauer*, pp. 180–181; Bauer, "Unbewältigte," Mar. 25, 1961, in: Foljanty, Johst (eds.), *Fritz Bauer*, vol. 1, p. 703; Pendas, *The Frankfurt*, p. 143; Bauer, "Unbewältigte," Mar. 25, 1961, in: Foljanty, Johst (eds.), *Fritz Bauer*, vol. 1, p. 703. On the IfZ report see: Pendas, *The Frankfurt*, pp. 145–147; Joachim Kügler, Interview by Werner Renz, May 5, 1998. FBInst, part 3; Bauer, "Unbewältigte," Mar. 25, 1961, in: Foljanty, Johst (eds.), *Fritz Bauer*, vol. 1, p. 703.

21. Zwerenz, "Mutterseelenallein," *Forschungsjournal Soziale Bewegungen*, 2015/4 (28), p. 300; Steinke, *Fritz Bauer*, pp. 190, 157; Wojak, *Fritz Bauer*, p. 452; Johannes Warlo, Interview by Almut Schoenfeld, July 20, 2020; Fritz Bauer, Postcard to Heinz Meyer-Velde, Oct. 6, 1961. FBInst, Nachlass Heinz Meyer-Velde 13, no pages; Fritz Bauer, Postcard to Heinz Meyer-Velde, c. Dec 1961. FBInst, Nachlass Heinz Meyer-Velde 13, no pages; Fritz Bauer, Postcard to Heinz Meyer-Velde, c. 1962. FBInst, Nachlass Heinz Meyer-Velde 14, no pages.

22. Meyer-Velde, "'Dann machen's,'" in: Backhaus, Boll, Gross (eds.), *Fritz Bauer*, p. 246; Einsele, "Worte," in: Oberstaatsanwaltschaft, Frankfurt am Main Oberlandesgericht (ed.), *Fritz Bauer*, pp. 19–22; Alexander Kluge, Interview by Jack Fairweather, Sept. 3, 2021. Helm was initially arrested for breaking into multiple U.S. military barracks, after which he claimed to have witnessed a murder. While being escorted away from the alleged crime scene, he shot the American and German detectives who were driving him. He was initially sentenced to death ("Spass mit Charly," *Der Spiegel*, Oct. 29, 1948, online source; Garland, "Anatomy," *Military Police*, Spring 2010, pp. 37–44). Kuper, *Hamlet*, p. 371; Alexander Kluge, Interview by Jack Fairweather, Sept. 3, 2021. Horkheimer—considerably more worried about being attacked by former Nazis than was Bauer—had taken to walking whenever he could (Alexander Kluge, Interview by Jack Fairweather, Sept. 3, 2021).

23. Schlesak, *The Druggist*, p. 130; Kurt Jurasek, Deposition, Jan. 14, 1960. HHStAW, 461, 37638/24, vol. 23, pp. 3811–3820; Hans Münch, Deposition, Apr. 4, 1960. HHStAW, 461, 37638/28, vol. 27, pp. 4602–4619; Bernhard Walter, Deposition, Oct. 15, 1960. HHStAW, 461, 37638/40, vol. 39, pp. 6738–6740; Ludwig Wörl, Deposition, Feb. 1, 1962. HHStAW, 461, 37638/62, vol. 61, pp. 11373–11384; Wilhelm-Wojciech Prokop, Letter to Hermann Langbein, June 9, 1960. HHStAW, 461, 37638/39, vol. 38, p. 6952; Langbein, *People*, p. 485.

24. Bauer, "Die 'ungesühnte,'" in: Perels, Wojak (eds.), *Die Humanität*, p. 135; Whisnant, *Male*, p. 187; Bauer, "Zur sexualstrafrechtlichen," Oct. 20, 1967, in: Foljanty, Johst (eds.), *Fritz Bauer*, vol. 2, pp. 1727–1728. Bauer's contribution to the essay collection, *Sexuality and Punishment*, pointed out that only four other countries in Western Europe continued to punish gay men and yet the more liberal laws in places like Denmark hadn't led to an explosion of vice. All German law had succeeded in doing was imposing an arbitrary and pernicious distinction whereby men who were considered "respectable fellow citizens under Danish law" be-

came so-called "'sex criminals'" in West Germany (Bauer, "Sexualstrafrecht," 1963, in: Foljanty, Johst [eds.], *Fritz Bauer,* vol. 2, pp. 1101–1114). Other contributors included Hans Giese and Theodor Adorno (Bauer et al., "Sexualität," pp. 11–26). Police arrests peaked in the early 1960s, although that did not prevent the establishment of a vibrant gay bar scene in West Berlin and Hamburg in particular (Whisnant, *Male,* pp. 157, 161). Schwartz, "Homosexualität," in: Rauschenberger, Steinbacher (eds.), *Fritz Bauer,* p. 168; Petersen, "Generalstaatsanwalt," Feb. 27, 1963, in: Foljanty, Johst (eds.), *Fritz Bauer,* vol. 2, pp. 1022–1025; Steinke, *Fritz Bauer,* pp. 145–147.

25. Petersen, "Generalstaatsanwalt," Feb. 27, 1963, in: Foljanty, Johst (eds.), *Fritz Bauer,* vol. 2, p. 1022.

26. Weingärtner, "Dr. Bauer," *Rheinischer Merkur,* Mar. 8, 1963, cited in: Steinke, *Fritz Bauer,* p. 147.

27. Steinke, *Fritz Bauer,* p. 190; Johannes Warlo, Interview by Almut Schoenfeld, July 20, 2020. "My driver died," Bauer wrote to a friend, "about which I am very sad and unhappy" (Fritz Bauer, Letter to Birgitta Wolf, Dec. 14, 1962. HIS, Nothilfe Birgitta Wolf, NBW 001, p. 116). Nelhiebel, "Eine Kugel," *Weltexpresso,* June 30, 2018, online source; Steinke, *Fritz Bauer,* pp. 181–182. Other cases ground to a halt as his staff encountered equally troubling obstacles. One of his prosecutors, Johannes Warlo, had filed an arrest warrant for euthanasia doctor Reinhold Vorberg, only for the local judge to tip Vorberg off so that he could flee to Spain. Bauer had flown to Madrid himself to get the German embassy to supply the Vorbergs' address and enlisted the Vatican's help to secure his extradition (Johannes Warlo, Interview by Almut Schoenfeld, July 20, 2020; Wojak, *Fritz Bauer,* pp. 383–384; Steinke, Renz, "Gespräch," in: Backhaus, Boll, Gross [eds.], *Fritz Bauer,* pp. 171–186).

28. Fritz Bauer, Letter to Thomas Harlan, Nov. 7, 1962, in: Renz (ed.), *"Von Gott,"* p. 48; Stengel, *Hermann Langbein,* p. 481; Fritz Bauer, Letter to Thomas Harlan, Nov. 7, 1962, in: Renz (ed.), *"Von Gott,"* p. 48; Fritz Bauer, Letter to Thomas Harlan, June 23, 1963, in: Renz (ed.), *"Von Gott,"* p. 49; Trojanowska, Doniesienie, July 13, 1961. IPN, Bu 003273/17, vol. II, pp. 49–51; Trojanowska, Doniesienie, May 3, 1962. IPN, Bu 003273/17, vol. II, pp. 153–160; Trojanowska, Doniesienie, July 13, 1961. IPN, Bu 003273/17, vol. II, pp. 49–51; Author unknown, Information concerning Thomas Harlan, June 1962. IPN, Bu 1585/2945, p. 10; Janina Trojanowska, Doniesienie, Jan. 22, 1962. IPN, Bu 003273/17, vol. II, p. 108. Harlan had helped to publish the Argentina material in Poland during the Eichmann trial to limited effect (Harlan, *Hitler,* pp. 97–98; Stengel, *Hermann Langbein,* pp. 388–389; Daniel Passent, Interview with Jack Fairweather and Katarzyna Chiżyńska, Sept. 9, 2021).

29. Fritz Bauer, Letter to Thomas Harlan, Nov. 7, 1962, in: Renz (ed.), *"Von Gott,"* p. 48.

30. Wittmann, *Beyond,* pp. 64–67, p. 102; Bauer, "In unserem," 1965, in: Foljanty, Johst (eds.), *Fritz Bauer,* vol. 2, p. 1423; Heinrich Bischoff, Interrogation, Nov. 24, 1961. HHStAW, 461, 37638/58, vol. 57, pp. 10587–10597; Hans Stark, Interrogation, Apr. 23, 1959. HHStAW, 461, 37638/7, vol. 6, pp. 937–960; Franz-Johann Hofmann, Interrogation, Oct. 24, 1961. HHStAW, 461, 37638/57, vol. 56, p. 10337; Author unknown, Note, Aug. 22, 1960. HHStAW, 461, 37638/245, vol. 3, p. 489; Schlesak, *The Druggist,* p. 168; Henry Ormond, Plädoyer, May 24, 1965. FBInst, Auschwitz-Prozess, DVD; Wittmann, *Beyond,* p. 79; Bauer, "Wurzeln,"

1960, in: Foljanty, Johst (eds.), *Fritz Bauer,* vol. 1, pp. 667, 681; Bauer, "Unbewältigte," Mar. 25, 1961, in: Foljanty, Johst (eds.), *Fritz Bauer,* vol. 1, p. 700; Wittmann, *Beyond,* p. 102; Renz, "Auschwitz . . . des Tonbandschnittes," *Jahrbuch der Juristischen Zeitgeschichte,* 2010/19 (1), p. 178; Lifton, *Nazi,* pp. 303–308.

31. Hans Münch, Deposition, Mar. 17, 1960. HHStAW, 461, 37638/28, vol. 27, pp. 4602–4619; Lifton, *The Nazi,* pp. 303–308.

32. Hans Münch, Deposition, Mar. 8, 1960. HHStAW, 461, 37638/28, vol. 27, pp. 4612–4613; Trentmann, *Out of,* p. 55; Lifton, *The Nazi,* pp. 308–311, 320–325.

33. Detlef Nebbe, Testimony, Sept. 14, 1964. FBInst, Tonbandmitschnitte des Auschwitz-Prozesses (1963–1965), online source; Roman Orzeł, Oświadczenia, vol. 44, no date. PMA-B, pp. 142–143; Bilan, "Excerpt," in: Setkiewicz, *The SS,* p. 49; Naumann, *Auschwitz,* p. 176.

34. Bilan, "Excerpt," in: Setkiewicz, *The SS,* p. 49; Antonina Piątkowska, Wspomnienia, vol. 125, no date. PMA-B, p. 122; Roman Orzeł, Oświadczenia, vol. 44, no date. PMA-B, p. 143; Broad, "Reminiscences," in: Bezwińska, Czech (eds.), *KL Auschwitz,* pp. 131–132; Hersz Kugelmann, Testimony, Aug. 21, 1964. FBInst, Tonbandmitschnitte des Auschwitz-Prozesses (1963–1965), online source; Długoborski, Piper (eds.), *Auschwitz,* vol. 3, pp. 109–111, 140–141, 150–157.

35. Długoborski, Piper (eds.), *Auschwitz,* vol. 3, pp. 149, 141–142; Dow Paisikovic, Aug. 12, 1964. Oświadczenia, vol. 44. PMA-B, pp. 92, 93; Henryk Tauber, Testimony, May 24, 1945. PI, Chronicles of Terror (IPN, GK 196/93, pp. 128–155), online source; Roman Orzeł, Oświadczenia, vol. 44, no date. PMA-B, p. 142. Zyklon B itself had no scent, but because of the danger involved, the manufacturers, Tesch & Stabenow, owned by Degesch, added an almond smell that mimicked the natural aroma of cyanide. For more information on the use of Zyklon B, see: Długoborski, Piper (eds.), *Auschwitz,* vol. 3, pp. 165–170.

36. Wachsmann, *KL,* pp. 380–391; Konrad Morgen, Testimony, Mar. 9, 1964. FBInst, Tonbandmitschnitte des Auschwitz-Prozesses (1963–1965), online source; Konrad Morgen, Testimony, Mar. 8, 1962. HHStAW, 461, 37638/64, vol. 63, pp. 11, 714–721, 722.

37. Broad, *Reminiscences,* in: Bezwińska, Czech (eds.), *KL Auschwitz,* pp. 139–198; Deutschkron, *Auschwitz,* p. 195; Kremer, *Diary,* in: Bezwińska, Czech (eds.), *KL Auschwitz,* pp. 199–281; Wachsmann, *KL,* pp. 338–340. Kremer had been tried in Kraków in 1947 and sentenced to life. Upon his release in 1958, he was convicted again in West Germany but freed for time served (Stengel, *Hermann Langbein,* pp. 377–383). Kremer, *Diary,* Sept. 5–6, Oct. 18, 1942, in: Bezwińska, Czech (eds.), *KL Auschwitz,* p. 215; Kremer, "Diary," *Diary,* Sept. 6, 1942, in: Bezwińska, Czech (eds.), *KL Auschwitz,* pp. 216–217; Kremer, "Diary," Sept. 20, 1942, in: Bezwińska, Czech (eds.), *KL Auschwitz,* p. 220; Kremer, "Diary," Nov. 14, 1942, in: Bezwińska, Czech (eds.), *KL Auschwitz,* p. 230.

38. The defendant Stefan Baretzki was identified in one picture. Erich Kulka, Letter to Henry Ormond, Oct. 3, 1963. HHStAW, 461, 37638/257, vol. 16, pp. 3537–3538; Brink, *Das Auschwitz-Album,* in: Wojak (ed.), *Auschwitz-Prozess,* pp. 148–156; Stengel, *Hermann Langbein,* pp. 207–209. Some of the photographs were published in the fourth Czech edition of Kraus and Kulka's book *The Death Factory* in 1956, and in the German translation in 1958. They were also submitted as evidence in the Eichmann trial but attracted limited interest at the time (Kraus, "Ota Kraus," in: Rauschenberger, Puttkamer von, Steinbacher [eds.], *Investigating,* pp. 171–192).

39. Hermann Langbein, Letter to Henry Ormond, Apr. 30, 1963. ÖStA, Nachlass Hermann Langbein, E/1797: 106, p. 1, cited in: Stengel, *Hermann Langbein*, p. 495; Levi, *The Drowned*, p. 83. The one person to have survived the gas chambers was a sixteen-year-old girl whose face had been pressed against the damp concrete floor, where the moisture had helped to neutralize the cyanide compound. She had been pulled out of the tangle of bodies still breathing and brought to a side room where she gradually came to her senses. She was shot a short while later (Nyiszli, *Auschwitz*, pp. 56–58). Długoborski, Piper (eds.), *Auschwitz*, vol. 3, pp. 69–70, 106–107; Chare, Williams, *Matters*, p. 124–146; Stengel, *Die Überlebenden*, pp. 213, 286; Greif, *We Wept*, pp. 178–179, 54–56, Abraham Dragon, Interview by Gideon Greif, cited in: Greif, *We Wept*, p. 178; Levi, *The Drowned*, p. 50; Greif, *We Wept*, p. 44. Primo Levi suggested the Sonderkommando was "an extreme case of collaboration."

40. Chare, Williams, *Matters*, p. 134.

41. Kulka, "Die Kamera," *Die Tat*, Feb. 2, 1963, p. 10; Didi-Huberman, *Images*, pp. 110–111; Struk, *Photographing*, p. 424; Chare, Williams, *Matters*, pp. 183–207.

42. Kilian, "Ein leiser," *Mitteilungen der Lagergemeinschaft Auschwitz*, Dec. 2014/34, pp. 32–33. Some survivors-turned-witnesses faced open hostility. Henryk Tauber, a Polish Jew who had testified to the Soviet authorities about the crematoria of Auschwitz where he had been forced to work, narrowly survived being murdered by his German landlord while living for a time in Munich. Two other Polish Jewish Sonderkommando survivors had to fend off attackers from their newly opened jewelery shop in Frankfurt (Kilian, "Ein leiser," *Mitteilungen der Lagergemeinschaft Auschwitz*, 2014/34, pp. 26–39). Arnošt Basch, Letter to Hermann Langbein, Jan. 31, 1964. ÖStA, Nachlass Hermann Langbein, E/1797: 40, cited in: Stengel, *Die Überlebenden*, p. 286.

43. Stengel, *Hermann Langbein*, p. 492; Hermann Langbein, Letter to Henry Ormond, May 4, 1962. ÖStA, Nachlass Hermann Langbein, E/1797: 106, no pages; Müller, *Eyewitness*, pp. 111–112; Davies, "Translation," *A Journal of Culture and History*, 2021/27 (1), pp. 3–4; Filip Müller, Testimony, Oct. 5, 1964. FBInst, Tonbandmitschnitte des Auschwitz-Prozesses (1963–1965), online source.

44. Müller, *Eyewitness*, pp. 113–114.

45. Müller, *Eyewitness*, p. 114.

46. Sylvia Düx-Heiseler, Interview by Jack Fairweather and Florine Miez, Oct. 2, 2020. Müller had previously supplied a statement published in Kraus and Kulka's *The Death Factory* in 1946. He also testified at the Kraków Auschwitz trial in 1947 (Kilian, "Ein leiser," *Mitteilungen der Lagergemeinschaft Auschwitz*, 2014/34, pp. 26–39). In consultation with Langbein, Ormond also invited Sonderkommando members Dov Paisikovic and Milton Buki to testify (Stengel, "Mediators," in: Bourhis Le, Tcherneva, Voisin [eds.], *Seeking*, p. 345). Hermann Langbein, Letter to Henry Ormond, Apr. 30, 1963. ÖStA, Nachlass Hermann Langbein, E/1797: 106, no pages.

47. Gerhard Wiese, Interview by Jack Fairweather and Florine Miez, Oct. 2, 2020; Wittmann, *Beyond*, pp. 95–142; Renz, "Auschwitz," 2013, FBInst, Tonbandmitschnitte des Auschwitz-Prozesses (1963–1965), online source; Pendas, *The Frankfurt*, pp. 105–119.

48. Steinke, *Fritz Bauer*, pp. 148–150; Joachim Kügler, Interview by Werner Renz, May 5, 1998. FBInst, part 1, 2; Pendas, *The Frankfurt*, pp. 105–119; Gerhard

Wiese, Interview by Jack Fairweather and Florine Miez, Oct. 2, 2020; Hanns Grossmann, Note, May 3, 1961. HHStAW, 461 37638/247, vol. 5, p. 865; Pendas, *The Frankfurt*, p. 143; Pendas, *The Frankfurt*, pp. 145–147; Joachim Kügler, Interview by Werner Renz, May 5, 1998. FBInst, part 3; Bauer, "Unbewältigte," Mar. 25, 1961, in: Foljanty, Johst (eds.), *Fritz Bauer*, vol. 1, p. 703; Hanns Grossmann, Indictment, Apr. 16, 1963. HHStAW, 461, 37638/79–37638/81, vols. 80–82, pp. 14,605–15,304.

49. Joachim Kügler, Interview by Werner Renz, May 5, 1998. FBInst, part 2; Renz, "Auschwitz . . . des Tonbandschnittes," *Jahrbuch der Juristischen Zeitgeschichte*, 2010/19 (1), p. 178; Bauer, "Nach den Wurzeln," in: Foljanty, Johst (eds.), *Fritz Bauer*, vol. 2, p. 1167; Steinke, *Fritz Bauer*, pp. 148–150; Joachim Kügler, Interview by Werner Renz, May 5, 1998. FBInst, part 2.

21
RECKONING

1. Hechelhammer, *Spion*, pp. 193–194, 127, 168, 178–180, 185–186, 215; Müller, *Reinhard Gehlen*, p. 1023.
2. Hechelhammer, *Spion*, pp. 209–210; Felfe, *Im Dienst*, pp. 371–375. Special thanks to Harriet Phillips for researching Felfe material.
3. Hechelhammer, *Spion*, pp. 211–213; Felfe, *Im Dienst*, pp. 155, 331–332.
4. Müller, *Reinhard Gehlen*, pp. 1020–1021.
5. Müller, *Reinhard Gehlen*, pp. 1027, 1167–1168, 1141, 1109–1110, 1023, 1025, 1204. He also fobbed off Adenauer's adviser Reinhold Mercker, whom the chancellor sent to Pullach to investigate Gehlen's leadership. Mercker recommended that the chancellery set up a special office to oversee the organization (Müller, *Reinhard Gehlen*, p. 1028).
6. Kalb, *Coming*, pp. 164–167, 173; Thomas, *Protest*, pp. 40–41.
7. Doerry, Janssen (eds.), *Die Spiegel-Affäre*, pp. 1032–1035; Müller, *Reinhard Gehlen*, pp. 1032–1035; Thomas, *Protest*, pp. 42–43; Trentmann, *Out of*, pp. 397–398; Ahlers, "Der Hintergrund," *Der Spiegel*, May 25, 1965, online source.
8. Müller, *Reinhard Gehlen*, pp. 1032–1042, 1049; Bönisch, Latsch, Wiegrefe, "Unrühmliche," *Der Spiegel*, Sept. 16, 2012, online source; Bästlein, *Der Fall*, pp. 81–92.
9. Dorothee Gehlen-Koss, Interview by Jack Fairweather, Sept. 18, 2021.
10. Ibid.; Kalb, *Coming*, p. 174; Müller, *Reinhard Gehlen*, pp. 1150–1151.
11. Hechelhammer, *Spion*, pp. 215–217, 225–227; Felfe, *Im Dienst*, pp. 382–383; "Umarmt und geküsst," *Der Spiegel*, July 23, 1963, online source; Höhne, Zolling, *The General*, p. 292; Hechelhammer, *Spion*, p. 226; "Globke," *Welt am Sonntag*, July 14, 1963, p. 1; Bästlein, *Der Fall*, pp. 126–132; Schwarz, *Juden*, pp. 26–248; Bästlein, *Der Fall*, pp. 133–153; "Der Fall Globke," Buxus Stiftung, Fritz-Bauer-Archiv, no date, online source.
12. Hechelhammer, *Spion*, pp. 227–228; Müller, *Reinhard Gehlen*, pp. 1055–1057; Dönhoff, "Gehlens," *Die Zeit*, July 26, 1963, online source; Hechelhammer, *Spion*, pp. 230–231; Sälter, *NS-Kontinuitäten*, pp. 305–307.
13. Sälter, *NS-Kontinuitäten*, p. 305; Müller, *Reinhard Gehlen*, pp. 1052–1053.
14. Sälter, *NS-Kontinuitäten*, pp. 308–309, 313–314.
15. Biermann, *Konrad Adenauer*, p. 552.
16. Biermann, *Konrad Adenauer*, pp. 552–553.

17. Sälter, *NS-Kontinuitäten,* pp. 315–319, 16–17; Hechelhammer, *Spion,* pp. 231–232.

18. Hans-Henning Crome, Interview by Kerstin von Lingen, Dec. 3, 2010. USHMM, online source; Henke, *Geheime . . . Die politische Inlandsspionage des BND,* pp. 198–199; Sälter, *NS-Kontinuitäten,* pp. 314–319.

19. Sälter, *NS-Kontinuitäten,* pp. 629–632. For a summary of Jehoschua Rosenfeld's testimony against Schweizer see: Author unknown, Note, no date. HHStAW, 461, 32438/279, pp. 8886–8889.

22

TRIAL

1. Renz, "Auschwitz," FBInst, Tonbandmitschnitte des Auschwitz-Prozesses (1963–1965), Sept. 2013, online source; Hanns Grossmann, Closing argument, May 7, 1965. FBInst, Tonbandmitschnitte des Auschwitz-Prozesses (1963–1965), online source; Bedford, *As It Was,* p. 218; Pendas, *The Frankfurt,* p. 122; "Wettervorhersage," *Frankfurter Rundschau,* Dec. 20, 1963, p. 1; "Verhandlung," *Frankfurter Allgemeine Zeitung,* Dec. 21, 1963, p. 39.

2. "Letzter Kommandant," *Frankfurter Rundschau,* June 19, 1963, p. 2; "Verhandlung," *Frankfurter Allgemeine Zeitung,* Dec. 21, 1963, p. 39; Wittmann, *Beyond,* pp. 126–127; Kügler, "Es hat," in: Wojak, Meinl (eds.), *Im Labyrinth,* p. 300; Gerhard Wiese, Interview by Jack Fairweather and Florine Miez, Oct. 2, 2020; 3. Strafkammer des LG Frankfurt am Main, Eröffnungsbeschluss, Oct. 7, 1963. HHStAW, 461, 37638/89, vol. 88, p. 17074, cited in: Pendas, *The Frankfurt,* pp. 119–120.

3. Renz, "Auschwitz," FBInst, Tonbandmitschnitte des Auschwitz-Prozesses (1963–1965), Sept. 2013, online source; Stengel, *Die Überlebenden,* pp. 177–179. "Frankly speaking, I would rather prefer a former Nazi as the presiding judge to a Jew," stated a Jewish Claims Council official (Ernst Katzenstein [Jewish Claims Conference], Letter to Saul Kagan, Oct. 14, 1963. AJA, Best. WJC, box C, 180, file 5, cited in: Stengel, *Die Überlebenden,* p. 178). Joachim Kügler, Interview by Werner Renz, May 5, 1998. FBInst, part 2, part 3. For Bauer's views on judges with incriminated pasts, presumably including those he had investigated, see: Bauer, "Selbstreinigung," July 13, 1962, in: Foljanty, Johst (eds.), *Fritz Bauer,* vol. 2, pp. 900–903. For Bauer's investigation of Hofmeyer see: Eichmüller, "Die Verfolgung" [Database at Institut für Zeitgeschichte München]; Matias Ristic, Interview by Jack Fairweather. Special thanks to Matias Ristic for discussing his research. Wolf, *The Undivided,* p. 105. Hofmeyer had also served on a hereditary health court, where he routinely ordered the sterilization of men, women, and children (Haneke, "Der Richter," *Frankfurter Allgemeine Zeitung,* Mar. 31, 2019, p. 5; Ristic, "Hans Hofmeyer," *Kritische Justiz,* 2020/53, pp. 98–113).

4. Gerhard Wiese, Interview by Ronen Steinke, cited in: Steinke, *Fritz Bauer,* p. 150; Stengel, "Mediators," in: Bourhis Le, Tcherneva, Voisin (eds.), *Seeking,* p. 345; Wittmann, *Beyond,* pp. 64–67. The role of civil counsel was a quirk of the system intended to provide victims with an active voice during proceedings (Pendas, *The Frankfurt,* pp. 204–205).

5. Bedford, *As It Was,* p. 218; Pendas, *The Frankfurt,* p. 122; "Wettervorhersage," *Frankfurter Rundschau,* Dec. 20, 1963, p. 1; Lilienthal, "Hermann Krumey," no

date. Gedenkportal Korbach, p. 31; Dittmann, "Fritz Bauer," *Forschungsjournale Soziale Bewegungen,* 2015/4 (28), pp. 210–212; Heinz Meyer-Velde, Letter to Fritz Bauer, Oct. 18, 1963. FBInst, Nachlass Heinz Meyer-Velde 24, no pages; Bauer, Letter to Thomas Harlan, autumn 1963, in: Renz (ed.), *"Von Gott,"* p. 53; "Hakenkreuz-Plakate," *Frankfurter Rundschau,* June 1963, cited in: Wojak, *Fritz Bauer,* p. 440; "Nazi Antisemitic," *Jewish Telegraphic Agency,* July 31, 1963, online source; Wojak, *Fritz Bauer,* p. 457.

6. Barbara Necek (dir.), *Le procès,* 2019; Krüger, *Broken,* pp. 145, 157; Hess, *W nie-mieckim,* pp. 87–88; "Verhandlung," *Frankfurter Allgemeine Zeitung,* Dec. 21, 1963, p. 39; Krüger, *Broken,* pp. 155–157; Renz, "Auschwitz," FBInst, Tonband-mitschnitte des Auschwitz-Prozesses (1963–1965), Sept. 2013, online source; Krüger, *Broken,* pp. 156–157.

7. "The Crime," *The Daily Mirror,* Mar. 23, 1964, p. 9; "Verhandlung," *Frankfurter Allgemeine Zeitung,* Dec. 21, 1963, p. 39; Hoyer, "Ich wusste," *Frankfurter Rund-schau,* Dec. 21, 1963, p. 6; Bedford, *As It Was,* p. 218; Pendas, *The Frankfurt,* pp. 123–126; Hoyer, "Ich wusste," *Frankfurter Rundschau,* Dec. 21, 1963, p. 6.

8. The six jurors were housewives Else Häbich, Erna Grob, and Gertrud Flach; warehouse worker Gustav Baum; technical employee Wilhelm Hartung; and la-borer Adolf Holzhäuser. The five substitute jurors were housewives Elise Knodel and Anna Mayer; coal merchant Ernst Kadenbach; clerk Emma Kotzur; and bai-liff Ferdinand Link (1. Verhandlungstag, Dec. 20, 1963. FBInst, Der Auschwitz-Prozess, DVD, p. 4720). Hoyer, "Ich wusste," *Frankfurter Rundschau,* Dec. 21, 1963, p. 6; "Verhandlung," *Frankfurter Allgemeine Zeitung,* Dec. 21, 1963, p. 39; Bedford, *As It Was,* p. 219.

9. Hoyer, "Ich wusste," *Frankfurter Rundschau,* Dec. 21, 1963, p. 6; Pendas, *The Frankfurt,* pp. 93–95; "Verhandlung," *Frankfurter Allgemeine Zeitung,* Dec. 21, 1963, p. 39; Pendas, *The Frankfurt,* pp. 125–130.

10. Pendas, *The Frankfurt,* pp. 123–124, 130–131; Protokoll der Hauptverhandlung, Dec. 20, 1963. FBInst, Der Auschwitz-Prozess, DVD, pp. 4717–4744; "Let-ter," *Frankfurter Rundschau,* Dec. 21, 1963, cited in: Wittmann, *Beyond,* p. 184.

11. Langbein, *Auschwitz,* p. 671; Pendas, *The Frankfurt,* pp. 130, 134; Hoyer, "Ich wusste," *Frankfurter Rundschau,* Dec. 21, 1963, p. 6; Naumann, *Auschwitz,* p. 27; "Nichts," *Stuttgarter Zeitung,* Jan. 10, 1964, cited in: Pendas, *The Frankfurt,* pp. 134–135; Mevissen, "Der Adjutant," *Abendpost,* Jan. 10, 1964, cited in: Pen-das, *The Frankfurt,* p. 135.

12. Naumann, *Auschwitz,* p. 31.

13. Ibid.

14. Ibid.

15. Ibid.

16. Naumann, *Auschwitz,* pp. 31–32.

17. Naumann, *Auschwitz,* p. 36.

18. Ibid.

19. Ibid.

20. Broad, "Reminiscences," in: Bezwińska, Czech (eds.), *KL Auschwitz,* pp. 139–198; Naumann, *Auschwitz,* p. 39; Pendas, *The Frankfurt,* p. 134; Naumann, *Auschwitz,* p. 54.

21. "Genickschüsse," *Abendpost,* Jan. 1, 1964, no pages; Naumann, *Auschwitz,* p. 41.

22. Naumann, *Auschwitz*, p. 51; Pendas, *The Frankfurt*, p. 134; Naumann, *Auschwitz*, p. 62.

23. Naumann, *Auschwitz*, pp. 63, 48.

24. For an analysis of the defendants' strategy to elicit sympathy from the press see: Pendas, *The Frankfurt*, p. 133; Verg, "Wie konnte," *Hamburger Abendblatt*, Dec. 2, 1963, cited in: Pendas, *The Frankfurt*, p. 133; Bockelmann, "Straflosigkeit," *Frankfurter Allgemeine Zeitung*, Jan. 23, 1964, cited in: Bauer, "Nach den Wurzeln," Feb. 5, 1964, in: Foljanty, Johst (eds.), *Fritz Bauer*, p. 1162. Bockelmann's comments were part of a wider argument with Bauer over his ideas for criminal justice reform.

25. Bauer, "Nach den Wurzeln," Feb. 5, 1964, in: Foljanty, Johst (eds.), *Fritz Bauer*, pp. 1160–1167; Henry Ormond, Diary, Feb. 18, 1964, no pages. Material in possession of Walter Witte. The survivor on the stage with Bauer was Berthold Simonsohn.

26. For the role of historians and IfZ see: Renz, "Auschwitz . . . Tonbandschnittes," *Jahrbuch der Juristischen Zeitgeschichte*, 2010/19 (1), p. 178; Pendas, *The Frankfurt*, pp. 142–147; Wojak, *Fritz Bauer*, p. 383; "Starb," *Abendpost*, Feb. 14, 1964. HHStAW 505, 5824, p. 129. Bedford, "The Auschwitz," *The Observer*, Jan. 26, 1964, p. 12.

27. No title, *Die Tat*, May 2, 1964, cited in: Lilienthal, "Hermann Krumey," no date. Gedenkportal Korbach, p. 31; Wojak, *Fritz Bauer*, pp. 373–376; Klee, *Was sie*, pp. 42–50; Grunenberg, "Der merkwürdige," *Die Zeit*, Feb. 21, 1964, no pages; Werner Heyde, Letter to Fritz Bauer, no date. Jumi S-H VIII411 E 167/59, vol. 8, cited in: Godau-Schüttke, *Die Heyde-Sawade Affäre*, pp. 235–237; "Handvoll," *Der Spiegel*, Feb. 18, 1964, online source. The trial against the remaining euthanasia doctor, Hans Hefelmann, did begin on February 18 as planned but was almost immediately delayed because the defendant claimed he was unfit to stand trial (Wojak, *Fritz Bauer*, p. 381).

28. Joachim Kügler, Note, Feb. 14, 1964. HHStAW, 461, 37638/258, vol. 18, pp. 3746–3748; Henry Ormond, Closing argument, May 24, 1965. FBInst, Der Auschwitz-Prozess, DVD; Renz, "Auschwitz," FBInst, Tonbandmitschnitte des Auschwitz-Prozesses (1963–1965), Sept. 2013, online source; Lauer-Seidelmann, *Kamerun*, p. 164; Schlesak, *The Druggist*, p. 187.

29. Zwerenz, Zwerenz, "Mutterseelenallein," *Forschungsjournal Soziale Bewegungen*, 2015/4 (28), p. 298.

30. Naumann, *Auschwitz*, p. 84; Otto Wolken, Testimony, Feb. 24, 1964. FBInst, Tonbandmitschnitte des Auschwitz-Prozesses (1963–1965), online source.

31. Naumann, *Auschwitz*, pp. 84–88; Bedford, *As It Was*, pp. 233–234; Otto Wolken, Testimony, Feb. 24, 1964. FBInst, Tonbandmitschnitte des Auschwitz-Prozesses (1963–1965), online source.

32. Otto Wolken, Testimony, Feb. 24, 1964. FBInst, Tonbandmitschnitte des Auschwitz-Prozesses (1963–1965), online source; Naumann, *Auschwitz*, p. 85.

33. Otto Wolken, Testimony, Feb. 24, 1964. FBInst, Tonbandmitschnitte des Auschwitz-Prozesses (1963–1965), online source.

34. Naumann, *Auschwitz*, p. 88; Bedford, *As It Was*, p. 234; Krüger, *Broken*, pp. 149–151.

35. Naumann, *Auschwitz*, p. 88; Bedford, *As It Was*, p. 234.

36. Naumann, *Auschwitz*, p. 88; Bedford, *As It Was*, p. 234.

37. Krüger, *Broken,* pp. 150, 153–154, 163.
38. Krüger, *Broken,* pp. 154–155.
39. "SS-mańskie," Journal unknown, Feb. 25, 1964, no pages; "Dr Wolken," Journal unknown, Feb. 27, 1964, no pages.
40. Naumann, *Auschwitz,* p. 90.
41. Ibid.
42. Naumann, *Auschwitz,* pp. 90–91.
43. Stengel, *Die Überlebenden,* p. 153; Hans Münch, Testimony, Mar. 2 and Mar. 5, 1964. FBInst, Tonbandmitschnitte des Auschwitz-Prozesses (1963–1965), online source; "Die Erinnerung," *Der Spiegel,* Sept. 27, 1998, online source.
44. Konrad Morgen, Testimony, Mar. 9, 1964. FBInst, Tonbandmitschnitte des Auschwitz-Prozesses (1963–1965), online source; Wachsmann, *KL,* pp. 380–391.
45. For an analysis of Morgen's testimony and its consequences for the trial see: Wittmann, *Beyond,* pp. 160–174. Konrad Morgen, Testimony, Mar. 9, 1964. FBInst, Tonbandmitschnitte des Auschwitz-Prozesses (1963–1965), online source.
46. Konrad Morgen, Testimony, Mar. 9, 1964. FBInst, Tonbandmitschnitte des Auschwitz-Prozesses (1963–1965), online source.
47. Konrad Morgen, Testimony, Mar. 9, 1964. FBInst, Tonbandmitschnitte des Auschwitz-Prozesses (1963–1965), online source.
48. Hans Münch, Testimony, Mar. 2 and Mar. 5, 1964. FBInst, Tonbandmitschnitte des Auschwitz-Prozesses (1963–1965), online source; Joachim Caesar, Testimony, Mar. 5, 1964. FBInst, Tonbandmitschnitte des Auschwitz-Prozesses (1963–1965), online source; Konrad Morgen, Testimony, Mar. 9, 1964. FBInst, Tonbandmitschnitte des Auschwitz-Prozesses (1963–1965), online source; Helmut Bartsch, Testimony, Mar. 13, 1964. FBInst, Tonbandmitschnitte des Auschwitz-Prozesses (1963–1965), online source.
49. Joachim Kügler, Interview by Werner Renz, May 5, 1998. FBInst, part 1, part 2; Wolfgang Kaven, Interview by Ronen Steinke, cited in: Steinke, *Fritz Bauer,* p. 190. For Bauer's illness and incapacitation see: Fritz Bauer, Letter to Thomas Harlan, spring 1964, cited in: Renz (ed.), *"Von Gott,"* p. 67. Bauer, Telegram to Thomas Harlan, Mar. 13, 1964, cited in: Renz (ed.), *"Von Gott,"* p. 64.
50. Fritz Bauer, Letter to Thomas Harlan, Mar. 1964, cited in: Renz (ed.), *"Von Gott,"* p. 64.
51. "I need someone to 'cry' to about the bleakness" (Fritz Bauer, Letter to Thomas Harlan, Mar. 1964, in: Renz [ed.], *"Von Gott,"* p. 65).
52. Langbein, *Auschwitz,* p. 25; Stengel, *Die Überlebenden,* pp. 239–240; Kret, *Ostatni,* p. 168; Heska-Kwaśniewicz, Sadzikowska (eds.), *Głosy,* p. 155; Mauz, *Die Gerechten,* p. 273; Wittmann, *Beyond,* pp. 147, 189, 207–208; Pendas, *The Frankfurt,* pp. 164, 189; Stengel, *Die Überlebenden,* pp. 186, 245, 265–266; Kieta, "Proces," *Przekrój,* 1964/20 (997), p. 4; Stengel, *Die Überlebenden,* pp. 47–48, 54.
53. Naumann, *Auschwitz,* pp. 131–134; Dounia Wasserstrom, Testimony, Mitschrift des Beisitzenden Richters Perseke, Apr. 23 and 24, 1964. FBInst, Der Auschwitz-Prozess, DVD, pp. 6492–6493. On Wasserstrom's biography, her contact with Hermann Langbein, her testimony in court, and the defense trying to discredit her in their closing statement see: Stengel, *Die Überlebenden,* pp. 321–326.
54. Wittmann, *Beyond,* p. 88; Stengel, *Die Überlebenden,* p. 324; Dounia Wasserstrom, Testimony. Mitschrift des Beisitzenden Richters Perseke, Apr. 23–24, 1964. FBInst, Der Auschwitz-Prozess, DVD, p. 6493.

55. Dounia Wasserstrom, Testimony, Mitschrift des Beisitzenden Richters Perseke, Apr. 23–24, 1964. FBInst, Der Auschwitz-Prozess, DVD, p. 6493.

56. Pendas, *The Frankfurt*, p. 26; Dounia Wasserstrom, Testimony. Mitschrift des Beisitzenden Richters Perseke, Apr. 23–24, 1964. FBInst, Der Auschwitz-Prozess, DVD, p. 6493; Naumann, *Auschwitz*, p. 138.

57. Naumann, *Auschwitz*, p. 138.

58. Naumann, *Auschwitz*, p. 138.

59. Naumann, *Auschwitz*, pp. xii, xxviii, 127, 186, 190, 251. For Wörl's involvement as witness in Nazi trials see: Stengel, *Die Überlebenden*, pp. 133–134. KriPo München, Letter to Stuttgarter Staatsanwaltschaft, Sept. 19, 1958. HHStAW, 461, 37638/1, vol. 1, p. 84. Ludwig Wörl, Testimony, Mitschrift des Beisitzenden Richters Perseke, Apr. 6, 1964. FBInst, Der Auschwitz-Prozess, DVD, pp. 6338–6368; Naumann, *Auschwitz*, pp. 114–116; Hachmann, "Schwerer," *Frankfurter Rundschau*, Apr. 7, 1964, no pages, cited in: Pendas, *The Frankfurt*, p. 163.

60. Hachmann, "Schwerer," *Frankfurter Rundschau*, Apr. 7, 1964, no pages, cited in: Pendas, *The Frankfurt*, p. 163.

61. Ibid.; "Tumult," *Abendpost*, Apr. 7, 1964, no pages, cited in: Pendas, *The Frankfurt*, p. 163. For an analysis of this interjection and how it was reported on see: Pendas, *The Frankfurt*, p. 260.

62. Peter Kalb, Interview by Florine Miez, Sept. 20, 2020. Józef Kret spent eight days in the waiting room before he was finally summoned to testify (Kret, *Ostatni*, pp. 161–162). Stengel, *Die Überlebenden*, pp. 145–146; Langbein, *Auschwitz*, pp. 32–33; Imre Gönczi, Interview by Dagi Knellessen, Sept. 24, 2005, online source; Seweryn, *Usługiwałem*, pp. 276–277; Barbara Necek (dir.), *Le procès*, 2019; Daniel Bergmann, Interview by Harriet Phillips, Aug. 30, 2021. One Polish witness, Józef Mikusz, even bought himself a switchblade at the train station just in case he was attacked (Mikusz Family [Danuta Mikusz-Oslislo, Jan Mikusz, Tadeusz Mikusz], Interview by Katarzyna Chiżyńska, July 15, 2021; Stengel, *Die Überlebenden*, p. 434). Another Polish witness, Stanisław Kamiński, was attacked in the elevator by the widow of Commandant Höss, who had been asked to testify (Peter Kalb, Interview by Florine Miez, Sept. 20, 2020). Stengel, *Die Überlebenden*, p. 435.

63. Langbein, Testimony, Mar. 6, 1964. FBInst, Tonbandmitschnitte des Auschwitz-Prozesses (1963–1965), online source; Stengel, *Hermann Langbein*, pp. 507–508, 525–527; Stengel, *Die Überlebenden*, pp. 146–146, 437; Stengel, *Hermann Langbein*, pp. 517–518; Naumann, *Auschwitz*, pp. 118–119.

64. For Bauer's views on the strain suffered by the witnesses see: Bauer, "Unbewältigte," Mar. 25, 1961, in: Foljanty, Johst (eds.), *Fritz Bauer*, vol. 1, p. 703. Bauer claimed he had been surprised by the level of witness harassment at the trial (Bauer, "Heute," in: Foljanty, Johst [eds.], *Fritz Bauer*, vol. 2, pp. 1234–1235). Wittmann, *Beyond*, pp. 143, 169; Pendas, *The Frankfurt*, pp. 250–251; Wittmann, *Beyond*, pp. 176–179. Walser, *My Auschwitz*, cited in: Wittmann, *Beyond*, pp. 177–178; Mauz, *Die Gerechten*, pp. 266–267.

65. "Ein Prozess," *Darmstädter Echo*, Apr. 30, 1964, cited in: Stengel, *Hermann Langbein*, p. 522; Langbein, "Die Phantasie," *Frankfurter Rundschau*, May 30, 1964, cited in: Wittmann, *Beyond*, pp. 187–188.

66. Henry Ormond, Antrag auf Augenscheinseinnahme, June 8, 1964. Tonbandmitschnitte des Auschwitz-Prozesses (1963–1965), online source; Henry Ormond,

Antrag auf Augenscheinseinnahme, June 22, 1964. Tonbandmitschnitte des Auschwitz-Prozesses (1963–1965), online source; Pendas, *The Frankfurt,* pp. 168–179.

67. Henry Ormond, Antrag auf Augenscheinseinnahme, June 8, 1964. Tonband-mitschnitte des Auschwitz-Prozesses (1963–1965), online source; Henry Ormond, Antrag auf Augenscheinseinnahme, June 22, 1964. Tonbandmitschnitte des Auschwitz-Prozesses (1963–1965), online source; Pendas, *The Frankfurt,* pp. 168–179.

68. Wittmann, *Beyond,* pp. 64–67; Bauer, "Unbewältigte," Mar. 25, 1961, in: Foljanty, Johst (eds.), *Fritz Bauer,* vol. 1, pp. 699–705; *Fritz Bauer,* Letter to Thomas Harlan, Mar. 28, 1964, in: Renz (ed.), *"Von Gott,"* p. 68; Fritz Bauer, Letter to Thomas Harlan, Apr. 9, 1964, in: Renz (ed.), *"Von Gott,"* p. 69.

69. Fritz Bauer, Letter to Thomas Harlan, Mar. 28, 1964, in: Renz (ed.), *"Von Gott,"* p. 68.

70. Fritz Bauer, Postcard to Heinz Meyer-Velde, no date. FBInst, Nachlass Heinz Meyer-Velde 12, no date; Fritz Bauer, Letter to Thomas Harlan, Apr. 1964, in: Renz (ed.), *"Von Gott,"* p. 69.

71. Fritz Bauer, Letter to Thomas Harlan, Apr. 1964, in: Renz (ed.), *"Von Gott,"* p. 69.

72. Harlan, *Hitler,* p. 161.

73. Harlan, *Hitler,* p. 161; Harlan, "Fritz Bauer," *Forschungsjournal Soziale Bewegungen,* 2015/4 (28), p. 284.

74. Ibid.

75. Harlan, *Hitler,* p. 161; Harlan, "Fritz Bauer," *Forschungsjournal Soziale Bewegungen,* 2015/4 (28), p. 284.

76. Harlan, "Fritz Bauer," *Forschungsjournal Soziale Bewegungen,* 2015/4 (28), pp. 284–285.

77. Thomas Harlan, Letter to Krystyna Żywulska, May 14, 1964, cited in: Renz, "Wider die Sittenwächter," in: Borowski et al. (eds.), *Jahrbuch,* p. 90.

78. Thomas Harlan, Letter to Krystyna Żywulska, May 14, 1964, cited in: Renz, "Wider die Sittenwächter," in: Borowski et al. (eds.), *Jahrbuch,* p. 90.

79. Thomas Harlan, Letter to Krystyna Żywulska, May 15, 1964, cited in: Renz, "Wider die Sittenwächter," in: Borowski et al. (eds.), *Jahrbuch,* p. 91; Bauer, Letter to Thomas Harlan, May 1964, in: Renz (ed.), *"Von Gott,"* p. 75.

23
FUGUE

1. Bauer, Letter to Thomas Harlan, May 1964, in: Renz (ed.), *"Von Gott,"* p. 75; Wittmann, *Beyond,* pp. 176–179; Brink, *Auschwitz,* pp. 18–19; Steinke, *Fritz Bauer,* p. 136.

2. Six defendants who had served on the ramp remained at liberty in May 1964: Stark, Höcker, Frank, Lucas, Broad, and Dylewski (Renz, "Auschwitz . . . des Tonbandschnittes," *Jahrbuch der Juristischen Zeitgeschichte,* 2010/19 [1], p. 181). Naumann, *Auschwitz,* pp. 14–15; Müller, *Eyewitness,* p. 11; Smoleń, "Kariera," *Zeszyty oświęcimskie* 5, 1961, pp. 103–108; Naumann, *Auschwitz,* p. 15; Langbein, *People,* p. 397. Stark's father took his own life in 1948, due to the guilt—or so Stark claimed—that he had allowed Stark to join the SS (Naumann, *Auschwitz,* p. 14). Margarete Stark, Eidesstattliche Erklärung, Darmstadt, June 11, 1959.

HHStAW, 461, 37638/11, vol. 10, p. 1603. For brief biography of Stark see: Georg Friedrich Vogel, Closing argument May 7, 1965. Der Auschwitz-Prozess, DVD, pp. 32,945–32,948. Bauer understood the challenging nature of Stark's case. He himself had argued repeatedly for leniency to be shown to young offenders but with the caveat that they start by recognizing their crimes. Stark had shown some recognition of guilt. Following his arrest, he asked why they hadn't come for him sooner, before he had a wife and kids. But he'd become more cautious over the course of his pretrial questioning and ended up admitting to only one execution in the penal block and introducing Zyklon B into a gas chamber (Bauer, "Gedanken," July/Aug. 1959, in: Foljanty, Johst [eds.], Fritz Bauer, vol. 2, pp. 565–567; Langbein, People, pp. 498, 509; Stark, Interrogation, Sept. 3, 1962, Der Auschwitz-Prozess, DVD, pp. 4583–4592).

3. Józef Kral, Testimony, May 15, 1964. FBInst, Tonbandmitschnitte des Auschwitz-Prozesses (1963–1965), online source; Stengel, Die Überlebenden, pp. 262–264; Hans Stark, Aufnahmemitteilung, May 15, 1964. HHStAW, 461, 37638/92, vol. 91, p. 17,898.

4. Langbein, Auschwitz, p. 351; Stengel, Die Überlebenden, p. 264; Seweryn, Usługiwałem, p. 274; Naumann, Auschwitz, pp. 147–148; Stengel, Die Überlebenden, pp. 261–267. The Ukrainian witnesses accused Kral of not intervening to stop other kapos killing prisoners; Omelan Kowal, Testimony, May 21, 1964. FBInst, Tonbandmitschnitte des Auschwitz-Prozesses (1963–1965), online source; Boris Witoszyńsky, Testimony, May 21, 1964. FBInst, Tonbandmitschnitte des Auschwitz-Prozesses (1963–1965), online source.

5. Seweryn, Usługiwałem, pp. 275–277. On one occasion, a witness was run over when a car mounted the sidewalk, leading Seweryn to suspect a deliberate attack (Seweryn, Usługiwałem, p. 277).

6. Steinke, Fritz Bauer, p. 149.

7. Langbein, Auschwitz, p. 33; Wisely, "From Humiliation," S: I. M. O. N., 2021/8, p. 22; Peter Kalb, Interview by Katharina Stengel, Nov. 26, 2009, cited in: Stengel, Hermann Langbein, p. 514; Peter Kalb, Interview by Florine Miez, Sept. 20, 2020; Peter Kalb, Interview by Florine Miez, Oct. 15, 2020; Peter Kalb, Interview by Harriet Phillips, Dec. 8, 2023; Renz, "Auschwitz," 2013. FBInst, Tonbandmitschnitte des Auschwitz-Prozesses (1963–1965), online source, note 234; Gerhard Wiese, Interview by Almut Schoenfeld, May 2020. Nuns from the Sisters of Mary convent in Darmstadt-Eberstadt offered to host witnesses for recuperation after their testimony (Adam, Salomon, Was wird, p. 80).

8. Hermann Holtgreve, Testimony, July 31, 1964. FBInst, Tonbandmitschnitte des Auschwitz-Prozesses (1963–1965), online source; Otto Dov Kulka, Testimony, July 30, 1964. FBInst, Tonbandmitschnitte des Auschwitz-Prozesses (1963–1965), online source. For attacks on Otto Dov Kulka see: Stengel, "Wir sind," in: Steinbacher, Rauschenberger (eds.), Der Auschwitz-Prozess, pp. 28–29. Kulka called the police at Frankfurt Airport when he spotted, to his horror, the defendant Franz Lucas checking in for a flight. Kulka thought the former SS doctor was trying to flee the country, but once the police arrived it turned out he was simply flying home to Hamburg for the weekend (Kulka, Soudcové, p. 59). For Kügler's outrage at defendants and former SS who testified as witnesses see: Schlesak, The Druggist, pp. 127–130; Hantl: Tadeusz Paczuła, Testimony, Apr. 30, 1964. FBInst, Tonbandmitschnitte des Auschwitz-Prozesses (1963–1965), online source; Kaduk: Władysław Fejkiel, Testimony, May 29, 1964. FBInst,

Tonbandmitschnitte des Auschwitz-Prozesses (1963–1965), online source; Ontl: Friedrich Ontl, Testimony, June 4, 1964. FBInst, Tonbandmitschnitte des Auschwitz-Prozesses (1963–1965), online source; Kaduk: Heinrich Dürmayer, Testimony, June 22, 1964. FBInst, Tonbandmitschnitte des Auschwitz-Prozesses (1963–1965), online source; Schatz: Friedrich Hirsch, Testimony, Aug. 7, 1964. FBInst, Tonbandmitschnitte des Auschwitz-Prozesses (1963–1965), online source; Siebald: Anton Siebald, Testimony, Sept. 17, 1964. FBInst, Tonbandmitschnitte des Auschwitz-Prozesses (1963–1965), online source; Broch: Karl Broch, Testimony, Nov. 11, 1964. FBInst, Tonbandmitschnitte des Auschwitz-Prozesses (1963–1965), online source; Hofer: Josef Hofer, Testimony, Dec. 4, 1964. FBInst, Tonbandmitschnitte des Auschwitz-Prozesses (1963–1965), online source; Boger: Edward Burakowski, Testimony, Apr. 26, 1965. FBInst, Tonbandmitschnitte des Auschwitz-Prozesses (1963–1965), online source; Franz Ruprecht, Testimony, July 23, 1964. FBInst, Tonbandmitschnitte des Auschwitz-Prozesses (1963–1965), online source; and Carl Krauch, Testimony, Feb. 19, 1965. FBInst, Tonbandmitschnitte des Auschwitz-Prozesses (1963–1965), online source. Multiple sources (e.g., Joachim Kügler, Interview by Werner Renz, May 5, 1998. FBInst, part 1) refer to Kügler calling Mulka a member of a uniformed murder squad, however, none cites a date or court transcript. During the testimony of witness Hans Spicker on September 24, 1964, Kügler points out he accused Mulka of being a member of a uniformed murder squad on July 24, 1964, and it wasn't until August 3 that Mulka referred to this incident to justify his decision to no longer answer questions from the prosecution. Kügler intimates that this is because Richard Böck, a former SS man who was testifying on August 3, made statements that incriminated Mulka (Richard Böck, Testimony, Aug. 3, 1964. FBInst, Tonbandmitschnitte des Auschwitz-Prozesses [1963–1965], online source). Special thanks to Harriet Phillips for researching Kügler's impact on the trial. Kügler, "Es hat," in: Wojak, Meinl (eds.), *Im Labyrinth*, pp. 302–303; Joachim Kügler, Interview by Werner Renz, May 5, 1998. FBInst, part 1. Meanwhile, the Krumey trial, running in the Haus Gallus on off days from the Auschwitz proceedings, was in crisis after the lead prosecutor suffered a mental breakdown and the star witness, Joel Brand, died of a heart attack (Ziegler, "Merkwürdiges," *Die Zeit*, July 10, 1964, online source; Mauz, "Teufelskreis," *Der Spiegel*, Feb. 2, 1965, online source).

9.   The defendant Pery Broad had been obliged to admit under questioning that the gruesome account he'd given to the British in 1945 was, contrary to his initial claims, entirely accurate. The report was read out in its entirety, the first time the real views of a defendant were unmasked in court. One SS witness broke the code of silence and incriminated a former colleague. Another was arrested before he could even speak. Henry Ormond played a key role in tracking down the original version of Pery Broad's written account of his time in Auschwitz (Deutschkron, *Auschwitz*, pp. 195, 228–229, p. 231). Mauritius Berner, Testimony, Aug. 17, 1964. FBInst, Tonbandmitschnitte des Auschwitz-Prozesses (1963–1965), online source; Schlesak, *The Druggist*, p. 155; Fulbrook, *Reckonings*, p. 297; Naumann, *Auschwitz*, p. 190; Eilat Negev, Interview by Catherine Mullier, Feb. 5, 2021; Eilat Negev, Email to Jack Fairweather and Catherine Mullier, Jan. 15, 2021. Special thanks to the Berner family for their insights and to Catherine Mullier for research.

10. Mauritius Berner, Testimony, Aug. 17, 1964. FBInst, Tonbandmitschnitte des Auschwitz-Prozesses (1963–1965), online source.
11. Mauritius Berner, Testimony, Aug. 17, 1964. FBInst, Tonbandmitschnitte des Auschwitz-Prozesses (1963–1965), online source.
12. "He also said that it would have been a terrible fate, if they became Mengele's guinea pigs." (Eliat Negev, Email to Jack Fairweather and Catherine Mullier, Jan. 15, 2021). Mengele was only interested in conducting experiments on identical twins, and Helga and Nora were nonidentical.
13. Filip Müller, Testimony, Oct. 5, 1964. FBInst, Tonbandmitschnitte des Auschwitz-Prozesses (1963–1965), online source; Peter Kalb, Interview by Harriet Phillips, Dec. 8, 2023; Müller, *Eyewitness,* pp. 111–112.
14. Filip Müller, Testimony, Oct. 5, 1964. FBInst, Tonbandmitschnitte des Auschwitz-Prozesses (1963–1965), online source.
15. Filip Müller, Testimony, Oct. 5, 1964. FBInst, Tonbandmitschnitte des Auschwitz-Prozesses (1963–1965), online source.
16. Ibid.
17. Filip Müller, Testimony, Oct. 5, 1964. FBInst, Tonbandmitschnitte des Auschwitz-Prozesses (1963–1965), online source. For an analysis of the role of translation and the dynamic between Müller, his interpreter, and Judge Hofmeyer see: Davies, "Translation," *Holocaust Studies,* 2021/27 (1), pp. 118–130.
18. Ibid.
19. Filip Müller, Testimony, Oct. 5, 1964. FBInst, Tonbandmitschnitte des Auschwitz-Prozesses (1963–1965), online source; Deutschkron, *Auschwitz,* p. 291. SS guard Dylewski and camp dentist Frank were arrested on the same day that Müller testified; the Gestapo man Broad on November 6, 1964; and Mulka himself on December 3, 1964 (Langbein, Auschwitz, pp. 671–708).
20. Henry Ormond, Antrag auf Augenscheinseinnahme, June 8, 1964. Tonbandmitschnitte des Auschwitz-Prozesses (1963–1965), online source; Henry Ormond, Antrag auf Augenscheinseinnahme, June 22, 1964. Tonbandmitschnitte des Auschwitz-Prozesses (1963–1965), online source; Jan Sehn, Eugeniusz Szmulewski, Wizja lokalna w Oświęcimiu-Brzezince, Feb. 5, 1965. IPN, Bu 2586/404, p. 10; Pendas, *The Frankfurt,* pp. 169–175; Hans Hofmeyer, Letter to Marian Rybicki, Oct. 27, 1964. IPN, Kr 0/60/13, pp. 40–42; Pendas, *The Frankfurt,* pp. 176–178; Jan Sehn, Eugeniusz Szmulewski, Wizja lokalna w Oświęcimiu-Brzezince, Feb. 5, 1965. IPN, Bu 2586/404, p. 9; Henry Ormond, Antrag auf Augenscheinseinnahme, Jun. 8, 1964. Tonbandmitschnitte des Auschwitz-Prozesses (1963–1965), online source; Henry Ormond, Antrag auf Augenscheinseinnahme, Jun. 22, 1964. Tonbandmitschnitte des Auschwitz-Prozesses (1963–1965), online source; Institut für Demoskopie, *Verjährung,* cited in: Kröger, *Die Ahndung,* p. 276, cited in: Pendas, *The Auschwitz,* pp. 253, 256.

24

AUSCHWITZ

1. Walter Hotz, Report, Jan. 6, 1965. HHStAW, 461, 37638/93, vol. 92, p. 18295; Mauz, "Wo ist," *Der Spiegel,* Dec. 23, 1964, online source; Wisely, "Confession," *Holocaust Studies,* Jan. 24, 2020, online source. Lili Jacob testified that she had

seen Lucas on the ramp (Lili Zelmanovic, Testimony, Dec. 3, 1964. FBInst, Tonbandmitschnitte des Auschwitz-Prozesses [1963–1965], online source). Deutschkron, "The Auschwitz," *Maariv*, Dec. 13, 1964, no pages; Władysław Rutka, Meldunek specjalny, Dec. 21, 1964. IPN, Bu 0/1062/33, vol. 3, p. 114; Deutschkron, *Auschwitz*, pp. 292–294. Inge Deutschkron's account of the court visit was serialized in the Israeli newspaper *Maariv* and later published in the book *Auschwitz war nur ein Wort*. Some details appear in the articles but not in the book, and vice versa; I cite the more detailed version for each scene in question.

2.   Deutschkron, "The Auschwitz," *Maariv*, Dec. 13, 1964, no pages; Mauz, "Wo ist," *Der Spiegel*, Dec. 23, 1964, online source.

3.   Mauz, "Wo ist," *Der Spiegel*, Dec. 23, 1964, online source; Deutschkron, "'Let's get ready,'" *Maariv*, Dec. 14, 1964, no pages.

4.   Walter Hotz, Report, Jan. 6, 1965. HHStAW, 461, 37638/93, vol. 92, p. 18,295; Deutschkron, *Auschwitz*, p. 295. For a discussion on Polish attitudes to the Holocaust in the early 1960s see: Muchowski, "Społeczeństwo," *teksty drugie*, 2020/3, pp. 110–129.

5.   Mauz, "Wo ist," *Der Spiegel*, Dec. 23, 1964, online source; S. Wałach, Raport specjalny nr 1, Dec. 13, 1964. IPN, Kr 0/60/13, p. 80.

6.   Mauz, "Wo ist," *Der Spiegel*, Dec. 23, 1964, online source; List of field view participants and their hotel room numbers, no date. IPN, Kr 0/60/13, pp. 82–83; Komaniecka, *Pod obserwacją*, pp. 324–325.

7.   Mauz, "Wo ist," *Der Spiegel*, Dec. 23, 1964, online source; S. Wałach, Kronika wydarzeń, Dec. 13(?), 1964. IPN, Kr 0/60/13, pp. 148–149; Weiss, *My Place*, online source.

8.   Walter Hotz, Report, Jan. 6, 1965. HHStAW, 461, 37638/93, vol. 92, p. 18,296; Smoleń, "Wizjelokalne," *Muzea Walki*, 1970/III, pp. 204–205; Janusz Kidawa (dir.), *Wizja lokalna*, 1965; Gańczak, Jan Sehn, p. 193; List of questions for field view in Auschwitz-Birkenau, no date. IPN, Bu 2586/404, pp. 90–95; *Jan Sehn, Eugeniusz Szmulewski, Wizja lokalna w Oświęcimiu-Brzezince*, Feb. 5, 1965. IPN, Bu 2586/404, p. 30.

9.   Dwork, van Pelt, *Auschwitz*, p. 180; Długoborski, Piper (eds.), *Auschwitz*, vol. 1, pp. 35–36, 40, 53; Długoborski, Piper (eds.), *Auschwitz*, vol. 3, pp. 53ff; Długoborski, Piper (eds.), *Auschwitz*, vol. 3, p. 132; Długoborski, Piper (eds.), *Auschwitz*, vol. 1, p. 80. About 70,000 of 140,000–150,000 Polish prisoners died in Auschwitz, along with 47,000 non-Jewish prisoners of other nationalities (data based on information published on the Auschwitz-Birkenau State Museum website). The majority of non-Jewish prisoners were registered and housed in the main camp (Długoborski, Piper [eds.], *Auschwitz*, vol. 3, p. 230). S. Wałach, Raport specjalny nr 3, Dec. 14, 1964. IPN, Kr 0/60/13, p. 128.

10.   S. Wałach, Meldunek specjalny nr 2, Dec. 14, 1964. IPN, Bu 0/1062/33, vol. III, p. 83; Deutschkron, *Auschwitz*, p. 298.

11.   Jan Sehn, Eugeniusz Szmulewski, Wizja lokalna w Oświęcimiu-Brzezince, Feb. 5, 1965. IPN, Bu 2586/404, p. 30; S. Wałach, Meldunek specjalny nr 2, Dec. 14, 1964. IPN, Bu 0/1062/33, vol. III, p. 83; Długoborski, Piper (eds.), *Auschwitz*, vol. 3, pp. 71–72; Mauz, "Wo ist," *Der Spiegel*, Dec. 23, 1964, online source; Amos, *Journey*, pp. 5–6.

12.   Jan Sehn, Eugeniusz Szmulewski, Wizja lokalna w Oświęcimiu-Brzezince, Feb. 5, 1965. IPN, Bu 2586/404, p. 30; S. Wałach. Meldunek specjalny nr 2, Dec. 14,

1964. IPN, Bu 0/1062/33, vol. III, p. 83; Weiss, *My Place*, online source; Długoborski, Piper (eds.), *Auschwitz*, vol. 1, pp. 63–64; Setkiewicz, *Z dziejów*, p. 48ff; Długoborski, Piper (eds.), *Auschwitz*, vol. 3, pp. 7–10, 113ff.

13. Deutschkron, "The German," *Maariv*, Dec. 15, 1964, no pages.
14. Deutschkron, *Auschwitz*, p. 297; Kąkol, *Sąd*, p. 229; K. Helbin, Note, Dec. 15, 1964. IPN, Kr 0/60/13, pp. 209–211; Balewicz (ed.), *Wizja sądu*, no pages.
15. Deutschkron, "The German," *Maariv*, Dec. 15, 1964, no pages.
16. Kąkol, *Sąd*, p. 229.
17. Amos, *Journey*, pp. ?, 10; Janusz Kidawa (dir.), *Wizja lokalna*, 1965; Jan Sehn, Eugeniusz Szmulewski, Wizja lokalna w Oświęcimiu-Brzezince, Feb. 5, 1965. IPN, Bu 2586/404, p. 30; List of questions for field view in Auschwitz-Birkenau, no date. IPN, Bu 2586/404, pp. 90–95.
18. Deutschkron, "The German," *Maariv*, Dec. 15, 1964, no pages; Długoborski, Piper (eds.), *Auschwitz*, vol. III, pp. 113–115, 121; Amos, *Journey*, pp. 7–8; Smoleń, "Wizje lokalne," *Muzea Walki*, 1970/III, p. 205; Amos, *Journey*, p. 9. Approximately one million Jews perished in Auschwitz (data based on information published on the Auschwitz-Birkenau State Museum website).
19. Amos, *Journey*, p. 9.
20. Kąkol, *Sąd*, p. 230; Smoleń, "Wizje lokalne," *Muzea Walki*, 1970/III, p. 205.
21. Kąkol, *Sąd*, p. 230; Amos, *Journey*, p. 9.
22. Amos, *Journey*, p. 8; Kąkol, *Sąd*, p. 230; Balewicz (ed.), *Wizja sądu*, no pages.
23. Deutschkron, "The German," *Maariv*, Dec. 15, 1964.
24. Ibid.; Author unknown, Note, Dec. 14, 1964. IPN, Kr 0/60/13, pp. 98–99; S. Wałach, Meldunek specjalny nr 4, Dec. 14, 1964. IPN, Bu 0/1062/33, vol. III, p. 106.
25. S. Wałach, Raport specjalny nr 2, Dec. 14, 1964. IPN, Kr 0/60/13, pp. 87–88; S. Wałach, Meldunek specjalny nr 3, Dec. 14, 1964. IPN, Kr 0/60/13, pp. 125–128. Wałach's chronology is a little confused in places. Walter Hotz, Report, Jan. 6, 1965. HHStAW, 461, 37638/93, vol. 92, p. 18297; L. Czubała, Note, Dec. 16, 1964. IPN, Kr 0/60/13, p. 135; L. Karczmarz, Note, Dec. 15, 1964. IPN, Kr 0/60/13, pp. 131–132.
26. M. Bała, Z. Chowaniec, Streszczenie rozmów, Dec. 15, 1964. IPN, Kr 0/60/13, p. 219; K. Helbin, Note, Dec. 15, 1964. IPN, Kr 0/60/13, p. 209; S. Wałach, Meldunek specjalny nr 3, Dec. 14, 1964. IPN, Kr 0/60/13, p. 126.
27. S. Wałach, Meldunek specjalny nr 4, Dec. 15, 1964. IPN, Bu 0/1062/33, vol. 3, pp. 103–104; Emanuel Cwiertnia, Note, Dec. 15, 1964. IPN, Kr 0/60/13, p. 119; Janusz Kidawa (dir.), *Wizja lokalna*, 1965; Smoleń, "Wizje lokalne," *Muzea Walki*, 1970/III, p. 206.
28. Author unknown, Plan organizacji wizji lokalnej w Oświęcimiu, Dec. 10, 1964. IPN, Kr 0/60/13, p. 23; S. Wałach, Meldunek specjalny nr 2, Dec. 14, 1964. IPN, Bu 0/1062/33, vol. III, p. 83; Pendas, *The Frankfurt*, p. 181; Georg Severa, Testimony, Aug. 6, 1964. FBInst, Tonbandmitschnitte des Auschwitz-Prozesses (1963–1965), online source; Józef Kral, Testimony, May 15, 1964. FBInst, Tonbandmitschnitte des Auschwitz-Prozesses (1963–1965), online source. Pendas, *The Frankfurt*, p. 181; Janusz Kidawa (dir.), *Wizja lokalna*, 1965; Deutschkron, "The Visit," *Maariv*, Dec. 16, 1964, no pages; Naumann, *Auschwitz*, p. 336. The Goethe poem is about sexual assault.
29. S. Wałach, Meldunek specjalny nr 4, Dec. 15, 1964. IPN, Bu 0/1062/33, vol. 3, p. 104.

30. S. Wałach, Kronika wydarzeń, Dec. 16, 1964. IPN, Kr 0/60/13, p. 162; Józef Kral, Testimony, May 15, 1964. FBInst, Tonbandmitschnitte des Auschwitz-Prozesses (1963–1965), online source; Deutschkron, "The German," *Maariv,* Dec. 17, 1964, no pages; Smoleń, "Wizje lokalne," *Muzea Walki,* 1970/III, p. 207; Deutschkron, "The German," *Maariv,* Dec. 17, 1964, no pages.

31. Jan Sehn, Eugeniusz Szmulewski, Wizja lokalna w Oświęcimiu-Brzezince, Feb. 5, 1965. IPN, Bu 2586/404, pp. 32–33; S. Wałach, Raport specjalny nr 5, Dec. 16, 1964. IPN, Bu 0/1062/33, vol. 3, p. 129; Deutschkron, "The German," *Maariv,* Dec. 17, 1964, no pages; Deutschkron, "'It's Horrible,'" *Maariv,* Dec. 18, 1964, no pages; Deutschkron, "The German," *Maariv,* Dec. 17, 1964, no pages.

32. Deutschkron, "'It's Horrible,'" *Maariv,* Dec. 18, 1964, no pages; Deutschkron, "The German," *Maariv,* Dec. 17, 1964, no pages; Deutschkron, "'It's Horrible,'" *Maariv,* Dec. 18, 1964, no pages.

33. Deutschkron, "'It's Horrible,'" *Maariv,* Dec. 18, 1964, no pages; Mauz, *Die Gerechten,* p. 274; Walter Hotz, Report, Jan. 6, 1965. HHStAW, 461, 37638/93, vol. 92, p. 18,298; Władysław Rutka, Meldunek specjalny, Dec. 21, 1964. IPN, Bu 0/1062/33, vol. 3, pp. 115–116; Walter Hotz, Report, Jan. 6, 1965. HHStAW, 461, 37638/93, vol. 92, p. 18,300.

34. Lucas confessed in March 1965 (Wisely, "Confession," *Holocaust Studies,* Jan. 24, 2020, online source). Kieta, "Po co," *Przekrój,* 1965/31, p. 4.

35. Kieta, "Po co," *Przekrój,* 1965/31, p. 4; Renz, "Auschwitz . . . Tonbandschnittes," *Jahrbuch der Juristischen Zeitgeschichte,* 2010/19 (1), p. 182.

36. The Auschwitz exhibition Bauer had helped to conceive opened in November 1964 in the Paulskirche, a former Lutheran church next to the city hall, and ran until December 20. It attracted large crowds and controversy because the initial display included photographs of the defendants and descriptions of their roles drawn from Bauer's investigation. After defense lawyers complained that the exhibition was prejudicial to their clients, the panels were removed (Brink, *Auschwitz,* pp. 18–22). Renz, "Auschwitz . . . Tonbandschnittes," p. 182. Bauer attempted at the end of the trial to add a further charge for all the defendants under Article 73 of the German criminal code. The law stipulated that certain acts committed in close temporal and contextual proximity should be considered as a single action or offense rather than multiple distinct actions. Under the new charges, the defendants were accused of "psychologically aiding and abetting or co-perpetrating a unitary extermination program." The Chełmno trial of 1963 verdict had already come to the conclusion, confirmed by the Federal Supreme Court, that members of the camp's guard unit had assisted in the killings of Jews simply through their membership in the unit (Kurz, "Paradigmenwechsel," *Zeitschrift für Internationale Strafrechtsdogmatik,* 2013/8 [3], pp. 122–129). Hofmeyer, however, was to reject this argument in his own verdict (Frankfurt Public Prosecutor's Office, Statement, May 6, 1965. HHStAW, 461, 37638/112, vol. 111, no pages; Pendas, *The Frankfurt,* p. 197).

25

VERDICT

1. The lead prosecutor, Hanns Grossmann, did the introductory closing argument on May 7, followed by Vogel and Wiese, who presented their closing arguments

against the defendants they'd been responsible for. Kügler gave four closing arguments against ten defendants on May 13, 17, and 20, 1965. The scene described in this chapter is from his first closing argument (Joachim Kügler, Closing argument against Lucas, Schatz, Frank, Capesius, May 13, 1965. FBInst, Tonbandmitschnitte des Auschwitz-Prozesses [1963–1965], online source). Kügler and Vogel alternated until May 20, when the joint plaintiffs spoke. The defense presented its arguments on May 31 (FBInst, Tonbandmitschnitte des Auschwitz-Prozesses [1963–1965], online source). On the prosecution's closing arguments see: Pendas, *The Frankfurt*, pp. 192–193 (for Grossmann's closing argument see pp. 194–200; for Vogel's closing argument see pp. 200–204). Bedford, "The Auschwitz," *The Observer*. Jan. 26, 1964, p. 12; Joachim Kügler, Interview by Werner Renz, May 5, 1998. FBInst, part 2.

2. Joachim Kügler, Closing argument, May 13, 1965. FBInst, Tonbandmitschnitte des Auschwitz-Prozesses (1963–1965), online source.
3. Ibid.
4. Ibid.
5. Ibid.
6. Pendas, *The Frankfurt*, pp. 211–214; Hermann Stolting II, Closing argument, undated, pp. 1–8, cited in: Pendas, *The Frankfurt*, pp. 216, 223; Pendas, *The Frankfurt*, pp. 223–224, 216, 193, 223–224, 214–215. On defense closing arguments see: Pendas, *The Frankfurt*, pp. 211–226.
7. Robert Mulka, Closing statement, Aug. 6, 1965. FBInst, Tonbandmitschnitte des Auschwitz-Prozesses (1963–1965), online source; Franz Lucas, Closing statement, Aug. 6, 1965. FBInst, Tonbandmitschnitte des Auschwitz-Prozesses (1963–1965), online source; Hans Stark, Closing statement, Aug. 6, 1965. FBInst, Tonbandmitschnitte des Auschwitz-Prozesses (1963–1965), online source.
8. Hans Stark, Closing statement, Aug. 6, 1965. FBInst, Tonbandmitschnitte des Auschwitz-Prozesses (1963–1965), online source.
9. Bauer, "Heute," in: Foljanty, Johst (eds.), *Fritz Bauer*, vol. 2, pp. 1224–1241.
10. Naumann, *Auschwitz*, p. 412; Wittmann, *Beyond*, p. 209; Pendas, *The Frankfurt*, pp. 227–228; Naumann, *Auschwitz*, p. 411; Wittmann, *Beyond*, pp. 285–286; Naumann, *Auschwitz*, p. 413; Kügler, Interview by Werner Renz, May 5, 1998. FBInst, part 2; Stengel, *Hermann Langbein*, pp. 531–533 .
11. Hofmeyer spoke for almost eleven hours across two days (May 19–20, 1965). Hans Hofmeyer, Oral judgment, Aug. 19, 1965. FBInst, Tonbandmitschnitte des Auschwitz-Prozesses (1963–1965), online source. For an analysis of the oral judgment (a condensed version of the more than nine-hundred-page written judgment read out after the verdicts) see: Wittmann, *Beyond*, pp. 210–215; Pendas, *The Frankfurt*, pp. 227–248.
12. Hans Hofmeyer, Oral judgment, Aug. 19, 1965. FBInst, Tonbandmitschnitte des Auschwitz-Prozesses (1963–1965), online source; Stengel, *Die Überlebenden*, p. 418.
13. Hans Hofmeyer, Oral judgment, Aug. 19, 1965. FBInst, Tonbandmitschnitte des Auschwitz-Prozesses (1963–1965), online source; Wittmann, *Beyond*, pp. 210–215; Pendas, *The Frankfurt*, pp. 227–248; Bauer, "Im Namen," 1965, in: Perels, Wojak (eds.), *Die Humanität*, pp. 77–90; Müller, *Furchtbare Juristen*, p. 257, cited in: Krause, *Der Eichmann-Prozess*, p. 81; Bauer, "Im Namen," 1965, in: Perels, Wojak (eds.), *Die Humanität*, pp. 85–86. Part of Bauer's frustration stemmed

from Hofmeyer's rejection of the charges he had brought under Article 73 of the German legal code (Wittmann, *Beyond*, pp. 213–215; Pendas, *The Frankfurt*, pp. 197–198).

14. Bauer, citing a poll, noted that 63 percent of all men and 76 percent of all women were in favor of ending the prosecution of Nazi crimes (Bauer, "Im Namen," 1965, in: Perels, Wojak [eds.], *Die Humanität*, pp. 77–78). "Trial," *The New York Times*, July 12, 1964, p. 18; Walser, *Unser Auschwitz*, in: Meier (ed.), *Martin Walser*, pp. 70–80; Naumann, *Auschwitz*, p. vii;. For an analysis of German press response to the verdict, see: Wittmann, *Beyond*, pp. 246–253.

15. "Auschwitz," *The New York Times*, Dec. 27, 1964, p. 4; Benjamin Ferencz, "Letter," *The New York Times*, Aug. 29, 1965, no pages; Bedford, "Auschwitz," *The Observer*, Mar. 7, 1965, pp. 11–12; Bedford, *As It Was*, pp. 259–260.

16. Stengel, *Die Überlebenden*, pp. 429–430, p. 428; "Er beharrt," *Süddeutsche Zeitung*, Dec. 20, 2013, online source; Steinke, *Fritz Bauer*, p. 171; Freimüller, *Frankfurt*, pp. 252–253, 345–346; Micha Brumlik, Interview by Catherine Mullier, Mar. 17, 2021; Kugelmann, C., "Fritz Bauer," in: Rauschenberger (ed.), *Rückkehr*, pp. 217–222; Cilly Kugelmann, Interview by Harriet Phillips, Mar. 17, 2023; Hersz Kugelmann, Testimony, Aug. 21, 1964. FBInst, Tonbandmitschnitte des Auschwitz-Prozesses (1963–1965), online source. Hans Frankenthal gave an account of his exploitation by IG Farben's synthetic rubber factory in Monowitz, near Auschwitz, in a book on slave labor that he published in 1999, the year he died (Fulbrook, *Reckonings*, p. 371).

17. Wittmann, *Beyond*, pp. 261–262.

18. Wittmann, *Beyond*, p. 267.

26

PROTEST

1. Fritz Bauer, Letter to Thomas Harlan, 1965, in: Renz (ed.), *"Von Gott,"* p. 94; Atze, "An die Front," in: Wojak (ed.), *Auschwitz-Prozess*, pp. 783–794. The play, originally entitled *Anus Mundi*, was completed on April 19, 1965. Weiss does not appear to have shared a copy with Bauer (Atze, "An die Front," in: Wojak [ed.], *Auschwitz-Prozess*, p. 796). Fritz Bauer, Letter to Thomas Harlan, Oct. 29, 1965, in: Renz (ed.), *"Von Gott,"* p. 121. Bauer and Langbein were locked in a battle with Hofmeyer to preserve the recordings of the trial (Renz, "Stimmen," in: Renz, *Fritz Bauer*, pp. 109–126; Fritz Bauer, Letter to Thomas Harlan, Sept. 1965, in: Renz [ed.], *"Von Gott,"* p. 116).

2. Vogt, "'Die Ermittlung,'" *Literaturkritik*, 2017/4, online source; Atze, "An die Front," in: Wojak (ed.), *Auschwitz-Prozess*, pp. 795–804; Fritz Bauer, Letter to Thomas Harlan, Oct. 29, 1965, in: Renz (ed.), *"Von Gott,"* p. 123. Some criticized Weiss for avoiding any reference to the Jewish victims of the camp. Weiss explained that he wanted to show how the camp could exist "anywhere under certain circumstances" (Atze, "An die Front," in: Wojak [ed.], *Auschwitz-Prozess*, p. 799).

3. Bauer, "Auschwitz," 1965, in: Foljanty, Johst (eds.), *Fritz Bauer*, vol. 2, pp. 1386–1388; Braese et al. (eds.), *Deutsche*, pp. 74–76; Fritz Bauer, Letter to Thomas Harlan, Oct. 29, 1965, in: Renz (ed.), *"Von Gott,"* p. 123; Vogt, "'Die Ermittlung,'" *Literaturkritik*, 2017/4, online source. The director Peter Palitzsch and publisher

Siegried Unseld were also onstage (Bauer, "Auschwitz," 1965, in: Foljanty, Johst [eds.], *Fritz Bauer,* vol. 2, p. 1386).

4.   Fritz Bauer, Letter to Thomas Harlan, Feb. 1965, in: Renz (ed.), *"Von Gott,"* p. 83; Fritz Bauer, Letter to Thomas Harlan, Mar. 18, 1965, in: Renz (ed.), *"Von Gott,"* p. 85; Fritz Bauer, Letter to Thomas Harlan, Apr. 1965, in: Renz (ed.), *"Von Gott,"* p. 86; Fritz Bauer, Letter to Thomas Harlan, Apr. 5, 1965, in: Renz (ed.), *"Von Gott,"* p. 87; Fritz Bauer, Letter to Thomas Harlan, Apr. 21, 1965, in: Renz (ed.), *"Von Gott,"* p. 88; Fritz Bauer, Letter to Thomas Harlan, May 10, 1965, in: Renz (ed.), *"Von Gott,"* p. 90; Fritz Bauer, Letter to Thomas Harlan, May 15, 1965, in: Renz (ed.), *"Von Gott,"* p. 91; Fritz Bauer, Letter to Thomas Harlan, 1965, in: Renz (ed.), *"Von Gott,"* p. 95; Fritz Bauer, Letter to Thomas Harlan, July 10, 1965, in: Renz (ed.), *"Von Gott,"* pp. 98–100.

5.   Fritz Bauer, Letter to Thomas Harlan, June 13, 1965, in: Renz (ed.), *"Von Gott,"* pp. 96–97.

6.   Fritz Bauer, Letter to Thomas Harlan, July 17, 1965 in: Renz (ed.), *"Von Gott,"* p. 103; Thomas Harlan, Letter to Fritz Bauer, Sept. 20, 1965, in: Renz (ed.), *"Von Gott,"* p. 121.

7.   Bauer, "§175," 1965, in: Foljanty, Johst (eds.), *Fritz Bauer,* pp. 1388–1389; Whisnant, *Male,* pp. 188–191.

8.   Bauer, "§175," 1965, in: Foljanty, Johst (eds.), *Fritz Bauer,* p. 1389.

9.   Boll, Gross (eds.), *"Ich staune,"* pp. 317–344; Pollmann, "Arbeit," in: Rauschenberger, Steinbacher (eds.), *Fritz Bauer,* p. 265. At no point did Bauer draw attention to the Nazis' persecution of gay men. The first account of their persecution to reach a wide audience was in an essay collection by Willhart Schlegel in 1967 (Whisnant, *Male,* p. 194). Ernst Fraenkel, in: Wildt, *Die Angst,* cited in: Boll, Gross (eds.), *"Ich staune,"* p. 333.

10. Bauer, "Sexualität," *Die Zeit,* Feb. 11, 1966, p. 44, cited in: Whisnant, *Male,* p. 193.

11. Bauer, "Sexualität," *Die Zeit,* Feb. 11, 1966, p. 44.

12. Atze, "An die Front," in: Wojak (ed.), *Auschwitz-Prozess,* pp. 698–701; Fritz Bauer, Letter to Thomas Harlan, 1966, in: Renz (ed.), *"Von Gott,"* pp. 150–151; Alexander Kluge, Interview by Jack Fairweather, Sept. 3, 2021.

13. Henry Ormond, Notes, Klausurtagung Königsteiner Kreis, Apr. 1–3, 1966, no pages. Material in possession of Matias Ristic. Special thanks to Matias Ristic for his transcription of Henry Ormond's notes from the meeting. The statute of limitations for murder for Nazi crimes, which had been due to expire the year before, had been extended by another decade in part because of the evidence presented at the Auschwitz trial. Hofmeyer repeated these points at the 46th German Jurists' Conference, which took place in Essen from 27 to September 30, 1966 (Stengel, *Die Überlebenden,* p. 54). Fritz Bauer, Letter to Thomas Harlan, Oct. 1966 in: Renz (ed.), *"Von Gott,"* pp. 161–162; Lilienthal, "Hermann Krumey," no date. Gedenkportal Korbach, p. 31.

14. Fritz Bauer, Letter to Thomas Harlan, May 9, 1966 in: Renz (ed.), *"Von Gott,"* p. 140; Sälter, *NS-Kontinuitäten,* p. 321; Müller, *Reinhard Gehlen,* p. 1168. Among those given a generous retirement package was Emil Augsburg, the Einsatzgruppen member (Nowack, *Sicherheitsrisiko,* p. 445). Lommatzsch, *Hans Globke,* p. 172; Waske, "Die Verschwörung," *Die Zeit,* Dec. 2, 2012, online source; Schwenger, "Nach Lektüre," *Tagesspiegel,* Sept. 25, 2013, online source; Bästlein, *Der Fall,* pp. 43–45.

15. Wojak, *Fritz Bauer*, pp. 413–422; "Abschluss," *Darmstädter Echo*, Nov. 7, 1967, no pages; "Befahlen," *Darmstädter Echo*, Nov. 9, 1967, no pages, cited in: Wojak, *Fritz Bauer*, p. 423. For Bauer's struggles to try euthanasia doctors see: Wojak, *Fritz Bauer*, pp. 377–397. All three defendants in the first euthanasia trial were acquitted on May 23, 1967, on grounds of insufficient evidence (Wojak, *Fritz Bauer*, p. 389). In further trials of euthanasia doctors that began that year, three of the seven accused were declared unfit to stand trial (Wojak, *Fritz Bauer*, pp. 391–392).

16. Wojak, *Fritz Bauer*, p. 421; "Abschluss," *Darmstädter Echo*, Nov. 7, 1967, no pages.

17. "Abschluss," *Darmstädter Echo*, Nov. 7, 1967, no pages; "Kalk," *Der Spiegel*, Oct. 10, 1967, online source. Connected to the Babi Yar case was the murder of ninety Jewish children that clearly implicated the Wehrmacht. Two German army chaplains had tried to save the children, only for the commander of the Sixth Army, General Field Marshal Walter von Reichenau, to insist they "be brought to an expedient end" (Wojak, *Fritz Bauer*, pp. 420–421).

18. Shabecoff, "At Babi Yar," *The New York Times*, Feb. 13, 1968, p. 11. Bauer tried to garner greater interest by summoning Hans Globke to take the stand. Adenauer's confidant had largely kept out of the public spotlight other than to attend the former chancellor's funeral in 1967. It seemed Globke didn't want to testify; he skipped his first court-mandated attendance and was issued with a fine of one thousand deutschmarks (Ordnungsstrafheft, no date. HHStAW, 631a, 2071, pp. 1–4).

19. Johannes Warlo, Interview with Florine Miez, Oct. 2, 2020; Steinke, *Fritz Bauer*, p. 189; Johannes Warlo, Interview by Almut Schoenfeld, July 20, 2020; Steinke, *Fritz Bauer*, pp. 176–177, 180–182, 190; Hofmann, *Ein Versuch*, pp. 121–122. Bauer filed an application to extend the date of his retirement on July 17, 1967 (Wojak, *Fritz Bauer*, p. 547 note 38). Fritz Bauer, Letter to Thomas Harlan, Aug. 1967 in: Renz (ed.), *"Von Gott,"* p. 114.

20. Fritz Bauer, Letter to Thomas Harlan, Oct. 1966, in: Renz (ed.), *"Von Gott,"* p. 159; Fritz Bauer, Letter to Thomas Harlan, 1966, in: Renz (ed.), *"Von Gott,"* p. 136; Fritz Bauer, Letter to Thomas Harlan, July 13, 1965, in: Renz (ed.), *"Von Gott,"* p. 102; Fritz Bauer, Letter to Thomas Harlan, no date, 1966, in: Renz (ed.), *"Von Gott,"* p. 138; Fritz Bauer, Letter to Thomas Harlan, Sept. 24, 1966, in: Renz (ed.), *"Von Gott,"* pp. 156–157; Fritz Bauer, Letter to Thomas Harlan, June 27, 1966, in: Renz (ed.), *"Von Gott,"* p. 149; Fritz Bauer, Letter to Thomas Harlan, Nov. 14, 1966, in: Renz (ed.), *"Von Gott,"* p, 172; Fritz Bauer, Letter to Thomas Harlan, Jan. 6, 1967, in: Renz (ed.), *"Von Gott,"* p. 175; Fritz Bauer, Letter to Thomas Harlan, Oct. 20, 1967, in: Renz (ed.), *"Von Gott,"* p. 203; Fritz Bauer, Letter to Thomas Harlan, Nov. 1967, in: Renz (ed.), *"Von Gott,"* pp. 215–217; Steinke, *Fritz Bauer*, p. 185.

21. Steinke, *Fritz Bauer*, p. 183. For an example of Bauer's support for the protests see his comments in 1966: "People on the streets do not get upset about foolish speeches, but only about unpleasant truths" (Bauer, "Stellungnahme," 1966, in: Foljanty, Johst [eds.], *Fritz Bauer*, vol. 2, p. 1444). Trentmann, *Out of*, pp. 424–425, 419. The work of the Aktion Sühnezeichen had begun in the 1950s, but its first visit to Auschwitz came after the Auschwitz trial (Trentmann, *Out of*, pp. 209, 211, 233). For a discussion on Bauer's relationship to the student protests see: Rauschenberger, "Einführung," in: Rauschenberger, Steinbacher (eds.), *Fritz Bauer*, pp. 7–22. Steinke, *Fritz Bauer*, p. 184.

22. Brown, *West Germany*, pp. 333–334; Judt, *Postwar*, pp. 627–628; Brown, *West Germany*, p. 56. The protests in West Germany were small-scale in comparison to those in the United States and in France, where President Charles de Gaulle at one point asked his own army leadership if he still had their support.

23. Weinke, *Eine Gesellschaft*, pp. 101–102; Fritz Bauer, Letter to Thomas Harlan, Jan. 31, 1967, in: Renz (ed.), *"Von Gott,"* p. 178; Fritz Bauer, Letter to Gisela and Heinz Meyer-Velde, Jan. 29, 1967. FBInst, Nachlass Meyer-Velde 19, no pages; Fritz Bauer, cited in: Zwerenz, "Gespräche," *Streit-Zeit-Schrift*, Sept. 1968, pp. 92ff; Löw-Beer, "Fritz Bauer," in: Rauschenberger (ed.), *Rückkehr*, p. 229.

24. Meyer-Velde, " 'Dann machen's," in: Backhaus, Boll, Gross (eds.), *Fritz Bauer*, p. 246.

25. Ibid.

26. Ibid.

27. Fritz Bauer, Letter to Thomas Harlan, Apr. 1968, in: Renz (ed.), *"Von Gott,"* p. 218; Wojak, *Fritz Bauer*, pp. 435–436; Meyer-Velde, " 'Dann machen's," in: Backhaus, Boll, Gross (eds.), *Fritz Bauer*, p. 241; Fritz Bauer, Letter to Thomas Harlan, Sept. 1967, in: Renz (ed.), *"Von Gott,"* pp. 200–201; Hyde, *The Trials*, p. 201.

28. Hyde, *The Trials*, p. 201.

29. Wojak, *Fritz Bauer*, pp. 435–436; Meyer-Velde, *"Dann machen's,"* in: Backhaus, Boll, Gross (eds.), *Fritz Bauer*, p. 241; Fritz Bauer, Letter to Thomas Harlan, Sept. 1967, in: Renz (ed.), *"Von Gott,"* pp. 200–201. The push to repeal Article 175 reflected the careful advocacy of a small number of progressive doctors, attorneys, theologians, and politicians to reframe homosexuality rather than a grassroots campaign by activists. Bauer was one of several courageous voices that were crucial in persuading lawmakers to reconsider the law (Whisnant, *Male*, pp. 167–170, 198–201). Wojak, *Fritz Bauer*, p. 385.

30. Krüger, "Fremdling," *Die Zeit*, July 12, 1968, online source; Ole Grünbaum, Interview by Jack Fairweather and Sine Maria Vinther, Mar. 24, 2022..

31. Ole Grünbaum, Interview by Jack Fairweather and Sine Maria Vinther, Mar. 24, 2022.

32. Müller-Wirth, "Eine letzte," *Forschungsjournal Soziale Bewegungen*, 2015/4 (28), pp. 280–282; Ilona Ziok, (dir.), *Fritz Bauer*, 2010; Schenk, "Die Todesumstände," *Einsicht 08: Bulletin des Fritz Bauer Instituts*, 2012, pp. 38–39.

33. Joachim Gerchow, Abschliessendes Gutachten über das Ergebnis der Obduktion und weiterer Untersuchungen, Jan. 24, 1969, cited in: Schenk, "Die Todesumstände," *Einsicht 08: Bulletin des Fritz Bauer Instituts*, 2012, p. 40.

EPILOGUE

1. Steinke, *Fritz Bauer*, pp. 188–189; Harlan, *Hitler*, p. 117; "Nachruf," *Frankfurter Allgemeine Zeitung*, July 2, 1968, no pages.

2. Wojak, *Fritz Bauer*, p. 451; Harlan, *Heldenfriedhof*, p. 405; Meyer-Velde, " 'Dann machen's,' " in: Backhaus, Boll, Gross (eds.), *Fritz Bauer*, p. 253; Steinke, *Fritz Bauer*, p. 188. Adorno also selected to be played Beethoven's String Quartet No. 14 in C-sharp minor and String Quartet No. 15 in A minor (Kluge, *"Wer ein Wort,"* p. 7). Wojak, *Fritz Bauer*, pp. 454, 457–458, 454; Harlan, *Heldenfriedhof*, p. 406; Wojak, *Fritz Bauer*, p. 454.

3. Weinke, *Eine Gesellschaft*, p. 135; Steinke, *Fritz Bauer*, pp. 191–192. The new law, which passed on May 10, 1968, and came into force on October 1, 1968, obligated judges to give light sentences to Nazi perpetrators charged as accessory to murder which, together with a reduction in the statute of limitations for investigating such crimes, meant that it would only be possible to prosecute those with "special personal characteristics" of murderers (Steinke, *Fritz Bauer*, p. 191). The drop in prosecutions in Hesse was reflected across the country with a few notable exceptions. Franz Stangl, the commandant of the Treblinka and Sobibór death camps, was extradited from Brazil in 1967, tried in 1970, and sentenced to life. He died six months later (Fulbrook, *Reckonings*, p. 305). In 1975, fifteen staff members of the Majdanek concentration camp were tried in Düsseldorf; seven were acquitted or released on flimsy medical grounds, while the deputy camp commandant sued and won damages for his time in prison (Fulbrook, *Reckonings*, pp. 308–312). By the 1980s, the number of trials had dwindled, partly a result of both witnesses and perpetrators dying, but also because German law still failed to recognize the exceptional nature of Nazi crimes. Steinke, *Fritz Bauer*, pp. 193, 191, 193; Renz, "Auschwitz . . . des Tonbandschnittes," *Jahrbuch der Juristischen Zeitgeschichte*, 2010/19 (1), pp. 181–182; Renz, "Auschwitz," 2013, FBInst, Tonbandmitschnitte des Auschwitz-Prozesses (1963–1965), online source.

4. Sharples, *Postwar*, pp. 153, 157–158; Fulbrook, *Reckonings*, pp. 363–364. For the controversy surrounding the miniseries, see: Sharples, *Postwar*, pp. 134–137.

5. Following publication of his memoir, Müller was subject to a vicious smear campaign by neo-Nazis (Kilian, *"Ein leiser,"* *Mitteilungen der Lagergemeinschaft Auschwitz*, 2014/34, pp. 36–38). Fulbrook, *Reckonings*, pp. 460–461, 502–505. The persecution of gay men was belatedly recognized in 2002 with a law overturning prewar convictions under Article 175 and a new exhibition at the Dachau memorial museum (Fulbrook, *Reckonings*, pp. 376, 503). Fulbrook, *Reckonings*, pp. 502–505, 4–5, 498–499, 125; Sharples, *Postwar*, p. 83. Only a few more prosecutions of former Nazis were possible in light of the Demjanjuk ruling, such as that of the so-called "bookkeeper of Auschwitz," Oskar Gröning, in 2015 (Cowell, "Oskar Gröning," *The New York Times*, Mar. 12, 2018, online source). It is notable that the change in law came about when the vast majority of perpetrators had died. For a discussion of Bauer's legacy see: Renz, "Auf der Suche," *Recht und Politik*, 2018/54 (2), pp. 215–219.

6. Globke family, Interview by Jack Fairweather, Anna Schattschneider, and Harriet Phillips, Sept. 20, 2021; Dorothee Gehlen-Koss, Interview by Jack Fairweather, Sept. 18, 2021; Welzer, Tschuggnall, *Opa War*, p. 226. Even when confronted with the truth by the perpetrators themselves, families refused to alter their perceptions of their loved ones. SS doctor Hans Münch, who'd presented himself as a "good" Nazi at his trial in Kraków in 1947 and subsequently appeared as a witness in Frankfurt, let his mask slip in a 1998 *Der Spiegel* interview in which he reminisced fondly over his time in Auschwitz and admitted to conducting research on the heads of Jewish children supplied to him by Josef Mengele. To avert criminal proceedings, Münch's son claimed his father was suffering from Alzheimer's (Fulbrook, *Reckonings*, pp. 419–420; "Die Erinnerung," *Der Spiegel*, Sept. 27, 1998, online source). Some children of former Nazis, like Niklas Frank, the son of the former governor-general of occupied Poland, have publicly excoriated their parents.

7.   Bauer, "Die Wurzeln," 1961, in: Foljanty, Johst (eds.), *Fritz Bauer,* vol. 1, p. 795; Bauer, "Nach den, Wurzeln," Feb. 5, 1964, in: Foljanty, Johst (eds.), *Fritz Bauer,* vol. 2, pp. 1160–1167.
8.   Bauer, "Heute," Dec. 8, 1964, in: Foljanty, Johst (eds.), *Fritz Bauer,* vol. 2, pp. 1224–1241.

Sources

ARCHIVES

Abs—Archiv bezpečnostních složek
AdsD—Archiv der sozialen Demokratie
A-DZOK—Dokumentationszentrum
  Oberer Kuhberg
AJA—American Jewish Archive
ARAB—Arberarrörelsens Arkiv och
  Bibliotek
BA—Bundesarchiv [BA B—Bundesarchiv
  Berlin; BA K—Bundesarchiv Koblenz;
  BA Bayreuth—Lastenausgleichsarchiv
  Bayreuth; BA, MfS—Stasi-Unterlagen-
  Archiv]
BA-MA—Bundesarchiv-Militärarchiv
  Freiburg im Breisgau
BG Archive—The Ben-Gurion
  Archive
BND-Archiv—Bundesnachrichtendienst
  Archive, Berlin
BStU—Bundesbeauftragter für die
  Unterlagen des
  Staatssicherheitsdienstes der
  ehemaligen Deutschen
  Demokratischen Publik
Buxus Stiftung (Fritz Bauer Archiv)
Centrum för Näringslivshistoria
College of William and Mary, Digital
  Archive
Deutsches Exilarchiv
FBInst—Fritz Bauer Institut
HHStAW—Hessisches Hauptstaatsarchiv
  Wiesbaden

HIS—Hamburger Institut für
  Sozialforschung
HStAS—Hauptstaatsarchiv Stuttgart
IfZ—Institut für Zeitgeschichte
IPN—Instytut Pamięci Narodowej
ISA—Israel State Archives
KAS—Konrad Adenauer Stiftung
Kinemathek
Krigsarkivet
KSA—Københavns stadsarkiv
M. E. Grenander Department of Special
  Collections and Archives. State
  University of New York at
  Albany
MGFA—Militärgeschichtliches
  Forschungsamt
Mossad Archive
NARA—National Archives at College
  Park, MD
NLA HA—Niedersächsisches
  Landesarchiv, Hannover
NLA WO—Niedersächsisches
  Landesarchiv, Wolfenbüttel
ÖStA—Österreichisches Staatsarchiv
PAAA—Politisches Archiv des
  Auswärtigen Amts
PI—Pilecki Institute / Instytut Pileckiego
PMA-B—Państwowe Muzeum
  Auschwitz-Birkenau
RA Denmark—Riksarkivet, Danish
  National Archive

RA Sweden—Riksarkivet, Swedish National Archive
StAAH—Staatsarchiv Hansestadt Hamburg
StadtA KB—Stadtarchiv Korbach
StAL—Staatsarchiv Ludwigsburg
StAS—Stadtarchiv Stuttgart
Stockholms Stadsarkiv
TNA—The National Archives, London
Universitätsbibliothek Frankfurt am Main

USHMM—United States Holocaust Memorial Museum
VVN-BdA—Vereinigung der Verfolgten des Naziregimes-Bund der Antifaschistinnen und Antifaschisten
WJC—World Jewish Congress
YVA—Yad Vashem Archives
ZSt—Zentrale Stelle
ГА РФ—Государственный архив Российской Федерации [State Archive of the Russian Federation]

SELECT BIBLIOGRAPHY

Abmayr, Hermann G. "Wir wollten die Nazis heraushauen," Mar. 1, 2023. Kontext: Wochenzeitung: https://www.kontextwochenzeitung.de/zeitgeschehen/622/wir-wollten-die-nazis-heraushauen-8725.html [Aug. 29, 2024].

"Abschluss der Vernehmungen." *Darmstädter Echo,* Nov. 7, 1967. No pages.

Adam, Mariane; Salomon, Ella. *Was wird der Morgen bringen?* Transl. Moshe Fogel. Stuttgart: Anker im Christlichen Verlagshaus, 1995.

Adenauer, Konrad. (Küsters, Hanns Jürgen [ed.]). *Teegespräche 1959–1961.* Berlin: Siedler, 1988.

Adler, H.G.; Langbein, Hermann; Lingens-Reiner, Ella (eds.). *Auschwitz—Zeugnisse und Berichte.* Cologne / Frankfurt am Main: Europäische Verlagsanstalt, 1962.

"Adolf Eichmann erwähnt Globkes Namen. *Frankfurter Rundschau,* June 22, 1961, p. 1.

"Adolf Hitler kommt nicht an." *Frankfurter Rundschau,* Mar. 1, 1956, p. 3.

Agrell, Wilhelm. *Stockholm som spioncentral: Spåren efter tre hemliga städer.* Lund: Historiska Media, 2020.

Aharoni, Zvi; Dietl, Wilhelm. *Operation Eichmann: Pursuit and Capture.* Transl. Helmut Bögler. London: Weidenfeld Military, 1997.

Ahlers, Conrad. "Vor der Abrechnung." *Frankfurter Rundschau,* Apr. 11, 1961. Cited in: Krause, *Der Eichmann-Prozess,* p. 258.

Albrecht-Heider, Christoph; Ahäuser, Jürgen (eds.). *Frankfurter Rundschau Geschichte,* vol. 2. Frankfurt am Main: Frankfurter Rundschau Druck- und Verlagshaus, 2012.

Åmark, Klas. *Att bo granne med ondskan Sveriges förhållande till nazismen, Nazityskland och Förintelsen.* Stockholm: Alberg Bonnier, 2011.

Amos, Elon. *Journey Through a Haunted Land: The New Germany.* London: André Deutsch, 1967.

"Amtseinführung des Generalstaatsanwalts." *Braunschweiger Zeitung,* Aug. 2, 1950. No pages.

Andersen, Richard. *Danmark I 30'erne—En historisk mosaik.* Copenhagen: Gyldendal, 1976.

Anglo-Jewish Association. *Germany's New Nazis.* New York: Philosophical Library, 1952.

"Ansprache von Bundeskanzler Dr. Adenauer in Bergen-Belsen am 2. Februar 1960." In: Bundesregierung (ed.), *Die antisemitischen,* pp. 66–67.

Anthony, Tamara. *Ins Land der Väter oder der Täter? Israel und die Juden in Deutschland nach der Schoah.* Berlin: Metropol, 2004.

Arad, Yitzhak. "'Operation Reinhard:' Extermination Camps of Belzec, Sobibor and Treblinka." *Yad Vashem Studies* XVI, 1984, pp. 205–239: https://www.yadvashem.org/odot_pdf/Microsoft%20Word%20-%203576.pdf [Aug. 19, 2024].

Archer, William D. *The Merten Affair.* PhD thesis. California State University, Sacramento, 2016: https://csu-csus.esploro.exlibrisgroup.com/esploro/outputs/graduate/The-Merten-Affair/99257831048501671?institution=01CALS_USL [June 9, 2022].

Arendt, Hannah. "Adolf Eichmann and the Banality of Evil." *The New York Times,* Feb. 8, 1963. No pages.

Arnold, Klaus Jochen; Lübbers, Gert C. "The Meeting of the Staatssekretäre on 2 May 1941 and the Wehrmacht: A Document up for Discussion." *Journal of Contemporary History,* 2007/42 (4), pp. 613–626.

Atze, Marcel. *"An die Front des Auschwitz-Prozesses: Zur zeitgenössischen Rezeption der 'Strafsache gegen Mulka und andere.'"* In: Wojak (ed.), *Auschwitz-Prozess,* pp. 647–807.

"Auschwitz Trial." *The New York Times,* Dec. 27, 1964, p. 4.

Ausmeier, Peter. *Klagges: Ein Verbrecher im Hintergrund; Ein Prozessbericht.* Braunschweig: Volksfreund Druck- und Verlagsanstalt GmbH, 1950.

Ausschuss für deutsche Einheit (ed.). *Globke und die Ausrottung der Juden: Über die verbrecherische Vergangenheit des Staatssekretärs im Amt des Bundeskanzlers Adenauer.* Berlin (East): Ausschuss f. Dt. Einheit, 1960.

Backhaus, Fritz; Boll, Monika; Gross, Raphael (eds.). *Fritz Bauer: Der Staatsanwalt. NS-Verbrechen vor Gericht.* Frankfurt am Main / New York: Campus Verlag, 2014.

Bak, Sofie Lene. *Nothing to Speak Of—Wartime Experiences of the Danish Jews 1943–1945.* Copenhagen: Transl. Virginia Raynolds Laursen. The Danish Jewish Museum, 2011.

Bak, Sofie Lene; Christensen, Claus Bundgård; Lund, Joachim, Sørensen, Jakob. *Turen går til besættelsestidens København.* Copenhagen: Politikens Forlag, 2015.

Balewicz, Stanisław (ed.). *Wizja sądu frankfurckiego w Oświęcimiu w fotogramach Adama Bujaka w 20-lecie wyzwolenia Oświęcimia.* Kraków: Galeria Krzysztofory. Zarząd Okręgu ZBoWiD Klub Oświęcimiaków w Krakowie, 1965. No pages.

Bareli, Gideon. "Letter to the reader." *HaOlam HaZe,* Aug, 15, 1962, p. 2.

Barkai, Avraham. "Jüdisches Leben unter der Verfolgung." In: Meyer, Brenner (eds.), *Deutsch-jüdische,* vol. 4, pp. 225–248, cited in: Wojak, *Fritz Bauer,* p. 119.

Bascomb, Neal. *Hunting Eichmann: How a Band of Survivors and a Young Spy Agency Chased Down the World's Most Notorious Nazi.* Boston / New York: Houghton Mifflin Harcourt, 2009. Ebook.

Bästlein, Klaus. *Der Fall Globke: Propaganda und Justiz in Ost und West.* Berlin: Metropol Verlag, 2018.

———. "Nazi-Blutrichter als Stützen des Adenauer-Regimes: Die DDR-Kampagnen gegen NS-Richter und -Staatsanwälte, die Reaktionen der bundesdeutschen Justiz und ihre gescheiterte Selbstreinigung 1957–1968." In: Grabitz (ed.), *Die Normalität,* pp. 408–430.

Bauer, Fritz. "Antinazistische Prozesse und politisches Bewusstsein. Dienen NS-Prozesse der politischen Aufklärung?" Jan.–Feb. 1964. In: Foljanty, Johst (eds.), *Fritz Bauer,* vol. 2, pp. 1390–1404.

———. "'Auschwitz auf dem Theater': Ein Podiumsgespräch in den Württembergischen Staatstheatern Stuttgart aus Anlass der Uraufführung des

szenischen Oratoriums 'Die Ermittlung' von Peter Weiss [Auszug]," 1965. In:
   Foljanty, Johst (eds.), *Fritz Bauer,* vol. 2, pp. 1386–1388.

———. "§175 in Deutschland. Wie sie leben, was sie fürchten, wie sie sich tarnen,"
   1965. In: Foljanty, Johst (eds.), *Fritz Bauer,* vol. 2, pp. 1388–1389.

———. "Auschwitz-Kommandant Richard Baer: Der SS-Staat in Person," Jan. 13, 1961.
   In: Foljanty, Johst (eds.), *Fritz Bauer,* vol. 1, pp. 684–687.

———. "Brief aus Dänemark," Sept. 1945. In: Foljanty, Johst (eds.), *Fritz Bauer,* vol. 1,
   pp. 173–176.

———. "Das Ende waren die Gaskammern," Sept. 15, 1960. In: Foljanty, Johst (eds.),
   Fritz Bauer, vol. 1, pp. 650–654.

———. "Das Nansen-Amt," June 23, 1938. In: Foljanty, Johst (eds.), *Fritz Bauer,* vol. 1,
   pp. 84–86.

———. "Das neue Geschwätz vom Dolchstoss," Mar. 11, 1946. In: Foljanty, Johst
   (eds.), *Fritz Bauer,* vol. 1, pp. 188–190.

———. "Das politische Gespräch." [Interview]. Norddeutscher Rundfunk, Aug. 20,
   1963. In: Foljanty, Johst (eds.), *Fritz Bauer,* vol. 2, pp. 1048–1061.

———. "Der Generalstaatsanwalt hat das Wort Das Plädoyer des Anklägers Dr.Bauer
   im Prozess gegen Remer," July 20, 1952. In: Foljanty, Johst (eds.), *Fritz Bauer,* vol. 1,
   pp. 323–336.

———. "Der Kampf ums Recht," Oct. 1950. In: Foljanty, Johst (eds.), *Fritz Bauer,*
   vol. 1, pp. 297–303.

———. "Der Nürnberger Prozess," Oct. 17, 1946. In: Foljanty, Johst (eds.), *Fritz Bauer,*
   vol. 1, pp. 223–240.

———. "Der Todestag des Dritten Reiches," May 6, 1946. In: Foljanty, Johst (eds.),
   Fritz Bauer, vol. 1, pp. 192–194.

———. "Deutsche mit Nazi-Vergangenheit konfrontiert," 1961. In: Foljanty, Johst
   (eds.), *Fritz Bauer,* vol. 1, pp. 691–694.

———. "Die Abrechnung mit den Kriegsverbrechern." *Sozialistische Tribüne,* Feb. 2,
   1945, pp. 11–13.

———. "Die erste Etappe," Aug. 19, 1946. In: Foljanty, Johst (eds.), *Fritz Bauer,* vol. 1,
   pp. 201–203.

———. "Die Kriegsverbrechen und das Schuldproblem (II)," Dec. 21, 1964. In:
   Foljanty, Johst (eds.), *Fritz Bauer,* vol. 2, pp. 1250–1254.

———. *Die Kriegsverbrecher vor Gericht.* Zürich: Europa, 1945.

———. "Die Kriminalität der Jugendlichen," May, 1951. In: Foljanty, Johst (eds.), *Fritz
   Bauer,* vol. 1, pp. 304–307.

———. "Die Rückkehr in die Freiheit—Probleme der Resozialisierung," 1960. In:
   Foljanty, Johst (eds.), *Fritz Bauer,* vol. 1, pp. 658–663.

———. "Die russische Planwirtschaft," Sept. 1945. In: Foljanty, Johst (eds.), *Fritz
   Bauer,* vol. 1, pp. 167–172.

———. "Die Splitterrichter," Mar. 26, 1946. In: Foljanty, Johst (eds.), *Fritz Bauer,* vol. 1,
   pp. 190–192.

———. "Die Stärke der Demokratie," Feb. 1954. In: Foljanty, Johst (eds.), *Fritz Bauer,*
   vol. 1, pp. 368–372.

———. "Die Strafe in der modernen Rechtspflege," Sept. 24, 1949. In: Foljanty, Johst
   (eds.), *Fritz Bauer,* vol. 1, pp. 290–292.

———. "Die 'ungesühnte Nazijustiz,'" 1960. In: Perels, Wojak (eds.), *Die Humanität,*
   pp. 119–142.

———. "Die Verjährung der nazistischen Massenverbrechen," 1964. In: Foljanty, Johst (eds.), *Fritz Bauer,* vol. 2, pp. 1209–1215.

———. "Die Wirtschaftsgesetzgebung in der Ostzone," Apr. 14, 1947. In: Foljanty, Johst (eds.), *Fritz Bauer,* vol. 1, pp. 244–250.

———. "Die Wurzeln faschistischen und nationalsozialistischen Handelns," 1961. In: Foljanty, Johst (eds.), *Fritz Bauer,* vol. 1, pp. 770–796.

———. "Ein neues Strafrecht," Oct. 23, 1954. In: Foljanty, Johst (eds.), *Fritz Bauer,* vol. 1, pp. 376–377.

———. "Eine Weltmoral entsteht," 1945. In: Foljanty, Johst (eds.), *Fritz Bauer,* vol. 1, pp. 179–183.

———. "Europäische Zollunion," Sept. 8, 1947. In: Foljanty, Johst (eds.), *Fritz Bauer,* vol. 1, pp. 272–274.

———. Extracts from letters to Melitta Wiedemann, no date. *Gewerkschafliche Monatshefte,* 1968/19, pp. 490–492. Cited in: Steinke, *Fritz Bauer,* p. 127.

———. "Freunde, nicht diese Töne," June 3, 1946. In: Foljanty, Johst (eds.), *Fritz Bauer,* vol. 1, pp. 197–198.

———. "Freund oder Feind?" Feb. 11, 1946. In: Foljanty, Johst (eds.), *Fritz Bauer,* vol. 1, pp.186–187.

———. "Generalstaatsanwalt Dr. Fritz Bauer, Frankfurt am Main, schrieb nach der Lektüre des neuen Buches von Ludwig Marcuse das Folgende," 1962. In: Foljanty, Johst (eds.), *Fritz Bauer,* vol. 2, pp. 957–962.

———. "Glückliche Insel Dänemark," Dec. 24, 1936. In: Backhaus, Boll, Gross (eds.), *Fritz Bauer,* pp. 106–113.

———. "Graf Helmuth James von Moltke," Dec. 9, 1946. In: Foljanty, Johst (eds.), *Fritz Bauer,* vol. 1, p. 206.

———. "Heute Abend Kellerklub: Die Jugend im Gespräch mit Fritz Bauer," Dec. 8, 1964. In: Foljanty, Johst (eds.), *Fritz Bauer,* vol. 2, pp. 1224–1241.

———. "Ideal- oder Realkonkurrenz bei nationalsozialistischen Verbrechen?" Oct. 20, 1967, In: Foljanty, Johst (eds.), *Fritz Bauer,* vol. 2, pp. 1568–1577.

———. "Im Kampf um des Menschen Rechte," Apr. 1955. In: Foljanty, Johst (eds.), *Fritz Bauer,* vol. 1, pp. 446–456.

———. "Im Namen des Volkes: Die strafrechtliche Bewältigung der Vergangenheit," 1965. In: Perels, Wojak (eds.), *Die Humanität,* pp. 77–90.

———. "In unserem Namen Justiz und Strafvollzug," 1965. In: Foljanty, Johst (eds.), *Fritz Bauer,* vol. 2, pp. 1418–1427.

———. "Juden in Europas Norden," Sept. 22, 1938. In: Foljanty, Johst (eds.), *Fritz Bauer,* vol. 1, pp. 86–89.

———. *Krigsförbrytarna inför domstol.* Stockholm: Natur och Kultur, 1944.

———. "Lebendige Vergangenheit," June 9, 1963. In: Foljanty, Johst (eds.), *Fritz Bauer,* vol. 2, pp. 1069–1075.

———. "Mörder unter uns!" *Deutsche Nachrichten,* 1947/3, p. 2.

———. "Nach den Wurzeln des Bösen fragen," Feb. 5, 1964. In: Foljanty, Johst (eds.), *Fritz Bauer,* vol. 2, pp. 1160–1167.

———. No title. [Note about exile.] In: Sender Freies Berlin (ed.), *Um uns die Fremde,* pp. 31–32, 69.

———. "NS-Verbrechen vor deutschen Gerichten: Versuch einer Zwischenbilanz," 1964. In: Foljanty, Johst (eds.), *Fritz Bauer,* vol. 2, pp. 1185–1187.

———. "Penge." *København.* Martins Forlag, 1941.

———. "Prozesse und politisches Bewusstsein: Dienen NS-Prozesse der politischen Aufklärung?" Jan.–Feb. 1964. In: Foljanty, Johst (eds.), *Fritz Bauer,* vol. 2, pp. 1390–1405.

———. "Recht oder Unrecht . . . mein Vaterland," June 24, 1946. In: Foljanty, Johst (eds.), *Fritz Bauer,* vol. 1, pp. 199–201.

———. "Rezept für Kartoffelpuffer," 1968. In: Foljanty, Johst (eds.), *Fritz Bauer,* vol. 2, pp. 1679–1680.

———. "Scham bei der Lektüre." Die Zeit, Sept. 29, 1967, p. 3.

———. "§175 in Deutschland. Wie sie leben, was sie fürchten, wie sie sich tarnen," 1965. In: Foljanty, Johst (eds.), *Fritz Bauer,* vol. 2, pp. 1388–1389.

———. "Selbstreinigung klappt nicht Belastete Richter immer noch in Amt und Würden—Die Hartnäckigen wollen nicht in Pension gehen," July 13, 1962. In: Foljanty, Johst (eds.), *Fritz Bauer,* vol. 2, pp. 900–903.

———. "Sexualität, Sitte und ein neues Recht: Reform ist keine Aufgabe für Juristen allein—Es wird zuviel kriminalisiert," Feb. 11, 1966. In: Foljanty, Johst (eds.), *Fritz Bauer,* vol. 2, pp. 1438–1444.

———. "Sexualstrafrecht heute," 1963. In: Foljanty, Johst (eds.), *Fritz Bauer,* vol. 2, pp. 1101–1113.

———. "Sexualtabus und Sexualethik im Spiegel des Strafgesetzes," 1967. In: Foljanty, Johst (eds.), *Fritz Bauer,* vol. 2, pp. 1524–1539.

———. "Sozialismus und Sozialisierung," May 12, 1947. In: Foljanty, Johst (eds.), *Fritz Bauer,* vol. 1, pp. 255–261.

———. "Staat und Sexus," 1963. In: Foljanty, Johst (eds.), *Fritz Bauer,* vol. 2, pp. 1008–1016.

———. "Stellungnahme zum Thema 'Der Staat und die Intellektuellen,'" 1966. In: Foljanty, Johst (eds.), *Fritz Bauer,* vol. 2, pp. 1444–1445.

———. "Unbewältigte Vergangenheit—Ein Jurist nimmt Stellung." / Aktuelles zum Wochenende. [Interview]. Deutschlandfunk, 1961. Broadcast Mar. 25, 1961. In: Foljanty, Johst (eds.), *Fritz Bauer,* vol. 1, pp. 699–705.

———. "Ungehorsam und Widerstand in Geschichte und Gegenwart," June 21, 1968. In: Foljanty, Johst (eds.), *Fritz Bauer,* vol. 2, pp. 1622–1633.

———. "Unser Erleben im Lichte zeitgemässer Dichter u. Denker." *Gemeinde-Zeitung für die israelitischen Gemeinden Württembergs,* Jan. 16, 1936, p. 159.

———. "USA heute," June 2, 1947. In: Foljanty, Johst (eds.), *Fritz Bauer,* vol. 1, pp. 262–263.

———. "Warum Gefängnisse?" June 1949. In: Foljanty, Johst (eds.), *Fritz Bauer,* vol. 1, pp. 286–290.

———. "Widerstand heisst Verantwortlichkeit," July 1956. In: Foljanty, Johst (eds.), *Fritz Bauer,* vol. 1, pp. 464–471.

———. "Wiedergutmachung und Neuaufbau," Sept. 4, 1945. In: Foljanty, Johst (eds.), *Fritz Bauer,* vol. 1, pp. 161–162.

———. "Wurzeln nazistischen Denkens und Handelns," 1960. In: Foljanty, Johst (eds.), *Fritz Bauer,* vol. 1, pp. 664–682.

———. "Zum 7. Mai 1945," May 1945. In: Foljanty, Johst (eds.), *Fritz Bauer,* vol. 1, pp. 159–160.

———. "Zwei Welten—Eine Welt—Keine Welt," Oct. 20, 1947. In: Foljanty, Johst (eds.), *Fritz Bauer,* vol. 1, pp. 275–277.

Bauer, Fritz; Bürger-Prinz, Hans; Giese, Hans; Jäger, Herbert. *Sexualität und*

Verbrechen: Beiträge zur Strafrechtsreform. Frankfurt am Main: Fischer Bücherei KG, 1963.

Baumann, Imanuel; Reinke, Herbert; Stephan, Andrej; Wagner, Patrik (eds.). *Schatten der Vergangenheit: Das BKA und seine Gründungsgeneration in der frühen Bundesrepublik.* Köln: Luchterhand, 2011.

Bauz, Ingrid; Brüggemann, Sigrid; Maier, Roland (eds.). *Die Geheime Staatspolizei in Württemberg und Hohenzollern.* Stuttgart: Schmetterling Verlag, 2018.

[Becker, Hans Detlev]. "Des Kanzlers lieber General." *Der Spiegel,* Sept. 21, 1954: https://www.spiegel.de/politik/des-kanzlers-lieber-general-a-8f03b312-0002-0001 -0000-000028957469 [Feb. 16, 2022].

Bedford, Sybille. "The Auschwitz Trial." *The Observer,* Jan. 26, 1964, pp. 11–12.

———. *As It Was: Pleasures, Landscapes and Justice.* London: Sinclair-Stevenson, 1990.

Beevor, Antony. *The Fall of Berlin 1945.* New York: Penguin Books, 2003.

"Befahlen Wehrmachtsstäbe den Mord von Babij-Jar?" *Darmstädter Echo,* Nov. 9, 1967. No pages. Cited in: Wojak, *Fritz Bauer,* p. 423.

Bembenek, Lothar. "Die Geschichte der Wiesbadener Deportationsfotos." In: Ulrich, Streich (eds.), *Gedenkort,* pp. 18–21.

Benz, Wolfgang. "Die jüdische Emigration." In: Krohn et al. (eds.), *Handbuch,* pp. 5–16, cited in: Wojak, *Fritz Bauer,* p. 119.

Bergman, Ronen. *Rise and Kill First: The Secret History of Israel's Targeted Assassinations.* New York: Random House, 2018.

Bergmann, Werner. "Antisemitism in the Postwar Period: The Case of Friedrich Nieland." Transl. Insa Kummer. In: *Key Documents of German-Jewish History: A Digital Source Edition,* Sept. 22, 2016: https://dx.doi.org/10.23691/jgo:article-113 .en.v1 [Aug. 12, 2024].

———. "Antisemitismus als politisches Ereignis: Die antisemitische Schmierwelle im Winter 1959/1960." In: Bergmann, Erb (eds.), *Antisemitismus in der politischen,* pp. 253–277.

———. "Sind die Deutschen antisemitisch? Meinungsumfragen von 1946–1987 in der Bundesrepublik Deutschland." In: Bergmann, Erb (eds.), *Antisemitismus,* pp. 108–130.

Bergmann, Werner; Erb, Rainer (eds.). *Antisemitismus in der politischen Kultur nach 1945.* Wiesbaden: VS Verlag für Sozialwissenschaften, 1990.

Bergstrøm, Vilhelm. (Lauridsen, John T. [ed.]). *En Borger I Danmark Under Krigen-Dagbog 1939–1945,* vol. 1. Gylling: Gadsforlag. 2005.

"Berichterstatter in Eichmanns Zelle." *Frankfurter Rundschau,* Mar. 3, 1961, p. 16.

Berkhoff, Karel C. "Aussage der Zeugin Dina Proničeva, Kiew. Abschrift eines Auszugs aus dem Protokoll des Darmstädter Prozesses." *Osteuropa,* 2021/1–2, pp. 47–57.

Bernaerts, Arnd. *War Changes Climate: The Naval War Effect.* No place: Trafford, 2006: http://www.warchangesclimate.com/trafford/B.pdf [Mar. 14, 2022].

Bertelsen, Aage. *Oktober 43.* Viborg: Gyldendals Papaerback, 1952.

Beyme, Klaus von. *Bruchstücke der Erinnerung eines Sozialwissenschaftlers.* Wiesbaden: Springer VS, 2016.

Bezwińska, Jadwiga; Czech, Danuta (eds.). *KL Auschwitz Seen by the SS: Rudolf Höss, Pery Broad, Johann Paul Kremer.* Transl. Constantine FritzGibbon, Krystyna Michalik. Oświęcim: The Auschwitz-Birkenau State Museum, 2005.

Biegel, Gerd. *75 "Jahre nach dem Ende des Zweiten Weltkriegs: Introduction and parts*

1–7." Unpublished essay by Prof. Dr. h.c. Gerd Biegel. Material in possession of the author, 2020.

Biermann, Werner. *Konrad Adenauer: Ein Jahrhundertleben.* Berlin: Rowohlt Berlin, 2017.

Bilan, Wladimir. "Excerpt from the Memoirs." In: Setkiewicz, *The SS,* pp. 46–68.

Binder, Magdalena; Duraj, Halina; Duraj, Paweł; Jóźwiak, Bogumił (eds.). *Świadkowie wojny i okupacji.* Poddębice: ARW Prof-Art. Sieradz, 2010.

Birn, Ruth Bettina. "Ein deutscher Staatsanwalt in Jerusalem. Zum Kenntnisstand der Anklagebehörde im Eichmann-Prozess und der Strafverfolgungsbehörden der Bundesrepublik." In: Renz (ed.), *Interessen,* pp. 93–117.

Blessing, Otto. "Kulturpolizei?" *Frankfurter Rundschau,* Dec. 1, 1949, p. 2.

Blüdnikow, Bent; Rothstein, Klaus (eds.). *Dage I oktober 43—Vidnesbyrd.* København: Forlaget Centrum / Det Mosaiske Troessamfund, 1993.

Bockelmann, Paul. "Straflosigkeit für nicht mehr gefährliche Schwerverbrecher?" *Frankfurter Allgemeine Zeitung,* Jan. 23, 1964. No pages. Cited in: Bauer, "Nach den Wurzeln," Feb. 5, 1964, in: Foljanty, Johst (eds.), *Fritz Bauer,* vol. 2, pp. 1160–1167.

Böhler, Jochen. *Auftakt zum Vernichtungskrieg. Die Wehrmacht in Polen 1939. (Die Zeit des Nationalsozialismus).* Frankfurt am Main: Fischer, 2006.

Boker, John R. Jr. "Report of Initial Contacts with General Gehlen's Organization, May 1, 1952." In: Ruffner (ed.), *Forging,* pp. 19–34.

Boll, Monika. "Als politischer Flüchtling anerkannt, als homosexueller observiert— Das dänische Exil." In: Backhaus, Boll, Gross (eds.), *Fritz Bauer,* pp. 51–73.

Bönisch, Georg; Latsch, Gunther; Wiegrefe, Klaus. "Unrühmliche Rolle." *Der Spiegel,* Sept. 16, 2012: https://www.spiegel.de/politik/unruehmliche-rolle-a-ecdf58fd -0002-0001-0000-000088656052?context=issue [Aug. 29, 2024].

"Bonn Observers." *Frankfurter Rundschau,* May 28–29, 1960, p. 2.

Bor, Peter. *Gespräche mit Halder.* Wiesbaden: Limes Verlag, 1950.

Bormuth, Maria. *"Ein Mann, der mit einem anderen Mann Unzucht treibt [. . .], wird mit Gefängnis bestraft."* Celle: Stiftung niedersächsische Gedenkstätten, 2019.

Borowski, Maria; Feddersen, Jan; Gammerl, Benno; Nicolaysen, Rainer; Schmelzer, Christian (eds.). *Jahrbuch Sexualitäten 2017.* Göttingen: Wallstein Verlag, 2017.

Borries, Bodo von. "The Third Reich in German History Textbooks since 1945." *Journal of Contemporary History* 2003/38 (1), pp. 45–62.

"Böse Erinnerungen." *Der Spiegel,* Apr. 3, 1956: https://www.spiegel.de/politik/boese -erinnerungen-a-ef2aa1ad-0002-0001-0000-000031882318?context=issue [Jan. 20, 2022].

Böttcher, Hans-Ernst. "Richard Schmid: Ein Radikaler im öffentlichen Dienst." In: Fröhlich, Kohlstruck (eds.), *Engagierte,* pp. 143–153.

Bourhis Le, Eric; Tcherneva, Irina; Voisin, Vanessa (eds.). *Seeking Accountability for Nazi and War Crimes in East and Central Europe: A People's Justice?* Suffolk: Boydell & Brewer, 2022.

Bower, Thomas M. *The Pledge Betrayed. America and Britain and the Denazification of Post-War Germany.* New York: Doubleday, 1982.

Braese, Stephan; Gehle, Holger; Kiesel, Doron; Loew, Hanno. (eds.). *Deutsche Nachkriegsliteratur und der Holocaust.* Frankfurt am Main / New York: Campus Verlag, 1998.

Brandt, Willy. *Links und frei: Mein Weg 1930–1950.* Hamburg: Hofmann und Campe, 1982.

"Braunschweig ist der grösste Landgerichtsbezirk." *Braunschweiger Presse:* Nov. 5, 1949, p. 3.

"Braunschweiger Richter bedroht." *Hannoversche Presse*, Mar. 19, 1952, p. 1.

Bregenzer, Albrecht; Pötzel, Norbert; Ruggaber, Lotte (eds.). *Unser Land und seine Sozialdemokraten: Die Sozialdemokratie in Baden und Württemberg.* Stuttgart: SPD-Landesverband Baden Württemberg, 1980.

Breitman, Richard (ed.). *German History in Documents and Images.* Vol. 7: *Nazi Germany, 1933–1945*, document 6, no date: https://germanhistorydocs.ghi-dc.org/ sub_doclist.cfm?sub_id=173&section_id=13 [July 24, 2024].

———. *U.S. Intelligence and the Nazis.* Cambridge: Cambridge University Press, 2005.

Breyer, Wolfgang. *Dr. Max Merten—Ein Militärbeamter der deutschen Wehrmacht im Spannungsfeld zwischen Legende und Wahrheit.* Mannheim: Universität Mannheim Philosophische Fakultät, 2003.

Bringer, Carl. " 'Der General'—Erinnerungen an Fritz Bauer" In: Backhaus, Boll, Gross (eds.), *Fritz Bauer,* pp. 209–211.

Brink, Cornelia. *Auschwitz in der Paulskirche: Erinnerungspolitik in Fotoausstellungen der 60er Jahre.* Marburg: Jonas Verlag, 2000.

———. "Das Auschwitz-Album vor Gericht." In: Wojak (ed.), *Auschwitz-Prozess,* pp. 148–156.

Broad, Pery. "Reminiscences." In: Bezwińska, Czech (eds.), *KL Auschwitz,* pp. 103–148.

Brockhaus, F. A. *Der Neue Brockhaus: Allbuch in fünf Bänden und einem Atlas.* Vol. 1, A–D. 3rd ed. Wiesbaden: F. A. Brockhaus, 1958.

Brown, Timothy Scott. *West Germany and the Global Sixties: The Antiauthoritarian Revolt, 1962–1978.* Cambridge: Cambridge University Press, 2013.

Browning, Christopher R. *Ordinary Men: Reserve Police Battalion 101 and the Final Solution in Poland.* New York: HarperPerennial, 1998.

Brüggemann, Jens. *Männer von Ehre? Die Wehrmachtgeneralität im Nürnberger Prozess 1945/46. Zur Entstehung einer Legende.* Paderborn: Verlag Ferdinand Schöningh, 2018.

Bruun-Petersen, Jens; Poulsen, John. *Internationale tog Via Jylland.* Smørum: Bane Bøger, 2002.

Buber, Martin. (Friedman, Maurice [ed.]). *The Knowledge of Man: Selected Essays.* Transl. Maurice Friedman, Ronald Gregor Smith. New York: Harper & Row, 1965.

"Buchbesprechung, Fritz Bauer: 'Krigsförbrytarna infördomstol.' " *Politische Information,* Oct. 15, 1944. No pages.

Buchwitz, Otto. *50 Jahre Funktionär der deutschen Arbeiterbewegung.* Berlin: Dietz Verlag, 1949.

Buck, Meike. "Der 20. Juli vor Gericht: Der Prozess gegen Otto Ernst Remer vor dem Braunschweiger Landgericht 1952." In: Graf, Fiedler, Hermann (eds.), *75 Jahre,* pp. 104–107.

Bundesregierung Bonn (ed.). *Die antisemitischen und nazistischen Vorfälle: Weissbuch und Erklärung der Bundesregierung.* Bundesregierung: Bonn, 1960.

Burghardt, Boris. "Vor 60 Jahren: Fritz Bauer und der Braunschweiger Remer-Prozess; Ein Strafverfahren als Vehikel der Geschichtspolitik." *Journal der Juristischen Zeitgeschichte* 2012/6 (2), pp. 47–59.

Burkhardt, Bernd. "Hitler = Krieg: Jugend im Widerstand—die Stuttgarter Gruppe 'G.' " In: Fuchs (ed.), *Stuttgart . . . Anpassung,* pp. 379–387.

Buschke, Heiko. "Der Braunschweiger Remer-Prozess 1952." In: Buschke (ed.), *Deutsche,* pp. 187–209.

Buschke, Heiko (ed.). *Deutsche Presse, Rechtsextremismus und nationalsozialistische Vergangenheit in der Ära Adenauer.* Frankfurt am Main / New York: Campus Verlag, 2003.

Cervini, Eric. *The Deviant's War: The Homosexuals vs. The United States of America.* New York: Farrar, Straus and Giroux, 2020. Ebook.

Cesarani, David. *After Eichmann: Collective Memory and the Holocaust Since 1961.* London & New York: Routledge, 2005.

———. *Becoming Eichmann: Rethinking the Life, Crimes, and Trial of a "Desk Murderer."* Cambridge: Da Capo Press, 2004.

Cesarani, David; Sundquist, Eric J. (eds.). *After the Holocaust: Challenging the Myth of Silence.* London & New York: Routledge, 2011.

Chare, Nicolas; Williams, Dominic. *Matters of Testimony: Interpreting the Scrolls of Auschwitz.* New York / Oxford: Berghahn Books, 2015.

Chen, Yossi. *Clouds and Winds but No Rain: After Unpunished Nazi Criminals.* No place: Mossad Historical Department, 2007.

Christensen, Claus Bundgård; Olesen, Niels Wium; Lund, Joachim; Sørensen, Jakob. *Danmark besat—Krig og hverdag 1940–45:* Copenhagen: Informations Forlag, 2012.

Christensen, Poul. "Likvideringen af en stikker," no date. Lokalhistorie fra Nordvestfyn: https://www.poulc-strib.dk/likvideringen-af-en-stikker/ [July 17, 2024].

Čirkić, Jasmina. *Rotwelsch in der deutschen Gegenwartssprache.* PhD thesis. Johannes Gutenberg Universität Mainz, 2006.

Clausen, Thomas; Larsen, Leif. *De Forrådte—Tyske Hitlerflygtninge I Danmark:.* Denmark: Gyldendal, 1997.

Cohen, Boaz. "Rachel Auerbach, Yad Vashem and Israeli Holocaust Memory." *Polin: Studies in Polish Jewry,* 2007/20, pp. 121–197: https://www.researchgate.net/profile/Boaz-Cohen-2/publication/333683232_Rachel_Auerbuch_Yad_Vashem_and_Israeli_Holocaust_Memory_Polin_Studies_in_Polish_Jewry_20_121-197/links/5dcbb5cba6fdcc57504408fd/Rachel-Auerbuch-Yad-Vashem-and-Israeli-Holocaust-Memory-Polin-Studies-in-Polish-Jewry-20-121-197.pdf?origin=publication_detail [May 10, 2021].

Cohen-Abravanel, Shlomo. *Art Undercover.* Tel Aviv: Center for Special Studies in Memory of the Fallen of the Israel Intelligence Community, 1995.

Conze, Eckart. *Das Amt und die Vergangenheit: Deutsche Diplomaten im Dritten Reich und in der Bundesrepublik.* München: Blessing, 2010.

Cowell, Alan. "Oskar Gröning, the 'Bookkeeper of Auschwitz,' Is Dead at 96." *The New York Times,* Mar. 12, 2018: https://www.nytimes.com/2018/03/12/obituaries/oskar-groning-the-bookkeeper-of-auschwitz-is-dead-at-96.html [July 6, 2024].

Creuzberger, Stefan; Geppert, Dominik (eds.). *Die Ämter und ihre Vergangenheit: Ministerien und Behörden im geteilten Deutschland 1949–1972.* Paderborn: Brill / Schöningh, 2018.

Critchfield, James H. *Partners at the Creation: The Men Behind Postwar Germany's Defense and Intelligence Establishments.* Maryland: Naval Institute Press, 2003.

Dähnhardt, Willy; Nielsen, Birgit S. "Einleitung: Dänemark als Asylland." In: Dähnhardt, Nielsen (eds.), *Exil,* pp. 14–54.

Dähnhardt, Willy; Nielsen, Birgit S. (eds.). *Exil in Dänemark: Deutschsprachige*

Wissenschaftler, Künstler und Schriftsteller im dänischen Exil. Heide: Boyens Medien, 1993.

Dan, Uri. "Bonn Wants Eichmann's Testimony in Preparation for the 'Auschwitz Trial.'" *Maariv,* Oct. 22, 1961. No pages.

Danielsen, Niels, J. *Dansk viden om Holocaust—Belyst gennem en undersøgelse af udenlandsk radio, svensk presse og danske illegale blade frem til oktober 1943.* MA thesis, Aarhus University, 2004.

Danyel, Jürgen (ed.). *Die geteilte Vergangenheit: Zum Umgang mit Nationalsozialismus und Widerstand in beiden deutschen Staaten.* Berlin: Akademie Verlag, 1995.

"Das ist kein Spass mehr!" *Der Münchner Merkur,* June 25, 1962. No pages. Cited in: Kalb, *Coming,* p. 166.

"Das Wetter." *Stuttgarter Neues Tagblatt,* Mar. 22, 1933, p. 3.

Datner, Szymon. *55 dni Wehrmachtu w Polsce (1.IX—25.X.1939).* Warszawa: Wydawnictwo Ministerstwa Obrony Narodowej, 1967.

Davies, Peter. "Translation and the Language of Testimony: Filip Müller's Testimony at the Frankfurt Auschwitz Trial." *Holocaust Studies: A Journal of Culture and History,* 2021/27 (1), pp. 118–130.

"'Dear Hannah Arendt.'" Correspondence between Leni Yahil and Hannah Arendt, 1961–1971," Sept. 24, 2010. Eurozine: https://www.eurozine.com/dear-hannah -arendt/?_id=loc.mss.eadmss.ms001004&_start=287&_lines=125 [Aug. 5, 2024].

Delmer, Sefton. "Hitler General Now Spying for Dollars." *Daily Express,* Mar. 17, 1952. No pages. Cited in: Kellerhof, von Kostka, *Capital,* pp. 143–144.

Denham, Henry. *Inside the Nazi Ring—a Naval Attache in Sweden 1940–1945.* London: John Murray, 1984.

"Der Goldene Sonntag." *NS-Kurier,* Dec. 18, 1933, p. 8.

"Der Mann muss weg." *Der Spiegel,* Oct. 15, 1957: https://www.spiegel.de/politik/der -mann-muss-weg-a-45f2504b-0002-0001-0000-000041758794 [Oct. 20, 2022].

"Der organisierte Judenmord in Ungarn. Zur Verhaftung des früheren SS-Obersturmbannführers Krumey." *Frankfurter Rundschau,* Apr. 4, 1957. No pages. HHStAW, 461, 33694. Krumey, Hermann u.a.: Handakten, vol. 1, p. 13.

"Der 39. Deutsche Juristentag." *Juristen Zeitung,* Oct. 15, 1951, pp. 663–667: http:// www.jstor.org/stable/20802128 [July 17, 2022].

"Der Vergaser." *Der Spiegel,* Dec. 2, 1958: https://www.spiegel.de/politik/der-vergaser -a-ac504151-0002-0001-0000-000042620985 [June 28, 2023].

"Det fria tyska kulturförbundet." *Aftonbladet,* June 4, 1944, p. 21.

Deutschkron, Inge. (Kosmala, Beate [ed.]). *Auschwitz war nur ein Wort. Berichte über den Frankfurter Auschwitz-Prozess 1963–1965.* Transl. Beate Kosmala. Berlin: Metropol, 2018.

———. *Israel und die Deutschen: Das besondere Verhältnis.* Köln: Verlag Wissenschaft und Politik, 1970.

———. "'It's Horrible, Horrible'—the German Judge Mumbled After Visiting the Auschwitz Museum. The Court's Investigation in the Extermination Camp Made a Great Impression on the German Defense Attorneys, Who Used to Doubt the Guilt of Their Clients." *Maariv,* Dec. 18, 1964. No pages.

———. "'Let's Get Ready for the Selection:' Auschwitz Defendants' Lawyers Joked on Their Way to the Extermination Camp." *Maariv,* Dec. 14, 1964. No pages.

———. "The Auschwitz Passengers Had a Good Time." *Maariv,* Dec. 13, 1964. No pages.

———. "The German Court Is Looking for 'Proofs' in the Death Camp. Judges,

Prosecutors and Defense Attorneys Tour Auschwitz." *Maariv*, Dec. 15, 1964. No pages.

———. "The German Defense Attorney Wept at the Sight of the Piles of Shoes in Auschwitz. The Investigation in the Camp Is Over: The Trial Will Resume in Frankfurt on Monday." *Maariv*, Dec. 17, 1964. No pages.

———. "The Visit to Auschwitz Confirmed the Incriminating Testimonies of the Prosecution's Witnesses. The Nazi's Lawyers Attempt a Delay Tactic. The Prosecutor Confirms 'We Know Where Mengele Is.'" *Maariv*, Dec. 16, 1964. No pages.

Didi-Huberman, Georges. *Images in Spite of All: Four Photographs from Auschwitz*. Tansl. Shane B. Lillis. Chicago: University of Chicago Press, 2008.

"Die Affäre um Dr. Bauer: Der Ausdruck 'jüdischer Amtsrichter' ist eine Beleidigung." *NS-Kurier*, Sept. 26–27, 1931, p. 3.

"Die Deutschen in Schweden: Freie Deutsche erheben ihre Stemme." *Politische Information*, Nov. 15, 1944, pp. 2–3.

"Die Erinnerung der Täter," *Der Spiegel*, Sept. 27, 1998: https://www.spiegel.de/politik/die-erinnerung-der-taeter-a-931ad134-0002-0001-0000-000008001833 [Aug. 29, 2024].

Die Linkspartei PDS (ed.). *Konferenz zum 60. Jahrestag der Befreiung vom Faschismus: Die juristische Aufarbeitung von NS-Verbrechen und deren Widerspiegelung in der Gedenkkultur*. Magdeburg: Die Linkspartei PDS, 2005: https://silo.tips/download/konferenz-zum-60-jahrestag-der-befreiung-vom-faschismus# [Dec. 3, 2022].

Diercks, Herbert; KZ-Gedenkstätte Neuengamme (eds.). *Schuldig: NS-Verbrechen vor deutschen Gerichten—Beiträge zur Geschichte der nationalsozialistischen Verfolgung in Norddeutschland 9*. Bremen: Edition Temmen, 2005.

Dirks, Liane. *Und die Liebe? frag ich sie: Die ungeschriebene Geschichte der Krystyna Zywulska*. Zürich: Ammann Verlag & Co, 1998.

Dittmann, Udo. "Der private Fritz Bauer: Erinnerungen von Rosemarie Ausmeier an Fritz Bauer." *Schriftenreihe des "Fritz Bauer Freundeskreises,"* 2013, pp. 1–11: http://fritz-bauer-freundeskreis.de/wp-content/uploads/2020/11/2013-02-15-Rosemarie-Ausmeier_Erinnerungen-an-Fritz-Bauer.pdf [Apr. 25, 2024].

———. "Fritz Bauer und die Aufarbeitung der NS-'Euthanasie.'" *Forschungsjournal Soziale Bewegungen*, 2015/4 (28), pp. 208–228.

Długoborski, Wacław; Piper, Franciszek (eds.). *Auschwitz 1940–1945. Węzłowe zagadnienia z dziejów obozu*, vols. 1–5. Oświęcim: PMA-B, 1995.

Doerry, Martin; Janssen, Hauke (eds). *Die Spiegel-Affäre: Ein Skandal und seine Folgen*. München: Deutsche Verlags-Anstalt, 2013.

Domagała-Pereira, Katarzyna; Dudek, Bartosz. "'Meine Lebensaufgabe:' Auschwitz vor Gericht." *Deutsche Welle*, Dec. 6, 2019: https://amp.dw.com/de/auschwitz-vor-gericht-meine-lebensaufgabe/a-51554227 [Nov. 12, 2023].

Dönhoff, Marion. "*Gehlens Geheimdienst*." *Die Zeit*, July 26, 1963: https://www.zeit.de/1963/30/gehlens-geheimdienst [Aug. 28, 2024].

Douglas, Lawrence. "Rivka Yoselewska on the Stand: The Structure of Legality and the Construction of Heroic Memory at the Eichmann Trial." In: Freeman, Lewis (eds.), *Law*, pp. 285–300.

"Dr Wolken demaskuje Baretzkiego: Zeznania świadka w procesie oświęcimskim." Journal unknown, Feb. 27, 1964. No pages.

"Dr. Bauer: Keine schematische Strafverfolgung; Braunschweig hat wieder einen Generalstaatsanwalt." *Braunschweiger Presse*, Aug. 2, 1950, p. 7.

"Drei Monate Gefängnis für Remer." *Hannoversche Allgemeine Zeitung,* Mar. 17, 1952, p. 2.

Drummer, Heike; Zwilling, Jutta. "Die Befreiung Frankfurts durch die Amerikaner," Jan. 1, 2012. Institut fuer Stadtgeschichte: https://www.frankfurt1933-1945.de/ beitraege/besatzung/beitrag/die-befreiung-frankfurts-durch-die-amerikaner [Aug. 16, 2024].

Dülffer, Jost; Henke, Klaus-Dietmar; Krieger, Wolfgang; Müller, Rolf-Dieter (eds). *Die Geschichte der Organisation Gehlen und des BND 1945–1968: Umrisse und Einblicke Dokumentation der Tagung am 2. Dezember 2013.* Marburg: Unabhängige Historikerkommission zur Erforschung der Geschichte des Bundesnachrichtendienstes 1945–1968, 2014.

Durrell, Gerald. *The Whispering Land.* London: Penguin Books, 1961.

Dwork, Deborah; van Pelt, Robert Jan. *Auschwitz. 1270 to the Present.* New York: W. W. Norton & Co., 2002.

Edelberg, Peter. *Storbyen trækker—Homoseksualitet, prostitution og pornografi i Danmark 1945–1976.* Copenhagen: Jurist- og Økonomiforbundets Forlag, 2002.

Ehrenburg, Ilja. *Visum der Zeit.* Leipzig: Verlag Philipp Reclam, 1982.

Ehrhardt, Frank (ed.). *Aufbauzeit, Perlonkleid & Tanzvergnügen: Alltag in Braunschweig in den 50er Jahren.* Braunschweig: Arbeitskreis Andere Geschichte e.V., 1998.

Eichmüller, Andreas. "Die juristische Aufarbeitung von NS-Verbrechen in Hessen: Die Ära von Generalstaatsanwalt Fritz Bauer (1956–1968)." *Einsicht 12: Bulletin des Fritz Bauer Institutes,* Herbst 2014, pp. 42–49: https://www.fritz-bauer-institut.de/ publikation/einsicht-12 [May 25, 2024].

———. "Die Strafverfolgung von NS-Verbrechen durch westdeutsche Justizbehörden seit 1945. Eine Zahlenbilanz." *Vierteljahrshefte für Zeitgeschichte,* 2008/56 (4), pp. 621–640.

"Eine Million Delikte." *Der Spiegel,* Nov. 28, 1950: https://www.spiegel.de/politik/eine -million-delikte-a-a2566ad0-0002-0001-0000-000044451207?context=issue [Aug. 26, 2024].

"Ein Prozess als Herausforderung zum Nachdenken." *Darmstädter Echo,* Apr. 30, 1964. No pages. Cited in: Stengel, *Hermann Langbein,* p. 522.

Einsele, Helga. "Worte der Erinnerung." In: Oberstaatsanwaltschaft, Frankfurt am Main Oberlandesgericht (ed.), *Fritz Bauer,* pp. 19–22.

"Ein Sonntag zum Spazierengehen." *Ludwigsburger Kreiszeitung,* Feb. 27, 1933. No pages.

Einstein, Walter; Bauer, Fritz. Note on founding Juedischer Jugendring in Stuttgart. *Gemeinde-Zeitung für die israelitischen Gemeinden Württembergs,* Apr. 18, 1930, p. 26.

"Ein unbedeutender Mann." *Der Spiegel,* Feb. 15, 1961: https://www.spiegel.de/spiegel/ print/d-43159747.html [July 7, 2020].

"Er beharrt darauf, dass sein Antrieb Recht, nicht Rache ist." *Süddeutsche Zeitung,* Dec. 20, 2013: https://www.sueddeutsche.de/politik/fritz-bauer-holocaust-1 .1848015-2 [Feb. 21, 2023].

"Ergebnisse des einzelnen Wahlbezirke in Ludwigsburg und der Bezirksgemeinden." *Ludwigsburger Kreiszeitung,* Mar. 5, 1933. No pages.

"Ermittlungsverfahren." *Frankfurter Rundschau,* Jan. 6, 1961. No pages.

"Fahndung nach Eichmann-Mitarbeiter." *Frankfurter Allgemeine Zeitung,* Jan. 28, 1961/24, p. 3.

Fairweather, Jack. *The Volunteer: One Man, an Underground Army, and the Secret Mission to Destroy Auschwitz*. New York: HarperCollins Publishers, 2019.

Falk, Georg D. *Entnazifizierung und Kontinuität: Der Wiederaufbau der hessischen Justiz am Beispiel des Oberlandesgerichts Frankfurt am Main*. Marburg: Historische Kommission für Hessen, 2017.

"Feindliches Ausland." *Der Spiegel*, July 30, 1995: https://www.spiegel.de/politik/feindliches-ausland-a-35891a2a-0002-0001-0000-000009205805?context=issue [Apr. 7, 2024].

Felfe, Heinz. *Im Dienst des Gegners*. Berlin: Verlag der Nation, 1988.

Felstiner, John. *Paul Celan: Poet, Survivor, Jew*. New Haven / London. Yale University Press, 2001.

Feltrinelli, Carlo. "Il racconto: Il libro segreto sul nazismo di Feltrinelli." *La Reppublica*, Mar. 11, 2022: https://www.repubblica.it/cultura/2022/03/10/news/il_racconto_il_libro_segreto_sul_nazismo_di_feltrinelli-340931336/ [Dec. 6, 2022].

———. *Senior Service*. No place: Feltrinelli, 2014. Ebook.

Ferencz, Benjamin B. "Letter to the Editor." *The New York Times*, Aug. 29, 1965. No pages.

Foljanty, Lena; Johst, David (eds.). *Fritz Bauer: Kleine Schriften (1921–1961)*, vols. 1–2. Frankfurt am Main / New York: Campus Verlag, 2018.

Förster, Jürgen. "Wehrmacht, Krieg und Holocaust." In: Müller, Volkmann (eds.), *Die Wehrmacht*, pp. 948–966.

Foth, Carlos. "Die Nürnberger Gesetze und der Globke-Prozeß in der DDR." *Bulletin für Faschismus- und Weltkriegsforschung: Die Nürnberger Prinzipien—ein Umbruch im Völkerrecht*, 2006/27, pp. 44–70.

———. "Günther Wieland und die internationale Abteilung beim Generalstaatsanwalt der DDR." In: Wieland, *Naziverbrechen*, pp. 394–439.

———. "Mein Anteil an der Ahndung von NS-Straftaten." In: Die Linkspartei PDS (ed.), *Konferenz zum 60. Jahrestag*, no pages.

Foth, Carlos; Ender, Gerhard. *Staatsanwälte zur Übergabe der Globke-Dokumente: Ein Beitrag aus dem Archiv des Deutschen Fernsehfunks, dem ehemaligen staatlichen Fernsehen der DDR*, Jan. 19, 1961: https://www.ardmediathek.de/video/aktuelle-kamera/staatsanwaelte-zur-bergabe-der-globke-dokumente/ard-de/Y3JpZDovL2hyLW9ubGluZS8xMTY0ODk/ [Apr. 5, 2021].

"Frankfurter Spiegel." *Frankfurter Rundschau*, Mar. 1, 1956, p. 3.

Franz, Corinna. "Prinzipien und Pragmatismus: Konrad Adenauers Umgang mit der NS-Vergangenheit." In: Creuzberger, Geppert (eds.), *Die Ämter*, pp. 17–45.

Frederick, Hans. *Das Ende einer Legende: Die abenteuerlichen Erlebnisse des Towaritsch Alexander Busch*. München: Politisches Archiv, 1971.

Freeman, Michael; Lewis, Andrew (eds.). *Law and Literature: Current Legal Issues 1999*, vol. 2. Oxford: Oxford University Press, 1999.

Frei, Norbert. *Adenauer's Germany and the Nazi Past*. New York: Columbia University Press, 1983.

Freimüller, Tobias. *Frankfurt und die Juden: Neuanfänge und Fremdheitserfahrungen 1945–1990*. Göttingen: Wallstein Verlag, 2020.

Frieze, Donna-Lee (ed.). *Totally Unofficial: The Autobiography of Raphael Lemkin*. New Haven / London: Yale University Press, 2013.

Fritz Bauer Institut und Staatliches Museum Auschwitz-Birkenau (eds.). *Der Auschwitz-Prozess. Tonbandmitschnitte, Protokolle und Dokumente*. Direktmedia Verlag: 2004. DVD.

Fritzsche, Peter. *Hitler's First Hundred Days: When Germans Embraced the Third Reich.* New York: Basic Books, 2020. Ebook.

Fröhlich, Claudia. "Der Braunschweiger Remer-Prozess 1952: Zum Umgang mit dem Widerstand gegen den NS-Staat in der frühen Bundesrepublik." In: Diercks, KZ-Gedenkstätte Neuengamme (ed.), *Schuldig,* pp. 17–28.

———. "Remigration und Neuanfang: Fritz Bauer als Richter und Generalstaatsanwalt in Braunschweig 1949–1956." In: Backhaus, Boll, Gross (eds.), *Fritz Bauer,* pp. 127–144.

———. *"Wider die Tabuisierung des Ungehorsams": Fritz Bauers Widerstandsbegriff und die Aufarbeitung von NS-Verbrechen.* Frankfurt am Main: Campus Verlag, 2006.

Fröhlich, Claudia; Kohlstruck, Michael (eds.). *Engagierte Demokraten: Vergangenheitspolitik in kritischer Absicht.* Münster: Westfälisches Dampfboot, 1999.

"Früherer hoher SS-Führer aus Korbach in Haft: Verdacht der Beihilfe zum Mord an 400.000 Juden." *Frankfurter Neue Presse,* Apr. 4, 1957. No pages. HHStAW, 461, 33694. Krumey, Hermann u.a.: Handakten, vol. 1, p. 16.

Fuchs, Karlheinz. "Arbeitslosigkeit in Stuttgart." In: Fuchs (ed.), *Stuttgart . . . Die Machtergreifung,* pp. 267–271.

———. "Auseinandersetzungen in Stuttgart." In: Fuchs (ed.), *Stuttgart . . . Die Machtergreifung,* pp. 262–265.

———. "Bühne frei fürs Deutsche Volkstum: Die Machtergreifung an den Stuttgarter Theatern." In: Fuchs (ed.), *Stuttgart . . . Die Machtergreifung,* pp. 367–373.

———. "Die 'März-Ereignisse' in der Stuttgarter Presse: Verboten, durchsucht, verhaftet." In: Fuchs (ed.), *Stuttgart . . . Die Machtergreifung,* pp. 355–357.

———. "Die neuen Herren." In: Fuchs (ed.), *Stuttgart . . . Die Machtergreifung,* pp. 316–319.

———. "Im Schweizer Exil." In: Fuchs (ed.), *Stuttgart . . . Anpassung,* p. 410.

———. "Tote waren 'unerwünscht': Das Konzentrationslager Heuberg." In: Fuchs (ed.), *Stuttgart . . . Die Machtergreifung,* pp. 408–422.

———. "Zeugnisse zur Schutzhaft." In: Fuchs (ed.), *Stuttgart . . . Die Machtergreifung,* pp. 399–407.

Fuchs, Karlheinz (ed.). "Am 6. März war es so weit Matthäus Eisenhofers Erinnerungen an die Machtergreifung im Funk." In: Fuchs (ed.), *Stuttgart . . . Die Machtergreifung,* pp. 358–367.

———. *Stuttgart im Dritten Reich: Anpassung, Widerstand, Verfolgung; Die Jahre von 1933 bis 1939.* Stuttgart: Projekt Zeitgeschichte im Kulturamt, 1984.

———. *Stuttgart im Dritten Reich: Die Machtergreifung; Von der republikanischen zur braunen Stadt.* Stuttgart: Projekt Zeitgeschichte im Kulturamt, 1983.

Fulbrook, Mary. *A History of Germany Traces the Dramatic Social, Cultural, and Political Tensions in Germany Since 1918.* No place: John Wiley & Sons, 2011.

———. *Reckonings. Legacies of Nazi Persecution and the Quest for Justice.* Oxford: Oxford University Press, 2018.

G. -Dr, "Världshistorien är världsdomen," [Nov. 1944]. Centrum för Näringslivshistoria. Natur och Kultur, vol. Ö1b, Pressklipp 1920–20, pp. 9–11.

Gańczak, Filip. *Jan Sehn: Tropiciel nazistów.* Wołowiec: Czarne, 2020.

Gańczak, Filip; Litka, Piotr. *Profesor Jan Sehn 1909–1965: Prawnik, sędzia śledczy, łowca nazistów.* Warszawa: IPN, Instytut Ekspertyz Sądowych, 2019.

Garland, Patrick V. "Anatomy of a Murder." *Military Police,* Spring 2010, pp. 37–44: https://docslib.org/doc/6111700/military-police-an-of-cial-u-s [Sept. 23, 2022].

Garvey, Kerry J. *The Byline of Europe: An Examination of Foreign Correspondents' Reporting from 1930 to 1941.* PhD thesis. Illinois State University, 2017: https://ir .library.illinoisstate.edu/cgi/viewcontent.cgi?article=1671&context=etd [July 17, 2024].

"Gefängnis in der Büchsenstrasse, Stuttgart," 2018. Hotel Silber: https://virtuell .geschichtsort-hotel-silber.de/das-netz-der-gestapo/stuttgart/gefaengnis-in-der -buechsenstrasse/ [Mar. 7, 2022].

Gehlen, Reinhard. *Der Dienst: Erinnerungen 1942–1971.* Mainz: v. Hase & Koehler, 1971.

———. *The Service: The Memoirs of General Reinhard Gehlen.* Transl. David Irving. New York: World Publishing, 1972.

Gellhorn, Martha. "Eichmann and the Private Conscience." *The Atlantic Monthly,* Feb. 1962: https://www.theatlantic.com/past/docs/issues/62feb/eichmann.htm [Apr. 27, 2024].

"Genickschüsse an der 'schwarzen Wand' des Lagers Auschwitz." *Abendpost,* Jan. 1, 1964. No pages.

"Gennem byen—efterhaanden stigende temperatur." *Aftenbladet (København),* June 1, 1935, p. 2.

Gerlach, Adolf. "Ein jüdischer Amtsrichter missbraucht sein Amt zu Parteizwecken/ Der 'Informator' der Tagwacht." *NS-Kurier,* June 5, 1931, p. 3.

Gerlach, Christian. "Männer des 20. Juli und der Krieg gegen die Sowjetunion." In: Heer, Hannes; Naumann, Klaus (eds.). *Vernichtungskrieg: Verbrechen der Wehrmacht 1941–1944.* Hamburg: Hamburger Edition, 1997.

"German observers." *Frankfurter Allgemeine Zeitung,* May 28, 1960, p. 1.

Geyer, Hans-Joachim. *Am Anfang stand das Ende.* Berlin: Kongress Verlag, 1954.

Gieseke, Jens. *The History of the Stasi: East Germany's Secret Police, 1945–1990.* Transl. David Burnett. New York / Oxford: Berghahn Books, 2014.

Gilbert, Martin. *Auschwitz and the Allies.* New York: Henry Holt & Company, 1982.

Glienke, Stephan A. "Die Ausstellung 'Ungesühnte Nazijustiz' 1960 in Berlin im Spannungsfeld von Aufarbeitung und Kaltem Krieg." Aktives Museum, Berlin. *Mitglieder-Rundbrief* 83, Aug. 2020, pp. 8–16.

———. *Die Ausstellung "Ungesühnte Nazijustiz" (1959–1962): Zur Geschichte der Aufarbeitung nationalsozialistischer Justizverbrechen.* Baden-Baden: Nomos Verlagsgesellschaft, 2008.

———. "Die Ausstellung Ungesühnte Nazijustiz (1959–1962)." In: Weisbrod, Bernd (ed.). *Demokratische Übergänge: Das Ende der Nachkriegszeit und die neue Verantwortung. Tagungsdokumentation der Jahrestagung des Zeitgeschichtlichen Arbeitskreises Niedersachsen, Göttingen, 26./27. November 2004.* Göttingen: Universität Göttingen, 2005, pp. 31–37.

Globke, Hans. "Aufzeichnung," 1956. Cited in: Hehl, "Der Beamte," in: Gotto (ed.), *Der Staatssekretär,* pp. 247–259.

"Globke: Ein zweiter Fall Felfe nicht möglich." *Welt am Sonntag,* July 14, 1963, p. 1.

"Globke und die Juden. [Interview]." *Der Spiegel,* May 9, 1961: https://www.spiegel.de/ politik/globke-und-die-juden-a-bbc1e15b-0002-0001-0000-000043161087 [Nov. 18, 2022].

Glotz, Peter; Langenbucher, Wolfgang R. (eds.). *Vorbilder für Deutsche: Korrektur einer Heldengalerie.* München: R. Piper & Co. Verlag, 1974.

Gmünder, Bruno (ed.). *Frankfurt Offenbach Mainz Wiesbaden von hinten: Lese- und*

Reisebuch für Schwule, Gays und andere Freunde. Berlin: bruno gmünder verlag, 1984.

Gnielka, Thomas. "Die Henker von Auschwitz: Ein Prozess und seine Vorgeschichte." *Metall,* 1961/16, p. 6.

Godau-Schüttke, Klaus-Detlev. *Die Heyde-Sawade-Affäre: Wie Juristen und Mediziner den NS-Euthanasieprofessor Heyde nach 1945 deckten und straflos blieben.* Baden-Baden: Nomos Verlag, 1998.

"Gøg and Gokk paaèn igen." *Politiken,* June 5, 1935, p. 20.

Goldhagen, Daniel Jonah. *Hitler's Willing Executioners: Ordinary Germans and the Holocaust.* New York: Vintage, 1997.

Goñi, Uki. *The Real Odessa: How Nazi War Criminals Escaped Europe.* London: Granta Publications, 2022.

Goschler, Constantin; Wala, Michael. *"Keine neue Gestapo": Das Bundesamt für Verfassungsschutz und die NS-Vergangenheit.* Reinbeck bei Hamburg: Rowohlt Verlag, 2015.

Gotto, Klaus (ed.). *Der Staatssekretär Adenauers: Persönlichkeit und Wirken Hans Globkes.* Stuttgart: Klett-Cotta, 1980.

Gouri, Haim. *Facing the Glass Booth: The Jerusalem Trial of Adolf Eichmann.* Transl. Michael Swirsky. Detroit: Wayne State University Press, 2004.

Grabitz, Helge (ed.). *Die Normalität des Verbrechens: Bilanz und Perspektiven der Forschung zu den nationalsozialistischen Gewaltverbrechen; Festschrift für Wolfgang Scheffler zum 65. Geburtstag.* Berlin: Ed. Hentrich, 1994.

Graf, Sabine; Fiedler, Gudrun; Hermann, Michael (eds.). *75 Jahre Niedersachsen: Einblicke in seine Geschichte anhand von 75 Dokumenten.* Göttingen: Wallstein 2021.

Grebing, Helga (ed.). *Lehrstücke in Solidarität: Briefe u. Biographien dt. Sozialisten 1945–1949.* Stuttgart: Deutsche Verlags-Anstalt, 1983.

Greif, Gideon. *We Wept Without Tears: Testimonies of the Jewish Sonderkommando from Auschwitz.* New Haven / London: Yale University Press, 2005.

Grieben Reiseführer Band 58. *Kopenhagen und Umgebung.* Berlin: Grieben-Verlag, 1936.

Grigg, Joseph. W. " 'Fuehrer' Says U.S. Policies Bound to Fail." *The Washington Post,* Mar. 31, 1952, p. 2.

Groenewold, Kurt; Ignor, Alexander; Koch, Arnd (eds.). *Lexikon der Politischen Strafprozesse,* 2018: https://www.lexikon-der-politischen-strafprozesse.de/glossar/eichmann-adolf/ [Jan. 5, 2022].

Grunenberg, Nina. "Der merkwürdige Fall Heyde." *Die Zeit,* Feb. 21, 1964. No pages.

Gumber, Karl. "Hans Globke—Anfänge und erste Jahre im Bundeskanzleramt." In: Gotto (ed.), *Der Staatssekretär,* pp. 73–98.

Gutmark, Jacob; Streich, Brigitte; Ulrich, Axel. "Die Deportation der Wiesbadener Juden." In: Ulrich, Streich (eds.), *Gedenkort,* pp. 22–31.

Haag, Lina. Eine Handvoll Staub. *Widerstand einer Frau 1933–1945.* Frankfurt am Main: Fischer, 1995.

Hachmann, Horst. "Schwerer Zusammenstoss beim Auschwitz-Prozess." *Frankfurter Rundschau,* Apr. 7, 1964. No pages. Cited in: Pendas, *The Frankfurt,* p. 163.

Hachmeister, Lutz. *Der Gegnerforscher: Die Karriere des SS-Führers Franz Alfred Six.* München: C. H Beck, 1998.

Hafner, Georg M.; Schapira, Esther. *Die Akte Alois Brunner: Warum einer der grössten*

Naziverbrecher noch immer auf freiem Fuss ist. Frankfurt am Main / New York: Campus Verlag, 2000.

Hahn, Joachim. *Jüdisches Leben in Esslingen: Geschichte, Quellen und Dokumentation.* Esslingen am Neckar: Stadtarchiv, 1994.

Hájková, Anna. "Israeli Historian Otto Dov Kulka Tells Auschwitz Story of a Czech Family That Never Existed." *Tablet Magazine,* Oct. 30, 2014: https://www.tabletmag .com/sections/arts-letters/articles/otto-dov-kulka [Aug. 28, 2024].

"Hakenkreuz-Plakate sichergestellt." *Frankfurter Rundschau,* June 1963. No pages. Cited in: Wojak, *Fritz Bauer,* p. 440.

Halder, Franz. *Kriegstagebuch,* vols. 1–3. Stuttgart: Kohlhammer, 1962–1964.

Hammer, Walter. *Musste das sein? Vom Leidensweg der aus Dänemark ausgelieferten deutschen Emigranten.* Brandenburg: W. Hammer, 1948.

Hancock, Eleanor. " 'Only the Real, the True, the Masculine Held Its Value': Ernst Röhm, Masculinity, and Male Homosexuality." *Journal of the History of Sexuality,* 1998/8 (4), pp. 616–641.

"Handvoll Asche." *Der Spiegel,* Feb. 18, 1964: https://www.spiegel.de/politik/handvoll -asche-a-b5c08400-0002-0001-0000-000046163172 [Nov. 4, 2022].

Haneke, Alexander. "Der Richter und sein Geheimnis." *Frankfurter Allgemeine Zeitung,* Mar. 31, 2019, p. 5.

Hansen, Niels. *Aus dem Schatten der Katastrophe: Die deutsch-israelischen Beziehungen in der Ära Adenauer und David Ben Gurion.* Düsseldorf: Droste, 2002.

"Hans Globke." *Der Spiegel,* Feb. 18, 1973: https://www.spiegel.de/politik/hans-globke -a-708b24bb-0002-0001-0000-000042650973?context=issue [Aug. 26, 2024].

Harding, Thomas. *Hanns and Rudolf: The German Jew and the Hunt for the Kommandant of Auschwitz.* Great Britain: Random House, 2013. Ebook.

———. "Hiding in N. Virginia, a Daughter of Auschwitz." *The Washington Post,* Sept. 7, 2013: https://www.washingtonpost.com/lifestyle/magazine/hiding-in -n-virginia-a-daughter-of-auschwitz/2013/09/06/1314d648-04fd-11e3-a07f -49ddc7417125_story.html [July 17, 2024].

Harel, Isser. *The House on Garibaldi Street.* Abingdon: Routledge, 2013. Ebook.

Harlan, Thomas. "Fritz Bauer und die Erziehung der Deutschen zur Mündigkeit." *Forschungsjournal Soziale Bewegungen,* 2015/4 (28), pp. 282–288.

———. *Heldenfriedhof.* Frankfurt: Eichborn, 2006.

———. *Hitler war meine Mitgift: Ein Gespräch mit Jean-Pierre Stephan.* Reinbeck: Rowohlt Taschenbuch Verlag, 2011.

———. *Veit.* Reinbek bei Hamburg: Rowohlt Verlag, 2011.

"Harlan Junior: 'Ich Will zu den Juden.' " *AJR Information,* June 1955, p. 3: https://ajr .org.uk/wp-content/uploads/2018/02/1955_june.pdf [July 16, 2024].

Hastings, Max. *The Secret War: Spies, Codes and Guerrillas 1939–1945.* New York: HarperCollins, 2016.

Hausner, Gideon. *Justice in Jerusalem.* New York: Schocken Books, 1966.

Hechelhammer, Bodo. "Die 'Dossiers': Reinhard Gehlens geheime Sonderkartei." In: Dülffer et al. (eds), *Die Geschichte,* pp. 83–92.

———. *Spion ohne Grenzen: Heinz Felfe: Agent in sieben Geheimdiensten.* München: Piper, 2019.

Hechelhammer, Bodo; Meinl, Susanne. *Geheimobjekt Pullach: Von der NS- Mustersiedlung zur Zentrale des BND.* Berlin: Chr. Links, 2014.

Hedtoft, Hans. "Introduktion." In: Bertelsen, Aage. *Oktober 43.* Viborg: Gyldendals Paperback, 1952, pp. 7–9.

Hehl von, Ulrich. "Der Beamte im Reichsinnenministerium: Die Beurteilung Globkes in der Diskussion der Nachkriegszeit Eine Dokumentation." In: Gotto (ed.), *Der Staatssekretär*, pp. 230–282.

Heidenreich, Ronny; Münkel, Daniela; Stadelmann-Wenz, Elke. *Geheimdienstkrieg in Deutschland: Die Konfrontation von DDR-Staatssicherheit und Organisation Gehlen 1953*. Berlin: Ch. Links Verlag, 2016.

Heimsath, Katja. *"Trotz allem glaube ich an das Gute im Menschen": Das Tagebuch der Anne Frank und seine Rezeption in der Bundesrepublik Deutschland*. Hamburg: Hamburg University Press, 2013.

Heitefuss, Dieter. *Braunschweig: Gestern und Heute; Städtebauliche Veränderungen in 65 Jahren: Fachwerkstadt—Kriegszerstörungen—Wiederaufbau*. Braunschweig: Verlag Dieter Heitefuss, 1993.

Helfer, Martha B.; Donahue, William Collins (eds.). *Nexus 3: Essays in German Jewish Studies*. New York: Boydell & Brewer. Camden House, 2017.

Hemi, Yosef; Lahis, Noa (eds.). *Bureau 06: The Investigation of Adolf Eichmann in the Israel Police*. Jerusalem: Israel Police, 2020.

Henke, Klaus-Dietmar. *Geheime Dienste: Die politische Inlandsspionage der Organisation Gehlen 1946–1953*. Berlin: Ch. Links, 2018.

———. *Geheime Dienste: Die politische Inlandsspionage des BND in der Ära Adenauer*. Berlin: Ch. Links, 2022.

Henne, Thomas; Riedlinger, Arne (eds.). *Das Lüth-Urteil aus (rechts-) historischer Sicht: Die Konflikte um Veit Harlan und die Grundrechtsjudikatur des Bundesverfassungsgerichts*. Berlin: Berliner Wissenschafts-Verlag, 2005.

Herbert, Ulrich. *Best: Biographische Studien über Radikalismus, Weltanschauung und Vernunft*. München: C. H. Beck, 2016.

Herman, Ora. *The Furnace and the Reactor: Behind the Scenes at the Eichmann Trial*. Tel Aviv: Hakibbutz Hameuchad, 2017.

Hertel, Hans (ed). *Tilbageblik på 30'erne—Litteratur, teater, kulturdebat 1930–39—en antologi*. Copenhagen: Aschehoug, 1997.

Heska-Kwaśniewicz, Krystyna; Sadzikowska, Lucyna (eds.). *Głosy z "ostatniego kręgu": Korespondencja z Konzentrationslager Auschwitz Józefa Kreta i Zofii Hoszowskiej-Kretowej*. Katowice: Studio NOA, 2000.

Hess, Annette. *W niemieckim domu*. Transl. Barbara Niedźwiecka. Kraków: Wydawnictwo Literackie, 2019.

Hett, Benjamin Carter. *The Death of Democracy: Hitler's Rise to Power and the Downfall of the Weimar Republic*. New York: Henry Holt and Co., 2018.

Hett, Benjamin Carter; Wala, Michael. *Otto John: Patriot oder Verräter; Eine deutsche Biographie*. Hamburg: Rowohlt, 2019. Ebook.

Hickok, Guy. "Nazi Camp Prisoners Begin to Complain." *The Brooklyn Daily Eagle*, Apr. 9, 1933, pp. 1, 12.

Hirschfeld, Gerhard (ed.). *The Policies of Genocide*. London: German Historical Institute, 1986.

Hirschfeld, Magnus. *Geschlechtskunde auf Grund dreissigjähriger Forschung und Erfahrung bearbeitet*. Vol. 1: *Die körperseelischen Grundlagen*. Stuttgart: Julius Püttmann Verlagsbuchhandlung, 1926.

Hocke, Gustav René. "Streifzüge durch das neue und alte Hamburg: Verfall und Aufstieg einer Weltstadt." In: Schoeller (ed.), *Diese merkwürdige*, pp. 305–310.

Hoffmann, Friedrich. *Die Verfolgung der nationalsozialistischen Gewaltverbrechen in Hessen*. Baden-Baden: Nomos, 2001.

Hoffmann, Peter. *Stauffenberg: A Family History, 1905–1944*. Montreal / Kingston: McGill-Queen's University Press, 2008. Ebook.

Hoffschildt, Rainer. "140.000 Verurteilungen nach '§ 175.'" *Invertito*, 2002/4, pp. 140–149.

———. *Statistik der Kriminalisierung und Verfolgung homosexueller Handlungen unter Männern durch Justiz und Polizei in der Bundesrepublik Deutschland von der Nachkriegszeit bis 1994*. Hannover: Selbstverlag, 2016.

Hofmann, Kerstin. *"Ein Versuch nur—immerhin ein Versuch": Die Zentrale Stelle in Ludwigsburg unter der Leitung von Erwin Schüle und Adalbert Rückerl (1958–1984)*. Berlin: Metropol, 2018.

Hofmeyer, Hans. "Prozessrechtliche Probleme und Schwierigkeiten bei der Durchführung der Prozesse." In: Ständige Deputation des deutschen Juristentages (ed.). *Verhandlungen des sechsundvierzigsten deutschen Juristentages*. München / Berlin: C. H. Beck, 1967, pp. C38–C44.

Hogenkamp, Susanne. *Die württembergische Sozialdemokratie von 1928 bis 1933/34*. PhD thesis. Universität Stuttgart, 2017: https://elib.uni-stuttgart.de/bitstream/ 11682/9933/3/diss05052018.pdf [Jan. 3, 2022].

Höhne, Heinz; Zolling, Hermann. *Network: The Truth About General Gehlen and His Spy Ring*. London: Secker & Warburg, 1972.

———. *The General Was a Spy: The Truth About General Gehlen and His Spy Ring*. Transl. Martin Secker. London: Pan Books, 1973.

Horstmann, Thomas; Litzinger, Heike (eds.). *An den Grenzen des Rechts: Gespräche mit Juristen über die Verfolgung von NS-Verbrechen, mit einem Vorwort von Micha Brumlik*. Frankfurt am Main / New York: Campus Verlag, 2006.

Höss, Rudolf. *Commandant of Auschwitz*. Transl. Constantine FitzGibbon. London: Phoenix Press, 2000.

Hoyer, Hans-Jürgen. "Ich wusste nicht, was Auschwitz ist." *Frankfurter Rundschau*, Dec. 21, 1963, p. 6.

Hubner-Funk, Sibylle. "Jugend als Symbol des politischen Neubeginns." In: Bergmann, Erb (eds.), *Antisemitismus*, pp. 218–237.

Hürtler, Johannes. *Hitlers Heerführer*. München: Oldenbourg Wissenschaftsverlag GmbH, 2007.

Hütter, Jörg. "'Sie sind ja schon wieder hier!' Ein ehemaliger Rosa-Winkel-Häftling berichtet." *taz Bremen*, June 27–28, 1998: https://www.joerg-hutter.de/karl_b _.htm#The [Aug. 15, 2024].

Hyde, Harford Montgomery (ed.). *The Trials of Oscar Wilde*. London / Edinburgh / Glasgow: Hodge, 1948.

Igounet, Valérie. *Histoire du négationnisme en France*. Paris: Seuil, 2000. Ebook.

"Im Hinterhaus. [Tagebuch]." *Der Spiegel*, Oct. 9, 1956: https://www.spiegel.de/kultur/ im-hinterhaus-a-c35f0a6d-0002-0001-0000-000043064277 [Mar. 7, 2024].

Institut für Demoskopie. *Verjährung von NS-Verbrechen: Ergebnisse einer Schnellumfrage*. Allensbach am Bodensee: Institut für Demoskopie, 1965.

"Ist benachrichtigt." *Der Spiegel*, Apr. 14, 1968: https://www.spiegel.de/politik/ist -benachrichtigt-a-55df460b-0002-0001-0000-000046050198 [Aug. 25, 2024].

Jacobsen, Annie. *Operation Paperclip: The Secret Intelligence Program That Brought Nazi Scientists to America*. New York: Little, Brown & Company, 2015. Ebook.

Jähner, Harald. *Aftermath: Life in the Fallout of the Third Reich, 1945–1955*. Transl. Shaun Whiteside. London: WH Allen, 2021.

Jaide, Walter. *Das Verhältnis der Jugend zur Politik: Empirische Untersuchungen zur politischen Anteilnahme und Meinungsbildung junger Menschen der Geburtsjahrgänge 1940–1946*. Berlin-Spandau: Luchterhand, 1963.

Janssen, Karl-Heinz. "Der Fall John." *Die Zeit*, Sept. 6, 1985: https://www.zeit.de/1985/37/der-fall-john/komplettansicht [Oct. 25 2022].

Jarausch, Konrad H. *After Hitler: Recivilising Germans, 1945–1995*. Transl. Brandon Hunziker. New York: Oxford University Press, 2006.

Jaspers, Karl; Arendt, Hannah (Köhler, Lotte; Saner, Hans [eds.]). *Briefwechsel 1926–1969*. München: Piper, 1985.

Jeffries, Stuart. *Grand Hotel Abyss: The Lives of the Frankfurt School*. London / New York: Verso, 2016.

"Joel Brand, 58, Hungarian Jew in Eichmann's Truck Deal, Dies." *The New York Times*, July 15, 1964. No pages.

Jørgensen, Claus Ingemann. "Ich hätte in Kopenhagen bleiben sollen," 1965. [Interview with Fritz Bauer]. In: Foljanty, Johst (eds.), *Fritz Bauer*, vol. 2, pp. 1333–1338.

"Judgment at Nuremberg." *The Times*, Sept. 30, 1946, p. 4.

Judt, Tony. *Postwar: A History of Europe Since 1945*. London: Penguin Books, 2006.

Junger, Ernst. *Storm of Steel*. London: Penguin, 2004.

Kąkol, Kazimierz. *Sąd nierychliwy: Frankfurcki proces oprawców z Oświęcimia*. Warszawa: Książka i Wiedza, 1966.

Kalb, Martin. *Coming of Age: Constructing and Controlling Youth in Munich, 1942–1973*. New York: Berghahn Books, 2016.

"Kalk von den Wänden." *Der Spiegel*, Oct. 10, 1967: https://www.spiegel.de/politik/kalk-von-den-waenden-a-22990f2f-0002-0001-0000-000046289911 [May 25, 2024].

Kardorff von, Ursula von. *Berliner Aufzeichnungen 1942–1945*. München: C. H. Beck, 1992.

Kästner, Erich. "Streiflichter aus Nürnberg." *Die Neue Zeitung*, Nov. 23, 1945. In: Radlmaier (ed.), *Der Nürnberger*, pp. 65–73.

Kater, Michael H. *After the Nazis: The Story of Culture in West Germany*. New Haven: Yale University Press, 2023.

Kellerhoff, Sven Felix; von Kostka, Bernd. *Capital of Spies: Intelligence Agencies in Berlin During the Cold War*. Havertown: Casemate Publishers, 2021.

Kempner, Robert M. W. "Begegnungen mit Hans Globke: Berlin—Nürnberg—Bonn." In: Gotto (ed.), *Der Staatssekretär*, pp. 213–229.

Kesselring, Agilolf. *Die Organisation Gehlen und die Neuformierung des Militärs in der Bundesrepublik*. Berlin: Ch. Links Verlag, 2017.

Kienle, Markus. *Das Konzentrationslager Heuberg bei Stetten am kalten Markt*. Ulm: Verlag Klemm & Oelschläger, 1998.

Kienzle, Michael; Mende, Dirk. "6 Namen zur Stuttgarter Literatur—Max Barth, Bernhard Blume, Anni Geiger-Gog und Gregor Gog, Paul Wanner, Walter Erich Schäfer." In: Fuchs (ed.), *Stuttgart . . . Die Machtergreifung*, pp. 60–83.

Kieta, Mieczysław. "Po co ten proces-mamut? Mówią obrońcy w procesie oświęcimskim." *Przekrój*, 1965/31 (1060), p. 4.

———. "Proces trwa. Zeznają polscy świadkowie." *Przekrój*, 1964/20 (997), p. 4.

Kilian, Andreas. "Ein leiser Abschied: Zum Gedenken an Filip Müller." *Mitteilungen der Lagergemeinschaft Auschwitz: Freundeskreis der Auschwitzer; Mitteilungsblatt*, 2014/34, pp. 26–39.

Kilp, Maria Anna. *Ach wie ist das Leben schön, Hammelsgasse 6–10. U-Haft in Frankfurt/M 1903–1973*. Frankfurt am Main: Fachhochschule Frankfurt, 1986.

Kinsey, Alfred C. *Sexual Behavior in the Human Male*. Philadelfia / London: W.B. Saunders Company: 1949.

Kirchhoff, Hans; Rünitz, Lone. *Udsendt til Tyskland—Dansk flygtningepolitik under besættelsen*. Odense: Syddansk Universitetsforlag, 2007.

Kjeldbæk, Esben. "Café Mokka—En terrorist aktion." In: Lauridsen (ed.), *Over stregen*, pp. 164–177.

Klamberg, Mark. "Raphaël Lemkin in Stockholm—Significance for His Work on 'Axis Rule in Occupied Europe.'" *Genocide Studies and Prevention: An International Journal*, 2019/13 (1), pp. 64–87.

Klee, Ernst. *Was sie taten—was sie wurden: Ärzte, Juristen und andere Beteiligte am Kranken- oder Judenmord*. Frankfurt am Main: Fischer, 1986.

Klehr, Gebhard. "Arthur Hirsch, vom Unternehmer zum Heizer Hospitalstr. 21 B," no date. Gegen das Vergessen. Stolpersteine für Stuttgart: https://www.stolpersteine -stuttgart.de/index.php?docid=532&mid=30 [Aug. 25, 2021].

Kliem, Peter G.; Noack, Klaus. *Berlin Anhalter Bahnhof*. Frankfurt am Main / Berlin / Wien: Ullstein, 1984.

Klitgaard, Mogens. *Der sidder en mand i en sporvogn*. Copenhagen: Branner, 1937.

Kluge, Alexander. *"Wer ein Wort des Trostes spricht, ist ein Verräter": 48 Geschichten für Fritz Bauer*. Berlin: Suhrkamp, 2013.

Kochanski, Halik. *The Eagle Unbowed: Poland and the Poles in the Second World War*. Cambridge, MA: Harvard University Press, 2014.

Kochavi, Arieh J. *Prelude to Nuremberg: Allied War Crimes Policy and the Question of Punishment*. Chapel Hill: The University of North Carolina Press, 2000. Ebook.

Kolk, Jürgen. *Mit dem Symbol des Fackelreiters: Walter Hammer (1888–1966); Verleger der Jugendbewegung, Pionier der Widerstandsforschung*. PhD thesis. Freie Universität Berlin, 2011.

Komaniecka, Monika. *Pod obserwacją i na podsłuchu: Rzeczowe środki pracy operacyjnej aparatu bezpieczeństwa w województwie krakowskim w latach 1945– 1990*. Kraków: IPN, 2014.

Kopp, Manfred. "Im Labyrinth der Schuld. US Army Interrogation Center in Oberursel, 1945–1952." *Sonderdruck aus dem Jahrbuch des Hochtaunuskreis*, 2010 (18), pp. 232–244: https://www.ursella.info/Sonderdruck/files/Kopp_tot _Hechelma.pdf [Apr. 26, 2022].

Kostka von, Bernd; Kellerhoff, Sven Felix. *Capital of Spies. Intelligence Agencies in Berlin During the Cold War*. Transl. Linden Lyons. Philadelphia / Oxford: Casemate, 2021.

Krabbe, Oluf H. (ed.). *Borgerlig Straffelov af 15. april 1930*. København: G.E.C. Gads forlag, 1931.

Kramer, Helmut. "Als hätten sie nie das Recht gebeugt." *Ossietzky: Zweiwochenschrift für Politik, Kultur, Wirtschaft*, 2002/23: https://web.archive.org/web/201304030 64102/http://sopos.org/aufsaetze/3dde4e00d2bcb/1.phtml [May 30, 2022].

———. "Die NS-Justiz in Braunschweig und ihre Bewältigung ab 1945." In: Kramer (ed.), *Braunschweig*, pp. 29–60.

———. "'Gerichtstag halten wir über uns selbst': Das Verfahren Fritz Bauers zur Beteiligung der Justiz am Anstaltsmord." In: Loewy (ed.), *NS-"Euthanasie,"* pp. 81– 133.

Kramer, Helmut (ed.). *Braunschweig unterm Hakenkreuz: Bürgertum, Justiz und Kirche—Eine Vortragsreihe und ihr Echo.* Braunschweig: Magni-Buchladen, 1981.

Kratz, Philipp. *Eine Stadt und die Schuld: Wiesbaden und die NS-Vergangenheit seit 1945.* Göttingen: Wallstein Verlag, 2019.

Kraus, Michael. "Ota Kraus and Erich Kulka—Contending with the Holocaust: 'To Unmask What Has Happened Here, So That It Can Never Again Be Repeated!'" In: Rauschenberger, Puttkamer von, Steinbacher (eds.), *Investigating,* pp. 172–193.

Krause, Peter. *Der Eichmann-Prozess in der deutschen Presse.* Frankfurt am Main: Campus Verlag, 2002.

Kraushaar, Elmar. "Unzucht vor Gericht: Die 'Frankfurter Prozesse' und die Kontinuität des §175 in den fünfziger Jahren." In: Kraushaar (ed.), *Hundert,* pp. 60–69.

Kraushaar, Elmar (ed.). *Hundert Jahre schwul: Eine Revue.* Berlin: Rowohlt Verlag, 1997.

Kremer, Johann Paul. "Diary." In: Bezwińska, Czech (eds.), *KL Auschwitz,* pp. 149–215.

Kret, Józef. *Ostatni krąg.* Kraków: Wydawnictwo Literackie, 1973.

"Krigsförbrytare hängda i Charkov." *Dagens Nyheter,* Dec. 20, 1943, p. 11.

Kristensen, Tom. *Havoc.* Transl. Carl Malmberg. Introd. Morten Høi Jensen. New York: New York Review Books Classics, 2018. Ebook.

Kröger, Ullrich. *Die Ahndung von NS-Verbrechen vor westdeutschen Gerichten und ihre Rezeption in der deutschen Öffentlichkeit 1958 bis 1965.* Hamburg: Universität Hamburg, 1973.

Krohn, Klaus-Dieter; Mühlen von zur, Patrik; Paul, Gerhard; Winckler, Lutz; Kohlhaas, Elisabeth (eds.). *Handbuch der deutschsprachigen Emigration 1933–1945.* Darmstadt: Wiss. Buchges, 1998.

Kröller, Wilhelm. *Die Chronik der Stadt Wiesbaden über das Schicksalsjahr 1945.* Dezember 1945. Stadtarchiv Wiesbaden NL 72/7.

Krüger, Horst. *Broken House.* Transl. Shaun Whiteside. London: The Bodley Head, 2021.

Kugelmann, Cilly. "Fritz Bauer hinter dem Schwimmbad." In: Rauschenberger (ed.), *Rückkehr,* pp. 217–222.

Kügler, Joachim. "Es hat das Leben verändert." In: Wojak, Meinl (eds.), *Im Labyrinth,* pp. 297–314.

Kuhlbrodt, Dietrich. "'Jud Süss, der antisemitische Paradefilm von 1940: Zugleich ein Fall der Hamburger Nachkriegsjustiz." *Miteilungen des Hamburgischen Richtervereins,* 1991/10. No pages.

Kulka, Erich. "Die Kamera als Kronzeuge." *Die Tat,* Feb. 2, 1963, p. 10.

———. *Soudcové, žalobci, obhájci.* Praha: XYZ, 2019.

Kunde, Karl. *Die Odyssee Eines Arbeiters.* Stuttgart: Edition Cordeliers, 1985.

Kuper, Peter. *Hamlet oder die Liebe zu Amerika.* Berlin: März Verlag, 1982.

Kurz, Jörg. "Mord in Raten—Juden in Stuttgart ab 1933," no date. Gegen das Vergessen. Stolpersteine für Stuttgart: https://www.stolpersteine-stuttgart.de/index.php?docid=191 [Sept. 16, 2021].

Kurz, Thilo. "Paradigmenwechsel bei der Strafverfolgung des Personals in den deutschen Vernichtungslagern?" *Zeitschrift für Internationale Strafrechtsdogmatik,* 2013/8 (3), pp. 122–129: https://www.zis-online.com/dat/artikel/2013_3_739.pdf [May 19, 2024].

Lababut, Benjamín. *When We Cease to Understand the World*. Transl. Adrian Nathan West. London: Pushkin Press, 2020.

Lachendo, Jacek. *Auschwitz After Liberation*. Transl. William Brand. Oświęcim: Auschwitz-Birkenau State Museum, 2018.

Langbein, Hermann. *Auschwitz przed sądem: Proces we Frankfurcie nad Menem 1963–1965; Dokumentacja*. Transl. V. Grotowicz. Wrocław-Warszawa-Oświęcim: VIA NOVa, IPN, PMA-B, 2011.

———. "Die Phantasie Versagt." *Frankfurter Rundschau*, May 30, 1964. No pages. Cited in: Wittmann, *Beyond*, pp. 187–188.

———. *People in Auschwitz*. Transl. Harry Zohn. Chapel Hill: University of North Carolina Press, 2004.

Lauer-Seidelmann, Irmgard. *Kamerun—das sind wir. Das Gallus—ein Frankfurter Stadtteil*. Verlag Lindemann, 2012.

Lauridsen, John T. (ed.). *Over stregen—under besættelsen*. Copenhagen: Gyldendal, 2007.

Lechner, Silvester. *Das KZ Oberer Kuhberg und die NS-Zeit in der Region Ulm/Neu-Ulm*. Stuttgart: Silberburg-Verlag, 1988.

Leide, Henry. *NS-Verbrecher und Staatssicherheit: Die geheime Vergangenheitspolitik der DDR*. Göttingen: Vandenhoeck & Ruprecht, 2006.

Lemke, Michael. "Instrumentalisierter Antifaschismus und SED-Kampagnepolitik im deutschen Sonderkonflikt 1960–1968." In: Danyel (ed.), *Die geteilte*, pp. 61–86.

Lemkin, Raphael. *Axis Rule in Occupied Europe: Laws of Occupation, Analysis of Government, Proposals for Redress*. Washington: Carnegie Endowment for International Peace, 1944.

Lenz, Otto. "Eidesstattliche Versicherung," Jan. 3, 1946. Cited in: Hehl von, "Der Beamte," in: Gotto (ed.), *Der Staatssekretär*, pp. 260–262.

Lepiarz, Jacek. "Bezkarni naziści w powojennej RFN. 'Amnezja i brak empatii dla ofiar.'" *Deutsche Welle*, Aug. 31, 2019: https://www.dw.com/pl/bezkarni-nazi %C5%9Bci-w-powojennej-rfn-amnezja-i-brak-empatii-dla-ofiar/a-50232957 [Aug. 1, 2024].

Leth, Göran. (Andersson, Lars; Tydén, Mattias [eds.]). *"Mediernas svek i skuggan av Förintelsen" i Sverige och Nazityskland Skuldfrågor och moraldebatt*. Stockholm: Dialogos, 2007.

"Letter to the Editor." *Frankfurter Rundschau*, Dec. 21, 1963. No pages. Cited in: Wittmann, *Beyond*, p. 184.

"Letzter Kommandant von KZ Auschwitz im Gefängnis gestorben." *Frankfurter Rundschau*, June 19, 1963, p. 2.

Levi, Primo. *The Black Hole of Auschwitz*. Transl. Sharon Wood. (Belpoliti, Marco [ed.]). Cambridge: Polity, 2005.

———. *The Drowned and the Saved*. Transl. Raymond Rosenthal. New York: Summit Books, 1988.

Liebert, Frank. "Vom Karrierestreben zum 'Nötigungsnotstand'—'Jud Süss,' Veit Harlan und die westdeutsche Nachkriegsgesellschaft (1945–50)." In: Henne, Riedlinger (eds.), *Das Lüth-Urteil*, pp. 111–146.

Lifton, Robert. *The Nazi Doctors: Medical Filing and the Psychology of Genocide*. New York: Basic, 1986.

Lilienthal, Georg. "Rassenhygiene im Dritten Reich. Krise und Wende." *Medizinhistorisches Journal*, 1979/1–2, pp. 114–134.

Lilienthal, Marion. "Hermann Krumey—Manager der Judenvernichtung."

Gedenkportal Korbach für die Opfer des Nationalsozialismus 1933–1945, no date. Gedenkportal Korbach, pp. 1–34: http://www.gedenkportal-korbach.de/pdf.php ?pdf=krumey [Oct. 20, 2022].

Lindgren, Astrid. *War Diaries, 1939–1945*. Transl. Sarah Death. New Haven / London: Yale University Press, 2018.

Lipstadt, Deborah. *The Eichmann Trial*. New York: Schocken Books, 2011. Ebook.

"Lkw und Geld gegen Menschen eingehandelt? Ehemaliger SS-Obersturmbannführer Krumey in Korbach verhaftet—Drogist und Kreistagsabgeordneter." *Abendpost*, Apr. 4, 1957. No pages. HHStAW, 461, 33694. Krumey, Hermann u.a.: Handakten, vol. 1, p. 17.

Loewy, Hanno (ed.). *NS-"Euthanasie" vor Gericht: Fritz Bauer und die Grenzen juristischer Bewältigung*. Frankfurt am Main: Campus Verlag, 1996.

Lommatzsch, Erik. *Hans Globke (1898–1973): Beamter im Dritten Reich und Staatssekretär Adenauers*. Frankfurt am Main: Campus Verlag, 2009.

Longerich, Peter. *Heinrich Himmler*. Transl. Jeremy Noakes, Lesley Sharpe. Oxford: Oxford University Press, 2012.

Lorenz, Einhart. "Dänemark." In: Krohn et al. (eds.), *Handbuch*, pp. 204–208, cited in: Wojak, *Fritz Bauer*, p. 124.

Löw-Beer, Nele. "Fritz Bauer und Helga Einsele—eine Freundschaft." In: Rauschenberger (ed.), *Rückkehr*, pp. 227–230.

Lund, Joachim. "Transnational Police Networks and the Fight Against Communism in Germany and Denmark, 1933–1940." *Working Paper / Department of Business and Politics*, 2016/91, pp. 1–24.

"Lunefuld april." *Aftenbladet (København)*, Apr. 16, 1936, p. 2.

M. W. "Zum Himmel." *Braunschweiger Zeitung*, Jan. 3, 1950, p. 8.

Madajczyk, Piotr. "Kim był albo w co został zamieszany Reinhard Strecker?" *Rocznik Polsko-Niemiecki*, 2018/26, pp. 131–142.

Mann, Thomas. "Letter to Germany." *Prevent W.W.III Magazine*, Dec. 1945, p. 25.

Manvell, Roger. *Goering: The Rise and Fall of the Notorious Nazi Leader*. New York: Skyhorse, 2011.

Markowska, Krystyna; Bielasik, Leszek; Weigel, Stanisław; Delegatura Powiatu w Poddębicach. *Zbrodnie Wehrmachtu na terenie powiatu poddębickiego w czasie i rejonie bitwy nas Bzurą: Sesja popularno-naukowa. Uniejów, Oct. 12, 1974*. No pages.

Marley, D. Leigh Aman; Roosevelt, Franklin D.; World Committee for the Victims of German Fascism. *The Brown Book of the Hitler Terror and the Burning of the Reichstag*. First American ed. New York: A.A. Knopf, 1933.

Marwecki, Daniel. *Germany and Israel: Whitewashing and Statebuilding*. Oxford: Oxford University Press, 2020.

Mauz, Gerhard. *Die Gerechten und die Gerichteten*. Stuttgart / Hamburg: Dt. Bücherbund, 1968.

———. "Ein Gedränge ohne Ausweg." *Der Spiegel*, Feb. 24, 1969. No pages. Cited in: Steinke, *Fritz Bauer*, p. 143.

———. "Teufelskreis aus Blut und Tinte." *Der Spiegel*, Feb. 2, 1965: https://www.spiegel .de/spiegel/print/d-46169395.html [Aug. 16, 2021].

———. "Wo ist denn unser Angeklagter?" *Der Spiegel*, Dec. 23, 1964: https://www .spiegel.de/politik/wo-ist-denn-unser-angeklagter-a-e882fcf6-0002-0001-0000 -000046176416 [Aug. 16, 2021].

Maxwill, Peter. "Rechtsradikale SRP Geheim ins Reich." *Der Spiegel*, Mar. 2, 2012:

https://www.spiegel.de/geschichte/rechtsradikale-srp-a-947501.html# [Aug. 26, 2024].

McCormick [O'Hare], Anne. "Nuremberg on the Eve of the Verdicts." *The New York Times,* Sept. 29, 1946, p. 21.

McDonough, Frank. *The Weimar Years: Rise and Fall 1918–1933.* London: Bloomsbury Publishing, 2023. Ebook.

Meehan, Patricia. *A Strange Enemy People: Germans Under the British, 1945–50.* London: Peter Owen Publishers, 2001.

Meier, Andreas (ed.). *Martin Walser: Unser Auschwitz; Auseinandersetzung mit der deutschen Schuld.* Hamurg: Rowohlt, 2015. Ebook.

"Meine liebe Prinzessin." *Der Spiegel,* Jan. 30, 1951: https://www.spiegel.de/politik/ meine-liebe-prinzessin-a-d320bf2e-0002-0001-0000-000029191990 [June 25, 2024].

Mellenthin, Knut. "Chronologie des Holocaust, 1933," no date. *Chronologie des Holocaust Hamburg*: https://www.holocaust-chronologie.de/chronologie/1933 [Aug. 28, 2024].

Mendelsohn, John (ed.). *The Holocaust: Selected Documents in Eighteen Volumes,* vol. 3. New York: Garland, 1982.

"Merkt euch den Namen Hirschfeld." *Der Spiegel,* Dec. 29, 1949: https://www.spiegel .de/politik/merkt-euch-den-namen-hirschfeld-a-290cf9c2-0002-0001-0000 -000044439435?context=issue [Mar. 9, 2024].

Merseburger, Peter. *Der schwierige Deutsche: Kurt Schumacher.* Stuttgart: Deutsche Verlags-Anstalt, 1995.

———. *Willy Brandt 1913–1992: Visionär und Realist.* München: Pantheon, 2013.

Meusch, Matthias. *Von der Diktatur zur Demokratie: Fritz Bauer und die Aufarbeitung der NS-Verbrechen in Hessen 1956–1968.* Wiesbaden: Historische Kommission für Nassau, 2001.

Mevissen, Paul. "Der Adjutant des Teufels." *Abendpost,* Jan. 10, 1964. No pages. Cited in: Pendas, *The Frankfurt,* p. 135.

Meyer, George. *Adolf Heusinger: Dienst eines deutschen Soldaten 1915–1964.* Hamburg / Berlin / Bonn: E.S. Mittler & Sohn, 2001.

Mcyer, Michael A.; Brenner, Michael (eds.). *Deutsch-jüdische Geschichte in der Neu zeit.* Vol. 4: *Aufbruch und Zerstörung 1918–1945.* München: C. H. Beck Verlag, 1997.

Meyer-Velde, Heinz Friedrich. " 'Dann machen's doch selbst besser.': Interview by Monika Boll." In: Backhaus, Boll, Gross (eds.), *Fritz Bauer,* pp. 235–253.

Middleton, Drew. "Neo-Nazism: 'A Cloud Like a Man's Hand'; Revival of Interest in Hitler's Creed Creates Fear of a Future Storm over Germany." *The New York Times,* July 1, 1951. No pages.

Mielke, Helmut. "Die Zeit von 1932–1945." In: Bregenzer, Pötzel, Ruggaber (eds.), *Unser Land,* pp. 60–67.

Milton, Giles. *Checkmate in Berlin: The Cold War Showdown That Shaped the Modern World.* New York: Henry Holt and Co., 2021. Ebook.

Minerbi, Sergio I. *The Eichmann Trial Diary: An Eyewitness Account of the Trial That Revealed the Holocaust.* Transl. Robert L. Miller. New York: Enigma Books, 2011.

Miquel von, Marc. *Ahnden oder amnestieren? Westdeutsche Justiz und Vergangenheitspolitik in den sechziger Jahren.* Göttingen: Wallstein Verlag, 2004.

Mix, Karl-Georg. *Deutsche Flüchtlinge in Dänemark 1945–1949.* Stuttgart: Franz Steiner Verlag, 2005.

Moeller, Robert G. "Reconstructing the Family in Reconstruction Germany: Women and Social Policy in the Federal Republic, 1949–1955." In: Moeller (ed.), *West Germany*, pp. 109–133.

———. *War Stories: The Search for a Usable Past in the Federal Republic of Germany*. Berkeley: University of California Press, 2001.

Moeller, Robert G. (ed.). *West Germany Under Construction: Politics, Society, and Culture in the Adenauer Era*. Ann Arbor: University of Michigan Press, 1997.

Molitor, Jan [Josef Müller-Marein]. "Die Schatten der Toten vom 20. Juli . . ." *Die Zeit*, Mar. 13, 1952 (11), pp. 2–2a.

[Molotov] Молотов. "Нота народного комиссара иностранных дел тов. В.М. Молотова." *Известия*, Jan. 7, 1942, p. 2. Cited in: Zeltser, "The Subject," no date, online source.

Monika, Boll; Gross, Raphael (eds.). *"Ich staune, dass Sie in dieser Luft atmen können": Jüdische Intellektuelle in Deutschland nach 1945*. Frankfurt am Main: FISCHER Taschenbuch, 2013.

Moses, A. Dirk. *German Intellectuals and the Nazi Past*. Cambridge: Cambridge University Press, 2007.

Muchowski, Jakub. "Społeczeństwo postronnych śledzi sprawę Eichmanna. Recepcja procesu w Polsce lat 60." *teksty drugie*, 2020/3, pp. 110–129.

Mühlhausen, Walter. "Im Kampf um die Republik—Der junge Fritz Bauer." In: Backhaus, Boll, Gross (eds.), *Fritz Bauer*, pp. 31–47.

Müller, Filip. *Eyewitness Auschwitz: Three Years in the Gas Chambers*. New York: Stein and Day, 1979.

Müller, Peter F.; Mueller, Michael. *Gegen Freund und Feind: Der BND; Geheime Politik und schmutzige Geschäfte*. Reinbek: Rowohlt, 2002.

Müller, Roland. "Der Branddirektor als Brandstifter: Der Judenpogrom im November 1938." In: Fuchs (ed.), *Stuttgart . . . Anpassung*, pp. 488–507.

———. "Ein geräuschloser Umbau: Die Machtübernahme im Stuttgarter Rathaus." In: Fuchs (ed.), *Stuttgart . . . Die Machtergreifung*, pp. 331–350.

Müller, Rolf-Dieter. *Reinhard Gehlen: Geheimdienstchef im Hintergrund der Bonner Republik: Die Biografie*. Vol. 1: *1902–1950*. Berlin: Ch. Links, 2017.

Müller, Rolf-Dieter (ed.). *Die Wehrmacht: Mythos und Realität*. München: Oldenbourg, 1999.

Müller, Rolf-Dieter; Volkmann, Hans Erich (eds.). *Die Wehrmacht: Mythos und Realität*. München: Oldenbourg, 1999.

Müller-Doohm, Stefan. *Adorno: A Biography*. Transl. Rodney Livingstone. Cambridge: Polity Press, 2005.

Müller-Wirth, Christof. "Eine letzte Begegnung mit Generalstaatsanwalt Dr. Fritz Bauer am 28. Juni 1968 im Schlosshotel in Karlsruhe." *Forschungsjournal Soziale Bewegungen*, 2015/4 (28), pp. 280–282.

Munier, Julia Noah. *Lebenswelten und Verfolgungsschicksale homosexueller Männer in Baden und Württemberg im 20. Jahrhundert*. Stuttgart: Verlag W. Kohlhammer, 2021.

Nachtmann, Walter. "Intensive Beziehungen: Hitlers fünf Stuttgart-Besuche zwischen 1933 und 1938." In: Fuchs (ed.), *Stuttgart . . . Anpassung*, pp. 16–25.

———. " "Wir haben nicht gewusst, dass . . . ": Gespräch mit Dr. jur. Albert Locher." In: Fuchs (ed.), *Stuttgart . . . Anpassung*, pp. 50–57.

Näslund, Erik. *Rolf de Maré: Art Collector, Ballet Director, Museum Creator*. Alton: Dance Books, 2009.

Nationalrat der Nationalen Front des Demokratischen Deutschland Dokumentationszentrum der Staatlichen Archivverwaltung der DDR (ed.). *Braunbuch. Kriegs- und Naziverbrecher in der Bundesrepublik und in Westberlin.* Berlin: Staatsverlag der Deutschen Demokratischen Republik, 1968: https://web .archive.org/web/20071214171543/http://www.braunbuch.de/index.shtml [June 18, 2024].

Naucke, Wolfgang. "Muster der Wende: In der 'Heyde/Sawade-Affäre' steckt auch eine Karl-Binding-Affäre." *Frankfurter Allgemeine Zeitung,* June 23, 1999, p. 10: https:// www.faz.net/aktuell/feuilleton/politik/rezension-sachbuch-muster-der-wende -11315430.html?printPagedArticle=true#pageIndex_2 [Mar. 16, 2021].

Naumann, Bernd. *Auschwitz: Bericht uber die Strafsache gegen Mulka und andere.* Athenäum Verlag, 1965.

——. "Ohrfeigen für die Sterbenden." *Frankfurter Allgemeine Zeitung,* Apr. 14, 1964. No pages. Cited in: Pendas, *The Frankfurt,* p. 164.

"Nazi Anti-Semitic Literature Is Printed in U.S. for Neo-Nazis in Germany." *Jewish Telegraphic Agency,* July 31, 1963: http://pdfs.jta.org/1963/1963-07-31_144.pdf [July 23, 2021].

"Nazi Officer Admits Participation in Killing 813 Lithuania Jews." *Jewish Telegraphic Agency,* July 14, 1958: https://www.jta.org/archive/nazi-officer-admits -participation-in-killing-813-lithuania-jews [Oct. 13, 2023].

"Naziblutrichter im Bonner Dienst." *Neues Deutschland,* Jan. 26, 1956, p. 2.

Nelhiebel, Kurt. "Eine Kugel kam geflogen . . ." *Weltexpresso,* June 30, 2018: https:// weltexpresso.de/index.php/zeitgesehen/13370-eine-kugel-kam-geflogen [Jan. 12, 2023].

Neumann, Herbert. "Mit der lustigen Witwe heiterte der Truppenjesus die SS-Leute auf. Frankfurter Juristen erinnern sich unter dem 'Holocaust'-Eindruck an den ersten Auschwitz-Prozess." *Frankfurter Allgemeine Zeitung,* Jan. 27, 1979, p. 51.

Newsome, W. Jake. *Homosexuals After the Holocaust: Sexual Citizenship and the Politics of Memory in Germany and the United States, 1945–2008.* PhD thesis. University at Buffalo, 2016.

"Nichts als Pappendeckel." *Der Spiegel,* Dec. 1, 1949: https://www.spiegel.de/spiegel/ print/d-44439124.html [Mar. 2, 2022].

"Nichts gehört, nichts gemeldet, nichts befohlen." *Stuttgarter Zeitung,* Jan. 10, 1964. No pages. Cited in: Pendas, *The Frankfurt,* pp. 134–135.

Niven, Bill. *Hitler and Film: The Führer's Hidden Passion.* New Haven / London: Yale University Press, 2018.

"No Soy Mengele." *El Imparcial,* Mar. 24, 1961, p. 1.

No title. *Die Tat,* May 2, 1964. No pages. Cited in: Lilienthal, "Hermann Krumey," no date. Gedenkportal Korbach, p. 31.

No title. *Frankfurter Allgemeine Zeitung,* Jan. 5, 1961. No pages.

No title. *Frankfurter Rundschau,* Apr. 4, 1957, p. 2.

No title. *Frankfurter Rundschau,* Apr. 9, 1956, p. 4.

No title. *Frankfurter Rundschau,* Dec. 22, 1960, p. 4.

No title. *Frankfurter Rundschau,* July 27, 1956, pp. 4, 7.

No title. *Frankfurter Rundschau,* June 1–2, 1957, p. 5.

No title. *Frankfurter Rundschau,* June 23, 1961, p. 1.

No title. *Frankfurter Rundschau,* June 24–26, 1961, p. 2.

No title. *Haboker,* June 10, 1960, p. 1.

No title. *HaOlam HaZe,* July 5, 1961, pp. 7–8.

Noack, Frank. *Veit Harlan: The Life and Work of a Nazi Filmmaker.* Lexington: University of Kentucky, 2016.

Nowack, Sabrina. *Sicherheitsrisiko NS-Belastung: Personalüberprüfungen im Bundesnachrichtendienst in den 1960er Jahren.* Berlin: C. H. Link, 2016.

"Nuremberg Trial Hailed by Truman." *The New York Times,* Oct. 13, 1946, p. 36.

Nyiszli, Miklos. *Auschwitz: A Doctor's Eyewitness Account.* Transl. Tibere Kremer, Richard Seaver. New York: Arcade, 2011. Ebook.

Oberschulamt Tübingen. "Württembergisches Schutzhaftlager Ulm." Ein frühes Konzentrationslager im Nationalsozialismus (1933–1935). Informationen und Arbeitshilfen für den Besuch der Ulmer KZ-Gedenkstätte mit Schülern. Tübingen: Oberschulamt, 2004: https://www.yumpu.com/de/document/read/5275481/wurttembergisches-schutzhaftlager-ulm-oberer-kuhberg-telebus [Jan. 8, 2022].

Oberstaatsanwaltschaft, Frankfurt am Main Oberlandesgericht (ed.). *Fritz Bauer: Eine Denkschrift.* Frankfurt am Main: no publisher, 1993.

Orbach, Danny. *Fugitives: A History of Nazi Mercenaries During the Cold War.* New York: Pegasus Books, 2022. Ebook.

Osterloh, Jörg (ed.). *". . . der schrankenlosesten Willkür ausgeliefert": Häftlinge der frühen Konzentrationslager 1933–1936/37.* Frankfurt am Main / New York: Campus Verlag, 2017.

Osterloh, Jörg; Vollnhals, Clemens (eds.). *NS-Prozesse und deutsche Öffentlichkeit.* Göttingen: Vandenhoeck & Ruprecht, 2011.

Pahl, Magnus. *Fremde Heere Ost: Hitlers militärische Feindaufklärung.* Berlin: Ch. Links Verlag, 2012.

Palmier, Jean-Michel. *Weimar in Exile: The Anti-Fascist Emigration in Europe and America.* Transl. David Fernbach. London: Verso, 2017.

Parikas, Dodos. "Identitet och pengar." In: Silverstolpe, Söderström (eds.), *Sympatiens,* pp. 554–575.

Parini, Jay. *John Steinbeck: A Biography.* London: Heinemann, 1994.

Parker, Stephen. *Bertolt Brecht: A Literary Life.* London: Methuen Drama, 2014. Ebook.

Passent, Daniel. "Zbrodniarz na łamach." *Polityka,* Mar. 10, 2007: https://www.polityka.pl/tygodnikpolityka/kraj/212323,1,zbrodniarz-na-lamach.read [Dec. 8, 2020].

Pasternak-Slater, Ann. "Kasztner's Ark." *Areté,* 2004/15, pp. 12–16.

Paulus, G. "Remer beschloss, Politiker zu werden." *Braunschweiger Zeitung,* Sept. 6, 1949, p. 8. FBInst, Nachlass Fritz Bauer 54.

Pauly, Walter. "'Kämpferische Wissenschaft.' Studien zur Universität Jena im Nationalsozialismus, hg. v. Hossfeld, Uwe / John, Jürgen / Lemuth, Oliver / Stutz, Rüdiger. Böhlau, Köln 2003. 1160 S., Ill. [Review]." koeblergerhard.de: https://www.koeblergerhard.de/ZRG122Internetrezensionen/KaempferischeWissenschaft.htm [Feb. 25, 2022].

Pedersen, Minna Steffen. "Matteotti-Komiteen Og Hitler-Flygtningen." *Årbog for arbejderbevægelsens historie,* 1990/20, pp. 305–319.

Pelt, Robert Jan van. *The Case for Auschwitz: Evidence from the Irving Trial.* Bloomington: Indiana University Press, 2002.

Pendas, Devin O. *The Frankfurt Auschwitz Trial, 1963–1965: Genocide, History, and the Limits of the Law.* Cambridge: Cambridge University Press, 2006.

Perels, Joachim; Wojak Irmtrud (eds.). *Die Humanität der Rechtsordnung: Ausgewählte Schriften.* Frankfurt am Main: Campus Verlag, 1998.

Petersen, Hans Herman. "Generalstaatsanwalt Dr. Fritz Bauer, der Deutsche, der die Jagd auf die Top-Nazis leitet, sagt, dass ein neuer Hitler nicht abgewiesen würde," 1963. In: Foljanty, Johst (eds.), *Fritz Bauer,* vol. 2, pp. 1022–1024.

Petersen, Hans Uwe (ed.). *Hitlerflüchtlinge im Norden: Asyl und poltisches Exil 1933–1945.* Kiel: Neuer Malik Verlag, 1999.

Petersen, Ole Hyltoft. "Kulturdebatten i 1930'erne." In: Hertel (ed), *Tilbageblik,* pp. 170–188.

Pietrzak, Jan. "Mord na bezbronnych mieszkańcach Poddębic 13 września 1939 roku." *Nad Wartą. Weekend,* 2019/401, p. 14.

"Pingvinerne i Tivoli." *Politiken,* June 2, 1935, p. 10.

Plötz, Kirsten; Velke, Marcus. *Aufarbeitung von Verfolgung und Repression lesbischer und schwuler Lebensweisen in Hessen 1945–1985.* Berlin: Verein der Freundinnen und Freunde des Schwulen Museums in Berlin e.V., 2018.

Poiger, Uta. *Jazz, Rock, and Rebels: Cold War Politics and American Culture in a Divided Germany.* Berkeley: University of California Press, 2000.

Poliakov, Léon. *Harvest of Hate: The Nazi Program for the Destruction of the Jews of Europe.* Transl. unknown. New York: Waldon Press, 1979.

Poliakov, Léon; Wulf, Joseph. *Das Dritte Reich und seine Diener.* Frankfurt am Main / Berlin / Wien: Ullstein, 1983.

Pollmann, Anna. "Arbeit am Begriff: Auschwitz, Vietnam und die Kategorie des Genozids." In: Rauschenberger, Steinbacher (eds.), *Fritz Bauer,* pp. 252–267.

Pöpken, Christian. *Vergangenheitspolitik durch Strafrecht: Der Oberste Gerichtshof der Britischen Zone und die Ahndung von Verbrechen gegen die Menschlichkeit.* Baden-Baden: Nomos, 2021.

Porter, Anna. *Kasztner's Train: The True Story of Rezső Kasztner, Unknown Hero of the Holocaust.* Vancouver / Toronto: Douglas & McIntyre, 2007.

Power, Samantha. *"A Problem from Hell": America and the Age of Genocide.* New York: Basic Books, 2002.

Pretzel, Andreas. *NS-Opfer unter Vorbehalt: Homosexuelle Männer in Berlin nach 1945.* Berlin / Hamburg / Münster: Lit Verlag, 2002.

"Prosecutor Released in Anti-Jewish Case." *The Washington Post,* Dec. 21, 1958, p. A4.

Radlmaier, Steffen (ed.). *Der Nürnberger Lernprozess: Von Kriegsverbrechern und Starreportern.* Frankfurt am Main: Eichborn Verlag, 2001.

Raloff, Karl. *Ein bewegtes Leben: vom Kaiserreich zur Bundesrepublik.* Hannover: Niedersächsische Landeszentrale für Politische Bildung, 1995.

Rauschenberger, Katharina. "Einführung." In: Rauschenberger, Steinbacher (eds.), *Fritz Bauer,* pp. 7–22.

———. "Recht schaffen und politisch handeln Fritz Bauer und Henry Ormond—ein Vergleich." In: Rauschenberger (ed.), *Rückkehr,* pp. 39–64.

Rauschenberger, Katharina (ed.). *Rückkehr in Feindesland? Fritz Bauer in der deutsch-jüdischen Nachkriegsgeschichte.* Frankfurt am Main / New York: Campus Verlag, 2013.

Rauschenberger, Katharina; Puttkamer von, Joachim; Steinbacher, Sybille (eds.). *Investigating, Punishing, Agitating: Nazi Perpetrator Trials in the Eastern Bloc.* Göttingen: Wallstein Verlag, 2023.

Rauschenberger, Katharina; Steinbacher, Sybille (eds.). *Fritz Bauer und "Achtundsechzig": Positionen zu den Umbrüchen in Justiz, Politik und Gesellschaft.* Göttingen: Wallstein, 2020.

Redies, Rainer. "Karl Ruggaber, als Sozialdemokrat verfolgt," no date. Cannstatter

Stolperstein-Initiative: https://www.stolpersteine-cannstatt.de/biografien/karl
-ruggaber-als-sozialdemokrat-verfolgt [Dec. 31, 2021].

Reese, Mary Ellen. *General Reinhard Gehlen: The CIA Connection.* Fairfax, VA: George
Mason University Press, 1990.

Reichsbahndirektion München (ed.). *Reichsbahn-Kursbuch Amerikanisches
Besatzungsgebiet. Jahresfahrplan 1948/49: Sommerabschnitt gültig vom 9. Mai 1948
an.* Offenbach: Publisher unknown, 1948.

Reitlinger, Gerald. *The Final Solution: The Attempt to Exterminate the Jews of Europe
1939–1945.* Northvale / London: Jason Aronson Incorporated, 1987.

"Remer greift Widerstandskämpfer an." *Frankfurter Allgemeine Zeitung,* May 5, 1951.
No pages.

"Remer Prozess. Rehabilitierung des Rechts auf Widerstand," no date. Buxus Stiftung:
https://wimbv.fritz-bauer-forum.de/remer-prozess/ [Feb. 20, 2024].

Renz, Werner. "Auf der Suche nach Recht und Gerechtigkeit: Anmerkungen zum 50;
Todestag von Fritz Bauer." *Recht und Politik,* 2018/54 (2), pp. 215–219: https://
braunschweig-spiegel.de/wp-content/uploads/2018/07/1-Zum-50.-Todestag-von
-Fritz-Bauer_RuP.pdf [June 15, 2023].

———. "Auschwitz als Augenscheinsobjekt: Ortstermin in Auschwitz." In: Renz, *Fritz
Bauer,* pp. 77–90.

———. "Auschwitz vor Gericht: Der Frankfurter Auschwitz-Prozess (1963–1965)."
FBInst, Tonbandmitschnitte des Auschwitz-Prozesses (1963–1965), Sept. 2013:
https://www.auschwitz-prozess.de/materialien/T_02_Der_Frankfurter_Auschwitz
-Prozess/ [Dec. 6, 2023].

———. "Der 1. Frankfurter Auschwitz-Prozess: Zwei Vorgeschichten." *Zeitschrift für
Geschichtswissenschaft,* 2002/50 (7), pp. 1–33.

———. *Fritz Bauer und das Versagen der Justiz: Nazi-Prozesse und ihre "Tragödie."*
Hamburg: CEP Europäische Verlagsanstalt, 2015.

———. "Geschichtsklitterung oder Fritz Bauer und die Hagiografie." Manuscript,
FBInst, 2015, pp. 1–36: http://www.dieter-schenk.info/Neues%20Material/2015/
Oktober/Fritz%20Bauer%20Geschichtskl.pdf [May 31, 2022].

———. "Stimmen der Opfer und der Täter: Der Tonbandmitschnitt." In: Renz, *Fritz
Bauer,* pp. 109–126.

———. "Wider die Sittenwächter: Fritz Bauers Kritik am überkommenen
Sexualstrafrecht der 1950er und 1960er Jahre." In: Borowski et al. (eds.), *Jahrbuch,*
pp. 70–93.

Renz, Werner (ed.). *Interessen um Eichmann: Israelische Justiz, deutsche Strafverfolgung
und alte Kameradschaften.* Frankfurt am Main: Campus Verlag, 2012.

———. *"Von Gott und der Welt verlassen": Fritz Bauers Briefe an Thomas Harlan.*
Frankfurt am Main / New York: Campus Verlag, 2015.

Riedlinger, Arne. "Vom Boykottaufruf zur Verfassungsbeschwerde: Erich Luth und die
Kontroverse urn Harlans Nachkriegsfilme (1950–58)." In: Henne, Riedlinger
(eds.), *Das Lüth-Urteil,* pp. 147–186.

Riess, Volker. "Fritz Bauer und die Zentrale Stelle: Personen zwischen Konsens und
Dissens." In: Rauschenberger (ed.), *Rückkehr,* pp. 131–149.

Rigoll, Dominik. *Staatsschutz in Westdeutschland: Von der Entnazifizierung zur
Extremistenabwehr.* Göttingen: Wallstein Verlag, 2013.

Ristic, Matias. "Hans Hofmeyer—Widersprüche eines Richters 'von Format' oder: Ein
Blick auf den Auschwitz-Prozess-Vorsitzenden im Lichte bislang
unberücksichtigter Rechtsprechung." *Kritische Justiz,* 2020/53 (1), pp. 98–113.

Rossino, Alexander B. *Hitler Strikes Poland: Blitzkrieg, Ideology, and Atrocity.* Lawrence: University Press of Kansas, 2005.

Rossmann, Erich. *Ein Leben für Sozialismus und Demokratie.* Stuttgart / Tübingen: Rainer Wunderlich Verlag, 1946.

Ruffner, Kevin C. (ed.). *Forging an Intelligence Partnership: CIA and the Origins of the BND, 1945–49; A Documentary History,* vol. 1. Washington, DC: CIA History Staff Center for the Study of Intelligence. European Division. Directorate of Operations, 1999.

"Ruhiger Wahlberlauf. Der Wahlsonntag in Berlin und im Reich." *Badische Presse,* Mar. 6, 1933, p. 4.

Rupieper, Hermann-Josef. *Die Wurzeln der westdeutschen Nachkriegsdemokratie: Der amerikanische Beitrag 1945–1952.* Wiesbaden: Springer-Verlag, 2013.

Rydström, Jens. *Sinners and Citizens: Beastiality and Homosexuality in Sweden, 1880– 1950.* Chicago: The University of Chicago Press, 2003.

Saidon, Gabriel. *Letters from Lothar.* Ciudad Autónoma de Buenos Aires: Editorial Dunken, 2019.

Sälter, Gerhard. *NS-Kontinuitäten im BND: Rekrutierung, Diskurse, Vernetzungen.* Berlin: Ch. Links Verlag, 2022.

———. *Phantome des Kalten Krieges: Die Organisation Gehlen und die Wiederbelebung des Gestapo-Feindbildes "Rote Kapelle."* Berlin: Ch. Links Verlag, 2016.

Sands, Philippe. *East West Street: On the Origins of "Genocide" and "Crimes Against Humanity."* London: W&N, 2016.

Sauer, Kai. "Situation im BS-Land 1945," no date. Leben in Braunschweig: https:// www.braunschweig.de/leben/stadtportraet/stadtteile/timmerlah/Timmerlah _Pastoren_Situation_im_BS-Land_1945.php [Aug. 18, 2023].

"Scharfe Attacken im Remer-Prozess." *Die Welt,* Mar. 8, 1952, p. 1.

Schenk, Dieter. *Auf dem rechten Auge blind: Die braunen Wurzeln des BKA.* Köln: Kiepenheuer und Witsch, 2001.

———. "Die Todesumstände von Generalstaatsanwalt Fritz Bauer (1903–1968)." *Einsicht 08: Bulletin des Fritz Bauer Instituts,* Herbst 2012, pp. 38–43: https://www .fritz-bauer-institut.de/publikation/einsicht-08 [May 25, 2024].

Schiefelbein, Dieter. "Wiederbeginn der juristischen Verfolgung homosexueller Männer in der Bundesrepublik Deutschland. Die Homosexuellen-Prozesse in Frankfurt am Main 1950/51." *Zeitschrift für Sexualforschung,* 1992/5 (1), pp. 59–73.

Schlesak, Dieter. *The Druggist of Auschwitz: A Documentary Novel.* Transl. John Hargraves. New York: Picador, 2012.

"Schlicht und zweckmässig: Der Schwurgerichtssaal im neuen Gewande." *Braunschweiger Presse,* Nov. 17, 1949, p. 6.

Schmid, Richard. "Nachruf auf Fritz Bauer 1903–1968." *Kritische Justiz,* 1968/1, pp. 60–61.

Schmidt, Hans. "Hochhäuser im Silberlicht: Frankfurt in den fünfziger Jahren." In: Gmünder, (ed.), *Frankfurt,* pp. 33–42.

Schmidt-Lüer, Susanne. "Gedenken an den Auschwitz-Prozess im Bürgerhaus Gallus," Apr. 6, 2014. Evangelisches Frankfurt Nachrichten und Debatten: http://www .evangelischesfrankfurtarchiv.de/2014/04/gedenken-an-den-auschwitz-prozess-im -buergerhaus-gallus/ [Nov. 27, 2023].

Schoeller, Wilfried F. (ed.). *Diese merkwürdige Zeit: Leben nach der Stunde Null; Ein Textbuch aus der "Neuen Zeitung."* Frankfurt am Main: Büchergilde, 2005.

Schrag, Steven D. *ASHCAN: Nazis, Generals and Bureaucrats as Guests at the Palace*

Hotel, Mondorf les Bains, Luxembourg, May–August 1945. PhD thesis. University of Toledo, 2015.

Schröder, Stefan. "Geschubse an der Tafel." *Wiesbadener Nachrichten,* Dec. 12, 2020, p. 18.

Schwartz, Michael. "Homosexualität, Sexualstrafrecht und Sittlichkeit: Gesellschaftliche Kontroversen und Reformdebatten in der frühen Bundesrepublik." In: Rauschenberger, Steinbacher (eds.), *Fritz Bauer,* pp. 166–188.

———. *Homosexuelle, Seilschaften, Verrat: Ein transnationales Stereotyp im 20. Jahrhundert.* Berlin / Boston: de Gruyter, 2019.

Schwarz, Erika. *Juden im Zeugenstand: Die Spur des Hans Globke im Gedächtnis der Überlebenden der Shoa.* Berlin: Hentrich & Hentrich, 2009.

Schweigard, Jörg. *Stuttgart in den Roaring Twenties: Politik, Gesellschaft, Kunst und Kultur in Stuttgart 1919–1933.* Karlsruhe: G. Braun Buchverlag, 2012.

Schwelien, Joachim. "Der Amtsgehilfe des Todes." *Frankfurter Allgemeine Zeitung,* Apr. 21, 1961. No pages. Cited in: Krause, *Der Eichmann-Prozess,* p. 171.

Schwenger, Hannes. "Nach Lektüre vernichten." *Tagesspiegel,* Sept. 25, 2013: https://www.tagesspiegel.de/kultur/nach-lekture-vernichten-3520453.html [Aug. 23, 2024].

Segev, Tom. *A State at Any Cost: The Life of David Ben-Gurion.* Transl. Haim Watzman. UK: Apollo, 2019.

Sellner, Jan. "In diesem Haus kam Fritz Bauer zur Welt." *Stuttgarter Zeitung,* Aug. 25, 2023, p. 20.

Sender Freies Berlin (ed.). *Um uns die Fremde: Die Vertreibung des Geistes 1933–1945.* Berlin: Haude & Spenersche, 1968.

Servatius, Robert. *Verteidiger in Jerusalem: Ein Zeitbild.* Schiffbruch Teil V. Köln: Selbstverlag, 1979.

Sethe, Paul. No title. *Frankfurter Allgemeine Zeitung,* May 8, 1951. Cited in: Wojak, *Fritz Bauer,* p. 262.

Setkiewicz, Piotr. *The SS Garrison in KL Auschwitz.* Transl. William Brand. *Voices of Memory 13.* Oświęcim: Auschwitz-Birkenau State Museum, 2018.

———. *Z dziejów obozów IG Farben Werk Auschwitz 1941–1945.* Oświęcim: PMA-B, 2006.

Seweryn, Józef. *Usługiwałem esesmanom w Auschwitz: Wspomnienia więźnia komanda SS-Unterkunftskammer.* Warszawa / Kraków: mireki, 2017.

Shabecoff, Philip. "At Babi Yar Trial. Only 4 Spectators." *The New York Times,* Feb. 13, 1968, p. 11.

———. "17 Auschwitz Aides Get Prison Terms; 6 Must Serve Life." *The New York Times,* Aug. 19, 1965, pp. 1, 8.

Sharples. Caroline. *Postwar Germany and the Holocaust: Perspectives on the Holocaust.* London: Bloomsbury Academic, 2015.

Shavit, Ari. *My Promised Land: The Triumph and Tragedy of Israel.* New York: Random House, 2013.

Shub, Anatole. "Auschwitz Trial Ends in Sentencing of 17 Nazis." *The Washington Post,* Aug. 20, 1965, p. A13: https://www.proquest.com/docview/142579129 [Mar. 21, 2024].

"Sie mögen schuldig sein." *Der Spiegel,* Feb. 27, 1951: https://www.spiegel.de/politik/sie-moegen-schuldig-sein-a-5819dd84-0002-0001-0000-000029193343 [June 25, 2024].

Silver, Arnold M. "Memories of Oberursel: Questions, Questions, Questions." *Studies*

in Intelligence, 1994/37 (5), pp. 81–90: https://www.cia.gov/static/e5bbb497912
673cd3ed4471821a3d75e/Questions-Questions-Questions.pdf [May 9, 2022].

Silverstolpe, Fredrik; Söderström, Göran (eds.). *Sympatiens hemlighetsfulla makt:
Stockholms homosexuella 1860–1960.* Stockholm: Stockholmia Förlag, 1999.

"Sins of the Grandfathers: How Delving into Family Secrets Has Helped Third
Generation Lift the Burden of Guilt over Nazi Atrocities." *Daily Mail,* May 19,
2011: https://www.dailymail.co.uk/news/article-1387334/How-delving-family
-secrets-helped-generation-lift-burden-guilt-Nazi-atrocities.html [July 19, 2024].

Smoleń, Kazimierz. "Kariera." *Zeszyty oświęcimskie* 5, 1961, pp. 103–108.

———. "Wizje lokalne sądu frankfurckiego na terenie byłego obozu koncentracyjnego
w Oświęcimiu—Brzezince." *Muzea Walki: Rocznik muzeów historii walk
rewolucyjnych i narodowo-wyzwoleńczych,* 1970/III, pp. 196–210.

Sohn, Werner. *Im Spiegel der Nachkriegsprozesse: Die Errichtung der NS-Herrschaft im
Freistaat Braunschweig.* Braunschweig: Appelhans, 2003.

Söhner, Jasmin; Zombory, Máté. "Accusing Globke, 1960–1963: Agency and the Iron
Curtain." In: Bourhis Le, Tcherneva, Voisin (eds.), *Seeking,* pp. 351–386.

"Søndag—vejrudsigt søndag." *Politiken,* Mar. 15, 1936, p. 1.

Sontheimer, Michael; Wensierski, Peter. "Als die Polizei 'Gammler' jagte." *Der Spiegel,*
Mar. 8, 2018: https://www.spiegel.de/geschichte/berlin-in-den-1960ern-als-die
-polizei-gammler-an-der-gedaechtniskirche-jagte-a-1196555.html [Mar. 14, 2023].

"Spass mit Charly." *Der Spiegel,* Oct. 29, 1948: https://www.spiegel.de/politik/spass
-mit-charly-a-6bc85065-0002-0001-0000-000044419619 [Aug. 26, 2024].

"SS-mańskie 'zabawy w polowanie' . . . Wstrząsające zeznania świadka na procesie
oprawców z Oświęcimia." Journal unknown, Feb. 25, 1964. No pages.

"SS-Obersturmbannführer arrested in Frankfurt." *Frankfurter Rundschau,* Apr. 2, 1957.
No pages. HHStAW, 461, 33694. Krumey, Hermann u.a.: Handakten, vol. 1, p. 12.

"Staatsanwalt hält Paragraph 175 verfassungswidrig." *Allgemeine Gerichts-Zeitung,*
1952/15 (3), p. 5.

Stahel, David. *Operation Barbarossa and Germany's Defeat in the East.* London:
Cambridge University Press, 2009.

Ständigen deputation des Deutschen Juristentages (ed.). *Verhandlungen des
sechundvierzigsten Deutschen Juristentages. Essen 1966,* vols. 1–2. München /
Berlin: Beck, 1967.

Stangneth, Bettina. *Eichmann Before Jerusalem: The Unexamined Life of a Mass
Murderer.* Transl. Ruth Martin. London: The Bodley Head, 2014.

Stangneth, Bettina; Winkler, Willi. "Der Mann, der Adolf Eichmann enttarnte."
Süddeutsche Zeitung, Aug. 20, 2021: https://projekte.sueddeutsche.de/artikel/
gesellschaft/der-mann-der-adolf-eichmann-enttarnte-e114499/ [Apr. 7, 2024].

"Starb Prof. Heyde auf 'Befehl'?" *Abendpost,* Feb. 14, 1964. HHStAW 505, 5824, p. 129.

Stargardt, Nicholas. *The German War: A Nation Under Arms, 1939–1945.* No place:
Vintage Digital, 2015.

Statista Research Department. "Zahl der vertriebenen Deutschen nach dem Zweiten
Weltkrieg nach Herkunft in den Jahren 1944 bis 1948," Apr. 30, 2015. Statista:
https://de.statista.com/statistik/daten/studie/1060100/umfrage/zahl-der
-vertriebenen-deutschen-nach-herkunft/ [Aug. 26, 2024].

Steiger, Christian. *Rosemarie Nitribitt: Autopsie eines deutschen Skandals.*
Königswinter: HEEL Verlag, 2007.

Steinbacher, Sybille. *Wie der Sex nach Deutschland kam: Der Kampf um Sittlichkeit und
Anstand in der frühen Bundesrepublik.* München: Siedler, 2011.

Steinbacher, Sybille; Rauschenberger, Katharina (eds.). *Der Auschwitz-Prozess auf Tonband: Akteure, Zwischentöne, Überlieferung.* Göttingen: Wallstein Verlag, 2020.

Steincke, Karl Kristian. "Emigrantspørgsmålet i Danmark I." *Social-Demokraten,* Apr. 27, 1937, p. 11.

Steinke, Ronen. *Fritz Bauer: The Jewish Prosecutor Who Brought Eichmann and Auschwitz to Trial.* Transl. Sinéad Crowe. Bloomington: Indiana University Press, 2020.

———. "Fritz Bauer und die ungesühnte Nazijustiz: Zum Umgang des einstigen hessischen Generalstaatsanwalts mit NS-Justizverbrechen." *Kritische Justizm,* 2016/49 (1), pp. 129–136.

Steinthal, Th. "Politiken's Korrespondent paa Besøg i nazistisk Fangelejr for politiske modstandere." *Politiken,* Apr. 23, 1933, pp. 1–6.

"Stellungnahme Zinns im Fall Globke." *Frankfurter Rundschau,* Jan. 28–29, 1961, p. 2.

Stengel, Katharina. "Boten der verdrängten Wahrheit." *Damals: Magazin für Geschichte,* 2020/07, pp. 24–29.

———. *Die Überlebenden vor Gericht: Auschwitz-Häftlinge als Zeugen in NS-Prozessen (1950–1976).* Göttingen: Vandenhoeck & Ruprecht, 2022.

———. *Hermann Langbein: Ein Auschwitz-Überlebender in den erinnerungspolitischen Konflikten der Nachkriegszeit.* Frankfurt am Main: Campus Verlag, 2012.

———. "Mediators Behind the Scenes: The World Jewish Congress and the International Auschwitz Committee During the Preparations for the First Auschwitz Trial in Frankfurt." In: Bourhis Le, Eric; Tcherneva, Irina; Voisin, Vanessa (eds.). *Seeking Accountability for Nazi and War Crimes in East and Central Europe: A People's Justice?* Rochester Studies in East and Central Europe, vol. 29. Rochester: Boydell & Brewer, 2022.

———. " 'Wir sind heute Zeugen': Die Aussagen von Erich und Dov Kulka— Perspektiven der Verfolgten." In: Steinbacher; Rauschenberger (eds.), *Der Auschwitz-Prozess,* pp. 15–34.

Stephan, Jean-Pierre. "Fritz Bauers Briefe an Thomas Harlan: Eine deutsche Freundschaft." *Einsicht 09: Bulletin des Fritz Bauer Instituts,* 2013, pp. 36–44: https://www.fritz-bauer-institut.de/fileadmin/editorial/publikationen/einsicht/einsicht-09.pdf [June 22, 2024].

[Stepanenko] Степаненко. "Что происходит в Киеве." *Правда,* Nov. 29, 1941, p. 3.

Stern, Walter; Gajdosch, Franz. *U.S. Army Camp King: Die Amerikaner in Oberursel.* Manuscript. Camp History 543. Sammlung Gajdosch. Oberursel, 1990–2006.

Stevnsborg, Henrik. *Politiet 1938–47—Bekaempelsen af spionage, sabotage og nedbrydende virksomhed.* Copenhagen: Gads Forlag, 1992.

Stiefele, Werner. "Banditentum, gesetzlich geschützt; Die Arisierung jüdischer Geschäfte in Stuttgart." In: Fuchs, (ed.), *Stuttgart . . . Anpassung,* pp. 538–555.

Stilz, Eberhard (ed.). *Das Oberlandesgerichts Stuttgart: 125 Jahre: 1979–2004.* Villingen-Schwenningen: Neckar-Verlag, 2004.

Stræde, Therkel. *Octobre 1943: Le sauvetage des juifs danois menacés d'extermination.* Copenhagen: Ministere Royal des Affaires Etrangères du Danemark, 1993.

Strasas, Michael. "4.000 demonstrieren am Landsberger Hauptplatz—für die Begnadigung der letzten zum Tode verurteilten Kriegsverbrecher," *Landsberger-Zeitgeschichte,* Jan. 7, 1951. Erinnern—Forschen—Dokumentieren. Europäische Holocaustgedenkstätte Stiftung e.V. Landsberg, 2016: https://www.kaufering -memorial.de/publikationen/4000-demonstrieren-am-landsberger-hauptplatz -fuer-die-begnadigung-der-letzten-zum-tode-verurteilten-kriegsverbrecher/ [June 23, 2024].

Strecker, Reinhard (ed.). *Dr. Hans Globke: Aktenauszüge; Dokumente*. Hamburg: Rütten & Loening Verlag, 1961.

Streit, Christian. "The German Army and the Policies of Genocide." In: Hirschfeld (ed.), *The Policies*, pp. 1–14.

Strik-Strikfeldt, Wilfried. *Gegen Stalin und Hitler: General Wlassow und die russische Freiheitsbewegung*. Mainz: von Hase & Koehler, 1970.

Strobel, Robert. "Globke und die Judengesetze. Ein ZEIT-Interview mit dem Staatssekretär im Bundeskanzleramt." *Die Zeit*, Feb. 17, 1961: https://www.zeit.de/1961/08/globke-und-die-judengesetze/komplettansicht [June 16, 2021].

———. "Wieder wühlt er in den Akten. Eichmann: Ein Mann mit der Seele einer Schreibmaschine." *Die Zeit*, June 30, 1961: https://www.zeit.de/1961/27/wieder-wuehlt-er-in-den-akten [May 3, 2024].

Struk, Janina. *Photographing the Holocaust: Interpretations of the Evidence*. London: Routledge, 2021.

Svanberg, Ingvar; Tydén, Mattias. *Sverige och förintelsen: Debatt och dokument om Europas judar 1933–1945*. Stockholm: Arena, 1997.

Szende, Stefan. *Der letzte Jude aus Polen*. Zürich / New York: Europa, 1945.

Szymusik, Adam. "Progressive Asthenia in Former Prisoners of the Auschwitz-Birkenau Concentration Camp." *Medical Review—Auschwitz*, Aug. 15, 2017. Originally published as: "Astenia poobozowa u byłych więźniów obozu koncentracyjnego w Oświęcimiu." *Przegląd Lekarski—Oświęcim*, 1964, pp. 23–29: https://www.mp.pl/auschwitz/journal/english/170054,progressive-asthenia-in-former-prisoners-of-the-auschwitz-birkenau-concentration-camp [July 24, 2024].

Taylor, Edmond. "Eyewitness View of Prison Life in Germany: Tribune Man Visits Large Camp." *Chicago Daily Tribune*, Apr. 7, 1933 (92/83), p. 12.

Teschke, John P. *Hitler's Legacy: West Germany Confronts the Aftermath of the Third Reich*. New York: Lang, 1999.

"The Crime of Murder Does Not Sleep." *The Daily Mirror*, Mar. 23, 1964, p. 9.

"The Nuremberg Sentences." *The New York Times*, Oct. 2, 1946, p. 28.

Thomas, Nick. *Protest Movements in 1960s West Germany: A Social History of Dissent and Democracy*. Oxford: Berg, 2003.

Tiefenthal, Rolf. "Doppelter Exodus." In: Backhaus, Boll, Gross (eds.), *Fritz Bauer*, pp. 75–81.

Tobin, Patrick. *Crossroads at Ulm: Postwar West Germany and the 1958 Ulm Einsatzkommando Trial*. PhD thesis. University of North Carolina, 2013.

———. "No Time for 'Old Fighters': Postwar West Germany and the Origins of the 1958 Ulm Einsatzkommando Trial." *Central European History*, 2011/44 (4), pp. 684–710.

Tödt, Heinz Eduard. *Wagnis und Fügung: Anfänge einer theologischen Biographie; Kindheit in der Republik, Jugend im Dritten Reich, fünf Jahre an den Fronten des Zweiten Weltkriegs, fünf Jahre Gefangenschaft in sowjetrussischen Lagern*. Münster: LIT Verlag, 2013.

Tormin, Walter. *Die Geschichte der SPD in Hamburg 1945 bis 1950: Forum Zeitgeschichte 4*. Hamburg: Research Center for the History of National Socialism in Hamburg, 1994.

Trentmann, Frank. *Out of the Darkness: The Germans, 1942–2022*. No place: Allen Lane, 2023.

"Treugelöbnis der Schufo: Mitgliederversammlung des Reichsbanners," *Schwäbische Tagwacht*, June 28, 1932. No pages. Cited in: Steinke, *Fritz Bauer*, p. 58.

"Trial of Ex-Nazis Has Wide Impact; 83% of West German Adults Found to Be Aware of It." *The New York Times,* July 12, 1964, p. 18.

"Tumult im Gerichtssaal: 'Schlagt das Schwein Kaduk tot!'" *Abendpost,* Apr. 7, 1964. No pages. Cited in: Pendas, *The Frankfurt,* p. 163.

Turner, Christopher. *Adventures in the Orgasmatron: How the Sexual Revolution Came to America.* New York: Farrar, Straus and Giroux, 2011. Ebook.

Tusa, Ann; Tusa, John. *The Nuremberg Trial.* New York: Skyhorse Publishing, 2010.

Uhlman, Fred. *The Making of an Englishman: Erinnerungen eines deutschen Juden.* Zürich: Diogenes, 1960.

Ulrich, Axel; Streich, Brigitte (eds.). *Gedenkort Schlachthoframpe: Wiesbaden, Kulturamt der Landeshauptstadt Wiesbaden—Stadtarchiv,* 2009: https://www .wiesbaden.de/medien-zentral/dok/kultur/Internet_Einzelseiten_Katalog _Schlachthof_1_.pdf [Feb. 18, 2022].

"Umarmt und geküsst." *Der Spiegel,* July 27, 1963: https://www.spiegel.de/politik/ umarmt-und-gekuesst-a-d070f73b-0002-0001-0000-000046171283 [Nov. 9, 2022].

USHMM. "Poland 1945: Territorial Losses and Gains," no date. USHMM, Holocaust Encyclopedia: https://encyclopedia.ushmm.org/content/en/article/poland-in -1945#:~:text=Thus%2C%20Poland%20received%20more%20than,and%20a %20Baltic%20Sea%20coastline [Aug. 26, 2024].

Uslar von, Thilo. "Der ehrenwerte Karmasin." *Die Zeit,* June 24, 1966. No pages. Cited in: Lilienthal, "Hermann Krumey," no date. Gedenkportal Korbach, pp. 1–34.

"Vädret." *Svenska Dagbladet,* Jan. 28, 25, 1943, p. 10.

"Vädret." *Svenska Dagbladet,* Nov. 25, 1943, p. 10.

"Vädret." *Svenska Dagbladet,* Nov. 26, 1943, p. 12.

Vered, Ruti. "Displays in the Market." *HaOlam HaZe,* March 5, 1958. No pages.

Verg, Erik. "Wie konnte ein Deutscher zum Dienst nach Auschwitz kommen?" Hammerburger *Abendblatt,* Dec. 21, 1963. No pages. Cited in: Pendas, *The Frankfurt,* p. 133.

"Verhandlung gegen Mulka und Andere." *Frankfurter Allgemeine Zeitung,* Dec. 21, 1963, p. 39.

Vilhjálmsson, Vilhálmur Örn. *Medaljens bagside—Jødiske flygtningeskæbner i Danmark 1933-1945.* Copenhagen: Forlaget Vandkunsten, 2004.

Vogel, Rolf. "Der Prozess in Jerusalem." *Deutsche Zeitung,* Apr. 22–23, 1961, p. 3.

Vogel, Rolf (ed.). *Der Deutsch-Israelische Dialog: Dokumentation eines erregenden Kapitels deutscher Aussenpolitik.* München: Saur, 1987.

Vogt, Jochen. "'Die Ermittlung' von Peter Weiss im Kontext oder: Frankfurt am Main 1963/65. Eine Rückblende." *Literaturkritik,* 2017/4: https://literaturkritik.de/public/ rezension.php?rez_id=23188 [Sept. 22, 2021].

Wachsmann, Nikolaus. *KL: A History of the Nazi Concentration Camps.* London: Little, Brown, 2015.

"Wahlkundgebungen der Eisernen Front." *Ludwigsburger Kreiszeitung,* Feb. 27, 1933, no pages.

Walk, Joseph, et al. (eds.). "Stuttgart." Encyclopaedia of Jewish Communities: Germany, vol. 2. Transl. Selwyn Rose. No pages. (Transl. from: Walk, Joseph, et al. [eds.]. *Pinkas Hakehillot: Encyclopaedia of Jewish Communities: Germany,* vol. 2. Jerusalem: Yad Vashem, 1972, p. 141): https://www.jewishgen.org/yizkor/pinkas _germany/ger2_00141.html [Dec. 21, 2021].

Walker, Jonathan. *Poland Alone: Britain, SOE and the Collapse of the Polish Resistance, 1944.* Great Britain: The History Press Limited, 2008.

Walser, Martin. "Unser Auschwitz." In: Meier (ed.), *Martin Walser*, no pages.

Waske, Stefanie. "Die Verschwörung gegen Brandt." *Die Zeit*, Dec. 2, 2012: https://web
.archive.org/web/20130201181034/https://www.zeit.de/2012/49/Spionage-CDU
-CSU-Willy-Brandt/komplettansicht [Aug. 23, 2024].

Wassermann, Rudolf. "Fritz Bauer (1903–1968)." In: Glotz, Peter; Langenbucher,
Wolfgang R. (eds.). *Vorbilder für Deutsche: Korrektur einer Heldengalerie.*
München: R. Piper& Co. Verlag, 1974, pp. 296–309.

Weber, Hartmut (ed.). *Kabinettssitzung am 27. Januar 1960. H. Gedenkfeier am
Mahnmal des früheren Konzentrationslagers Bergen-Belsen am 2. Februar 1960. Die
Kabinettsprotokolle der Bundesregierung Band 13. 1960.* München: R. Oldenbourg
Verlag, 2003: https://kabinettsprotokolle.bundesarchiv.de/ [Apr. 7, 2024].

"Wegen der Tötung von Juden verhaftet: Der ehemalige SS-Obersturmbannführer
Krumey wird vor Gericht gestellt." *Frankfurter Allgemeine Zeitung*, Apr. 4, 1957. No
pages. HHStAW, 461, 33694. Krumey, Hermann u.a.: Handakten, vol. 1, no pages.

Weingärtner, Paul. "Dr. Bauer und die Deutschen." *Rheinischer Merkur*, Mar. 8, 1963.
No pages. Cited in: Steinke, *Fritz Bauer*, p. 147.

Weinke, Annette. "'Bleiben die Mörder unter uns?': Öffentliche Reaktionen auf die
Gründung und Tätigkeit der Zentralen Stelle Ludwigsburg." In: Osterloh, Vollnhals
(eds.), *NS-Prozesse*, pp. 263–282.

———. "Der Prozess gegen Adolf Eichmann, Israel 1961." In: Groenewold, Ignor,
Koch (eds.), *Lexikon*, online source.

———. *Die Verfolgung von NS-Tätern im geteilten Deutschland
Vergangenheitsbewältigung 1949–1969 oder: Eine deutsch-deutsche
Beziehungsgeschichte im Kalten Krieg.* Paderborn: Ferdinand Schoningh, 2002.

———. *Eine Gesellschaft ermittelt gegen sich selbst: Die Geschichte der Zentralen Stelle
Ludwigsburg 1958–2008.* Darmstadt: WGB, 2009.

Weinmann, Günther. "Das Oberlandesgericht Stuttgart von 1933 bis 1945." In: Stilz
(ed.), *Das Oberlandesgerichts*, pp. 37–60.

Weiss, Peter. *My Place.* Transl. Roger Hillman, Aug. 1, 2008: https://transit.berkeley
.edu/2008/hillman/ [Dec. 7, 2023].

———. *Notizbücher 1960–1971*, vols. 1–2. Frankfurt am Main: Suhrkamp, 1982.

Weissberg, Alex. *Desperate Mission: Joel Brand's Story as Told by Alex Weissberg.* Transl.
Constantine Fitzgibbon, Andrew Foster-Melliar. New York: Criterion Books, 1958.

Weizsäcker von, Richard. Speech by Federal President During the Ceremony
Commemorating the 40th Anniversary of the End of War in Europe and of
National-Socialist Tyranny (Bundestag, Bonn), May 8, 1985, pp. 1–12: https://
www.bundespraesident.de/SharedDocs/Downloads/DE/Reden/2015/02/150202
-RvW-Rede-8-Mai-1985-englisch.pdf?__blob=publicationFile [July 26, 2024].

Welzer, Harald; Moller, Sabine; Tschuggnall, Karoline. *"Opa war kein Nazi":
Nationalsozialismus und Holocaust im Familiengedächtnis.* Fischer E-Books, 2014.

Wenge, Nicola. "Das System des Quälens, der Einschüchterung, der Demütigung . . .
Die frühen württembergischen Konzentrationslager Heuberg und Oberer
Kuhberg." In: Osterloh (ed.), ". . . der schrankenlosesten," pp. 123–150.

"Wer zahlt?" *Der Spiegel*, Oct. 18, 1960: https://www.spiegel.de/politik/wer-zahlt-a
-c54970b3-0002-0001-0000-000043067088 [Jan. 6, 2022].

Werner, Röder. "Die politische Emigration." In: Krohn et al. (eds.), *Handbuch*,
pp. 16–30, cited in: Wojak, *Fritz Bauer*, p. 121.

West, Fritz. *So ist Stuttgart: Ein Unterhaltsamer Begleiter für in- und Ausländer von
Fritz West.* Stuttgart: W. Kohlhammer Verlag, 1933.

"Wettervorhersage." *Frankfurter Rundschau,* Dec. 20, 1963, p. 1.

Whisnant, Clayton J. *Male Homosexuality in West Germany: Between Persecution and Freedom, 1949–1969.* London: Macmillan, 2012.

———. *Queer Identities and Politics in Germany: A History, 1880–1945.* New York: Harrington Park Press, 2016.

"Who Is Dr. Globke?" *Frankfurter Rundschau,* Nov. 9, 1949. No pages. NARA, Hans Globke 640446, box 42, folder 6, pp. 21–26.

"Wie Pfarrer Pohls Geheimnis gelüftet wurde." *Westfälischer Anzeiger,* Sept. 9, 2021: https://www.wa.de/nordrhein-westfalen/pfarrer-pohl-und-die-ergreifung-von -nazi-verbrecher-adolf-eichmann-tochter-sigrid-wobst-erinnert-sich-90969139 .html [Sept. 22, 2022].

Wiegrefe, Klaus. "Aktenklau für die Adenauer-Republik." *Der Spiegel,* Sept. 2, 2010: https://www.spiegel.de/politik/deutschland/kalter-krieg-beim-eichmann-prozess -aktenklau-fuer-die-adenauer-republik-a-715292.html [Aug. 11, 2024].

———. "Der Fluch der bösen Tat." *Der Spiegel,* Apr. 11, 2011: https://www.spiegel.de/ spiegel/print/d-77962916.html [July 29, 2024].

———. "Who Ordered the Construction of the Berlin Wall?" Transl. Christopher Sultan. *Der Spiegel,* May 30, 2009: https://www.spiegel.de/international/germany/ the-khrushchev-connection-who-ordered-the-construction-of-the-berlin-wall -a-628052.html [Aug. 11, 2024].

Wieland, Günther. *Naziverbrechen und deutsche Strafjustiz.* Berlin: Organon, 2004.

Wilbrink, Joost. "Epoch III," 2005. dbtrains.com: http://www.dbtrains.com/en/ epochIII.7 [July 30, 2024].

Wildt, Michael. "Die Angst vor dem Volk: Ernst Fraenkel in der deutschen Nachkriegsgesellschaft." In: Boll, Gross, *"Ich staune,"* pp. 317–344.

Wilkinson, Tracy. "Hansi Brand; Worked to Help Jews Escape from the Holocaust." *Los Angeles Times,* Apr. 19, 2000: https://www.latimes.com/archives/la-xpm-2000 -apr-19-me-21281-story.html [June 2, 2024].

Will, Martin. *Ephorale Verfassung: Das Parteiverbot der rechtsextremen SRP von 1952; Thomas Dehlers Rosenburg und die Konstituierung der Bundesrepublik Deutschland.* Tübingen: Mohr Siebeck, 2018.

Williams, Charles. *Adenauer: The Father of the New Germany.* Boston: Little, Brown & Company, 2000.

Wilson, Jason. *Buenos Aires: A Cultural and Literary Companion.* Oxford: Signal Books, 1999.

Wirth, Christof. "Eine letzte Begegnung mit Generalstaatsanwalt Dr. Fritz Bauer am 28. Juni 1968 im Schlosshotel in Karlsruhe." *Forschungsjournal Soziale Bewegungen,* 2015/4 (28), pp. 280–281.

Wisely, Andrew. "Confession That Isn't: The Fear Claims of Dr. Franz Lucas Between Accusation and Acquittal in the Frankfurt Auschwitz Trial (1963–65)." *Holocaust Studies,* Jan. 24, 2020: https://doi.org/10.1080/17504902.2020.1718921 [Sept. 23, 2022].

———. *The Trial of a Nazi Doctor.* Oxford / New York: Berghahn Books, 2024.

Wisely, Andrew Clark. "From Humiliation to Humanity: Reconciling Helen Goldman's Testimony with the Forensic Strictures of the Frankfurt Auschwitz Trial." *S: I. M. O. N.,* 2021/8 (1), pp. 4–35: https://simon.vwi.ac.at/public/journals/ 1/fullissues/SIMON-01-2021-Buch.pdf [Mar, 14, 2024].

Wistrich, Robert S. *Who's Who in Nazi Germany.* London: Weidenfeld and Nicolson, 1982.

Withuis, Jolande; Mooij, Annet. *The Politics of War Trauma: The Aftermath of World War II in Eleven European Countries*. Amsterdam: Amsterdam University Press, 2010.

Witte, Walter. *Alles zu seiner Zeit: Rechtsanwalt Henry Ormond (1901–1973)*. Unpublished typescript, no date. FBInst.

Wittmann, Rebecca. *Beyond Justice: The Auschwitz Trial*. Cambridge, MA: Harvard University Press, 2005.

Woelk, Emma. "Authenticity, Distance, and the East German Volksstück: Yiddish in Thomas Christoph Harlan's 'Ich Selbst und Kein Engel.'" In: Helfer, Donahue (eds.), *Nexus 3*, pp. 171–186.

Wojak, Irmtrud. "Fritz Bauer: 'Im Kampf um des Menschen Rechte.'" *Forschungsjournal Soziale Bewegungen*, 2015/4 (28), pp. 125–135.

———. *Fritz Bauer 1903–1968: The Man Who Found Eichmann and Put Auschwitz on Trial*. Transl. Adam Blauhut, Karen Margalis. Bochum: Buxus Edition, 2018.

Wojak, Irmtrud (ed.). *Auschwitz-Prozess. 4 Ks 2/63 Frankfurt am Main*. Köln: Snoeck, 2004.

Wojak, Irmtrud; Meinl, Susanne (eds.). *Im Labyrinth der Schuld: Täter—Opfer—Ankläger*. Frankfurt am Main: Campus Verlag, 2003.

Wolf, Horst. "Auschwitz—Fabrik des Todes." *Frankfurter Rundschau*, Dec 17, 1963, p. 3.

Wolf, Norbert. "Der Remer-Prozess." *Forschungsjournal Soziale Bewegungen*, 2015/4 (28), pp. 197–207.

Wolf, René. *The Undivided Sky: The Holocaust on East and West German Radio in the 1960s*. London: Palgrave / Macmillan, 2010.

Wolf, Thomas. *Die Entstehung des BND: Aufbau, Finanzierung, Kontrolle*. Berlin: Ch. Links Verlag, 2018.

Wolfert, Raimund. *Homosexuellenpolitik in der jungen Bundesrepublik: Kurt Hiller, Hans Giese und das Frankfurter Wissenschaftlich-humanitäre Komitee*. Göttingen: Wallstein, 2015.

Wolff, Wilfried. *Max Hodann (1894–1946): Sozialist und Sexualreformer*. Hamburg: von Bockel Verlag, 1993.

Wucher, Albert. "Die Eigene Chance." *Süddeutsche Zeitung*, July 24, 1961. No pages. Cited in: Krause, *Der Eichmann-Prozess*, p. 270.

Yablonka, Hanna. *The State of Israel vs. Adolf Eichmann*. Transl. Ora Cummings; David Herman. New York: Schocken Books, 2004.

"You and the Atom Bomb." *Tribune*, Oct. 19, 1945. Cited in: The Orwell Foundation: https://www.orwellfoundation.com/the-orwell-foundation/orwell/essays-and -other-works/you-and-the-atom-bomb/ [Aug. 28, 2024].

Zaeske Architekten. "Neubau und Sanierung einer Stadtvilla Bodenstedtstrasse, Wiesbaden," no date. Zaeske: https://www.zaeske-architekten.de/projekte/stadtvilla -bodenstedtstrasse-4 [Feb. 18, 2022].

Zapf, Lilli. *Die Tübinger Juden: Eine Dokumentation*. Tübingen: Katzmann, 1974.

"Zeitliste. 150 Jahre Palmengarten," 2021. Stadt Frankfurt: https://www.palmengarten .de/de/150-jahre-palmengarten.html [Feb. 20, 2023].

Zeltser, Arkadi. "The Subject of 'Jews in Babi Yar' in the Soviet Union in the Years 1941–1945." Transl. Michael Sigal. Yad Vashem: https://www.yadvashem.org/ research/about/mirilashvili-center/articles/babi-yar.html [June 24, 2024].

Ziegler, Gerhard. "Merkwürdiges im Frankfurter SS-Prozess." *Die Zeit*, July 10, 1964: https://www.zeit.de/1964/28/merkwuerdiges-im-frankfurter-ss-prozess/ komplettansicht. [Mar. 8, 2022].

———. "Name ohne Glanz. Der neue Generalstaatsanwalt in Hessen." *Die Zeit,* Feb. 7, 1969. No pages. Cited in: Steinke, *Fritz Bauer,* p. 191.

Zimmerman, Joshua D. *The Polish Underground and the Jews, 1939–1945.* New York: Cambridge University Press, 2015.

"Zonen-Staatsanwälte bei Bauer. "*Frankfurter Allgemeine Zeitung,* Jan. 18, 1961/15, p. 4.

"Zum Generalstaatsanwalt ernannt." *Frankfurter Rundschau,* Mar. 24–25, 1956, p. 4.

"Zwei einzig Volk." *Der Spiegel,* Dec. 7, 1965: https://www.spiegel.de/kultur/zwei -einzig-volk-a-f5070d66-0002-0001-0000-000046275409?context=issue [Jan. 9, 2023].

Zweig, Ronald. *The Gold Train: The Destruction of the Jews and the Looting of Hungary.* New York: William Morrow, 2002.

Zwerenz, Gerhard. "Gespräche mit Fritz Bauer." *Streit-Zeit-Schrift,* Sept. 1968, pp. 89–93.

Zwerenz, Gerhard; Zwerenz, Ingrid. "Mutterseelenallein durch Frankfurt am Main." *Forschungsjournal Soziale Bewegungen,* 2015/4 (28), pp. 296–301.

Index

Note: *Italic page numbers* indicate photographs.

About the Author

JACK FAIRWEATHER is the author of the Costa Book of the Year Award–winner *The Volunteer*, a #1 bestseller in the UK that's been hailed as a modern classic and compared to *Schindler's List*. He served as a correspondent for *The Washington Post* and *The Daily Telegraph*, where he was the paper's Baghdad and Persian Gulf bureau chief.

Also by Jack Fairweather

#1 SUNDAY TIMES BESTSELLER

the volunteer

the true story of the resistance hero who infiltrated Auschwitz

'Fascinating'
Simon Sebag Montefiore

'Remarkable'
Peter Frankopan

'Extraordinary'
The Times

'Superbly written'
Sebastian Junger

COSTA BOOK OF THE YEAR 2019

JACK FAIRWEATHER

Available now